AMERICAN PROTEST LITERATURE

The John Harvard Library

AMERICAN

LITERATURE

Edited by

ZOE TRODD

Foreword by

JOHN STAUFFER

Afterword by

HOWARD ZINN

The Belknap Press of Harvard University Press

Cambridge, Massachusetts, and London, England

2006

Copyright © 2006 by the President and Fellows of Harvard College
All rights reserved
Printed in the United States of America

Pages 519–527 constitute an extension of the copyright page.

Library of Congress catalog card number 2006049690
CIP Data available from the Library of Congress

ISBN-13: 978-0-674-02352-9
ISBN-10: 0-674-02352-8

Contents

3. LITTLE BOOKS THAT STARTED A BIG WAR
Abolition and Antislavery

4. THIS LAND IS HERLAND
Women's Rights and Suffragism

7. DUST TRACKS ON THE ROAD
The Great Depression

THE LITERATURE

THE LEGACY

8. THE DUNGEON SHOOK
Civil Rights and Black Liberation

THE LITERATURE

THE LEGACY

11. FROM SAIGON TO BAGHDAD
The Vietnam War and Beyond

JOHN STAUFFER

Foreword

American Protest Literature is an extraordinary collection of protest documents ranging from the Revolution to the present. Organized around eleven reform movements, it highlights the rich variety of protest art. This volume greatly enhances our understanding of the link between art and protest, and the role of history and historical memory in creating protest literature.

History is the activist's muse, and in this collection, Zoe Trodd brilliantly debunks the myth of America as a series of "fresh starts" and new beginnings. But she does much more: the book is ideal for anyone interested in the origins and forms of social change. Trodd's introduction and headnotes provide original insights and essential context for each document. And the structure of the book is unique. Most studies and anthologies of protest focus on one era or movement; very few explore, as Trodd does, the relationship between political movements and their art forms. In her careful selection of a wide variety of documents, from poem to pamphlet to photograph, from the familiar to the obscure, Trodd creatively opens up the canon and gives definition and weight to a genre which has been little studied and understood. The book makes a major contribution to our understanding of the politics of form and the influence of art on society.

This book has its origins in a course I began teaching at Harvard in 2002, called "American Protest Literature." Trodd was involved with the course at the outset, as was Timothy Patrick McCarthy, who has frequently taught it with me. At the time there were few examples or models on which to draw, and the scholarship on protest literature was extremely limited, despite excellent studies of specific movements and texts, such as the proletarian novel. At the outset I hoped the course would provide an overview of protest literature and appeal to students from a variety of disciplines. What I didn't fully realize was how timely the topic was. Over the past four years, course enrollment has grown from fewer than 100 to more than 300 undergraduates. I have received numerous queries about the course from faculty and students across the country and even from abroad, and similar courses have since emerged at other schools.

Such interest in the course surprised me, for today we lack the kind of idealism that existed among students in the 1960s, when large numbers of young people believed that their words and actions could change the world. The growing interest stems, I think, more from the desire to understand the nature of protest and its literature than from the hope of transforming society. How are voices of dissent shaped and articulated, and how do forms of protest function as aesthetic, performative, rhetorical, and ideological expressions within culture? *American Protest Literature* offers answers to these questions.

In defining protest literature, Trodd builds on themes from my course. While writing my lectures, I was surprised to find that there was no common understanding of protest literature; the term has been used to mean virtually all literature (or an entire genre) or no literature. Ralph Ellison considered all novels to be a form of protest: "Implicitly the novel protests," he wrote in 1969. "It protests the agonies of growing up. It protests the problem of trying to find a way into a complex, intricately structured society in a way which would allow this particular man to behave in a manly way and which would allow him to seize some instrumentalities of political power." Conversely, some literary critics, especially self-described "New Critics," have treated literature as a hermetic text, divorced from politics and ideology, and so the very term "protest literature" was something of an oxymoron.[1]

I define protest literature broadly to mean the uses of language to transform the self and change society. By language I refer not only to words, but to visual art, music, and film. Protest literature functions as a catalyst, guide, or mirror of social change. It not only critiques some aspect of society, but also suggests, either implicitly or explicitly, a solution to society's ills.

There are countless examples of individuals' being inspired or transformed by language. Frederick Douglass discovered the "rich treasure" of *The Columbian Orator*, a collection of speeches, essays, and poems by classic writers, which enabled him to "give tongue" to his thoughts. Upton Sinclair was so inspired by *Uncle Tom's Cabin* (1852) that he used it "as a model for what [he] wished to do" in protesting working conditions in the meatpacking industry in his novel *The Jungle* (1906). And the character of Niel Herbert in Willa Cather's *A Lost Lady* (1923), after discovering "a complete set of the Bohn classics," and reading Ovid, Goethe, and Byron, began treating characters "as living creatures." These characters shaped "his conception of the people about him" and made him wish to become an architect.[2]

In the broadest sense, then, literature inspires people to redefine themselves. The difference between literature and protest literature is that while the former empowers and transforms individuals, the latter strives to give voice to a collective consciousness, uniting isolated or inchoate discontent. Protest literature taps into an ideological vein of dissent and announces to people that they are not alone in their frustrations. Protest literature is part of its milieu, inextricably linked to its time and place. But it also stands at a remove from prevailing social values, offering a critique of society from the outside.

Protest literature employs three rhetorical strategies in the quest to convert audiences. The first two are empathy and shock value. Empathy is central to all humanitarian reform, and protest literature encourages its readers to participate in the experiences of the victims, to "feel their pain." Shock value inspires outrage, agitation, and a desire to correct social ills. The third characteristic of protest literature is "symbolic action," to borrow a term from Kenneth Burke. Symbolic action implies indeterminacy of meaning, rich ambiguity, and open-endedness in the text, which goes beyond the author's intent. It invites dialogue, debate, and interpretation among readers. It points to a distinction between what an author displays and what he betrays. It prevents protest literature from becoming an advertisement, or propaganda, whose purpose is strictly teleological. Advertisements and propaganda send a clear message and seek to convert their audiences. Symbolic action produces open-ended symbols, giving a text subtlety and nuance, providing an aesthetic experience for the reader.[3]

We can see how symbolic action works in the most enduring work of protest literature in American culture. In *Uncle Tom's Cabin,* Harriet Beecher Stowe intended Uncle Tom to be a symbol of Christ. But Stowe was also a "reluctant abolitionist," and her ambivalence about abolitionism is reflected in her narrative. Her reluctance to associate with abolitionist organizations was an asset to her art, enabling her to create symbolic action in Tom and in the ending of her novel. Tom is more than simply a symbol of Christ: he represents national redemption, feminine purity, black male heroism, and emasculated deference to white authority. Moreover, as Lawrence Buell has noted, while Stowe defines Tom as "the Martyr" rather than "the Christ," as the story develops his actions keep "crossing the line" between Christ and martyr, history and scripture, "type and antitype." It is also significant that Stowe characterizes Tom both as unique and as a representative black man. These contrasting and contradictory symbols have enriched the novel, contributing to its influence and resonance throughout the twentieth century and into the twenty-first. Similarly, the novel ends in ambiguity, suggesting that the problem of slavery can be solved both by establishing racial equality in America and by shipping blacks to the African colony of Liberia. The ending thus prevents the book from becoming an unambiguous advertisement for the abolitionist cause.[4]

How does protest literature affect society? This question forces us to grapple with the link between ideas and material forces. The study of religious belief offers a helpful guide. In fact, one might say that protest literature is analogous to a religious revival. Revivals are a collective conversion experience. In conversion, an individual undergoes a rite of passage to become a new man or woman. This experience can take many forms; in the language of evangelical Christianity, the convert is "born again" through Christ. Conversions are often isolated events and do not lead to any kind of social action. However, they occur most frequently within the context of a religious revival, in which a charismatic evangelist preaches the word of God to a group of people. A revivalist is essentially a protest artist, creating protest literature with words, images, and oratory to effect conversion. As the religious historian William McLoughlin notes in his important study *Revivals, Awakenings, and Reform,* "most religious converts move from states of anxiety and inhibition to states of functionally constructive personal and social action." This same tendency toward social action applies to converts of protest literature.[5]

While revivals alter the lives of individuals, awakenings "alter the world view of a whole people or culture." Awakenings are periods of cultural revitalization, lasting a generation or more, that emerge during a time of social stress and cultural confusion. During awakenings there are "jarring disjunctions between norms and experience, old beliefs and new realities, dying patterns and emerging patterns of behavior." Awakenings result in the restructuring of society, norms, and values. Protest literature, much like revivals, can lead to permanent social change when the protest occurs during an awakening. It is during times of upheaval and discontent that the masses are willing to abandon the existing order for the chaos that always comes with social revitalization. As Thomas Paine put it in 1776, "These are the times that try men's souls." His famous comment perfectly captures the sense of religious awakening, in which the answer to society's "sick soul" is revolution.[6]

Paine coupled his call for revolution with an appeal to the spirit. And in his twinning of reform and religion he was a representative American protest artist. Virtually all substantive reform movements in America draw on spiritual beliefs and religious language to clarify a problem and envision a better world. According to the anthropologist Anthony Wallace, a central feature of cultural revitalization movements is the appearance of a prophet, who undergoes a religious experience, "epitomizes the crisis within the culture," and speaks to the masses. As the awakening gains momentum, the prophet attracts more and more members, especially young people, who are flexible in their worldviews and willing to experiment with new lifestyles. Prophecy—the belief that you are heeding God's will—is a crucial component of American reform. When the writer is a prophet, protest literature becomes a sacred text, appealing to God as the ultimate source of authority. The prophetic voice extends throughout American protest literature, from Tom Paine, Nat Turner, Stowe and almost every abolitionist, through Elizabeth Cady Stanton, Martin Luther King, Jr., and James Baldwin. Although Tom Paine is often viewed as a secular figure, in his Revolutionary pamphlets he defines himself as a prophet: "The King of America . . . reigns above, and doth not make havock of mankind like [England]," he writes in *Common Sense* (1776), which greatly mobilized public opinion. He justifies independence by appealing to "divine law, the word of God." Even the labor movement, which is often characterized in wholly secular terms, was originally tied to religious belief and the prophetic tradition. Prophecy encouraged workers and labor leaders to challenge industrial power, condemn "natural" economic laws, and oppose the conformist Christianity of most respectable clergymen. As J. A. Crawford, the Illinois district president of the United Mine Workers, wrote: "The first labor organization mentioned in history, either profane or divine, was the one founded just outside of the historic Garden of Eden, by God himself; the charter members being Adam and Eve."[7]

But protest literature does not lead *directly* to social change, much as charismatic preachers and prophets cannot convert the masses simply through the power of their evangelizing. If a work of art or an individual had such power, then history would be the criticism of representative texts and the biographies of "great men." The causes of revivals, awakenings, and social change are far more complex than charismatic revivalists and effective protest literature. While great revivalists and protest literature act as catalysts for social change, it is impossible to measure any direct, linear causality. Too many other forces and contingencies are at play.

In fact there have been comparatively few awakenings, or periods of cultural revitalization in America. This means that most protest literature, like most evangelism, does not transform the masses. Most historians point to only four awakenings: the first three led, respectively, to the Revolution, the Civil War, and America's entry into World War I; and the fourth was centered on the civil rights movement and the Vietnam war. And historians have highlighted the problems of periodizing eras of cultural revitalization.

The point is that patience is a prerequisite for protest and conversion. As Trodd shrewdly notes, activists need to know their movement's history and literature. The "successful" protest movements—abolitionism, women's rights, and civil rights—occurred within a context of religious awakening and required generations to achieve measurable change. For the activists, things often got worse before improving. And when transformation did occur, the outcome was often unintended. Upton Sinclair was one of the few writers for whom we can trace a direct causal link between his book and the course of history. He wrote *The Jungle* to attack working conditions in hopes of a socialist revolution, a transformation of the means of production. But his middle-class readers interpreted his book as a consumerist critique of the meat industry. And so while the novel did little to improve working conditions, it mobilized public opinion and helped pass the Food and Drugs Act of 1906. Sinclair thought he had failed in his purpose: "I aimed at the public's heart," he wrote, "and by accident I hit it in the stomach."[8]

While protest literature seeks to ameliorate social evils, its primary effect is to empower and transform individuals. This is a crucial first step toward a broader social transformation, as W. E. B. Du Bois, one of the great champions of protest literature, noted. In a 1930 essay, he was distressed to find that many of his fellow African Americans believed that "unless the protest is successful or seems to have a reasonable chance of success, it is worse than worthless." Such attitudes were defeatist, he wrote, and in response he articulated two essential purposes of protest. The first was to let the opposition know where you stood on an issue; even if your effort to change things failed, the protest was "successful," for you had staked out your position. The second, more important, reason to protest was "for the effect it has on yourself": "Even if the offending politician does not hear of your opposition; does not feel your lone vote, you know and you feel, and it is an awful thing to have to be ashamed of one's self." Even when protest literature misses its mark, by empowering its author it is an antidote to shame, passivity, and submissiveness.[9]

The eleven protest movements that Trodd traces in the book fit within a tradition that might be called progressive protest literature. Implicit in this tradition is the assumption that protest literature is never reactionary, and the Divinity on whom activists rely is never conservative. McLoughlin shares a similar sensibility about revivals and awakenings: "There is no conservative tradition in America because God is not a conservative. God is an innovator. American culture is thus always in the making but never complete. It will be completed, according to one of our most cherished cultural myths, at the end of human time, the beginning of God's Kingdom, the coming of the millennium. Exactly how and when that will occur is itself constantly subject to new light." But there is a "conservative tradition" of "traditionalist movements" within culture that seeks to restore order and authority. These movements are made up of "reactionaries who look back to a golden time."[10]

These traditionalist movements constitute an alternative protest tradition and literature. This alternative tradition includes the literature of Loyalists during the American Revolution; proslavery advocates; the Confederate States of America and various neo-Confederate legacies; the Klan and its votaries; social Darwinists and champions of laissez-faire capitalism; and antifeminists. Each of these movements critiqued society and suggested a resolution to its ills. Each movement created its own protest literature and history to explain its purpose. In many cases the movement traced its genealogy back to a text and tradition shared by progressive protest. In 1861 seceding Southerners acted on their faith in the Declaration of Independence. Were not "the men of 1776" "Secessionists"? asked one. Secessionists rallied to "the standard of Liberty and Equality for white men" against "our Abolition enemies" who threatened their freedom. And both sides of the protest tradition, the conservatives and progressives, "read the same Bible, and pray[ed] to the same God; and each invoke[d] His aid against the other," to quote Abraham Lincoln. Although the conservative tradition of protest literature does not appear in these pages, it highlights what progressives were up against. By ignoring this alternative tradition, it is easy to conclude that progress is inevitable and that the social visions that fill these pages will eventually prevail. Although the conservative tradition of protest has been a powerful countervailing force in American history, the achievements of the movements recorded in this volume should inspire confidence in the power of words and moral reform. To cite just one example, on the eve of the American Revolution "slavery was legal and almost unquestioned throughout the New World," as David Brion Davis has emphasized. With few exceptions, people could not envision a world without slavery, and so they accepted the institution as a fact of life. Even slaves, while seeking freedom, did not condemn slavery as an *institution*. Yet one hundred years later, slavery became illegal in the United States, and by 1888 "the institution had been oulawed throughout the Western Hemisphere." While new forms of bondage such as "sex slaves" have recently proliferated, slavery remains illegal and today's abolitionists do not need to convince people that the institution is inhuman and evil. This is an extraordinary moral achievement, which stems from the collective and *willed* protest of countless slaves, ex-slaves, and abolitionists. Trodd elegantly describes and illuminates the literature that led to such achievements.[11]

Notes

1. Ralph Ellison, *Going to the Territory* (New York: Vintage Books, 1987), 62; John Crowe Ransom, "Criticism, Inc.," in *Norton Anthology of Literary Theory* (New York: W. W. Norton, 2001), 1105–1117.
2. Frederick Douglass, *My Bondage and My Freedom,* ed. John Stauffer (1855; New York: The Modern Library, 2003), 82; Upton Sinclair, *The Jungle,* ed. Clare Virginia Eby (1906; New York: W. W. Norton, 2003), 350; Willa Cather, *A Lost Lady* (1923; New York: Vintage Classics, 1990), 67–68.
3. Kenneth Burke, *The Philosophy of Literary Form* (1941; Berkeley: University of California Press, 1973), 1–38. While some recent theorists have argued that empathetic awareness erases differences between two people, the fact that empathy is always an ideal, and can never be realized, obviates such concerns. The very act of trying to identify with another self, and enter into her thoughts, stimulates humanitarian feelings and actions.
4. Lawrence Buell, *New England Literary Culture. From Revolution through Renaissance* (Cambridge: Cambridge University Press, 1986), 189.
5. William McLoughlin, *Revivals, Awakenings, and Reform: An Essay on Religion and Social Change in America, 1607–1977* (Chicago: University of Chicago Press, 1978), 8.
6. McLoughlin, xiii, 10; Anthony F. C. Wallace, "Revitalization Movements," *American Anthropologist,* 58:2 (April 1956): 264–281; Thomas Paine, "The Crisis, No. 1,"

in *The Norton Anthology of American Literature,* 3rd ed. (New York: W. W. Norton, 1989), I: 624. Paine's pamphlet was also referred to as *The American Crisis.*

7. Wallace, 273–280; McLoughlin, 16; Paine, *Common Sense,* ed. Isaac Kramnick (1776; New York: Penguin Books, 1986), 98; Herbert Gutman, *Work, Culture, and Society in Industrializing America: Essays in American Working Class and Social History* (New York: Vintage Books, 1977), 94.

8. Sinclair, *The Jungle,* 299, 350, 351; quotations on 350, 351 from Sinclair, "What Life Means to Me" (1906).

9. W. E. B. Du Bois, "Protest," *The Crisis* (1930) reprinted in Du Bois, *Writings* (New York: Library of America, 1986), 1231–1232.

10. McLoughlin, 14, 18.

11. David Brion Davis, *Inhuman Bondage: The Rise and Fall of Slavery in the New World* (New York: Oxford University Press, 2006), 1–3, 330–331, quotation from p. 1; Kevin Bales, *Disposable People: New Slavery in the Global Economy* (Berkeley: University of California Press, 1999).

Introduction

"We know how gods are made," wrote Jack London in 1915. "Comes now the time to make a world." That world would be made, London adds, by protest writers for "not merely have they reported the human ills. They have proposed the remedy," and they will persist "until all the world beautiful be made over in their image." Raging and reasoning, prophesying and provoking, reporting ills and proposing remedies, protest writers aim to "make over" their world. The protest literature they create provides a revolutionary language and a renewed vision of the possible. It gives distinctive shape to long-accumulating grievances, claims old rights, and demands new ones. It creates space for argument, introduces doubt, deepens perception, and shatters the accepted limits of belief. American protest writers recognize the failed promises of the democratic experiment and redraw its blueprints—believing, as Ralph Ellison puts it, that "in this great, inventive land man's idlest dreams are but the blueprints and mockups of emerging realities."[1]

Protest writers also try to close the gap between blueprint and reality, between what should be and what is: "Poets, prophets, and reformers are all picture-makers, and this ability is the secret of their power and achievements," writes Frederick Douglass; "they see what ought to be by the reflection of what is, and endeavor to remove the contradiction." In protest literature, this contradiction between what is and what ought to be is often based on a critique of America's founding documents. Observing whole groups abandoned by the omissions and loopholes of these documents, protest artists revise them. "You can dehydrate soups and teas . . . and all you need to do is add a drop of water and it is reconstituted into its real substance. Maybe, that's what those words in those great documents are," suggests the poet Lorenzo Thomas, and protest writers offer their own words as the drops of water that reconstitute America's dehydrated social contract.[2]

Living in a partially achieved nation, protest writers adopt what Ellison calls "a role beyond that of entertainer." Sometimes the protest artist's role is to be "the man who told you something you already know," as Woody Guthrie said. At other times the protest writer is the one who awakens the nation from its slumber: "It would be great to start a poem, 'America! Awake! Awake! Awake!' And then list all the things it could actually awake to," observes Allen Ginsberg. Other protest artists emerge as participant-witnesses and whimsical philosophers, purposeful preacher-poets and leaders of a congregational call-and-response, self-fashioned martyrs and outlaws, narrators of America's unrecorded history, or Sisyphus figures endlessly pushing a boulder up the American mountain.[3]

These protest artists appear in *American Protest Literature* across eleven protest movements. Each part of the anthology presents five literary or documentary sources for the movement and five pieces of that literature's legacy, including documents of concrete social or political change. Each part tells a story and can be read straight through, but sources connect across different movements as well, so the book can be read along less straightforward routes. Many sources are hard to find elsewhere, and some material is original to this book: a new protest poem by Robert Pinsky and material from interviews with Amiri Baraka, Tony Kushner, Barbara Ehrenreich, Kevin Bales, "Country" Joe McDonald, Clinton Fein, Lisa Roth of the John Brown Anti-Klan Committee, Robert Pinsky, Senator Edward Kennedy, Tim O'Brien, John Balaban, and Doric Wilson.

This anthology sets different kinds of documents in conversation with each other: some sources, like the text and photographs of *Let Us Now Praise Famous Men* (1941), were ignored when first published but taken up during a later protest moment. Others evolved in new climates: new stanzas were added to "Solidarity Forever" (1915) and the New Black Panther Party adopted the Black Panther Party's "Ten Point Program" (1966) and included new demands in their 2001 version. Still others took on a life unintended by their creators: Upton Sinclair's *The Jungle* (1906) gave rise to the 1906 Food and Drugs and Meat Inspection Acts, though it was intended to usher in a new socialist world; and Eddie Adams eventually regretted destroying General Loan's reputation with his 1968 photograph of Loan executing a man on the street in Saigon, noting in 1983 that the image was never meant to mobilize public opinion against the Vietnam war.

Taken together, the artists in this anthology answer the warning issued by John Dewey in 1940: "We have taken democracy for granted; we have thought and acted as if our forefathers had founded it once and for all," and have been negligent "in creating a school that should be the constant nurse of democracy." But protest artists set out to rebuild the schools of American democracy. The touchstone of their literature is democracy, and the touchstone of American democracy is their democratic fictions.[4]

The Politics of Connection

The schools of American democracy are built collaboratively. For example, though the Fourteenth and Fifteenth Amendments excluded women and thus divided abolitionists and suffragists, antislavery activists like Douglass, Wendell Phillips, William Lloyd Garrison, Theodore Parker, Henry Ward Beecher, and Parker Pillsbury had all worked for women's rights, just as women's rights activists had worked to end slavery. Lydia Maria Child asserted that "a struggle for the advancement of any principle of freedom would inevitably tend to advance all free principles, for they are connected like a spiral line, which, if the top be put in motion, revolves even to the lowest point," and Elizabeth Cady Stanton instructed: "Let us remember that all reforms are interdependent . . . The object of an individual life is not to carry one fragmentary measure in human progress, but to utter the highest truth clearly seen in all directions." Douglass agreed, telling the Woman Suffrage Association: "All good causes are mutually helpful." After the Civil War, suffragists shifted from comparing women with slaves to comparing women with degraded workers, and worked with labor activists and members of the First International.[5]

Equally, while feminists believed administrators of the 1964 Civil Rights Act and the Equal Employment Opportunity Commission didn't take sex discrimination seriously, and in response formed the National Organization for Women, they took inspiration from civil rights activists. Shirley Chisholm often compared feminism to the civil rights movement, noting that shame of race had become pride, and so should shame of sex. As late as 1992, the feminist group Third Wave was borrowing the language of civil rights for their voter registration drive, Freedom Summer. Connecting other late 20th-century protest movements, woman activists in the American Indian Movement (AIM) formed the feminist organization Women of All Red Nations, and ACT UP, an AIDS activist group, inspired the formation of the Women's Health Action Mobilization. AIM activists and gay rights activists worked with the Black Panthers and in the antiwar movement, and civil rights activists protested the Vietnam war. Civil rights and Black Nationalist leaders functioned as correctives to one another. Malcolm X said in 1964 that he and Martin Luther King, Jr., had "nothing to debate about. We are both indicting. I would say to him: You indict and give them hope. I'll indict and give them no hope." In early 1965, he told Coretta Scott King: "If white people realize what the alternative is, perhaps they will be more willing to hear Dr. King." In 1965 King made plans to meet with Malcolm, realizing their views were not so different, but Malcolm was killed two days before their scheduled meeting.[6]

Building alliances across movements, protest writers seek further connection and invite readers to join a community in literature. "We spend our life trying to be less lonesome," writes John Steinbeck. "One of our ancient methods is to tell a story begging the listener to say—and to feel—'Yes, that's the way it is, or at least that's the way I feel it. You're not as alone as you thought.'" Protest literature builds solidarity, connecting writer, reader, subject, and world, and fosters a common human identity, as Audre Lorde explains: "I am a black feminist lesbian poet, and I identify myself as such because if there is one other black feminist lesbian poet in isolation somewhere within the reach of my voice, I want her to know she is not alone."[7]

Sensing that the hardest journey of all might be toward another self, protest artists often call for empathy, suggesting sharing another's suffering in order to help end it. Some imagine themselves as their subjects, often painfully so: Lewis Hine needed "spiritual antiseptic" to survive, and Sinclair described the "tears and anguish" that went into *The Jungle*. Others ask the reader to become the subject: James Agee says that he wrote repetitiously because he wanted the reader of *Let Us Now Praise Famous Men* to experience the boredom of tenant farmers' work, and Ida B. Wells hands off responsibility to her reader in the last paragraph of *Southern Horrors* (1892): "Nothing is more definitely settled than he must act for himself . . . by a combination of all these agencies can be effectually stamped out lynch law . . . 'The gods help those who help themselves.'" The phrase "by . . . all these agencies can be effectively stamped out lynch law" reverses the expected syntax, causing the stumbling reader to work harder— and accept a part in the stamping out.

But other protest artists ask whether empathetic engagement will really prompt action. "The ultimate question," acknowledges Ginsberg, is "how to make poetry that will make people cry." But "is tender heart enough? . . . If you have tender heart, will you have clear enough vision to define the problem?" Richard Wright, for example, was troubled by the "tender-heart" response to his *Uncle Tom's Children* (1938). "When the reviews of that book began to appear, I realized that I had made an awfully naïve mistake," he remembered in 1940. "I found that I had written a book which even bankers' daughters could read and weep over and feel good about. I swore to myself that if I ever wrote another book, no one would weep over it; that it would be so hard and deep that they would have to face it without the consolation of tears." As early as 1937 Wright protested this "consolation of tears," writing bitterly in a newspaper column: "Negro, with 3 week old baby, begs food on streets . . . if you are the type to weep you can have a good cry over this and then feel good, 'purged,' you know."[8]

Noting this question of the ultimate value of a "tender heart" by itself, some protest artists connect knowledge and emotion: feelings lead to a search for knowledge, and in turn this knowledge deepens emotional response. When a reader is emotionally exhausted, knowledge will remain. Stanton demanded thought: "Do all you can, *no matter what,* to get people to think on your reform," she advises; "then, if the reform is good, it will come about in due season." Others combine shock value with empathy: Abel Meeropol praised Billie Holiday's rendition of "Strange Fruit" (1939), which could "jolt the audience out of its complacency anywhere," John Balaban explains that his early poems about Vietnam were meant to "shock and sicken" his American audience, and Tim O'Brien claims that the shock value in his work "*awakens* the reader, and shatters the abstract language of war." He adds: "So many images of war don't endure for the reader—it's the effect of a TV clip followed by a Cheerios ad. But my fiction asks readers not to shirk or look away." Equally, Steinbeck claims to have done his "damndest to rip a reader's nerves to rags" with *The Grapes of Wrath* (1939). The breast-feeding tableau in Steinbeck's novel is intended to shock, as are the suicide moment in *Life in the Iron Mills* (1861), the meatpacking scenes in *The Jungle,* and Agee's descriptions of masturbation in *Let Us Now Praise Famous Men.*[9]

While some writers insist that imaginative empathy must transform the self before the self can change society, others—still questioning the practical value of empathetic connection—maintain that taking action to change society will eventually transform the self. Child claimed that ideas needed to change first: "public sentiment cannot be made *by* political machinery; though political parties *can* be changed by public sentiment." She warns, "Great political changes may be forced by the pressure of external circumstances, without a corresponding change in the moral sentiment of a nation, but in all such cases, the change is worse than useless." But Stanton believed the political changed the personal, and Chisholm believed that equality before the law would begin a process of attitude change: women would no longer feel inferior, and men would find it harder to perpetuate myths of male superiority.[10]

One final politics of connection in protest literature is a connection to the self. Protest writers transform the country's inner life, and often their own. For example, *Looking Backward* (1888) changed Edward Bellamy, who began to focus on reform after its publication, writing to the *Atlantic Monthly* editor Horace Scudder in 1890: "My eyes have been opened to the evils and faults of our social state and I have begun to cherish a clear hope of better things." Similarly, Nick Ut's Vietnam war image "Napalm" (1972) changed his life. After taking his famous photograph of Kim Phuc he drove her ten miles to Cu Chi hospital, which was full of dying soldiers. Ut begged the nurses to treat her, finally succeeding after telling them he was a reporter. Phuc, who lives in Toronto, is now part of his family. They visit and speak by phone, and she calls him "Uncle Nick."[11]

The Politics of Form

These combinations of empathy, shock value, and knowledge—and protest literature's connections across movements, and between writers, readers, and subjects—are central to protest writers' politics of form. The blueprints of

American protest literature combine aesthetics and ideologies, offering a poetics of engagement and making form central to political protest. Identifying this politics of form, *American Protest Literature* takes up Terry Eagleton's suggestion that "'commitment' . . . reveals itself in how far the artist reconstructs the artistic forms at his disposal, turning authors, readers and spectators into collaborators."[12]

Commitment to a politics of form is revealed in other ways. For example, in *Uncle Tom's Cabin* (1852), Harriet Beecher Stowe equalizes black and white women when she describes both *as* the food they prepare: the black slave Aunt Chloe is shown trussing chicken with a face "so glossy as to suggest . . . she might have been washed over with white of eggs, like one of her own tea rusks," and the white Quaker Rachel Halliday first appears "sorting some dried peaches" with a face "round and rosy . . . suggestive of a ripe peach." Steinbeck makes literary form political by putting a predetermining interchapter before each narrative chapter in *The Grapes of Wrath,* to express the migrants' loss of agency. Tim O'Brien's politics of form in his collection of Vietnam stories, *The Things They Carried* (1990), is the looping from story to story. "Though each protest medium has its place, *this* form of Vietnam literature matches its looping subject—the circular war," explains O'Brien in an interview. O'Brien also connects his form to traumatic memories: "To tell stories in a linear way would be deceitful. War and trauma don't end in a literal sense, they reverberate across time, and my repetitions are a way to get at this psychological truth." Another Vietnam writer, John Balaban, claims poetry as the best form for protest literature, because its immediacy brings with it an obligation to take action.[13]

In developing a relationship between literary form and political content, protest artists try to balance the exigencies of protest against those of aesthetics. Though "propaganda itself is preferable to shallow, truckling imitation," said the Harlem Renaissance writer Alain Locke in 1928, beauty is literature's "best priest," psalms "more effective than sermons." Similarly balancing politics and form in 1938, Glenway Wescott said of Walker Evans's photographs: "For me this is better propaganda than it would be if it were not aesthetically enjoyable. It is because I enjoy looking that I go on looking until the pity and the shame are impressed upon me, unforgettably." While Evans and other protest artists do take on a "role beyond . . . entertainer," as Ellison put it, they also offer pleasure in the moment of confrontation: something to dance, march, and courageously sing to.[14]

This creation of protest as art accompanies a protest *against* art. Some artists put words and images in tension to make this protest: at one point Wright's text for *12 Million Black Voices* (1941) describes green fields and budding honeysuckle, while on the facing page an image of dry, dusty land marks their absence. On the next page, Wright hints at the reason for this disjunction: "To paint a picture of how we live . . . is to compete with the mighty artists . . . the newspapers . . . They have painted one picture: charming, idyllic, romantic; but we live another." Similarly, Roy DeCarava and Langston Hughes's image-text, *The Sweet Flypaper of Life* (1955), stages a battle between the visual and the written. While Hughes's text celebrates Harlem as bustling and full, DeCarava's images show isolated figures and empty spaces. The written word has failed its subject, and protest artists try to reclaim the act of representation—sometimes pointing out the long history of words as protest. In *12 Million Black Voices*, Wright observes: "We stole words from the grudging lips of the Lords of the Land . . . we proceeded to build our language . . . by assigning to common, simple words new meanings, meanings which enabled us to speak of revolt in the actual presence of the Lords of the Land without their being aware!" Like many protest artists, Wright offers a redefinition of the nature of protest, and of literature.

The Politics of Appropriation

Wright's image of stealing "words from the grudging lips of the Lords of the Land" points to another important strategy in protest literature: appropriation. American protest literature has a long tradition of transforming images, ideas, and language placed in new contexts into a living protest legacy. Protest artists appropriate the master's tools and dismantle the master's house—for example, the abolitionists used technical diagrams of slave ships to protest slavery; James Allen recontextualized photographs celebrating lynchings for *Without Sanctuary* (2000); and anti-lynching protest writers stole the rhetoric and imagery of Christianity from lynch mobs. Creating figures of black Christs, writers like W. E. B. Du Bois and Langston Hughes meet white supremacists in their own performance space.

One such appropriation of the master's tools comes in Claude McKay's poem "The Lynching" (1920). Written during the resurgence of the Ku Klux Klan, with its particularly stylized lynching rituals, McKay's adaptation of the Italian sonnet form allows him to set a slow pace that echoes the prolonged torture of lynching practices. Ida B. Wells uses a similar strategy of appropriation. Fashioning her anti-lynching protest from material generated by lynchers themselves, she quotes white newspapers at length in her anti-lynching protest pamphlets, explaining: "Out of their own mouths shall the murderers be condemned." She explained this strategy to Douglass. Waiting with him to speak at a meeting, she observed that he was nervous and she was composed. "That is because you are an orator, Mr. Douglass," she said. "I am only a mouthpiece through which to tell the story of lynching . . . I do not have to embellish it; it makes its own way."[15]

But though they appropriate the master's tools, protest writers also imagine their words as weapons, their pens as swords. Douglass claims that words are only useful "as they stimulate to blows," and Wright imagines "using words as a weapon, using them as one would use a club." Audre Lorde calls herself "a Black woman warrior poet," and Gwendolyn Brooks describes Hughes as a "hatchet." Amiri Baraka depicts poems as daggers, fists, and poison gas in "Black Art" (1966), and words as "fire darts" in "For Malcolm" (1965). Equally, Agee called the camera a gun, Riis said he photographed the poor like a "war correspondent," and for years Guthrie had a sign on his guitar that read, "This Machine Kills Fascists." In 1970, the Black Panther Party member Emory Douglas told artists to "take up their paints and brushes in one hand and their gun in the other," adding: "all of the Fascist American empire must be blown up in our pictures." For some protest writers, pens, cameras, guitars, and paintbrushes are weapons—tools that violently dismantle the master's house.[16]

The Politics of Memory

Many protest writers also appropriate pieces of earlier reform movements as they redraw America's blueprints. Recycling earlier protest literature, fitting old tunes with new words in new circumstances, protest writers debunk the myth of American history and literature as a series of fresh starts—of America as a perpetual New World. With their acknowledged and reshaped ancestry, protest writers challenge the particularly pervasive idea that protest movements are without memory, never putting down roots. Though they seek and find new countries, then set sail for better ones, protest writers carry fragments along.

This book begins with the American Revolution, at the moment when a language of independence, equality, and universal rights defined a new genre. Claiming this heritage of dissent, the protest artists who came after made America a protest nation and protest literature the most American of forms. "We do not even know that the literature of America is above everything else a literature of protest and of rebellion," complained the socialist writer Floyd Dell in 1920; "not knowing the past, we cannot learn by its mistakes . . . We only slowly come to learn that what we sometimes contemptuously call 'American' is not American at all: that it is, astonishingly enough, *we* who are American: that Debs and Haywood are as American as Franklin and Lincoln." Similarly emphasizing an American tradition of patriotic protest, and connecting his own protest movement to the Revolution, Wendell Phillips said of abolitionism in 1859: "it may be treason, but the fact is it runs in the blood. We were traitors in 1776."[17]

After abolitionism, American protest literature builds on the writings of Phillips and other abolitionists. Ellison observes that "the Constitution and the Bill of Rights made up the acting script which future Americans would follow in the process of improvising the futuristic drama of American democracy," and protest writers have certainly tried to close the loopholes in those documents. But after the Civil War and Reconstruction, the Emancipation Proclamation and the Thirteenth through Fifteenth Amendments became a new acting script: post-Emancipation writers acknowledge the limitations in practice of the rights won—demanding that America close the gap between ideals and reality—while claiming those ideals for new groups in American society, too.[18]

For example, Sinclair set out to write the *Uncle Tom's Cabin* of wage slavery, comparing chattel slavery to wage slavery in *The Jungle,* and claimed that abolitionism was an early form of socialism. Eugene V. Debs looked to the abolitionists as his heroes, demanding a John Brown for wage slavery. "John Brown's Body" was rewritten by Ralph Chaplin as "Solidarity Forever," and hip-hop artists traced a line from overseer to officer. The John Brown Anti-Klan Committee and the Black Panthers called on Brown. Michael Harrington, who took up Jacob Riis's idea of "the other half," was often introduced as "the author of *The Other America,* the book that sparked the war on poverty," echoing Lincoln's purported comment that Stowe's book had started a big war, and the Vietnam-era folksinger "Country" Joe McDonald reverses Lincoln's comment in claiming (with tongue in cheek) to be the singer that *stopped* the Vietnam war.

Beyond the foundational eras of the Revolution and abolitionism, protest writers connect with other moments in the history of American protest. Ginsberg wanted to speak the unspeakable, and calls on Walt Whitman as his forebear. The documentary style of Sinclair and Agee influenced the Vietnam-era New Journalism of Michael Herr and Norman Mailer. Farm Security Administration photographers returned to Hine's survey tradition, and the rural Alabama children in Evans's images seem the visual descendants of Hine's factory children. Nineteenth-century feminists also looked to their predecessors and forward to their successors: in 1902 Susan B. Anthony anticipated a new "generation of . . . strong, courageous, capable young women" who would take her place and complete her work. Second-wave feminists then looked back to Anthony and feminism's first wave, diving into what Adrienne Rich calls "the earth-deposits of our history."[19]

These historical connections gave protest writers courage. "If the house is not yet finished, Don't be discouraged, builder!" writes Hughes in "Freedom's Plow" (1943). "The plan and the pattern is here, woven from the beginning

xxviii   Introduction

into the warp and woof of America." Historical connections also offered correction. In 1853 the radical abolitionist Gerrit Smith said that *Uncle Tom's Cabin* shouldn't stand alone. "I have just read *The White Slave,* written by Richard Hildreth of Boston," he wrote to Douglass. "I am very much pleased with this Book. If not as highly dramatic and entertaining as *Uncle Tom's Cabin,* it is, perhaps, even more philosophical and instructive. Both Books should be in every family." What James Baldwin would later dub "Everybody's Protest Novel" wasn't the only protest novel. Used as a model by Bellamy and Sinclair, as a negative spur by Baldwin and Carl Wittman, and eventually transformed by Bill T. Jones, Stowe's novel needed corrective dialogue with other protest literature to make it whole.[20]

Whether it looks backward in order to move America forward, builds connections across movements, demands empathy from readers, transforms its creators, crafts a politics of form, appropriates the master's tools, or makes words into weapons, American protest literature tries to remake "a world beautiful," as London puts it. The protest cycle beats on, boats against the current.

Notes

1. Jack London, introduction to Upton Sinclair, ed., *The Cry for Justice* (Philadelphia: John C. Winston, 1915), 10–11; Ralph Ellison, *Juneteenth* (New York: Vintage, 1999), 17.

2. Frederick Douglass, "Pictures," unpublished manuscript (?late 1864), Frederick Douglass Papers, Library of Congress; Lorenzo Thomas, "How to See though Poetry" (2002), in *Civil Disobediences* (Minneapolis: Coffee House Press, 2004), 345.

3. Ellison, "The Novel as a Function of American Democracy" (1967), in *The Collected Essays of Ralph Ellison,* 767; Woody Guthrie, in John Greenaway, *American Folk-Songs of Protest* (Philadelphia: University of Pennsylvania Press, 1953), 289; Allen Ginsberg, "Revolutionary Poetics" (1989), in *Civil Disobediences,* 245, 265–266.

4. John Dewey, *Education Today* (New York: Putnam, 1940), 357.

5. Lydia Maria Child, in the *National Anti-Slavery Standard,* March 6, 1840; Elizabeth Cady Stanton, *The Women's Bible* (1898; Boston: Northeastern University Press, 1993), 11; Douglass, in *The Woman's Journal,* April 14, 1888.

6. Malcolm X, in George Plimpton, "Miami Notebook: Cassius Clay and Malcolm X," *Harper's,* June 1964: 57; and in *Malcom X on Afro-American History* (New York: Pathfinder Press, 1970), 44.

7. John Steinbeck (1955), in *Writers at Work* (New York: Viking, 1976), 183; Audre Lorde, "Sisterhood and Survival," *The Black Scholar,* March/April 1986: 5–7.

8. Ginsberg, "Revolutionary Poetics," 263; Wright, "How 'Bigger' Was Born," in *Native Son,* 531; Wright, *The Daily Worker,* August 4, 1937.

9. Stanton (1888), in Theodore Stanton, ed., *Elizabeth Cady Stanton* (New York: Harper, 1922), 252; Balaban, interview with Zoe Trodd (07/13/05); O'Brien, interview with Zoe Trodd (07/12/05).

10. Child, *Letters from New York* (London: Richard Bentley, 1846), 157; Child, "Dissolution of the Union," *Liberator,* May 20, 1842.

11. Edward Bellamy, in Daphne Patai, "Edward Bellamy," in Mari Jo and Paul Buhle, eds., *The American Radical* (New York: Routledge, 1994), 73.

12. Terry Eagleton, *Marxism and Literary Criticism* (Berkeley: University of California Press, 1976), 12.

13. Harriet Beecher Stowe, *Uncle Tom's Cabin* (1852; rept. New York: Penguin Books, 1988), 66–67, 215; O'Brien, interview with Zoe Trodd (07/12/05); Balaban, interview with Zoe Trodd (07/13/05).

14. Alain Locke, "Art or Propaganda?" *Harlem 1,* November 1928: 12–13; Glenway Wescott, *U.S. Camera,* 1, 1938: 67.

15. Ida B. Wells, *A Red Record* (1895), in Jacqueline Jones Royster, ed., *Southern Horrors and Other Writings: The Anti-Lynching Campaign of Ida B. Wells, 1892–1900* (Boston: Bedford Books, 1997), 82; Wells, in Alfreda M. Duster, ed., *Crusade for Justice: The Autobiography of Ida B. Wells* (Chicago: University of Chicago Press, 1970), 231.

16. Douglass, "Men of Color to Arms" (1863), in *Frederick Douglass: Selected Speeches and Writings* (Chicago: Lawrence Hill Books, 1999), 526; Wright, *Black Boy* (1945; rept. New York: Harper, 1993), 248; Lorde, "The Transformation of Silence into Action," in *Sister Outsider: Essays and Speeches* (Trumansburg, N.Y.: Crossing Press, 1984), 41. Gwendolyn Brooks, "Langston Hughes" (1963), in *Blacks* (Chicago: Third World Press, 1987), 396; Jacob Riis, *The Making of an American* (New York: Macmillan, 1901), 272; Emory Douglas, "Art," *Nation,* October 19, 1970: 382.

17. Floyd Dell, "Our America," *The Liberator,* III, January 1920: 46; Wendell Phillips (1859), in Zoe Trodd and John Stauffer, eds., *Meteor of War: The John Brown Story* (New York: Brandywine Press, 2004), 13.

18. Ellison, *Collected Essays,* 855. For an argument that these documents were the equivalent of a new Constitution, see Eric Foner, "The Second American Revolution," *In These Times,* September 16–22, 1987.

19. Susan B. Anthony, letter to Elizabeth Cady Stanton, 1902, in Daniel Katz, ed., *Why Freedom Matters* (New York: Workman, 2003), 137; Rich, "Power" (1974), in *The Dream of a Common Language* (New York: Norton, 1978), 3.

20. Gerrit Smith, in *Frederick Douglass' Paper,* January 28, 1853.

1

DECLARING

INDEPENDENCE

The
American
Revolution

A Political Litany

1775

American protest literature begins in bitter laughter; at the King with a "tooth-full of brains" and at the bloody noses of British captains. To Philip Freneau (1752–1832), America's first great satirist in the protest tradition, the world was too serious *not* to laugh at. His satirical poetry offered social commentary with the clarity of a pamphlet; like Revolutionary-era pamphleteers, he created a language for his political subject matter. He satirized pompous oratory and pretentious imitations of the English poets, and addressed Americans in a colloquial style: "To the Americans" (1775) calls the country to war: "so virtuous is your cause, I say, / Hell must prevail, if Britain gains the day."

Freneau fought as a militiaman during the war and was captured by a British prison ship in 1780. His poem about the incident, "The British Prison Ship," along with "A Political Litany," "American Liberty," and "George the Third's Soliloquy," earned him a reputation as the poet of the American Revolution. In 1790, James Madison and Thomas Jefferson asked him to launch a newspaper countering John Fenno's Hamiltonian paper. Freneau's *National Gazette* espoused Jeffersonian Republicanism and made him the first great campaigning editor in America, the forebear of William Lloyd Garrison and Frederick Douglass. He remained as editor until 1793.

Further reading: Jacob Axelrad, *Philip Freneau, Champion of Democracy* (1967); Gilbert Highet, *The Anatomy of Satire* (1962).

Libera nos, Domine—Deliver us, O Lord, *not only from British Dependence, but also,*

From a junto that labor with absolute power,
Whose schemes disappointed have made them look sour;
From the lords of the council, who fight against freedom
Who still follow on where delusion shall lead them.

From groups at St. James's who slight our petitions,
And fools that are waiting for further submissions—
From a nation whose manners are rough and severe,
From scoundrels and rascals,—do keep us all clear.

From pirates sent out by command of the king
To murder and plunder, but never to swing;

From *Wallace,* and *Greaves,* and *Vipers* and *Roses,*
Who, if heaven pleases, we'll give bloody noses.

From the valiant *Dunmore,* with his crew of banditti,
Who plunder Virginians at *Williamsburg* city,
From hot-headed *Montague,* mighty to swear,
The little fat man with his pretty white hair.

From bishops in Britain, who butchers are grown,
From slaves, that would die for a smile from the throne,
From assemblies that vote against *Congress proceedings,*
(Who now see the fruit of their stupid misleadings).

From *Tryon,* the mighty, who flies from our city,
And swelled with importance, disdains the committee:
(But since he is pleased to proclaim us his foes,
What the devil care we where the devil he goes.)

From the caitiff, lord *North,* who would bind us in chains,
From our noble king Log, with his tooth-full of brains,
Who dreams, and is certain (when taking a nap)
He has conquered our lands as they lay on his map.

From a kingdom that bullies, and hectors, and swears,
We send up to heaven our wishes and prayers
That we, disunited, may freemen be still,
And Britain go on—to be damned if she will.

From Common Sense

<u>1776</u>

Thomas Paine (1732–1809) wanted to make a new world. He envisaged an egalitarian, republican society, and in his pamphlet *Common Sense* sketched a map of that utopia. By 1791 his utopia seemed real: he observed in *The Rights of Man* that mankind need no longer say, "Had we . . . a place to stand upon, we might raise the world."

Common Sense captured the colonists' imaginations. They had begun fighting in June 1775 but by the year's end were still unsure *what* they were fighting for. Some sought separation, others reconciliation. Only a third of the members of the 1775 winter Congress favored independence. But in January 1776 *Common Sense* declared that America's struggle was for independence and democracy. The most popular of some two thousand pamphlets published during the Revolution, it sold 500,000 copies within the year. Its influence on the Declaration of Independence seemed so evident that many believed Paine had written that, too.

Paine's rage against British violations expelled any idea that colonists might remain loyal to the throne. He uses the language of universal rights and individual sovereignty to argue against reconciliation and prophetic language to invoke "the divine law," linking America's independence to God's will and depicting hereditary succession as a kind of original sin. "Had the Spirit of prophecy directed the birth of a publication, it could not have fallen upon a more fortunate period," wrote one reader in the *Boston Gazette.* "*Common Sense,* like a ray of revelation, has come in seasonably to clear our doubts." It was a spiritual reawakening: "We were blind, but on reading these enlightening words the scales have fallen from our eyes," claimed another in the *Connecticut Gazette.* Another wrote to the *Providence Gazette* to praise Paine's "facts," "reasoning," and plain "stile," but also his "wonders and miracles."

Mingling miracle, reason, and plain "stile," Paine forged a new political language. He roots his arguments in common experience and addresses his audience directly. His "common sense" means plain reason, common sentiment, and natural empathy, and he appeals to both feeling and reason, using analogies, logic, and comedy, countering objections, explaining economics, and appealing to his readers' consciences.

Born in England, Paine arrived in Philadelphia in 1774 to work as a printer. *Common Sense,* his first success, made *him* as much as it made America. Commentators heralded "the Age of Paine," and in 1805 John Adams doubted "whether any man in the world has had more influence . . . for the last thirty years." But when Paine returned to America in 1802 after a spell in Europe, the "Age of Paine" was over. A Federalist ideology had made his radicalism a thing of the past and he died in obscurity on June 8, 1809. The poet of the Revolution, Philip Freneau, attempted to rehabilitate Paine, writing in a poem of

1815: "To tyrants and the tyrant crew, / Indeed, he was the bane; / He writ, and gave them all their due, / And signed it— / THOMAS PAINE."

Further reading: Eric Foner, *Tom Paine and Revolutionary America* (1976); Gordon Wood, *The Radicalism of the American Revolution* (1992).

Perhaps the sentiments contained in the following pages, are not yet sufficiently fashionable to procure them general favor; a long habit of not thinking a thing wrong, gives it a superficial appearance of being right, and raises at first a formidable outcry in defence of custom. But tumult soon subsides. Time makes more converts than reason . . . The cause of America is, in a great measure, the cause of all mankind. Many circumstances have, and will arise, which are not local, but universal, and through which the principles of all lovers of mankind are affected, and in the event of which, their affections are interested. The laying a country desolate with fire and sword, declaring war against the natural rights of all mankind, and extirpating the defenders thereof from the face of the earth, is the concern of every man to whom nature hath given the power of feeling; of which class, regardless of party censure, is the AUTHOR . . .

In the following pages I offer nothing more than simple facts, plain arguments, and common sense; and have no other preliminaries to settle with the reader, than that he will divest himself of prejudice and prepossession, and suffer his reason and his feelings to determine for themselves; that he will put on, or rather that he will not put off the true character of a man, and generously enlarge his views beyond the present day.

Volumes have been written on the subject of the struggle between England and America . . . The sun never shined on a cause of greater worth. 'Tis not the affair of a city, a country, a province, or a kingdom, but of a continent—of at least one eighth part of the habitable globe. 'Tis not the concern of a day, a year, or an age; posterity are virtually involved in the contest, and will be more or less affected, even to the end of time, by the proceedings now. Now is the seed time of continental union, faith and honor. The least fracture now will be like a name engraved with the point of a pin on the tender rind of a young oak; The wound will enlarge with the tree, and posterity read it in full grown characters . . .

As much hath been said of the advantages of reconciliation, which, like an agreeable dream, hath passed away and left us as we were, it is but right, that we should examine the contrary side of the argument, and inquire into some of the many material injuries which these colonies sustain, and always will sustain, by being connected with, and dependant on Great Britain. To examine that connection and dependence, on the principles of nature and common sense, to see what we have to trust to, if separated, and what we are to expect, if dependant.

I have heard it asserted by some, that as America hath flourished under her former connection with Great Britain, that the same connection is necessary towards her future happiness, and will always have the same effect. Nothing can be more fallacious than this kind of argument. We may as well assert, that because a child has thrived upon milk, that it is never to have meat; or that the first twenty years of our lives is to become a precedent for the next twenty. But even this is admitting more than is true, for I answer roundly, that America would have flourished as much, and probably much more, had no European power had any thing to do with her. The commerce by which she hath enriched herself are the necessaries of life, and will always have a market while eating is the custom of Europe.

But she has protected us, say some. That she hath engrossed us is true, and defended the continent at our expense as well as her own is admitted, and she would have defended Turkey from the same motive, viz., the sake of trade and dominion.

Alas! we have been long led away by ancient prejudices and made large sacrifices to superstition. We have boasted the protection of Great Britain, without considering, that her motive was interest not attachment; that she did not protect us from our enemies on our account, but from her enemies on her own account, from those who had no quarrel with us on any other account, and who will always be our enemies on the same account. Let Britain wave her pretensions to the continent, or the continent throw off the dependance, and we should be at peace with France and Spain were they at war with Britain. The miseries of Hanover last war, ought to warn us against connections . . .

It is repugnant to reason, to the universal order of things, to all examples from the former ages, to suppose, that this continent can longer remain subject to any external power. The most sanguine in Britain does not think so. The utmost stretch of human wisdom cannot, at this time compass a plan short of separation, which can promise the continent even a year's security. Reconciliation is now a fallacious dream. Nature hath deserted the connection, and Art cannot supply her place. For, as Milton wisely expresses, "never can true reconcilement grow where wounds of deadly hate have pierced so deep."

Every quiet method for peace hath been ineffectual. Our prayers have been rejected with disdain; and only tended to convince us, that nothing flatters vanity, or confirms obstinacy in kings more than repeated petitioning—and nothing hath contributed more than that very measure to make the kings of Europe absolute: Witness Denmark and Sweden. Wherefore since nothing but blows will do, for God's sake, let us come to a final separation, and not leave the next generation to be cutting throats, under the violated unmeaning names of parent and child . . .

But where says some is the king of America? I'll tell you Friend, he reigns above, and doth not make havoc of mankind like the Royal of Britain. Yet that we may not appear to be defective even in earthly honors, let a day be solemnly set apart for proclaiming the charter; let it be brought forth placed on the divine law, the word of God; let a crown be placed thereon, by which the world may know, that so far as we approve of monarchy, that in America the law is king. For as in absolute governments the king is law, so in free countries the law ought to be king; and there ought to be no other. But lest any ill use should afterwards arise, let the crown at the conclusion of the ceremony be demolished, and scattered among the people whose right it is.

A government of our own is our natural right: And when a man seriously reflects on the precariousness of human affairs, he will become convinced, that it is infinitely wiser and safer, to form a constitution of our own in a cool deliberate manner, while we have it in our power, than to trust such an interesting event to time and chance. If we omit it now, some Massenello may hereafter arise, who laying hold of popular disquietudes, may collect together the desperate and the discontented, and by assuming to themselves the powers of government, may sweep away the liberties of the continent like a deluge. Should the government of America return again into the hands of Britain, the tottering situation of things, will be a temptation for some desperate adventurer to try his fortune; and in such a case, what relief can Britain give? Ere she could hear the news the fatal business might be done, and ourselves suffering like the wretched Britons under the oppression of the Conqueror. Ye that oppose independence now, ye know not what ye do; ye are opening a door to eternal tyranny, by keeping vacant the seat of government.

There are thousands, and tens of thousands, who would think it glorious to expel from the continent, that barbarous and hellish power, which hath stirred up the Indians and Negroes to destroy us; the cruelty hath a double guilt, it is dealing brutally by us, and treacherously by them. To talk of friendship with those in whom our reason forbids us to have faith, and our affections (wounded through a thousand pores) instruct us to detest, is madness and folly. Every day wears out the little remains of kindred between us and them, and can there be any reason to hope, that as the relationship expires, the affection will increase, or that we shall agree better, when we have ten times more and greater concerns to quarrel over than ever?

Ye that tell us of harmony and reconciliation, can ye restore to us the time that is past? Can ye give to prostitution its former innocence? Neither can ye reconcile Britain and America. The last cord now is broken, the people of England are presenting addresses against us. There are injuries which nature cannot forgive; she would cease to be nature if she did. As well can the lover forgive the ravisher of his mistress, as the continent forgive the murders of Britain. The Almighty hath implanted in us these inextinguishable feelings for good and wise purposes. They are the guardians of his image in our hearts. They distinguish us from the herd of common animals. The social compact would dissolve, and justice be extirpated from the earth, or have only a casual existence were we callous to the touches of affection. The robber and the murderer, would often escape unpunished, did not the injuries which our tempers sustain, provoke us into justice.

O ye that love mankind! Ye that dare oppose, not only the tyranny, but the tyrant, stand forth! Every spot of the old world is overrun with oppression. Freedom hath been hunted round the globe. Asia, and Africa, have long expelled her. Europe regards her like a stranger, and England hath given her warning to depart. O! receive the fugitive, and prepare in time an asylum for mankind . . .

The infant state of the Colonies, as it is called, so far from being against, is an argument in favor of independence. We are sufficiently numerous, and were we more so, we might be less united. It is a matter worthy of observation, that the more a country is peopled, the smaller their armies are. In military numbers, the ancients far exceeded the moderns: and the reason is evident, for trade being the consequence of population, men become too much absorbed thereby to attend to anything else. Commerce diminishes the spirit, both of patriotism and military defence. And history sufficiently informs us, that the bravest achievements were always accomplished in the non-age of a nation. With the increase of commerce England hath lost its spirit. The city of London, notwithstanding its numbers, submits to continued insults with the patience of a coward. The more men have to lose, the less willing are they to venture. The rich are in general slaves to fear, and submit to courtly power with the trembling duplicity of a spaniel.

Youth is the seed-time of good habits, as well in nations as in individuals. It might be difficult, if not impossible, to form the Continent into one government half a century hence. The vast variety of interests, occasioned by an increase of trade and population, would create confusion. Colony would be against colony. Each being able might scorn each other's assistance: and while the proud and foolish gloried in their little distinctions, the wise would lament that the union had not been formed before. Wherefore, the present time is the true time for establishing it. The intimacy which is contracted in infancy, and the friendship which is formed in misfortune, are, of all others, the most lasting and unalterable. Our present union is marked with both these characters: we are young, and we have been distressed; but our concord hath withstood our troubles, and fixes a memorable area for posterity to glory in.

From The Dominion of Providence
over the Passions of Men

1776

Religion gave birth to America, or so observed Alexis de Tocqueville in 1840. Certainly by 1776, John Witherspoon thought this birth was overdue: the colonies were "in danger of becoming rotten." Though initially reluctant to politicize his pulpit, in July 1774 he had taken part in a state convention and recommended war. Then on May 17, 1776, a day of public prayer for the Continental Congress, Witherspoon gave his first political sermon. In "The Dominion of Providence," one of the most influential Revolutionary-era sermons, he offers an explication of a Biblical text, and a practical application of the text's truth. This application of doctrine to the manners of men was a model for protest literature, formulating both problem and solution. Witherspoon joins religious liberty to political and economic liberty, explains that liberty is God-given, and tells Americans it is their duty to resist oppression. Benjamin Franklin's August 1776 draft of the Great Seal motto echoed Witherspoon's sermon: "Rebellion to tyrants is obedience to God."

Witherspoon was elected to the Continental Congress in June 1776 and was the only practicing clergyman to sign the Declaration of Independence. As an active member of Congress until 1782, he sat on more than 100 legislative committees, but continued to give Sunday sermons, believing that ministers should shape a moral citizenry and that religion would sustain the republic.

Further reading: Jeffrey Morrison, *John Witherspoon and the Founding of the American Republic* (2005); Ellis Sandoz, *A Government of Laws* (1990).

While we give praise to God the supreme disposer of all events, for his interposition in our behalf, let us guard against the dangerous error of trusting in, or boasting of an arm of flesh. I could earnestly wish, that while our arms are crowned with success, we might content ourselves with a modest ascription of it to the power of the Highest. It has given me great uneasiness to read some ostentatious, vaunting expressions in our news-papers, though happily I think, much restrained of late. Let us not return to them again. If I am not mistaken, not only the holy scriptures in general, and the truths of the glorious gospel in particular, but the whole course of providence, seem intended to abase the pride of man, and lay the vain-glorious in the dust. How many instances does history furnish us with, of those who after exulting over, and despising their enemies, were signally and shamefully defeated. The truth is, I believe, the remark may be applied universally, and we may say, that through the whole frame of nature, and the whole system of human life, that which promises most, performs the least. The flowers of finest colour seldom have the sweetest fragrance. The trees of quickest groweth or fairest form, are seldom of the greatest value or duration. Deep waters move with least noise. Men who think most are seldom talkative. And I think it holds as much in war as in any thing, that every boaster is a coward.

Pardon me, my brethren, for insisting so much upon this, which may seem but an immaterial circumstance. It is in my opinion of very great moment. I look upon ostentation and confidence to be a sort of outrage upon Providence, and when it becomes general, and infuses itself into the spirit of a people, it is a forerunner of destruction. How does Goliath the champion armed in a most formidable manner, express his disdain of David the stripling with his sling and his stone, 1 Samuel xvii. 42, 43, 44, 45. "And when the Philistine looked about and saw David, he disdained him: for he was but a youth, and ruddy, and of a fair countenance. And the Philistine said unto David, Am I a dog, that thou comest to me with staves? And the Philistine cursed David by his gods, and the Philistine said to David, come to me, and I will give thy flesh unto the fowls of the air, and to the beasts of the field." But how just and modest the reply? "Then said David to the Philistine, thou comest to me with a sword and with a spear, and with a shield, but I come unto thee in the name of the Lord of hosts, the God of the armies of Israel, whom thou hast defied." I was well pleased with a remark of this kind thirty years ago in a pamphlet, in which it was observed, that there was a great deal of profane ostentation in the names given to ships of war, as the Victory, the Valient, the Thunderer, the Dreadnought, the Terrible, the Firebrand, the Furnace, the Lightning, the Infernal, and many more of the same kind. This the author considered as a symptom of the national character and manners very unfavorable, and not likely to obtain the blessing of the God of heaven.

From what has been said you may learn what encouragement you have to put your trust in God, and hope for his assistance in the present important conflict. He is the Lord of hosts, great in might, and strong in battle. Whoever hath his countenance and approbation, shall have the best at last. I do not mean to speak prophetically, but agreeably to the analogy of faith, and the principles of God's moral government. Some have observed that true religion, and in her train, dominion, riches, literature, and arts, have taken their course in a slow and gradual manner, from east to west, since the earth was settled after the flood, and from thence forebode the future glory of America. I leave this as a matter rather of conjecture than certainty, but observe, that if your cause is just, if your principles are pure, and if your conduct is prudent, you need not fear the multitude of opposing hosts.

If your cause is just—you may look with confidence to the Lord and intreat him to plead it as his own. You are all my witnesses, that this is the first time of my introducing any political subject into the pulpit. At this season however, it is not only lawful but necessary, and I willingly embrace the opportunity of declaring my opinion without any hesitation, that the cause in which America is now in arms, is the cause of justice, of liberty, and of human nature. So far as we have hitherto proceeded, I am satisfied that the confederacy of the colonies, has not been the effect of pride, resentment, or sedition, but of a deep and general conviction, that our civil and religious liberties, and consequently in a great measure the temporal and eternal happiness of us and our posterity, depended on the issue. The knowledge of God and his truths have from the beginning of the world been chiefly, if not entirely, confined to those parts of the earth, where some degree of liberty and political justice were to be seen, and great were the difficulties with which they had to struggle from the imperfection of human society, and the unjust decisions of usurped authority. There is not a single instance in history in which civil liberty was lost, and religious liberty preserved entire. If therefore we yield up our temporal property, we at the same time deliver the conscience into bondage.

You shall not, my brethren, hear from me in the pulpit, what you have never heard from me in conversation, I mean railing at the king personally, or even his ministers and the parliament, and people of Britain, as so many barbarous savages. Many of their actions have probably been worse than their intentions. That they should desire unlimited dominion, if they can obtain or preserve it, is neither new nor wonderful. I do not refuse submission to their unjust claims, because they are corrupt or profligate, although probably many of them are so, but because they are men, and therefore liable to all the selfish bias inseparable from human nature. I call this claim unjust, of making laws to bind us in all cases whatsoever, because they are separated from us, independent of us, and have an interest in opposing us. Would any man who could prevent it, give up his estate, person, and family, to the disposal of his neighbour, although he had liberty to chuse the wisest and the best master? Surely not. This is the true and proper hinge of the controversy between Great-Britain and America. It is however to be added, that such is their distance from us, that a wise and prudent administration of our affairs is as impossible as the claim of authority is unjust. Such is and must be their ignorance of the state of things here, so much time must elapse before an error can be seen and remedied, and so much injustice and partiality must be expected from the arts and misrepresentation of interested persons, that for these colonies to depend wholly upon the legislature of Great-Britain, would be like many other oppressive connexions, injury to the master, and ruin to the slave.

The management of the war itself on their part, would furnish new proof of this, if any were needful. Is it not manifest with what absurdity and impropriety they have conducted their own designs? We had nothing so much to fear as dissension, and they have by wanton and unnecessary cruelty forced us into union. At the same time to let us see what we have to expect, and what would be the fatal consequence of unlimited submission, they have uniformly called those acts *lenity,* which filled this whole continent with resentment and horror. The ineffable disdain expressed by our fellow subject, in saying, "That he would not harken to America, till she was at his feet," has armed more men, and inspired more deadly rage, than could have been done by laying waste a whole province with fire and sword. Again we wanted not numbers, but time, and they sent over handful after handful till we were ready to oppose a multitude greater than they have to send. In fine, if there was one place stronger than the rest, and more able and willing to resist, there they made the attack, and left the others till they were duly informed, completely incensed, and fully furnished with every instrument of war.

I mention these things, my brethren, not only as grounds of confidence in God, who can easily overthrow the wisdom of the wise, but as decisive proofs of the impossibility of these great and growing states, being safe and happy when every part of their internal polity is dependant on Great Britain. If, on account of their distance, and ignorance of our situation, they could not conduct their own quarrel with propriety for one year, how can they give direction and vigor to every department of our civil constitutions from age to age? There are fixed bounds to every human thing. When the branches of a tree grow very large and weighty, they fall off from the trunk. The sharpest sword will not pierce when it cannot reach. And there is a certain distance from the seat of government, where an attempt to rule will either produce tyranny and helpless subjection, or provoke resistance and effect a separation.

I have said, if your principles are pure—the meaning of this is, if your present opposition to the claims of the British ministry does not arise from a seditious and turbulent spirit, or a wanton contempt of legal authority; from a blind and factious attachment to particular persons or parties; or from a selfish rapacious disposition, and a desire to turn public confusion to private profit—but from a concern for the interest of your country, and the safety of yourselves and your posterity. On this subject I cannot help observing, that though it would be a miracle if there were not many selfish persons among us, and discoveries now and then made of mean and interested transactions, yet they have been comparatively inconsiderable both in number and effect. In general, there has been so great a degree of public spirit, that we have much more reason to be thankful for its vigor and prevalence, than to wonder at the few appearances of dishonesty or disaffection. It would be very uncandid to ascribe the universal ardor that has prevailed among all ranks of men, and the spirited exertions in the most distant colonies, to any thing else than public spirit. Nor was there ever perhaps in history so general a commotion from which religious differences have been so entirely excluded. Nothing of this kind has as yet been heard, except of late in the absurd, but malicious and detestable attempts of our few remaining enemies to introduce them. At the same time I must also, for the honor of this country observe, that though government in the ancient forms has been so long unhinged, and in some colonies not sufficient care taken to substitute another in its place; yet has there been, by common consent, a much greater degree of order and public peace, than men of reflection and experience foretold or expected. From all these circumstances I conclude favorably of the principles of the friends of liberty, and do earnestly exhort you to adopt and act upon those which have been described, and resist the influence of every other.

Once more, if to the justice of your cause, and the purity of your principles, you add prudence in your conduct, there will be the greatest reason to hope, by the blessing of God, for prosperity and success. By prudence in conducting this important struggle, I have chiefly in view union, firmness, and patience. Every body must perceive the absolute necessity of union. It is indeed in every body's mouth, and therefore instead of attempting to convince you of its importance, I will only caution you against the usual causes of division. If persons of every rank, instead of implicitly complying with the orders of those whom they themselves have chosen to direct, will needs judge every measure over again, when it comes to be put in execution; if different classes of men intermix their little private views, or clashing interest with public affairs, and marshal into parties, the merchant against the landholder, and the landholder against the merchant; if local provincial pride and jealousy arise, and you allow yourselves to speak with contempt of the courage, character, manners, or even language of particular places, you are doing a greater injury to the common cause, than you are aware of. If such practices are admitted among us, I shall look upon it as one of the most dangerous symptoms, and if they become general, a presage of approaching ruin . . .

Upon the whole, I beseech you to make a wise improvement of the present threatening aspect of public affairs, and to remember that your duty to God, to your country, to your families, and to yourselves, is the same. True religion is nothing else but an inward temper and outward conduct suited to your state and circumstances in providence at any time. And as peace with God and conformity to him, adds to the sweetness of created comforts while we possess them, so in times of difficulty and trial, it is in the man of piety and inward principle, that we may expect to find the uncorrupted patriot, the useful citizen, and the invincible soldier. God grant that in America true religion and civil liberty may be inseparable, and that the unjust attempts to destroy the one, may in the issue tend to the support and establishment of both.

The Declaration of Independence

"The Declaration of Independence makes a difference," wrote Herman Melville in 1849. This concept of "making" was central to the Declaration: if declaring independence created an independent nation, then words were making a new world. It was not a wholly new form of literature: in 1774 the Continental Congress drew up a statement of rights that included "A List of Infringements," and British writers had long published grievances against monarchs. But when Thomas Jefferson (1743–1826) undertook to draft the Declaration on behalf of the Continental Congress in 1776, his purpose, as he later explained, was not to invent a new form but rather to find terms "so plain and firm as to command their assent." Self-evident principles would be easily accepted, and so the preamble offered no new or complex justification, but rather a simple 202-word statement. The preamble's progression feels inevitable: within the sentences, single-syllable words progress toward three- and four-syllable words. The grievances then move thematically toward emotive heights. The Declaration's concision and rhythms embody the necessary revolution.

Jefferson was a master of rhetoric who likened great literature to music. He includes alliteration, a chiasmus, and a blend of short and long words in the penultimate paragraph. He also marked his draft with pause marks, emphasizing the dissolving of political bands, the separate and equal station of the powers of earth, and the laws of nature's God. These marks were included on the official broadside, for those reading it aloud. The Declaration appeared in the *Philadelphia Evening Post* on July 6, 1776, and public readings took place from July 8 onward.

Even more important for the protest tradition, Jefferson offers himself as the people's prophet: he uses "we," "our," and "us" (eleven times in the grievances), and later claimed that the Declaration was an "expression of the American mind." When Benjamin Franklin changed Jefferson's "sacred and undeniable" to "self-evident," he secularized the text. But, through its appeals to "Nature's God," the Declaration founded a prophetic tradition that includes Nat Turner, John Brown, Walt Whitman, Martin Luther King, Jr., and James Baldwin. Imagining new worlds in order to change society, the American prophetic tradition has been crucial to the protest tradition.

The Declaration made a new nation but—in spite of its importance to the prophetic tradition—it made no new world. Jefferson's draft included a denunciation of the slave trade but the final Declaration's failure to condemn slavery left America's "original sin" (as James Madison put it) lurking between its lines. The abolitionist Wendell Phillips would later write to Frederick Douglass that "the fathers, in 1776, signed . . . with the halter about their necks."

Further reading: James Darsey, *The Prophetic Tradition and Radical Rhetoric in America* (1997); Jay Fliegelman, *Declaring Independence* (1993).

When in the Course of human events, it becomes necessary for one people to dissolve the political bands which have connected them with another, and to assume among the powers of the earth, the separate and equal station to which the Laws of Nature and of Nature's God entitle them, a decent respect to the opinions of mankind requires that they should declare the causes which impel them to the separation.

We hold these truths to be self-evident, that all men are created equal, that they are endowed by their Creator with certain unalienable Rights, that among these are Life, Liberty and the pursuit of Happiness.—That to secure these rights, Governments are instituted among Men, deriving their just powers from the consent of the governed,—That whenever any Form of Government becomes destructive of these ends, it is the Right of the People to alter or to abolish it, and to institute new Government, laying its foundation on such principles and organizing its powers in such form, as to them shall seem most likely to effect their Safety and Happiness. Prudence, indeed, will dictate that Governments long established should not be changed for light and transient causes; and accordingly all experience hath shewn, that mankind are more disposed to suffer, while evils are sufferable, than to right themselves by abolishing the forms to which they are accustomed. But when a long train of abuses and usurpations, pursuing invariably the same Object evinces a design to reduce them under absolute Despotism, it is their right, it is their duty, to throw off such Government, and to provide new Guards for their future security.— Such has been the patient sufferance of these Colonies; and such is now the necessity which constrains them to alter their former Systems of Government. The history of the present King of Great Britain is a history of repeated injuries and usurpations, all having in direct object the establishment of an absolute Tyranny over these States. To prove this, let Facts be submitted to a candid world.

He has refused his Assent to Laws, the most wholesome and necessary for the public good.

He has forbidden his Governors to pass Laws of immediate and pressing importance, unless suspended in their operation till his Assent should be obtained; and when so suspended, he has utterly neglected to attend to them.

He has refused to pass other Laws for the accommodation of large districts of people, unless those people would relinquish the right of Representation in the Legislature, a right inestimable to them and formidable to tyrants only.

He has called together legislative bodies at places unusual, uncomfortable, and distant from the depository of their public Records, for the sole purpose of fatiguing them into compliance with his measures.

He has dissolved Representative Houses repeatedly, for opposing with manly firmness his invasions on the rights of the people.

He has refused for a long time, after such dissolutions, to cause others to be elected; whereby the Legislative powers, incapable of Annihilation, have returned to the People at large for their exercise; the State remaining in the mean time exposed to all the dangers of invasion from without, and convulsions within.

He has endeavoured to prevent the population of these States; for that purpose obstructing the Laws for Naturalization of Foreigners; refusing to pass others to encourage their migrations hither, and raising the conditions of new Appropriations of Lands.

He has obstructed the Administration of Justice, by refusing his Assent to Laws for establishing Judiciary powers.

He has made Judges dependent on his Will alone, for the tenure of their offices, and the amount and payment of their salaries.

He has erected a multitude of New Offices, and sent hither swarms of Officers to harrass our people, and eat out their substance.

He has kept among us, in times of peace, Standing Armies without the Consent of our legislatures.

He has affected to render the Military independent of and superior to the Civil power.

He has combined with others to subject us to a jurisdiction foreign to our constitution, and unacknowledged by our laws; giving his Assent to their Acts of pretended Legislation:

For Quartering large bodies of armed troops among us:

For protecting them, by a mock Trial, from punishment for any Murders which they should commit on the Inhabitants of these States:

For cutting off our Trade with all parts of the world:

For imposing Taxes on us without our Consent:

For depriving us in many cases, of the benefits of Trial by Jury:

For transporting us beyond Seas to be tried for pretended offences:

For abolishing the free System of English Laws in a neighbouring Province, establishing therein an Arbitrary government, and enlarging its Boundaries so as to render it at once an example and fit instrument for introducing the same absolute rule into these Colonies:

For taking away our Charters, abolishing our most valuable Laws, and altering fundamentally the Forms of our Governments:

For suspending our own Legislatures, and declaring themselves invested with power to legislate for us in all cases whatsoever.

He has abdicated Government here, by declaring us out of his Protection and waging War against us.

He has plundered our seas, ravaged our Coasts, burnt our towns, and destroyed the lives of our people.

He is at this time transporting large Armies of foreign Mercenaries to compleat the works of death, desolation and tyranny, already begun with circumstances of Cruelty & perfidy scarcely paralleled in the most barbarous ages, and totally unworthy the Head of a civilized nation.

He has constrained our fellow Citizens taken Captive on the high Seas to bear Arms against their Country, to become the executioners of their friends and Brethren, or to fall themselves by their Hands.

He has excited domestic insurrections amongst us, and has endeavoured to bring on the inhabitants of our frontiers, the merciless Indian Savages, whose known rule of warfare, is an undistinguished destruction of all ages, sexes and conditions.

In every stage of these Oppressions We have Petitioned for Redress in the most humble terms: Our repeated Petitions have been answered only by repeated injury. A Prince whose character is thus marked by every act which may define a Tyrant, is unfit to be the ruler of a free people.

Nor have We been wanting in attentions to our British brethren. We have warned them from time to time of attempts by their legislature to extend an unwarrantable jurisdiction over us. We have reminded them of the circumstances of our emigration and settlement here. We have appealed to their native justice and magnanimity, and we have conjured them by the ties of our common kindred to disavow these usurpations, which, would inevitably interrupt our connections and correspondence. They too have been deaf to the voice of justice and of consanguinity. We must, therefore, acquiesce in the necessity, which denounces our Separation, and hold them, as we hold the rest of mankind, Enemies in War, in Peace Friends.

We, therefore, the Representatives of the United States of America, in General Congress, Assembled, appealing to the Supreme Judge of the world for the rectitude of our intentions, do, in the Name, and by Authority of the good People of these Colonies, solemnly publish and declare, That these United Colonies are, and of Right ought to be Free and Independent States; that they are Absolved from all Allegiance to the British Crown, and that all political connection between them and the State of Great Britain, is and ought to be totally dissolved; and that as Free and Independent States, they have full Power to levy War, conclude Peace, contract Alliances, establish Commerce, and to do all other Acts and Things which Independent States may of right do. And for the support of this Declaration, with a firm reliance on the protection of divine Providence, we mutually pledge to each other our Lives, our Fortunes and our sacred Honor.

J. HECTOR ST. JOHN DE CRÈVECOEUR

From Letters from an American Farmer

1782

J. Hector St. John de Crèvecoeur (1735–1813) adopted the persona of a farmer-corre-spondent (one of the self-sufficient "cultivators of the earth," as Thomas Jefferson put it) and portrayed the consciousness of an emerging American society. Without a mediating narrator, *Letters* seemingly offers direct access to American life from what Crèvecoeur calls "an eye witness": the reader looks over the recipient's shoulder, an audience for the developing American self.

But in the excerpt printed here, the narrator is a "witness" to a scene of gothic horror: he encounters a slave in the woods, suspended in a cage. The slave is the strange fruit on America's tree of knowledge, a macabre vision of the country's original sin. Previously the narrator has pondered the possibilities for indefinite westward expansion and resisted what he calls "useless retrospect" in favor of "anticipated fields of future civilizations." But slavery breaks the future's spell. Now he cannot cease from retrospect. He loses faith in America, and at the end of the book abandons its civilization. The laws of nature have taught him that "self-preservation is the rule," a dark vision.

The new nation had offered a middle ground between the decadent Old World and the savage wilderness of the frontier, but after the encounter with slavery the narrator imagines this "center . . . tumbled down," and sees himself as "one of the stones of a ru-ined arch." America's original sin scatters the ruins of Old World hierarchies across the New World garden, and the country is no longer a source of regeneration for the peoples of Europe. In the years that followed, Native American and black writers would echo Crèvecoeur's vision of the center that would not hold, and protest the American dream gone bad.

Further reading: Duncan MacLeod, *Slavery, Race, and the American Revolution* (1974); Henry Nash Smith, *Virgin Land* (1950).

While all is joy, festivity, and happiness in Charles-Town, would you imagine that scenes of misery overspread in the country? Their ears by habit are be-come deaf, their hearts are hardened; they neither see, hear, nor feel for the woes of their poor slaves, from whose painful labours all their wealth proceeds. Here the horrors of slavery, the hardship of incessant toils, are unseen; and no one thinks with compassion of those showers of sweat and of tears which from the bodies of Africans, daily drop, and moisten the ground they till. The cracks of the whip urging these miserable beings to excessive labour, are far too distant from the gay Capital to be heard. The chosen race eat, drink, and live happy, while the unfortunate one grubs up the ground, raises indigo, or husks the rice; exposed to a sun full as scorching as their native one; without the support of good food, without the cordials of any chearing liquor. This great contrast has often afforded me subjects of the most afflicting meditation. On the one side, behold a people enjoying all that life affords most bewitching and pleasurable, without labour, without fatigue, hardly subjected to the trouble of wishing. With gold, dug from Peruvian mountains, they order vessels to the coasts of Guinea; by virtue of that gold, wars, murders, and devastations are committed in some harmless, peaceable African neighbourhood, where dwelt innocent people, who even knew not but that all men were black. The daughter torn from her weeping mother, the child from the wretched parents, the wife from the loving husband; whole families swept away and brought through storms and tempests to this rich metropolis! There, arranged like horses at a fair, they are branded like cattle, and then driven to toil, to starve, and to languish for a few years on the different plantations of these citizens. And for whom must they work? For persons they know not, and who have no other power over them than that of violence; no other right than what this accursed metal has given them! Strange order of things! Oh, Nature, where art thou?—Are not these blacks thy children as well as we? On the other side, nothing is to be seen but the most diffusive misery and wretchedness, unrelieved even in thought or wish! Day after day they drudge on without any prospect of ever reaping for themselves; they are obliged to devote their lives, their limbs, their will, and every vital exertion to swell the wealth of masters; who look not upon them with half the kindness and affection with which they consider their dogs and horses. Kindness and affection are not the portion of those who till the earth, who carry the burdens, who convert the logs into useful boards. This reward, simple and natural as one would conceive it, would border on humanity; and planters must have none of it!

If negroes are permitted to become fathers, this fatal indulgence only tends to increase their misery: the poor companions of their scanty pleasures are likewise the companions of their labours; and when at some critical seasons they could wish to see them relieved, with tears in their eyes they behold them perhaps doubly oppressed, obliged to bear the burden of nature—a fatal present—as well as that of unabated tasks. How many have I seen cursing the irresistible propensity, and regretting, that by having tasted of those harmless joys, they had become the authors of double misery to their wives. Like their masters, they are not permitted to partake of those ineffable sensations with which nature inspires the hearts of fathers and mothers; they must repel them all, and become callous and passive. This unnatural state often occasions the most acute, the most pungent of their afflictions; they have no time, like us, tenderly to rear their helpless offspring, to nurse them on their knees, to enjoy the delight of being parents. Their paternal fondness is embittered by considering, that if their children live, they must live to be slaves like themselves; no time is allowed them to exercise their pious office, the mothers must fasten them on their backs, and, with this double load, follow their husbands in the fields, where they too often hear no other sound than that of the voice or whip of the task-master, and the cries of their infants, broiling in the sun. These unfortunate creatures cry and weep like their parents, without a possibility of relief; the very instinct of the brute, so laudable, so irresistible, runs counter here to their master's interest; and to that god, all the laws of nature must give way. Thus planters get rich; so raw, so unexperienced am I in this mode of life, that were I to be possessed of a plantation, and my slaves treated as in general they are here, never could I rest in peace; my sleep would be perpetually disturbed by a retrospect of the frauds committed in Africa, in order to entrap them; frauds surpassing in enormity every thing which a common mind can possibly conceive. I should be thinking of the barbarous treatment they meet with on ship-board; of their anguish, of the despair necessarily inspired by their situation, when torn from their friends and relations; when delivered into the hands of a people differently coloured, whom they cannot understand; carried in a strange machine over an ever agitated element, which they had never seen before; and finally delivered over to the severities of the whippers, and the excessive labours of the field. Can it be possible that the force of custom should ever make me deaf to all these reflections, and as insensible to the injustice of that trade, and to their miseries, as the rich inhabitants of this town seem to be? What then is man; this being who boasts so much of the excellence and dignity of his nature, among that variety of unscrutable mysteries, of unsolvable problems, with which he is surrounded? The reason why man has been thus created, is not the least astonishing! . . .

Every where one part of the human species are taught the art of shedding the blood of the other; of setting fire to their dwellings; of levelling the works of their industry: half of the existence of nations regularly employed in destroying other nations. What little political felicity is to be met with here and there, has cost oceans of blood to purchase; as if good was never to be the portion of unhappy man. Republics, kingdoms, monarchies, founded either on fraud or successful violence, increase by pursuing the steps of the same policy, until they are destroyed in their turn, either by the influence of their own crimes, or by more successful but equally criminal enemies. If from this general review of human nature, we descend to the examination of what is called civilized society; there the combination of every natural and artificial want, makes us pay very dear for what little share of political felicity we enjoy. It is a strange heterogeneous assemblage of vices and virtues, and of a variety of other principles, for ever at war, for ever jarring for ever producing some dangerous, some distressing extreme. Where do you conceive then that nature intended we should be happy? Would you prefer the state of men in the woods, to that of men in a more improved situation? Evil preponderates in both; in the first they often eat each other for want of food, and in the other they often starve each other for want of room. For my part, I think the vices and miseries to be found in the latter, exceed those of the former; in which real evil is more scarce, more supportable, and less enormous. Yet we wish to see the earth peopled; to accomplish the happiness of kingdoms, which is said to consist in numbers. Gracious God! to what end is the introduction of so many beings into a mode of existence in which they must grope amidst as many errors, commit as many crimes, and meet with as many diseases, wants, and sufferings!

The following scene will I hope account for these melancholy reflections, and apologize for the gloomy thoughts with which I have filled this letter: my mind is, and always has been, oppressed since I became a witness to it. I was not long since invited to dine with a planter who lived three miles from ——, where he then resided. In order to avoid the heat of the sun, I resolved to go on foot, sheltered in a small path, leading through a pleasant wood. I was leisurely travelling along, attentively examining some peculiar plants which I had collected, when all at once I felt the air strongly agitated; though the day was perfectly calm and sultry. I immediately cast my eyes toward the cleared ground, from which I was but at a small distance, in order to see whether it was not occasioned by a sudden shower; when at that instant a sound resembling a deep rough voice, uttered, as I thought, a few inarticulate monosyllables. Alarmed and surprized, I precipitately looked all round, when I perceived at about six rods distance something resembling a cage, suspended to the limbs of a tree; all the branches of which appeared covered with large birds of prey, fluttering about, and anxiously endeavouring to perch on the cage. Actuated by an involuntary motion of my hands, more than by any design of my mind, I fired at them; they all flew to a short distance, with a most hideous noise: when, horrid to think and painful to repeat, I perceived a negro, suspended in the cage, and left there to expire! I shudder when I recollect that the birds had already picked out his eyes, his cheek bones were bare; his arms had been attacked in several places, and his body seemed covered with a multitude of wounds. From the edges of the hollow sockets and from the lacerations with which he was disfigured, the blood slowly dropped, and tinged the ground beneath. No sooner were the birds flown, than swarms of insects covered the whole body of this unfortunate wretch, eager to feed on his mangled flesh and to drink his blood. I found myself suddenly arrested by the power of affright and terror; my nerves were convulsed; I trembled, I stood motionless, involuntarily contemplating the fate of this negro, in all its dismal latitude. The living spectre, though deprived of his eyes, could still distinctly hear, and in his uncouth dialect begged me to give him some water to allay his thirst. Humanity herself would have recoiled back with horror; she would have balanced whether to lessen such reliefless distress, or mercifully with one blow to end this dreadful scene of agonizing torture! Had I had a ball in my gun, I certainly should have despatched him; but finding myself unable to perform so kind an office, I sought, though trembling, to relieve him as well as I could. A shell ready fixed to a pole, which had been used by some negroes, presented itself to me; filled it with water, and with trembling hands I guided it to the quivering lips of the wretched sufferer. Urged by the irresistible power of thirst, he endeavoured to meet it, as he instinctively guessed its approach by the noise it made in passing through the bars of the cage. "Tanke, you white man, tanke you, pute some poy'son and give me." "How long have you been hanging there?" I asked him. "Two days, and me no die; the birds, the birds; aaah me!" Oppressed with the reflections which this shocking spectacle afforded me, I mustered strength enough to walk away, and soon reached the house at which I intended to dine. There I heard that the reason for this slave being thus punished, was on account of his having killed the overseer of the plantation. They told me that the laws of self-preservation rendered such executions necessary; and supported the doctrine of slavery with the arguments generally made use of to justify the practice; with the repetition of which I shall not trouble you at present. Adieu.

The Working Men's Party
Declaration of Independence

1829

The Declaration of Independence has been an inspiration to radicals throughout American history. They've used it to call for change, invoke the right of continuous revolution, and preempt charges of un-Americanism by setting themselves in the tradition of 1776. Women's rights activists, labor leaders, and abolitionists rewrote its script for their own protests, and in 1861 Abraham Lincoln pointed to its principle of liberty for all, adding, in a tragic irony, "I would rather be assassinated on this spot than surrender it."

The first important application of the Declaration came in 1829, when George Evans (1805–56) published "The Working Men's Party Declaration of Independence" in the *Working Man's Advocate* of New York and the *Mechanic's Free Press* of Philadelphia. The Working Men's Party was the world's first labor party, founded in New York in October 1829 by Robert Dale Owen, Frances Wright, Thomas Skidmore, and the printer and editor George Evans, when employers attempted to extend the workday from ten to eleven hours. The group won state legislative seats in New Hampshire and Connecticut, and established the ten-hour day in Philadelphia and other cities. Some members then formed the Equal Rights Party of New York State, which demanded "our equal and constitutional rights according to the fundamental truths in the Declaration of Independence."

"The Working Men's Declaration" quotes directly from the Declaration's opening, but with additions. It lists a new set of grievances and concludes with a demand for "equal means to *obtain* equal moral happiness," rather than "pursuit of happiness." Others have followed Evans's approach toward modifying the Declaration: in 1945, Ho Chi Minh quoted the 1776 document in his own Declaration and changed the opening to read, "all the peoples on the earth are equal from birth," correcting the omission of women; and in 1966 the Black Panthers quoted the Declaration in their "Ten Points," adding boldface for emphasis.

"When, in the course of human events, it becomes necessary" for one class of a community to assert their natural and unalienable rights in opposition to other classes of their fellow men, "and to assume among" them a political "station of equality to which the laws of nature and of nature's God," as well as the principles of their political compact "entitle them; a decent respect to the opinions of mankind," and the more paramount duty they owe to their own fellow citizens, "requires that they should declare the causes which impel them" to adopt so painful, yet so necessary, a measure.

"We hold these truths to be self evident that all men are *created equal;* that they are endowed by their creator with certain unalienable rights; that among these are *life, liberty,* and the *pursuit of happiness;* that to secure these rights" against the undue influence of other classes of society, prudence, as well as the claims of self defence, dictates the necessity of the organization of a party, who shall, by their representatives, prevent dangerous combinations to subvert these indefeasible and fundamental privileges. "All experience hath shown, that mankind" in general, and *we as a class in particular,* "are more disposed to suffer, while evils are sufferable, than to right themselves," by an opposition which the pride and self interest of unprincipled political aspirants, with more unprincipled zeal or religious bigotry, will willfully misrepresent. "But when a long train of abuses and usurpations" take place, all invariably tending to the oppression and degradation of one class of society, and to the unnatural and iniquitous exaltation of another by political leaders, "it is their right it is their due" to use every constitutional means to *reform* the abuses of such a government and to provide new guards for their future security. The history of the political *parties* in this state, is a history of political *iniquities,* all tending to the enacting and enforcing oppressive and unequal laws. To prove this, let facts be submitted to candid and impartial fellow citizens of all parties.

1. The laws for levying taxes are all based on erroneous principles, in consequence of their operating most oppressively on one of society, and being scarcely felt by the other.
2. The laws regarding the duties of jurors, witnesses, and militia trainings, are still more unequal and oppressive.
3. The laws for private incorporations are all partial in their operations; favoring one class of society to the expense of the other, who have no equal participation.
4. The laws incorporating religious societies have a pernicious tendency, by promoting the erection of magnificent places of public worship, by the rich, excluding others, and which others cannot imitate; consequently engendering spiritual pride in the clergy and people, and thereby creating odious distinctions in society, destructive to its social peace and happiness.
5. The laws establishing and patronizing seminaries of learning are unequal, favoring the rich, and perpetuating imparity, which natural causes have produced, and which judicious laws ought, and can, remedy.
6. The laws and municipal ordinances and regulations, generally, besides those specially enumerated, have heretofore been ordained on such principles, as have deprived nine tenths of the members of the body politic, who

are *not* wealthy, of the *equal means* to enjoy *"life, liberty, and the pursuit of happiness"* which the *rich* enjoy exclusively; but the federative compact intended to secure to all, indiscriminately. The lien law in favor of landlords against tenants, and all other honest creditors, is one illustration among innumerable others which can be adduced to prove the truth of these allegations.

We have trusted to the influence of the justice and good sense of our political leaders, to prevent the continuance of these abuses, which destroy the natural bands of equality so essential to the attainment of moral happiness, "but they have been deaf to the voice of justice and of consanguinity."

Therefore, we, the working class of society, of the city of New York, "appealing to the supreme judge of the world," and to the reason, and consciences of the impartial of all parties, "for the rectitude of our intentions, do, in the spirit, and by the authority" of that political liberty which has been promised to us equally with our fellow men, solemnly publish and declare, and invite all under like pecuniary circumstances, together with every liberal mind, to join us in the declaration, "that we are, & of right ought to be," entitled to equal means to obtain equal moral happiness, and social enjoyment, and that all lawful and constitutional measures ought to be adopted to the attainment of those objects. "And for the support of this declaration, we mutually pledge to each other" our faithful aid to the end of our lives.

Seneca Falls Declaration of Sentiments

1848

It was the year of international revolution. On July 13, 1848, four women—Lucretia Mott, Martha Wright, Mary Ann McClintock, and Elizabeth Cady Stanton—took tea in Waterloo, N.Y., and imagined a woman's rights convention. In 1840 Mott and Stanton had been forced to sit in the curtained-off section for women at the World Anti-Slavery Convention and there had first resolved to hold their own convention. Now, eight years on, they announced a convention for July 19–20.

Three days later the women met to write speeches and resolutions. They examined antislavery and temperance convention proceedings, but found no inspiration. Then someone read aloud the 1776 Declaration. They decided to keep its three-part structure but make additions to the preamble and write eighteen new grievances. Like Thomas Jefferson, they mixed matter-of-fact and emotive points. Eleven resolutions offer solutions to their grievances.

Stanton also wrote a fiery address, which she gave on the convention's first day. There was no need to justify women's equality of rights, she explained, but rather they were gathered to take "possession of what rightfully belongs to us." She threw this task before the 300 people in attendance, and the delegates debated the eleven resolutions. Only the ninth, on suffrage, was contentious. Stanton insisted: "The right is ours. Have it we must," and Frederick Douglass spoke in favor. It passed narrowly, and 68 women and 32 men signed the Declaration. Newspapers published the document, Stanton wrote long replies to all newspaper articles that referred to it, and on October 23, 1850, one thousand people attended the First National Woman's Rights Convention in Worcester, Mass. The woman's movement had gained the national spotlight.

When, in the course of human events, it becomes necessary for one portion of the family of man to assume among the people of the earth a position different from that which they have hitherto occupied, but one to which the laws of nature and of nature's God entitle them, a decent respect to the opinions of mankind requires that they should declare the causes that impel them to such a course.

We hold these truths to be self-evident: that all men and women are created equal; that they are endowed by their Creator with certain inalienable rights; that among these are life, liberty, and the pursuit of happiness; that to secure these rights governments are instituted, deriving their just powers from the consent of the governed. Whenever any form of government becomes destructive of these ends, it is the right of those who suffer from it to refuse allegiance to it, and to insist upon the institution of a new government, laying its foundation on such principles, and organizing its powers in such form, as to them shall seem most likely to effect their safety and happiness.

Prudence, indeed, will dictate that governments long established should not be changed for light and transient causes; and, accordingly, all experience has shown that mankind are more disposed to suffer, while evils are sufferable, than to right themselves by abolishing the forms to which they were accustomed. But when a long train of abuses and usurpations, pursuing invariably the same object, evinces a design to reduce them under absolute despotism, it is their duty to throw off such government and to provide new guards for their future security. Such has been the patient sufferance of the women under this government, and such is now the necessity which constrains them to demand the equal station to which they are entitled.

The history of mankind is a history of repeated injuries and usurpations on the part of man toward woman, having in direct object the establishment of an absolute tyranny over her. To prove this, let facts be submitted to a candid world.

He has never permitted her to exercise her inalienable right to the elective franchise. He has compelled her to submit to law in the formation of which she had no voice. He has withheld from her rights which are given to the most ignorant and degraded men, both natives and foreigners. Having deprived her of this first right as a citizen, the elective franchise, thereby leaving her without representation in the halls of legislation, he has oppressed her on all sides. He has made her, if married, in the eye of the law, civilly dead. He has taken from her all right in property, even to the wages she earns. He has made her morally, an irresponsible being, as she can commit many crimes with impunity, provided they be done in the presence of her husband. In the covenant of marriage, she is compelled to promise obedience to her husband, he becoming, to all intents and purposes, her master—the law giving him power to deprive her of her liberty and to administer chastisement. He has so framed the laws of divorce, as to what shall be the proper causes and, in case of separation, to whom the guardianship of the children shall be given, as to be wholly regardless of the happiness of the women—the law, in all cases, going upon a false supposition of the supremacy of man and giving all power into his hands. After depriving her of all rights as a married woman, if single and the owner of property, he has taxed her to support a government which recognizes her only when her property can be made profitable to it. He has monopolized nearly all the profitable employments, and from those she is permitted to follow, she receives but a scanty remuneration. He closes against her all the avenues to wealth and distinction which he considers most honorable to himself. As a teacher of theology, medicine, or law, she is not known. He has denied her the facilities for obtaining a thorough education, all colleges being closed against her. He allows her in church, as well as state, but a subordinate position, claiming apostolic authority for her exclusion from the ministry, and, with some exceptions, from any public participation in the affairs of the church. He has created a false public sentiment by giving to the world a different code of morals for men and women, by which moral delinquencies which exclude women from society are not only tolerated but deemed of little account in man. He has usurped the prerogative of Jehovah himself, claiming it as his right to assign for her a sphere of action, when that belongs to her conscience and to her God. He has endeavored, in every way that he could, to destroy her confidence in her own powers, to lessen her self-respect, and to make her willing to lead a dependent and abject life. Now, in view of this entire disfranchisement of one-half the people of this country, their social and religious degradation, in view of the unjust laws above mentioned, and because women do feel themselves aggrieved, oppressed, and fraudulently deprived of their most sacred rights, we insist that they have immediate admission to all the rights and privileges which belong to them as citizens of the United States.

In entering upon the great work before us, we anticipate no small amount of misconception, misrepresentation, and ridicule; but we shall use every instrumentality within our power to effect our object. We shall employ agents, circulate tracts, petition the state and national legislatures, and endeavor to enlist the pulpit and the press in our behalf. We hope this Convention will be followed by a series of conventions embracing every part of the country.

Resolutions. *Whereas,* the great precept of nature is conceded to be that "man shall pursue his own true and substantial happiness." Blackstone in his *Commentaries* remarks that this law of nature, being coeval with mankind and dictated by God himself, is, of course, superior in obligation to any other. It is binding over all the globe, in all countries and at all times; no human laws are of any validity if contrary to this, and such of them as are valid derive all their force, and all their validity, and all their authority, mediately and immediately, from this original; therefore,

Resolved, That such laws as conflict, in any way, with the true and substantial happiness of woman, are contrary to the great precept of nature and of no validity, for this is "superior in obligation to any other." *Resolved,* that all laws which prevent woman from occupying such a station in society as her conscience shall dictate, or which place her in a position inferior to that of man, are contrary to the great precept of nature and therefore of no force or authority. *Resolved,* that woman is man's equal, was intended to be so by the Creator, and the highest good of the race demands that she should be recognized as such. *Resolved,* that the women of this country ought to be enlightened in regard to the laws under which they live, that they may no longer publish their degradation by declaring themselves satisfied with their present position, nor their ignorance, by asserting that they have all the rights they want. *Resolved,* that inasmuch as man, while claiming for himself intellectual superiority, does accord to woman moral superiority, it is preeminently his duty to encourage her to speak and teach, as she has an opportunity, in all religious assemblies. *Resolved,* that the same amount of virtue, delicacy, and refinement of behavior that is required of woman in the social state also be required of man, and the same transgressions should be visited with equal severity on both man and woman. *Resolved,* that the objection of indelicacy and impropriety, which is so often brought against woman when she addresses a public audience, comes with a very ill grace from those who encourage, by their attendance, her appearance on the stage, in the concert, or in feats of the circus. *Resolved,* that woman has too long rested satisfied in the circumscribed limits which corrupt customs and a perverted application of the Scriptures have marked out for her, and that it is time she should move in the enlarged sphere which her great Creator has assigned her. *Resolved,* that it is the duty of the women of this country to secure to themselves their sacred right to the elective franchise. *Resolved,* that the equality of human rights results necessarily from the fact of the identity of the race in capabilities and responsibilities. *Resolved,* that the speedy success of our cause depends upon the zealous and untiring efforts of both men and women for the overthrow of the monopoly of the pulpit, and for the securing to woman an equal participation with men in the various trades, professions, and commerce. *Resolved,* therefore, that, being invested by the Creator with the same capabilities and same consciousness of responsibility for their exercise, it is demonstrably the right and duty of woman, equally with man, to promote every righteous cause by every righteous means; and especially in regard to the great subjects of morals and religion, it is self-evidently her right to participate with her brother in teaching them, both in private and in public, by writing and by speaking, by any instrumentalities proper to be used, and in any assemblies proper to be held; and this being a self-evident truth growing out of the divinely implanted principles of human nature, any custom or authority adverse to it, whether modern or wearing the hoary sanction of antiquity, is to be regarded as a self-evident falsehood, and at war with mankind.

From Resistance to Civil Government

1849

In July 1846, Ralph Waldo Emerson visited Henry David Thoreau (1817–1862) in a Concord jail. "What are you doing in there?" asked Emerson. "What are you doing out there?" replied Thoreau, who was spending the night for nonpayment of poll tax. He had been arrested on his way to the shoemaker's and quietly continued with his errand upon release. But the incident was not easily forgotten. He had experienced a conversion in jail, like Eugene Debs or Malcolm X, explaining: "When I came out of prison . . . a change had . . . come over the scene."

In the 1840s radical abolitionists advocated tax refusal as protest against slavery. Thoreau's essay is a protest against slavery, as well as Manifest Destiny and the expansionist war with Mexico. It embraces the Declaration but not the Constitution, and develops Jefferson's theory of government in its opening. Thoreau is not averse to violence, asking: "What if blood should flow as a result to your resistance?" Later, shocked by the Fugitive Slave Law of 1850, he condemned it in an 1854 lecture. The era was not one "of repose," he acknowledged in a journal entry of 1854, adding that when Massachusetts returned the fugitive Anthony Burns to slavery he realized "we must fight." He eventually welcomed John Brown's violent antislavery raid, saying in an 1859 speech: "I do not wish to kill nor to be killed, but I can foresee circumstances in which both these things would be by me unavoidable." Brown perhaps personified Thoreau's doctrine of civil disobedience: "Is it not possible that an individual may be right and a government wrong?" asked Thoreau.

Thoreau's ideas influenced others. Mahatma Gandhi called him a "teacher" and said this essay offered "scientific confirmation" for his own actions, and Martin Luther King, Jr., placed himself in Thoreau's "legacy of creative protest," adding that Thoreau "came alive in our civil rights movement."

How does it become a man to behave toward this American government today? I answer, that he cannot without disgrace be associated with it. I cannot for an instant recognize that political organization as my government which is the slave's government also.

All men recognize the right of revolution; that is, the right to refuse allegiance to, and to resist, the government, when its tyranny or its inefficiency are great and unendurable. But almost all say that such is not the case now. But such was the case, they think, in the Revolution of '75. If one were to tell me that this was a bad government because it taxed certain foreign commodities brought to its ports, it is most probable that I should not make an ado about it, for I can do without them. All machines have their friction; and possibly this does enough good to counterbalance the evil. At any rate, it is a great evil to make a stir about it. But when the friction comes to have its machine, and oppression and robbery are organized, I say, let us not have such a machine any longer. In other words, when a sixth of the population of a nation which has undertaken to be the refuge of liberty are slaves, and a whole country is unjustly overrun and conquered by a foreign army, and subjected to military law, I think that it is not too soon for honest men to rebel and revolutionize. What makes this duty the more urgent is the fact that the country so overrun is not our own, but ours is the invading army . . . This people must cease to hold slaves, and to make war on Mexico, though it cost them their existence as a people . . .

There are thousands who are in opinion opposed to slavery and to the war, who yet in effect do nothing to put an end to them; who, esteeming themselves children of Washington and Franklin, sit down with their hands in their pockets, and say that they know not what to do, and do nothing; who even postpone the question of freedom to the question of free trade, and quietly read the prices-current along with the latest advices from Mexico, after dinner, and, it may be, fall asleep over them both. What is the price-current of an honest man and patriot today? They hesitate, and they regret, and sometimes they petition; but they do nothing in earnest and with effect. They will wait, well disposed, for others to remedy the evil, that they may no longer have it to regret. At most, they give only a cheap vote, and a feeble countenance and God-speed, to the right, as it goes by them. There are nine hundred and ninety-nine patrons of virtue to one virtuous man. But it is easier to deal with the real possessor of a thing than with the temporary guardian of it . . .

It is not a man's duty, as a matter of course, to devote himself to the eradication of any, even the most enormous, wrong; he may still properly have other concerns to engage him; but it is his duty, at least, to wash his hands of it, and, if he gives it no thought longer, not to give it practically his support. If I devote myself to other pursuits and contemplations, I must first see, at least, that I do not pursue them sitting upon another man's shoulders. I must get off him first, that he may pursue his contemplations too. See what gross inconsistency is tolerated. I have heard some of my townsmen say, "I should like to have them order me out to help put down an insurrection of the slaves, or to march to Mexico;—see if I would go"; and yet these very men have each, directly by their allegiance, and so indirectly, at least, by their money, furnished a substitute. The soldier is applauded who refuses to serve in an unjust war by those who do not refuse to sustain the unjust government which makes the war; is applauded by those whose own act and authority he disregards and sets at naught; as if the state were penitent to that degree that it hired one to scourge it while it sinned, but not to that degree that it left off sinning for a moment. Thus, under the name of Order and Civil Government, we are all made at last to pay homage to and support our own meanness. After the first blush of sin comes its indifference; and from immoral it becomes, as it were, unmoral, and not quite unnecessary to that life which we have made . . .

How can a man be satisfied to entertain an opinion merely, and enjoy it? Is there any enjoyment in it, if his opinion is that he is aggrieved? If you are cheated out of a single dollar by your neighbor, you do not rest satisfied with knowing that you are cheated, or with saying that you are cheated, or even with petitioning him to pay you your due; but you take effectual steps at once to obtain the full amount, and see that you are never cheated again. Action from principle, the perception and the performance of right, changes things and relations; it is essentially revolutionary, and does not consist wholly with anything which was. It not only divides States and churches, it divides families; ay, it divides the individual, separating the diabolical in him from the divine.

Unjust laws exist: shall we be content to obey them, or shall we endeavor to amend them, and obey them until we have succeeded, or shall we transgress them at once? Men generally, under such a government as this, think that they ought to wait until they have persuaded the majority to alter them. They think that, if they should resist, the remedy would be worse than the evil. But it is the fault of the government itself that the remedy is worse than the evil. It makes it worse. Why is it not more apt to anticipate and provide for reform? Why does it not cherish its wise minority? Why does it cry and resist before it is hurt? Why does it not encourage its citizens to be on the alert to point out its faults, and do better than it would have them? Why does it always crucify Christ, and excommunicate Copernicus and Luther, and pronounce Washington and Franklin rebels? . . .

If the injustice is part of the necessary friction of the machine of government, let it go, let it go: perchance it will wear smooth—certainly the machine will wear out. If the injustice has a spring, or a pulley, or a rope, or a crank, exclusively for itself, then perhaps you may consider whether the remedy will not be worse than the evil; but if it is of such a nature that it requires you to be the agent of injustice to another, then, I say, break the law. Let your life be a counter-friction to stop the machine. What I have to do is to see, at any rate, that I do not lend myself to the wrong which I condemn.

As for adopting the ways which the State has provided for remedying the evil, I know not of such ways. They take too much time, and a man's life will be gone. I have other affairs to attend to. I came into this world, not chiefly to make this a good place to live in, but to live in it, be it good or bad. A man has not everything to do, but something; and because he cannot do everything, it is not necessary that he should do something wrong. It is not my business to be petitioning the Governor or the Legislature any more than it is theirs to petition me; and if they should not bear my petition, what should I do then? But in this case the State has provided no way: its very Constitution is the evil. This may seem to be harsh and stubborn and unconciliatory; but it is to treat with the utmost kindness and consideration the only spirit that can appreciate or deserves it. So is all change for the better, like birth and death, which convulse the body.

I do not hesitate to say, that those who call themselves Abolitionists should at once effectually withdraw their support, both in person and property, from the government of Massachusetts, and not wait till they constitute a majority of one, before they suffer the right to prevail through them. I think that it is enough if they have God on their side, without waiting for that other one. Moreover, any man more right than his neighbors constitutes a majority of one already.

I meet this American government, or its representative, the State government, directly, and face to face, once a year—no more—in the person of its tax-gatherer; this is the only mode in which a man situated as I am necessarily meets it; and it then says distinctly, Recognize me; and the simplest, the most effectual, and, in the present posture of affairs, the indispensablest mode of treating with it on this head, of expressing your little satisfaction with and love for it, is to deny it then. My civil neighbor, the tax-gatherer, is the very man I have to deal with—for it is, after all, with men and not with parchment that I quarrel—and he has voluntarily chosen to be an agent of the government. How shall he ever know well what he is and does as an officer of the government, or as a man, until he is obliged to consider whether he shall treat me, his neighbor, for whom he has respect, as a neighbor and well-disposed man, or as a maniac and disturber of the peace, and see if he can get over this obstruction to his neighborliness without a ruder and more impetuous thought or speech corresponding with his action. I know this well, that if one thousand, if one hundred, if ten men whom I could name—if ten honest men only—ay, if one HONEST man, in this State of Massachusetts, ceasing to hold slaves, were actually to withdraw from this copartnership, and be locked up in the county jail therefor, it would be the abolition of slavery in America. For it matters not how small the beginning may seem to be: what is once well done is done forever. But we love better to talk about it: that we say is our mission, Reform keeps many scores of newspapers in its service, but not one man. If my esteemed neighbor, the State's ambassador, who will devote his days to the settlement of the question of human rights in the Council Chamber, instead of being threatened with the prisons of Carolina, were to sit down the prisoner of Massachusetts, that State which is so anxious to foist the sin of slavery upon her sister—though at present she can discover only an act of inhospitality to be the ground of a quarrel with her—the Legislature would not wholly waive the subject the following winter.

Under a government which imprisons any unjustly, the true place for a just man is also a prison. The proper place today, the only place which Massachusetts has provided for her freer and less desponding spirits, is in her prisons, to be put out and locked out of the State by her own act, as they have already put themselves out by their principles. It is there that the fugitive slave, and the Mexican prisoner on parole, and the Indian come to plead the wrongs of his race should find them; on that separate, but more free and honorable, ground, where the State places those who are not with her, but against her—the only house in a slave State in which a free man can abide with honor. If any think that their influence would be lost there, and their voices no longer afflict the ear of the State, that they would not be as an enemy within its walls, they do not know by how much truth is stronger than error, nor how much more eloquently and effectively he can combat injustice who has experienced a little in his own person. Cast your whole vote, not a strip of paper merely, but your whole influence. A minority is powerless while it conforms to the majority; it is not even a minority then; but it is irresistible when it clogs by its whole weight. If the alternative is to keep all just men in prison, or give up war and slavery, the State will not hesitate which to choose. If a thousand men were not to pay their tax-bills this year, that would not be a violent and bloody measure, as it would be to pay them, and enable the State to commit violence and shed innocent blood. This is, in fact, the definition of a peaceable revolution, if any such is possible. If the tax-gatherer, or any other public officer, asks me, as one has done, "But what shall I do?" my answer is, "If you really wish to do anything, resign your office." When the subject has refused allegiance, and the officer has resigned his office, then the revolution is accomplished. But even suppose blood should flow. Is there not a sort of blood shed when the conscience is wounded? Through this wound a man's real manhood and immortality flow out, and he bleeds to an everlasting death. I see this blood flowing now . . .

From Provisional Constitution

1858

In 1816, Thomas Jefferson suggested that the Constitution be "handed on, with periodical repairs, from generation to generation." A generation later, while revolutionary constitutions were being drawn up across the U.S. and Europe, the radical abolitionist John Brown (1800–1859) wrote a new constitution, emphasizing in Article XLVI that it looked "to Amendment and Repeal"—to what Jefferson called "repairs."

Brown's constitution was for the provisional government of a slave-free nation. In April 1858 he began to organize a constitutional convention in Chatham, Ontario. Some of Chatham's free blacks attended the May 8–10 convention, and the remainder of the 46 delegates were Brown's men. Frederick Douglass, who didn't attend, kept a copy of the constitution until he died. At the convention, Brown outlined his plans to attack western Virginia, arm slaves, and establish a slave-free state. The delegates ratified the constitution and elected Brown commander-in-chief, and Brown appointed a committee to fill executive, legislative, judicial, and military offices.

The convention was emotionally charged. Brown spoke passionately, and his enemies cited these speeches and the constitution as evidence of his fanaticism. But many abolitionists admired his principles and enjoyed the document's parody of the U.S. Constitution, complete with a three-branch government. The constitution was ready for distribution when Brown attacked Harpers Ferry in October 1859, and interviewers questioned him about it after the raid.

Some believe that the ensuing Civil War was a second American revolution, producing amendments that added up to a new Constitution. But many in the protest tradition didn't agree. For example, calling for more than "repairs," Huey Newton and the Black Panther Party announced a constitutional convention in 1970: "Black people have no future within the present structure of power and authority in the United States under the present Constitution," Newton said; "we must have a new Constitution that will strictly guarantee our Human Rights to Life, Liberty and the Pursuit of Happiness."

Preamble:

Whereas slavery, throughout its entire existence in the United States, is none other than a most barbarous, unprovoked, and unjustifiable war of one portion of its citizens upon another portion—the only conditions of which are perpetual imprisonment and hopeless servitude or absolute extermination—in utter disregard and violation of those eternal and self-evident truths set forth in our Declaration of Independence:

Therefore we, citizens of the United States, and the oppressed people who, by a recent decision of the Supreme Court, are declared to have no rights which the white man is bound to respect, together with all other people degraded by the laws thereof, do, for the time being, ordain and establish for ourselves the following Provisional Constitution and Ordinances, the better to protect our persons, property, lives, and liberties, and to govern our actions:

Article I. Qualifications for membership

All persons of mature age, whether proscribed, oppressed, and enslaved citizens, or of the proscribed and oppressed races of the United States, who shall agree to sustain and enforce the Provisional Constitution and Ordinances of this organization, together with all minor children of such persons, shall be held to be fully entitled to protection under the same.

Article II. Branches of Government

The provisional government of this organization shall consist of three branches, viz.: legislative, executive, and judicial.

Article XLVI. These Articles Not for the Overthrow of Gov'm't

The foregoing Articles shall not be construed so as in any way to encourage the overthrow of any State Government of the United States: and look to no dissolution of the Union, but simply to Amendment and Repeal. And our flag shall be the same that our Fathers fought under in the Revolution.

Article XLVIII. Oath

Every officer, civil or military, connected with this organization, shall, before entering upon the duties of his office, make solemn oath or affirmation, to abide by and support this Provisional Constitution and these Ordinances. Also, every Citizen and Soldier, before being fully recognized as such, shall do the same.

From Declaration of Interdependence
by the Socialist Labor Party

1895

Daniel De Leon (1852–1914) examined "'76 in '95," as he explains in his Declaration's introduction. He recognized the Revolution's limitations, but noted elsewhere that these did not "detract from the genuineness of the revolutionary spirit of 1776." In 1893 De Leon had imagined an America "under the folds of the Socialist banner . . . whose brilliance and magnificence will be beyond the dreams of poetry." He believed in the transcendent potential of socialism and often infused his writing with millennialist language, as in his Declaration's conclusion.

As editor of the Socialist Labor Party (SLP) newspaper, *The People,* from 1892 until his death in 1914, De Leon tried to apply Marxist theories to the American system. The SLP organized as the Workingmen's Party in 1876, was renamed in 1877, and reorganized itself around Marxism in 1890, after De Leon joined the party and began to develop the Socialist Industrial Union program. Reformers like Jacob Riis frustrated him. "As a poodle may have his hair cut . . . yet he remains the same old poodle, so capitalism may be trimmed with factory laws, tenement laws, divorce laws and gambling laws, but it remains the same old capitalism," he wrote mockingly in 1906. "Socialism . . . means to get rid of the poodle." But he was sometimes charged with vagueness about how to achieve his vision. He responded, "To have asked the exponents of American independence to prove independence practical under King George would have been unjust; yet, the opponents of socialism ask socialists to prove socialism practical under capitalism."

In 1776, John Adams had acknowledged "the toil, and blood, and treasure, that it will cost us to maintain this declaration," but concluded that "posterity will triumph." In spite of the efforts of radicals like De Leon, posterity had still not triumphed by 1963, when Martin Luther King, Jr., called again on the Declaration: "I have a dream that one day this nation will . . . live out the true meaning of its creed." De Leon's America, "beyond the dreams of poetry," was still only a dream.

When, in the course of human progression, the despoiled class of wealth producers becomes fully conscious of its rights and determined to take them, a decent respect to the judgment of posterity requires that it should declare the causes which impel it to change the social order.

More truly can we say of our plutocracy than our forefathers did of the

British crown that "its history is one of repeated injuries and usurpations, all having in direct object the establishment of an absolute tyranny over these states." Let the facts speak.

The foundation of the Union was co-eval with the birth of the modern system of production by machinery. No sooner was the federal Constitution adopted than the spirit of capitalism began to manifest its absorbing tendency and corrupting influence. Every new invention was looked upon, not as a means of promoting the welfare of all, but as an instrument of private profit. Every tract of fertile land belonging to the states was appropriated by individuals, regardless of the rights of future generations. Every public franchise of any value was given away to "enterprising" persons and companies.

Thus was already formed in those early days, a privileged class, whose wealth was derived from the labor of others; this growing monopoly of the means of production and exchange, by placing a steadily, increasing number of disinherited workers in its dependence for employment, strengthened its hold upon the public powers, which it used more and more unscrupulously for its own aggrandizement.

Even such a public calamity as war was turned by that selfish and unpatriotic class to its own enrichment . . . So did the promises and purposes of the Revolution immediately prove abortive. While the fundamental law declared that the Union was formed "to establish justice, insure domestic tranquility, promote the general welfare, and secure the blessings of liberty," free scope was given to an economic system replete with injustice, pregnant with the seeds of domestic strife, destructive, of every true element of happiness, and fatally tending to class tyranny.

Under that system men, proclaimed free and equal, were soon made to realize that they were only labor power in human form, to be sold in the market for what it could fetch, and to be consumed in the production of wealth for the exclusive benefit of those who already had wealth. Under that system the value of a man, and, therefore, his remuneration, were not to be measured by the extent to which his industry and intelligence benefited his fellows. They were to be gauged by the necessities of his competitors on the "labor market"; so that, as the competition increased, the tendency of his wages was constantly downward, until it reached the minimum required to keep alive his flesh-and-bone machine while it was hired to an employer, who thus became the absolute owner of the net product, or, "surplus value," created by that human machine.

Under that system the toiling masses, hungry and despised, turned the wilderness into a garden, the stones, the clay, the trees into resplendent cities, the ore and the coal into new organs of motion, through which human strength, speed and skill were multiplied a thousand-fold, the lightning itself into an obedient messenger; they built factories, ships, docks and warehouses; constructed railroads, bridged rivers and pierced mountains; then descended into their nameless graves, leaving all in the hands of their despoilers, to further oppress and degrade the inheritors of their misery.

Under this system society, so called, became a worse pandemonium than it had ever been. Each looked upon his neighbor as a legitimate prey or a dangerous antagonist. The laborer viewed with dismay, the appearance of another laborer, while the employer of both plotted the ruin of a rival employer. And this horrible struggle for life among the weak, for dominion among the powerful, ever more intense as the means of life became greater and as the dominion of man over nature grew more extensive, was glorified by sophists as the providential law of human progress!

. . . The time at last came when the powerful had more to gain by combination among themselves than by internecine war. They became class-conscious, and, therefore, interdependent, as against the individualistic and, therefore, turbulent class from which they had now emerged. The era of capitalistic competition was fast passing away, to be succeeded by the era of plutocratic concentration . . . The powers of government so long used legislatively to confer privileges upon the capitalist class were at last used arbitrarily, and even murderously, to establish the absolute dominion of the plutocracy. And, blind to the true cause of its sufferings, lacking in the knowledge and spirit of interdependence, hopelessly divided against itself, the multitude stupidly sanctioned at the polls the economic despotism and political corruption which its own venal misleaders affected to denounce in bombastic phrases at public assemblies.

. . . But throughout the civilized world the wage workers are asserting their interdependence—the natural dependence of every man upon his fellows, of every nation upon all other nations; and under the banner of international socialism millions of them are now marching to the conquest of the public powers.

They recognize that the social body is an organism, and, as such, is subject in its life, health and development to the general law which governs organic nature; that the more highly it is developed, the more interdependent are all its members; that the very extent of this mutual dependence of parts determines the amount of freedom and the degree of perfection with which they respectively perform their natural functions, ever so diverse, yet all tending usefully and harmoniously to the common end.

They realize also that the capitalist is no more a legitimate member of the social organism than a parasite in the human body is a necessary part of the organ upon which it feeds, and upon the proper working of which all the other organs depend for support and vigor. And they are determined to expel him.

The class struggle has reached its climax. With the triumph of the united toilers over their combined despoilers will end class privilege and class rule.

Americans, fall into line! Onward to the Cooperative Commonwealth!

To the industrious the tools of industry; to the laborer the fruits of his labor; to mankind the earth!

2

UNVANISHING
THE INDIAN

Native
American
Rights

Speech to Governor William Harrison
at Vincennes

1810

In August 1810, as the Shawnee chief Tecumseh (1768–1813) sat next to Governor Harrison in Vincennes, the capital of the Indiana Territory, he gradually pushed Harrison to the seat's edge. Harrison protested, and Tecumseh remarked that this was what settlers were doing to Indians.

Native history is no tale of passive victimization; Tecumseh marked the climax of a vigorous resistance. In 1805 his brother Tenskwatawa emerged as the Shawnee Prophet. Tecumseh remained in Tenskwatawa's shadow until 1809, when the Treaty of Fort Wayne ceded three million acres of land for less than two cents an acre. It was signed by Indians on both sides of the Wabash River in the brothers' absence. Tecumseh expressed outrage and proclaimed himself head of all Indians, and Harrison, who had been appointed governor of Indiana in 1800, asked him to visit Vincennes.

Tecumseh arrived with 75 warriors and announced that he was building a pan-tribal confederacy. Like the protest writers of the American Revolution, Tecumseh imagined one nation united against an aggressor. Building on Tenskwatawa's messianic religious movement, he told the Choctaw in August 1811: "The annihilation of our race is at hand unless we unite in one common cause," and the Osages later that year: "Brothers, we all belong to one family." His was the broadest intertribal confederacy yet attempted, prompting Harrison's observation that he could be "the founder of an empire." He was, Harrison added, "one of those uncommon geniuses which spring up occasionally to produce revolutions."

Part of Tecumseh's genius was his oratory. Tecumseh's 1810 speech reprinted here asks the white audience to recall Christ's suffering, making Harrison the Pontius Pilate of Indian removal. In fact, Harrison had written himself into this Passion Play in 1806, echoing the temptation of Christ when he told the Delaware Indians: "If [Tenskwatawa] is really a prophet, ask him to cause . . . the dead to rise from their graves." Native American protest writers would echo Tecumseh's attack on Christianity and his identification with Christ all the way to John Lame Deer's declaration in 1972: "The trouble is not with Christianity . . . but with what you have made out of it . . . You have made the religion of the protest leader and hippie Jesus into the religion of missionaries, army padres, Bureau of Indian Affairs officials."

After Vincennes, both Harrison and Tecumseh could see war on the horizon. Tecumseh was killed in battle in October 1813, and his death seemed the end of the Indian Movement. But his legacy of a pan-Indian philosophy would fuel the 1890 Ghost Dance, a movement cut down at Wounded Knee, and the 1970s American Indian Movement. Tecumseh and the Indian Movement also influenced both the budding abolitionist movement of the 1830s and the early woman's rights movement.

Further reading: Gregory Dowd, *A Spirited Resistance* (1991); Anthony J. Hall, *The Bowl with One Spoon* (2003).

Houses are built for you to hold councils in; Indians hold theirs in the open air. I am a Shawnee. My forefathers were warriors. Their son is a warrior. From them I take only my existence. From my tribe I take nothing. I have made myself what I am. And I would that I could make the red people as great as the conception in my own mind, when I think of the Great Spirit that rules over us all . . . I would not then come to Governor Harrison to ask him to tear up the treaty. But I would say to him, "Brother, you have the liberty to return to your own country."

You wish to prevent the Indians from doing as we wish them, to unite and let them consider their lands as the common property of the whole. You take the tribes aside and advise them not to come into this measure . . . You want by your distinctions of Indian tribes, in allotting to each a particular, to make them war with each other. You never see an Indian endeavor to make the white people do this. You are continually driving the red people, when at last you will drive them onto the great lake, where they can neither stand nor work.

Since my residence at Tippecanoe, we have endeavored to level all distinction, to destroy village chiefs, by whom all mischiefs are done. It is they who sell the land to the Americans. Brother, this land that was sold, and the goods that were given for it, was only done by a few . . . In the future we are prepared to punish those who propose to sell land to the Americans. If you continue to purchase them, it will make war among the different tribes, and, at last I do not know what will be the consequences among the white people. Brother, I wish you would take pity on the red people and do as I have requested. If you will not give up the land and do cross the boundary of our present settlement, it will be very hard, and produce a great trouble between us.

The way, the only way to stop this evil is for the red men to unite in claiming a common and equal right in the land, as it was at first, and should be now— for it was never divided, but belongs to all. No tribe has the right to sell, even to each other, much less to strangers . . . Sell a country! Why not sell the air, the great sea, as well as the earth? Did not the Great Spirit make them all for the use of his children?

How can we have confidence in the white people? When Jesus Christ came upon the earth you killed Him and nailed Him to the cross. You thought He was dead, and you were mistaken. You have Shakers among you and you laugh and make light of their worship.

Everything I have told is the truth. The Great Spirit has inspired me.

An Indian's Looking-Glass
for the White Man

<u>1833</u>

Reaching to the heart of American racism, the Native American writer William Apess (1798–1839) imagines all the nations assembled together, each skin with "its national crimes written upon it." The idea that crimes might be written upon the body appeared throughout 19th-century literature, from *Typee* (1846) to *The Scarlet Letter* (1850) to *The Red Badge of Courage* (1895). Apess's essay is also important for its idea of cultural mirroring. He is often dismissed as a Salvationist writer who based his work on the providential narrative and the spiritual confession, seeming to mirror white culture. But his Methodist rhetoric criticized the dominant religious culture, his rhetoric of American nationalism conveyed his egalitarian vision, and he affirmed Indian cultural and political identity by using Euroamerican forms of history in order to express their limitations—as in his "Eulogy on King Philip" (1836), which revises American history. This 1836 speech, about the leader of a 1675 uprising against European settlers in New England, challenged the image of the vanishing Indian and wrote Native Americans back into history.

Apess also used Euroamerican literary conventions to reappropriate what he considered to be a cultural "looking-glass," for he knew the limitations of cultural mirroring. "An Indian's Looking-Glass" condemns Massachusetts's antimiscegenation law, and the essay's central metaphor suggests that mirroring keeps cultures apart, as two distinct shapes. In addition, his formulation of an Indian's "looking-glass for the white man" means both a mirror *for* whites and a mirror for Indians to see themselves *for* whites, in an early instance of what W. E. B. Du Bois would later call "double-consciousness."

Further reading: Philip Deloria, *Playing Indian* (1998); Gerald Vizenor, *The Heirs of Columbus* (1991).

Having a desire to place a few things before my fellow creatures who are traveling with me to the grave, and to that God who is the maker and preserver both of the white man and the Indian, whose abilities are the same and who are to be judged by one God, who will show no favor to outward appearances but will judge righteousness. Now I ask if degradation has not been heaped long enough upon the Indians? And if so, can there not be a compromise? Is it right to hold and promote prejudices? If not, why not put them all away? I mean here, among those who are civilized. It may be that many are ignorant of the situation of many of my brethren within the limits of New England. Let me for a few moments turn your attention to the reservations in the different states of New England, and, with but few exceptions, we shall find them as follows: the most mean, abject, miserable race of beings in the world—a complete place of prodigality and prostitution.

Let a gentleman and lady of integrity and respectability visit these places, and they would be surprised; as they wandered from one hut to the other they would view, with the females who are left alone, children half-starved and some almost as naked as they came into the world. And it is a fact that I have seen them as much so—while the females are left without protection, and are seduced by white men, and are finally left to be common prostitutes for them and to be destroyed by that burning, fiery curse, that has swept millions, both of red and white men, into the grave with sorrow and disgrace—rum. One reason why they are left so is because their most sensible and active men are absent at sea. Another reason is because they are made to believe they are minors and have not the abilities given them from God to take care of themselves, without it is to see to a few little articles, such as baskets and brooms. Their land is in common stock, and they have nothing to make them enterprising.

Another reason is because those men who are Agents, many of them are unfaithful and care not whether the Indians live or die; they are much imposed upon by their neighbors, who have no principle. They would think it no crime to go upon Indian lands and cut and carry off their most valuable timber, or anything else they chose; and I doubt not but they think it clear gain. Another reason is because they have no education to take care of themselves; if they had, I would risk them to take care of their own property.

Now I will ask if the Indians are not called the most ingenious people among us. And are they not said to be men of talents? And I would ask: Could there be a more efficient way to distress and murder them by inches than the way they have taken? And there is no people in the world but who may be destroyed in the same way. Now, if these people are what they are held up in our view to be, I would take the liberty to ask why they are not brought forward and pains taken to educate them, to give them all a common education, and those of the brightest and first-rate talents put forward and held up to office. Perhaps some unholy, unprincipled men would cry out, "The skin was not good enough"; but stop, friends—I am not talking about the skin but about principles. I would ask if there cannot be as good feelings and principles under a red skin as there can be under a white. And let me ask: Is it not on the account of a bad principle that we who are red children have had to suffer so much as we have? And let me ask: Did not this bad principle proceed from the whites or their forefathers? And I would ask: Is it worthwhile to nourish it any longer? If not, then let us have a change, although some men no doubt will spout their corrupt principles against it, that are in the halls of legislation and elsewhere. But I presume this kind of talk will seem surprising and horrible. I do not see why it should so long as they (the whites) say that they think as much of us as they do of themselves.

This I have heard repeatedly, from the most respectable gentlemen and ladies—and having heard so much precept, I should now wish to see the example. And I would ask who has a better right to look for these things than the naturalist himself—the candid man would say none.

I know that many say that they are willing, perhaps the majority of the people, that we should enjoy our rights and privileges as they do. If so, I would ask, Why are not we protected in our persons and property throughout the Union? Is it not because there reigns in the breast of many who are leaders a most unrighteous, unbecoming, and impure black principle, and as corrupt and unholy as it can be—while these very same unfeeling, self-esteemed characters pretend to take the skin as a pretext to keep us from our unalienable and lawful rights? I would ask you if you would like to be disfranchised from all your rights, merely because your skin is white, and for no other crime. I'll venture to say, these very characters who hold the skin to be such a barrier in the way would be the first to cry out, "Injustice! awful injustice!"

But, reader, I acknowledge that this is a confused world, and I am not seeking for office, but merely placing before you the black inconsistency that you place before me—which is ten times blacker than any skin that you will find in the universe. And now let me exhort you to do away that principle, as it appears ten times worse in the sight of God and candid men than skins of color—more disgraceful than all the skins that Jehovah ever made. If black or red skins or any other skin of color is disgraceful to God, it appears that he has disgraced himself a great deal—for he has made fifteen colored people to one white and placed them here upon this earth.

Now let me ask you, white man, if it is a disgrace for to eat, drink, and sleep with the image of God, or sit, or walk and talk with them. Or have you the folly to think that the white man, being one in fifteen or sixteen, are the only beloved images of God? Assemble all nations together in your imagination, and then let the whites be seated among them, and then let us look for the whites, and I doubt not it would be hard finding them; for to the rest of the nations, they are still but a handful. Now suppose these skins were put together, and each skin had its national crimes written upon it—which skin do you think would have the greatest? I will ask one question more. Can you charge the Indians with robbing a nation almost of their whole continent, and murdering their women and children, and then depriving the remainder of their lawful rights, that nature and God require them to have? And to cap the climax, rob another nation to till their grounds and welter out their days under the lash with hunger and fatigue under the scorching rays of a burning sun? I should look at all the skins, and I know that when I cast my eye upon that white skin, and if I saw those crimes written upon it, I should enter my protest against it immediately and cleave to that which is more honorable. And I can tell you that I am satisfied with the manner of my creation, fully—whether others are or not.

But we will strive to penetrate more fully into the conduct of those who profess to have pure principles and who tell us to follow Jesus Christ and imitate him and have his Spirit. Let us see if they come anywhere near him and his ancient disciples. The first thing we are to look at are his precepts, of which we will mention a few. "Thou shalt love the Lord thy God with all thy heart, with all thy soul, with all thy mind, and with all thy strength. The second is like unto it. Thou shalt love thy neighbor as thyself. On these two precepts hang all the law and the prophets" (Matt. 22:37, 38, 39, 40). "By this shall all men know that they are my disciples, if ye have love one to another" (John 13:35). Our Lord left this special command with his followers, that they should love one another.

Again, John in his Epistles says, "He who loveth God loveth his brother also" (1 John 4:21). "Let us not love in word but in deed" (1 John 3:18). "Let your love be without dissimulation. See that ye love one another with a pure heart fervently" (1 Peter 1:22). "If any man say, I love God, and hateth his brother, he is a liar" (1 John 4:20). "Whosoever hateth his brother is a murderer, and no murderer hath eternal life abiding in him" [1 John 3:15]. The first thing that takes our attention is the saying of Jesus, "Thou shalt love," etc. The first question I would ask my brethren in the ministry, as well as that of the membership: What is love, or its effects? Now, if they who teach are not essentially affected with pure love, the love of God, how can they teach as they ought? Again, the holy teachers of old said, "Now if any man have not the spirit of Christ, he is none of his" (Rom. 8:9). Now, my brethren in the ministry, let me ask you a few sincere questions. Did you ever hear or read of Christ teaching his disciples that they ought to despise one because his skin was different from theirs? Jesus Christ being a Jew, and those of his Apostles certainly were not whites—and did not he who completed the plan of salvation complete it for the whites as well as for the Jews, and others? And were not the whites the most degraded people on the earth at that time? And none were more so, for they sacrificed their children to dumb idols! And did not St. Paul labor more abundantly for building up a Christian nation among you than any of the Apostles? And you know as well as I that you are not indebted to a principle beneath a white skin for your religious services but to a colored one.

What then is the matter now? Is not religion the same now under a colored skin as it ever was? If so, I would ask, why is not a man of color respected? You may say, as many say, we have white men enough. But was this the spirit of Christ and his Apostles? If it had been, there would not have been one white preacher in the world—for Jesus Christ never would have imparted his grace or word to them, for he could forever have withheld it from them. But we find that Jesus Christ and his Apostles never looked at the outward appearances. Jesus in particular looked at the hearts, and his Apostles through him, being discerners of the spirit, looked at their fruit without any regard to the skin, color, or nation; as St. Paul himself speaks, "Where there is neither Greek nor Jew, circumcision nor uncircumcision, Barbarian nor Scythian, bond nor free—but Christ is all, and in all" (Col. 3:11). If you can find a spirit like Jesus Christ and his Apostles prevailing now in any of the white congregations, I should like to know it. I ask: Is it not the case that everybody that is not white is treated with contempt and counted as barbarians? And I ask if the word of God justifies the white man in so doing. When the prophets prophesied, of whom did they speak? When they spoke of heathens, was it not the whites and others who were counted Gentiles? And I ask if all nations with the exception of the Jews were not counted heathens. And according to the writings of some, it could not mean the Indians, for they are counted Jews. And now I would ask: Why is all this distinction made among these Christian societies? I would ask: What is all this ado about missionary societies, if it be not to Christianize those who are not Christians? And what is it for? To degrade them worse, to bring them into society where they must welter out their days in disgrace merely because their skin is of a different complexion. What folly it is to try to make the state of human society worse than it is. How astonished some may be at this—but let me ask: Is it not so? Let me refer you to the churches only. And, my brethren, is there any agreement? Do brethren and sisters love one another? Do they not rather hate one another? Outward forms and ceremonies, the lusts of the flesh, the lusts of the eye, and pride of life is of more value to many professors than the love of God shed abroad in their hearts, or an attachment to his altar, to his ordinances, or to his children. But you may ask: Who are the children of God? Perhaps you may say, none but white. If so, the word of the Lord is not true.

I will refer you to St. Peter's precepts (Acts 10): "God is no respecter of persons," etc. Now if this is the case, my white brother, what better are you than God? And if no better, why do you, who profess his Gospel and to have his spirit, act so contrary to it? Let me ask why the men of a different skin are so despised. Why are not they educated and placed in your pulpits? I ask if his services well performed are not as good as if a white man performed them. I ask if a marriage or a funeral ceremony or the ordinance of the Lord's house would not be as acceptable in the sight of God as though he was white. And if so, why is it not to you? I ask again: Why is it not as acceptable to have men to exercise their office in one place as well as in another? Perhaps you will say that if we admit you to all of these privileges you will want more. I expect that I can guess what that is—Why, say you, there would be intermarriages. How that would be I am not able to say—and if it should be, it would be nothing strange or new to me; for I can assure you that I know a great many that have intermarried, both of the whites and the Indians—and many are their sons and daughters and people, too, of the first respectability. And I could point to some in the famous city of Boston and elsewhere. You may look now at the disgraceful act in the statute law passed by the legislature of Massachusetts, and behold the fifty-pound fine levied upon any clergyman or justice of the peace that dare to encourage the laws of God and nature by a legitimate union in holy wedlock between the Indians and whites. I would ask how this looks to your lawmakers. I would ask if this corresponds with your sayings—that you think as much of the Indians as you do of the whites. I do not wonder that you blush, many of you, while you read; for many have broken the ill-fated laws made by man to hedge up the laws of God and nature. I would ask if they who have made the law have not broken it—but there is no other state in New England that has this law but Massachusetts; and I think, as many of you do not, that you have done yourselves no credit.

But as I am not looking for a wife, having one of the finest cast, as you no doubt would understand while you read her experience and travail of soul in the way to heaven, you will see that it is not my object. And if I had none, I should not want anyone to take my right from me and choose a wife for me; for I think that I or any of my brethren have a right to choose a wife for themselves as well as the whites—and as the whites have taken the liberty to choose my brethren, the Indians, hundreds and thousands of them, as partners in life, I believe the Indians have as much right to choose their partners among the whites if they wish. I would ask you if you can see anything inconsistent in your conduct and talk about the Indians. And if you do, I hope you will try to become more consistent. Now, if the Lord Jesus Christ, who is counted by all to be a Jew—and it is well known that the Jews are a colored people, especially those living in the East, where Christ was born—and if he should appear among us, would he not be shut out of doors by many, very quickly? And by those too who profess religion?

By what you read, you may learn how deep your principles are. I should say they were skin-deep. I should not wonder if some of the most selfish and ignorant would spout a charge of their principles now and then at me. But I would ask: How are you to love your neighbors as yourself? Is it to cheat them? Is it to wrong them in anything? Now, to cheat them out of any of their rights is robbery. And I ask: Can you deny that you are not robbing the Indians daily, and many others? But at last you may think I am what is called a hard and unchari-table man. But not so. I believe there are many who would not hesitate to ad-vocate our cause; and those too who are men of fame and respectability—as well as ladies of honor and virtue. There is a Webster, an Everett, and a Wirt, and many others who are distinguished characters—besides a host of my fel-low citizens, who advocate our cause daily. And how I congratulate such noble spirits—how they are to be prized and valued; for they are well calculated to promote the happiness of mankind. They well know that man was made for society, and not for hissing-stocks and outcasts. And when such a principle as this lies within the hearts of men, how much it is like its God—and how it honors its Maker—and how it imitates the feelings of the Good Samaritan, that had his wounds bound up, who had been among thieves and robbers.

Do not get tired, ye noble-hearted—only think how many poor Indians want their wounds done up daily; the Lord will reward you, and pray you stop not till this tree of distinction shall be leveled to the earth, and the mantle of prejudice torn from every American heart—then shall peace pervade the Union.

Indian Names

1834

In 1833 Lydia Sigourney (1791–1865) was no longer a vanishing woman: she signed her name to a publication. She had published anonymously until then, because her husband objected to her public authorship. Soon after claiming her own name, she claimed Indian names on behalf of the vanishing Indian, in the poem reprinted here.

Though forgotten now, Sigourney was hugely popular in her time. Her writings interwove conservative republicanism with compassionate Christianity, and Indian removal seemed a violation of both. The "YE" of Sigourney's first line addresses Jacksonian America. Andrew Jackson negotiated nine treaties between 1814 and 1824 that gave the United States control of three-quarters of Florida and Alabama, and parts of Kentucky, Georgia, Mississippi, Tennessee, and North Carolina. In 1830 he pushed the Indian Removal Act through Congress, which gave him the power to negotiate removal treaties with tribes east of the Mississippi. When some nations resisted, he forced them to leave: 46,000 Native Americans were removed by 1837, and in 1838 some 4,000 Cherokee people died on the "Trail of Tears" as they were marched west. Another powerful source of protest literature in this period was the first American Indian newspaper, *The Cherokee Phoenix,* published by the Cherokee Nation, which protested the Indian Removal Act of 1830 and the encroachment of settlers.

Within the American protest literature tradition, writers have echoed Sigourney's strategy of naming. Robert Dana's "At the Vietnam War Memorial" (1984) makes "words . . . obscene beside these names," and June Jordan's "Kissing God Goodbye" (1997) reclaims women's names. Others in the protest tradition have renamed themselves, protesting old identities and claiming new ones, like Malcolm X, who discarded his "slave name" Little. Like Sigourney, Malcolm knew, as he said in 1963, "There's a whole lot in a name."

Further reading: Brian Dippie, *The Vanishing American* (1982); Michael Green, *The Politics of Indian Removal* (1982).

> *"How can the Red men be forgotten, while so many of our states and territories, bays, lakes and rivers, are indelibly stamped by names of their giving?"*

YE say, they all have passed away,
That noble race and brave,
That their light canoes have vanished

From off the crested wave;
That 'mid the forests where they roamed
There rings no hunter's shout;
But their name is on your waters,
Ye may not wash it out.
'Tis where Ontario's billow
Like Ocean's surge is curl'd,
Where strong Niagara's thunders wake
The echo of the world,
Where red Missouri bringeth
Rich tributes from the west,
And Rappahannock sweetly sleeps
On green Virginia's breast.
Ye say, their cone-like cabins,
That clustered o'er the vale,
Have fled away like withered leaves
Before the autumn gale:
But their memory liveth on your hills
Their baptism on your shore,
Your everlasting rivers speak
Their dialect of yore.
Old Massachusetts wears it
Within her lordly crown,
And broad Ohio bears it
Amid her young renown;
Connecticut hath wreathed it
Where her quiet foliage waves,
And bold Kentucky breathed it hoarse
Through all her ancient caves.
Wachuset hides its lingering voice
Within his rocky heart,
And Alleghany graves its tone
Throughout his lofty chart;
Monadnock on his forehead hoar
Doth seal the sacred trust,
Your mountains build their monument,
Though ye destroy their dust.

From From the Deep Woods
to Civilization

1916

Charles Eastman (1858–1939) called himself "an Indian . . . an American." A self-described quarter-white Indian in civilization and a Christian in the woods, he possessed both "savage gentleness and native refinement." Resisting the limitation of Native identity, his autobiography shifts between the first and third person and employs multiple voices (from his grandmother's to whites'). These multiple voices protest white attempts to limit Native identity to that of the noble, vanishing Indian, like Eastman's character in the autobiography who "refused to allow the census taker to enumerate his people." The protest echoes William Apess's suspicion of identity fixing and anticipates Mary Crow Dog's dislike of being "frozen in ghostly attitudes."

Eastman's autobiography incorporates Native and white literary forms, as well as Native and white voices. It borrows from the bildungsroman, the education narrative, the spiritual confession, and the conversion narrative. But he also subverts these conventional forms: he describes no baptism or dramatic conversion, and when seeking light he goes into the dark woods. Finally, Eastman doesn't choose one culture or another but finds a borderland space. In his account, an Indian converts a white man to Christianity, a white guides him through the wilderness, reading can be hunting, book learning a warpath. In a land of color lines, there are also crossroads.

Further reading: Helen Hunt Jackson, *A Century of Dishonor* (1881); Raymond Wilson, *Ohiyesa* (1983).

It appears remarkable to me now that my father, thorough Indian as he was, should have had such deep and sound conceptions of a true civilization. But there is the contrast—my father's mother! whose faith in her people's philosophy and training could not be superseded by any other allegiance.

To her such a life as we lead to-day would be no less than sacrilege. "It is not a true life," she often said. "It is a sham. I cannot bear to see my boy live a made-up life!"

Ah, grandmother! you had forgotten one of the first principles of your own teaching, namely: "When you see a new trail, or a footprint that you do not know, follow it to the point of knowing."

"All I want to say to you," the old grandmother seems to answer, "is this: Do not get lost on this new trail."

"I find," said my father to me, "that the white man has a well-grounded religion, and teaches his children the same virtues that our people taught to theirs. The Great Mystery has shown to the red and white man alike the good and evil, from which to choose. I think the way of the white man is better than ours, because he is able to preserve on paper the things he does not want to forget. He records everything—the sayings of his wise men, the laws enacted by his counselors."

I began to be really interested in this curious scheme of living that my father was gradually unfolding to me out of his limited experience.

"The way of knowledge," he continued, "is like our old way in hunting. You begin with a mere trail—a footprint. If you follow that faithfully, it may lead you to a clearer trail—a track—a road. Later on there will be many tracks, crossing and diverging one from the other. Then you must be careful, for success lies in the choice of the right road. You must be doubly careful, for traps will be laid for you, of which the most dangerous is the spirit-water, that causes a man to forget his self-respect," he added, unwittingly giving to his aged mother material for her argument against civilization . . .

My chief object has been, not to entertain, but to present the American Indian in his true character before Americans. The barbarous and atrocious character commonly attributed to him has dated from the transition period, when the strong drink, powerful temptations, and commercialism of the white man led to deep demoralization. Really it was a campaign of education on the Indian and his true place in American history.

I have been, on the whole, happily surprised to meet with so cordial a response. Again and again I have been told by recognized thinkers, "You present an entirely new viewpoint. We can never again think of the Indian as we have done before." A great psychologist wrote me after reading "The Soul of the Indian": "My God! why did we not know these things sooner?" Many of my hearers have admitted that morality and spirituality are found to thrive better under the simplest conditions than in a highly organized society, and that the virtues are more readily cultivated where the "struggle for existence" is merely a struggle with the forces of nature, and not with one's fellow-men.

The philosophy of the original American was demonstrably on a high plane, his gift of eloquence, wit, humor and poetry is well established; his democracy and community life was much nearer the ideal than ours to-day; his standard of honor and friendship unsurpassed, and all his faults are the faults of generous youth.

It was not until I felt that I had to a degree established these claims, that I consented to appear on the platform in our ancestral garb of honor. I feel that I was a pioneer in this new line of defense of the native American, not so much of his rights in the land as of his character and religion. I am glad that the drift is now toward a better understanding, and that he is become the acknowledged hero of the Boy Scouts and Camp Fire Girls, as well as of many artists, sculptors, and sincere writers.

I was invited to represent the North American Indian at the First Universal Races Congress in London, England, in 1911. It was a great privilege to attend that gathering of distinguished representatives of 53 different nationalities, come together to mutually acquaint themselves with one another's progress and racial ideals. I was entertained by some well known men, but there was little time for purely social enjoyment. What impressed me most was the perfect equality of the races, which formed the background of all the discussions. It was declared at the outset that there is no superior race, and no inferior, since individuals of all races have proved their innate capacity by their standing in the universities of the world, and it has not seldom happened that men of the undeveloped races have surpassed students of the most advanced races in scholarship and ability . . .

From the time I first accepted the Christ ideal it has grown upon me steadily, but I also see more and more plainly our modern divergence from that ideal. I confess I have wondered much that Christianity is not practised by the very people who vouch for that wonderful conception of exemplary living. It appears that they are anxious to pass on their religion to all races of men, but keep very little of it themselves. I have not yet seen the meek inherit the earth, or the peacemakers receive high honor.

Why do we find so much evil and wickedness practised by the nations composed of professedly "Christian" individuals? The pages of history are full of licensed murder and the plundering of weaker and less developed peoples, and obviously the world to-day has not outgrown this system. Behind the material and intellectual splendor of our civilization, primitive savagery and cruelty and lust hold sway, undiminished, and as it seems, unheeded. When I let go of my simple, instinctive nature religion, I hoped to gain something far loftier as well as more satisfying to the reason. Alas! it is also more confusing and contradictory. The higher and spiritual life, though first in theory, is clearly secondary, if not entirely neglected, in actual practice. When I reduce civilization to its lowest terms, it becomes a system of life based upon trade. The dollar is the measure of value, and *might* still spells *right;* otherwise, why war?

Yet even in deep jungles God's own sunlight penetrates, and I stand before my own people still as an advocate of civilization. Why? First, because there is no chance for our former simple life any more; and second, because I realize that the white man's religion is not responsible for his mistakes. There is every evidence that God has given him all the light necessary by which to live in peace and good-will with his brother; and we also know that many brilliant civilizations have collapsed in physical and moral decadence. It is for us to avoid their fate if we can.

I am an Indian; and while I have learned much from civilization, for which I am grateful, I have never lost my Indian sense of right and justice. I am for development and progress along social and spiritual lines, rather than those of commerce, nationalism, or material efficiency. Nevertheless, so long as I live, I am an American.

From Black Elk Speaks

<u>1932</u>

Black Elk (1863–1950) narrated his life story as the fulfillment of a duty. He intended his collaboration with the white Christian poet John G. Neihardt (1881–1973) to save his vision for future generations. "The tree will bloom again and the people will know the true facts," he observed. "When [Neihardt's] words have passed, the memory of them will stand long in the west like a flaming rainbow." As "Flaming Rainbow," his proffered Lakota name, Neihardt made Black Elk's dream visible.

Neihardt explained that his contribution involved not translation but "*transformation.*" Though he believed history was a series of loops (explaining in a letter, "we do not proceed toward perfection upon an ascending straight line"), he imposed a chronology: "Black Elk did not sit and tell me his story in a chronological order . . . The beginning and the ending are mine." The line "a people's dream died there" isn't in the original typescript. "And so it was all over," Neihardt writes, seeming to vanish the Indian.

But the book does embody an intersection of cultures, times, genres, and voices. The white man's squares, lines, and bounded horizons intersect with the circles of peace and warfare and the movement of the day. The Lakota Indians order time by event in their reminiscences, time runs upstream, men move backward up a hill, and Black Elk watches himself grow younger. Prophecy disrupts chronology, too, bringing the future into the present. The book features ritual performances, chants, drawings, dream-talks, and kill-talks alongside Christian symbols, echoes of the King James Bible, and elements of the confession, memoir, and apology. Like William Apess and Charles Eastman, Black Elk emphasizes his plural identity and creates a composite first-person voice. He creates readers' voices too, addressing them directly.

This narration, involving Black Elk, his translating son, Neihardt, Neihardt's transcribing daughter, participating tribal members, and readers, challenges what Black Elk calls the rule of "everybody for himself," and makes the world an event in process. The book protests America's negative utopia of borders and finds a borderland where possible worlds and multiple voices coexist. Though ignored on its original publication in 1932, the book's message appealed to later readers. Reissued in 1961, Black Elk's narrative was embraced as spiritual vision, ecological protest, and countercultural philosophy.

Further reading: Brian Holloway, *Interpreting the Legacy* (2003); Arnold Krupat, *Ethnocriticism* (1992).

I kept on curing the sick for three years more, and many came to me and were made over; but when I thought of my great vision, which was to save the nation's hoop and make the holy tree to bloom in the center of it, I felt like crying, for the sacred hoop was broken and scattered. The life of the people was in the hoop, and what are many little lives if the life of those lives be gone?

But late in my twenty-third summer (1886), it seemed that there was a little hope. There came to us some Wasichus who wanted a band of Ogalalas for a big show that the other Pahuska* had. They told us this show would go across the big water to strange lands, and I thought I ought to go, because I might learn some secret of the Wasichu that would help my people somehow. In my great vision, when I stood at the center of the world, the two men from the east had brought me the daybreak-star herb and they had told me to drop it on the earth; and where it touched the ground it took root and bloomed four-rayed. It was the herb of understanding. Also, where the red man of my vision changed into a bison that rolled, the same herb grew and bloomed when the bison had vanished, and after that the people in my vision found the good red road again. Maybe if I could see the great world of the Wasichu, I could understand how to bring the sacred hoop together and make the tree to bloom again at the center of it.

I looked back on the past and recalled my people's old ways, but they were not living that way any more. They were traveling the black road, everybody for himself and with little rules of his own, as in my vision. I was in despair, and I even thought that if the Wasichus had a better way, then maybe my people should live that way. I know now that this was foolish, but I was young and in despair . . .

We wanted a much bigger war-party so that we could meet the soldiers and get revenge. But this was hard, because the people were not all of the same mind, and they were hungry and cold. We had a meeting there, and were all ready to go out with more warriors, when Afraid-of-His-Horses came over from Pine Ridge to make peace with Red Cloud, who was with us there.

Our party wanted to go out and fight anyway, but Red Cloud made a speech to us something like this: "Brothers, this is a very hard winter. The women and children are starving and freezing. If this were summer, I would say to keep on fighting to the end. But we cannot do this. We must think of the women and children and that it is very bad for them. So we must make peace, and I will see that nobody is hurt by the soldiers."

The people agreed to this, for it was true. So we broke camp next day and went down from the O-ona-gazhee to Pine Ridge, and many, many Lakotas were already there. Also, there were many, many soldiers. They stood in two lines with their guns held in front of them as we went through to where we camped.

And so it was all over.

* Long Hair, Buffalo Bill.

I did not know then how much was ended. When I look back now from this high hill of my old age, I can still see the butchered women and children lying heaped and scattered all along the crooked gulch as plain as when I saw them with eyes still young. And I can see that something else died there in the bloody mud, and was buried in the blizzard. A people's dream died there. It was a beautiful dream.

And I, to whom so great a vision was given in my youth,—you see me now a pitiful old man who has done nothing, for the nation's hoop is broken and scattered. There is no center any longer, and the sacred tree is dead.

Author's Postscript

After the conclusion of the narrative, Black Elk and our party were sitting at the north edge of Cuny Table, looking off across the Badlands ("the beauty and the strangeness of the earth," as the old man expressed it). Pointing at Harney Peak that loomed black above the far sky-rim, Black Elk said: "There, when I was young, the spirits took me in my vision to the center of the earth and showed me all the good things in the sacred hoop of the world. I wish I could stand up there in the flesh before I die, for there is something I want to say to the Six Grandfathers."

So the trip to Harney Peak was arranged, and a few days later we were there. On the way up to the summit, Black Elk remarked to his son, Ben: "Something should happen to-day. If I have any power left, the thunder beings of the west should hear me when I send a voice, and there should be at least a little thunder and a little rain." What happened is, of course, related to Wasichu readers as being merely a more or less striking coincidence. It was a bright and cloudless day, and after we had reached the summit the sky was perfectly clear. It was a season of drouth, one of the worst in the memory of the old men. The sky remained clear until about the conclusion of the ceremony.

"Right over there," said Black Elk, indicating a point of rock, "is where I stood in my vision, but the hoop of the world about me was different, for what I saw was in the spirit."

Having dressed and painted himself as he was in his great vision, he faced the west, holding the sacred pipe before him in his right hand. Then he sent forth a voice; and a thin, pathetic voice it seemed in that vast space around us:

"Hey-a-a-hey! Hey-a-a-hey! Hey-a-a-hey! Hey-a-a-hey! Grandfather, Great Spirit, once more behold me on earth and lean to hear my feeble voice. You lived first, and you are older than all need, older than all prayer. All things belong to you—the two-leggeds, the four-leggeds, the wings of the air and all green things that live. You have set the powers of the four quarters to cross each other. The good road and the road of difficulties you have made to cross;

and where they cross, the place is holy. Day in and day out, forever, you are the life of things.

"Therefore I am sending a voice, Great Spirit, my Grandfather, forgetting nothing you have made, the stars of the universe and the grasses of the earth.

"You have said to me, when I was still young and could hope, that in difficulty I should send a voice four times, once for each quarter of the earth, and you would hear me.

"To-day I send a voice for a people in despair.

"You have given me a sacred pipe, and through this I should make my offering. You see it now.

"From the west, you have given me the cup of living water and the sacred bow, the power to make live and to destroy. You have given me a sacred wind and the herb from where the white giant lives—the cleansing power and the healing. The daybreak star and the pipe, you have given from the east; and from the south, the nation's sacred hoop and the tree that was to bloom. To the center of the world you have taken me and showed the goodness and the beauty and the strangeness of the greening earth, the only mother—and there the spirit shapes of things, as they should be, you have shown to me and I have seen. At the center of this sacred hoop you have said that I should make the tree to bloom.

"With tears running, O Great Spirit, Great Spirit, my Grandfather—with running tears I must say now that the tree has never bloomed. A pitiful old man, you see me here, and I have fallen away and have done nothing. Here at the center of the world, where you took me when I was young and taught me; here, old, I stand, and the tree is withered, Grandfather, my Grandfather!

"Again, and maybe the last time on this earth, I recall the great vision you sent me. It may be that some little root of the sacred tree still lives. Nourish it then, that it may leaf and bloom and fill with singing birds. Hear me, not for myself, but for my people; I am old. Hear me that they may once more go back into the sacred hoop and find the good red road, the shielding tree!"

We who listened now noted that thin clouds had gathered about us. A scant chill rain began to fall and there was low, muttering thunder without lightning. With tears running down his cheeks, the old man raised his voice to a thin high wail, and chanted: "In sorrow I am sending a feeble voice, O Six Powers of the World. Hear me in my sorrow, for I may never call again. O make my people live!"

For some minutes the old man stood silent, with face uplifted, weeping in the drizzling rain.

In a little while the sky was clear again.

From Bury My Heart at Wounded Knee

1970

Dee Brown (1908–2002) wrote a protest of history and a history as protest. He describes the opening of the West from the Native viewpoint, even imagining himself as an "old Indian" at one point. Each chapter of *Bury My Heart at Wounded Knee* deals with a different tribe or battle, but tells the same story: another tragedy, another massacre. Brown attacks stereotypes, and traces how expressions like "the only good Indian is a dead Indian" came about. He focuses on the ideas of "noble savagery" and "manifest destiny," showing that there was nothing destined about the destruction of Indian tribes: it was a result of specific programs and policies.

Bury My Heart sold over five million copies within two years of its publication. It appealed to environmentalists: Brown describes Indian bones "sealed under a million miles of freeways, parking lots, and slabs of tract housing." After Brown came ecological protest fiction, like Leslie Marmon Silko's *Almanac of the Dead* (1991). In addition, during what Brown describes as "an age without heroes," his book struck a chord with white counterculturists, to whom Indians seemed "the most heroic of Americans," as Brown puts it. Playing Indian, hippies wore moccasins, visited sweat lodges, and experimented with communal living—prompting protest from some Native Americans. "Our religion and ceremonies have become fads . . . among many whites seeking something that they hope will give meaning to their empty lives," complained Mary Crow Dog. Brown's book also spoke to the situation in Vietnam. In 1960 John F. Kennedy described "a new frontier," and politicians and generals soon called Vietnam "Indian country," imagining search-and-destroy missions as games of cowboys-and-Indians. *Bury My Heart* coincided with antiwar protest that focused on the violence inherent in American culture and sought earlier examples of empire mentality.

Part of a tradition of protest history that includes William Apess's "Eulogy on King Phillip" (1836) and Charles Eastman's *The Indian Today* (1915), the book challenges Americans to rethink their history, which, as Brown observes, "has a way of intruding upon the present." In 1972 American Indian Movement (AIM) activists used that history to challenge the present. They staged the "Trail of Broken Treaties," a march that followed the Trail of Tears, and then in 1973 began a 71-day standoff with federal officers at Wounded Knee, on the Lakota reservation in South Dakota. Brown had ended his book with a scene of the 1890 massacre of Lakota Indians at Wounded Knee: not just protesting history, AIM was trying to change it.

[From the introduction]

Most Indian leaders spoke freely and candidly in councils with white officials, and as they became more sophisticated in such matters during the 1870's and 1880's, they demanded the right to choose their own interpreters and record-ers. In this latter period, all members of the tribes were free to speak, and some of the older men chose such opportunities to recount events they had wit-nessed in the past, or to sum up the histories of their peoples. Although the In-dians who lived through this doom period of their civilization have vanished from the earth, millions of their words are preserved in official records. Many of the more important council proceedings were published in government documents and reports.

Out of all these sources of almost forgotten oral history, I have tried to fash-ion a narrative of the conquest of the American West as the victims experi-enced it, using their own words whenever possible. Americans who have al-ways looked westward when reading about this period should read this book facing eastward.

This is not a cheerful book, but history has a way of intruding upon the pres-ent, and perhaps those who read it will have a clearer understanding of what the American Indian is, by knowing what he was. They may be surprised to hear words of gentle reasonableness coming from the mouths of Indians ste-reotyped in the American myth as ruthless savages. They may learn something about their own relationship to the earth from a people who were true conser-vationists. The Indians knew that life was equated with the earth and its re-sources, that America was a paradise, and they could not comprehend why the intruders from the East were determined to destroy all that was Indian as well as America itself.

And if the readers of this book should ever chance to see the poverty, the hopelessness, and the squalor of a modern Indian reservation, they may find it possible to truly understand the reasons why . . .

[From the final chapter]

In the first seconds of violence, the firing of carbines was deafening, filling the air with powder smoke. Among the dying who lay sprawled on the frozen ground was Big Foot. Then there was a brief lull in the rattle of arms, with small groups of Indians and soldiers grappling at close quarters, using knives, clubs, and pistols. As few of the Indians had arms, they soon had to flee, and then the big Hotchkiss guns on the hill opened up on them, firing almost a shell a second, raking the Indian camp, shredding the tepees with flying shrap-nel, killing men, women, and children.

"We tried to run," Louise Weasel Bear said, "but they shot us like we were a buffalo. I know there are some good white people, but the soldiers must be mean to shoot children and women. Indian soldiers would not do that to white children."

"I was running away from the place and followed those who were running away," said Hakiktawin, another of the young women. "My grandfather and grandmother and brother were killed as we crossed the ravine, and then I was shot on the right hip clear through and on my right wrist where I did not go any further as I was not able to walk, and after the soldier picked me up where a little girl came to me and crawled into the blanket."*

When the madness ended, Big Foot and more than half of his people were dead or seriously wounded; 153 were known dead, but many of the wounded crawled away to die afterward. One estimate placed the final total of dead at very nearly three hundred of the original 350 men, women, and children. The soldiers lost twenty-five dead and thirty-nine wounded, most of them struck by their own bullets or shrapnel.

After the wounded cavalrymen were started for the agency at Pine Ridge, a detail of soldiers went over the Wounded Knee battlefield, gathering up Indians who were still alive and loading them into wagons. As it was apparent by the end of the day that a blizzard was approaching, the dead Indians were left lying where they had fallen. (After the blizzard, when a burial party returned to Wounded Knee, they found the bodies, including Big Foot's, frozen into grotesque shapes.)

The wagonloads of wounded Sioux (four men and forty-seven women and children) reached Pine Ridge after dark. Because all available barracks were filled with soldiers, they were left lying in the open wagons in the bitter cold while an inept Army officer searched for shelter. Finally the Episcopal mission was opened, the benches taken out, and hay scattered over the rough flooring.

It was the fourth day after Christmas in the Year of Our Lord 1890. When the first torn and bleeding bodies were carried into the candlelit church, those who were conscious could see Christmas greenery hanging from the open rafters. Across the chancel front above the pulpit was strung a crudely lettered banner: PEACE ON EARTH, GOOD WILL TO MEN.

* McGregor, pp. 111, 140.

What Is the American Indian Movement?

1973

"My aimlessness ended when I encountered AIM." In *Lakota Woman* (1990), Mary Crow Dog explained that the American Indian Movement (AIM) of the 1960s and 1970s hit reservations "like the Ghost Dance fever" that swept Native American culture in 1890. In July 1968, Clyde Bellcourt, Eddie Benai, Dennis Banks, and George Mitchell founded Concerned Indians Americans—quickly renamed because of the acronym—to address the weakening of Indian culture and the problems created by relocation. The group had its origins in the National Indian Youth Council, founded by Vine Deloria in 1960, and in the Indian fishing-rights struggles taking place in Washington and Oregon. In 1973 Birgil Kills Straight, of the Oglala Lakota Nation, and Richard LaCourse, Director of the American Indian Press Association, wrote this document to explain the philosophy of AIM. The organization called for Native self-determination and the renewal of spirituality and traditional culture. It worked on education, housing, and police violence in its first years, wrote Native culture legislation, which was adopted, and successfully sued the federal government for the protection of Native Nations' rights. In 1978 it organized "The Longest Walk," a protest march from California to Washington, D.C.; marchers erected a tepee on White House grounds until proposed anti-Indian legislation was defeated.

Two of AIM's most high-profile protests came in 1972 and 1973. On November 3, 1972, before the presidential election, a four-mile-long procession retraced in reverse the steps of dying Indians, driven from their homes by President Jackson's Indian removal policy in 1838. The march began in Minneapolis and ended with an occupation of the Bureau of Indian Affairs headquarters in Washington, D.C. AIM members presented a twenty-point proposal, which included demands for the restitution of constitutional treaty-making powers and the restoration of 110 million acres of land. The FBI classified AIM as an extremist organization, and in March 1973 AIM began a 71-day battle with U.S. armed forces at Wounded Knee, on the Pine Ridge Reservation in South Dakota.

AIM members, many of whom were Vietnam veterans, identified with antiwar protestors, connecting American imperialism abroad and at home. But they resisted comparison to the civil rights movement, noting that *they* weren't seeking desegregation. Their policies seemed closer to the Black Panther Party's assertions of black nationalism than Martin Luther King, Jr.'s, calls for racial integration. "We took some of our rhetoric from the blacks," acknowledged Crow Dog, "but there were differences . . . They want *in*. We Indians want *out!*"

Things will never be the same again and that is what the American Indian Movement is about. They are respected by many, hated by some, but they are never ignored. They are the catalyst for Indian Sovereignty. They intend to raise questions in the minds of all, questions that have gone to sleep in the minds of Indians and non-Indians alike.

From the outside, AIM people are tough people, they had to be. AIM was born out of the dark violence of police brutality and voiceless despair of Indian people in the courts of Minneapolis, Minnesota. AIM was born because a few knew that it was enough, enough to endure for themselves and all others like them who were people without power or rights. AIM people have known the insides of jails; the long wait; the no appeal of the courts for Indians, because many of them were there.

From the inside AIM people are cleansing themselves; many have returned to the old traditional religions of their tribes, away from the confused notions of a society that has made them slaves of their own unguided lives. AIM is first, a spiritual movement, a religious re-birth, and then the re-birth of dignity and pride in a people. AIM succeeds because they have beliefs to act upon.

The American Indian Movement is attempting to connect the realities of the past with the promise of tomorrow. They are people in a hurry, because they know that the dignity of a person can be snuffed by despair and a belt in a cell of a city jail. They know that the deepest hopes of the old people could die with them. They know that the Indian way is not tolerated in White America, because it is not acknowledged as a decent way to be. Sovereignty, Land, and Culture cannot endure if a people is not left in peace.

The American Indian Movement is then, the Warriors Class of this century, who are bound to the bond of the Drum, who vote with their bodies instead of their mouths. THEIR BUSINESS IS HOPE.

American Indians and Vietnamese

1973

The myth of the Western frontier pervaded the American vision of the Vietnam war: soldiers and politicians alike made dangerous connections between Native Americans and Vietnamese: Western movies of 1965–1972 were often about Vietnam, and Vietnam was represented as a Western. The producer of *The Green Berets* (1968) admitted: "when you're making a picture, the Indians are the bad guys." Disillusionment with this equation echoed across veteran memoirs and interviews. "When I went to Vietnam, I believed in Jesus Christ and John Wayne. After Vietnam, both went down the tubes," said one veteran, and another recalled a moment in combat when he screamed: "This ain't a John Wayne movie!" Doctors eventually dubbed a post-Vietnam stress disorder the "John Wayne syndrome."

During the war, protestors turned this myth against those perpetuating it. One remarked, "this is not the first time that American soldiers have murdered women and children . . . how about Wounded Knee?" and Michael Herr noted, "might as well say that Vietnam was where the Trail of Tears was headed all along." Some activists suggested that the FBI tried out tactics against the American Indian Movement that were later used in Indochina, making contemporary Indian wars preparation for Vietnam. The government did bring the war home; one agency ran a campaign linking the Black Panthers and the Vietcong. But activists turned this connection around too. The Student Nonviolent Coordinating Committee connected lynching to Vietnam, Huey Newton set the Vietnam war in a history of racist policies toward African Americans, and a 1969 letter to *Life* magazine observed: "We have thousands of My Lais every day right here."

This composite drawing by Roland Winkler, juxtaposing North American Indians with Vietnamese, with a flag in the shape of the Statue of Liberty superimposed, appropriated and protested the frontier soundtrack to Vietnam. It appeared in *Akwesasne Notes* in 1974. This journal was the official publication of the Mohawk Nation Council, and supported the 1969 Alcatraz occupation, the 1972 Trail of Broken Treaties, and the 1973 Wounded Knee occupation, reaching a circulation of 50,000 during the 1970s. Its motto echoed the protest message of Winkler's poster: "in the spirit of unity and diversity."

71

MARY CROW DOG

From Lakota Woman

<u>1990</u>

"Now we've burned our bridge behind us," joked someone. American Indian Movement (AIM) activists at the 1973 siege of Wounded Knee had just burned a wooden bridge so that federal agents couldn't cross it. This figural and literal bridge burning in *Lakota Woman* expresses the impossibility of bridging a cultural gulf. But Mary Crow Dog, born Mary Brave Bird in 1953 and raised on reservations in South Dakota, also challenges the divide, weaving together Native and white literary traditions in her life story. She draws on the conversion narrative to dramatize her journey from "half-breed" to "traditional Sioux," subverts the great-deeds model of autobiography, and absorbs multiple voices.

Throughout she observes the clash of myth and reality. Whites expect a Wild West Show, people try to look like Marlboro ads, and a sheriff seems to walk right out of a Western. Protesting this fictional culture, AIM activists set fire to an imitation pioneer cabin. But throughout the Wounded Knee occupation, the past returns in full force. The activists fight on the anniversary of Custer's battle and ghosts rise from a mass grave. This connection to the past seems natural to Crow Dog's husband, for his family has "no shortage of legends": he repeats the 1884 courthouse surrender and makes the Sun Dance repeat the old ritual. Mary Crow Dog knows no "big deeds of some ancestors," however, and must create her own legends: her legendary article (the worst thing in the school's history), shoplifting (a new version of counting coup), and the birth of her baby at Wounded Knee.

In her late 20th-century autobiography there is a double erasure: whites have already replaced an Indian site with a church and left Indian graves unmarked. Now, after the AIM resistance, they flatten the trading post. "Everything is gone," writes Crow Dog. But she knows that whites "cannot extinguish . . . a memory we will pass on to generations still unborn." Her story comprises layers of old stories but also living legends that mean she can affirm: "still I go on . . . Life goes on."

Our land itself is a legend, especially the area around Grass Mountain where I am living now. The fight for our land is at the core of our existence, as it has been for the last two hundred years. Once the land is gone, then we are gone too. The Sioux used to keep winter counts, picture writings on buffalo skin, which told our people's story from year to year. Well, the whole country is one vast winter count. You can't walk a mile without coming to some family's sacred vision hill, to an ancient Sun Dance circle, an old battle-ground, a place where something worth remembering happened. Mostly a death, a proud death or a drunken death. We are a great people for dying. "It's a good day to die!" that's our old battle cry. But the land with its tar paper shacks and outdoor privies, not one of them straight, but all leaning this way or that way, is also a land to live on, a land for good times and telling jokes and talking of great deeds done in the past. But you can't live forever off the deeds of Sitting Bull or Crazy Horse. You can't wear their eagle feathers, freeload off their legends. You have to make your own legends now. It isn't easy.

Leonard always thought that the dancers of 1890 had misunderstood Wovoka and his message. They should not have expected to bring the dead back to life, but to bring back their ancient beliefs by practicing Indian religion. For Leonard, dancing in a circle holding hands was bringing back the sacred hoop—to feel, holding on to the hand of your brother and sister, the rebirth of Indian unity, feel it with your flesh, through your skin. He also thought that reviving the Ghost Dance would be making a link to our past, to the grandfathers and grandmothers of long ago. So he decided to ghost-dance again at the place where this dance had been killed and where now it had to be resurrected. He knew all the songs and rituals that his father Henry had taught him, who himself had learned them from his grandfather. All through the night women were making old-style Ghost Dance shirts out of curtains, burlap bags, or whatever they could find. They painted them in the traditional way and they were beautiful.

On the evening before the dance, Leonard addressed the people. We got it down on tape. This is what he said: "Tomorrow we'll ghost-dance. You're not goin' to say 'I got to rest.' There'll be no rest, no intermission, no coffee break. We're not going to drink water. So that'll take place whether it snows or rains. We're goin' to unite together, no matter what tribe we are. We won't say, 'I'm a different tribe,' or, 'He's a black man, he's a white man.' We're not goin' to have this white man's attitude.

"If one of us gets into the power, the spiritual power, we'll hold hands. If he falls down, let him. If he goes into convulsions, don't be scared. We won't call a medic. The spirit's goin' to be the doctor.

"There's a song I'll sing, a song from the spirit. Mother Earth is the drum, and the clouds will be the visions. The visions will go into your mind. In your mind you might see your brothers, your relations that have been killed by the white man.

"We'll elevate ourselves from this world to another world from where you can see. It's here that we're goin' to find out. The Ghost Dance spirit will be in us. The peace pipe is goin' to be there. The fire is goin' to be there; tobacco is goin' to be there. We'll start physically and go on spiritually and then you'll get into the power. We're goin' to start right here, at Wounded Knee, in 1973.

Everybody's heard about the Ghost Dance but nobody's ever seen it. The United States prohibited it. There was to be no Ghost Dance, no Sun Dance, no Indian religion.

"But the hoop has not been broken. So decide tonight—for the whole unborn generations. If you want to dance with me tomorrow, you be ready!"

For the dance, Leonard had selected a hollow between hills where the feds could neither see the dancers nor shoot at them. And he had made this place waken—sacred. And so the Sioux were ghost-dancing again, for the first time in over eighty years. They danced for four days starting at five o'clock in the morning, dancing from darkness into the night. And that dance took place around the first day of spring, a new spring for the Sioux Nation. Like the Ghost Dancers of old, many men danced barefoot in the snow around a cedar tree. Leonard had about thirty or forty dancers. Not everybody who wanted to was able to dance. Nurses and medics had to remain at their stations. Life had to be sustained and the defenses maintained.

On the first day, one of the women fell down in the snow and was helped back to what used to be the museum. They smoked the pipe and Leonard cedared her, fanning her with his eagle wing. Slowly she came to. The woman said she could not verbalize what had happened to her, but that she was in the power and had received a vision. It took her a long time to say that much because she was in a trance with only the whites of her eyes showing. On one of the four days a snowstorm interrupted the dancing, but it could not stop it. Later, Wallace Black Elk thanked the dancers for their endurance and Russel Means made a good speech about the significance of the rebirth of the Ghost Dance.

The Oglala holy man Black Elk, who died some fifty years ago, in his book said this about Wounded Knee: "I can still see the butchered women and children lying heaped and scattered all along the crooked gulch as plain as when I saw them with eyes still young. And I can see something else died there in the bloody mud, and was buried in the blizzard. A people's dream died there. It was a beautiful dream.

"And I, to whom so great a vision was given in my youth—you see me now a pitiful old man who has done nothing, for the nation's hoop is broken and scattered. There is no center any longer, and the sacred tree is dead."

In that ravine, at Cankpe Opi, we gathered up the broken pieces of the sacred hoop and put them together again. All who were at Wounded Knee, Buddy Lamont, Clearwater, and our medicine men, we mended the nation's hoop. The sacred tree *is not dead!*

The Exaggeration of Despair

1996

Sherman Alexie (b. 1966) calls himself "a world-class coyote, foolish clown," but his pen is a smoking gun aimed at America's absurdist fictions. "Ha, ha!" he wrote in 2003, after joining Poets against the War: "The United States is the freedom-loving country where Americans fought each other over the right to own slaves! Ha!" Sardonic laughter ripples through his poems, short stories, and novels, which are designed to entertain and pro-voke. "Humor is the most effective political tool . . . people will listen to anything if they're laughing," he once explained. Alexie, a Spokane–Coeur d'Alene Indian, laughs at Indians and whites alike, denying readers the consolation of tears.

Alexie's trademark humor protests the caricature of the noble, tragic Indian (though he often uses stereotypes himself). He calls the Indian writer an ambassador, politician, and activist, with a responsibility to tell the truth, and he forces readers to redefine "Indian-ness" and grapple with the complexities of modern identities, quipping in 1998, "I've met thousands of Indians, and I have yet to know of anyone who has stood on a moun-tain waiting for a sign." He challenges Native Americans to resist stereotypes, explaining: "When I see words like *the Creator, Father Sky* . . . I almost feel like we're colonizing our-selves."

"The Exaggeration of Despair" confronts cultural imperialism and Native self-coloniza-tion head-on. Most of the poem, a catalogue of degradations that draws on the proliferat-ing power of the oral tradition, is enclosed in parentheses. This enclosure represents what Alexie frequently refers to as a "reservation of the mind": the degradation is real but shouldn't define Indian culture, from within or without. The poem's couplets also express his belief that "King Lear takes place on my reservation daily." If it must be tragic, Indian culture is a complex, Shakespearean tragedy of dialogic couplets. Alexie claims the "king-dom of culture" that W. E .B. Du Bois envisioned in 1903: "I sit with Shakespeare and he winces not."

I open the door

(this Indian girl writes that her brother tried to hang himself
with a belt just two weeks after her other brother did hang himself

and this Indian man tells us that back in boarding school,
five priests took him into a back room and raped him repeatedly

and this homeless Indian woman begs for quarters, and when I ask
her about her tribe, she says she's horny and bends over in front of me

and this homeless Indian man is the uncle of an Indian man
who writes for a large metropolitan newspaper, and so now I know them both

and this Indian child cries when he sits to eat at our table
because he had never known his own family to sit at the same table

and this Indian woman was born to an Indian woman
who sold her for a six-pack and a carton of cigarettes

and this Indian poet shivers beneath the freeway
and begs for enough quarters to buy pencil and paper

and this fancydancer passes out at the powwow
and wakes up naked, with no memory of the evening, all of his regalia gone)

I open the door

(and this is my sister, who waits years for a dead eagle from the Park Service,
    receives it
and stores it with our cousins, who then tell her it has disappeared

though the feathers reappear in the regalia of another cousin
who is dancing for the very first time

and this is my father, whose own father died on Okinawa, shot
by a Japanese soldier who must have looked so much like him

and this is my father, whose mother died of tuberculosis
not long after he was born, and so my father must hear coughing ghosts

and this is my grandmother who saw, before the white men came,
three ravens with white necks, and knew our God was going to change)

I open the door
and invite the wind inside.

3

LITTLE BOOKS
THAT STARTED
A BIG WAR

Abolition
and
Antislavery

DAVID WALKER

From Appeal to the Coloured Citizens

1829

In 1830, runaway slaves were discovered with copies of David Walker's *Appeal.* Walker (1785–1830), a free black born in North Carolina who settled in Boston and wrote for America's first independent black newspaper, *Freedom's Journal,* had died that year, but black communities continued to read his words. The *Boston Evening Transcript* noted that his pamphlet seemed "a star in the east, guiding [slaves] to freedom." A North Carolina select committee called the *Appeal* incendiary and subversive.

Walker's pamphlet *was* incendiary, combining essay, manifesto, narrative, and sermon into a raging indictment of white hypocrisy. It is an ironic elegy, a drama, and a direct address that, like most early abolitionist protest, relies on moral principles rather than economic or political arguments. Walker appeals to higher laws and expresses faith in spiritual regeneration. The first abolitionist pamphlet to address blacks, it was meant to be read by black ministers to their slave congregations: he includes finger pointers (☞)— signals of emphasis for those reading aloud, like Thomas Jefferson's pause marks in his draft of the Declaration of Independence.

The pamphlet's formal construction and use of language are themselves a form of protest: one 1831 reviewer noted: "Let those who believe in the mental inferiority of the blacks read it." While emotive, Walker's pamphlet also draws on Enlightenment principles of justice, incorporates history, and calls on America to reconcile its rhetoric with reality. Shifting from equality as a general principle to racial equality as a specific principle, he makes the republican "we" a democratic "I." And, while Tom Paine moved between "we" and "I" in *Common Sense* and Jefferson used "we" in the Declaration, Walker uses "I" and "you."

The *Appeal* produced "more commotion . . . than any volume of its size," the abolitionist Henry Garnet observed in 1848. Frederick Douglass added in 1883 that it "startled the land like a trump of coming judgment" and launched the abolitionist movement. Walker's *Appeal* also influenced protest novels, which grew out of pamphlet print culture: in *Uncle Tom's Cabin* (1852) Harriet Beecher Stowe makes 43 direct addresses to the reader, her version of Walker's ☞.

Further reading: Peter Hinks, *To Awaken My Afflicted Brethren* (1997); Patrick Rael, *Black Identity* (2002).

Preamble

I am fully aware, in making this appeal to my much afflicted and suffering brethren, that I shall not only be assailed by those whose greatest earthly desires are, to keep us in abject ignorance and wretchedness, and who are of the firm conviction that Heaven has designed us and our children to be slaves and beasts of burden to them and their children. I say, I do not only expect to be held up to the public as an ignorant, impudent and restless disturber of the public peace, by such avaricious creatures, as well as a mover of insubordination—and perhaps put in prison or to death, for giving a superficial exposition of our miseries, and exposing tyrants. But I am persuaded, that many of my brethren, particularly those who are ignorantly in league with slaveholders or tyrants, who acquire their daily bread by the blood and sweat of their more ignorant brethren—and not a few of those too, who are too ignorant to see an inch beyond their noses, will rise up and call me cursed—Yea, the jealous ones among us will perhaps use more abject subtlety, by affirming that this work is not worth perusing, that we are well situated, and there is no use in trying to better our condition, for we cannot. I will ask one question here.—Can our condition be any worse?—Can it be more mean and abject? If there are any changes, will they not be for the better though they may appear for the worst at first? Can they get us any lower? Where can they get us? They are afraid to treat us worse, for they know well, the day they do it they are gone. But against all accusations which may or can be preferred against me, I appeal to Heaven for my motive in writing—who knows what my object is, if possible, to awaken in the breasts of my afflicted, degraded and slumbering brethren, a spirit of inquiry and investigation respecting our miseries and wretchedness in this Republican Land of Liberty!!!!!! . . .

Article II

The whites want slaves, and want us for their slaves, but some of them will curse the day they ever saw us. As true as the sun ever shone in its meridian splendor, my colour will root some of them out of the very face of the earth. They shall have enough of making slaves of, and butchering, and murdering us in the manner which they have. No doubt some may say that I write with a bad spirit, and that I being a black, wish these things to occur. Whether I write with a bad or a good spirit, I say if these things do not occur in their proper time, it is because the world in which we live does not exist, and we are deceived with regard to its existence.—It is immaterial however to me, who believe, or who refuse—though I should like to see the whites repent peradventure God may have mercy on them, some however, have gone so far that their cup must be filled . . .

Men of colour, who are also of sense, for you particularly is my APPEAL designed. Our more ignorant brethren are not able to penetrate its value. I call upon you therefore to cast your eyes upon the wretchedness of your brethren, and to do your utmost to enlighten them—go to work and enlighten your brethren!—Let the Lord see you doing what you can to rescue them and yourselves from degradation. Do any of you say that you and your family are free and happy, and what have you to do with the wretched slaves and other people? So can I say, for I enjoy as much freedom as any of you, if I am not quite as well off as the best of you. Look into our freedom and happiness, and see of what kind they are composed!! They are of the very lowest kind—they are the very dregs!—they are the most servile and abject kind, that ever a people was in possession of! If any of you wish to know how FREE you are, let one of you start and go through the southern and western States of this country, and unless you travel as a slave to a white man (a servant is a slave to the man whom he serves) or have your free papers, (which if you are not careful they will get from you) if they do not take you up and put you in jail, and if you cannot give good evidence of your freedom, sell you into eternal slavery, I am not a living man: or any man of colour, immaterial who he is, or where he came from, if he is not the fourth from the negro race!! (as we are called) the white Christians of America will serve him the same they will sink him into wretchedness and degradation for ever while he lives. And yet some of you have the hardihood to say that you are free and happy! May God have mercy on your freedom and happiness!! I met a coloured man in the street a short time since, with a string of boots on his shoulders; we fell into conversation, and in course of which, I said to him, what a miserable set of people we are! He asked, why?—Said I, we are so subjected under the whites, that we cannot obtain the comforts of life, but by cleaning their boots and shoes, old clothes, waiting on them, shaving them &c. Said he, (with the boots on his shoulders) "I am completely happy!!! I never want to live any better or happier than when I can get a plenty of boots and shoes to clean!!!" Oh! how can those who are actuated by avarice only, but think, that our creator made us to be an inheritance to them for ever, when they see that our greatest glory is centered in such mean and low objects? Understand me, brethren, I do not mean to speak against the occupations by which we acquire enough and sometimes scarcely that, to render ourselves and families comfortable through life. I am subjected to the same inconvenience, as you all.—My objections are, to our glorying and being happy in such low employments; for if we are men, we ought to be thankful to the Lord for the past, and for the future, Be looking forward with thankful hearts to higher attainments than wielding the razor and cleaning boots and shoes. The man whose aspirations are not above, and even below these, is indeed, ignorant and wretched enough. I advanced it therefore to you, not as a problematical, but as an unshaken and for ever immovable fact, that your full glory and happiness, as well as all other coloured people under Heaven, shall never be fully consummated, but with the entire emancipation of your enslaved brethren all over the world. You may therefore, go to work and do what you can to rescue, or join in with tyrants to oppress them and yourselves, until the Lord shall come upon you all like a thief in the night. For I believe it is the will of the Lord that our greatest happiness shall consist in working for the salvation of our whole body. When this is accomplished a burst of glory will shine upon you, which will indeed astonish you and the world. Do any of you say this never will be done? I assure you that God will accomplish it—if nothing else will answer, he will hurl tyrants and devils into atoms and make way for his people. But O my brethren! I say unto you again, you must go to work and prepare the way of the Lord. There is a great work for you to do, as trifling as some of you may think of it. You have to prove to the Americans and the world, that we are MEN, and not brutes, as we have been represented, and by millions treated.

Article III

See how they treat us in open violation of the Bible!! They no doubt will be greatly offended with me, but if God does not awaken them, it will be, because they are superior to other men, as they have represented themselves to be. Our divine Lord and Master said, "all things whatsoever ye would that men should do unto you, do ye even so unto them." But an American minister, with the Bible in his hand, holds us and our children in the most abject slavery and wretchedness. Now I ask them, would they like for us to hold them and their children in abject slavery and wretchedness? No says one, that never can be done—you are too abject and ignorant to do it—you are not men—you were made to be slaves to us, to dig up gold and silver for us and our children. Know this, my dear sirs, that although you treat us and our children now, as you do your domestic beast—yet the final result of all future events are known but to God Almighty alone, who rules in the armies of heaven and among the inhabitants of the earth, and who dethrones one earthly king and sits up another, as it seemeth good in his holy sight. We may attribute these vicissitudes to what we please, but the God of armies and of justice rules in heaven and in earth, and the whole American people shall see and know it yet, to their satisfaction . . .

Perhaps they will laugh at or make light of this; but I tell you Americans! that unless you speedily alter your course, you and your Country are gone!!!!!! For God Almighty will tear up the very face of the earth!!! Will not that very remarkable passage of Scripture be fulfilled on Christian Americans? Hear it Americans!! "He that is unjust, let him be unjust still:—and he which is filthy, let him be filthy still: and he that is righteous, let him be righteous still: and he that is holy, let him be holy still." I hope that the Americans may hear, but I am afraid that they have done us so much injury, and are so firm in the belief that our Creator made us to be an inheritance to them for ever, that their hearts will be hardened, so that their destruction may be sure. This language, perhaps is too harsh for the American's delicate ears. But Oh Americans! Americans!! I warn you in the name of the Lord, (whether you will hear, or forbear,) to repent and reform, or you are ruined!!! Do you think that our blood is hidden from the Lord, because you can hide it from the rest of the world, by sending out missionaries, and by your charitable deeds to the Greeks, Irish, &c.? Will he not publish your secret crimes on the house top? Even here in Boston, pride and prejudice have got to such a pitch, that in the very houses erected to the Lord, they have built little places for the reception of coloured people, where they must sit during meeting, or keep away from the house of God, and the preachers say nothing about it—much less go into the hedges and highways seeking the lost sheep of the house of Israel, and try to bring them in to their Lord and Master. There are not a more wretched, ignorant, miserable, and abject set of beings in all the world, than the blacks in the Southern and Western sections of this country, under tyrants and devils. The preachers of America cannot see them, but they can send out missionaries to convert the heathens, notwithstanding. Americans! unless you speedily alter your course of proceeding, if God Almighty does not stop you, I say it in his name, that you may go on and do as you please for ever, both in time and eternity—never fear any evil at all!!!!!!!! . . .

Did not God make us as it seemed best to himself? What right, then, has one of us, to despise another and to treat him cruel, on account of his colour, which none but the God who made it can alter? Can there be a greater absurdity in nature, and particularly in a free republican country? But the Americans, having introduced slavery among them, their hearts have become almost seared, as with an hot iron, and God has nearly given them up to believe a lie in preference to the truth!!! and I am awfully afraid that pride, prejudice, avarice and blood, will, before long, prove the final ruin of this happy republic, or land of liberty!!! Can any thing be a greater mockery of religion than the way in which it is conducted by the Americans? It appears as though they are bent only on daring God Almighty to do his best—they chain and handcuff us and our children and drive us around the country like brutes, and go into the house of the God of justice to return Him thanks for having aided him in their infernal cruelties inflicted upon us. Will the Lord suffer this people to go on much longer, taking his holy name in vain? Will he not stop them, PREACHERS and all? O Americans! Americans!! I call God—I call angels—I call men, to witness, that your DESTRUCTION is at hand, and will be speedily consummated unless you REPENT.

Article IV

. . . See your Declaration Americans!!! Do you understand your own language?
Hear your language, proclaimed to the world, July 4th, 1776—☞"We hold
these truths to be self evident—that ALL MEN ARE CREATED EQUAL!! that
they are endowed by their Creator with certain unalienable rights; that among
these are life, liberty, and the pursuit of happiness!!" Compare your own language above, extracted from your Declaration of Independence, with your cruelties and murders inflicted by your cruel and unmerciful fathers and yourselves on our fathers and on us—men who have never given your fathers
or you the least provocation!!!!!! Hear your language further! ☞"But when
a long train of abuses and usurpation, pursuing invariably the same object,
evinces a design to reduce them under absolute despotism, it is their right, it is
their duty, to throw off such government, and to provide new guards for their
future security."

Now, Americans! I ask you candidly, was your sufferings under Great Britain,
one hundredth part as cruel and tyranical as you have rendered ours under
you?

From Uncle Tom's Cabin

<u>1852</u>

"Once upon a time a great-hearted woman . . . roused a continent to arms"—so wrote Upton Sinclair of Harriet Beecher Stowe (1811–1896). Sinclair himself roused a continent in 1906 with *The Jungle* (termed the "*Uncle Tom's Cabin* of Wage Slavery"). He was not the first to make this claim: Stowe had done more than any politician to advance the abolitionist cause, Joshua Giddings told Congress in December 1852 (by which time *Uncle Tom's Cabin* had sold 500,000 copies—eventually selling more than any book in the 19th century save the Bible), and Abraham Lincoln allegedly greeted Stowe in 1862 with the words, "So you're the little woman who wrote the book that started this great war!" Frederick Douglass remained convinced Stowe had changed history, noting in 1881: "More than to reason or religion are we indebted to [her] influence . . . on the public mind."

But, as with much great protest literature, the relationship between text and history was symbiotic. "Nothing could have better suited the moral and humane requirements of the hour," wrote Douglass in the same piece, and one 1852 reviewer explained that Stowe's popularity was due to "organized agitation" which kept America "ready to blaze forth." The book came after more than twenty years of abolitionist agitation and organizing, and in addition it spoke powerfully to an audience already roused to anger by the 1850 Fugitive Slave Law, which empowered federal authorities to capture fugitive slaves in free states and return them to their owners.

The debate over Stowe as trigger or product of history reflects the novel's complicated origins. One stimulus for its composition was indeed the Fugitive Slave Law. In response to urging from her sister-in-law to "make this whole nation feel what an accursed thing slavery is," Stowe announced: "I will write something." Stowe's second prompt was apparently God. She often claimed that "the Lord Himself wrote *Uncle Tom's Cabin*," and as God's instrument she joins social critique to spiritual renewal, suggesting that the combination of Anglo-Saxon femininity (Eva) and black Christianity (Tom) will achieve heaven on earth. She drew on the Bible, the sermon, the confession, and the conversion narrative: sensing that a protest novel should demonstrate affinity with readers' attitudes, she challenged the dominant discourse while using its tools. The third stimulus was the death of Stowe's child, when, as she said in 1852, she felt what a slave mother "may feel when her child is torn away." She sought consolation in working out "some great good to others."

In the excerpt reprinted here, Senator and Mrs. Bird, discussing the Fugitive Slave Law, are interrupted by the arrival of the runaway slave Eliza, who arouses Mrs. Bird's sympathy as they share experiences of losing children. Stowe asks readers to experience the same empathetic pain: "See . . . to your sympathies," she instructs in her final chapter. Sure enough, one 1852 reviewer claimed that *Uncle Tom's Cabin* had done more to "arouse the sluggish nation [than] all the orations . . . and documents," adding: "Its appeal to our sympathies is genuine." And in August 1852 Charles Sumner told Congress: "The feelings of women were enlisted . . . [*Uncle Tom's Cabin* is] the testimony of the people against the principle of that law." Then he defined a literary tradition: "Poetry and Literature came to aid the Cause of Freedom." The American protest novel was born.

Further reading: Joan Hedrick, *Harriet Beecher Stowe* (1994); Harriet Beecher Stowe, *A Key to Uncle Tom's Cabin* (1853).

Chapter IX. In Which It Appears That a Senator Is But a Man

. . . Mr. and Mrs. Bird went into the kitchen, followed by the two eldest boys, the smaller fry having, by this time, been safely disposed of in bed.

The woman was now sitting up on the settle, by the fire.

She was looking steadily into the blaze, with a calm, heart-broken expression, very different from her former agitated wildness.

"Did you want me?" said Mrs. Bird, in gentle tones. "I hope you feel better now, poor woman!"

A long-drawn, shivering sigh was the only answer; but she lifted her dark eyes, and fixed them on her with such a forlorn and imploring expression, that the tears came into the little woman's eyes.

"You needn't be afraid of anything; we are friends here, poor woman! Tell me where you came from, and what you want," said she.

"I came from Kentucky," said the woman.

"When?" said Mr. Bird, taking up the interogatory.

"Tonight."

"How did you come?"

"I crossed on the ice."

"Crossed on the ice!" said every one present.

"Yes," said the woman, slowly, "I did. God helping me, I crossed on the ice; for they were behind me—right behind—and there was no other way!"

"Law, Missis," said Cudjoe, "the ice is all in broken-up blocks, a swinging and a tetering up and down in the water!"

"I know it was—I know it!" said she, wildly; "but I did it! I wouldn't have thought I could,—I didn't think I should get over, but I didn't care! I could but die, if I didn't. The Lord helped me; nobody knows how much the Lord can help 'em, till they try," said the woman, with a flashing eye.

"Were you a slave?" said Mr. Bird.

"Yes, sir; I belonged to a man in Kentucky."

"Was he unkind to you?"

"No, sir; he was a good master."

"And was your mistress unkind to you?"

"No, sir—no! my mistress was always good to me."

"What could induce you to leave a good home, then, and run away, and go through such dangers?"

The woman looked up at Mrs. Bird, with a keen, scrutinizing glance, and it did not escape her that she was dressed in deep mourning.

"Ma'am," she said, suddenly, "have you ever lost a child?"

The question was unexpected, and it was thrust on a new wound; for it was only a month since a darling child of the family had been laid in the grave.

Mr. Bird turned around and walked to the window, and Mrs. Bird burst into tears; but, recovering her voice, she said,

"Why do you ask that? I have lost a little one."

"Then you will feel for me. I have lost two, one after another,—left 'em buried there when I came away; and I had only this one left. I never slept a night without him; he was all I had. He was my comfort and pride, day and night; and, ma'am, they were going to take him away from me,—to *sell* him,—sell him down south, ma'am, to go all alone,—a baby that had never been away from his mother in his life! I couldn't stand it, ma'am. I knew I never should be good for anything, if they did; and when I knew the papers were signed, and he was sold, I took him and came off in the night; and they chased me,—the man that bought him, and some of Mas'r's folks,—and they were coming down right behind me, and I heard 'em. I jumped right on to the ice; and how I got across, I don't know,—but, first I knew, a man was helping me up the bank."

The woman did not sob nor weep. She had gone to a place where tears are dry; but every one around her was, in some way characteristic of themselves, showing signs of hearty sympathy . . .

Mrs. Bird and her husband reentered the parlor. She sat down in her little rocking-chair before the fire, swaying thoughtfully to and fro. Mr. Bird strode up and down the room, grumbling to himself, "Pish! pshaw! confounded awkward business!" At length, striding up to his wife, he said,

"I say, wife, she'll have to get away from here, this very night. That fellow will be down on the scent bright and early tomorrow morning: if 't was only the woman, she could lie quiet till it was over; but that little chap can't be kept still by a troop of horse and foot, I'll warrant me; he'll bring it all out, popping his head out of some window or door. A pretty kettle of fish it would be for me, too, to be caught with them both here, just now! No; they'll have to be got off tonight." . . .

"Your heart is better than your head, in this case, John," said the wife, laying her little white hand on his. "Could I ever have loved you, had I not known you better than you know yourself?"

And the little woman looked so handsome, with the tears sparkling in her eyes, that the senator thought he must be a decidedly clever fellow, to get such a pretty creature into such a passionate admiration of him; and so, what could he do but walk off soberly, to see about the carriage. At the door, however, he stopped a moment, and then coming back, he said, with some hesitation—

"Mary, I don't know how you'd feel about it, but there's that drawer full of things—of—of—poor little Henry's." So saying, he turned quickly on his heel, and shut the door after him.

His wife opened the little bed-room door adjoining her room and, taking the candle, set it down on the top of a bureau there; then from a small recess she took a key, and put it thoughtfully in the lock of a drawer, and made a sudden pause, while two boys, who, boy like, had followed close on her heels, stood looking, with silent, significant glances, at their mother. And oh! mother that reads this, has there never been in your house a drawer, or a closet, the opening of which has been to you like the opening again of a little grave? Ah! happy mother that you are, if it has not been so.

Mrs. Bird slowly opened the drawer. There were little coats of many a form and pattern, piles of aprons, and rows of small stockings; and even a pair of little shoes, worn and rubbed at the toes, were peeping from the folds of a paper. There was a toy horse and wagon, a top, a ball,—memorials gathered with many a tear and many a heart-break! She sat down by the drawer, and, leaning her head on her hands over it, wept till the tears fell through her fingers into the drawer; then suddenly raising her head, she began, with nervous haste, selecting the plainest and most substantial articles, and gathering them into a bundle . . .

What a situation, now, for a patriotic senator, that had been all the week before spurring up the legislature of his native state to pass more stringent resolutions against escaping fugitives, their harborers and abettors!

Our good senator in his native state had not been exceeded by any of his brethren at Washington, in the sort of eloquence which has won for them immortal renown! How sublimely he had sat with his hands in his pockets, and scouted all sentimental weakness of those who would put the welfare of a few miserable fugitives before great state interests!

He was as bold as a lion about it, and "mightily convinced" not only himself, but everybody that heard him;—but then his idea of a fugitive was only an idea of the letters that spell the word,—or at the most, the image of a little newspaper picture of a man with a stick and bundle with "Ran away from the subscriber" under it. The magic of the real presence of distress,—the imploring human eye, the frail, trembling human hand, the despairing appeal of helpless agony,—these he had never tried. He had never thought that a fugitive might be a hapless mother, a defenceless child,—like that one which was now wearing his lost boy's little well-known cap; and so, as our poor senator was not stone or steel,—as he was a man, and a downright noble-hearted one, too,—he was, as everybody must see, in a sad case for his patriotism. And you need not exult over him, good brother of the Southern States; for we have some inklings that many of you, under similar circumstances, would not do much better.

Chapter XI. In Which Property Gets into an Improper State of Mind

"Why, George, this state of mind is awful; it's getting really desperate George. I'm concerned. Going to break the laws of your country!"

"My country again! Mr. Wilson, *you* have a country; but what country have *I*, or any one like me, born of slave mothers? What laws are there for us? We don't make them,—we don't consent to them,—we have nothing to do with them; all they do for us is to crush us, and keep us down. Haven't I heard your Fourth-of-July speeches? Don't you tell us all, once a year, that governments derive their just power from the consent of the governed? Can't a fellow *think* that hears such things? Can't he put this and that together, and see what it comes to? . . . look at me, now. Don't I sit before you, every way, just as much a man as you are? Look at my face,—look at my hands,—look at my body," and the young man drew himself up proudly; "why am I *not* a man, as much as anybody? Well, Mr. Wilson, hear what I can tell you. I had a father—one of your Kentucky gentlemen—who didn't think enough of me to keep me from being sold with his dogs and horses, to satisfy the estate, when he died. I saw my mother put up at sheriff's sale, with her seven children. They were sold before her eyes, one by one, all to different masters; and I was the youngest. She came and kneeled down before old Mas'r, and begged him to buy her with me, that she might have at least one child with her; and he kicked her away with his heavy boot. I saw him do it; and the last that I heard was her moans and screams, when I was tied to his horse's neck, to be carried off to his place . . . Do you call these the laws of *my* country? Sir, I haven't any country, anymore than I have any father. But I'm going to have one. I don't want anything of *your* country, except to be let alone,—to go peaceably out of it; and when I get to Canada, where the laws will own me and protect me, *that* shall be my country, and its laws I will obey. But if any man tries to stop me, let him take care, for I am desperate. I'll fight for my liberty to the last breath I breathe. You say your fathers did it; if it was right for them, it is right for me!"

This speech, delivered partly while sitting at the table, and partly walking up and down the room,—delivered with tears, and flashing eyes, and despairing gestures,—was altogether too much for the good-natured old body to whom it was addressed, who had pulled out a great yellow silk pocket-handkerchief, and was mopping up his face with great energy . . .

Chapter XLV. Concluding Remarks

The writer has given only a faint shadow, a dim picture, of the anguish and despair that are, at this very moment, riving thousands of hearts, shattering thousands of families, and driving a helpless and sensitive race to frenzy and despair. There are those living who know the mothers whom this accursed traffic has driven to the murder of their children; and themselves seeking in death a shelter from woes more dreaded than death. Nothing of tragedy can be written, can be spoken, can be conceived, that equals the frightful reality of scenes daily and hourly acting on our shores, beneath the shadow of American law, and the shadow of the cross of Christ.

And now, men and women of America, is this a thing to be trifled with, apologized for, and passed over in silence? Farmers of Massachusetts, of New Hampshire, of Vermont, of Connecticut, who read this book by the blaze of your winter-evening fire,—strong-hearted, generous sailors and ship-owners of Maine,—is this a thing for you to countenance and encourage? Brave and generous men of New York, farmers of rich and joyous Ohio, and ye of the wide prairie states,—answer, is this a thing for you to protect and countenance? And you, mothers of America,—you who have learned, by the cradles of your own children, to love and feel for all mankind,—by the sacred love you bear your child; by your joy in his beautiful, spotless infancy; by the motherly pity and tenderness with which you guide his growing years; by the anxieties of his education; by the prayers you breathe for his soul's eternal good;—I beseech you, pity the mother who has all your affections, and not one legal right to protect, guide, or educate, the child of her bosom! By the sick hour of your child; by those dying eyes, which you can never forget; by those last cries, that wrung your heart when you could neither help nor save; by the desolation of that empty cradle, that silent nursery,—I beseech you, pity those mothers that are constantly made childless by the American slave-trade! And say, mothers of America, is this a thing to be defended, sympathized with, passed over in silence? . . . If the mothers of the free states had all felt as they should, in times past, the sons of the free states would not have been the holders, and, proverbially, the hardest masters of slaves; the sons of the free states would not have connived at the extension of slavery, in our national body; the sons of the free states would not, as they do, trade the souls and bodies of men as an equivalent to money, in their mercantile dealings. There are multitudes of slaves temporarily owned, and sold again, by merchants in northern cities; and shall the whole guilt or obloquy of slavery fall only on the South?

Northern men, northern mothers, northern Christians, have something more to do than denounce their brethren at the South; they have to look to the evil among themselves.

But, what can any individual do? Of that, every individual can judge. There is one thing that every individual can do,—they can see to it that *they feel right.* An atmosphere of sympathetic influence encircles every human being; and the man or woman who *feels* strongly, healthily and justly, on the great interests of humanity, is a constant benefactor to the human race. See, then, to your sympathies in this matter! Are they in harmony with the sympathies of Christ? or are they swayed and perverted by the sophistries of worldly policy? . . . What do you owe to these poor unfortunates, oh Christians? Does not every American Christian owe to the African race some effort at reparation for the wrongs that the American nation has brought upon them? Shall the doors of churches and school-houses be shut upon them? Shall states arise and shake them out? Shall the church of Christ hear in silence the taunt that is thrown at them, and shrink away from the helpless hand that they stretch out; and, by her silence, encourage the cruelty that would chase them from our borders? If it must be so, it will be a mournful spectacle. If it must be so, the country will have reason to tremble, when it remembers that the fate of nations is in the hands of One who is very pitiful, and of tender compassion.

From The Meaning of July Fourth
for the Negro

1852

As the last phrases of the Declaration of Independence died away, at a commemorative recital during an abolition meeting in Rochester, N.Y., Frederick Douglass (1817–1895) rose to speak. He fancied that some might advise: "would you . . . rebuke less; your cause would be much more likely to succeed." But just as the Declaration had thundered across meeting halls since 1776, so Douglass would hurl thunder now. A former slave, a prominent abolitionist, and the most famous African American of his day, Douglass issued an apocalyptic warning in a speech that is a virtuoso blend of the Bible with 18th-century philosophy, echoing Thomas Paine at one point: "there was a time when, to pronounce against England . . . tried men's souls." It also takes up the divisions of black and white in antebellum America: the nation is "your nation," the fathers are "your fathers."

Douglass had chosen to give his Rochester speech on July 5. Protesters have often chosen July 4 as their independence day: Nat Turner planned his revolt for July 4, 1831; Henry David Thoreau went to Walden Pond on July 4, 1845; William Lloyd Garrison burned the Constitution on July 4, 1854; Walt Whitman published *Leaves of Grass* on July 4, 1855; and John Brown timed his raid for July 4, 1858 and 1859 (though he had to postpone twice). But in New York, blacks had traditionally celebrated a day late, to protest the long delay in the realization of the Declaration's ideals.

Douglass's choice to speak on July 5 reminded his white audience that slavery was disrupting American progress. But more than denouncing history, Douglass wanted to change it. The Revolution loomed large in antebellum discourse and Douglass believed that fugitive slaves "acted out the declaration of independence." Invoking the spirit of the Revolution, Douglass's words on July 5 were words of action. He also offered the action of words. Douglass was a speaker with few equals, employing sarcasm, pathos, song, and mimicry, beginning quietly and building to crashing heights. His performative stage presence began to solve the problem of historical exclusion from the meaning of July 4: by the end of his speech, there are no more "walled cities," the Pacific is at his feet, and there is hope for abolition.

Further reading: David Blight, *Frederick Douglass' Civil War* (1989); Peter Walker, *Moral Choices* (1978).

. . . Fellow-citizens, above your national, tumultuous joy, I hear the mournful wail of millions! whose chains, heavy and grievous yesterday, are, to-day, rendered more intolerable by the jubilee shouts that reach them. If I do forget, if I do not faithfully remember those bleeding children of sorrow this day, "may my right hand forget her cunning, and may my tongue cleave to the roof of my mouth!" To forget them, to pass lightly over their wrongs, and to chime in with the popular theme, would be treason most scandalous and shocking, and would make me a reproach before God and the world. My subject, then, fellow-citizens, is American slavery. I shall see this day and its popular characteristics from the slave's point of view. Standing there identified with the American bondman, making his wrongs mine, I do not hesitate to declare, with all my soul, that the character and conduct of this nation never looked blacker to me than on this 4th of July! Whether we turn to the declarations of the past, or to the professions of the present, the conduct of the nation seems equally hideous and revolting. America is false to the past, false to the present, and solemnly binds herself to be false to the future. Standing with God and the crushed and bleeding slave on this occasion, I will, in the name of humanity which is outraged, in the name of liberty which is fettered, in the name of the constitution and the Bible which are disregarded and trampled upon, dare to call in question and to denounce, with all the emphasis I can command, everything that serves to perpetuate slavery—the great sin and shame of America! "I will not equivocate; I will not excuse"; I will use the severest language I can command; and yet not one word shall escape me that any man, whose judgment is not blinded by prejudice, or who is not at heart a slaveholder, shall not confess to be right and just . . .

At a time like this, scorching irony, not convincing argument, is needed. O! had I the ability, and could reach the nation's ear, I would, today, pour out a fiery stream of biting ridicule, blasting reproach, withering sarcasm, and stern rebuke. For it is not light that is needed, but fire; it is not the gentle shower, but thunder. We need the storm, the whirlwind, and the earthquake. The feeling of the nation must be quickened; the conscience of the nation must be roused; the propriety of the nation must be startled; the hypocrisy of the nation must be exposed; and its crimes against God and man must be proclaimed and denounced.

What, to the American slave, is your 4th of July? I answer; a day that reveals to him, more than all other days in the year, the gross injustice and cruelty to which he is the constant victim. To him, your celebration is a sham; your boasted liberty, an unholy license; your national greatness, swelling vanity; your sounds of rejoicing are empty and heartless; your denunciation of tyrants, brass fronted impudence; your shouts of liberty and equality, hollow mockery; your prayers and hymns, your sermons and thanksgivings, with all your religious parade and solemnity, are, to Him, mere bombast, fraud, deception, impiety, and hypocrisy—a thin veil to cover up crimes which would disgrace a nation of savages. There is not a nation on the earth guilty of practices more shocking and bloody than are the people of the United States, at this very hour.

Go where you may, search where you will, roam through all the monarchies and despotisms of the Old World, travel through South America, search out every abuse, and when you have found the last, lay your facts by the side of the everyday practices of this nation, and you will say with me, that, for revolting barbarity and shameless hypocrisy, America reigns without a rival . . .

Behold the practical operation of this internal slave-trade, the American slave-trade, sustained by American politics and American religion. Here you will see men and women reared like swine for the market. You know what is a swine-drover? I will show you a man-drover. They inhabit all our Southern States. They perambulate the country, and crowd the highways of the nation, with droves of human stock. You will see one of these human flesh jobbers, armed with pistol, whip, and bowie-knife, driving a company of a hundred men, women, and children, from the Potomac to the slave market at New Orleans. These wretched people are to be sold singly, or in lots, to suit purchasers. They are food for the cotton-field and the deadly sugar-mill. Mark the sad procession, as it moves wearily along, and the inhuman wretch who drives them. Hear his savage yells and his blood-curdling oaths, as he hurries on his affrighted captives! There, see the old man with locks thinned and gray. Cast one glance, if you please, upon that young mother, whose shoulders are bare to the scorching sun, her briny tears falling on the brow of the babe in her arms. See, too, that girl of thirteen, weeping, yes! weeping, as she thinks of the mother from whom she has been torn! The drove moves tardily. Heat and sorrow have nearly consumed their strength; suddenly you hear a quick snap, like the discharge of a rifle; the fetters clank, and the chain rattles simultaneously; your ears are saluted with a scream, that seems to have torn its way to the centre of your soul. The crack you heard was the sound of the slave-whip; the scream you heard was from the woman you saw with the babe. Her speed had faltered under the weight of her child and her chains! that gash on her shoulder tells her to move on. Follow this drove to New Orleans. Attend the auction; see men examined like horses; see the forms of women rudely and brutally exposed to the shocking gaze of American slave-buyers. See this drove sold and separated forever; and never forget the deep, sad sobs that arose from that scattered multitude. Tell me, citizens, where, under the sun, you can witness a spectacle more fiendish and shocking. Yet this is but a glance at the American slave-trade, as it exists, at this moment, in the ruling part of the United States.

I was born amid such sights and scenes. To me the American slave-trade is a terrible reality. When a child, my soul was often pierced with a sense of its horrors. I lived on Philpot Street, Fell's Point, Baltimore, and have watched from the wharves the slave ships in the Basin, anchored from the shore, with their cargoes of human flesh, waiting for favorable winds to waft them down the Chesapeake. There was, at that time, a grand slave mart kept at the head of Pratt Street, by Austin Woldfolk. His agents were sent into every town and county in Maryland, announcing their arrival, through the papers, and on flaming "hand-bills," headed cash for Negroes. These men were generally well dressed men, and very captivating in their manners; ever ready to drink, to treat, and to gamble. The fate of many a slave has depended upon the turn of a single card; and many a child has been snatched from the arms of its mother by bargains arranged in a state of brutal drunkenness.

The flesh-mongers gather up their victims by dozens, and drive them, chained, to the general depot at Baltimore. When a sufficient number has been collected here, a ship is chartered for the purpose of conveying the forlorn crew to Mobile, or to New Orleans. From the slave prison to the ship, they are usually driven in the darkness of night; for since the antislavery agitation, a certain caution is observed.

In the deep, still darkness of midnight, I have been often aroused by the dead, heavy footsteps, and the piteous cries of the chained gangs that passed our door. The anguish of my boyish heart was intense; and I was often consoled, when speaking to my mistress in the morning, to hear her say that the custom was very wicked; that she hated to hear the rattle of the chains and the heart-rending cries. I was glad to find one who sympathized with me in my horror.

Fellow-citizens, this murderous traffic is, to-day, in active operation in this boasted republic. In the solitude of my spirit I see clouds of dust raised on the highways of the South; I see the bleeding footsteps; I hear the doleful wail of fettered humanity on the way to the slave-markets, where the victims are to be sold like horses, sheep, and swine, knocked off to the highest bidder. There I see the tenderest ties ruthlessly broken, to gratify the lust, caprice and rapacity of the buyers and sellers of men. My soul sickens at the sight.

> Is this the land your Fathers loved,
> The freedom which they toiled to win?
> Is this the earth whereon they moved?
> Are these the graves they slumber in?

But a still more inhuman, disgraceful, and scandalous state of things remains to be presented. By an act of the American Congress, not yet two years old, slavery has been nationalized in its most horrible and revolting form. By that act, Mason and Dixon's line has been obliterated; New York has become as Virginia; and the power to hold, hunt, and sell men, women and children, as slaves, remains no longer a mere state institution, but is now an institution of the whole United States. The power is co-extensive with the star-spangled banner, and American Christianity. Where these go, may also go the merciless slave-hunter. Where these are, man is not sacred. He is a bird for the sportsman's gun. By that most foul and fiendish of all human decrees, the liberty and person of every man are put in peril. Your broad republican domain is hunting ground for *men*. Not for thieves and robbers, enemies of society, merely, but for men guilty of no crime. Your law-makers have commanded all good citizens to engage in this hellish sport. Your President, your Secretary of State, your *lords, nobles,* and ecclesiastics enforce, as a duty you owe to your free and glorious country, and to your God, that you do this accursed thing. Not fewer than forty Americans have, within the past two years, been hunted down and, without a moment's warning, hurried away in chains, and consigned to slavery and excruciating torture. Some of these have had wives and children, dependent on them for bread; but of this, no account was made. The right of the hunter to his prey stands superior to the right of marriage, and to *all* rights in this republic, the rights of God included! For black men there is neither law nor justice, humanity nor religion. The Fugitive Slave *Law* makes mercy to them a crime; and bribes the judge who tries them. An American judge gets ten dollars for every victim he consigns to slavery, and five, when he fails to do so. The oath of any two villains is sufficient, under this hell-black enactment, to send the most pious and exemplary black man into the remorseless jaws of slavery! His own testimony is nothing. He can bring no witnesses for himself. The minister of American justice is bound by the law to hear but *one* side; and *that* side is the side of the oppressor. Let this damning fact be perpetually told. Let it be thundered around the world that in tyrant-killing, king-hating, people-loving, democratic, Christian America the seats of justice are filled with judges who hold their offices under an open and palpable *bribe,* and are bound, in deciding the case of a man's liberty, *to hear only his accusers!*

In glaring violation of justice, in shameless disregard of the forms of administering law, in cunning arrangement to entrap the defenceless, and in diabolical intent this Fugitive Slave Law stands alone in the annals of tyrannical legislation. I doubt if there be another nation on the globe having the brass and the baseness to put such a law on the statute-book. If any man in this assembly thinks differently from me in this matter, and feels able to disprove my statements, I will gladly confront him at any suitable time and place he may select.

I take this law to be one of the grossest infringements of Christian Liberty, and, if the churches and ministers of our country were not stupidly blind, or most wickedly indifferent, they, too, would so regard it.

At the very moment that they are thanking God for the enjoyment of civil and religious liberty, and for the right to worship God according to the dictates of their own consciences, they are utterly silent in respect to a law which robs religion of its chief significance and makes it utterly worthless to a world lying in wickedness . . .

Americans! your republican politics, not less than your republican religion, are flagrantly inconsistent. You boast of your love of liberty, your superior civilization, and your pure Christianity, while the whole political power of the nation (as embodied in the two great political parties) is solemnly pledged to support and perpetuate the enslavement of three millions of your countrymen. You hurl your anathemas at the crowned headed tyrants of Russia and Austria and pride yourselves on your Democratic institutions, while you yourselves consent to be the mere *tools* and *bodyguards* of the tyrants of Virginia and Carolina. You invite to your shores fugitives of oppression from abroad, honor them with banquets, greet them with ovations, cheer them, toast them, salute them, protect them, and pour out your money to them like water; but the fugitives from oppression in your own land you advertise, hunt, arrest, shoot, and kill. You glory in your refinement and your universal education; yet you maintain a system as barbarous and dreadful as ever stained the character of a nation—a system begun in avarice, supported in pride, and perpetuated in cruelty. You shed tears over fallen Hungary, and make the sad story of her wrongs the theme of your poets, statesmen, and orators, till your gallant sons are ready to fly to arms to vindicate her cause against the oppressor; but, in regard to the ten thousand wrongs of the American slave, you would enforce the strictest silence, and would hail him as an enemy of the nation who dares to make those wrongs the subject of public discourse! You are all on fire at the mention of liberty for France or for Ireland; but are as cold as an iceberg at the thought of liberty for the enslaved of America. You discourse eloquently on the dignity of labor; yet, you sustain a system which, in its very essence, casts a stigma upon labor. You can bare your bosom to the storm of British artillery to throw off a three-penny tax on tea; and yet wring the last hard earned farthing from the grasp of the black laborers of your country. You profess to believe "that, of one blood, God made all nations of men to dwell on the face of all the earth," and hath commanded all men, everywhere, to love one another; yet you notoriously hate (and glory in your hatred) all men whose skins are not colored like your own. You declare before the world, and are understood by the world to declare that you *"hold these truths to be self-evident, that all men are created equal; and are endowed by their Creator with certain inalienable rights; and that among these are, life, liberty, and the pursuit of happiness"*; and yet, you hold securely, in a bondage which, according to your own Thomas Jefferson, *"is worse than ages of that which your fathers rose in rebellion to oppose,"* a seventh part of the inhabitants of your country.

Fellow-citizens, I will not enlarge further on your national inconsistencies. The existence of slavery in this country brands your republicanism as a sham, your humanity as a base pretense, and your Christianity as a lie. It destroys your moral power abroad: it corrupts your politicians at home. It saps the foundation of religion; it makes your name a hissing and a bye-word to a mocking earth. It is the antagonistic force in your government, the only thing that seriously disturbs and endangers your Union. It fetters your progress; it is the enemy of improvement; the deadly foe of education; it fosters pride; it breeds insolence; it promotes vice; it shelters crime; it is a curse to the earth that supports it; and yet you cling to it as if it were the sheet anchor of all your hopes. Oh! be warned! be warned! a horrible reptile is coiled up in your nation's bosom; the venomous creature is nursing at the tender breast of your youthful republic; *for the love of God, tear away,* and fling from you the hideous monster, and *let the weight of twenty millions crush and destroy it forever!* . . .

Allow me to say, in conclusion, notwithstanding the dark picture I have this day presented, of the state of the nation, I do not despair of this country. There are forces in operation which must inevitably work the downfall of slavery.

"The arm of the Lord is not shortened," and the doom of slavery is certain. I, therefore, leave off where I began, with hope. While drawing encouragement from "the Declaration of Independence," the great principles it contains, and the genius of American Institutions, my spirit is also cheered by the obvious tendencies of the age. Nations do not now stand in the same relation to each other that they did ages ago. No nation can now shut itself up from the surrounding world and trot round in the same old path of its fathers without interference. The time was when such could be done. Long established customs of hurtful character could formerly fence themselves in, and do their evil work with social impunity. Knowledge was then confined and enjoyed by the privileged few, and the multitude walked on in mental darkness. But a change has now come over the affairs of mankind. Walled cities and empires have become unfashionable. The arm of commerce has borne away the gates of the strong city. Intelligence is penetrating the darkest corners of the globe. It makes its pathway over and under the sea, as well as on the earth. Wind, steam, and lightning are its chartered agents. Oceans no longer divide, but link nations together. From Boston to London is now a holiday excursion. Space is comparatively annihilated.—Thoughts expressed on one side of the Atlantic are distinctly heard on the other.

The far off and almost fabulous Pacific rolls in grandeur at our feet. The Celestial Empire, the mystery of ages, is being solved. The fiat of the Almighty, "Let there be Light," has not yet spent its force.

Prison Letters

<u>1859</u>

On October 16, 1859, John Brown (1800–1859) launched an attack against the institution of slavery. With a band of sixteen whites and five blacks, he captured the town of Harpers Ferry and its federal arsenal, about 60 miles northwest of Washington, D.C., intending that blacks use arms from the arsenal to rise up and claim their freedom. Brown, an abolitionist, tanner, farmer, and failed businessman, had planned the raid while living in a black community at North Elba, N.Y., and his training ground was the guerrilla warfare of Bleeding Kansas, where he fought with his sons against proslavery settlers.

Federal forces overwhelmed Brown and his men after 36 hours of battle at Harpers Ferry, and Brown was indicted on counts of assault, murder, conspiracy, and treason. After his trial, Brown asked the jailer, "Have you any objections to my writing to my wife and telling her that I am to be hanged on the second of December?" It was one of many letters that he'd write in prison, letters that W. E. B. Du Bois called "the mightiest Abolition document that America has known." In his funeral address for Brown, the abolitionist Wendell Phillips claimed: "His words . . . are stronger even than his rifles." With words, Brown fought and won the battle for public opinion. "Having taken possession of Harper's Ferry," Phillips quipped in a speech on December 15, "he began to edit the New York *Tribune* and the New York *Herald* for the next three weeks."

Brown's friends planned attempts to rescue him from prison. But the abolitionist preacher Henry Ward Beecher pronounced: "a gibbet would . . . round up Brown's failure with a heroic success." Brown read this passage in prison and wrote in the margins: "good." He saw the potential value of his execution to the abolitionist cause and claimed divine authority for his protest, in the prophetic tradition of David Walker and Harriet Beecher Stowe. He compares himself to Peter, Samson, and Moses in various letters, and in one echoes Jesus: "may God forgive them, for they know not what they do." Brown's rhetoric resonated with the religiosity embedded in American political culture. This, and his talent for self-dramatization, allowed Northern abolitionists to repackage his image for their cause, comparing him to apostles, martyrs, and Christ himself. Throughout the 20th century, Brown remained a symbol of violent redemption.

Brown's letters, sampled here, are part of an important tradition in protest writing. Writers have used prison letters to construct their self-image and to address an implied audience, allowing a rhetorically powerful marriage of public and private: Brown wrote to the newspaper-reading public as well as his family. The image of incarceration (appearing in the protest literature of Rebecca Harding Davis, Upton Sinclair, John Steinbeck, and in *The Defiant Ones*) also protests America's self-made prisons, while demonstrating that words cannot be put behind bars.

Further reading: David Reynolds, *John Brown, Abolitionist* (2005); Zoe Trodd and John Stauffer, *Meteor of War* (2004).

Charlestown, Jefferson Co., Va., 31st. Oct. 1859.

My dear Wife, and Children every one

I suppose you have learned before this by the newspapers that two weeks ago today we were fighting for our lives at Harpers ferry: that during the fight Watson was mortally wounded; Oliver killed, Wm Thompson killed, & Dauphin slightly wounded. That on the following day I was taken prisoner immediately after which I received several Sabre cuts in my head; & Bayonet stabs in my body. As nearly as I can learn Watson died of his wound on Wednesday the 2d or on Thursday the 3d day after I was taken. Dauphin was killed when I was taken; & Anderson I suppose also. I have since been tried, & found guilty of treason, &c; and of murder in the first degree. I have not yet received my sentence. No others of the company with who you were acquainted were so far as *I can learn* either killed or taken. Under all these terrible calamities; I feel quite cheerful in the assurance that God reigns; & will overrule all for his glory; & the best possible good. I feel *no* conciusness of *guilt* in the matter: nor even mortifycation on account of my imprisonment; & irons; & I feel perfectly assured that very soon no member of my family will feel any possible disposition to "blush on my account." Already dear friends at a distance with kindest sympathy are cheering me with the assurance that *posterity* at least: will do me justice. I shall commend you all together with my beloved; but bereaved daughters in law to their sympathies which I have no doubt will soon reach you. I also commend you all to him "whose mercy endureth forever": to the God of my *fathers* "whose I am; & whom I serve." "He will never leave you or forsake you" unless you forsake him. Finally my dearly beloved be of good comfort. Be as it has been consistent with the holy religion of Jesus Christ in which I remain a most firm, & humble believer. Never forget the poor nor think any thing you bestow on them to be lost, to you even though they may be as *black* as Ebedmelch, the Ethiopian eunuch one to whom Phillip preached Christ. Be sure to entertain strangers for thereby some have—"Remember them that are in bonds as bound with them." I am in charge of a jailor *like* the one who took charge of "Paul & Silas;" & you may rest assured that both *kind hearts* and *kind faces* are more or less about me: whilst thousands are thirsting for my blood. "These *light* afflictions which are but *for a moment* shall work out for us a far *more exceeding & eternal* weight of glory." I hope to be able to write you again. My wounds are doing well. Copy this & send it to your sorrow stricken brothers, *Ruth;* to comfort them. Write me a few words in regard to the welfare of all. God Almighty bless you all: & make you "joyful in the midst of all your tribulations." Write to John Brown, Charlestown, Jefferson Co, Va, care of Capt John Avis

Your Affectionate Husband, & Father. John Brown

Nov. 3d 1859

P.S. Yesterday Nov 2d I was sentenced to be hanged on 2 Decem next. Do not grieve on my account. I am still quite cheerful.

Charlestown, Jefferson County, Va., Nov. 8, 1859.

Dear Wife and Children, Every One,

I will begin by saying that I have in some degree recovered from my wounds, but that I am quite weak in my back and sore about my left kidney. My appetite has been quite good for most of the time since I was hurt. I am supplied with almost everything I could desire to make me comfortable, and the little I do lack (some articles of clothing which I lost) I may perhaps soon get again. I am, besides, quite cheerful, having (as I trust) "the peace of God, which passeth all understanding," to "rule in my heart," and the testimony (in some degree) of a good conscience that I have not lived altogether in vain. I can trust God with both the time and the manner of my death, believing, as I now do, that for me at this time to seal my testimony for God and humanity with my blood will do vastly more toward advancing the cause I have earnestly endeavored to promote, than all I have done in my life before. I beg of you all meekly and quietly to submit to this, not feeling yourselves in the least *degraded* on the account. Remember, dear wife and children all, that Jesus of Nazareth suffered a most excruciating death on the cross as a felon, under the most aggravating circumstances. Think also of the prophets and apostles and Christians of former days, who went through greater tribulations than you or I, and try to be reconciled. May God Almighty comfort all your hearts, and soon wipe away all tears from your eyes! To him be endless praise! Think, too, of the crushed millions who "have no comforter." I charge you all never in your trials to forget the griefs "of the poor that cry, and of those that have none to help them." I wrote most earnestly to my dear and afflicted wife not to come on for the present, at any rate. I will now give her reasons for doing so. First, it would use up all the scanty means she has, or is at all likely to have, to make herself and children comfortable hereafter. For let me tell you that the sympathy that is now aroused in your behalf may not always follow you. There is but little more of the romantic about helping poor widows and their children than there is about trying to relieve poor "niggers." Again, the little comfort it might afford us to meet again would be dearly bought by the pains of a final separation. We must part; and I feel assured for us to meet under such dreadful circumstances would only add to our distress. If she comes on here, she must be only a gazing-stock throughout the whole journey, to be remarked upon in every look, word, and action, and by all sorts of creatures, and by all sorts of papers, throughout the whole country. Again, it is my most decided judgment that in quietly and submissively staying at home vastly more of generous sympathy will reach her, without such dreadful sacrifice of feeling as she must put up with if she comes on. The visits of one or two female friends that have come on here have produced great excitement, which is very annoying; and they cannot possibly do me any good. Oh, Mary! do not come, but patiently wait for the meeting of those who love God and their fellow-men, where no separation must follow. "They shall go no more out forever." I greatly long to hear from some one of you, and to learn anything that in any way affects your welfare. I sent you ten dollars the other day; did you get it? I have also endeavored to stir up Christian friends to visit and write to you in your deep affliction. I have no doubt that some of them, at least, will heed the call. Write to me, care of Captain John Avis, Charlestown, Jefferson County, Virginia.

"Finally, my beloved, be of good comfort." May all your names be "written in the Lamb's book of life!"—may you all have the purifying and sustaining influence of the Christian religion!—is the earnest prayer of

Your affectionate husband and father, John Brown

P.S.—I cannot remember a night so dark as to have hindered the coming day, nor a storm so furious and dreadful as to prevent the return of warm sunshine and a cloudless sky. But, beloved ones, do remember that this is not your rest,—that in this world you have no abiding place or continuing city. To God and his infinite mercy I always commend you.

Charlestown, Jefferson Co. Va. 17th Nov. 1859

J B Musgrave Esqr
My Dear Young Friend

I have just received your most kind; & welcome letter of the 15th inst but did not get any other from you. I am under many obligations *to you & to your Father* for all the kindness you have shown me, especially since my disaster. *May God* & your own consciousness ever be your rewarders. Tell your Father that I am quite cheerful that I do not feel myself in the least degraded by my imprisonment, my chain, or the *near prospect* of the Gallows. *Men* cannot *imprison,* or *chain;* or *hang* the *soul.* I go joyfuly in behalf of Millions that "have no rights" that this "great, & glorious"; "this Christian Republic," "is bound to respect." Strange *change in morals political;* as well as *Christian;* since 1776. I look forward to *other changes* to take place *in "Gods good time;"* fully believing that "the fashion of this world passeth away." (I am unable *now* to tell you where my friend is; that you inquire after. Perhaps my Wife who I suppose is still with Mrs. Spring, may have some information of him. I think it quite uncertain however.) Farewell; may God abundantly bless You all.

Your Friend, John Brown

Jail, Charlestown, Wednesday, Nov. 23, 1859

Rev. McFarland,

Dear Friend:

Although you write to me as a stranger, the spirit you show towards me and the cause for which I am in bonds, makes me feel towards you as a dear friend. I would be glad to have you, or any of my liberty-loving ministerial friends here, to talk and pray with me. I am not a stranger to the way of salvation by Christ. From my youth I have studied much on that subject, and at one time hoped to be a minister myself; but God had another work for me to do. To me it is given in behalf of Christ, not only to believe on him, but also to *suffer* for his sake. But while I trust that I have some experimental and saving knowledge of religion, it would be a great pleasure to me to have some one better qualified than myself to lead my mind in prayer and meditation, now that my time is so near a close. You may wonder, are there no ministers of the gospel here? I answer, No. There are no ministers of *Christ* here. These ministers who profess to be Christian, and hold slaves or advocate slavery, I cannot abide them. My knees will not bend in prayer with them while their hands are stained with the blood of souls. The subject you mention as having been preaching on, the day before you wrote to me, is one which I have often thought of since my imprisonment. I think I feel as happy as Paul did when he lay in prison. He knew if they killed him it would greatly advance the cause of Christ; that was the reason he rejoiced so. On that same ground "I do rejoice, yea, and will rejoice." Let them hang me; I forgive them, and may God forgive them, for they know not what they do. I have no regret for the transaction for which I am condemned. I went against the laws of men, it is true; but "whether it be right to obey *God* or *men*, judge ye." Christ told me to remember them that are in bonds, as *bound with them*, to do towards them as I would wish them to do towards me in similar circumstances. My conscience bade me do that. I tried to do it, but failed. Therefore I have no regret on that score. I have no sorrow either as to the result, only for my poor wife and children. They have suffered much, and it is hard to leave them uncared for. But God will be a husband to the widow, and a father to the fatherless.

I have frequently been in Wooster; and if any of my old friends from Akron are there, you can show them this letter. I have but a few more days, and I feel anxious to be away, "where the wicked cease from troubling, and the weary are at rest." Farewell.

Your friend, and the friend of all friends of liberty, John Brown.

Charlestown, Prison, Jefferson Co. Va. 30th Nov. 1859.

My Dearly beloved Wife, Sons: & Daughters, *every one*

. . . I am writing the hour of my public *murder* with great composure of mind, & cheerfulness; feeling the strongest assurance that in no other possible way could I be used to so much advance the cause of God; & of humanity; & that nothing that either I or all my family have sacrificed or suffered: *will be lost.* The reflection that a *wise, & merciful, as well as Just, & holy God:* rules not only the affairs of *this world;* but of all worlds; is a rock to set our feet upon; under all circumstances; *even* those more severely *trying ones:* into which our own follies; & [w]rongs have placed us. I have now no doubt but that our seeming *disaster:* will ultimately result in the most *glorious success.* So my dear *shattered; & broken* family; be of good cheer; & believe & trust in God; "with all your heart; & with all your soul;" for *he* doeth *All things well."* Do not feel ashamed on my account; nor *for one moment* despair of the cause; or grow *weary* of *well doing.* I bless God; I never felt stronger confidence in the certain & near approach of a *bright Morning; & glorious day;* then I have felt; & do now feel; since my confinement here. I am endeavouring to "return" like a "poor Prodigal" *as I am;* to my Father: against whom I have *always* sined: *in the hope;* that he may kindly, & forgivingly "meet me: though; *a verry great way off."* Oh my dear Wife & Children would "to God" you could know how I have been "traveling in birth for you" all; that no one of you "may fail of the grace of God, through Jesus Christ:" that no one of you may be blind to the truth: & glorious "light of *his* word;" in which Life; & Immortality; are brought to light." I beseech you *every one* to make the bible your *dayly & Nightly study;* with a *childlike honest, candid, teachable spirit:* out of love and respect for your Husband; & Father: & I beseech *the God* of *my Fathers;* to open all your eyes to a discovery of *the truth.* You *cannot imagine* how much *you* may *soon need* the consolations of the Christian religion.

Circumstances like my own; for more than a month past; convince me beyound *all doubt* of our great need: of something more to rest our hopes on; than merely our own vague theories framed up, while our *prejudices* are excited; *or* our *Vanity* worked up to its highest pitch. Oh do not trust your eternal all uppon the boisterous Ocean, without *even a Helm;* or *Compass* to aid you in steering. I do *not ask any* of you; to throw *away your reason:* I only *ask* you, to make a candid, & sober *use of your reason:* My dear younger children will you listen to this last poor admonition of one who can *only* love you? Oh be determined at once to give your whole hearts to God; & let *nothing shake; or alter;* that resolution. You need have no fear *of* REGRETING *it.* Do not be in vain; and thoughtless: but *sober minded.* And let me entreat you all to love *the whole remnant* or our once great family: "with a pure *heart fervently.*" Try to *build again:* your broken walls: & to make *the utmost* of every *stone* that is left. Nothing can so tend to make life a blessing as the consciousness that you *love: & are beloved:* & "love ye the stranger" *still.* It is a ground of the utmost comfort to *my mind:* to know that so many of you as have had *the opportunity;* have given full proof of your fidelity to the great family of man. *Be faithful* until *death.* From the exercise of habitual love to man: *it cannot* be very *hard:* to *learn to love* his *maker.* I must *yet* insert a reason for my firm belief in the Divine inspiration of the Bible: notwithstanding I am (perhaps naturally) skeptical. (certainly not, *credulous.*) I wish you all to consider *it most thoroughly;* when you read that blessed book; & see whether you *can not* discover such evidence yourselves. It is the purity of *heart, feeling, or motive:* as well as *word, & action* which is every where insisted on; that distinguish it from *all other teachings;* that *commends it* to *my conscience:* whether *my heart* be "willing, & obedient" *or not.* The inducements that it holds out; are another reason *of my conviction* or its *truth: & genuineness;* that I cannot here *omit;* in this my *last argument,* for the Bible *Eternal life:* is that my soul *is "panting after" this moment.* I mention this; as reason for endeavouring to leave a valuable copy of the Bible to be carefully *preserved* in remembrance of *me:* to so many of my posterity; *instead* of some *other* thing: of equal *cost.* I beseech you all to live in habitual contentment with verry *moderate* circumstances: & gains, of *worldly store:* & most earnestly to teach this: to your *children; & Childrens, Children;* after you: by *example: as well;* as precept. Be determined to know by experience *as soon as may be:* whether bible instruction is of *Divine origin* or not; *which says; "Owe no man anything but* to love one another." John Rogers wrote to his children, "Abhor that arrant whore of Rome." John Brown writes to his children to abhor with *undiing hatred,* also: that "sum of all vilanies;" Slavery. *Remember* that "he that is *slow* to *anger* is *better* than the mighty: and he that ruleth his *spirit;* than he that taketh a city." Remember also: *that* "they that be *wise* shall *shine:* and they that *turn* many to *righteousness:* as the stars forever; & ever." And now dearly beloved *Farewell* To God & the word of his grace I comme[n]d you all.

Your Affectionate Husband & Father, John Brown

Charlestown, Va, 2d, December, 1859.

I John Brown am now quite *certain* that the crimes of this *guilt land: will* never be purged *away;* but with Blood. I had as *I now think; vainly* flattered myself that without *verry much* bloodshed; it might be done.

From Incidents in the Life of a Slave Girl

1861

In 1849 the abolitionist clergyman Theodore Parker explained that America finally had a "series of literary productions that could be written by none but Americans, and only here . . . the Lives of Fugitive Slaves." *Incidents,* written by Harriet Jacobs (1813–1897) and published under the pseudonym Linda Brent, is one of America's most important slave narratives, and one of the few by a woman. It's also one of the most profound protests against national amnesia and social alienation ever written. The autobiography has at its center a tiny garret space, where Brent hides for seven years, calling it a "loophole of retreat." She makes a mark for each day that passes—like the marks on the headboard in Charlotte Perkins Gilman's madwoman-in-the-attic story "The Yellow Wallpaper" (1892). Though Brent eventually escapes from the garret, while trapped there she is a marginalized woman, pushed into the cracks of the national house, like Gilman's protagonist.

Brent is trapped in the edifice of slavery, which she describes as a living death. The loophole is slavery's social death made into a real living grave. She is also trapped in the loophole of America's founding documents, which failed to abolish slavery; the garret space evokes the historical ellipsis between ideal and fulfillment. But, mixing slave narrative and sentimental novel, classic gothic and captivity narrative, Jacobs makes the slaveholder, Dr. Flint, a character in an epistolary novel. The loophole becomes a protective space: Brent creates a circular mail system that outlines a place beyond the crevice, and these letters transform the garret from a no-man's-land into a creative refuge. Brent remains in the garret space but the alter ego of her letters lives a parallel history in the North. And, in telling her story as Linda Brent, Jacobs constructed another alter ego: liberated from her garret space, the real Harriet Jacobs would be hard to pin down.

Further reading: Johnnie Stover, *Rhetoric and Resistance* (2003); Kari Winter, *Subjects of Slavery* (1992).

XXI. The Loophole of Retreat

A small shed had been added to my grandmother's house years ago. Some boards were laid across the joists at the top, and between these boards and the roof was a very small garret, never occupied by any thing but rats and mice. It was a pent roof, covered with nothing but shingles, according to the southern custom for such buildings. The garret was only nine feet long, and seven wide.

The highest part was three feet high, and sloped down abruptly to the loose board floor. There was no admission for either light or air. My uncle Philip, who was a carpenter, had very skillfully made a concealed trap door, which communicated with the storeroom. He had been doing this while I was waiting in the swamp. The storeroom opened upon a piazza. To this hole I was conveyed as soon as I entered the house. The air was stifling; the darkness total. A bed had been spread on the floor. I could sleep quite comfortably on one side; but the slope was so sudden that I could not turn on the other without hitting the roof. The rats and mice ran over my bed; but I was weary, and I slept such sleep as the wretched may, when a tempest has passed over them. Morning came. I knew it only by the noises I heard; for in my small den day and night were all the same. I suffered for air even more than for light. But I was not comfortless. I heard the voices of my children.

There was joy and there was sadness in the sound. It made my tears flow. How I longed to speak to them! I was eager to look on their faces; but there was no hole, no crack, through which I could peep. This continued darkness was oppressive. It seemed horrible to sit or lie in a cramped position day after day, without one gleam of light. Yet I would have chosen this, rather than my lot as a slave, though white people considered it an easy one; and it was so compared with the fate of others. I was never cruelly over-worked; I was never lacerated with the whip from head to foot; I was never so beaten and bruised that I could not turn from one side to the other; I never had my heel-strings cut to prevent my running away; I was never chained to a log and forced to drag it about, while I toiled in the fields from morning till night; I was never branded with hot iron, or torn by bloodhounds. On the contrary, I had always been kindly treated, and tenderly cared for, until I came into the hands of Dr. Flint. I had never wished for freedom till then. But though my life in slavery was comparatively devoid of hardships, God pity the woman who is compelled to lead such a life!

My food was passed up to me through the trap-door my uncle had contrived; and my grandmother, my uncle Phillip, and aunt Nancy would seize such opportunities as they could, to mount up there and chat with me at the opening. But of course this was not safe in the daytime. It must all be done in darkness. It was impossible for me to move in an erect position, but I crawled about my den for exercise. One day I hit my head against something, and found it was a gimlet.

My uncle had left it sticking there when he made the trap-door. I was as rejoiced as Robinson Crusoe could have been in finding such a treasure. It put a lucky thought into my head. I said to myself, "Now I will have some light. Now I will see my children." I did not dare to begin my work during the daytime, for fear of attracting attention. But I groped round; and having found the side next the street, where I could frequently see my children, I stuck the gimlet in and waited for evening. I bored three rows of holes, one above another; then I bored out the interstices between. I thus succeeded in making one hole about an inch long and an inch broad. I sat by it till late into the night, to enjoy the little whiff of air that floated in. In the morning I watched for my children. The first person I saw in the street was Dr. Flint. I had a shuddering, superstitious feeling that it was a bad omen. Several familiar faces passed by. At last I heard the merry laughing of children, and presently two sweet little faces were looking up at me, as though they knew I was there, and were conscious of the joy they imparted. How I longed to *tell* them I was there!

My condition was now a little improved. But for weeks I was tormented by hundreds of little red insects, fine as a needle's point, that pierced through my skin, and produced an intolerable burning. The good grandmother gave me herb teas and cooling medicines, and finally I got rid of them. The heat of my den was intense, for nothing but thin shingles protected me from the scorching summer's sun. But I had my consolations. Through my peeping-hole I could watch the children, and when they were near enough, I could hear their talk.

Aunt Nancy brought me all the news she could hear at Dr. Flint's. From her I learned that the doctor had written to New York to a colored woman, who had been born and raised in our neighborhood, and had breathed his contaminating atmosphere. He offered her a reward if she could find out any thing about me. I know not what was the nature of her reply; but he soon after started for New York in haste, saying to his family that he had business of importance to transact. I peeped at him as he passed on his way to the steamboat. It was a satisfaction to have miles of land and water between us, even for a little while; and it was a still greater satisfaction to know that he believed me to be in the Free States. My little den seemed less dreary than it had done. He returned, as he did from his former journey to New York, without obtaining any satisfactory information. When he passed our house next morning, Benny was standing at the gate. He had heard them say that he had gone to find me, and he called out, "Dr. Flint, did you bring my mother home? I want to see her." The doctor stamped his foot at him in a rage, and exclaimed, "Get out of the way, you little damned rascal! If you don't, I'll cut off your head."

Benny ran terrified into the house, saying, "You can't put me in jail again. I don't belong to you now." It was well that the wind carried the words away from the doctor's ear. I told my grandmother of it, when we had our next conference at the trap-door; and begged of her not to allow the children to be impertinent to the irascible old man.

Autumn came, with a pleasant abatement of heat. My eyes had become accustomed to the dim light, and by holding my book or work in a certain position near the aperture I contrived to read and sew. That was a great relief to the tedious monotony of my life. But when winter came, the cold penetrated through the thin shingle roof, and I was dreadfully chilled. The winters there are not so long, or so severe, as in northern latitudes; but the houses are not built to shelter from cold, and my little den was peculiarly comfortless. The kind grandmother brought me bed-clothes and warm drinks. Often I was obliged to lie in bed all day to keep comfortable; but with all my precautions, my shoulders and feet were frostbitten. O, those long, gloomy days, with no object for my eye to rest upon, and no thoughts to occupy my mind, except the dreary past and the uncertain future! I was thankful when there came a day sufficiently mild for me to wrap myself up and sit at the loophole to watch the passers by. Southerners have the habit of stopping and talking in the streets, and I heard many conversations not intended to meet my ears. I heard slave-hunters planning how to catch some poor fugitive. Several times I heard allusions to Dr. Flint, myself, and the history of my children, who, perhaps, were playing near the gate. One would say, "I wouldn't move my little finger to catch her, as old Flint's property." Another would say, "I'll catch *any* nigger for the reward. A man ought to have what belongs to him, if he *is* a damned brute." The opinion was often expressed that I was in the Free States. Very rarely did any one suggest that I might be in the vicinity. Had the least suspicion rested on my grandmother's house, it would have been burned to the ground. But it was the last place they thought of. Yet there was no place, where slavery existed, that could have afforded me so good a place of concealment.

Dr. Flint and his family repeatedly tried to coax and bribe my children to tell something they had heard said about me. One day the doctor took them into a shop, and offered them some bright little silver pieces and gay handkerchiefs if they would tell where their mother was. Ellen shrank away from him, and would not speak; but Benny spoke up, and said, "Dr. Flint, I don't know where my mother is. I guess she's in New York; and when you go there again, I wish you'd ask her to come home, for I want to see her; but if you put her in jail, or tell her you'll cut her head off, I'll tell her to go right back."

XXIII. Still in Prison

When spring returned, and I took in the little patch of green the aperture commanded, I asked myself how many more summers and winters I must be condemned to spend thus. I longed to draw in a plentiful draught of fresh air, to stretch my cramped limbs, to have room to stand erect, to feel the earth under my feet again. My relatives were constantly on the lookout for a chance of escape; but none offered that seemed practicable, and even tolerably safe. The hot summer came again, and made the turpentine drop from the thin roof over my head.

During the long nights I was restless for want of air, and I had no room to toss and turn. There was but one compensation; the atmosphere was so stifled that even mosquitoes would not condescend to buzz in it. With all my detestation of Dr. Flint, I could hardly wish him a worse punishment, either in this world or that which is to come, than to suffer what I suffered in one single summer. Yet the laws allowed *him* to be out in the free air, while I, guiltless of crime, was pent up here, as the only means of avoiding the cruelties the laws allowed him to inflict upon me! I don't know what kept life within me. Again and again, I thought I should die before long; but I saw the leaves of another autumn whirl through the air, and felt the touch of another winter. In summer the most terrible thunderstorms were acceptable, for the rain came through the roof, and I rolled up my bed that it might cool the hot boards under it. Later in the season, storms sometimes wet my clothes through and through, and that was not comfortable when the air grew chilly. Moderate storms I could keep out by filling the chinks with oakum.

But uncomfortable as my situation was, I had glimpses of things out of doors, which made me thankful for my wretched hiding-place. One day I saw a slave pass our gate, muttering, "It's his own, and he can kill it if he will." My grandmother told me that woman's history. Her mistress had that day seen her baby for the first time, and in the lineaments of its fair face she saw a likeness to her husband. She turned the bondwoman and her child out of doors, and forbade her ever to return. The slave went to her master, and told him what had happened. He promised to talk with her mistress, and make it all right. The next day she and her baby were sold to a Georgia trader.

Another time I saw a woman rush wildly by, pursued by two men. She was a slave, the wet nurse of her mistress's children. For some trifling offence her mistress ordered her to be stripped and whipped. To escape the degradation and the torture, she rushed to the river, jumped in, and ended her wrongs in death.

Senator Brown, of Mississippi, could not be ignorant of many such facts as these, for they are of frequent occurrence in every Southern State. Yet he stood up in the Congress of the United States, and declared that slavery was "a great moral, social, and political blessing; a blessing to the master, and a blessing to the slave!"

I suffered much more during the second winter than I did during the first. My limbs were benumbed by inaction, and the cold filled them with cramp. I had a very painful sensation of coldness in my head; even my face and tongue stiffened, and I lost the power of speech . . . Dark thoughts passed through my mind as I lay there day after day. I tried to be thankful for my little cell, dismal as it was, and even to love it, as part of the price I had paid for the redemption of my children. Sometimes I thought God was a compassionate Father, who would forgive my sins for the sake of my sufferings. At other times, it seemed to me there was no justice or mercy in the divine government. I asked why the curse of slavery was permitted to exist, and why I had been so persecuted and wronged from youth upward. These things took the shape of mystery, which is to this day not so clear to my soul as I trust it will be hereafter.

The Emancipation Proclamation
and the Thirteenth, Fourteenth,
and Fifteenth Amendments to the Constitution

1863, 1865–1870

Abraham Lincoln's hand purportedly trembled when he tried to sign the Emancipation Proclamation freeing slaves, on January 1, 1863. But after signing his name he commented aloud: "I never, in my life, felt more certain that I was doing right than I do in signing this paper." He added, in an echo of God at the moment of creation—*and it was so*—"That will do." Upon hearing the news, Frederick Douglass called the Proclamation "the first step." Then, in his 1876 speech at the Freedmen's Memorial Monument, Douglass recalled the "happy hour" when "we forgot all delay, and forgot all tardiness." This mention of a delay recalled Lincoln's attempts to persuade slaveholders in the border states to eliminate slavery gradually in return for compensation. In addition, the emancipation document applied only to seceded states, not to border states or parts of the Confederacy already under Northern control. The process of emancipation then proceeded in stages: the Thirteenth, Fourteenth, and Fifteenth Amendments were three more steps after Lincoln's "first step."

Others returned to the question of delay to ask if progress had really followed that first step. In the early 1960s, the NAACP adopted the motto "Free by '63," and in August 1963, Martin Luther King, Jr., cried: "Five score years ago, a great American . . . signed the Emancipation Proclamation . . . But one hundred years later . . . the life of the Negro is still sadly crippled by the manacles of segregation." African Americans were still not free.

From the Emancipation Proclamation

Whereas, on the twenty second day of September, in the year of our Lord one thousand eight hundred and sixty two, a proclamation was issued by the President of the United States, containing, among other things, the following, to wit:

"That on the first day of January, in the year of our Lord one thousand eight hundred and sixty-three, all persons held as slaves within any State or designated part of a State, the people whereof shall then be in rebellion against the United States, shall be then, thenceforward, and forever free; and the Executive Government of the United States, including the military and naval authority thereof, will recognize and maintain the freedom of such persons, and will do no act or acts to repress such persons, or any of them, in any efforts they may make for their actual freedom.

"That the Executive will, on the first day of January aforesaid, by proclamation, designate the States and parts of States, if any, in which the people thereof, respectively, shall then be in rebellion against the United States; and the fact that any State, or the people thereof, shall on that day be, in good faith, represented in the Congress of the United States by members chosen thereto at elections wherein a majority of the qualified voters of such State shall have participated, shall, in the absence of strong countervailing testimony, be deemed conclusive evidence that such State, and the people thereof, are not then in rebellion against the United States."

Now, therefore I, Abraham Lincoln, President of the United States, by virtue of the power in me vested as Commander-in-Chief, of the Army and Navy of the United States . . . do order and declare that all persons held as slaves within said designated States, and parts of States, are, and henceforward shall be free; and that the Executive government of the United States, including the military and naval authorities thereof, will recognize and maintain the freedom of said persons.

And I hereby enjoin upon the people so declared to be free to abstain from all violence, unless in necessary self-defence; and I recommend to them that, in all cases when allowed, they labor faithfully for reasonable wages.

And I further declare and make known, that such persons of suitable condition, will be received into the armed service of the United States to garrison forts, positions, stations, and other places, and to man vessels of all sorts in said service.

And upon this act, sincerely believed to be an act of justice, warranted by the Constitution, upon military necessity, I invoke the considerate judgment of mankind, and the gracious favor of Almighty God.

In witness whereof, I have hereunto set my hand and caused the seal of the United States to be affixed.

Done at the City of Washington, this first day of January, in the year of our Lord one thousand eight hundred and sixty three, and of the Independence of the United States of America the eighty-seventh.

Amendment XIII

Section 1. Neither slavery nor involuntary servitude, except as a punishment for crime whereof the party shall have been duly convicted, shall exist within the United States, or any place subject to their jurisdiction.

Section 2. Congress shall have power to enforce this article by appropriate legislation.

Amendment XIV

Section 1. All persons born or naturalized in the United States, and subject to the jurisdiction thereof, are citizens of the United States and of the State wherein they reside. No State shall make or enforce any law which shall abridge the privileges or immunities of citizens of the United States; nor shall any State deprive any person of life, liberty, or property, without due process of law; nor deny to any person within its jurisdiction the equal protection of the laws.

Section 2. Representatives shall be apportioned among the several States according to their respective numbers, counting the whole number of persons in each State, excluding Indians not taxed. But when the right to vote at any election for the choice of electors for President and Vice-President of the United States, Representatives in Congress, the Executive and Judicial officers of a State, or the members of the Legislature thereof, is denied to any of the male inhabitants of such State, being twenty-one years of age, and citizens of the United States, or in any way abridged, except for participation in rebellion, or other crime, the basis of representation therein shall be reduced in the proportion which the number of such male citizens shall bear to the whole number of male citizens twenty-one years of age in such State.

Section 3. No person shall be a Senator or Representative in Congress, or elector of President and Vice-President, or hold any office, civil or military, under the United States, or under any State, who, having previously taken an oath, as a member of Congress, or as an officer of the United States, or as a member of any State legislature, or as an executive or judicial officer of any State, to support the Constitution of the United States, shall have engaged in insurrection or rebellion against the same, or given aid or comfort to the enemies thereof. But Congress may by a vote of two-thirds of each House, remove such disability.

Section 4. The validity of the public debt of the United States, authorized by law, including debts incurred for payment of pensions and bounties for services in suppressing insurrection or rebellion, shall not be questioned. But neither the United States nor any State shall assume or pay any debt or obligation incurred in aid of insurrection or rebellion against the United States, or any claim for the loss or emancipation of any slave; but all such debts, obligations and claims shall be held illegal and void.

Section 5. The Congress shall have the power to enforce, by appropriate legislation, the provisions of this article.

Amendment XV

Section 1. The right of citizens of the United States to vote shall not be denied or abridged by the United States or by any State on account of race, color, or previous condition of servitude.

Section 2. The Congress shall have the power to enforce this article by appropriate legislation.

Solidarity Forever

1915

"Listen just for once to the throbbing of your own heart, and you will hear that it is beating quick-step marches to Camp Freedom," instructed the socialist Eugene Debs in 1905. This "quick-step" was often to the tune of "John Brown's Body," a marching song that took its parodic inspiration from a Scotsman in the Massachusetts Volunteer Militia who shared the abolitionist John Brown's name. In 1861 Julia Ward Howe wrote her own words to the tune, publishing them as "The Battle Hymn of the Republic," and in 1863 Edna Dean Proctor rewrote the song as "The President's Proclamation," but the most famous rewrite was by Ralph Chaplin (1887–1961), the righthand man of the labor activist William Haywood. "Solidarity Forever," the soundtrack to the workers' protest movement, was sung at meetings, in jails, and on picket lines.

Workers began distributing strike songbooks during the 1890s, and in 1909 the Industrial Workers of the World (IWW) issued *The Little Red Song Book,* which has gone through more than thirty editions and was the 20th century's bestselling radical book. By 1915 it included "Solidarity Forever." The song was often sung with only the first stanza and chorus intact, with new stanzas added to refer to specific situations. The IWW believed that discontent needed to be articulated through song and speech before action could begin, and used songs to initiate strikes, recruit members, articulate their goals, and build solidarity. The IWW songwriter and organizer Joe Hill explained: "If a person can put a few cold, common sense facts into a song, and dress them up in a cloak of humor to take the dryness off of them, he will succeed in reaching a great number of workers."

Labor reformers and socialists looked back to abolitionism for a model. Workers sang a union song to the tune of "John Brown's Body" for the first time in 1894: "We're headed straight for Washington with leaders brave and true . . . And truth goes marching on." Debs often referred to Brown, asking in 1907, "Who shall be the John Brown of Wage-Slavery?" and Kenneth Porter called on Brown during the Spanish Civil War, writing in 1936: "John Brown . . . goes marching on, his tread is on the plains of Aragon." In 1953, a huge crowd in Beijing greeted W. E. B. Du Bois with a rendition of "John Brown's Body."

When the union's inspiration through the workers' blood shall run,
There can be no power greater anywhere beneath the sun;
Yet what force on earth is weaker than the feeble strength of one?
But the union makes us strong. (chorus)

Solidarity forever!
Solidarity forever!
Solidarity forever!
For the union makes us strong.

Is there aught we hold in common with the greedy parasite,
Who would lash us into serfdom and would crush us with his might?
Is there anything left to us but to organize and fight?
For the union makes us strong. (chorus)

It is we who plowed the prairies; built the cities where they trade;
Dug the mines and built the workshops, endless miles of railroad laid;
Now we stand outcast and starving midst the wonders we have made;
But the union makes us strong. (chorus)

All the world that's owned by idle drones is ours and ours alone.
We have laid the wide foundations; built it skyward stone by stone.
It is ours, not to slave in, but to master and to own,
While the union makes us strong. (chorus)

They have taken untold millions that they never toiled to earn,
But without our brain and muscle not a single wheel can turn.
We can break their haughty power, gain our freedom when we learn
That the union makes us strong. (chorus)

In our hands is placed a power greater than their hoarded gold,
Greater than the might of armies, magnified a thousand-fold.
We can bring to birth a new world from the ashes of the old,
For the union makes us strong. (chorus)

From Everybody's Protest Novel

1949

James Baldwin (1924–1987) was the 20th century's preeminent protest essayist. With conversational, highly personal essays that nonetheless offered a critique of the surrounding culture, he built on the sermonic protest essays of David Walker, Frederick Douglass, and W. E. B. Du Bois, laid the ground for the civil rights movement, and paved the way for New Journalists like Norman Mailer and Michael Herr. And he remodeled American protest literature. In the essay excerpted here, he describes protest literature variously as sociology, fantasy, mirror, missionary text, and motto, acknowledging elsewhere the "war between . . . social and artistic responsibilities" that spoil protest writing. His alternative is a new voice that speaks the "we" of different people: protest essays that forged a complex collective.

Harriet Beecher Stowe's *Uncle Tom's Cabin* (1852), examined here by Baldwin in the essay that launched his career, mixes political radicalism with aesthetic convention. Stowe aimed the novel at Southerners, invoking paternalism, and at sentimental Northern reformers, adopting a romantic racialist attitude. Twentieth-century critics attacked Stowe's racism and cheap ploys for sympathy, suggesting that she appealed to emotion for emotion's sake, and even her first readers queried the connection between sympathy and action: "there is many a man that weeps over *Uncle Tom* who votes the Whig or the Democrat ticket," warned the abolitionist Wendell Phillips. Stowe's insistence upon patience, and her prophecy of an apocalyptic millennium that would redeem the South, seemed to leave the reader with little left to do. Critics also attacked the novel's sprawling structure, melodrama, and cardboard figures. Some, like Baldwin, have asked if the novel's catalogue of violence desensitized readers—a problem Stowe acknowledged: "[The trader's] heart was exactly where yours, sir, and mine could be brought," she warns in the novel. "You can get used to such things, too, my friend."

In *Uncle Tom's Cabin,* that cornerstone of American social protest fiction, St. Clare, the kindly master, remarks to his coldly disapproving Yankee cousin, Miss Ophelia, that, so far as he is able to tell, the blacks have been turned over to the devil for the benefit of the whites in this world—however, he adds thoughtfully, it may turn out in the next. Miss Ophelia's reaction is, at least, vehemently right-minded: "This is perfectly horrible!" she exclaims. "You ought to be ashamed of yourselves!"

Miss Ophelia, as we may suppose, was speaking for the author; her exclamation is the moral, neatly framed, and incontestable like those improving mottoes sometimes found hanging on the walls of furnished rooms. And, like these mottoes, before which one invariably flinches, recognizing an insupportable, almost an indecent glibness, she and St. Clare are terribly in earnest. Neither of them questions the medieval morality from which their dialogue springs: black, white, the devil, the next world—posing its alternatives between heaven and the flames—were realities for them as, of course, they were for their creator. They spurned and were terrified of the darkness, striving mightily for the light; and considered from this aspect, Miss Ophelia's exclamation, like Mrs. Stowe's novel, achieves a bright, almost a lurid significance, like the light from a fire which consumes a witch. This is the more striking as one considers the novels of Negro oppression written in our own, more enlightened day, all of which say only: "This is perfectly horrible! You ought to be ashamed of yourselves!" (Let us ignore, for the moment, those novels of oppression written by Negroes, which add only a raging, near-paranoiac postscript to this statement and actually reinforce, as I hope to make clear later, the principles which activate the oppression they decry.)

Uncle Tom's Cabin is a very bad novel, having, in its self-righteous, virtuous sentimentality, much in common with *Little Women*. Sentimentality, the ostentatious parading of excessive and spurious emotion, is the mark of dishonesty, the inability to feel; the wet eyes of the sentimentalist betray his aversion to experience, his fear of life, his arid heart; and it is always, therefore, the signal of secret and violent inhumanity, the mask of cruelty. *Uncle Tom's Cabin*—like its multitudinous, hard-boiled descendants—is a catalogue of violence. This is explained by the nature of Mrs. Stowe's subject matter, her laudable determination to flinch from nothing in presenting the complete picture; an explanation which falters only if we pause to ask whether or not her picture is indeed complete; and what constriction or failure of perception forced her to so depend on the description of brutality—unmotivated, senseless—and to leave unanswered and unnoticed the only important question: what it was, after all, that moved her people to such deeds.

But this, let us say, was beyond Mrs. Stowe's powers; she was not so much a novelist as an impassioned pamphleteer; her book was not intended to do anything more than prove that slavery was wrong; was, in fact, perfectly horrible. This makes material for a pamphlet but it is hardly enough for a novel; and the only question left to ask is why we are bound still within the same constriction. How is it that we are so loath to make a further journey than that made by Mrs. Stowe, to discover and reveal something a little closer to the truth?

But that battered word, truth, having made its appearance here, confronts one immediately with a series of riddles and has, moreover, since so many gospels are preached, the unfortunate tendency to make one belligerent. Let us say, then, that truth, as used here, is meant to imply a devotion to the human being, his freedom and fulfillment; freedom which cannot be legislated, fulfillment which cannot be charted. This is the prime concern, the frame of reference; it is not to be confused with a devotion to Humanity which is too easily equated with a devotion to a Cause; and Causes, as we know, are notoriously bloodthirsty. We have, as it seems to me, in this most mechanical and interlocking of civilizations, attempted to lop this creature down to the status of a time-saving invention. He is not, after all, merely a member of a Society or a Group or a deplorable conundrum to be explained by Science. He is—and how old-fashioned the words sound!—something more than that, something resolutely indefinable, unpredictable. In overlooking, denying, evading his complexity—which is nothing more than the disquieting complexity of ourselves—we are diminished and we perish; only within this web of ambiguity, paradox, this hunger, danger, darkness, can we find at once ourselves and the power that will free us from ourselves. It is this power of revelation which is the business of the novelist, this journey toward a more vast reality which must take precedence over all other claims. What is today parroted as his Responsibility—which seems to mean that he must make formal declaration that he is involved in, and affected by, the lives of other people and to say something improving about this somewhat self-evident fact—is, when he believes it, his corruption and our loss; moreover, it is rooted in, interlocked with and intensifies this same mechanization. Both *Gentleman's Agreement* and *The Postman Always Rings Twice* exemplify this terror of the human being, the determination to cut him down to size. And in *Uncle Tom's Cabin* we may find foreshadowing of both: the formula created by the necessity to find a lie more palatable than the truth has been handed down and memorized and persists yet with a terrible power.

It is interesting to consider one more aspect of Mrs. Stowe's novel, the method she used to solve the problem of writing about a black man at all. Apart from her lively procession of field hands, house niggers, Chloe, Topsy, etc.—who are the stock, lovable figures presenting no problem—she has only three other Negroes in the book. These are the important ones and two of them may be dismissed immediately, since we have only the author's word that they are Negro and they are, in all other respects, as white as she can make them. The two are George and Eliza, a married couple with a wholly adorable child—whose quaintness, incidentally, and whose charm, rather put one in mind of a darky bootblack doing a buck and wing to the clatter of condescending coins. Eliza is a beautiful, pious hybrid, light enough to pass—the heroine of *Quality* might, indeed, be her reincarnation—differing from the genteel mistress who has overseered her education only in the respect that she is a servant. George is darker, but makes up for it by being a mechanical genius, and is, moreover, sufficiently un-Negroid to pass through town, a fugitive from his master, disguised as a Spanish gentleman, attracting no attention whatever beyond admiration. They are a race apart from Topsy. It transpires by the end of the novel, through one of those energetic, last-minute convolutions of the plot, that Eliza has some connection with French gentility. The figure from whom the novel takes its name, Uncle Tom, who is a figure of controversy yet, is jet-black, wooly-haired, illiterate; and he is phenomenally forbearing. He has to be; he is black; only through this forbearance can he survive or triumph. (*Cf.* Faulkner's preface to *The Sound and the Fury:* These others were not Compsons. They were black:—They endured.) His triumph is metaphysical, unearthly; since he is black, born without the light, it is only through humility, the incessant mortification of the flesh, that he can enter into communion with God or man. The virtuous rage of Mrs. Stowe is motivated by nothing so temporal as a concern for the relationship of men to one another—or, even, as she would have claimed, by a concern for their relationship to God—but merely by a panic of being hurled into the flames, of being caught in traffic with the devil. She embraced this merciless doctrine with all her heart, bargaining shamelessly before the throne of grace: God and salvation becoming her personal property, purchased with the coin of her virtue. Here, black equates with evil and white with grace; if, being mindful of the necessity of good works, she could not cast out the blacks—a wretched, huddled mass, apparently, claiming, like an obsession, her inner eye—she could not embrace them either without purifying them of sin. She must cover their intimidating nakedness, robe them in white, the garments of salvation; only thus could she herself be delivered from ever-present sin, only thus could she bury, as St. Paul demanded, "the carnal man, the man of the flesh." Tom, therefore, her only black man, has been robbed of his humanity and divested of his sex. It is the price for that darkness with which he has been branded.

Uncle Tom's Cabin, then, is activated by what might be called a theological terror, the terror of damnation; and the spirit that breathes in this book, hot, self-righteous, fearful, is not different from that spirit of medieval times which sought to exorcize evil by burning witches; and is not different from that terror which activates a lynch mob. One need not, indeed, search for examples so historic or so gaudy; this is a warfare waged daily in the heart, a warfare so vast, so relentless and so powerful that the interracial handshake or the interracial marriage can be as crucifying as the public hanging or the secret rape. This panic motivates our cruelty, this fear of the dark makes it impossible that our lives shall be other than superficial; this, interlocked with and feeding our glittering, mechanical, inescapable civilization which has put to death our freedom.

From The Defiant Ones

1958

The movie *The Defiant Ones,* directed by Stanley Kramer (1913–2001), is part of an interracial escape-narrative tradition that draws on the conventions of the slave narrative. Noah and John, an interracial pair, escape from a Southern prison chain gang, break the chains that still hold them together, and form an emotional bond instead: "You're dragging on the chain," says one, after the physical chain is broken. Similarly, another interracial buddy film, *American History X* (1998), which dramatizes a white racist's friendship with a black jailmate, ends with Abraham Lincoln's lines: "We are not enemies, but friends . . . Though passion may have strained, it must not break our bonds of affection."

The interracial pairs of this filmic tradition often bond through facing a common enemy (prison guards, sports teams, criminals, foreign armies), in a frontier space where interracial friendship is possible, like that of Frederick Douglass's "The Heroic Slave" (1853) or Mark Twain's *Huckleberry Finn* (1885). And, like 19th-century texts, these interracial films often emphasize physical challenge or violence to the body, so focusing on the characters' shared masculinity: "Let's learn to play this thing like men," says a character in *Remember the Titans* (2000). This shared masculinity pushes race to the background; the lesson is that "underneath we're all guys," as Moss in *Home of the Brave* (1949) puts it. Another way that these films' characters form friendships is through their shared outsider status: in *Remember the Titans,* the first whites on the football team to befriend their black teammates are either gay or self-described "white trash."

The films also echo the 19th-century tradition of black sacrifice. In *The Defiant Ones,* the two men climb out of a pit in an early scene, John on Noah's shoulders—embodying Ralph Ellison's 1946 vision of "American life . . . acted out upon the body of a Negro giant," a country built on the backs of slaves. Then, at the film's end, as the fugitives attempt a railroad journey to freedom, Noah sacrifices his freedom to help John. But, perhaps signaling that sentiment had moved past the acceptance of Ishmael's survival on Queequeg's coffin in *Moby Dick* (1850) or Tom's sacrifice for white America's soul in *Uncle Tom's Cabin* (1852), black cinema audiences booed.

From Disposable People:
New Slavery in the Global Economy

1999

Sometimes the sociologist and antislavery activist Kevin Bales (b. 1952) disguises himself as a slave trader in order to liberate slaves. It is disturbingly "easy to get into the role," he confessed in an interview. But because of his work, "governments and people talk about slavery and not slave-like practices," as he acknowledges. Bales is the world's leading expert on contemporary slavery and the president of Free the Slaves, the U.S. sister organization of Anti-Slavery International (the world's oldest human rights organization). He has spent fifteen years researching contemporary slavery, liberating slaves, advising the UN on slavery and trafficking, and trying to understand the role of globalization, the population explosion, and the complicity of governments. His work, and *Disposable People,* have been catalysts for the growing U.S. movement against slavery.

His were the first estimates of the problem's extent: there are 27 million slaves alive today, most likely half enslaved from freedom and half in hereditary slavery. Slavery is no longer racialized, except in Mauritania. He notes: "Though race, caste, tribe, and religion do initially look like markers of slavery, differences just make people vulnerable and slave traders prey on the vulnerable." This new slavery therefore bears little comparison with 19th-century slavery. In addition, while an Alabama slave cost $1000–1200 in 1850 (the equivalent of $40,000 today), a Mali farmworker now costs $40. Today's slaves are disposable.

Setting himself in the abolitionist tradition nonetheless, Bales explains, "We're in a better position than earlier abolitionists: we don't have to win moral arguments or even economic arguments. Slavery is worth just $13 billion a year." There's also no legal argument to be won: the 1948 Universal Declaration of Human Rights guarantees that "no one shall be held in slavery." The task for contemporary abolitionists, Bales says, is to raise awareness. It's true that "Americans don't want to believe that modern-day slavery is occurring," he observes, but in fact "Americans end up being more willing than Europeans to engage with the issue *because* it resonates with their history of slavery."

Bales often thinks about freedom: whether it's an innate or cultural concept, whether the transformation from slave to free is immediate or gradual. Sometimes he uses a form of Socratic dialogue to make slaves realize that they *are* slaves. In the moment of acknowledging publicly "I am a slave," they sometimes feel "free, though their bodies remain enslaved," says Bales, echoing Frederick Douglass, who famously observed: "however long I might remain a slave in form, the day had passed forever when I could be a slave in fact." But sometimes, Bales notes, slaves have "no notion of how to be free, but sense that they are in a bad place—perhaps relative to slaveholders, though sometimes this is an absolute sense, as though freedom is intrinsic." And even when the understanding of the fact of slavery comes suddenly, freedom remains a process. Most slavery is sedentary, not mobile; many slaves and masters live in proximity after liberation. "Change the mindset of a whole village and you're done," says Bales with a sigh. He never liberates a slave until there is a fully funded post-liberation plan. "We remember that America botched Emancipation," he says.

Yet in spite of his interest in the question of freedom, Bales emphasizes that he's trying to help slaves "find their own way into freedom." He notes that many "exhibit a philosophical orientation to their freedom far more developed than that of most 'free' people," adding: "One of the failings of much literature of slavery is that slaves are locked into the victim/survivor box, and there seems to be an expectation that they should restrict their emotional state to pathetic and grateful. But slaves and ex-slaves speak with many voices."

Slavery is not a horror safely consigned to the past; it continues to exist throughout the world, even in developed countries like France and the United States. Across the world slaves work and sweat and build and suffer. Slaves in Pakistan may have made the shoes you are wearing and the carpet you stand on. Slaves in the Caribbean may have put sugar in your kitchen and toys in the hands of your children. In India they may have sewn the shirt on your back and polished the ring on your finger. They are paid nothing.

Slaves touch your life indirectly as well. They made the bricks for the factory that made the TV you watch. In Brazil slaves made the charcoal that tempered the steel that made the springs in your car and the blade on your lawnmower. Slaves grew the rice that fed the woman that wove the lovely cloth you've put up as curtains. Your investment portfolio and your mutual fund pension own stock in companies using slave labor in the developing world. Slaves keep your costs low and returns on your investments high.

Slavery is a booming business and the number of slaves is increasing. People get rich by using slaves. And when they've finished with their slaves, they just throw these people away. This is the new slavery, which focuses on big profits and cheap lives. It is not about owning people in the traditional sense of the old slavery, but about controlling them completely. People become completely disposable tools for making money . . .

In spite of this difference between the new and the old slavery, I think everyone would agree that what I am talking about is slavery: the total control of one person by another for the purpose of economic exploitation. Modern slavery hides behind different masks, using clever lawyers and legal smoke screens, but when we strip away the lies, we find someone controlled by violence and denied all of their personal freedom to make money for someone else. As I traveled around the world to study the new slavery, I looked behind the legal masks and I saw people in chains. Of course, many people think there is no such thing as slavery anymore, and I was one of those people just a few years ago.

First Come, First Served

I first encountered the vestiges of the old slavery when I was four years old. What happened is one of my strongest memories. It was the 1950s in the American South and my family was having dinner in a cafeteria. As we started down the serving line I saw another family standing behind a chain, waiting as others moved through with their trays. With the certainty of a four-year-old, I knew that they had arrived first and should be ahead of us. The *fairness* of first come, first served had been drummed into me. So I unhooked the chain and said, "You were here first, you should go ahead." The father of this African American family looked down at me with eyes full of feeling, just as my own father came up and put his hand on my shoulder. Suddenly the atmosphere was thick with unspoken emotion. Tension mixed with bittersweet approval as both fathers grappled with the innocent ignorance of a child who had never heard of segregation. No one spoke, until finally the black father said, "That's OK, we're waiting on someone; go ahead."

My parents were not radicals, but they had taught me the value of fairness and equal treatment. They believed that the idea of our equality was one of the best things about America, and they never approved of the racism of segregation. But sometimes it takes a child's simplicity to cut through the weight of custom. The intensity of that moment stayed with me, though it was years before I began to understand what those two sets of parents were feeling. As I grew up I was glad to see such blatant segregation coming to an end. The idea that there might still be actual slavery—quite apart from segregation—never crossed my mind. Everyone knew that in the United States slavery had ended in 1865.

Of course, the gross inequalities in American society brought the slavery of the past to mind. I realized that the United States, once a large-scale slave society, was still suffering from a botched emancipation program. Soon after Abraham Lincoln's celebrated proclamation, Jim Crow laws and oppression took over to keep ex-slaves from economic and political power. I came to understand that emancipation was a *process*, not an event—a process that still had a way to go. As a young social researcher, I generally held jobs concerned with the residue of this unfinished process: I studied bad housing, health differences between the races, problems in integrated schools, and racism in the legal system. But I still saw all this as the vestiges of slavery, as problems that were tough but not intractable.

It was only after I moved to England in the early 1980s that I became aware of real slavery. At a large public event I came across a small table set up by Anti-Slavery International. I picked up some leaflets in passing, and I was amazed by what I read. There was no flash-of-light experience, but I developed a gnawing desire to find out more. I was perplexed that this most fundamental human right was still not assured—and that no one seemed to know or care about it. Millions of people were actively working against the nuclear threat, against apartheid in South Africa, against famine in Ethiopia, yet *slavery* wasn't even on the map. The more this realization dug into me, the more I knew I had to do something. Slavery is an obscenity. It is not just stealing someone's labor; it is the theft of an entire life. It is more closely related to the concentration camp than to questions of bad working conditions. There seems nothing to debate about slavery: it must stop. My question became: What can I do to bring an end to slavery? I decided to use my skills as a social researcher, and I embarked on the project that led to this book . . .

My best estimate of the number of slaves in the world today is 27 million.

This number is much smaller than the estimates put forward by some activists, who give a range as high as 200 million, but it is the number I feel I can trust; it is also the number that fits my strict definition of slavery. The biggest part of that 27 million, perhaps 15 to 20 million, is represented by *bonded labor* in India, Pakistan, Bangladesh, and Nepal. Bonded labor or debt bondage happens when people give themselves into slavery as security against a loan or when they inherit a debt from a relative (we'll look at this more closely later). Otherwise slavery tends to be concentrated in Southeast Asia, northern and western Africa, and parts of South America (but there are some slaves in almost every country in the world, including the United States, Japan, and many European countries). there are more slaves alive today than all the people stolen from Africa in the time of the transatlantic slave trade. Put another way, today's slave population is greater than the population of Canada, and six times greater than the population of Israel . . .

Everyone *knows* what slavery is—yet almost no one knows. The old slavery is so much a part of human history and of our shared understanding of the world that for most people slavery simply means one person legally owning another person. And as everyone *knows,* that sort of slavery was abolished long ago. It is something about which we might feel guilty or angry (an ugly episode in human history) and also a little smug and superior (since it is all in the past now, and *we're* more civilized than that). This is a terrible ignorance that leads us to overlook suffering and death. We couldn't be more wrong if we believed that because the Black Death ended in the Middle Ages, we don't have to worry about epidemics anymore. In fact, new diseases are evolving all the time; slavery is also evolving and changing, erupting whenever the conditions are right . . .

We are seeing the beginning of a new abolitionist movement, facing challenges as difficult and entrenched as those faced in the early nineteenth century. One of those challenges is that we don't *want* to believe that slavery exists. Many people in developed countries feel good about the fact that slavery was abolished "back then" and are shocked and disappointed that it will have to be abolished all over again. In fact, the work to be done today doesn't diminish the achievements of the nineteenth-century abolitionists one bit. They fought to stop legal slavery, and they won that fight. We must stop illegal slavery . . .

Hollow Mockery and Brass-Fronted Impudence

In 1852, preparing for the big Fourth of July celebrations, the city fathers of Rochester, New York, thought to ask one of their more famous citizens, Frederick Douglass, to give the keynote speech. Douglass was an escaped slave from the southern states who had become a leader in the fight for abolition. Perhaps the city fathers expected Douglass to be grateful to be living in freedom, or to favorably compare America's great tradition of liberty to the rule of European kings and tyrants. They were in for a surprise. When the whole town assembled for the celebration on Independence Day, Douglass mounted the platform and spoke:

> What to the American slave is your Fourth of July? . . . a day that reveals to him more than all other days, the gross injustice and cruelty to which he is a constant victim . . . your celebration is a sham; your boasted liberty an unholy license; your national greatness, swelling vanity; . . . your denunciation of tyrants, brass-fronted impudence; your shouts of liberty and equality, hollow mockery; your prayers and hymns, your sermons and thanksgivings, your religious parade are . . . bombast, fraud, deception, impiety and hypocrisy.

I suspect that Douglass wasn't invited to the barbecue that followed. He poured into the ears of his audience biting ridicule and sarcasm, beneath which lay a single, simple question: If there are still slaves, how can you be proud of your freedom?

We have to answer the same question today. Whether we like it or not, we are now a global people. We must ask ourselves: Are we willing to live in a world with slaves? If not, we are obligated to take responsibility for things that are connected to us, even when far away. Unless we work to understand the links that tie us to slavery and then take action to break those links, we are puppets, subject to forces we can't or won't control. Not to take action is simply to give up and let other people jerk the strings that tie us to slavery. Of course, there are many kinds of exploitation in the world, many kinds of injustice and violence that merit our concern. But slavery is exploitation, violence, and injustice all rolled together in their most potent combination. If there is one fundamental violation of our humanity we cannot allow, it is slavery. If there is one basic truth that virtually every human being can agree on, it is that slavery must end. What good is our economic and political power, if we can't use it to free slaves? If we can't choose to stop slavery, how can we say that we are free?

4

THIS LAND IS HERLAND

Women's Rights
and
Suffragism

From Shall Women Have the Right to Vote?

1851

"Balderdash, clap-trap, moonshine, rant." Such was the *New York Herald*'s judgment of the first Woman's Rights Convention, held in October 1850. Elizabeth Cady Stanton dated the birth of the women's rights movement to that first convention, but the *Herald* saw no historic milestone and dismissed the delegates: "Frederick Douglass, fugitive slave . . . Sojourner Truth, a deluded lady of color. Wendell Phillips, abolition demagogue." In 1855, the women's rights activist Lucy Stone responded to all such dismissals, "If the world scoff, let it scoff." The presence of Wendell Phillips (1811–1884) in this roll call was significant. Phillips, one of America's foremost antislavery leaders, had lent support to the women's movement as early as 1840: when Stanton and Lucretia Mott were put in a curtained section for female delegates at the World Anti-Slavery Convention, he and William Lloyd Garrison sat with them in protest. In the speech printed here he argues against the separate-spheres ideology, prompting comparisons to John Stuart Mill, who had championed women's rights in Britain.

The abolitionists Henry Ward Beecher, Theodore Parker, and Frederick Douglass were also active in the women's rights movement. Anticipating Charlotte Perkins Gilman's matriarchal utopia in her novel *Herland* (1915), Parker imagined how America might look if women were in charge: "I doubt that we should have spread slavery into nine new States . . . the Fugitive Slave Bill would never have been an Act." Though without this power, women had been involved with abolition since its early days, and their movement evolved in the wake of antislavery activism (just as aspects of modern feminism grew out of the civil rights movement a century later). Susan B. Anthony claimed women's right to speak publicly before she met any abolitionists, but the first Woman's Rights Convention was announced at an antislavery meeting, and antislavery women were leaders in women's rights. Black women like Sojourner Truth and Ida B. Wells were active in both the abolitionist and women's rights struggles. The political alliance with Garrisonian abolitionists gave activists a theory for social change and an example of theory in practice. The early feminist Abbie Kelley observed: "We have good cause to be grateful to the slave . . . In striving to strike his irons off, we found most surely that we were manacled ourselves."

Like male abolitionists, women's rights activists made the connection between slavery and the condition of women. In 1848 J. Elizabeth Jones declared: "Slaves we are, politically and legally"; in 1850 Stanton declared that married women had "not more absolute rights than a slave"; and in 1871 Victoria Woodhull argued that the Thirteenth Amendment had emancipated women. But women's rights activists were thrown by the Fourteenth Amendment: "If that word 'male' be inserted . . . it will take us a century at least to get it out," warned Stanton. Excluded from the Fifteenth Amendment, too, women recognized that the universal suffrage movement had failed, and in 1869 the Equal Rights Association became the National Woman Suffrage Association. In 1890 Stanton was still fighting: echoing those who knew that emancipation had failed blacks, she proclaimed women still "in a transition state from slavery to freedom."

Further reading: Karen Sánchez-Eppler, *Touching Liberty* (1993); Richard Symonds, *Inside the Citadel* (1999).

I rejoice to see so large an audience gathered to consider this momentous subject. It was well described by Mrs. Rose as the most magnificent reform that has yet been launched upon the world. It is the first organized protest against the injustice which has brooded over the character and the destiny of one-half of the human race. Nowhere else, under any circumstances, has a demand ever yet been made for the liberties of one whole half of our race . . . It strikes, indeed, a great and vital blow at the whole social fabric of every nation; but this, to my mind, is no argument against it. The time has been when it was the duty of the reformer to show cause why he appeared to disturb the quiet of the world. But during the discussion of the many reforms that have been advocated, and which have more or less succeeded, one after another,—freedom of the lower classes, freedom of food, freedom of the press, freedom of thought, reform in penal legislation, and a thousand other matters,—it seems to me to have been proved conclusively, that government commenced in usurpation and oppression; that liberty and civilization, at present, are nothing else than the fragments of rights which the scaffold and the stake have wrung from the strong hands of the usurpers. Every step of progress the world has made has been from scaffold to scaffold, and from stake to stake. It would hardly be exaggeration to say, that all the great truths relating to society and government have been first heard in the solemn protests of martyred patriotism, or the loud cries of crushed and starving labor. The law has been always wrong. Government began in tyranny and force, began in the feudalism of the soldier and bigotry of the priest; and the ideas of justice and humanity have been fighting their way, like a thunderstorm, against the organized selfishness of human nature. And this is the last great protest against the wrong of ages. It is no argument to my mind, therefore, that the old social fabric of the past is against us . . .

But I wish especially to direct your attention to the precise principle which this movement undertakes to urge upon the community. We do not attempt to settle what shall be the profession, education, or employment of woman. We have not that presumption. What we ask is simply this,—what all other classes have asked before: Leave it to woman to choose for herself her profession, her education, and her sphere. We deny to any portion of the species the right to prescribe to any other portion its sphere, its education, or its rights. We deny the right of any individual to prescribe to any other individual his amount of education, or his rights. The sphere of each man, of each woman, of each individual, is that sphere which he can, with the highest exercise of his powers, perfectly fill. The highest act which the human being can do, that is the act which God designed him to do. All that woman asks through this movement is, to be allowed to prove what she can do; to prove it by liberty of choice, by liberty of action, the only means by which it ever can be settled how much and what she can do . . .

Make the case our own. Is there any man here willing to resign his own right to vote, and trust his welfare and his earnings entirely to the votes of others? Suppose any class of men should condescendingly offer to settle for us our capacity or our calling,—to vote for us, to choose our sphere for us,—how ridiculously impertinent we should consider it! Yet few have the good sense to laugh at the consummate impertinence with which every bar-room brawler, every third-rate scribbler, undertakes to settle the sphere of the Martineaus and the De Staëls! With what gracious condescension little men continue to lecture and preach on "the female sphere" and "female duties!"

This Convention does not undertake the task of protecting woman. It contends that, in government, every individual should be endowed, as far as possible, with the means of protecting himself. This is far more the truth when we deal with classes. Every class should be endowed with the power to protect itself. Man has hitherto undertaken to settle what is best for woman in the way of education and in the matter of property. He has settled it for her, that her duties and cares are too great to allow her any time to take care of her own earnings, or to take her otherwise legitimate share in the civil government of the country. He has not undertaken to say that the sailor or the soldier, in active service, when he returns from his voyage or his camp, is not free to deposit his vote in the ballot-box. He has not undertaken to say that the manufacturer, whose factories cover whole townships, who is up early and lies down late, who has to borrow the services of scores to help him in the management of his vast estate,—he does not say that such a man cannot get time to study politics, and ought therefore to be deprived of his right to vote with his fellow-citizens. He has not undertaken to say that the lawyer may not vote, though his whole time is spent in the courts, until he knows nothing of what is going on in the streets. O no! But as for woman, her time *must* be all so entirely filled in taking care of her household, her cares must be so extensive, that neither those of soldiers nor sailors nor merchants can be equal to them; she has not a moment to qualify herself for politics! Woman cannot be spared long enough from the kitchen to put in a vote, though Abbott Lawrence can be spared from the counting-house, though General Gaines or Scott can be spared from the camp, though the Lorings and the Choates can be spared from the courts. This is the argument: Stephen Girard cannot go to Congress; he is too busy; therefore, no *man* ever shall. Because General Scott has gone to Mexico, and cannot be President, therefore no *man* shall be. Because A. B. is a sailor, gone on a whaling voyage, to be absent for three years, and cannot vote, therefore no male inhabitant ever shall. Logic how profound! how conclusive! Yet this is the exact reasoning in the case of woman. Take up the newspapers. See the sneers at this movement. "Take care of the children," "Make the clothes," "See that they are mended," "See that the parlors are properly arranged." Suppose we grant it all. Are there no women but housekeepers? no women but mothers? O yes, many! Suppose we grant that the cares of a household are so heavy that they are greater than the cares of the president of a college; that he who has the charge of some hundreds of youths is less oppressed with care than the woman with three rooms and two children; that though President Sparks has time for politics, Mrs. Brown has not. Grant that, and still we claim that you should be true to your theory, and allow to single women those rights which she who is the mistress of a household and mother of a family has no time to exercise . . .

Responsibility is one instrument—a great instrument—of education, both moral and intellectual. It sharpens the faculties. It unfolds the moral nature. It makes the careless prudent, and turns recklessness into sobriety. Look at the young wife suddenly left a widow, with the care of her children's education and entrance into life thrown upon her. How prudent and sagacious she becomes! How fruitful in resources and comprehensive in her views! How much intellect and character she surprises her old friends with! Look at the statesman bold and reckless in opposition; how prudent, how thoughtful, how timid, he becomes, the moment he is in office, and feels that a nation's welfare hangs on his decisions! Woman can never study those great questions that interest and stir most deeply the human mind, until she studies them under the mingled stimulus and check of this responsibility. And until her intellect has been tested by such questions, studied under such influences, we shall never be able to decide what it is.

One great reason, then, besides its justice, why we would claim the ballot for woman, is this: because the great school of this people is the jury-box and the ballot box. Tocqueville, after traveling in this country, went away with the conviction that, valuable as the jury trial was for the investigation of facts and defence of the citizens, its value even in these respects was no greater than as it was the school of civil education open to all the people. The education of the American citizen is found in his interest in the debates of Congress,—the earnest personal interest with which he seeks to fathom political questions. It is when the mind, profoundly stirred by the momentous stake at issue, rises to its most gigantic efforts, when the great crisis of some national convulsion is at hand,—it is then that strong political excitement lifts the people up in advance of the age, heaves a whole nation on to a higher platform of intellect and morality. Great political questions stir the deepest nature of one half the nation; but they pass far above and over the heads of the other half. Yet, meanwhile, theorists wonder that the first have their whole nature unfolded, and the others will persevere in being dwarfed. Now, this great, world-wide, practical, ever-present education we claim for woman. Never, until it is granted her, can you decide what will be her ability. Deny statesmanship to woman? What! to the sisters of Elizabeth of England, Isabella of Spain, Maria Theresa of Austria; ay, let me add, of Elizabeth Heyrick, who, when the intellect of all England was at fault, and wandering in the desert of a false philosophy,—when Brougham and Romilly, Clarkson and Wilberforce, and all the other great and philanthropic minds of England, were at fault and a dead-lock with the West India question and negro slavery,—wrote out, with the statesmanlike intellect of a Quaker woman, the simple yet potent charm,—Immediate, Unconditional Emancipation,—which solved the problem, and gave freedom to a race! How noble the conduct of those men! With an alacrity which does honor to their statesmanship, and proves that they recognized the inspired voice when they heard it, they sat down at the feet of that woman-statesman, and seven years under her instruction did more for the settlement of the greatest social question that had ever convulsed England, than had been done by a century, of more or less effort, before. O no! you cannot read history, unless you read it upside down, without admitting that woman, cramped, fettered, excluded, degraded as she has been, has yet sometimes, with one ray of her instinctive genius, done more to settle great questions than all the cumbrous intellect of the other sex has achieved.

It is, therefore, on the ground of natural justice, and on the ground again of the highest expediency, and yet again it is because woman, as an immortal and intellectual being, has a right to all the means of education,—it is on these grounds that we claim for her the civil rights and privileges which man enjoys . . . We throw down the gauntlet. We have counted the cost; we know the yoke and burden we assume. We know the sneers, the lying frauds of misstatement and misrepresentation, that await us. We have counted all; and it is but the dust in the balance and the small dust in the measure, compared with the inestimable blessings of doing justice to one-half of the human species, of curing this otherwise immedicable wound, stopping this overflowing fountain of corruption, at the very source of civilized life. Truly, it is the great question of the age . . . We know we are right. We only ask an opportunity to argue the question, to set it full before the people, and then leave it to the intellects and the hearts of our country, confident that the institutions under which we live, and the education which other reforms have already given to both sexes, have created men and women capable of solving a problem even more difficult, and meeting a change even more radical, than this.

From Women and Suffrage

1867

Lydia Maria Child (1802–1880) preferred, as she explained in 1841, "to *take* my freedom without disputing about my claim to it." Impatient with the debates on women's rights, she characterized both sides as "shallow philosophy." Instead of talking, women should "simply go forward and *do,*" she told the abolitionist William Lloyd Garrison in 1839.

Child was fearful of losing all connection to the past, telling a friend in 1843: "Let not the din of the noisy present drown the music of the past." Her work was not the "noisy present" of politics, but an "eternal anthem," and she argued that her art was activism enough: "My own appropriate mission is obviously that of a writer; and I am convinced that I can do more good . . . by infusing . . . *principles* . . . into all I write." But as the nation lurched toward war, Child saw that her genteel, sentimental style might effect change: "Slavery was abolished in England by rousing the *moral feelings* of the people." By 1856, she was exclaiming: "What a shame that women can't vote!" She joined abolitionists in the struggle for black suffrage, and in "Women and Suffrage," the endpoint of her long journey toward public activism, she calls for female suffrage too.

Child had spent years looking out from "the 'loopholes of retreat,'" as she once put it (an image also used in Harriet Jacobs's *Incidents* [1861], edited by Child). But in 1861 Child looked back on her years in retreat from public life, writing to Lucretia Mott: "There was a time when I grew tired of incessant strife . . . I make the best atonement that can be made, by working *now* with redoubled diligence." Amused at her own transformation, she wrote to others: "If I . . . go on at this rate, I shall be the rabidest radical that ever pelted a throne."

Further reading: Deborah Clifford, *Crusader for Freedom* (1992); Jean Fagan Yellin, *Women and Sisters* (1989).

Professor Lewis says, very truly, that the questions of black *men's* voting and of white *women's* voting are not analogous. And I confess to a reluctance to urge the question of female suffrage upon Congress at this time, when they have so many other difficult problems to solve. That the loyal blacks of the South should vote is a present and very imperious necessity—not only for their own protection, but also for the safety of the small minority of whites who are true to the Government. This is another of those remarkable leadings of Divine

Providence which have been so conspicuous throughout the war, whereby the people have been compelled to do justly for the sake of their own interest.

I will say, in passing, that there is a fallacy in the phrase "impartial suffrage," as used by many friends of the colored people. They propose that the elective franchise should not be taken away from any who have heretofore exercised it; but that hereafter only those should vote who can read and write. Thus thousands of foreigners, who cannot write their own names, or read their own votes, would be allowed to influence the elections of the country, while numerous native citizens, who are ignorant because our own laws have hitherto prevented them from obtaining the rudiments of learning, would be excluded from the polls. This is *not* impartial suffrage. Either *all* voters should be required to have some degree of education, or *none* should be subject to such limitations.

I have always thought that suffrage ought to rest on an educational basis. There is no hardship in such an arrangement, in a country where the means of obtaining the requisite qualification are offered to every one at the public expense. As a stimulus to education, it would be valuable beyond measure. Probably no motive would operate so strongly on the "poor whites" of the South; and their enlightenment is greatly needed as a check to that arrogant class who led them blindfold into a worse than needless war—a class whose patriarchal tendencies make them the natural enemies of a republic, and whose boast it has been that society among them was becoming "more and more oriental." This patriarchal element would, of course, ultimately destroy our free institutions, if unimpeded in its operations. It is important for the salvation of the nation that it should be kept in check until it disappears before the advances of a higher degree of civilization; and that can only be done by the moral and intellectual improvement of the people, black and white.

The suffrage of woman can better afford to wait than that of the colored people; and they speak truly who say that a majority of women would negative the claim, if left to their decision. In a recent debate in Congress several senators declared themselves ready to grant suffrage to women whenever a considerable number of them asked for it. I smiled at this adroit way of handing over a perplexing question to their sons or grandsons. But this state of mind in women proves nothing, except that human beings are creatures of habit. If a Chinese woman should let the feet of her infant daughter grow to the natural size, and furnish her with suitable shoes to walk in the street, would she not be regarded by her own sex as a shameless innovator? That Chinese men should regard such a proceeding as threatening the disintegration of patriarchal society would be a matter of course. Yet it would be a great improvement in the condition of China if the women were allowed to let their feet grow, and were at liberty to walk with them. When Frederick the Great emancipated the serfs, many of them petitioned to be exempted from the operation of his decree. He persisted in freeing them, for their own good; and at this day Prussia is all the stronger for it. One of the teachers of freedmen at the South informs us that both parents and children complain because there is no whipping in schools. "I really think I should behave better if you would whip me," said one of the boys. He had been brought up under "the patriarchal system," and could not easily get rid of the habits thus acquired.

In my former letter, I showed how women were gradually becoming accustomed to many pursuits that once seemed to them strange and inappropriate. It would be the same with their exercise of the rights of citizenship. Very few would vote at first; but year by year the number of those interested in public affairs would increase. They would doubtless make mistakes, as all beginners do. Some of them would be easily duped, and some would be over-conceited with a little superficial information. The present enlargement of woman's sphere of action is not without such results; and the same is true of the colored people. But I think candid observers would admit that the general gain to character is much greater than the loss.

It is the theory of our government that the people govern. Women constitute half of the people. It has been legally decided that they are citizens; and, as citizens, constituting so large a portion of the people, I think they plainly have a right to vote. I believe it would be good for them to exercise the right, because all human souls grow stronger in proportion to the increase of their responsibilities, and the high employment of their faculties. For ten or twelve years I lived in the midst of Quakers; and I could not but observe that their women were superior to women in general in habits of reflection and independent modes of thinking. I remember a Quaker cobbler who was much addicted to talking, not very wisely, about public affairs. His wife would look up from her knitting, now and then, and quietly remark, "I do not agree with thee, Reuben. Thee has not got on the right principle there, Reuben." If she had voted, it certainly would have been in a manner very different from him; but I don't think there would ever have been any nearer approach to a quarrel than that frequently expressed in her calm dissent from his opinions. This staid and self-relying character in Quaker women I attribute to the fact that they share equally with men in the management of all the business of the society. Frivolous pursuits make frivolous characters. Society has done grievous wrong to the souls of women by fencing them within such narrow enclosures. And then it adds insult to injury by mocking at the meanness it has made. The literature of all nations abounds with jibes, and jeers, and degrading comparisons concerning women. This is so common that men in general probably pass it by unnoticed; but to sensible women it is a perpetual offense. "More than a thousand women is one man worthy to see the light of life," says Euripides. "Stiff ale, stinging tobacco, and a girl in a smart dress are the best things," says the tradesman in Goethe's Faust. "There are exceedingly good points about the Turks; chibouks, coffee, and as many wives as they please. Under their system women become as gentle, as docile, and as tractable as any domestic animal," says Stephens, in his "Incidents of Travel." "Such a thing may happen as that the woman, not the man, may be in the right, (I mean when both are godly); but ordinarily it is otherwise," says John Bunyan. . . . And all this comes upon us in consequence of our having been systematically excluded from the professions, the trades, the arts, the sciences, the halls of legislation; in a word, from all the pursuits that are best calculated to enlarge the mind, to occupy it profitably, and to raise it above mean and petty subjects of thought. Professor Lewis asks whether, if wives and daughters voted, their influence would be as potent and healthy as it now is. I do not think the mere act of voting would make any difference, one way or the other; but I do think the education they would gradually acquire by taking a part in public affairs would make them more instructive and more interesting as household companions. I believe the domestic bond will never reach its possible hight of perfection till women occupy their thoughts and feelings with all that occupies the thoughts and feelings of men. The astronomer and the chemist would find home more satisfactory with wives who could understand their investigations and feel interested in their discoveries. The architect would find himself both enlivened and aided by a companion who had an eye for form and color, and a talent for inventing conveniences. If mothers, wives, and daughters were more generally interested in the ethics of politics, our statesmen would not so often waste their abilities on games of compromise, risking the interests of freedom on the hazard of their play.

How many such struggles we have witnessed as this concerning admitting Colorado and Nebraska into a free republic with a deep taint of despotism in their constitutions! And how very rare are legislators like Charles Sumner, who can never be induced, by any amount of reproach or persuasion, to sacrifice eternal principles to temporary expediency! What a stainless record he is leaving for history!

There is an obvious fallacy in Professor Lewis's statement that women *do* vote in the same way that all our people vote for President: that is, they choose their elector to vote *for* them. The circumstances of the times are always changing, requiring new men and new measures, and when men vote for electors to choose a President, they vote for such electors as are suited to the present emergency. But, admitting that, when a woman marries, and thus becomes "dead in the law," she chooses an elector to vote for her; what manifold changes may take place in affairs, and in his character, if they live together twenty or thirty years! How many chances there are that he will cease to represent her views, even if he does not vote for measures that she entirely disapproves. The Professor again observes: "Women choose their electors, or he is *provided* for them by one of the most precious ordinances of God and Nature." If a husband or a father should become an atheist or an infidel, while his wife and daughters of mature age wished to give their influence and a share of their earnings to the support of evangelical churches, would the Professor decide that the husband and father was their divinely-appointed representative, and that they ought to act only through him? In large portions of Christendom people believe that heads of the Church are divinely appointed to prescribe the faith of other men. I once asked an acquaintance how he came to turn Roman Catholic; and he replied, "It is so convenient to have a bishop to think *for* me." A young lady once told me that she went to all the churches in Boston by turns, because she did not want to decide till she knew what would be the religion of the man she married. Some time afterward she married a Roman Catholic; and, having chosen him to do her believing, she joined his church. What vitality can there be in a religion assumed under such circumstances? The fact is all conclusions are fallacious based on the hypothesis that one human soul can be merged in another soul. No human being can possibly think for me, or believe for me, any more than he can eat for me, or drink for me, or breathe for me. The family is a very sacred thing; but it appears to me that in a family of true order each one would think, feel, and act, as an individual, with respectful regard to the freedom of the other members, and a conscientious feeling of duty concerning the influence exerted on their characters and happiness. I do not see why difference in voting should necessarily produce dissension between husband and wife, any more than the mere difference of opinion which so frequently exists without such result. Nor do I see why the mere circumstance of depositing a vote need to make women boisterous, or expose them to rudeness. *They* are accustomed to press through crowds to go to theaters and operas, and meetings at Faneuil Hall; they go with the throng to hear orators and statesmen, and nobody treats them uncivilly, or considers their presence an unbecoming intrusion. Their appearance at the polls would soon cease to be a novelty, and the depositing of a vote might be done as easily and as quietly as leaving a card at a hotel.

I respect the fears of kind and conscientious conservatives, like Professor Lewis, although I do not share them. There is one abiding consolation for all that class of thinkers. God has so wisely arranged the laws of the universe that great changes *cannot* come till the way is prepared for them. History plainly shows his hand continually preparing the way for the complete individualizing of the masses. Paul spoke for a much larger audience than the churches of Galatia, when he said, "There is neither Jew nor Greek, there is neither bond nor free, there is neither male nor female: for ye are all one in Christ Jesus." With increasing knowledge the work goes on with accelerated speed; but the world is far enough yet from the great festival of ALL SOULS.

From Declaration and Protest of the Women of the United States

1876

On July 4, 1876, five women charged the rostrum at the Centennial celebrations in Philadelphia. Elizabeth Cady Stanton (1815–1902) and the National Woman Suffrage Association (NWSA) had written a declaration, based on the 1848 Seneca Falls "Declaration of Sentiments," and Susan B. Anthony (1820–1906) now presented it to Vice President Ferry. Pale-faced, he bowed and accepted it in silence. The women turned and left, scattering copies of their Declaration. Then they headed for George Washington's statue where, standing in the statesman's shadow, Anthony read the manifesto aloud.

The NWSA women had wanted to read it inside. Stanton recalled: "We thought it would be fitting . . . immediately after that of the Fathers was read, as an impeachment of them and their male descendants." But instead she asked for permission to present the document silently. The authorities refused, commenting: "to-morrow we propose to celebrate what we have done in the last hundred years; not what we have failed to do." Though Stanton's request was denied, the NWSA officers decided to act, inspired by what Stanton called "that heroic spirit which has ever animated lovers of liberty." They wanted "to place on record for the daughters of 1976, the fact that their mothers of 1876 had asserted their equality of rights."

While writing the Declaration, Stanton remembered the abolitionists: "All through our Civil War the slaves . . . had an abiding faith that the terrible conflict would result in freedom." Yet it was this new freedom of slaves that had brought the NWSA to the point of no return. In 1868 the Fourteenth Amendment defined "voters" as "male," and in 1870 the Fifteenth Amendment made no reference to sex. The "republican cry of manhood suffrage created an antagonism between black men and all women," Stanton realized. In 1869, debates over the Amendments split the women's movement, too. Stanton and Anthony organized the NWSA, and Lucy Stone and Julia Ward Howe established the more conservative American Woman Suffrage Association. The organizations didn't rejoin until 1890, when they became the National American Woman Suffrage Association.

Frederick Douglass once questioned why women were excepted from the principles of the Declaration of Independence, and suggested that history would have been less "bloody" had women been allowed more influence in world affairs. On the day that five women interrupted the celebrations in Philadelphia, history looked bloody indeed: amid the patriotic speeches and the NWSA protest, word reached the Centennial crowd that Sioux and Cheyenne warriors had defeated George Custer and his cavalry troops at Little Big Horn. And, in Hamburg, S.C., black Civil War veterans were violently prevented from marching in a July 4 parade. Several were killed in the incident and those responsible were later acquitted in a sham trial.

Further reading: Dee Brown, *The Year of the Century* (1966); Alana Jeydel, *Political Women* (2004).

While the Nation is buoyant with patriotism, and all hearts are attuned to praise, it is with sorrow we come to strike the one discordant note, on this hundredth anniversary of our country's birth. When subjects of Kings, Emperors, and Czars, from the Old World, join in our National Jubilee, shall the women of the Republic refuse to lay their hands with benedictions on the nation's head? Surveying America's Exposition, surpassing in magnificence those of London, Paris, and Vienna, shall we not rejoice at the success of the youngest rival among the nations of the earth? May not our hearts, in unison with all, swell with pride at our great achievements as a people; our free speech, free press, free schools, free church, and the rapid progress we have made in material wealth, trade, commerce, and the inventive arts? And we do rejoice, in the success thus far, of our experiment of self-government. Our faith is firm and unwavering in the broad principles of human rights, proclaimed in 1776, not only as abstract truths, but as the corner stones of a republic. Yet, we cannot forget, even in this glad hour, that while all men of every race, and clime, and condition, have been invested with the full rights of citizenship, under our hospitable flag, all women still suffer the degradation of disfranchisement.

Our history, the past hundred years, has been a series of assumptions and usurpations of power over woman, in direct opposition to the principles of just government, acknowledged by the United States at its foundation . . . And for the violation of these fundamental principles of our Government, we arraign our rulers on this 4th day of July, 1876,—and these are our ARTICLES OF IMPEACHMENT.

BILLS OF ATTAINDER have been passed by the introduction of the word "male" into all the State constitutions, denying to woman the right of suffrage, and thereby making sex a crime—an exercise of power clearly forbidden in Article 1st, Sections 9th and 10th of the United States Constitution.

THE WRIT OF HABEAS CORPUS, the only protection against *lettres de cachet*, and all forms of unjust imprisonment, which the Constitution declares "shall not be suspended, except when in cases of rebellion or invasion, the public safety demands it," is held inoperative in every State in the Union, in case of a married woman against her husband,—the marital rights of the husband being in all cases primary, and the rights of the wife secondary.

THE RIGHT OF TRIAL BY A JURY OF ONE'S PEERS was so jealously guarded that States refused to ratify the original Constitution, until it was guaranteed by the 6th Amendment. And yet the women of this nation have never been allowed a jury of their peers—being tried in all cases by men, native and foreign, educated and ignorant, virtuous and vicious . . . And not only are women denied a jury of their peers, but in some cases, jury trial altogether . . .

TAXATION WITHOUT REPRESENTATION, the immediate cause of the rebellion of the Colonies against Great Britain, is one of the grievous wrongs the women of this country have suffered during the century. Deploring war, with all the demoralization that follows in its train, we have been taxed to support standing armies, with their waste of life and wealth. Believing in temperance, we have been taxed to support the vice, crime, and pauperism of the Liquor Traffic . . . And, moreover, we are taxed to support the very legislators, and judges, who make laws, and render decisions adverse to woman . . .

UNEQUAL CODES FOR MEN AND WOMEN. Held by law a perpetual minor, deemed incapable of self-protection, even in the industries of the world, woman is denied equality of rights. The fact of sex, not the quantity or quality of work, in most cases, decides the pay and position; and because of this injustice thousands of fatherless girls are compelled to choose between a life of shame or starvation . . .

THE ADVANCE LEGISLATION FOR WOMAN has placed us in a most anomalous position. Women invested with the rights of citizens in one section—voters, jurors, office-holders—crossing an imaginary line, are subjects in the next. In some states, a married woman may hold property and transact business in her own name; in others, her earnings belong to her husband. In some states, a woman may testify against her husband, sue and be sued in the courts; in others, she has no redress in case of damage to person, property, or character. In divorce, on account of adultery in the husband, the innocent wife is held to possess no right to children, or property, unless by special decree of the court. But in no state of the Union has the wife the right to her own person, or to any part of the joint earnings of the co-partnership, during the life of her husband. In some States women may enter the law schools and practice in the courts; in others they are forbidden. In some universities, girls enjoy equal educational advantages with boys, while many of the proudest institutions in the land deny them admittance, though the sons of China, Japan and Africa are welcomed there. . . .

REPRESENTATION FOR WOMAN has had no place in the nation's thought. Since the incorporation of the thirteen original states, twenty four have been admitted to the Union, not one of which has recognized woman's right of self-government . . .

UNIVERSAL MANHOOD SUFFRAGE, by establishing an aristocracy of sex, imposes upon the women of this nation a more absolute and cruel despotism than monarchy; in that, woman finds a political master in her father, husband, brother, son. The aristocracies of the old world are based upon birth, wealth, refinement, education, nobility, brave deeds of chivalry; in this nation, on sex alone; exalting brute force above moral power, vice above virtue, ignorance above education, and the son above the mother who bore him.

THE JUDICIARY OF THE NATION has proved itself but the echo of the party in power, by upholding and enforcing laws that are opposed to the spirit and letter of the Constitution. When the slave power was dominant, the Supreme Court decided that a black man was not a citizen, because he had not the right to vote; and when the Constitution was so amended as to make all persons citizens, the same high tribunal decided that a woman, though a citizen, had not the right to vote. Such vascillating interpretations of constitutional law unsettle our faith in judicial authority, and undermine the liberties of the whole people.

THESE ARTICLES OF IMPEACHMENT AGAINST OUR RULERS we now submit to the impartial judgment of the people.

And to all these wrongs and oppressions woman has not submitted in silence and resignation. From the beginning of the century, when Abigail Adams, the wife of one President and the mother of another, said, "we will not hold ourselves bound to obey laws in which we have no voice or representation," until now, woman's discontent has been steadily increasing, culminating nearly thirty years ago in a simultaneous movement among the women of the nation, demanding the right of suffrage. In making our just demands, a higher motive than the pride of sex inspires us; we feel that national safety and stability depend on the complete recognition of the broad principles of our government. Woman's degraded, helpless position is the weak point in our institutions to-day; a disturbing force everywhere, severing family ties, filling our asylums with the deaf, the dumb, the blind, our prisons with criminals, our cities with drunkenness and prostitution, our homes with disease and death.

It was the boast of the founders of the republic, that the rights for which they contended, were the rights of human nature. If these rights are ignored in the case of one half the people, the nation is surely preparing for its own downfall. Governments try themselves. The recognition of a governing and a governed class is incompatible with the first principles of freedom. Woman has not been a heedless spectator of the events of this century, nor a dull listener to the grand arguments for the equal rights of humanity. From the earliest history of our country, woman has shown equal devotion with man to the cause of freedom, and has stood firmly by his side in its defence. Together, they have made this country what it is. Woman's wealth, thought and labor have cemented the stones of every monument man has reared to liberty.

And now, at the close of a hundred years, as the hour hand of the great clock that marks the centuries points to 1876, we declare our faith in the principles of self-government; our full equality with man in natural rights; that woman was made first for her own happiness, with the absolute right to herself—to all the opportunities and advantages life affords, for her complete development; and we deny that dogma of the centuries, incorporated in the codes of all nations—that woman was made for man—her best interests, in all cases, to be sacrificed to his will.

We ask of our rulers, at this hour, no special favors, no special privileges, no special legislation. We ask justice, we ask equality, we ask that all the civil and political rights that belong to citizens of the United States, be guaranteed to us and our daughters forever.

From Solitude of Self

1892

Elizabeth Cady Stanton's charm and humor often disarmed audiences, but in her speech resigning from the presidency of the National American Woman Suffrage Association (NAWSA), also given earlier that day to the United States House Committee on the Judiciary, she didn't soften her potentially dark vision of the human condition. Stanton's journey from personal suffering through rage and critique to battle seemed to have come full circle, back to the anguish of the solitary self. She infuses the speech with natural-rights philosophy, builds on John Locke, protests the exclusion of women from the American model of individual sovereignty, and echoes Ralph Waldo Emerson's "Self-Reliance" (1841), but also revives and darkens the Radical Abolitionist concept of sacred self-sovereignty and attacks the concept of losing the self to gain with God.

In 1892 she was distrustful of new alliances between organized religion and the suffrage movement, of purity legislation, and of the influence of Christian ideology on reform. Her speech engages current debates about protection versus independence, nature versus nurture, the political and the personal, and how the vote would change women (arguing against reformers who thought ideas needed to change first). She also confronts the Nationalist response to Edward Bellamy's vision of a state-run utopia, writes against the early strains of Progressive-era collectivism, and anticipates W. E. B. Du Bois's 1903 exploration of black "self-consciousness." The speech is a masterpiece—acknowledged by Stanton and Susan B. Anthony as the best of Stanton's life. And yet it offers no evidence, argument, or logical progression: this perhaps explains why a speech so steeped in the language of the liberal tradition, and with such contemporary currency, was seemingly "unanswerable"—in the margin of her copy, Anthony noted that the speech was "the strongest & most unanswerable argument & appeal ever made . . . for the full freedom & franchise of women."

The speech also resonates with Charlotte Perkins Gilman's "The Yellow Wallpaper," published the same month. Gilman's narrator lives within the "four walls of a prison cell" that Stanton describes in her speech. By the time of this speech Stanton, who was campaigning for liberalized divorce laws and reproductive self-determination, had been alienated from the mainstream of the women's rights movement: "I am a leader in thought, rather than numbers," she acknowledged in 1888. But just as Gilman's solitary narrator finds community in the wallpaper patterns, so Stanton's prominent use of metaphor hints at the interrelatedness of everything, and complicates her vision of solitude.

Further reading: Elizabeth Cady Stanton, *Eighty Years* (1898); Beth Waggenspack, *The Search for Self-Sovereignty* (1989).

The point I wish plainly to bring before you on this occasion is the individuality of each human soul; our Protestant idea, the right of individual conscience and judgment—our republican idea, individual citizenship. In discussing the rights of woman, we are to consider, first, what belongs to her as an individual, in a world of her own, the arbiter of her own destiny, an imaginary Robinson Crusoe with her woman Friday on a solitary island. Her rights under such circumstances are to use all her faculties for her own safety and happiness.

Secondly, if we consider her as a citizen, as a member of a great nation, she must have the same rights as all other members, according to the fundamental principles of our Government.

Thirdly, viewed as a woman, an equal factor in civilization, her rights and duties are still the same—individual happiness and development.

Fourthly, it is only the incidental relations of life, such as mother, wife, sister, daughter, that may involve some special duties and training. In the usual discussion in regard to woman's sphere, such men as Herbert Spencer, Frederic Harrison, and Grant Allen uniformity subordinate her rights and duties as an individual, as a citizen, as a woman, to the necessities of these incidental relations, some of which a large class of women may never assume. In discussing the sphere of man we do not decide his rights as an individual, as a citizen, as a man by his duties as a father, a husband, a brother, or a son, relations some of which he may never still. Moreover he would be better fitted for these very relations and whatever special work he might choose to do to earn his bread by the complete development of all his faculties as an individual.

Just so with woman. The education that will fit her to discharge the duties in the largest sphere of human usefulness will best fit her for whatever special work she may be compelled to do.

The isolation of every human soul and the necessity of self-dependence must give each individual the right to choose his own surroundings.

The strongest reason for giving women all the opportunities for higher education, for the full development of her faculties, forces of mind and body; for giving her the most enlarged freedom of thought and action; a complete emancipation from all forms of bondage, of custom, dependence, superstition; from all the crippling influences of fear, is the solitude and personal responsibility of her own individual life. The strongest reason why we ask for woman a voice in the government under which she lives; in the religion she is asked to believe; equality in social life, where she is the chief factor; a place in the trades and professions, where she may earn her bread, is because of her birthright to self-sovereignty; because, as an individual, she must rely on herself. No matter how much women prefer to lean, to be protected and supported, nor how much men desire to have them do so, they must make the voyage of life alone, and for safety in an emergency they must know something of the laws of navigation. To guide our own craft, we must be captain, pilot, engineer; with chart and compass to stand at the wheel; to watch the wind and waves and know when to take in the sail, and to read the signs in the firmament over all. It matters not whether the solitary voyager is man or woman. Nature having endowed them equally, leaves them to their own skill and judgment in the hour of danger, and, if not equal to the occasion, alike they perish.

To appreciate the importance of fitting every human soul for independent action, think for a moment of the immeasurable solitude of self. We come into the world alone, unlike all who have gone before us; we leave it alone under circumstances peculiar to ourselves. No mortal ever has been, no mortal ever will be like the soul just launched on the sea of life. There can never again be just such a combination of prenatal influences; never again just such environments as make up the infancy, youth, and manhood of this one. Nature never repeats herself, and the possibilities of one human soul will never be found in another. No one has ever found two blades of ribbon grass alike, and no one will ever find two human beings alike. Seeing, then, what must be the infinite diversity in human character, we can in a measure appreciate the loss to a nation when any large class of the people is uneducated and unrepresented in the government. We ask for the complete development of every individual, first, for his own benefit and happiness. In fitting out an army we give each soldier his own knapsack, arms, powder, his blanket, cup, knife, fork and spoon. We provide alike for all their individual necessities, then each man bears his own burden.

Again we ask complete individual development for the general good; for the consensus of the competent on the whole round of human interests; on all questions of national life, and here each man must bear his share of the general burden. It is sad to see how soon friendless children are left to bear their own burdens before they can analyze their feelings; before they can even tell their joys and sorrows, they are thrown on their own resources. The great lesson that nature seems to teach us at all ages is self-dependence, self-protection, self-support. What a touching instance of a child's solitude; of that hunger of the heart for love and recognition, in the case of the little girl who helped to dress a Christmas tree for the children of the family in which she served. On finding there was no present for herself she slipped away in the darkness and spent the night in an open field sitting on a stone, and when found in the morning was weeping as if her heart would break. No mortal will ever know the thoughts that passed through the mind of that friendless child in the long hours of that cold night, with only the silent stars to keep her company. The mention of her case in the daily papers moved many generous hearts to send her presents, but in the hours of her keenest suffering she was thrown wholly on herself for consolation.

In youth our most bitter disappointments, our brightest hopes and ambitions are known only to ourselves; even our friendship and love we never fully share with another; there is something of every passion in every situation we conceal. Even so in our triumphs and our defeats. The successful candidate for the Presidency and his opponent each have a solitude peculiarly his own, and good form forbids either to speak to his pleasure or regret. The solitude of the king on his throne and the prisoner in his cell differs in character and degree, but it is solitude nevertheless . . . Seeing then that life must ever be a march and a battle, that each soldier must be equipped for his own protection, it is the height of cruelty to rob the individual of a single natural right.

To throw obstacles in the way of a complete education is like putting out the eyes; to deny the rights of property, like cutting off the hands. To deny political equality is to rob the ostracized of all self-respect; of credit in the market place; of recompense in the world of work; of a voice in those who make and administer the law; a choice in the jury before whom they are tried, and in the judge who decides their punishment. Shakespeare's play of Titus and Andronicus contains a terrible satire on woman's position in the nineteenth century— "Rude men" (the play tells us) "seized the king's daughter, cut out her tongue, cut off her hands, and then bade her go call for water and wash her hands." What a picture of woman's position. Robbed of her natural rights, handicapped by law and custom at every turn, yet compelled to fight her own battles, and in the emergencies of life to fall back on herself for protection . . .

How the little courtesies of life on the surface of society, deemed so important from man towards woman, fade into utter insignificance in view of the deeper tragedies in which she must play her part alone, where no human aid is possible.

The young wife and mother, at the head of some establishment with a kind husband to shield her from the adverse winds of life, with wealth, fortune and position, has a certain harbor of safety, secure against the ordinary ills of life. But to manage a household, have a desirable influence in society, keep her friends and the affections of her husband, train her children and servants well, she must have rare common sense, wisdom, diplomacy, and a knowledge of human nature. To do all this she needs the cardinal virtues and the strong points of character that the most successful statesman possesses.

An uneducated woman, trained to dependence, with no resources in herself must make a failure of any position in life. But society says women do not need a knowledge of the world; the liberal training that experience in public life must give, all the advantages of collegiate education; but when for the lack of all this, the woman's happiness is wrecked, alone she bears her humiliation; and the solitude of the weak and the ignorant is indeed pitiable. In the wild chase for the prizes of life they are ground to powder . . . The chief reason for opening to every soul the doors to the whole round of human duties and pleasures is the individual development thus attained, the resources thus provided under all circumstances to mitigate the solitude that at times must come to everyone. I once asked Prince Krapotkin, a Russian nihilist, how he endured his long years in prison, deprived of books, pen, ink, and paper. "Ah," he said, "I thought out many questions in which I had a deep interest. In the pursuit of an idea I took no note of time. When tired of solving knotty problems I recited all the beautiful passages in prose or verse I had ever learned. I became acquainted with myself and my own resources. I had a world of my own, a vast empire, that no Russian jailor or Czar could invade." Such is the value of liberal thought and broad culture when shut off from all human companionship, bringing comfort and sunshine within even the four walls of a prison cell.

As women oftimes share a similar fate, should they not have all the consolation that the most liberal education can give? . . . Inasmuch, then, as woman shares equally the joys and sorrows of time and eternity, is it not the height of presumption in man to propose to represent her at the ballot box and the throne of grace, to do her voting in the state, her praying in the church, and to assume the position of high priest at the family altar?

Nothing strengthens the judgment and quickens the conscience like individual responsibility. Nothing adds such dignity to character as the recognition of one's self-sovereignty; the right to an equal place, everywhere conceded; a place earned by personal merit, not an artificial attainment, by inheritance, wealth, family, and position. Seeing, then, that the responsibilities of life rest equally on man and woman, that their destiny is the same, they need the same preparation for time and eternity. The talk of sheltering woman from the fierce storms of life is the sheerest mockery, for they beat on her from every point of the compass, just as they do on man, and with more fatal results, for he has been trained to protect himself, to resist, to conquer. Such are the facts in human experience, the responsibilities of individual sovereignty. Rich and poor, intelligent and ignorant, wise and foolish, virtuous and vicious, man and woman, it is ever the same, each soul must depend wholly on itself.

Whatever the theories may be of woman's dependence on man, in the supreme moments of her life he can not bear her burdens. Alone she goes to the gates of death to give life to every man that is born into the world. No one can share her fears, no one can mitigate her pangs; and if her sorrow is greater than she can bear, alone she passes beyond the gates into the vast unknown.

From the mountain tops of Judea, long ago, a heavenly voice bade His disciples "Bear ye one another's burdens," but humanity has not yet risen to that point of self-sacrifice, and if ever so willing, how few the burdens are that one soul can bear for another. In the highways of Palestine; in prayer and fasting on the solitary mountain top; in the Garden of Gethsemane; before the judgment seat of Pilate; betrayed by one of His trusted disciples at His last supper; in His agonies on the cross, even Jesus of Nazareth, in these last sad days on earth, felt the awful solitude of self. Deserted by man, in agony he cries, "My God! My God! why hast Thou forsaken me?" And so it ever must be in the conflicting scenes of life, in the long, weary march, each one walks alone. We may have many friends, love, kindness, sympathy, and charity to smooth our pathway in everyday life, but in the tragedies and triumphs of human experience each mortal stands alone.

Whatever may be said of man's protecting power in ordinary conditions, mid all the terrible disasters by land and sea, in the supreme moments of danger, alone woman must ever meet the horrors of the situation; the Angel of Death even makes no royal pathway for her. Man's love and sympathy enter only into the sunshine of our lives. In that solemn solitude of self, that links us with the immeasurable and the eternal, each soul lives alone forever. A recent writer says: I remember once, in crossing the Atlantic, to have gone upon the deck of the ship at midnight, when a dense black cloud enveloped the sky, and the great deep was roaring madly under the lashes of demoniac winds. My feeling was not of danger or fear (which is a base surrender of the immortal soul), but of utter desolation and loneliness; a little speck of life shut in by a tremendous darkness. Again I remember to have climbed the slopes of the Swiss Alps, up beyond the point where vegetation ceases, and the stunted conifers no longer struggle against the unfeeling blasts. Around me lay a huge confusion of rocks, out of which the gigantic toe peaks shot into the measureless blue of the heavens, and again my only feeling was the awful solitude.

And yet, there is a solitude, which each and every one of us has always carried with him more inaccessible than the ice-cold mountains, more profound than the midnight sea; the solitude of self. Our inner being, which we call ourself, no eye nor touch of man or angel has ever pierced. It is more hidden than the caves of the gnome; the sacred adytum of the oracle; the hidden chamber of Eleusinian mystery, for to it only omniscience is permitted to enter.

Such is individual life. Who, I ask you, can take, dare take, on himself the rights, the duties, the responsibilities of another human soul?

The Yellow Wallpaper

1892

Charlotte Perkins Gilman (1860–1935) presents the choice of nightmares for women: to break down or break out. As women entered the public sphere in the wake of the women's rights movement, a marked increase in the number of neurasthenia diagnoses put them back into confinement, reestablishing traditional gender roles. Killing off the infamous ideal of the "angel in the house" seemed to require creating the new role of fallen angel, a phantom replacement for the vanquished spirit of Victorian womanhood, like Gilman's narrator in "The Yellow Wallpaper," whose madness arises from an impasse—the restriction of female expression, and the incompatibility of marriage and work that Gilman had experienced firsthand. In a letter to Charles Stetson, whom she married in 1884 and divorced in 1894, Gilman explained: "As much as I love you I love WORK better, & cannot make the two compatible." And she had seen her mother confined by the cult of true womanhood, remembering her life as "one of the most painfully thwarted I have ever known."

The narrator's breakdown was similarly informed by Gilman's personal experience. After giving birth in 1885 she experienced severe depression and began a "rest-cure" prescribed by the nerve specialist S. Weir Mitchell, consisting of isolation and bed rest. "I came perilously near to losing my mind," she recalled. To save herself she "cast the noted specialist's advice to the winds and went to work again," eventually writing "The Yellow Wallpaper" to reach Mitchell "and convince him of the error of his ways." The narrator's tearing of the wallpaper is a subtle challenge to Mitchell's famous paper, "Wear and Tear, or Hints for the Overworked" (1871), which argued against work for women. And the secret diary in the story is another protest against restriction: sentenced to an intellectual imprisonment, the narrator seeks control of her own sentences.

Years later Gilman heard that Mitchell had read her story and changed his treatment. "If that is a fact," she wrote, "I have not lived in vain." And in 1915, in her novel *Herland*, Gilman imagined a matriarchal utopia: a territory of women broken out but not broken down.

Further reading: Sandra Gilbert and Susan Gubar, *The Madwoman in the Attic* (1984); Ann Lane, *To Herland* (1990).

It is very seldom that mere ordinary people like John and myself secure ancestral halls for the summer.

A colonial mansion, a hereditary estate, I would say a haunted house, and reach the height of romantic felicity but that would be asking too much of fate!

Still I will proudly declare that there is something queer about it.

Else, why should it be let so cheaply? And why have stood so long untenanted?

John laughs at me, of course, but one expects that in marriage.

John is practical in the extreme. He has no patience with faith, an intense horror of superstition, and he scoffs openly at any talk of things not to be felt and seen and put down in figures.

John is a physician, and—*perhaps* (I would not say it to a living soul, of course, but this is dead paper and a great relief to my mind) *perhaps* that is one reason I do not get well faster.

You see he does not believe I am sick!

And what can one do?

If a physician of high standing, and one's own husband, assures friends and relatives that there is really nothing the matter with one but temporary nervous depression—a slight hysterical tendency—what is one to do?

My brother is also a physician, and also of high standing, and he says the same thing.

So I take phosphates or phospites—whichever it is, and tonics, and journeys, and air, and exercise, and am absolutely forbidden to "work" until I am well again.

Personally, I disagree with their ideas.

Personally, I believe that congenial work, with excitement and change, would do me good.

But what is one to do?

I did write for a while in spite of them; but it *does* exhaust me a good deal—having to be so sly about it, or else meet with heavy opposition.

I sometimes fancy that in my condition if I had less opposition and more society and stimulus—but John says the very worst thing I can do is to think about my condition, and I confess it always makes me feel bad.

So I will let it alone and talk about the house.

The most beautiful place! It is quite alone, standing well back from the road, quite three miles from the village. It makes me think of English places that you read about, for there are hedges and walls and gates that lock, and lots of separate little houses for the gardeners and people.

There is a *delicious* garden! I never saw such a garden large and shady, full of box-bordered paths, and lined with long grape-covered arbors with seats under them.

There were greenhouses, too, but they are all broken now.

There was some legal trouble, I believe, something about the heirs and co-heirs; anyhow, the place has been empty for years.

That spoils my ghostliness, I am afraid, but I don't care—there is something strange about the house—I can feel it.

I even said so to John one moonlight evening, but he said what I felt was a *draught,* and shut the window.

I get unreasonably angry with John sometimes. I'm sure I never used to be so sensitive. I think it is due to this nervous condition.

But John says if I feel so, I shall neglect proper self-control; so I take pains to control myself—before him, at least, and that makes me very tired.

I don't like our room a bit. I wanted one downstairs that opened on the piazza and had roses all over the window, and such pretty old-fashioned chintz hangings! but John would not hear of it.

He said there was only one window and not room for two beds, and no near room for him if he took another.

He is very careful and loving, and hardly lets me stir without special direction.

I have a schedule prescription for each hour in the day; he takes all care from me, and so I feel basely ungrateful not to value it more.

He said we came here solely on my account, that I was to have perfect rest and all the air I could get. "Your exercise depends on your strength, my dear," said he, "and your food somewhat on your appetite; but air you can absorb all the time." So we took the nursery at the top of the house.

It is a big, airy room, the whole floor nearly, with windows that look all ways, and air and sunshine galore. It was nursery first and then playroom and gymnasium, I should judge; for the windows are barred for little children, and there are rings and things in the walls.

The paint and paper look as if a boys' school had used it. It is stripped off—the paper—in great patches all around the head of my bed, about as far as I can reach, and in a great place on the other side of the room low down. I never saw a worse paper in my life.

One of those sprawling flamboyant patterns committing every artistic sin.

It is dull enough to confuse the eye in following, pronounced enough to constantly irritate and provoke study, and when you follow the lame uncertain curves for a little distance they suddenly commit suicide—plunge off at outrageous angles, destroy themselves in unheard of contradictions.

The color is repellent, almost revolting; a smouldering unclean yellow, strangely faded by the slow-turning sunlight.

It is a dull yet lurid orange in some places, a sickly sulphur tint in others.

No wonder the children hated it! I should hate it myself if I had to live in this room long.

There comes John, and I must put this away,—he hates to have me write a word.

We have been here two weeks, and I haven't felt like writing before, since that first day.

I am sitting by the window now, up in this atrocious nursery, and there is nothing to hinder my writing as much as I please, save lack of strength.

John is away all day, and even some nights when his cases are serious.

I am glad my case is not serious!

But these nervous troubles are dreadfully depressing.

John does not know how much I really suffer. He knows there is no *reason* to suffer, and that satisfies him.

Of course it is only nervousness. It does weigh on me so not to do my duty in any way!

I meant to be such a help to John, such a real rest and comfort, and here I am a comparative burden already!

Nobody would believe what an effort it is to do what little I am able,—to dress and entertain, and order things.

It is fortunate Mary is so good with the baby. Such a dear baby!

And yet I *cannot* be with him, it makes me so nervous.

I suppose John never was nervous in his life. He laughs at me so about this wall-paper!

At first he meant to repaper the room, but afterwards he said that I was letting it get the better of me, and that nothing was worse for a nervous patient than to give way to such fancies.

He said that after the wall-paper was changed it would be the heavy bedstead, and then the barred windows, and then that gate at the head of the stairs, and so on.

"You know the place is doing you good," he said, "and really, dear, I don't care to renovate the house just for a three months' rental."

"Then do let us go downstairs," I said, "there are such pretty rooms there."

Then he took me in his arms and called me a blessed little goose, and said he would go down to the cellar, if I wished, and have it whitewashed into the bargain.

But he is right enough about the beds and windows and things.

It is an airy and comfortable room as any one need wish, and, of course, I would not be so silly as to make him uncomfortable just for a whim.

I'm really getting quite fond of the big room, all but that horrid paper.

Out of one window I can see the garden, those mysterious deepshaded arbors, the riotous old fashioned flowers, and bushes and gnarly trees.

Out of another I get a lovely view of the bay and a little private wharf belonging to the estate. There is a beautiful shaded lane that runs down there from the house. I always fancy I see people walking in these numerous paths and arbors, but John has cautioned me not to give way to fancy in the least. He says that with my imaginative power and habit of story-making, a nervous weakness like mine is sure to lead to all manner of excited fancies, and that I ought to use my will and good sense to check the tendency. So I try.

I think sometimes that if I were only well enough to write a little it would relieve the press of ideas and rest me.

But I find I get pretty tired when I try.

It is so discouraging not to have any advice and companionship about my work. When I get really well, John says we will ask Cousin Henry and Julia down for a long visit; but he says he would as soon put fireworks in my pillow case as to let me have those stimulating people about now.

I wish I could get well faster.

But I must not think about that. This paper looks to me as if it *knew* what a vicious influence it had!

There is a recurrent spot where the pattern lolls like a broken neck and two bulbous eyes stare at you upside down.

I get positively angry with the impertinence of it and the everlastingness. Up and down and sideways they crawl, and those absurd, unblinking eyes are everywhere. There is one place where two breaths didn't match, and the eyes go all up and down the line, one a little higher than the other.

I never saw so much expression in an inanimate thing before, and we all know how much expression they have! I used to lie awake as a child and get more entertainment and terror out of blank walls and plain furniture than most children could find in a toy-store.

I remember what a kindly wink the knobs of our big, old bureau used to have, and there was one chair that always seemed like a strong friend.

I used to feel that if any of the other things looked too fierce I could always hop into that chair and be safe.

The furniture in this room is no worse than inharmonious, however, for we had to bring it all from downstairs. I suppose when this was used as a playroom they had to take the nursery things out, and no wonder! I never saw such ravages as the children have made here.

The wall-paper, as I said before, is torn off in spots, and it sticketh closer than a brother—they must have had perseverance as well as hatred.

Then the floor is scratched and gouged and splintered, the plaster itself is dug out here and there, and this great heavy bed which is all we found in the room, looks as if it had been through the wars.

But I don't mind it a bit—only the paper.

There comes John's sister. Such a dear girl as she is, and so careful of me! I must not let her find me writing.

She is a perfect and enthusiastic housekeeper, and hopes for no better profession. I verily believe she thinks it is the writing which made me sick!

But I can write when she is out, and see her a long way off from these windows.

There is one that commands the road, a lovely shaded winding road, and one that just looks off over the country. A lovely country, too, full of great elms and velvet meadows.

This wall-paper has a kind of sub-pattern in a different shade, a particularly irritating one, for you can only see it in certain lights, and not clearly then.

But in the places where it isn't faded and where the sun is just so I can see a strange, provoking, formless sort of figure, that seems to skulk about behind that silly and conspicuous front design.

There's sister on the stairs!

Well, the Fourth of July is over! The people are all gone and I am tired out. John thought it might do me good to see a little company, so we just had mother and Nellie and the children down for a week.

Of course I didn't do a thing. Jennie sees to everything now.

But it tired me all the same.

John says if I don't pick up faster he shall send me to Weir Mitchell in the fall.

But I don't want to go there at all. I had a friend who was in his hands once, and she says he is just like John and my brother, only more so!

Besides, it is such an undertaking to go so far.

I don't feel as if it was worth while to turn my hand over for anything, and I'm getting dreadfully fretful and querulous.

I cry at nothing, and cry most of the time.

Of course I don't when John is here, or anybody else, but when I am alone.

And I am alone a good deal just now. John is kept in town very often by serious cases, and Jennie is good and lets me alone when I want her to.

So I walk a little in the garden or down that lovely lane, sit on the porch under the roses, and lie down up here a good deal.

I'm getting really fond of the room in spite of the wall-paper. Perhaps *because* of the wall-paper.

It dwells in my mind so!

I lie here on this great immovable bed—it is nailed down, I believe—and follow that pattern about by the hour. It is as good as gymnastics, I assure you. I start, we'll say, at the bottom, down in the corner over there where it has not been touched, and I determine for the thousandth time that I *will* follow that pointless pattern to some sort of a conclusion.

I know a little of the principle of design, and I know this thing was not arranged on any laws of radiation, or alternation, or repetition, or symmetry, or anything else that I ever heard of.

It is repeated, of course, by the breadths, but not otherwise.

Looked at in one way each breadth stands alone, the bloated curves and flourishes—a kind of "debased Romanesque" with *delirium tremens*—go waddling up and down in isolated columns of fatuity.

But, on the other hand, they connect diagonally, and the sprawling outlines run off in great slanting waves of optic horror, like a lot of wallowing seaweeds in full chase.

The whole thing goes horizontally, too, at least it seems so, and I exhaust myself in trying to distinguish the order of its going in that direction.

They have used a horizontal breadth for a frieze, and that adds wonderfully to the confusion.

There is one end of the room where it is almost intact, and there, when the crosslights fade and the low sun shines directly upon it, I can almost fancy radiation after all,—the interminable grotesques seem to form around a common centre and rush off in headlong plunges of equal distraction.

It makes me tired to follow it. I will take a nap I guess.

I don't know why I should write this.

I don't want to.

I don't feel able.

And I know John would think it absurd. But I *must* say what I feel and think in some way—it is such a relief!

But the effort is getting to be greater than the relief.

Half the time now I am awfully lazy, and lie down ever so much.

John says I mustn't lose my strength, and has me take cod liver oil and lots of tonics and things, to say nothing of ale and wine and rare meat.

Dear John! He loves me very dearly, and hates to have me sick. I tried to have a real earnest reasonable talk with him the other day, and tell him how I wish he would let me go and make a visit to Cousin Henry and Julia.

But he said I wasn't able to go, nor able to stand it after I got there; and I did not make out a very good case for myself, for I was crying before I had finished.

It is getting to be a great effort for me to think straight. Just this nervous weakness I suppose.

And dear John gathered me up in his arms, and just carried me upstairs and laid me on the bed, and sat by me and read to me till it tired my head.

He said I was his darling and his comfort and all he had, and that I must take care of myself for his sake, and keep well.

He says no one but myself can help me out of it, that I must use my will and self-control and not let any silly fancies run away with me.

There's one comfort, the baby is well and happy, and does not have to occupy this nursery with the horrid wall-paper.

If we had not used it, that blessed child would have! What a fortunate escape! Why, I wouldn't have a child of mine, an impressionable little thing, live in such a room for worlds.

I never thought of it before, but it is lucky that John kept me here after all, I can stand it so much easier than a baby, you see.

Of course I never mention it to them any more—I am too wise,—but I keep watch of it all the same.

There are things in that paper that nobody knows but me, or ever will.

Behind that outside pattern the dim shapes get clearer every day.

It is always the same shape, only very numerous.

And it is like a woman stooping down and creeping about behind that pattern. I don't like it a bit. I wonder—I begin to think—I wish John would take me away from here!

It is so hard to talk with John about my case, because he is so wise, and because he loves me so.

But I tried it last night.

It was moonlight. The moon shines in all around just as the sun does.

I hate to see it sometimes, it creeps so slowly, and always comes in by one window or another.

John was asleep and I hated to waken him, so I kept still and watched the moonlight on that undulating wall-paper till I felt creepy.

The faint figure behind seemed to shake the pattern, just as if she wanted to get out.

I got up softly and went to feel and see if the paper *did* move, and when I came back John was awake.

"What is it, little girl?" he said. "Don't go walking about like that—you'll get cold."

I thought it was a good time to talk, so I told him that I really was not gaining here, and that I wished he would take me away.

"Why darling!" said he, "our lease will be up in three weeks, and I can't see how to leave before.

"The repairs are not done at home, and I cannot possibly leave town just now. Of course if you were in any danger, I could and would, but you really are better, dear, whether you can see it or not. I am a doctor, dear, and I know. You are gaining flesh and color, your appetite is better, I feel really much easier about you."

"I don't weigh a bit more," said I, "nor as much; and my appetite may be better in the evening when you are here, but it is worse in the morning when you are away!"

"Bless her little heart!" said he with a big hug, "she shall be as sick as she pleases! But now let's improve the shining hours by going to sleep, and talk about it in the morning!"

"And you won't go away?" I asked gloomily.

"Why, how can I, dear? It is only three weeks more and then we will take a nice little trip of a few days while Jennie is getting the house ready. Really dear you are better!"

"Better in body perhaps—" I began, and stopped short, for he sat up straight and looked at me with such a stern, reproachful look that I could not say another word.

"My darling," said he, "I beg of you, for my sake and for our child's sake, as well as for your own, that you will never for one instant let that idea enter your mind! There is nothing so dangerous, so fascinating, to a temperament like yours. It is a false and foolish fancy. Can you not trust me as a physician when I tell you so?"

So of course I said no more on that score, and we went to sleep before long. He thought I was asleep first, but I wasn't, and lay there for hours trying to decide whether that front pattern and the back pattern really did move together or separately.

On a pattern like this, by daylight, there is a lack of sequence, a defiance of law, that is a constant irritant to a normal mind.

The color is hideous enough, and unreliable enough, and infuriating enough, but the pattern is torturing.

You think you have mastered it, but just as you get well underway in following, it turns a back somersault and there you are. It slaps you in the face, knocks you down, and tramples upon you. It is like a bad dream.

The outside pattern is a florid arabesque, reminding one of a fungus. If you can imagine a toadstool in joints, an interminable string of toadstools, budding and sprouting in endless convolutions—why, that is something like it.

That is, sometimes!

There is one marked peculiarity about this paper, a thing nobody seems to notice but myself and that is that it changes as the light changes.

When the sun shoots in through the east window—I always watch for that first long, straight ray—it changes so quickly that I never can quite believe it.

That is why I watch it always.

By moonlight—the moon shines in all night when there is a moon—I wouldn't know it was the same paper.

At night in any kind of light, in twilight, candle light, lamplight, and worst of all by moonlight, it becomes bars! The outside pattern I mean, and the woman behind it is as plain as can be.

I didn't realize for a long time what the thing was that showed behind, that dim sub-pattern, but now I am quite sure it is a woman.

By daylight she is subdued, quiet. I fancy it is the pattern that keeps her so still. It is so puzzling. It keeps me quiet by the hour.

I lie down ever so much now. John says it is good for me, and to sleep all I can.

Indeed he started the habit by making me lie down for an hour after each meal.

It is a very bad habit I am convinced, for you see I don't sleep.

And that cultivates deceit, for I don't tell them I'm awake—O no!

The fact is I am getting a little afraid of John.

He seems very queer sometimes, and even Jennie has an inexplicable look.

It strikes me occasionally, just as a scientific hypothesis,—that perhaps it is the paper!

I have watched John when he did not know I was looking, and come into the room suddenly on the most innocent excuses, and I've caught him several times *looking at the paper!* And Jennie too. I caught Jennie with her hand on it once.

She didn't know I was in the room, and when I asked her in a quiet, a very quiet voice, with the most restrained manner possible, what she was doing with the paper—she turned around as if she had been caught stealing, and looked quite angry—asked me why I should frighten her so!

Then she said that the paper stained everything it touched, that she had found yellow smooches on all my clothes and John's, and she wished we would be more careful!

Did not that sound innocent? But I know she was studying that pattern, and I am determined that nobody shall find it out but myself!

Life is very much more exciting now than it used to be. You see I have something more to expect, to look forward to, to watch. I really do eat better, and am more quiet than I was.

John is so pleased to see me improve! He laughed a little the other day, and said I seemed to be flourishing in spite of my wall-paper.

I turned it off with a laugh. I had no intention of telling him it was *because* of the wall-paper—he would make fun of me. He might even want to take me away.

I don't want to leave now until I have found it out. There is a week more, and I think that will be enough.

I'm feeling ever so much better! I don't sleep much at night, for it is so interesting to watch developments; but I sleep a good deal in the daytime.

In the daytime it is tiresome and perplexing.

There are always new shoots on the fungus, and new shades of yellow all over it. I cannot keep count of them, though I have tried conscientiously.

It is the strangest yellow, that wall-paper! It makes me think of all the yellow things I ever saw—not beautiful ones like buttercups, but old foul, bad yellow things.

But there is something else about that paper—the smell! I noticed it the moment we came into the room, but with so much air and sun it was not bad. Now we have had a week of fog and rain, and whether the windows are open or not, the smell is here.

It creeps all over the house.

I find it hovering in the dining-room, skulking in the parlor, hiding in the hall, lying in wait for me on the stairs.

It gets into my hair.

Even when I go to ride, if I turn my head suddenly and surprise it—there is that smell!

Such a peculiar odor, too! I have spent hours in trying to analyze it, to find what it smelled like.

It is not bad—at first, and very gentle, but quite the subtlest, most enduring odor I ever met.

In this damp weather it is awful, I wake up in the night and find it hanging over me.

It used to disturb me at first. I thought seriously of burning the house—to reach the smell.

But now I am used to it. The only thing I can think of that it is like is the *color* of the paper! A yellow smell.

There is a very funny mark on this wall, low down, near the mopboard. A streak that runs round the room. It goes behind every piece of furniture, except the bed, a long, straight, even *smooch*, as if it had been rubbed over and over.

I wonder how it was done and who did it, and what they did it for. Round and round and round—round and round and round—it makes me dizzy!

I really have discovered something at last.

Through watching so much at night, when it changes so, I have finally found out.

The front pattern *does* move—and no wonder! The woman behind shakes it!

Sometimes I think there are a great many women behind, and sometimes only one, and she crawls around fast, and her crawling shakes it all over.

Then in the very bright spots she keeps still, and in the very shady spots she just takes hold of the bars and shakes them hard.

And she is all the time trying to climb through. But nobody could climb through that pattern—it strangles so; I think that is why it has so many heads.

They get through, and then the pattern strangles them off and turns them upside down, and makes their eyes white!

If those heads were covered or taken off it would not be half so bad.

I think that woman gets out in the daytime!

And I'll tell you why—privately—I've seen her!

I can see her out of every one of my windows!

It is the same woman, I know, for she is always creeping, and most women do not creep by daylight.

I see her on that long road under the trees, creeping along, and when a carriage comes she hides under the blackberry vines.

I don't blame her a bit. It must be very humiliating to be caught creeping by daylight!

I always lock the door when I creep by daylight. I can't do it at night, for I know John would suspect something at once.

And John is so queer now, that I don't want to irritate him. I wish he would take another room! Besides, I don't want anybody to get that woman out at night but myself.

I often wonder if I could see her out of all the windows at once.

But, turn as fast as I can, I can only see out of one at one time.

And though I always see her, she *may* be able to creep faster than I can turn!

I have watched her sometimes away off in the open country, creeping as fast as a cloud shadow in a high wind.

*   *   *

If only that top pattern could be gotten off from the under one! I mean to try it, little by little.

I have found out another funny thing, but I shan't tell it this time! It does not do to trust people too much.

There are only two more days to get this paper off, and I believe John is beginning to notice. I don't like the look in his eyes.

And I heard him ask Jennie a lot of professional questions about me. She had a very good report to give.

She said I slept a good deal in the daytime.

John knows I don't sleep very well at night, for all I'm so quiet!

He asked me all sorts of questions, too, and pretended to be very loving and kind.

As if I couldn't see through him!

Still, I don't wonder he acts so, sleeping under this paper for three months.

It only interests me, but I feel sure John and Jennie are secretly affected by it.

Hurrah! This is the last day, but it is enough. John to stay in town over night, and won't be out until this evening.

Jennie wanted to sleep with me—the sly thing! but I told her I should undoubtedly rest better for a night all alone.

That was clever, for really I wasn't alone a bit! As soon as it was moonlight and that poor thing began to crawl and shake the pattern, I got up and ran to help her.

I pulled and she shook, I shook and she pulled, and before morning we had peeled off yards of that paper.

A strip about as high as my head and half around the room.

And then when the sun came and that awful pattern began to laugh at me, I declared I would finish it to-day!

We go away to-morrow, and they are moving all my furniture down again to leave things as they were before.

Jennie looked at the wall in amazement, but I told her merrily that I did it out of pure spite at the vicious thing.

She laughed and said she wouldn't mind doing it herself, but I must not get tired.

How she betrayed herself that time!

But I am here, and no person touches this but me,—not *alive!*

She tried to get me out of the room—it was too patent! But I said it was so quiet and empty and clean now that I believed I would lie down again and sleep all I could; and not to wake me even for dinner—I would call when I woke.

So now she is gone, and the servants are gone, and the things are gone, and there is nothing left but that great bedstead nailed down, with the canvas mattress we found on it.

We shall sleep downstairs to-night, and take the boat home to-morrow.

I quite enjoy the room, now it is bare again.

How those children did tear about here!

This bedstead is fairly gnawed!

But I must get to work.

I have locked the door and thrown the key down into the front path.

I don't want to go out, and I don't want to have anybody come in, till John comes.

I want to astonish him.

I've got a rope up here that even Jennie did not find. If that woman does get out, and tries to get away, I can tie her!

But I forgot I could not reach far without anything to stand on!

This bed will not move!

I tried to lift and push it until I was lame, and then I got so angry I bit off a little piece at one corner—but it hurt my teeth.

Then I peeled off all the paper I could reach standing on the floor. It sticks horribly and the pattern just enjoys it! All those strangled heads and bulbous eyes and waddling fungus growths just shriek with derision!

I am getting angry enough to do something desperate. To jump out of the window would be admirable exercise, but the bars are too strong even to try.

Besides I wouldn't do it. Of course not. I know well enough that a step like that is improper and might be misconstrued.

I don't like to *look* out of the windows even—there are so many of those creeping women, and they creep so fast.

I wonder if they all come out of that wall-paper as I did?

But I am securely fastened now by my well hidden rope—you don't get *me* out in the road there!

I suppose I shall have to get back behind the pattern when it comes night, and that is hard!

It is so pleasant to be out in this great room and creep around as I please!

I don't want to go outside. I won't, even if Jennie asks me to.

For outside you have to creep on the ground, and everything is green instead of yellow.

But here I can creep smoothly on the floor, and my shoulder just fits in that long smooch around the wall, so I cannot lose my way.

Why there's John at the door!

It is no use, young man, you can't open it!

How he does call and pound!

Now he's crying for an axe.

It would be a shame to break down that beautiful door!

"John dear!" said I in the gentlest voice, "the key is down by the front steps, under a plantain leaf!"

That silenced him for a few moments.

Then he said very quietly indeed, "Open the door, my darling!"

"I can't," said I. "The key is down by the front door under a plantain leaf!"

And then I said it again, several times, very gently and slowly, and said it so often that he had to go and see, and he got it of course, and came in. He stopped short by the door.

"What is the matter?" he cried. "For God's sake, what are you doing!"

I kept on creeping just the same, but I looked at him over my shoulder.

"I've got out at last," said I, "in spite of you and Jane. And I've pulled off most of the paper, so you can't put me back!"

Now why should that man have fainted? But he did, and right across my path by the wall, so that I had to creep over him every time!

Frederick Douglass

1908

Frederick Douglass crossed boundaries between slavery and freedom, America and Europe, abolition and women's rights. Just as suffragists stood with abolitionists, so Douglass joined the suffrage movement, often equating women's conditions with slavery. He even came to call women's rights a *more* important struggle, saying in 1888: "Mine was a great cause. Yours is a much greater cause, since it comprehends the liberation and elevation of one half of the whole human family." The first issue of Douglass's newspaper proclaimed: "Right is of no sex," and he was the only man to speak in favor of Elizabeth Cady Stanton's resolution on woman suffrage at Seneca Falls in 1848. But in 1865 he split from women's rights activists over the question of the Fourteenth and Fifteenth Amendments, which excluded women. He resumed fighting for women's rights in 1870.

Though his own marriage seemed to reinforce conventional gender roles, radical women embraced Douglass as a hero. Upon his death Stanton declared: "He was the only man I ever saw who understood the degradation of the disenfranchisement of women." Mary Church Terrell also paid tribute, in the speech reprinted here. Terrell was the first president of the National Association of Colored Women, formed in 1896, and one of the founders of the National Association for the Advancement of Colored People. Like Douglass, she was known for both her work on women's suffrage and her opposition to lynching and racial segregation. Terrell tried to bring black women into the women's movement and in 1953, at the age of 90, she led a successful antisegregation campaign in Washington, D.C.

Beyond his death, Douglass remained integral to the protest tradition. Writers often reached back to him for inspiration. "Ah, Douglass, we have fall'n on evil days," wrote the poet Paul Laurence Dunbar in 1903; "Oh, for thy voice high-sounding o'er the storm." And in 1947 the poet and essayist Robert Hayden imagined Douglass's living legacy: "the lives grown out of his life, the lives fleshing his dream of the needful, beautiful thing."

There are two reasons why I look back upon the meeting of which this is the sixtieth anniversary with genuine pleasure and glowing pride. In the first place, I am a woman like Elizabeth Cady Stanton. In the second place, I belong to the race of which Frederick Douglass was such a magnificent representative. Perhaps I should be too modest to proclaim from the housetops that I think I have a decided advantage over everybody else who participates in this anniversary to-day. Perhaps I should be too courteous and generous to call attention to the fact that I have one more reason for being proud of that record-breaking history making meeting, which was held in this city 60 years ago, than anybody else who takes part in these exercises to-day. But I simply cannot resist the temptation to show that this is one occasion on which a colored woman really has good and sufficient reasons for feeling several inches taller than her sisters of the more favored race. It so rarely happens that a colored woman in the United States can prove by convincing, indisputable facts that she has good reasons for being proud of the race with which she is identified that you will pardon me for the pride I feel on this occasion, I am sure.

The incomparable Frederick Douglass did many things of which I as a member of that race which he served so faithfully and well am proud. But there is nothing he ever did in his long and brilliant career in which I take keener pleasure and greater pride than I do in his ardent advocacy of equal political rights for women and the effective service he rendered the cause of woman suffrage sixty years ago. Even though some of us have passed that period in our lives, when we take much pleasure in those old romances which describe in such deliciously thrilling details those days of old, when knights were bold and had a chronic habit of rescuing fair ladies in high towers in distress, still I am sure there is nobody here to-day with soul so dead and heart so cold who does not admire a man who, in the everyday affairs of this prosaic world, rushes gallantly to the assistance of a woman fighting to the death for a principle as dear to her as life and actually succeeds in helping her establish and maintain it, in spite of the opposition of even her faithful coadjutors and her most faithful friends. This is precisely the service which Frederick Douglass rendered Elizabeth Cady Stanton at that Seneca Falls meeting sixty years ago.

When the defeat of that resolution which demanded equal political rights for women seemed imminent, because some of the most ardent advocates of woman suffrage deemed it untimely and unwise, when even dear, broad, brave Lucretia Mott tried to dissuade Mrs. Stanton, to whom it was the very heart and soul of the movement, from insisting upon it by declaring "Lizzie, thee will make us all ridiculous," I am glad that it was to a large extent due to Frederick Douglass' masterful arguments and matchless eloquence that it was carried, in spite of the opposition of its equally conscientious and worthy foes. And I am as proud of Elizabeth Cady Stanton, as a woman, as I am of Frederick Douglass, the Negro. Try as hard as we may, it is difficult for women of the present day to imagine what courage and strength of mind it required for Elizabeth Cady Stanton to demand equal political rights for her sex at that time.

It is safe to assert that there is not a single woman here to-day who would not have uttered the same words of warning and caution as did Lucretia Mott if she had been present, when a sister made demands which seemed so utterly impossible and rashly extravagant as were those urged by Elizabeth Cady Stanton at a meeting in which for the first time in the history of the world it was openly, boldly proclaimed without any qualifications and reservations whatsoever, that women on general principles had as much right to choose the rulers and make laws as had men, and that it was the duty of American women in particular to do everything in their power to secure the elective franchise for themselves. And this little episode with which we are all so familiar should not cause us to love those who opposed the resolution demanding equal political rights for women the less but should cause us to praise and admire those who insisted upon its adoption, the more.

It is difficult for us to exaggerate the importance of the bold step taken by the advocates of this resolution, when they dared to array themselves against their friends who they knew were as interested in woman suffrage as themselves and as willing to make sacrifices to effect it as were they themselves. And for that reason there are no words of praise too strong to bestow on that great woman and that illustrious man who finally succeeded in convincing their friends in that meeting that the course they advised was the wisest and the best. How glad we all are to-day that Martha C. Wright, Mary Ann McClintock, Lucretia Mott and Elizabeth Cady Stanton dared to offend the tender, delicate sensibilities and shock the proprieties of this staid, inconsistently proper and hypocritical old world.

But if Elizabeth Cady Stanton manifested sublime courage and audacious contempt for the ridicule and denunciation she knew would be heaped upon her as a woman, how much more were such qualities displayed by Frederick Douglass, the ex-slave. It is doubtful if Frederick Douglass' independence of spirit and sense of justice were ever put to a severer test than they were on that day, when for the first time in his life, he publicly committed himself to the cause of woman suffrage. I have always extracted great pleasure from the thought not only that Frederick Douglass, and he alone of all men present at the Seneca Falls meeting, was conspicuous for his enthusiastic advocacy of equal political rights for women, but that he found it in his heart to advocate it ever afterward with such ardor and zeal.

In no half-hearted way did he lay hold of the newly-proclaimed doctrine, nor did he ever try to conceal his views. When nearly all the newspapers, big and little, good, bad and indifferent were hurling jibes and jeers at the women and the men who participated in the Seneca Falls meeting, there was one newspaper, which was published in Rochester, N.Y., which not only heartily commended the leaders, in the new movement but warmly espoused their cause. This was Frederick Douglass' *North Star*. In the leading editorial July 28, 1848, after declaring, "we could not do justice to our own convictions nor to the excellent persons connected with the infant movement, if we did not in this connection offer a few remarks on the general subject which the convention met to consider and the objects it seeks to attain." As editor of the *North Star,* Mr. Douglass expresses his views as follows: "A discussion of the rights of animals would be regarded with far more complacency by many of what are called the wise and good of the land than would be a discussion of the rights of women. Many who have at last made the discovery that Negroes have some rights as well as other members of the human family have yet to be convinced that women have any. Standing as we do upon the watch tower of human freedom, we cannot be deterred from an expression of our approbation of any movement, however humble, to improve and elevate any member of the human family."

In his autobiography which was published in 1882 Mr. Douglass thus explains how he first became interested in the cause of woman suffrage: "Observing woman's agency, devotion and efficiency in pleading the cause of the slave, gratitude for this high service early moved me to give favorable attention to the subject of what is called 'Woman's Rights' and caused me to be denominated a woman's rights man." "I am glad to say," he adds, "that I have never been ashamed to be thus designated." To Mrs. Elizabeth Cady Stanton Mr. Douglass always attributed his first conversion to the cause of woman suffrage. And so eager was he that Mrs. Stanton should know that he had referred to this in his book that he wrote her a letter February 6, 1882, calling her attention to that fact. "You will observe," he said, "that I don't forget my walk with you from the house of Mr. Joseph Southwick, where you quietly brought to my notice your arguments for womanhood suffrage. That is forty years ago. You had just returned from your European tour. From that conversation with you I have been convinced of the wisdom of woman suffrage and I have never denied the faith."

If at any time Mr. Douglass seemed to waver in his allegiance to the cause of political enfranchisement of women, it was because he realized as no white person, no matter how broad and sympathetic he may be, has ever been able to feel or can possibly feel today just what it means to belong to my despised, handicapped and persecuted race. I am woman and I know what it means to be circumscribed, deprived, handicapped and fettered on account of my sex. But I assure you that no where in the United States have my feelings been so lacerated, my spirit so crushed, my heart so wounded, no where have I been so humiliated and handicapped on account of my sex as I have been on account of my race. I can readily understand, therefore, what feelings must have surged through Frederick Douglass' heart, and I can almost feel the intensity of the following words he uttered, when he tried to explain why he honestly thought it was more necessary and humane to give the ballot to the Negro than to women, for the law makers of this country were too narrow and ungenerous to deal justly both by the oppressed race and the handicapped, disfranchised sex at one and the same time. "I must say," declared Mr. Douglass, "that I cannot see how any one can pretend that there is the same urgency in giving the ballot to woman as to the Negro. With us," he said, "the matter is a question of life and death at best in fifteen states of the union. When women, because they are women, are hunted down through the streets of New York and New Orleans; their children torn from their arms and their brains dashed out on the pavement; when they are objects of insult and outrage at every turn; when they are in danger of having their houses burnt down over their heads; when their children are not allowed to enter school; then they will have an urgency to obtain the ballot equal to our own." "Is that not also true about black women?" somebody in the audience inquired. "Yes, yes, yes," replied Mr. Douglass, "but not because they are women, but because they are black."

Now I am not trying to minimize in the slightest degree the crime against American women, particularly intelligent women, perpetrated by the lawmakers of this country, who for years have refused to allow women to exercise the rights and privileges already guaranteed them in the constitution of the United States. For I have placed myself in that glorious company of eminent American jurists who insist that the 14th amendment extends its privileges and benefactions to women as well as to colored men. As a woman I can readily understand the keen disappointment experienced by those women who had worked so indefatigably, so conscientiously and so long to secure equal political rights for their sex. I can understand their bitterness of spirit, too, when the right of citizenship was coldly withheld from them and conferred upon a race just emerging from bondage, the masses of whose men were densely ignorant—could neither read nor write. But I know that along with such staunch and sterling advocates of woman suffrage as was Wendell Phillips, Wm. Lloyd Garrison, Gerrit Smith and others, Mr. Douglass was as firmly and honestly convinced that his position was scrupulous, wise and just as were the opponents of his view. Those who knew Frederick Douglass best know that he was neither a truckler nor a time-server and that he was incapable of doing a mean, dishonest act. They know also that he was genuinely interested in the cause of woman suffrage . . .

If Frederick Douglass were here in the flesh to-day, I am sure he would urge us to buckle on the armor and go forth with fresh courage and renewed zeal to throttle the giants of prejudice, proscription and persecution on account of either sex or race. In Mr. Douglass' own fight from the degradation, the blight and the curse of slavery to freedom, he has set us an example of determination, energy, resolution, faith and hope which we should do well to imitate to-day. Catching the spirit of that great and good man, let us resolve here and now that neither principalities nor powers, nor things present, nor things to come shall separate us from our beloved cause and deter us from discharging the obligations and duties to it which rest upon us to-day.

From Why Women Should Vote

1910

Jane Addams (1860–1935) is usually associated with Hull House, which she cofounded in Chicago in 1889 as one of the first settlement houses in the United States. Hull House provided welfare for the poor, was a meeting place for social reformists, and served as a women's sociological institution. But Addams was also a force in the suffrage movement.

Suffragists had sought alliances with labor activists since the end of the Civil War, when they shifted from comparisons with slaves to comparisons with degraded workers, and Addams was a socialist feminist, like Charlotte Perkins Gilman and Crystal Eastman. She combined Progressive-era reform with suffrage activism, to the advantage of both. Female suffrage and Progressive reform would save the American home, Addams argued, because working-class women would use the vote to support important reforms. As one suffrage poster put it: "Women are by nature and training housekeepers. Let them help in the city housekeeping." Such respect for domesticity countered any idea that suffrage was incompatible with traditional roles.

Addams moved within the realm of popular ideas, reassuring her audience in 1897: "I am not one of those who believe—broadly speaking—that women are better than men. We have not . . . done many unholy things that men have done; but then we must remember that we have not had the chance." Another strategy was to avoid any suggestion that activists were making history; instead, historical inevitability had swept women to the point of suffrage. America had changed, and without the vote women couldn't restore order to their domestic situations. Addams focused on effect, not cause, and offered pragmatism rather than ideals. "Why Women Should Vote" is not about why women should have the vote, but rather what effect their vote would have. She wanted to break from what she called the "high flown" 18th-century "formulae of liberty and equality." The self-sovereignty and solitude proposed by Elizabeth Cady Stanton in 1892 seemed a version of what Addams called "personal ambition"—"too archaic to accomplish anything now." Part of a new generation of woman's rights activists, Addams helped inch America closer to the Nineteenth Amendment.

For many generations it has been believed that woman's place is within the walls of her own home, and it is indeed impossible to imagine the time when her duty there shall be ended or to forecast any social change which shall release her from that paramount obligation.

This paper is an attempt to show that many women to-day are failing to discharge their duties to their own households properly simply because they do not perceive that as society grows more complicated, it is necessary that woman shall extend her sense of responsibility to many things outside of her own home if she would continue to preserve the home in its entirety. One could illustrate in many ways. A woman's simplest duty, one would say, is to keep her house clean and wholesome and to feed her children properly. Yet if she lives in a tenement house, as so many of my neighbors do, she cannot fulfill these simple obligations by her own efforts because she is utterly dependent upon the city administration for the conditions which render decent living possible. Her basement will not be dry, her stairways will not be fireproof, her house will not be provided with sufficient windows to give light and air, nor will it be equipped with sanitary plumbing, unless the Public Works Department sends inspectors who constantly insist that these elementary decencies be provided. Women who live in the country sweep their own dooryards and may either feed the refuse of the table to a flock of chickens or allow it innocently to decay in the open air and sunshine. In a crowded city quarter, however, if the street is not cleaned by the city authorities, no amount of private sweeping will keep the tenement free from grime; if the garbage is not properly collected and destroyed a tenement house mother may see her children sicken and die of diseases from which she alone is powerless to shield them, although her tenderness and devotion are unbounded. She cannot even secure untainted meat for her household, she cannot provide fresh fruit, unless the meat has been inspected by city officials, and the decayed fruit, which is so often placed upon sale in the tenement districts, has been destroyed in the interests of public health. In short, if woman would keep on with her old business of caring for her house and rearing her children she will have to have some conscience in regard to public affairs lying quite outside of her immediate household. The individual conscience and devotion are no longer effective.

Chicago one spring had a spreading contagion of scarlet fever just at the time that the school nurses had been discontinued because businessmen had pronounced them too expensive. If the women who sent their children to the schools had been sufficiently public-spirited and had been provided with an implement through which to express that public spirit they would have insisted that the schools be supplied with nurses in order that their own children might be protected from contagion. In other words, if women would effectively continue their old avocations they must take part in the slow upbuilding of that code of legislation which is alone sufficient to protect the home from the dangers incident to modern life. One might instance the many deaths of children from contagions diseases the germs of which had been carried in tailored clothing. Country doctors testify as to the outbreak of scarlet fever in remote neighborhoods each autumn, after the children have begun to wear the winter overcoats and cloaks which have been sent from infected city sweat-shops. That their mothers mend their stockings and guard them from "taking cold" is not a sufficient protection when the tailoring of the family is done in a distant city under conditions which the mother cannot possibly control. The sanitary regulation of sweatshops by city officials is all that can be depended upon to prevent such needless destruction. Who shall say that women are not concerned in the enactment and enforcement of such legislation if they would preserve their homes? . . .

One of the interesting experiences in the Chicago campaign for inducing the members of the Charter Convention to recommend municipal franchise for women in the provisions of the new charter was the unexpected enthusi-asm and help which came from large groups of foreign-born women. The Scandinavian women represented in many Lutheran Church societies said quite simply that in the old country they had had the municipal franchise upon the same basis as men for many years; all the women living under the British Government, in England, Australia or Canada, pointed out that Chi-cago women were asking now for what the British women had long ago. But the most unexpected response came from the foreign colonies in which women had never heard such problems discussed and took the prospect of the municipal ballot as a simple device—which it is—to aid them in their daily struggle with adverse city conditions. The Italian women said that the men en-gaged in railroad construction were away all summer and did not know any-thing about their household difficulties. Some of them came to Hull-House one day to talk over the possibility of a public wash-house. They do not like to wash in their own tenements; they had never seen a washing-tub until they came to America, and find it very difficult to use it in the restricted space of their little kitchens and to hang the clothes within the house to dry. They say that in the Italian villages the women all go to the streams together; in the town they go to the public wash-house; and washing, instead of being lonely and disagreeable, is made pleasant by cheerful conversation. It is asking a great deal of these women to change suddenly all their habits of living, and their contention that the tenement house kitchen is too small for laundry work is well taken. If women in Chicago knew the needs of the Italian colony they would realize that any change bringing cleanliness and fresh air into the Ital-ian household would be a very sensible and hygienic measure. It is, perhaps, asking a great deal that the members of the City Council should understand this, but surely a comprehension of the needs of these women and efforts to-ward ameliorating their lot might be regarded as matters of municipal obliga-tion on the part of voting women.

The same thing is true of the Jewish women in their desire for covered markets which have always been a municipal provision in Russia and Poland. The vegetables piled high upon the wagons standing in the open markets of Chicago become covered with dust and soot. It seems to these women a violation of the most rudimentary decencies and they sometimes say quite simply: "If women had anything to say about it they would change all that."

If women follow only the lines of their traditional activities, here are certain primary duties which belong to even the most conservative women, and which no one woman or group of women can adequately discharge unless they join the more general movements looking toward social amelioration through legal enactment . . .

We would all agree that social amelioration must come about through the efforts of many people who are moved thereto by the compunction and stirring of the individual conscience, but we are only beginning to understand that the individual conscience will respond to the special challenge largely in proportion as the individual is able to see the social conditions because he has felt responsible for their improvement . . . If woman's sense of obligation had enlarged as the industrial conditions changed she might naturally and almost imperceptibly have inaugurated movements for social amelioration in the line of factory legislation and shop sanitation. That she has not done so is doubtless due to the fact that her conscience is slow to recognize any obligation outside of her own family circle, and because she was so absorbed in her own household that she failed to see what the conditions outside actually were. It would be interesting to know how far the consciousness that she had no vote and could not change matters operated in this direction. After all, we see only those things to which our attention has been drawn, we feel responsibility for those things which are brought to us as matters of responsibility. If conscientious women were convinced that it was a civic duty to be informed in regard to these grave industrial affairs, and then to express the conclusions which they had reached by depositing a piece of paper in a ballot-box, one cannot imagine that they would shirk simply because the action ran counter to old traditions.

To those of my readers who would admit that although woman has no right to shirk her old obligations, that all of these measures could be secured more easily through her influence upon the men of her family than through the direct use of the ballot, I should like to tell a little story. I have a friend in Chicago who is the mother of four sons and the grandmother of twelve grandsons who are voters. She is a woman of wealth, of secured social position, of sterling character and clear intelligence, and may, therefore, quite fairly be cited as a "woman of influence." Upon one of her recent birthdays, when she was asked how she had kept so young, she promptly replied: "Because I have always advocated at least one unpopular cause." It may have been in pursuance of this policy that for many years she has been an ardent advocate of free silver, although her manufacturing family are all Republicans! I happened to call at her house on the day that Mr. McKinley was elected President against Mr. Bryan for the first time. I found my friend much disturbed. She said somewhat bitterly that she had at last discovered what the much-vaunted influence of woman was worth; that she had implored each one of her sons and grandsons; had entered into endless arguments and moral appeals to induce one of them to represent her convictions by voting for Mr. Bryan; that, although sincerely devoted to her, each one had assured her that his convictions forced him to vote the Republican ticket! She said that all she had been able to secure was the promise from one of the grandsons, for whom she had an especial tenderness because he bore her husband's name, that he would not vote at all. He could not vote for Bryan, but out of respect for her feeling he would refrain from voting for McKinley. My friend said that for many years she had suspected that women could influence men only in regard to those things in which men were not deeply concerned, but when it came to persuading a man to a woman's view in affairs of politics or business it was absolutely useless. I contended that a woman had no right to persuade a man to vote against his own convictions; that I respected the men of her family for following their own judgement regardless of the appeal which the honored head of the house had made to their chivalric devotion. To this she replied that she would agree with that point of view when a woman had the same opportunity as a man to register her convictions by vote. I believed then as I do now, that nothing is gained when independence of judgment is assailed by "influence," sentimental or otherwise, and that we test advancing civilization somewhat by our power to respect differences and by our tolerance of another's honest conviction.

This is, perhaps, the attitude of many busy women who would be glad to use the ballot to further public measures in which they are interested and for which they have been working for years. It offends the taste of such a woman to be obliged to use indirect "influence" when she is accustomed to well-bred, open action in other affairs, and she very much resents the time spent in persuading a voter to take her point of view, and possibly to give up his own, quite as honest and valuable as hers, although different because resulting from a totally different experience. Public-spirited women who wish to use the ballot, as I know them, do not wish to do the work of men nor to take over men's affairs. They simply want an opportunity to do their own work and to take care of those affairs which naturally and historically belong to women, but which are constantly being overlooked and slighted in our political institutions. In a complex community like the modern city all points of view need to be represented; the resultants of diverse experiences need to be pooled if the community would make for sane and balanced progress. If it would meet fairly each problem as it arises, whether it be connected with a freight tunnel having to do largely with business men, or with the increasing death rate among children under five years of age, a problem in which women are vitally concerned, or with the question of more adequate streetcar transfers, in which both men and women might be said to be equally interested, it must not ignore the judgments of its entire adult population. To turn the administration of our civic affairs wholly over to men may mean that the American city will continue to push forward in its commercial and industrial development, and continue to lag behind in those things which make a City healthful and beautiful. After all, woman's traditional function has been to make her dwelling-place both clean and fair. Is that dreariness in city life, that lack of domesticity which the humblest farm dwelling presents, due to a withdrawal of one of the naturally co-operating forces? If women have in any sense been responsible for the gentler side of life which softens and blurs some of its harsher conditions, may they not have a duty to perform in our American cities? In closing, may I recapitulate that if woman would fulfill her traditional responsibility to her own children; if she would educate and protect from danger factory children who must find their recreation on the street; if she would bring the cultural forces to bear upon our materialistic civilization; and if she would do it all with the dignity and directness fitting one who carries on her immemorial duties, then she must bring herself to the use of the ballot—that latest implement for self-government. May we not fairly say that American women need this implement in order to preserve the home?

From Herland

1915

Charlotte Perkins Gilman's *Herland* explores the idea that women might change the nature of government. Gilman believed that history might have been different if women had been more active agents in its development and recording, noting in 1911: "What have men made [history]? The story of warfare and conquest . . . Men . . . have given us a history which is one unbroken record of courage and red cruelty, of triumph and black shame." *Herland* is a new history, commenting on war, cremation, and the suffrage struggle. It's also a new myth. Like Elizabeth Cady Stanton's *Woman's Bible* (1895), it offers a new creation story: there have been no men in Herland for two thousand years, the original Herland mother walked the earth with the Virgin Mary, and the women reproduce through virgin birth. And it's a new fiction: a plotless novel about a timeless utopia. Gilman associated the teleology of plot with "maleness," demanding in 1911 a new kind of fiction that showed "the interrelation of women with women." The narrator of *Herland,* Van, comes to see that "Othello could not have extinguished Alima [a Herland woman] with a pillow, as if she were a mouse": if men can no longer master women, then masculine dramatic fictions fall flat.

Yet *Herland,* with its timeless society at a dead end, reveals the great problem of utopian fiction—that without conflict, accident, tragedy, and hardship, there are few narrative possibilities. In addition, Gilman knew that a vision of security might simply allay—rather than solve—her society's unrest. So for the sake of literature *and* protest, she signals that Herland is not humanity's final destination. Unlike Edward Bellamy's socialist utopian novel, *Looking Backward* (1888), which Gilman had read, *Herland* contains few one-sided conversations, and Gilman encourages active critical participation on behalf of the reader. It matters what the visitors say and think, and we judge both Herlanders and explorers. Equally, the Herland women are both observed *and* observers: at the end of the novel, excerpted here, the women build a globe, map countries, and write lists of peoples, remaking the outside world. The male explorers leave Herland as outcasts from utopia, but they carry the seeds of America's regeneration; like the Herland women with their maps and lists, they might now remake their world.

Of course I had been homesick at first, while we were prisoners, before I had Ellador. And of course I had, at first, rather idealized my country and its ways, in describing it. Also, I had always accepted certain evils as integral parts of our civilization and never dwelt on them at all. Even when I tried to tell her the worst, I never remembered some things—which, when she came to see them, impressed her at once, as they had never impressed me. Now, in my efforts at explanation, I began to see both ways more keenly than I had before; to see the painful defects of my own land, the marvelous gains of this.

In missing men we three visitors had naturally missed the larger part of life, and had unconsciously assumed that they must miss it too. It took me a long time to realize—Terry never did realize—how little it meant to them. When we say *men, man, manly, manhood,* and all the other masculine derivatives, we have in the background of our minds a huge vague crowded picture of the world and all its activities. To grow up and "be a man," to "act like a man"— the meaning and connotation is wide indeed. That vast background is full of marching columns of men, of changing lines of men, of long processions of men; of men steering their ships into new seas, exploring unknown mountains, breaking horses, herding cattle, ploughing and sowing and reaping, toiling at the forge and furnace, digging in the mine, building roads and bridges and high cathedrals, managing great businesses, teaching in all the colleges, preaching in all the churches; of men everywhere, doing everything—"the world."

And when we say *women,* we think *female*—the sex.

But to these women, in the unbroken sweep of this two-thousand-year-old feminine civilization, the word *woman* called up all that big background, so far as they had gone in social development; and the word *man* meant to them only *male*—the sex.

Of course we could *tell* them that in our world men did everything; but that did not alter the background of their minds. That man, "the male," did all these things was to them a statement, making no more change in the point of view than was made in ours when we first faced the astounding fact—to us— that in Herland women were "the world."

We had been living there more than a year. We had learned their limited history, with its straight, smooth, upreaching lines, reaching higher and going faster up to the smooth comfort of their present life. We had learned a little of their psychology, a much wider field than the history, but here we could not follow so readily. We were now well used to seeing women not as females but as people; people of all sorts, doing every kind of work . . . We talk fine things about women, but in our hearts we know that they are very limited beings— most of them. We honor them for their functional powers, even while we dishonor them by our use of it; we honor them for their carefully enforced virtue, even while we show by our own conduct how little we think of that virtue; we value them, sincerely, for the perverted maternal activities which make our wives the most comfortable of servants, bound to us for life with the wages wholly at our own decision, their whole business, outside of the temporary duties of such motherhood as they may achieve, to meet our needs in every way. Oh, we value them, all right, "in their place," which place is the home . . .

Little had we thought that our careful efforts at concealment had been so easily seen through, with never a word to show us that they saw. They had followed up words of ours on the science of optics, asked innocent questions about glasses and the like, and were aware of the defective eyesight so common among us.

With the lightest touch, different women asking different questions at different times, and putting all our answers together like a picture puzzle, they had figured out a sort of skeleton chart as to the prevalence of disease among us. Even more subtly with no show of horror or condemnation, they had gathered something—far from the truth, but something pretty clear—about poverty, vice, and crime. They even had a goodly number of our dangers all itemized, from asking us about insurance and innocent things like that.

They were well posted as to the different races, beginning with their poison-arrow natives down below and widening out to the broad racial divisions we had told them about. Never a shocked expression of the face or exclamation of revolt had warned us; they had been extracting the evidence without our knowing it all this time, and now were studying with the most devout earnestness the matter they had prepared . . . They had a great globe, quite fairly mapped out from the small section maps in that compendium of ours. They had different peoples of the earth roughly outlined, and their status in civilization indicated. The had charts and figures and estimates, based on the facts in that traitorous little book and what they had learned from us.

Somel explained: "We find that in all your historic period, so much longer than ours, that with all the interplay of services, the exchange of inventions and discoveries, and the wonderful progress we so admire, that in this widespread Other World of yours, there is still much disease, often contagious."

We admitted this at once.

"Also there is still, in varying degree, ignorance, with prejudice and unbridled emotion."

This too was admitted.

"We find also that in spite of the advance of democracy and the increase of wealth, that there is still unrest and sometimes combat."

Yes, yes, we admitted it all. We were used to these things and saw no reason for so much seriousness.

"All things considered," they said, and they did not say a hundredth part of the things they were considering, "we are unwilling to expose our country to free communication with the rest of the world—as yet. If Ellador comes back, and we approve her report, it may be done later—but not yet.

"So we have this to ask of you gentlemen (they knew that word was held a title of honor with us), that you promise not in any way to betray the location of this country until permission—after Ellador's return."

Jeff was perfectly satisfied. He thought they were quite right. He always did. I never saw an alien become naturalized more quickly than that man in Herland.

I studied it awhile, thinking of the time they'd have if some of our contagions got loose there, and concluded they were right. So I agreed.

Terry was the obstacle. "Indeed I won't!" he protested. "The first thing I'll do is to get an expedition fixed up to force an entrance into Ma-land."

"Then," they said quite calmly, "he must remain an absolute prisoner, always."

"Anesthesia would be kinder," urged Moadine.

"And safer," added Zava.

"He will promise, I think," said Ellador.

And he did. With which agreement we at last left Herland.

Nineteenth Amendment
and Equal Rights Amendments

1920, 1923, 1943

Susan B. Anthony never cast a ballot. But the Nineteenth Amendment, passed fourteen years after her death, was dubbed the "Anthony Amendment," in tribute to her fifty-year struggle. She and others had introduced a Woman Suffrage Amendment to the Constitution in 1878. Reintroduced annually, the wording was unchanged when it finally passed in 1919.

In 1913, Alice Paul (1885–1977) and Crystal Eastman helped form the National Women's Party (NWP). While the National American Woman Suffrage Association (NAWSA) lobbied from the center, Paul and the more militant NWP organized marches and boycotts and practiced civil disobedience. The NAWSA condemned Paul's militancy, but she remarked: "It is better to have a small, united group than an immense debating society." In early 1917, the NWP began the first-ever White House picket. Police charged the picketers with traffic obstruction, finally arresting Paul. She was sentenced to seven months and placed in solitary confinement. Shocking details of her force feeding while on hunger strike added momentum to the cause, and she was released after five weeks.

On January 9, 1918, President Wilson announced that suffrage extension was essential to the war effort, and the House passed an amendment the following day. It was defeated in the Senate in September 1918 and in February 1919. In January 1919 Paul burned Wilson's speeches in an urn outside the White House, calling it a "watchfire for freedom." In the spring of 1919, NWP women toured the country on a train named the "Prison Special," pausing at stations to lecture on their experiences as suffrage prisoners, and tossing suffrage pamphlets from the windows as the train rolled along. The Senate passed the amendment with two votes to spare on June 4, 1919. The necessary ratification by three-quarters of the states apparently came down to a single vote: 24-year-old Harry Burn apparently switched to "yes" after receiving a letter from his mother instructing, "Hurrah, and vote for suffrage!" and so on August 18, 1920, Tennessee became the 36th and deciding state to ratify.

In 1923 the suffragist Carrie Chapman Catt traced the journey to this point: "fifty-two years of pauseless campaign . . . a continuous, seemingly endless chain of activity. Young suffragists who helped forge the last links of that chain were not born when it began. Old suffragists who forged the first links were dead when it ended." But for Paul the Nineteenth Amendment was only the beginning. Believing that only an Equal Rights Amendment (ERA) would end legal sex discrimination, she presented the "Lucretia Mott Amendment" at the 75th anniversary celebration of Seneca Falls, in July 1923. Intro-

duced to Congress in December 1923, it didn't reach either floor. The ERA was reintroduced in every session until 1970 and never voted upon. In 1943, senators suggested
that it threatened states' rights and Paul rewrote it. The new version, dubbed the "Alice
Paul Amendment," passed in 1972, but only thirty-five states ratified it by the 1982 deadline—three short of the requirement. Paul lobbied for the ERA until her death in 1977.

Amendment XIX ["Susan B. Anthony Amendment"]

The right of citizens of the United States to vote shall not be denied or
abridged by the United States or by any State on account of sex. Congress shall
have power to enforce this article by appropriate legislation.

Equal Rights Amendment ["Lucretia Mott Amendment"]

Men and women shall have equal rights throughout the United States and in
every place subject to its jurisdiction. Congress shall have power to enforce
this article by appropriate legislation.

New Equal Rights Amendment ["Alice Paul Amendment"]

Equality of rights under the law shall not be denied or abridged by the United
States, or by any State, on account of sex. Congress and the several states shall
have power, within their respective jurisdiction, to enforce this article by appropriate legislation.

Now We Can Begin

1920

Crystal Eastman (1881–1928) brought the First World War home, making women's bodies and dissenters' consciences the domestic battleground. She campaigned for reproductive rights and birth-control education, declaring in 1918: "While American men are fighting to rid the old world of autocracy let American women set to and rid the new world of this intolerable old burden of sex ignorance." And in 1917 she cofounded the American Civil Liberties Union, declaring that she wanted to "maintain something . . . worth coming back to when the weary war is over."

As far as Eastman was concerned, the "weary war" for women's rights didn't end with the Nineteenth Amendment. She asserted in her "Program for Voting Women" that women should now "dedicate their new political power . . . to *ridding the world of war*," and in 1925 she called for women to put their newly won rights to work: "It is not so much that women have a different point of view in politics as that they give a different emphasis. And this is vastly important, for politics is so largely a matter of emphasis." She campaigned for equality in the home and anticipated Betty Friedan's 1963 critique of women's magazines: "there is nothing more irritating to a feminist than the average 'Woman's Page' of a newspaper," observed Eastman in 1926, "with its out-dated assumption that all women have a common trade interest in the household arts."

For all Eastman's attempts to create a postsuffrage program, by 1924 there was no longer a national women's movement. The suffrage campaign had held it together and the Equal Rights Amendment (ERA) was polarizing: Progressive reformers like Jane Addams feared it would jeopardize laws governing maximum hours and minimum wages for working women, while Eastman believed that labor legislation applying only to women undermined their equal rights. Eastman was a feminist and a socialist, and tried to cultivate her politics out of both elements, but felt, as she explains in "Now We Can Begin," that "the woman's battle [is] distinct in its objects and different in its methods from the workers' battle for industrial freedom."

Eastman epitomized the socialist, feminist, bohemian culture of Greenwich Village. At the time of her death in 1928, she was, according to one obituary, "a symbol of what the free woman might be." The poet Genevieve Taggard observed that Eastman "managed to dominate . . . an entire generation," and "epitomized the unity of life, the dance of it."

Most women will agree that August 23, the day when the Tennessee legislature finally enacted the Federal suffrage amendment, is a day to begin with, not a day to end with. Men are saying perhaps "Thank God, this everlasting woman's fight is over!" But women, if I know them, are saying, "Now at last we can begin." In fighting for the right to vote most women have tried to be either non-committal or thoroughly respectable on every other subject. Now they can say what they are really after; and what they are after, in common with all the rest of the struggling world, is freedom.

Freedom is a large word.

Many feminists are socialists, many are communists, not a few are active leaders in these movements. But the true feminist, no matter how far to the left she may be in the revolutionary movement, sees the woman's battle as distinct in its objects and different in its methods from the workers' battle for industrial freedom. She knows, of course, that the vast majority of women as well as men are without property, and are of necessity bread and butter slaves under a system of society which allows the very sources of life to be privately owned by a few, and she counts herself a loyal soldier in the working-class army that is marching to overthrow that system. But as a feminist she also knows that the whole of woman's slavery is not summed up in the profit system, nor her complete emancipation assured by the downfall of capitalism.

Woman's freedom, in the feminist sense, can be fought for and conceivably won before the gates open into industrial democracy. On the other hand, woman's freedom, in the feminist sense, is not inherent in the communist ideal. All feminists are familiar with the revolutionary leader who "can't see" the woman's movement. "What's the matter with the women? My wife's all right," he says. And his wife, one usually finds, is raising his children in a Bronx flat or a dreary suburb, to which he returns occasionally for food and sleep when all possible excitement and stimulus have been wrung from the fight. If we should graduate into communism tomorrow this man's attitude to his wife would not be changed. The proletarian dictatorship may or may not free women. We must begin now to enlighten the future dictators.

What, then, is "the matter with women"? What is the problem of women's freedom? It seems to me to be this: how to arrange the world so that women can be human beings, with a chance to exercise their infinitely varied gifts in infinitely varied ways, instead of being destined by the accident of their sex to one field of activity—housework and child-raising. And second, if and when they choose housework and child-raising, to have that occupation recognized by the world as work, requiring a definite economic reward and not merely entitling the performer to be dependent on some man.

This is not the whole of feminism, of course, but it is enough to begin with. "Oh, don't begin with economics," my friends often protest, "Woman does not live by bread alone. What she needs first of all is a free soul." And I can agree that women will never be great until they achieve a certain emotional freedom, a strong healthy egotism, and some un-personal sources of joy—that in this inner sense we cannot make woman free by changing her economic status. What we can do, however, is to create conditions of outward freedom in which a free woman's soul can be born and grow. It is these outward conditions with which an organized feminist movement must concern itself.

Freedom of choice in occupation and individual economic independence for women: How shall we approach this next feminist objective? First, by breaking down all remaining barriers, actual as well as legal, which make it difficult for women to enter or succeed in the various professions, to go into and get on in business, to learn trades and practice them, to join trades unions. Chief among these remaining barriers is inequality in pay. Here the ground is already broken. This is the easiest part of our program.

Second, we must institute a revolution in the early training and education of both boys and girls. It must be womanly as well as manly to earn your own living, to stand on your own feet. And it must be manly as well as womanly to know how to cook and sew and clean and take care of yourself in the ordinary exigencies of life. I need not add that the second part of this revolution will be more passionately resisted than the first. Men will not give up their privilege of helplessness without a struggle. The average man has a carefully cultivated ignorance about household matters—from what to do with the crumbs to the grocer's telephone number—a sort of cheerful inefficiency which protects him better than the reputation for having a violent temper. It was his mother's fault in the beginning, but even as a boy he was quick to see how a general reputation for being "no good around the house" would serve him throughout life, and half-consciously he began to cultivate that helplessness until today it is the despair of feminist wives.

A growing number of men admire the woman who has a job, and, especially since the cost of living doubled, rather like the idea of their own wives contributing to the family income by outside work. And of course for generations there have been whole towns full of wives who are forced by the bitterest necessity to spend the same hours at the factory that their husbands spend. But these bread-winning wives have not yet developed homemaking husbands. When the two come home from the factory the man sits down while his wife gets supper, and he does so with exactly the same sense of fore-ordained right as if he were "supporting her." Higher up in the economic scale the same thing is true. The business or professional woman who is married, perhaps engages a cook, but the responsibility is not shifted, it is still hers. She "hires and fires," she orders meals, she does the buying, she meets and resolves all domestic crises, she takes charge of moving, furnishing, settling. She may be, like her husband, a busy executive at her office all day, but unlike him, she is also an executive in a small way every night and morning at home. Her noon hour is spent in planning, and too often her Sundays and holidays are spent in "catching up."

Two business women can "make a home" together without either one being over-burdened or over-bored. It is because they both know how and both feel responsible. But it is a rare man who can marry one of them and continue the homemaking partnership. Yet if there are no children, there is nothing essentially different in the combination. Two self-supporting adults decide to make a home together: if both are women it is a pleasant partnership, more fun than work; if one is a man, it is almost never a partnership—the woman simply adds running the home to her regular outside job. Unless she is very strong, it is too much for her, she gets tired and bitter over it, and finally perhaps gives up her outside work and condemns herself to the tiresome half-job of housekeeping for two.

Cooperative schemes and electrical devices will simplify the business of homemaking, but they will not get rid of it entirely. As far as we can see ahead people will always want homes, and a happy home cannot be had without a certain amount of rather monotonous work and responsibility. How can we change the nature of man so that he will honorably share that work and responsibility and thus make the homemaking enterprise a song instead of a burden? Most assuredly not by laws or revolutionary decrees. Perhaps we must cultivate or simulate a little of that highly prized helplessness ourselves. But fundamentally it is a problem of education, of early training—we must bring up feminist sons.

Sons? Daughters? They are born of women—how can women be free to choose their occupation, at all times cherishing their economic independence, unless they stop having children? This is a further question for feminism. If the feminist program goes to pieces on the arrival of the first baby, it is false and useless. For ninety-nine out of every hundred women want children, and seventy-five out of every hundred want to take care of their own children, or at any rate so closely superintend their care as to make any other full-time occupation impossible for at least ten or fifteen years. Is there any such thing then as freedom of choice in occupation for women? And is not the family the inevitable economic unit and woman's individual economic independence, at least during that period, out of the question?

The feminist must have an answer to these questions, and she has. The immediate feminist program must include voluntary motherhood. Freedom of any kind for women is hardly worth considering unless it is assumed that they will know how to control the size of their families. "Birth control" is just as elementary an essential in our propaganda as "equal pay." Women are to have children when they want them, that's the first thing. That ensures some freedom of occupational choice; those who do not wish to be mothers will not have an undesired occupation thrust upon them by accident, and those who do wish to be mothers may choose in a general way how many years of their lives they will devote to the occupation of child-raising.

But is there any way of insuring a woman's economic independence while child-raising is her chosen occupation? Or must she sink into that dependent state from which, as we all know, it is so hard to rise again? That brings us to the fourth feature of our program—motherhood endowment. It seems that the only way we can keep mothers free, at least in a capitalist society, is by the establishment of a principle that the occupation of raising children is peculiarly and directly a service to society, and that the mother upon whom the necessity and privilege of performing this service naturally falls is entitled to an adequate economic reward from the political government. It is idle to talk of real economic independence for women unless this principle is accepted. But with a generous endowment of motherhood provided by legislation, with all laws against voluntary motherhood and education in its methods repealed, with the feminist ideal of education accepted in home and school, and with all special barriers removed in every field of human activity, there is no reason why woman should not become almost a human thing.

It will be time enough then to consider whether she has a soul.

CAPITALISM'S DISCONTENTS

Socialism
and
Industry

From Life in the Iron Mills

1861

Along with the photographer Lewis Hine, the author and journalist Rebecca Harding Davis (1831–1910) is the best example of an industrial-era protest artist who engaged the concept of empathy. Her character Hugh Wolfe in *Life in the Iron Mills* is a working-class sculptor who stops carving figures and makes *himself* art, carving himself to death with a piece of sharpened tin. Also demonstrating a theory of aesthetic empathy is the connection between Davis's narrator (who even acquires Hugh's Korl sculpture) and the millworker protagonists.

She challenges her readers to connect as well, addressing them directly. Unlike David Walker and Harriet Beecher Stowe, Davis didn't think of the author as prophet, as is evident in *Life in the Iron Mills*. Having asked us to engage, the rest is up to us: she leaves solutions open-ended, referring to an "unfinished work" on the last page. Davis never looked to revolutionary social reorganization and was suspicious of utopia: Wolfe is tortured by his imagination of life as "it might have been," that clear vision of the protest artist on behalf of a partially achieved nation. He finds peace only when he doesn't "think of what might be and was not."

Davis was anticipating the postwar reform crisis, when it would seem as though the apocalypse had come but the new age was nowhere in sight. She published her novella in the April 1861 issue of *Atlantic Monthly*, coinciding with the firing on Fort Sumter, and the story foreshadowed further changes in protest literature after the war: the shift away from religious language; the transition from romanticism to realism; the inclusion of unseemly, morally ambiguous heroes; and the production of fiction that didn't apologize for *being* fiction.

More than a century after Davis's novella was written, the feminist writer Tillie Olsen found a copy in an old volume of *Atlantic Monthly* in an Omaha junk shop. Its message to her was: "You, too, must write," and "literature can be made out of lives of despised people." She bought the novella for ten cents and persuaded the Feminist Press to republish it in 1972. Davis's Hugh Wolfe had made art out of factory junk. Now Olsen sifted through junk and found Davis's lost art.

Further reading: Jean Pfaelzer, *Parlor Radical* (1996); Jane Tompkins, *Sensational Designs* (1985).

A cloudy day: do you know what that is in a town of iron-works? The sky sank down before dawn, muddy, flat, immovable. The air is thick, clammy with the breath of crowded human beings. It stifles me. I open the window, and, looking out, can scarcely see through the rain the grocer's shop opposite, where a crowd of drunken Irishmen are puffing Lynchburg tobacco in their pipes. I can detect the scent through all the foul smells ranging loose in the air.

The idiosyncrasy of this town is smoke. It rolls sullenly in slow folds from the great chimneys of the iron-foundries, and settles down in black, slimy pools on the muddy streets. Smoke on the wharves, smoke on the dingy boats, on the yellow river,—clinging in a coating of greasy soot to the house-front, the two faded poplars, the faces of the passers-by. The long train of mules, dragging masses of pig-iron through the narrow street, have a foul vapor hanging to their reeking sides. Here, inside, is a little broken figure of an angel pointing upward from the mantel-shelf; but even its wings are covered with smoke, clotted and black. Smoke everywhere! A dirty canary chirps desolately in a cage beside me. Its dream of green fields and sunshine is a very old dream,—almost worn out, I think.

From the back-window I can see a narrow brick-yard sloping down to the river-side, strewed with rain-butts and tubs. The river, dull and tawny-colored, *(la belle riviere!)* drags itself sluggishly along, tired of the heavy weight of boats and coal-barges. What wonder? When I was a child, I used to fancy a look of weary, dumb appeal upon the face of the negro-like river slavishly bearing its burden day after day. Something of the same idle notion comes to me to-day, when from the street-window I look on the slow stream of human life creeping past, night and morning, to the great mills. Masses of men, with dull, besotted faces bent to the ground, sharpened here and there by pain or cunning; skin and muscle and flesh begrimed with smoke and ashes; stooping all night over boiling caldrons of metal, laired by day in dens of drunkenness and infamy; breathing from infancy to death an air saturated with fog and grease and soot, vileness for soul and body. What do you make of a case like that, amateur psychologist? You call it an altogether serious thing to be alive: to these men it is a drunken jest, a joke,—horrible to angels perhaps, to them commonplace enough. My fancy about the river was an idle one: it is no type of such a life. What if it be stagnant and slimy here? It knows that beyond there waits for it odorous sunlight,—quaint old gardens, dusky with soft, green foliage of apple-trees, and flushing crimson with roses,—air, and fields, and mountains. The future of the Welsh puddler passing just now is not so pleasant. To be stowed away, after his grimy work is done, in a hole in the muddy graveyard, and after that,—*not* air, nor green fields, nor curious roses.

Can you see how foggy the day is? As I stand here, idly tapping the window-pane, and looking out through the rain at the dirty back-yard and the coal-boats below, fragments of an old story float up before me,—a story of this house into which I happened to come to-day. You may think it a tiresome story enough, as foggy as the day, sharpened by no sudden flashes of pain or pleasure.—I know: only the outline of a dull life, that long since, with thousands of dull lives like its own, was vainly lived and lost: thousands of them,—massed, vile, slimy lives, like those of the torpid lizards in yonder stagnant water-butt.—Lost? There is a curious point for you to settle, my friend, who study psychology in a lazy, *dilettante* way. Stop a moment. I am going to be honest. This is what I want you to do. I want you to hide your disgust, take no heed to your clean clothes, and come right down with me,—here, into the thickest of the fog and mud and foul effluvia. I want you to hear this story. There is a secret down here, in this nightmare fog, that has lain dumb for centuries: I want to make it a real thing to you. You, Egoist, or Pantheist, or Arminian, busy in making straight paths for your feet on the hills, do not see it clearly,—this terrible question which men here have gone mad and died trying to answer. I dare not put this secret into words. I told you it was dumb. These men, going by with drunken faces, and brains full of unawakened power, do not ask it of Society or of God. Their lives ask it; their deaths ask it. There is no reply. I will tell you plainly that I have a great hope; and I bring it to you to be tested. It is this: that this terrible dumb question is its own reply; that it is not the sentence of death we think it, but, from the very extremity of its darkness, the most solemn prophecy which the world has known of the Hope to come. I dare make my meaning no clearer, but will only tell my story. It will, perhaps, seem to you as foul and dark as this thick vapor about us, and as pregnant with death, but if your eyes are free as mine are to look deeper, no perfume-tinted dawn will be so fair with promise of the day that shall surely come.

My story is very simple,—only what I remember of the life of one of these men,—a furnace-tender in one of Kirby & John's rolling-mills,—Hugh Wolfe. You know the mills? They took the great order for the lower Virginia railroads there last winter; run usually with about a thousand men. I cannot tell why I choose the half-forgotten story of this Wolfe more than that of myriads of these furnace-hands. Perhaps because there is a secret, underlying sympathy between that story and this day with its impure fog and thwarted sunshine,—or perhaps simply for the reason that this house is the one where the Wolfes lived. There were the father and son,—both hands, as I said, in one of Kirby & John's mills for making railroad-iron,—and Deborah, their cousin, a picker in some of the cotton-mills. The house was rented then to half a dozen families. The Wolfes had two of the cellar-rooms. The old man, like many of the puddlers and feeders of the mills, was Welsh,—had spent half of his life in the Cornish tin-mines. You may pick the Welsh emigrants, Cornish miners, out of the throng passing the windows, any day. They are a trifle more filthy; their muscles are not so brawny, they stoop more. When they are drunk, they neither yell, nor shout, nor stagger, but skulk along like beaten hounds. A pure, unmixed blood, I fancy, shows itself in the slight angular bodies and sharply-cut facial lines. It is nearly thirty years since the Wolfes lived here. Their lives were like those of their class: incessant labor, sleeping in kennel-like rooms, eating rank pork and molasses, drinking—God and the distillers only know what; with an occasional night in jail, to atone for some drunken excess. Is that all of their lives?—of the portion given to them and these their dupli-cates swarming the streets to-day?—nothing beneath?—all? So many a politi-cal reformer will tell you,—and many a private reformer, too, who has gone among them with a heart tender with Christ's charity, and come out outraged, hardened . . .

Mitchell started back, half-frightened, as, suddenly turning a corner, the white figure of a woman faced him in the darkness,—a woman, white, of giant pro-portions, crouching on the ground, her arms flung out in some wild gesture of warning.

"Stop! Make that fire burn there!" cried Kirby, stopping short.

The flame burst out, flashing the gaunt figure into bold relief.

Mitchell drew a long breath.

"I thought it was alive," he said, going up curiously.

The others followed.

"Not marble, eh?" asked Kirby, touching it.

One of the lower overseers stopped.

"Korl, Sir."

"Who did it?"

"Can't say. Some of the hands; chipped it out in off-hours."

"Chipped to some purpose, I should say. What a flesh-tint the stuff has! Do you see, Mitchell?"

"I see."

He had stepped aside where the light fell boldest on the figure, looking at it in silence. There was not one line of beauty or grace in it: a nude woman's form, muscular, grown coarse with labor, the powerful limbs instinct with some one poignant longing. One idea: there it was in the tense, rigid muscles, the clutching hands, the wild, eager face, like that of a starving wolf's. Kirby and Dr. May walked around it, critical, curious. Mitchell stood aloof, silent. The figure touched him strangely.

"Not badly done," said Doctor May. "Where did the fellow learn that sweep of the muscles in the arm and hand? Look at them! They are groping,—do you see?—clutching: the peculiar action of a man dying of thirst."

"They have ample facilities for studying anatomy," sneered Kirby, glancing at the half-naked figures.

"Look," continued the Doctor, "at this bony wrist, and the strained sinews of the instep! A working-woman,—the very type of her class."

"God forbid!" muttered Mitchell.

"Why?" demanded May. "What does the fellow intend by the figure? I cannot catch the meaning."

"Ask him," said the other, dryly. "There he stands,"—pointing to Wolfe, who stood with a group of men, leaning on his ash-rake.

The Doctor beckoned him with the affable smile which kind-hearted men put on, when talking to these people.

"Mr. Mitchell has picked you out as the man who did this,—I'm sure I don't know why. But what did you mean by it?"

"She be hungry."

Wolfe's eyes answered Mitchell, not the Doctor.

"Oh-h! But what a mistake you have made, my fine fellow! You have given no sign of starvation to the body. It is strong,—terribly strong. It has the mad, half-despairing gesture of drowning."

Wolfe stammered, glanced appealingly at Mitchell, who saw the soul of the thing, he knew. But the cool, probing eyes were turned on himself now,—mocking, cruel, relentless.

"Not hungry for meat," the furnace-tender said at last.

"What then? Whiskey?" jeered Kirby, with a coarse laugh.

Wolfe was silent a moment, thinking.

"I dunno," he said, with a bewildered look. "It mebbe. Summat to make her live, I think,—like you. Whiskey ull do it, in a way."

The young man laughed again. Mitchell flashed a look of disgust somewhere,—not at Wolfe.

"May," he broke out impatiently, "are you blind? Look at that woman's face! It asks questions of God, and says, 'I have a right to know.' Good God, how hungry it is!"

They looked a moment; then May turned to the mill-owner:—

"Have you many such hands as this? What are you going to do with them? Keep them at puddling iron?"

Kirby shrugged his shoulders. Mitchell's look had irritated him.

"*Ce n'est pas mon affaire.* I have no fancy for nursing infant geniuses. I suppose there are some stray gleams of mind and soul among these wretches. The Lord will take care of his own; or else they can work out their own salvation. I have heard you call our American system a ladder which any man can scale. Do you doubt it? Or perhaps you want to banish all social ladders, and put us all on a flat table-land,—eh, May?"

The Doctor looked vexed, puzzled. Some terrible problem lay hid in this woman's face, and troubled these men.

Kirby waited for an answer, and, receiving none, went on, warming with his subject.

"I tell you, there's something wrong that no talk of *'Liberte'* or *'Egalite'* will do away. If I had the making of men, these men who do the lowest part of the world's work should be machines,—nothing more,—hands. It would be kindness. God help them! What are taste, reason, to creatures who must live such lives as that?" He pointed to Deborah, sleeping on the ash-heap. "So many nerves to sting them to pain. What if God had put your brain, with all its agony of touch, into your fingers, and bid you work and strike with that?"

"You think you could govern the world better?" laughed the Doctor.

"I do not think at all."

"That is true philosophy. Drift with the stream, because you cannot dive deep enough to find bottom, eh?"

"Exactly," rejoined Kirby. "I do not think. I wash my hands of all social problems,—slavery, caste, white or black. My duty to my operatives has a narrow limit,—the pay-hour on Saturday night. Outside of that, if they cut korl, or cut each other's throats, (the more popular amusement of the two,) I am not responsible" . . . Something of a vague idea possessed the Doctor's brain that much good was to be done here by a friendly word or two: a latent genius to be warmed into life by a waited-for sunbeam. Here it was: he had brought it. So he went on complacently:—

"Do you know, boy, you have it in you to be a great sculptor, a great man?—do you understand?" (talking down to the capacity of his hearer: it is a way people have with children, and men like Wolfe)—"to live a better, stronger life than I, or Mr. Kirby here? A man may make himself anything he chooses. God has given you stronger powers than many men,—me, for instance."

May stopped, heated, glowing with his own magnanimity. And it was magnanimous. The puddler had drunk in every word, looking through the Doctor's flurry, and generous heat, and self-approval, into his will, with those slow, absorbing eyes of his.

"Make yourself what you will. It is your right."

"I know," quietly. "Will you help me?"

Mitchell laughed again. The Doctor turned now, in a passion,—

"You know, Mitchell, I have not the means. You know, if I had, it is in my heart to take this boy and educate him for"—

"The glory of God, and the glory of John May."

May did not speak for a moment; then, controlled, he said,—

"Why should one be raised, when myriads are left?—I have not the money, boy," to Wolfe, shortly . . .

Wolfe and the woman had stood in the shadow of the works as the coach drove off. The Doctor had held out his hand in a frank, generous way, telling him to "take care of himself, and to remember it was his right to rise." Mitchell had simply touched his hat, as to an equal, with a quiet look of thorough recognition. Kirby had thrown Deborah some money, which she found, and clutched eagerly enough. They were gone now, all of them. The man sat down on the cinder-road, looking up into the murky sky.

"'T be late, Hugh. Wunnot hur come?"

He shook his head doggedly, and the woman crouched out of his sight against the wall. Do you remember rare moments when a sudden light flashed over yourself, your world, God? when you stood on a mountain-peak, seeing your life as it might have been, as it is? one quick instant, when custom lost its force and every-day usage? when your friend, wife, brother, stood in a new light? your soul was bared, and the grave,—a foretaste of the nakedness of the Judgment-Day? So it came before him, his life, that night. The slow tides of pain he had borne gathered themselves up and surged against his soul. His squalid daily life, the brutal coarseness eating into his brain, as the ashes into his skin: before, these things had been a dull aching into his consciousness; to-night, they were reality. He gripped the filthy red shirt that clung, stiff with soot, about him, and tore it savagely from his arm. The flesh beneath was muddy with grease and ashes,—and the heart beneath that! And the soul? God knows.

Then flashed before his vivid poetic sense the man who had left him,—the pure face, the delicate, sinewy limbs, in harmony with all he knew of beauty or truth. In his cloudy fancy he had pictured a Something like this. He had found it in this Mitchell, even when he idly scoffed at his pain: a Man all-knowing, all-seeing, crowned by Nature, reigning,—the keen glance of his eye falling like a sceptre on other men. And yet his instinct taught him that he too—He! He looked at himself with sudden loathing, sick, wrung his hands with a cry, and then was silent. With all the phantoms of his heated, ignorant fancy, Wolfe had not been vague in his ambitions. They were practical, slowly built up before him out of his knowledge of what he could do. Through years he had day by day made this hope a real thing to himself,—a clear, projected figure of himself, as he might become.

Able to speak, to know what was best, to raise these men and women working at his side up with him: sometimes he forgot this defined hope in the frantic anguish to escape,—only to escape,—out of the wet, the pain, the ashes, somewhere, anywhere,—only for one moment of free air on a hill side, to lie down and let his sick soul throb itself out in the sunshine. But to-night he panted for life. The savage strength of his nature was roused; his cry was fierce to God for justice.

"Look at me!" he said to Deborah, with a low, bitter laugh, striking his puny chest savagely. "What am I worth, Deb? Is it my fault that I am no better? My fault? My fault?"

*   *   *

There was an inexpressible bitterness on his face, as he lay down on the bed, taking the bit of tin, which he had rasped to a tolerable degree of sharpness, in his hand,—to play with, it may be. He bared his arms, looking intently at their corded veins and sinews. Deborah, listening in the next cell, heard a slight clicking sound, often repeated. She shut her lips tightly, that she might not scream; the cold drops of sweat broke over her, in her dumb agony.

"Hur knows best," she muttered at last, fiercely clutching the boards where she lay.

If she could have seen Wolfe, there was nothing about him to frighten her. He lay quite still, his arms outstretched, looking at the pearly stream of moonlight coming into the window. I think in that one hour that came then he lived back over all the years that had gone before. I think that all the low, vile life, all his wrongs, all his starved hopes, came then, and stung him with a farewell poison that made him sick unto death. He made neither moan nor cry, only turned his worn face now and then to the pure light, that seemed so far off, as one that said, "How long, O Lord? how long?"

The hour was over at last. The moon, passing over her nightly path, slowly came nearer, and threw the light across his bed on his feet. He watched it steadily, as it crept up, inch by inch, slowly. It seemed to him to carry with it a great silence. He had been so hot and tired there always in the mills! The years had been so fierce and cruel! There was coming now quiet and coolness and sleep. His tense limbs relaxed, and settled in a calm languor. The blood ran fainter and slow from his heart. He did not think now with a savage anger of what might be and was not; he was conscious only of deep stillness creeping over him. At first he saw a sea of faces: the mill-men,—women he had known, drunken and bloated,—Janey's timid and pitiful,—poor old Debs: then they floated together like a mist, and faded away, leaving only the clear, pearly moonlight.

Whether, as the pure light crept up the stretched-out figure, it brought with it calm and peace, who shall say? His dumb soul was alone with God in judgment. A Voice may have spoken for it from far-off Calvary, "Father, forgive them, for they know not what they do!" Who dare say? Fainter and fainter the heart rose and fell, slower and slower the moon floated from behind a cloud, until, when at last its full tide of white splendor swept over the cell, it seemed to wrap and fold into a deeper stillness the dead figure that never should move again. Silence deeper than the Night! Nothing that moved, save the black, nauseous stream of blood dripping slowly from the pallet to the floor!

Nothing remains to tell that the poor Welsh puddler once lived, but this figure of the mill-woman cut in korl. I have it here in a corner of my library. I keep it hid behind a curtain,—it is such a rough, ungainly thing. Yet there are about it touches, grand sweeps of outline, that show a master's hand. Sometimes,— to-night, for instance,—the curtain is accidentally drawn back, and I see a bare arm stretched out imploringly in the darkness, and an eager, wolfish face watching mine: a wan, woful face, through which the spirit of the dead korl-cutter looks out, with its thwarted life, its mighty hunger, its unfinished work. Its pale, vague lips seem to tremble with a terrible question. "Is this the End?"—they say,—"nothing beyond?—no more?" Why, you tell me you have seen that look in the eyes of dumb brutes,—horses dying under the lash. I know.

The deep of the night is passing while I write. The gas-light wakens from the shadows here and there the objects which lie scattered through the room: only faintly, though; for they belong to the open sunlight. As I glance at them, they each recall some task or pleasure of the coming day. A half-moulded child's head; Aphrodite; a bough of forest-leaves; music; work; homely fragments, in which lie the secrets of all eternal truth and beauty. Prophetic all! Only this dumb, woful face seems to belong to and end with the night. I turn to look at it. Has the power of its desperate need commanded the darkness away? While the room is yet steeped in heavy shadow, a cool, gray light suddenly touches its head like a blessing hand, and its groping arm points through the broken cloud to the far East, where, in the flickering, nebulous crimson, God has set the promise of the Dawn.

From Looking Backward, 2000–1887

1888

Looking Backward, an instant bestseller written by Edward Bellamy (1850–1898), was to "the shaping of popular opinion for a new social order" what "*Uncle Tom's Cabin* was to the antislavery movement," according to John Dewey. The second novel to sell over a million copies in the United States (after *Uncle Tom's Cabin*), *Looking Backward* launched a political movement (Nationalism) and inspired the People's Party program. Oscar Wilde's famous dictum, that "when humanity lands there [Utopia], it looks out, and seeing a better country, sets sail," illuminates the strange moment in American literary history when Bellamy's novel captured the imagination of a country: the reading public landed on *Looking Backward,* looked out, saw its relevance to their political moment, and used it as a point of departure for their political parties and utopian societies.

As a thought experiment, suggesting one possible, egalitarian future, Bellamy's novel is oddly prescriptive: one character's name, E. Leete (elite) is ironically appropriate. All debates are rigged, no active judgments are required, and Bellamy's vision of history leaves no role for agency. Bellamy acknowledged the novel's stylistic flaws, writing in 1889 that "barely enough story was left to decently drape the skeleton of the argument." But the public had a large appetite for utopian fiction in the 1880s and 1890s. At least 160 writers offered fictional utopias during this period. Against a backdrop of unemployment and strikes—the Great Railroad Strike of 1877, and the May Day Strike of 1886, when 300,000 laborers struck for an eight-hour workday—Bellamy's vision of a happier society in the year 2000 evokes the myth of America's utopian founding. Consolation for the present, it locates a romanticized past in the future. Harriet Beecher Stowe had imagined a Christian millennium, while Bellamy's is secular, but both are within the national New World tradition. *Looking Backward*'s commercial success also reveals the limits of reform in the 1880s. It's a jingoist, nativist book. Women are innately different from men, crime is genetic, and aspects of Bellamy's utopia even anticipate later dystopian fictions (lack of solitude, brainwashing, and music that lulls people out of "uncanny feelings"—like Aldous Huxley's Soma in *Brave New World* [1932]).

But at the end of Bellamy's novel, the protagonist dreams he's back in the 19th century. Readers are jolted back to reality in a scene that anticipates a comment by the communist Louis Aragon in 1959: "Nothing is so dangerous as utopia. It lulls people to sleep and when they are awakened by reality . . . they suddenly find themselves tumbling down."

Further reading: Lawrence Goodwyn, *The Populist Moment* (1978); Arthur Lipow, *Authoritarian Socialism* (1982).

Chapter 1

I first saw the light in the city of Boston in the year 1857. . . . By way of attempting to give the reader some general impression of the way people lived together in those days, and especially of the relations of the rich and poor to one another, perhaps I cannot do better than to compare society as it then was to a prodigious coach which the masses of humanity were harnessed to and dragged toilsomely along a very hilly and sandy road. The driver was hunger, and permitted no lagging, though the pace was necessarily very slow. Despite the difficulty of drawing the coach at all along so hard a road, the top was covered with passengers who never got down, even at the steepest ascents. These seats on top were very breezy and comfortable. Well up out of the dust, their occupants could enjoy the scenery at their leisure, or critically discuss the merits of the straining team. Naturally such places were in great demand and the competition for them was keen, every one seeking as the first end in life to secure a seat on the coach for himself and to leave it to his child after him. By the rule of the coach a man could leave his seat to whom he wished, but on the other hand there were many accidents by which it might at any time be wholly lost. For all that they were so easy, the seats were very insecure, and at every sudden jolt of the coach persons were slipping out of them and falling to the ground, where they were instantly compelled to take hold of the rope and help to drag the coach on which they had before ridden so pleasantly. It was naturally regarded as a terrible misfortune to lose one's seat, and the apprehension that this might happen to them or their friends was a constant cloud upon the happiness of those who rode.

But did they think only of themselves? you ask. Was not their very luxury rendered intolerable to them by comparison with the lot of their brothers and sisters in the harness, and the knowledge that their own weight added to their toil? Had they no compassion for fellow beings from whom fortune only distinguished them? Oh, yes; commiseration was frequently expressed by those who rode for those who had to pull the coach, especially when the vehicle came to a bad place in the road, as it was constantly doing, or to a particularly steep hill. At such times, the desperate straining of the team, their agonized leaping and plunging under the pitiless lashing of hunger, the many who fainted at the rope and were trampled in the mire, made a very distressing spectacle, which often called forth highly creditable displays of feeling on the top of the coach. At such times the passengers would call down encouragingly to the toilers of the rope, exhorting them to patience, and holding out hopes of possible compensation in another world for the hardness of their lot, while others contributed to buy salves and liniments for the crippled and injured. It was agreed that it was a great pity that the coach should be so hard to pull, and there was a sense of general relief when the specially bad piece of road was gotten over. This relief was not, indeed, wholly on account of the team, for there was always some danger at these bad places of a general overturn in which all would lose their seats . . . I am well aware that this will appear to the men and women of the twentieth century an incredible inhumanity, but there are two facts, both very curious, which partly explain it. In the first place, it was firmly and sincerely believed that there was no other way in which Society could get along, except the many pulled at the rope and the few rode, and not only this, but that no very radical improvement even was possible, either in the harness, the coach, the roadway, or the distribution of the toil. It had always been as it was, and it always would be so. It was a pity, but it could not be helped, and philosophy forbade wasting compassion on what was beyond remedy.

Chapter 5

"I must know a little more about the sort of Boston I have come back to. You told me when we were upon the house-top that though a century only had elapsed since I fell asleep, it had been marked by greater changes in the conditions of humanity than many a previous millennium. With the city before me I could well believe that, but I am very curious to know what some of the changes have been. To make a beginning somewhere, for the subject is doubtless a large one, what solution, if any, have you found for the labor question? It was the Sphinx's riddle of the nineteenth century, and when I dropped out the Sphinx was threatening to devour society, because the answer was not forthcoming. It is well worth sleeping a hundred years to learn what the right answer was, if, indeed, you have found it yet."

"As no such thing as the labor question is known nowadays," replied Dr. Leete, "and there is no way in which it could arise, I suppose we may claim to have solved it. Society would indeed have fully deserved being devoured if it had failed to answer a riddle so entirely simple. In fact, to speak by the book, it was not necessary for society to solve the riddle at all. It may be said to have solved itself. The solution came as the result of a process of industrial evolution which could not have terminated otherwise. All that society had to do was to recognize and cooperate with that evolution, when its tendency had become unmistakable."

"I can only say," I answered, "that at the time I fell asleep no such evolution had been recognized."

"It was in 1887 that you fell into this sleep, I think you said."

"Yes, May 30th, 1887."

My companion regarded me musingly for some moments. Then he observed, "And you tell me that even then there was no general recognition of the nature of the crisis which society was nearing? Of course, I fully credit your statement. The singular blindness of your contemporaries to the signs of the times is a phenomenon commented on by many of our historians, but few facts of history are more difficult for us to realize, so obvious and unmistakable as we look back seem the indications, which must also have come under your eyes, of the transformation about to come to pass. I should be interested, Mr. West, if you would give me a little more definite idea of the view which you and men of your grade of intellect took of the state and prospects of society in 1887. You must, at least, have realized that the widespread industrial and social troubles, and the underlying dissatisfaction of all classes with the inequalities of society, and the general misery of mankind, were portents of great changes of some sort."

"We did, indeed, fully realize that," I replied. "We felt that society was dragging anchor and in danger of going adrift. Whither it would drift nobody could say, but all feared the rocks."

"Nevertheless," said Dr. Leete, "the set of the current was perfectly perceptible if you had but taken pains to observe it, and it was not toward the rocks, but toward a deeper channel."

"We had a popular proverb," I replied, "that 'hindsight is better than foresight,' the force of which I shall now, no doubt, appreciate more fully than ever. All I can say is, that the prospect was such when I went into that long sleep that I should not have been surprised had I looked down from your house-top to-day on a heap of charred and moss-grown ruins instead of this glorious city."

Dr. Leete had listened to me with close attention and nodded thoughtfully as I finished speaking. "What you have said," he observed, "will be regarded as a most valuable vindication of Storiot, whose account of your era has been generally thought exaggerated in its picture of the gloom and confusion of men's minds. That a period of transition like that should be full of excitement and agitation was indeed to be looked for; but seeing how plain was the tendency of the forces in operation, it was natural to believe that hope rather than fear would have been the prevailing temper of the popular mind."

"You have not yet told me what was the answer to the riddle which you found," I said. "I am impatient to know by what contradiction of natural sequence the peace and prosperity which you now seem to enjoy could have been the outcome of an era like my own." . . .

"Early in the last century the evolution was completed by the final consolidation of the entire capital of the nation. The industry and commerce of the country, ceasing to be conducted by a set of irresponsible corporations and syndicates of private persons at their caprice and for their profit, were intrusted to a single syndicate representing the people, to be conducted in the common interest for the common profit. The nation, that is to say, organized as the one great business corporation in which all other corporations were absorbed; it became the one capitalist in the place of all other capitalists, the sole employer, the final monopoly in which all previous and lesser monopolies were swallowed up, a monopoly in the profits and economies of which all citizens shared. The epoch of trusts had ended in The Great Trust. In a word, the people of the United States concluded to assume the conduct of their own business, just as one hundred odd years before they had assumed the conduct of their own government, organizing now for industrial purposes on precisely the same grounds that they had then organized for political purposes. At last, strangely late in the world's history, the obvious fact was perceived that no business is so essentially the public business as the industry and commerce on which the people's livelihood depends, and that to entrust it to private persons to be managed for private profit is a folly similar in kind, though vastly greater in magnitude, to that of surrendering the functions of political government to kings and nobles to be conducted for their personal glorification."

"Such a stupendous change as you describe," said I, "did not, of course, take place without great bloodshed and terrible convulsions."

"On the contrary," replied Dr. Leete, "there was absolutely no violence. The change had been long foreseen. Public opinion had become fully ripe for it, and the whole mass of the people was behind it. There was no more possibility of opposing it by force than by argument. On the other hand the popular sentiment toward the great corporations and those identified with them had ceased to be one of bitterness, as they came to realize their necessity as a link, a transition phase, in the evolution of the true industrial system. The most violent foes of the great private monopolies were now forced to recognize how invaluable and indispensable had been their office in educating the people up to the point of assuming control of their own business. Fifty years before, the consolidation of the industries of the country under national control would have seemed a very daring experiment to the most sanguine. But by a series of object lessons, seen and studied by all men, the great corporations had taught the people an entirely new set of ideas on this subject. They had seen for many years syndicates handling revenues greater than those of states, and directing the labors of hundreds of thousands of men with an efficiency and economy unattainable in smaller operations. It had come to be recognized as an axiom that the larger the business the simpler the principles that can be applied to it; that, as the machine is truer than the hand, so the system, which in a great concern does the work of the master's eye in a small business, turns out more

accurate results. Thus it came about that, thanks to the corporations themselves, when it was proposed that the nation should assume their functions,
the suggestion implied nothing which seemed impracticable even to the timid.
To be sure it was a step beyond any yet taken, a broader generalization, but the
very fact that the nation would be the sole corporation in the field would, it
was seen, relieve the undertaking of many difficulties with which the partial
monopolies had contended."

Postscript: The Rate of the World's Progress

Looking Backward, although in form a fanciful romance, is intended, in all seriousness, as a forecast, in accordance with the principles of evolution, of the
next stage in the industrial and social development of humanity, especially in
this country, and no part of it is believed by the author to be better supported
by the indications of probability than the implied prediction that the dawn
of the new era is already near at hand, and that the full day will swiftly follow. Does this seem at first thought incredible, in view of the vastness of the
changes presupposed? What is the teaching of history, but that great national
transformations, while ages in unnoticed preparation, when once inaugurated, are accomplished with a rapidity and resistless momentum propor-
tioned to their magnitude, not limited by it? . . . On no other stage are the
scenes shifted with a swiftness so like magic as on the great stage of history
when once the hour strikes. The question is not, then, how extensive the
scene-shifting must be to set the stage for the new fraternal civilization, but
whether there are any special indications that a social transformation is at
hand. The causes that have been bringing it ever nearer have been at work
from immemorial time. To the stream of tendency setting toward an ultimate
realization of a form of society which, while vastly more efficient for material
prosperity, should all satisfy and not outrage the moral instincts, every sigh of
poverty, every tear of pity, every humane impulse, every generous enthusiasm,
every true religious feeling, every act for which men have given effect to their
mutual sympathy by drawing more closely together for any purpose, have
contributed from the beginnings of civilization. That this long stream of influence, ever widening and deepening, is at last about to sweep away the barriers
it has so long sapped, is at least one obvious interpretation of the present universal ferment of men's minds as to the imperfections of present social arrangements. Not only are the toilers of the world engaged in something like a
world-wide insurrection, but true and humane men and women, of every degree, are in a mood of exasperation, verging on absolute revolt, against social
conditions that reduce life to a brutal struggle for existence, mock every dictate
of ethics and religion, and render well-nigh futile the efforts of philanthropy.

As an iceberg, floating southward from the frozen North, is gradually undermined by warmer seas, and, become at last unstable, churns the sea to yeast for miles around by the mighty rockings that portend its overturn, so the barbaric industrial and social system, which has come down to us from savage antiquity, undermined by the moderate humane spirit, riddled by the criticism of economic science, is shaking the world with convulsions that presage its collapse.

All thoughtful men agree that the present aspect of society is portentous of great changes. The only question is, whether they will be for the better or the worse. Those who believe in man's essential nobleness lean to the former view, those who believe in his essential baseness to the latter. For my part, I hold to the former opinion. *Looking Backward* was written in the belief that the Golden Age lies before us and not behind us, and is not far away. Our children will surely see it, and we too, who are already men and women, if we deserve it by our faith and by our works.

From How the Other Half Lives

1890

Jacob Riis (1849–1914), a crusading photographer and writer, wasn't the first to engage the conditions of the urban tenements, though he was the first to propose solutions—believing, as he said in 1901, that no question could "be asked of the Republic to which we shall not find the answer." Nor was he the first to discuss the "other half"; he used this phrase to access the established discourse of liberal reform. Most of his book's impact was due to its photographs. Americans had never seen pictures of poverty like this, or even encountered a book with any significant number of halftone photographic reproductions. Riis acknowledged their power, noting of "Five Cents Lodging" (reprinted here) that the recommendations of one written report to the Health Board made no impression until his negatives "came to reinforce them."

His methods were questionable. While Lewis Hine emphasized empathy, Riis preferred shock value. The invention of flash photography enabled invasive night raids, and his flash blinded subjects, flattening faces on the photographs' surfaces. He would pay subjects, interrupt them in their work, photograph them "in character," and label them as types—one image is captioned "typical toughs." He wrote as a genial guide, pointing out "picturesque costumes," the "spectacle" and "sights." His readers are cast as voyeurs, relishing exotic detail and feeling pity, and Riis told a reporter in 1888: "The beauty of looking into these places without actually being present there is that the excursionist is spared the vulgar sounds and odious scents and repulsive exhibitions."

Riis's imagined poor are incapable of self-help. His approach was to offer facts and anecdotes, and then call for practical solutions. Riis was no revolutionary, explaining in 1901: "I love to mend and make crooked things straight. When I was a carpenter I preferred to make an old house over to building a new." Rather than make over society, he called for systematic private charity, sanitary conditions, parks, playgrounds, and a labor bureau. The tenement was the problem, and tenement reform was the solution. His tight focus paid off: the tenement neighborhood of Mulberry Bend became a park in 1897, the New York Tenement House Law was rewritten in 1901, police-station lodgings were replaced by a better shelter for the homeless, public bathhouses were built, and the Five Points Mission and Children's Aid Society were formed.

Further reading: James Guimond, *American Photography* (1991); Richard Hofstadter, *The Age of Reform* (1955).

The Down Town Back-alleys and the Sweaters of Jewtown

Here comes a pleasure party, as gay as any on the avenue, though the carry-all is an ash-cart. The father is the driver and he has taken his brown-legged boy for a ride. How proud and happy they both look up there on their perch! The queer old building they have halted in front of is "The Ship," famous for fifty years as a ramshackle tenement filled with the oddest crowd. No one knows why it is called "The Ship," though there is a tradition that once the river came clear up here to Hamilton Street, and boats were moored along-side it. More likely it is because it is as bewildering inside as a crazy old ship, with its ups and downs of ladders parading as stairs and its unexpected pitfalls. But Hamilton Street, like Water Street, is not what it was. The missions drove from the latter the worst of its dives. A sailors' mission has lately made its appearance in Hamilton Street, but there are no dives there, nothing worse than the ubiquitous saloon and tough tenements.

Enough of them everywhere. Suppose we look into one? No.—Cherry Street. Be a little careful, please! The hall is dark and you might stumble over the children pitching pennies back there. Not that it would hurt them; kicks and cuffs are their daily diet. They have little else. Here where the hall turns and dives into utter darkness is a step, and another, another. A flight of stairs. You can feel your way, if you cannot see it. Close? Yes! What would you have? All the fresh air that ever enters these stairs comes from the hall-door that is forever slamming, and from the windows of dark bedrooms that in turn receive from the stairs their sole supply of elements God meant to be free, but man deals out with such niggardly hand. That was a woman filling her pail by the hydrant you just bumped against. The sinks are in the hallway, that all the tenants may have access—and all to be poisoned alike by their summer stenches. Hear the pump squeak! It is the lullaby of tenement-house babes. In summer, when a thousand thirsty throats pant for a cooling drink in this block, it is worked in vain. But the saloon, whose open door you passed in the hall, is always there. The smell of it has followed you up. Here is a door. Listen! That short hacking cough, that tiny, helpless wail—what do they mean? They mean that the soiled bow of white you saw on the door downstairs will have another story to tell—Oh! a sadly familiar story—before the day is at an end. The child is dying with measles. With half a chance it might have lived; but it had none. The dark bedroom killed it.

"It was took all of a suddint," says the mother, smoothing the throbbing little body with trembling hands. There is no unkindness in the rough voice of the man in the jumper, who sits by the window grimly smoking a clay pipe, with the little life ebbing out in his sight, bitter as his words sound: "Hush, Mary! if we cannot keep the baby, need we complain—such as we?"

Such as we! What if the words ring in your ears as we grope our way up the stairs and down from floor to floor, listening to the sounds behind the closed doors—some of quarreling, some of coarse songs, more of profanity. They are true. When the summer heats come with their suffering, they have meaning more terrible than words can tell.

Come over here. Step carefully over this baby—it is a baby, spite of its rags and dirt—under these iron bridges called fire-escapes, but loaded down, despite the incessant watchfulness of the firemen, with broken household goods, with washtubs and barrels, over which no man could climb from a fire. This gap between dingy brick walls is the yard. The strip of smoke-colored sky up there is the heaven of these people. Do you wonder the name does not attract them to churches? That baby's parents live in the rear tenement here. She is at least as clean as the steps we are now climbing. There are plenty of houses with half a hundred such in. The tenement is much like the one in front we just left, only fouler, closer, darker—we will not say more cheerless. The word is a mockery. A hundred thousand people lived in rear tenements in New York last year.

Evening has worn into night as we take up our homeward journey through the streets, now no longer silent. The thousands of lighted windows in the tenements glow like dull red eyes in a huge stone wall. From every door multitudes of tired men and women pour forth for a half-hour's rest in the open air before sleep closes the eyes weary with incessant working. Crowds of half-naked children tumble in the street and on the sidewalk, or doze fretfully on the stone steps. As we stop in front of a tenement to watch one of these groups, a dirty baby in a single brief garment—yet a sweet, human little baby despite its dirt and tatters—tumbles off the lowest step, rolls over once, clutches my leg with unconscious grip, and goes to sleep on the flagstones, its curly head pillowed on my boot.

How the Case Stands

There are three effective ways of dealing with the tenements in New York:

  I. By law.
  II. By remodeling and making the most out of the old houses.
  III. By building new, model tenements.

Private enterprise—conscience, to put it in the category of duties, where it belongs—must do the lion's share under these last two heads. Of what the law has effected I have spoken already. The drastic measures adopted in Paris, in Glasgow, and in London are not practicable here on anything like as large a scale. Still it can, under strong pressure of public opinion, rid us of the worst plague-spots. The Mulberry Street Bend will go the way of the Five Points when all the red tape that binds the hands of municipal effort has been unwound. Prizes were offered in public competition, some years ago, for the best plans of modern tenement-houses. It may be that we shall see the day when the building of model tenements will be encouraged by subsidies in the way of a rebate of taxes. Meanwhile the arrest and summary punishment of landlords, or their agents, who persistently violate law and decency, will have a salutary effect. If a few of the wealthy absentee landlords, who are the worst offenders, could be got within the jurisdiction of the city, and by arrest be compelled to employ proper overseers, it would be a proud day for New York. To remedy the over-crowding, with which the night inspections of the sanitary police cannot keep step, tenements may eventually have to he licensed, as now the lodging-houses, to hold so many tenants, and no more; or the State may have to bring down the rents that cause the crowding, by assuming the right to regulate them as it regulates the fares on the elevated roads. I throw out the suggestion, knowing quite well that it is open to attack. It emanated originally from one of the brightest minds that have had to struggle officially with this tenement-house question in the last ten years. In any event, to succeed, reform by law must aim at making it unprofitable to own a bad tenement. At best, it is apt to travel at a snail's pace, while the enemy it pursues is putting the best foot foremost . . .

Enough has been said to show that model tenements can be built success-fully and made to pay in New York, if the owner will be content with the five or six per cent. he does not even dream of when investing his funds in "govern-ments" at three or four. It is true that in the latter case he has only to cut off his coupons and cash them. But the extra trouble of looking after his tenement property, that is the condition of his highest and lasting success, is the penalty exacted for the sins of our fathers that "shall be visited upon the children, unto the third and fourth generation." We shall indeed be well off, if it stop there. I fear there is too much reason to believe that our own iniquities must be added to transmit the curse still further. And yet, such is the leavening influence of a good deed in that dreary desert of sin and suffering, that the erection of a sin-gle good tenement has the power to change, gradually but surely, the character of a whole bad block. It sets up a standard to which the neighborhood must rise, if it cannot succeed in dragging it down to its own low level.

And so this task, too, has come to an end. Whatsoever a man soweth, that shall he also reap. I have aimed to tell the truth as I saw it. If this book shall have borne ever so feeble a hand in garnering a harvest of justice, it has served its purpose. While I was writing these lines I went down to the sea, where thousands from the city were enjoying their summer rest. The ocean slum-bered under a cloudless sky. Gentle waves washed lazily over the white sand, where children fled before them with screams of laughter. Standing there and watching their play, I was told that during the fierce storms of winter it hap-pened that this sea, now so calm, rose in rage and beat down, broke over the bluff, sweeping all before it. No barrier built by human hands had power to stay it then. The sea of a mighty population, held in galling fetters, heaves un-easily in the tenements. Once already our city, to which have come the duties and responsibilities of metropolitan greatness before it was able to fairly mea-sure its task, has felt the swell of its resistless flood. If it rise once more, no hu-man power may avail to check it. The gap between the classes in which it surges, unseen, unsuspected by the thoughtless, is widening day by day. No tardy enactment of law, no political expedient, can close it. Against all other dangers our system of government may offer defence and shelter; against this not. I know of but one bridge that will carry us over safe, a bridge founded upon justice and built of human hearts.

I believe that the danger of such conditions as are fast growing up around us is greater for the very freedom which they mock. The words of the poet, with whose lines I prefaced this book, are truer to-day, have far deeper meaning to us, than when they were penned forty years ago:

—Think ye that building shall endure
Which shelters the noble and crushes the poor?

From The Jungle

1906

Jack London heralded *The Jungle* as "The *Uncle Tom's Cabin* of wage slavery," adding that Upton Sinclair (1878–1968) had improved upon the "beautiful theoretics of Bellamy's *Looking Backward.*" But the literary meat—ironically—was missing from Sinclair's novel. It has few lyrical passages, weak symbolism, and little character development. The manuscript was rejected by six publishers, and Sinclair eventually advertised it himself in the socialist magazine *Appeal to Reason,* which had sent him to investigate the Chicago meatpacking district in 1904. Only after he had received orders for 972 copies would Doubleday publish it.

The first two-thirds of the novel, about the poverty of the protagonist Jurgis and his family, form a convincing story. It is the last chapters that jar, when Sinclair shifts from encyclopedic realism to didacticism. As Jurgis finds secular salvation in socialism, Sinclair incorporates a speech that he'd given during his Chicago visit. He tries to dramatize the postbellum displacement of God, explaining that "the Socialist movement . . . was the new religion," but the new world is barely visualized and the spiritualized Jurgis almost ceases to exist materially. Sinclair sensed the novel's limitations, comparing his topic to Harriet Beecher Stowe's in a passage cut from the first edition: "This slave . . . is not beaten by picturesque villains . . . Who can make a romance out of the story of a man whose one life adventure is the scratching of a finger by an infected butcher knife . . .?" He added in an essay: "the life of the modern wage-slave is so much . . . less picturesque than that of the chattel-slave." He was also resisting what he called the "lie of Art for Art's Sake." He believed that all art was propaganda, that *The Jungle* marked the beginning of a proletarian literature in America, and that the proletarian writer thought "no more of 'art for art's sake' than a man on a sinking ship thinks of painting a beautiful picture in the cabin."

Within the protest tradition, the real problem with the novel is Sinclair's naturalist mode. Jurgis learns that life is "a war," and to show this learning process Sinclair conducts him through a series of representative experiences and narrates his inevitable decline. A vision of inexorability conveyed the logic of the capitalist jungle, but left readers feeling powerless to stop the machine. Instead they tinkered with parts: *The Jungle* helped pass the 1906 Food and Drugs and Meat Inspection Acts but fell short of ushering in the new world called for by its author. London saw the end of the capitalist jungle on the horizon, however, and invited readers to agency: "It will be read by every workingman . . . It will wake thousands of converts to our cause. Comrades, it is up to you!"

Further reading: David Chalmers, *The Muckrake Years* (1974); James Young, *Pure Food* (1989).

Chapter 9

. . . There was another interesting set of statistics that a person might have gathered in Packingtown—those of the various afflictions of the workers. When Jurgis had first inspected the packing plants with Szedvilas, he had marveled while he listened to the tale of all the things that were made out of the carcasses of animals, and of all the lesser industries that were maintained there; now he found that each one of these lesser industries was a separate little inferno, in its way as horrible as the killing beds, the source and fountain of them all. The workers in each of them had their own peculiar diseases. And the wandering visitor might be skeptical about all the swindles, but he could not be skeptical about these, for the worker bore the evidence of them about on his own person—generally he had only to hold out his hand.

There were the men in the pickle rooms, for instance, where old Antanas had gotten his death; scarce a one of these that had not some spot of horror on his person. Let a man so much as scrape his finger pushing a truck in the pickle rooms, and he might have a sore that would put him out of the world; all the joints in his fingers might be eaten by the acid, one by one. Of the butchers and floorsmen, the beef-boners and trimmers, and all those who used knives, you could scarcely find a person who had the use of his thumb; time and time again the base of it had been slashed, till it was a mere lump of flesh against which the man pressed the knife to hold it. The hands of these men would be criss-crossed with cuts, until you could no longer pretend to count them or to trace them. They would have no nails,—they had worn them off pulling hides; their knuckles were swollen so that their fingers spread out like a fan. There were men who worked in the cooking rooms, in the midst of steam and sickening odors, by artificial light; in these rooms the germs of tuberculosis might live for two years, but the supply was renewed every hour. There were the beef-luggers, who carried two-hundred-pound quarters into the refrigerator-cars; a fearful kind of work, that began at four o'clock in the morning, and that wore out the most powerful men in a few years. There were those who worked in the chilling rooms, and whose special disease was rheumatism; the time limit that a man could work in the chilling rooms was said to be five years. There were the wool-pluckers, whose hands went to pieces even sooner than the hands of the pickle men; for the pelts of the sheep had to be painted with acid to loosen the wool, and then the pluckers had to pull out this wool with their bare hands, till the acid had eaten their fingers off. There were those who made the tins for the canned meat; and their hands, too, were a maze of cuts, and each cut represented a chance for blood poisoning. Some worked at the stamping machines, and it was very seldom that one could work long there at the pace that was set, and not give out and forget himself and have a part of his hand chopped off. There were the "hoisters," as they were called, whose task it was to press the lever which lifted the dead cattle off the floor. They ran along upon a rafter, peering down through the damp and the steam; and as old Durham's architects had not built the killing room for the convenience of the hoisters, at every few feet they would have to stoop under a beam, say four feet above the one they ran on; which got them into the habit of stooping, so that in a few years they would be walking like chimpanzees. Worst of any, however, were the fertilizer men, and those who served in the cooking rooms. These people could not be shown to the visitor,—for the odor of a fertilizer man would scare any ordinary visitor at a hundred yards, and as for the other men, who worked in tank rooms full of steam, and in some of which there were open vats near the level of the floor, their peculiar trouble was that they fell into the vats; and when they were fished out, there was never enough of them left to be worth exhibiting,—sometimes they would be overlooked for days, till all but the bones of them had gone out to the world as Durham's Pure Leaf Lard!

Chapter 14

With one member trimming beef in a cannery, and another working in a sausage factory, the family had a first-hand knowledge of the great majority of Packingtown swindles. For it was the custom, as they found, whenever meat was so spoiled that it could not be used for anything else, either to can it or else to chop it up into sausage. With what had been told them by Jonas, who had worked in the pickle rooms, they could now study the whole of the spoiled-meat industry on the inside, and read a new and grim meaning into that old Packingtown jest—that they use everything of the pig except the squeal.

Jonas had told them how the meat that was taken out of pickle would often be found sour, and how they would rub it up with soda to take away the smell, and sell it to be eaten on free-lunch counters; also of all the miracles of chemistry which they performed, giving to any sort of meat, fresh or salted, whole or chopped, any color and any flavor and any odor they chose. In the pickling of hams they had an ingenious apparatus, by which they saved time and increased the capacity of the plant—a machine consisting of a hollow needle attached to a pump; by plunging this needle into the meat and working with his foot, a man could fill a ham with pickle in a few seconds. And yet, in spite of this, there would be hams found spoiled, some of them with an odor so bad that a man could hardly bear to be in the room with them. To pump into these the packers had a second and much stronger pickle which destroyed the odor— process known to the workers as "giving them thirty per cent." Also, after the hams had been smoked, there would be found some that had gone to the bad. Formerly these had been sold as "Number Three Grade," but later on

some ingenious person had hit upon a new device, and now they would extract the bone, about which the bad part generally lay, and insert in the hole a
white-hot iron. After this invention there was no longer Number One, Two,
and Three Grade—there was only Number One Grade. The packers were always originating such schemes—they had what they called "boneless hams,"
which were all the odds and ends of pork stuffed into casings; and "California
hams," which were the shoulders, with big knuckle joints, and nearly all the
meat cut out; and fancy "skinned hams," which were made of the oldest hogs,
whose skins were so heavy and coarse that no one would buy them—that is,
until they had been cooked and chopped fine and labeled "head cheese!"

It was only when the whole ham was spoiled that it came into the department of Elzbieta. Cut up by the two-thousand-revolutions-a-minute flyers, and
mixed with half a ton of other meat, no odor that ever was in a ham could
make any difference. There was never the least attention paid to what was cut
up for sausage; there would come all the way back from Europe old sausage
that had been rejected, and that was moldy and white—it would be dosed with
borax and glycerine, and dumped into the hoppers, and made over again for
home consumption. There would be meat that had tumbled out on the floor,
in the dirt and sawdust, where the workers had tramped and spit uncounted
billions of consumption germs. There would be meat stored in great piles in
rooms; and the water from leaky roofs would drip over it, and thousands of
rats would race about on it. It was too dark in these storage places to see well,
but a man could run his hand over these piles of meat and sweep off handfuls
of the dried dung of rats. These rats were nuisances, and the packers would
put poisoned bread out for them; they would die, and then rats, bread, and
meat would go into the hoppers together. This is no fairy story and no joke;
the meat would be shoveled into carts, and the man who did the shoveling
would not trouble to lift out a rat even when he saw one—there were things
that went into the sausage in comparison with which a poisoned rat was a tid-
bit. There was no place for the men to wash their hands before they ate their
dinner, and so they made a practice of washing them in the water that was to
be ladled into the sausage. There were the butt-ends of smoked meat, and the
scraps of corned beef, and all the odds and ends of the waste of the plants, that
would be dumped into old barrels in the cellar and left there. Under the system
of rigid economy which the packers enforced, there were some jobs that it only
paid to do once in a long time, and among these was the cleaning out of the
waste barrels. Every spring they did it; and in the barrels would be dirt and rust
and old nails and stale water—and cartload after cartload of it would be taken
up and dumped into the hoppers with fresh meat, and sent out to the public's
breakfast. Some of it they would make into "smoked" sausage—but as the
smoking took time, and was therefore expensive, they would call upon their

chemistry department, and preserve it with borax and color it with gelatine to make it brown. All of their sausage came out of the same bowl, but when they came to wrap it they would stamp some of it "special," and for this they would charge two cents more a pound.

Such were the new surroundings in which Elzbieta was placed, and such was the work she was compelled to do. It was stupefying, brutalizing work; it left her no time to think, no strength for anything. She was part of the machine she tended, and every faculty that was not needed for the machine was doomed to be crushed out of existence. There was only one mercy about the cruel grind—that it gave her the gift of insensibility. Little by little she sank into a torpor—she fell silent. She would meet Jurgis and Ona in the evening, and the three would walk home together, often without saying a word. Ona, too, was falling into a habit of silence—Ona, who had once gone about singing like a bird. She was sick and miserable, and often she would barely have strength enough to drag herself home. And there they would eat what they had to eat, and afterward, because there was only their misery to talk of, they would crawl into bed and fall into a stupor and never stir until it was time to get up again, and dress by candlelight, and go back to the machines. They were so numbed that they did not even suffer much from hunger, now; only the children continued to fret when the food ran short.

Yet the soul of Ona was not dead—the souls of none of them were dead, but only sleeping; and now and then they would waken, and these were cruel times. The gates of memory would roll open—old joys would stretch out their arms to them, old hopes and dreams would call to them, and they would stir beneath the burden that lay upon them, and feel its forever immeasurable weight. They could not even cry out beneath it; but anguish would seize them, more dreadful than the agony of death. It was a thing scarcely to be spoken—a thing never spoken by all the world, that will not know its own defeat.

They were beaten; they had lost the game, they were swept aside. It was not less tragic because it was so sordid, because it had to do with wages and grocery bills and rents. They had dreamed of freedom; of a chance to look about them and learn something; to be decent and clean, to see their child grow up to be strong. And now it was all gone—it would never be! They had played the game and they had lost. Six years more of toil they had to face before they could expect the least respite, the cessation of the payments upon the house; and how cruelly certain it was that they could never stand six years of such a life as they were living! They were lost, they were going down—and there was no deliverance for them, no hope; for all the help it gave them the vast city in which they lived might have been an ocean waste, a wilderness, a desert, a tomb. So often this mood would come to Ona, in the nighttime, when something wakened her; she would lie, afraid of the beating of her own heart, fronting the blood-red eyes of the old primeval terror of life. Once she cried aloud, and woke Jurgis, who was tired and cross. After that she learned to weep silently— their moods so seldom came together now! It was as if their hopes were buried in separate graves.

Chapter 28

It was like coming suddenly upon some wild sight of nature—a mountain forest lashed by a tempest, a ship tossed about upon a stormy sea. Jurgis had an unpleasant sensation, a sense of confusion, of disorder, of wild and meaningless uproar. The man was tall and gaunt, as haggard as his auditor himself; a thin black beard covered half of his face, and one could see only two black hollows where the eyes were. He was speaking rapidly, in great excitement; he used many gestures—he spoke he moved here and there upon the stage, reaching with his long arms as if to seize each person in his audience. His voice was deep, like an organ; it was some time, however, before Jurgis thought of the voice—he was too much occupied with his eyes to think of what the man was saying. But suddenly it seemed as if the speaker had begun pointing straight at him, as if he had singled him out particularly for his remarks; and so Jurgis became suddenly aware of his voice, trembling, vibrant with emotion, with pain and longing, with a burden of things unutterable, not to be compassed by words. To hear it was to be suddenly arrested, to be gripped, transfixed . . .

The sentences of this man were to Jurgis like the crashing of thunder in his soul; a flood of emotions surged up in him—all his old hopes and longings, his old griefs and rages and despairs. All that he had ever felt in his whole life seemed to come back to him at once, and with one new emotion, hardly to be described. That he should have suffered such oppressions and such horrors was bad enough; but that he should have been crushed and beaten by them, that he should have submitted, and forgotten, and lived in peace—ah, truly that was a thing not to be put into words, a thing not to be borne by a human creature, a thing of terror and madness! "What," asks the prophet, "is the murder of them that kill the body, to the murder of them that kill the soul?" And Jurgis was a man whose soul had been murdered, who had ceased to hope and to struggle—who had made terms with degradation and despair; and now, suddenly, in one awful convulsion, the black and hideous fact was made plain to him! There was a falling in of all the pillars of his soul, the sky seemed to split above him—he stood there, with his clenched hands upraised, his eyes bloodshot, and the veins standing out purple in his face, roaring in the voice of a wild beast, frantic, incoherent, maniacal. And when he could shout no more he still stood there, gasping, and whispering hoarsely to himself: "By God! By God! By God!"

Sadie Pfeifer *and* Making Human Junk

1908, 1915

"Light in floods!" cried Lewis Hine (1874–1940) at a 1909 social-work conference: "We have for our advance agent the light writer—the photograph." In 1890 the census had revealed that more than a million children aged 10–15 were at work; by 1910 they numbered two million. Some as young as five worked 18-hour days. In 1906 Congress rejected national laws prohibiting child labor and in 1908 the National Child Labor Committee (NCLC) employed Hine as their photographer. His images of child laborers often featured the "light" that he demanded: cracks appear in dark interiors, as in the first photograph reproduced here, "Sadie Pfeifer."

Some children in his photographs gaze into the light, out of the window, suggesting self-help. Hine did have the Progressive-era faith that knowledge equaled action, and demanded empathy from viewers and photographers alike: diagonal lines toward the lower

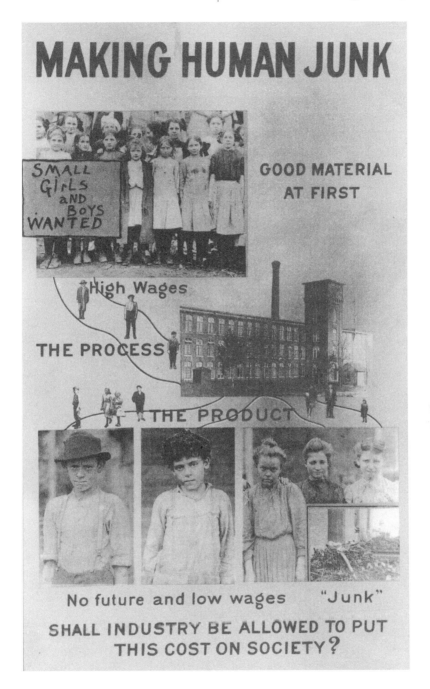

right of his images draw us in, and he often experienced such pain on his subjects' behalf that he had to administer himself "spiritual antiseptic," as he put it. But he also believed in the agency of workers and tried to connect them to their work, giving his subjects clear relationships to their environments within the photographs. When an interviewer asked him, "Do the workers you deal with understand what you are doing?" he answered, "I have found many so-called 'human machines' who had a genuine interest in the finer things of life. It is perfectly possible to direct that interest to their jobs."

He sought to personalize his subjects, seeking stories and context. This commitment to images in context made for difficult work. Where Jacob Riis would burst into buildings unannounced, Hine would disguise himself as a Bible salesman or a fire inspector to gain access to factories. His captioned photographs were then used in surveys and pamphlets, allowing words to reinforce images, and Hine to use advertising styles against advertisers, as in "Making Human Junk." He saw the potential of image-texts: "Reinforce [the photo-graph] with one of those social pen-pictures," he said, and "what a lever we have for the social uplift."

In 1910 Hine observed: "My child labor photos have already set the authorities to work to see if 'such things can be possible.'" Numbers of child workers only really declined af-ter the 1933 National Recovery Administration codes and the 1938 Fair Labor Standards Act. But by 1912, laws had changed in 34 states and the government had created a Children's Bureau. In 1916 Congress restricted the employment of children under four-teen and by 1928 all states had compulsory education laws. In 1929 the NCLC chairman commented that Hine's work "was more responsible than all other efforts in bringing the need to public attention." Before Hine, he added, the problem was "intellectually but not emotionally recognized."

Further reading: Alan Trachtenberg, *Reading American Photographs* (1989); *America and Lewis Hine* (1997).

From The People's Party Platform

1892

"We are today confronted by portentous indications . . . that this great experiment on which the last hopes of the race depend, is to prove . . . a disastrous failure." So Edward Bellamy warned the People's Party, in an open letter of 1892. "Let us bear in mind," he added, "that if it be a failure it will be a final failure. There can be . . . no fresh continents to offer virgin fields for new ventures." Bellamy's utopian novel *Looking Backward* (1888) had imagined a "great experiment": a society organized on a cooperative basis without class conflict or poverty. The novel launched a political movement, Nationalism, and its readers established "Bellamy" clubs for the discussion and implementation of his ideas: an end to pollution, sex discrimination, and poverty, and the establishment of a technocracy. There were 162 clubs across 27 states by 1890. But as the 1890 New York State election campaign approached, the Nationalist Clubs in New York divided into two groups: anti-socialists formed the Commonwealth Party, and socialist sympathizers invited unions to nominate a labor candidate. The movement lost force, especially when the two mainstream parties embraced aspects of the People's Party platform.

The People's Party (also known as the Populist Party) was organized in early 1892, to represent workers against the interests of railroads, bankers, and corporations. It attracted support from farmers in southern and midwestern states who felt victimized by the new industrial system, and was the most successful of the era's many agrarian political movements. At its July 1892 National Convention, the Party ratified its platform. Written by Ignatius Donnelly (1831–1901), an organizer with the Minnesota Farmers' Alliance, the platform adapted some of Bellamy's ideas in *Looking Backward.* Two years before he wrote the People's Party preamble and platform, Donnelly had written a dystopian novel, *Caesar's Column.* Set in 1988, it included Bellamy-like scenes of a corrupt capitalist society, only this time set in the future. The novel's protagonist eventually flees the American oligarchy and forms an agrarian community in Africa, led by a government called The People. Aspects of the People's Party platform echo its fictional constitution.

During the election of 1894, the People's Party lost control of the western states it had won in 1892, and the Democratic Party absorbed most of its members in 1896. But many of the Party's ideas—which included the abolition of national banks, a graduated income tax, an eight-hour workday, and civil service reform—entered the political mainstream and set the Progressive-era reform agenda. Others eventually appeared as part of Franklin D. Roosevelt's 1930s New Deal.

The conditions which surround us best justify our cooperation; we meet in the midst of a nation brought to the verge of moral, political, and material ruin. Corruption dominates the ballot-box, the Legislatures, the Congress, and touches even the ermine of the bench. The people are demoralized; most of the States have been compelled to isolate the voters at the polling places to prevent universal intimidation and bribery. The newspapers are largely subsidized or muzzled, public opinion silenced, business prostrated, homes covered with mortgages, labor impoverished, and the land concentrating in the hands of capitalists. The urban workmen are denied the right to organize for self-protection, imported pauperized labor beats down their wages, a hireling standing army, unrecognized by our laws, is established to shoot them down, and they are rapidly degenerating into European conditions. The fruits of the toil of millions are badly stolen to build up colossal fortunes for a few, unprecedented in the history of mankind; and the possessors of these, in turn, despise the Republic and endanger liberty. From the same prolific womb of governmental injustice we breed the two great classes—tramps and millionaires. The national power to create money is appropriated to enrich bondholders; a vast public debt payable in legal-tender currency has been funded into gold-bearing bonds, thereby adding millions to the burdens of the people.

Silver, which has been accepted as coin since the dawn of history, has been demonetized to add to the purchasing power of gold by decreasing the value of all forms of property as well as human labor, and the supply of currency is purposely abridged to fatten usurers, bankrupt enterprise, and enslave industry. A vast conspiracy against mankind has been organized on two continents, and it is rapidly taking possession of the world. If not met and overthrown at once it forebodes terrible social convulsions, the destruction of civilization, or the establishment of an absolute despotism.

We have witnessed for more than a quarter of a century the struggles of the two great political parties for power and plunder, while grievous wrongs have been inflicted upon the suffering people. We charge that the controlling influences dominating both these parties have permitted the existing dreadful conditions to develop without serious effort to prevent or restrain them. Neither do they now promise us any substantial reform. They have agreed together to ignore, in the coming campaign, every issue but one. They propose to drown the outcries of a plundered people with the uproar of a sham battle over the tariff, so that capitalists, corporations, national banks, rings, trusts, watered stock, the demonetization of silver and the oppressions of the usurers may all be lost sight of. They propose to sacrifice our homes, lives, and children on the altar of mammon; to destroy the multitude in order to secure corruption funds from the millionaires.

Assembled on the anniversary of the birthday of the nation, and filled with the spirit of the grand general and chief who established our independence, we seek to restore the government of the Republic to the hands of the "plain people," with which class it originated. We assert our purposes to be identical with the purposes of the National Constitution; to form a more perfect union and establish justice, insure domestic tranquility, provide for the common defense, promote the general welfare, and secure the blessings of liberty for ourselves and our posterity . . . Our country finds itself confronted by conditions for which there is not precedent in the history of the world; our annual agricultural productions amount to billions of dollars in value, which must, within a few weeks or months, be exchanged for billions of dollars' worth of commodities consumed in their production; the existing currency supply is wholly inadequate to make this exchange; the results are falling prices, the formation of combines and rings, the impoverishment of the producing class. We pledge ourselves that if given power we will labor to correct these evils by wise and reasonable legislation, in accordance with the terms of our platform. We believe that the power of government—in other words, of the people—should be expanded (as in the case of the postal service) as rapidly and as far as the good sense of an intelligent people and the teaching of experience shall justify, to the end that oppression, injustice, and poverty shall eventually cease in the land. . . .

We declare, therefore—First.—That the union of the labor forces of the United States this day consummated shall be permanent and perpetual; may its spirit enter into all hearts for the salvation of the republic and the uplifting of mankind. Second.—Wealth belongs to him who creates it, and every dollar taken from industry without an equivalent is robbery. "If any will not work, neither shall he eat." The interests of rural and civil labor are the same; their enemies are identical. Third.—We believe that the time has come when the railroad corporations will either own the people or the people must own the railroads; and should the government enter upon the work of owning and managing all railroads, we should favor an amendment to the constitution by which all persons engaged in the government service shall be placed under a civil-service regulation of the most rigid character, so as to prevent the increase of the power of the national administration by the use of such additional government employees.

FINANCE.—We demand a national currency, safe, sound, and flexible issued by the general government only, a full legal tender for all debts, public and private, and that without the use of banking corporations; a just, equitable, and efficient means of distribution direct to the people, at a tax not to exceed 2 per cent, per annum, to be provided as set forth in the sub-treasury plan of the Farmers' Alliance, or a better system; also by payments in discharge of its obligations for public improvements. We demand free and unlimited coinage of silver and gold at the present legal ratio of 16 to 1. We demand that the amount of circulating medium be speedily increased to not less than $50 per capita. We demand a graduated income tax. We believe that the money of the country should be kept as much as possible in the hands of the people, and hence we demand that all State and national revenues shall be limited to the necessary expenses of the government, economically and honestly administered. We demand that postal savings banks be established by the government for the safe deposit of the earnings of the people and to facilitate exchange. TRANSPORTATION.—Transportation being a means of exchange and a public necessity, the government should own and operate the railroads in the interest of the people. The telegraph and telephone, like the post-office system, being a necessity for the transmission of news, should be owned and operated by the government in the interest of the people. LAND.—The land, including all the natural sources of wealth, is the heritage of the people, and should not be monopolized for speculative purposes, and alien ownership of land should be prohibited. All land now held by railroads and other corporations in excess of their actual needs, and all lands now owned by aliens should be reclaimed by the government and held for actual settlers only.

From Food and Drugs Act *and*
Meat Inspection Act

1906

By 1905 the battle over pure-food regulation had reached a stalemate. Some 190 measures had been introduced since 1879, but pro-regulation campaigners and politicians remained at an impasse. The Food and Drugs Act and Meat Inspection Act of 1906 were enacted after a barrage of articles on the food and drug industry. By the late 1890s, the owners of low-cost, high-distribution magazines had discovered that they could boost sales by publishing sensational exposés of corruption and urban conditions. Ida Tarbell's *History of the Standard Oil Company* (1902) and Lincoln Steffens's *The Shame of Cities* (1904) were two of the most important exposés. Each of the main muckraking periodicals had expanded circulation to around 750,000 by 1905, and in 1904 Upton Sinclair was hired by the popular socialist weekly *Appeal to Reason* to research conditions in Chicago's stockyards and meatpacking districts. He spent seven weeks in Chicago and wrote *The Jungle,* which was serialized in *Appeal to Reason* in 1905.

The novel created a sense of crisis, generated support for regulatory reform, and united diverse interest groups. Ordinary consumers joined Progressive reformers and sent letters to President Theodore Roosevelt. Sinclair attended conferences on the Meat Inspection Act. Senate voting patterns shifted, and it became costly for opponents to continue blocking reform. The Pure Food Bill was taken out of committees, and Roosevelt sent a commission to Chicago. Their findings echoed and confirmed Sinclair's detailed descriptions in *The Jungle.* Roosevelt read the commission's report and released the first pages to Congress, demanding the passage of the bills. They passed, and more than sixty years later, Sinclair went to the White House again, this time to watch Lyndon Johnson sign the 1967 Wholesome Meat Act.

The only detail in Sinclair's novel that Roosevelt's commission couldn't confirm was his description of factory workers who are swallowed up in vats of lard. Sinclair had perhaps meant this as a metaphor for the all-consuming capitalist system, and in fact his main objective was to provoke outrage over working conditions. But a producer society had become a consumer society: as Sinclair dryly observed, he'd aimed at the nation's heart and hit its stomach.

Federal Food and Drugs Act

AN ACT For preventing the manufacture, sale, or transportation of adulterated or misbranded or poisonous or deleterious foods, drugs, medicines, and liquors, and for, IN THE CASE OF FOOD:

FIRST. If any substance has been mixed and packed with it so as to reduce or lower or injuriously affect its quality or strength.

SECOND. If any substance has been substituted wholly or in part for the article.

THIRD. If any valuable constituent of the article has been wholly or in part abstracted.

FOURTH. If it be mixed, colored, powdered, coated, or stained in a manner whereby damage or inferiority is concealed.

FIFTH. If it contain any added poisonous or other added deleterious ingredient which may render such article injurious to health: *Provided,* That when in the preparation of food products for shipment they are preserved by any external application applied in such manner that the preservative is necessarily removed mechanically, or by maceration in water, or otherwise, and directions for the removal of said preservative shall be printed on the covering or the package, the provisions of this Act shall be construed as applying only when said products are ready for consumption.

SIXTH. If it consists in whole or in part of a filthy, decomposed, or putrid animal or vegetable substance, or any portion of an animal unfit for food, whether manufactured or not, or if it is the product of a diseased animal, or one that has died otherwise than by slaughter.

Meat Inspection Act

For the purpose of preventing the use in commerce of meat and meat food products which are adulterated, the Secretary shall cause to be made, by inspectors appointed for that purpose, an examination and inspection of all cattle, sheep, swine, goats, horses, mules, and other equines before they shall be allowed to enter into any slaughtering, packing, meat-canning, rendering, or similar establishment . . . and all cattle, sheep, swine, goats, horses, mules, and other equines found on such inspection to show symptoms of disease shall be set apart and slaughtered separately from all other . . . and when so slaughtered the carcasses . . . shall be subject to a careful examination and inspection. The Secretary shall cause to be made by inspectors appointed for that purpose a post mortem examination and inspection of the carcasses and parts thereof of all cattle, sheep, swine, goats, horses, mules, and other equines to be prepared at any slaughtering, meat-canning, salting, packing, rendering, or similar establishment in any State . . . which are capable of use as human food; and the carcasses and parts thereof of all such animals found to be not adulterated shall be marked . . . as "Inspected and passed"; and . . . inspectors shall label . . . "Inspected and condemned" all carcasses and parts . . . of animals found to be adulterated; and all carcasses . . . condemned shall be destroyed for food purposes by the . . . establishment in the presence of an inspector, and the Secretary may remove inspectors from any such establishment which fails to . . . destroy any such condemned carcass.

Statement to the Court

1918

In 1894, the labor activist Eugene V. Debs (1855–1926) was jailed for his involvement in the Pullman strike. He emerged from prison a changed man, embraced socialism, helped form the Industrial Workers of the World, and began to cite examples of prophets and martyrs. "I am not gifted with prophetic vision, and yet I see the shadows vanishing," he observed. During one of his speeches in 1908, an audience member purportedly cried out, "There he is . . . the living link between God and man . . . Here is the God consciousness come down to earth."

In 1918 Debs seemed on the brink of martyrdom. On June 16, he arrived in Canton, Ohio, after a series of highly publicized antiwar speeches. There he spoke to a crowd of perhaps 1500, on a stage stripped of the American flag, and called upon the spirits of earlier dissenters. The speech marked the end of an era: membership in the Socialist party had grown to 100,000 but the First World War was dividing the international movement. Debs knew it was likely he'd be jailed for the speech but told the crowd, "They can not put the Socialist movement in jail." He was arrested on violation of the 1917 Espionage Act, one of more than 450 conscientious objectors imprisoned under this legislation.

Refusing any defense witnesses at his trial, held in Cleveland, Debs announced that he would plead his own cause to the jury. He used the plea to set himself in a tradition of patriotic protest (Thomas Jefferson, Tom Paine, and the abolitionists). The motion for a new trial was overruled, and in his last statement, reprinted here, Debs speaks as a prophet—from the perspective of the future. He mocks the trial, offering no evidence or legal arguments. The speech ranks with John Brown's "Statement to the Court" (1859), Emma Goldman's "Address to the Jury" (1917), and Bartolomeo Vanzetti's "Speech to the Court" (1927) as one of the greatest courtroom speeches of all time.

Debs was sentenced to ten years in prison and served nearly three. In 1920 he ran for United States President from the Atlanta Penitentiary and received a million votes. In one final irony, he was released on Christmas Day, 1921. His antiwar activism, along with that of Randolph Bourne, would be an inspiration for activists during the Vietnam war.

Your honor, years ago I recognized my kinship with all living beings, and I made up my mind that I was not one bit better than the meanest on earth. I said then, and I say now, that while there is a lower class, I am in it, and while there is a criminal element I am of it, and while there is a soul in prison, I am not free.

I listened to all that was said in this court in support and justification of this prosecution, but my mind remains unchanged. I look upon it as a despotic enactment in flagrant conflict with democratic principles and with the spirit of free institutions.

I have no fault to find with this court or with the trial. Everything in connection with this case has been conducted upon a dignified plane, and in a respectful and decent spirit.

Your honor, I have stated in this court that I am opposed to the social system in which we live; that I believe in a fundamental change—but if possible by peaceable and orderly means.

Let me call your attention to the fact this morning that in this system 5% of our people own and control two-thirds of our wealth; 65% of the people, embracing the working class who produce all wealth, have but 5% to show for it.

Standing here this morning, I recall my boyhood. At fourteen I went to work in a railroad shop; at sixteen I was firing a freight engine on a railroad. I remember all the hardships and privations of that earlier day, and from that time until now my heart has been with the working class. I could have been in Congress long ago. I have preferred to go to prison.

In the struggle—the unceasing struggle—between the toilers and producers and their exploiters, I have tried, as best I might, to serve those among whom I was born, and with whom I expect to share my lot to the end of my days.

I am thinking this morning of the men in the mills and the factories; of the men in the mines and on the railroads. I am thinking of the women who for a paltry wage are compelled to work out their barren lives; of the little children who in this system are robbed of their childhood and in their tender years are seized in the remorseless grasp of mammon and forced into the industrial dungeons, there to feed the monster machines while they themselves are being starved and stunted, body and soul. I see them dwarfed and diseased and their little lives broken and blasted because in this high noon of Christian civilization money is still so much more important than the flesh and blood of childhood. Gold is God and rules the affairs of men. The little girls, and there are a million of them in this country—this the most favored land beneath the bending skies, a land in which we have vast areas of rich and fertile soil, material resources in inexhaustible abundance, the most marvelous productive machinery on earth, millions of eager workers ready to apply their labor to that machinery to produce an abundance for every man, woman and child—and if there are still many millions of our people who are the victims of poverty, whose lives are a ceaseless struggle all the way from youth to age, until at last death comes to their rescue and stills the aching heart, and lulls the victims to dreamless sleep, it is not the fault of the Almighty, it can't be charged to nature; it is due entirely to an outgrown social system that ought to be abolished not only in the interest of the working class, but in the interest of a higher humanity.

When I think of these little children—the girls that are in the textile mills of all description in the east, in the cotton factories of the south—when I think of them at work in a vitiated atmosphere, when I think of them at work when they ought to be at play or at school, when I think that when they do grow up, if they live long enough to approach the marriage state, they are unfit for it. Their nerves are worn out, their tissue is exhausted, their vitality is spent. They have been fed to industry. Their lives have been coined into gold. Their offspring are born tired. That is why there are so many failures in modern life.

Your honor, the 5% of the people that I have made reference to constitute that element that absolutely rules our country. They privately own all our necessities. They wear no crowns; they wield no sceptres; they sit upon no thrones; and yet they are our economic masters and political rulers.

I believe, your honor, in common with all Socialists, that this nation ought to own and control its industries. I believe, as all Socialists do, that all things that are jointly needed and used ought to be jointly owned—that industry, the basis of life, instead of being the private property of the few and operated for their enrichment, ought to be the common property of all, democratically administered in the interest of all.

John D. Rockefeller has today an income of sixty million dollars a year, five million dollars a month, two hundred thousand dollars a day. He does not produce a penny of it. I make no attack on Mr. Rockefeller personally. I do not in the least dislike him. If he were in need and it were in my power to serve him, I should serve him as gladly as I would any other human being. I have no quarrel with Mr. Rockefeller personally, nor with any other capitalist. I am simply opposing a social order in which it is possible for one man who does absolutely nothing that is useful to amass a fortune of hundreds of millions of dollars, while millions of men and women who work all of the days of their lives secure barely enough for an existence.

This order of things cannot always endure. I have registered my protest against it. I recognize the feebleness of my effort, but, fortunately, I am not alone. There are multiplied thousands of others who, like myself, have come to realize that before we may truly enjoy the blessings of civilized life, we must reorganize society upon a mutual and cooperative basis; and to this end we have organized a great economic and political movement that spreads over the face of all the earth.

There are today upwards of sixty millions of Socialists, loyal, devoted adherents to this cause, regardless of nationality, race, creed, color, or sex. They are all making common cause. They are all spreading the propaganda of the new social order. They are waiting, watching, and working through all the hours of the day and the night. They are still in a minority. They have learned how to be patient and to bide their time. They feel—they know, indeed—that the time is coming, in spite of all opposition, all persecution, when this emancipating gospel will spread among all the peoples, and when this minority will become the triumphant majority and, sweeping into power, inaugurate the greatest social and economic change in history.

In that day we shall have the universal commonwealth . . . the harmonious cooperation of every nation with every other nation on earth.

Your honor, in a local paper yesterday there was some editorial exultation about my prospective imprisonment. I do not resent it in the least. I can understand it perfectly. In the same paper there appears an editorial that has in it a hint of the wrong to which I have been trying to call attention. *(Reading):* A Senator of the United States receives a salary of $7,500—$45,000 for the six years for which he is elected. One of the candidates for Senator from a state adjoining Ohio is reported to have spent through his committee $150,000 to secure the nomination. For advertising he spent $35,000, for printing $30,000; for traveling expenses, $10,000 and the rest in ways known to political managers.

The theory is that public office is as open to a poor man as to a rich man. One may easily imagine, however, how slight a chance one of ordinary resources would have in a contest against this man who was willing to spend more than three times his six year's salary merely to secure a nomination. Were these conditions to hold in every state, the Senate would soon become again what it was once held to be—a rich man's club.

Campaign expenses have been the subject of much restrictive legislation in recent years, but it has not always reached the mark. The authors of primary reform have accomplished some of the things they set out to do, but they have not yet taken the bank roll out of politics.

They will never take it out of politics, they never can take it out of politics, in this system.

Your honor, I wish to make acknowledgment of my thanks to the counsel for the defense. They have not only defended me with exceptional legal ability, but with a personal attachment and devotion of which I am deeply sensible, and which I can never forget.

Your honor, I ask no mercy and I plead for no immunity. I realize that finally the right must prevail. I never so clearly comprehended as now the great struggle between the powers of greed and exploitation on the one hand and upon the other the rising hosts of industrial freedom and social justice.

I can see the dawn of the better day for humanity. The people are awakening. In due time they will and must come to their own.

When the mariner, sailing over tropic seas, looks for relief from his weary watch, he turns his eyes toward the southern cross, burning luridly above the tempest-vexed ocean. As the midnight approaches, the southern cross begins to bend, the whirling worlds change their places, and with starry finger-points the Almighty marks the passage of time upon the dial of the universe, and though no bell may beat the glad tidings, the look-out knows that the midnight is passing and that relief and rest are close at hand.

Let the people everywhere take heart of hope, for the cross is bending, the midnight is passing, and joy cometh with the morning.

> "He's true to God who's true to man;
> wherever wrong is done,
> To the humblest and the weakest,
> 'neath the all-beholding sun.
> That wrong is also done to us, and
> they are slaves most base,
> Whose love of right is for themselves
> and not for all their race."

Your honor, I thank you, and I thank all of this court for their courtesy and their kindness, which I shall remember always.

I am prepared to receive your sentence.

Farewell, Capitalist America!

1929

In 1921, William Haywood (1869–1928), or Big Bill Haywood, a founding member and leader of the Industrial Workers of the World (IWW), bid farewell to America. In the passage excerpted here from his autobiography, he addresses the Statue of Liberty from a ship in New York's harbor. Haywood had declared the First World War a capitalist war fought by workers, and argued that treason against country was better than treason against class, though the IWW took no official position on the war and didn't obstruct the draft. In September 1917, Department of Justice agents raided forty-eight IWW meeting halls across the country. A total of 165 IWW leaders were accused of conspiring to encourage draft resistance and desertion, and arrested as violators of the 1917 Espionage Act. In April 1918, 101 of those leaders went on trial. It ended after five months, the longest criminal trial in American history to that date, and Haywood was sentenced to twenty years in prison. He raised bail but lost his appeals and, awaiting the Supreme Court's final decision on his case in April 1921, he accepted an invitation from the Bolshevik government to visit the Soviet Union, jumped bail, and fled to revolutionary Russia. He remained there until his death.

The night before Haywood left America for the Soviet Union he danced with a woman at an IWW event. When she tried to rejoin her husband, he reportedly begged her: "Stick with me. Don't leave me." Feeling betrayed by his flight, it was perhaps what his friends in the organized labor movement wanted to say to *him:* the public associated the IWW with Haywood and, though it led more workers out on strike during the 1920s than in the previous decade, the 1918 espionage trials and Haywood's flight crushed the organization.

Immediately after the Russian Revolution, Harrison George began a pamphlet entitled *Red Dawn.* He vividly portrayed the historic development of the Russian Revolution. I had it published in February 1918. Many thousands of copies were distributed. But when the new administration took over the headquarters in 1920, it reflected the opposition which had developed in the I.W.W. against the state character of the Soviets, and the remainder of George's pamphlet was destroyed.

About this time a lengthy letter reached us addressed to the I.W.W. by the Communist International. This letter spoke of the situation of capitalism after the imperialist war, outlined the points in common held by the I.W.W. and the

Communists, warned of the coming attacks on the workers, pictured the futility of reformism, analyzed the capitalist state and the rôle of the dictatorship of the proletariat and told how the Soviet state of workers and peasants was constructed. Such basic questions as "political" and "industrial" action, democratic centralization, the nature of the social revolution and of future society were gone into thoroughly. After I had finished reading it, I called Ralph Chaplin over to my desk and said to him: "Here is what we have been dreaming about; here is the I.W.W. all feathered out!"

The receipt of this letter was a momentous circumstance in my somewhat eventful life. While it was addressed to the I.W.W. as an organization, I felt, as I knew many other members did, that it was a tribute to ourselves, as each had helped to build this class conscious movement.

On July 4th, 1920, I spoke at Renton Park, Seattle, where an enormous crowd had gathered. After the meeting I was introduced to one of Wesley Everest's closest friends. He had served with Everest in the trenches and had been so badly injured in the back that it was impossible for him to move without assistance. The income from the Seattle meeting was something over $6,000.

From Seattle I went to Portland, Ore., where another large meeting was held. George F. Vanderveer, the attorney, was the chairman. At this meeting considerable over $1,000 was raised for the defense.

As soon as the consolidation of the Communist Party in the United States was effected, I became a member. John Martin was elected secretary of the General Defense Committee.

I came on to New York City and there urged members of the Central Executive Committee and other leaders who were known to me that some effort must be made to get the Party or an organization representing it out from underground, giving it as my opinion that little would be accomplished until we could freely publish our papers and take a place on the public platform.

I spoke at several meetings for the defense, the last of which was held in the Rand School. At this meeting two of my codefendants, who were out on bail, George Andreychine and Charles Ashleigh, were also speakers.

The suggestion had been made to me that I should go to Russia. There was little hope entertained of a favorable decision from the United States Supreme Court, and my friends thought it would be an unnecessary sacrifice for me to spend the rest of my life in prison. When I was told that I should go to Russia, I said: "It may not be so easy for me to get away, but I will make the effort."

I was booked with other friends on the S.S. *Oscar II,* which had been Henry Ford's "peace ship." After bidding my friends farewell, I stopped in the home of a Lettish family—my last night in the United States. From there I went early in the morning to a hotel in Hoboken where I had breakfast. I then went to the wharf and direct to the boat where I showed to the inspector what purported to be a passport. I went aboard and down into the hold where a berth had been reserved. I remained there until the ship was under way. When I came on deck we were passing the Statue of Liberty. Saluting the old hag with her uplifted torch, I said: "Good-by, you've had your back turned on me too long. I am now going to the land of freedom."

One of the stewards, who recognized me, was an I.W.W., and we were able to get better fare than is usually served to steerage passengers.

We traveled to Riga through battle-scarred country, marked with cemeteries, trenches, deserted fortifications and endless miles of barbed wire entanglements.

At Riga we were loaded into box cars. The train was guarded by Latvian soldiers until we reached the border. As we crossed the Russian line, there was a mighty burst of cheers and singing of the "International." The train moved along like a red flame. Red bunting, red banners, and red kerchiefs were flying to the breeze.

When we landed in the ancient city of Moscow, now again the capital of Russia, we were met at the station with automobiles and driven at once to the hotel. Michael Borodin asked me if I would like to go to the Kremlin to meet Lenin. I was suffering from diabetes and very tired after the long trip, and I told him I first needed a rest.

Some days later an interview was arranged for me with Comrade Lenin. It is not my purpose to describe here his personality or our meeting. I will just mention one phase of our conversation before closing this book.

I asked Comrade Lenin "if the industries of the Soviet Republic are run and administered by the workers?"

His reply was: "Yes, Comrade Haywood, that is Communism."

From Nickel and Dimed

2001

In 2003, the social critic Barbara Ehrenreich (b. 1941) had what she recently called an "Upton Sinclair moment"—referring to Sinclair's sense that his protest novel *The Jungle* (1906) had taken on a life of its own. Ehrenreich was attending a performance of a play based on *Nickel and Dimed:* "The reception beforehand was full of terrific, tough, working-class women of all ethnicities. I realized, hey, I've contributed to a working-class protest culture!" She also sets herself in the "Jacob Riis tradition," noting: "I'm with Riis . . . a big part of the problem is the ignorance of the non-poor."

Like Sinclair and Riis, Ehrenreich is part of an investigative reporting tradition. In 1999 and 2000 she chose to live as a low-skilled worker, earning the minimum wage as a waitress, a cleaner, a nursing-home aide, and a Wal-Mart associate. She described the experience in her bestselling book, *Nickel and Dimed,* which is also in the exposé tradition of Michael Harrington's *The Other America* (1962). Ehrenreich worked with Harrington in the 1980s, and in an interview cited his book as an influence. *Nickel and Dimed* shares observations on the global economy with Kevin Bales's *Disposable People* (1999), too, especially when Ehrenreich describes workers used like "so many disposable napkins."

Ehrenreich's experience as a minimum-wage worker was a journey: "I am always prepared to be surprised by my research and ready to go where it takes me, even if that doesn't fit with my starting assumptions and convictions," she says. She included her personal responses to the experience in the book after thinking about her feelings and deciding, "Hell, this is data too, I'm going to include it." But she struggles with a sense that too much "empathy" is bad for protest writers: "You can get too warm and cuddly. I need to create a distance." So she tries to write with "irony, sarcasm, and other forms of bitter humor." Like many protest writers, she considers language a weapon, remarking, "Sometimes I'm melodramatic enough to think of myself as a warrior."

Ehrenreich's first-person voice in *Nickel and Dimed* doesn't allow for much extended analysis, and she says that if she had been capable of offering documentary films or third-person novels, she might have done so. But on the other hand she was aiming her book at the general public, not lawmakers: "I had no specific policy proposals to make. They've been made so many times—universal health insurance, subsidized child care and housing, raising the minimum wage." In addition, Ehrenreich adds, "the first-person, present-tense narrative seemed right for what I had to report, and I ended up enjoying the immediacy of it."

Do the owners have any idea of the misery that goes into rendering their homes motel-perfect? Would they be bothered if they did know, or would they take a sadistic pride in what they have purchased—boasting to dinner guests, for example, that their floors are cleaned only with the purest of fresh human tears? In one of my few exchanges with an owner, a pert muscular woman whose desk reveals that she works part-time as a personal trainer, I am vacuuming and she notices the sweat. "That's a real workout, isn't it?" she observes, not unkindly, and actually offers me a glass of water, the only such offer I ever encounter. Flouting the rule against the ingestion of anything while inside a house, I take it, leaving an inch undrunk to avoid the awkwardness of a possible refill offer. "I tell all my clients," the trainer informs me, "'If you want to be fit, just fire your cleaning lady and do it yourself.'" "Ho ho," is all I say, since we're not just chatting in the gym together and I can't explain that this form of exercise is totally asymmetrical, brutally repetitive, and as likely to destroy the musculoskeletal structure as to strengthen it.

Self-restraint becomes more of a challenge when the owner of a million-dollar condo (that's my guess anyway, because it has three floors and a wide-angle view of the fabled rockbound coast) who is (according to a framed photograph on the wall) an acquaintance of the real Barbara Bush takes me into the master bathroom to explain the difficulties she's been having with the shower stall. Seems its marble walls have been "bleeding" onto the brass fixtures, and can I scrub the grouting extra hard? That's not your marble bleeding, I want to tell her, it's the worldwide working class—the people who quarried the marble, wove your Persian rugs until they went blind, harvested the apples in your lovely fall-themed dining room centerpiece, smelted the steel for the nails, drove the trucks, put up this building, and now bend and squat and sweat to clean it . . .

Let's talk about shit, for example. It happens, as the bumper sticker says, and it happens to a cleaning person every day. The first time I encountered a shit-stained toilet as a maid, I was shocked by the sense of unwanted intimacy. A few hours ago, some well-fed butt was straining away on this toilet seat, and now here I am wiping up after it. For those who have never cleaned a really dirty toilet, I should explain that there are three kinds of shit stains. There are remnants of landslides running down the inside of toilet bowls. There are the splash-back remains on the underside of toilet seats. And, perhaps most repulsively, there's sometimes a crust of brown on the rim of a toilet seat, where a turd happened to collide on its dive to the water. You don't want to know this? Well, it's not something I would have chosen to dwell on myself, but the different kinds of stains require different cleaning approaches. One prefers those that are interior to the toilet bowl, since they can be attacked by brush, which is a kind of action-at-a-distance weapon. And one dreads the crusts on the seats, especially when they require the intervention of a Dobie as well as a rag.

Or we might talk about that other great nemesis of the bathroom cleaner—pubic hair. I don't know what it is about the American upper class, but they seem to be shedding their pubic hair at an alarming rate. You find it in quantity in shower stalls, bathtubs, Jacuzzis, drains, and even, unaccountably, in sinks. Once I spent fifteen minutes crouching in a huge four-person Jacuzzi, maddened by the effort of finding the dark little coils camouflaged against the eggplant-colored ceramic background but fascinated by the image of the pubes of the economic elite, which must by this time be completely bald . . .

In the summer of 2000 I returned—permanently, I have every reason to hope—to my customary place in the socioeconomic spectrum. I go to restaurants, often far finer ones than the places where I worked, and sit down at a table. I sleep in hotel rooms that someone else has cleaned and shop in stores that others will tidy when I leave. To go from the bottom 20 percent to the top 20 percent is to enter a magical world where needs are met, problems are solved, almost without any intermediate effort. If you want to get somewhere fast, you hail a cab. If your aged parents have grown tiresome or incontinent, you put them away where others will deal with their dirty diapers and dementia. If you are part of the upper-middle-class majority that employs a maid or maid service, you return from work to find the house miraculously restored to order—the toilet bowls shit-free and gleaming, the socks that you left on the floor levitated back to their normal dwelling place. Here, sweat is a metaphor for hard work, but seldom its consequence. Hundreds of little things get done, reliably and routinely every day, without anyone's seeming to do them.

The top 20 percent routinely exercises other, far more consequential forms of power in the world. This stratum, which contains what I have termed in an earlier book the "professional-managerial class," is the home of our decision makers, opinion shapers, culture creators—our professors, lawyers, executives, entertainers, politicians, judges, writers, producers, and editors. When they speak, they are listened to. When they complain, someone usually scurries to correct the problem and apologize for it. If they complain often enough, someone far below them in wealth and influence may be chastised or even fired. Political power, too, is concentrated within the top 20 percent, since its members are far more likely than the poor—or even the middle class—to discern the all-too-tiny distinctions between candidates that can make it seem worthwhile to contribute, participate, and vote. In all these ways, the affluent exert inordinate power over the lives of the less affluent, and especially over the lives of the poor, determining what public services will be available, if any, what minimum wage, what laws governing the treatment of labor.

So it is alarming, upon returning to the upper middle class from a sojourn, however artificial and temporary, among the poor, to find the rabbit hole close so suddenly and completely behind me. You were *where,* doing *what?* Some odd optical property of our highly polarized and unequal society makes the poor almost invisible to their economic superiors. The poor can see the affluent easily enough—on television, for example, or on the covers of magazines. But the affluent rarely see the poor or, if they do catch sight of them in some public space, rarely know what they're seeing, since—thanks to consignment stores and, yes, Wal-Mart—the poor are usually able to disguise themselves as members of the more comfortable classes. Forty years ago the hot journalistic topic was the "discovery of the poor" in their inner-city and Appalachian "pockets of poverty." Today you are more likely to find commentary on their "disappearance," either as a supposed demographic reality or as a shortcoming of the middle-class imagination . . .

I grew up hearing over and over, to the point of tedium, that "hard work" was the secret of success: "Work hard and you'll get ahead" or "It's hard work that got us where we are." No one ever said that you could work hard—harder even than you ever thought possible—and still find yourself sinking ever deeper into poverty and debt.

When poor single mothers had the option of remaining out of the labor force on welfare, the middle and upper middle class tended to view them with a certain impatience, if not disgust. The welfare poor were excoriated for their laziness, their persistence in reproducing in unfavorable circumstances, their presumed addictions, and above all for their "dependency." Here they were, content to live off "government handouts" instead of seeking "self-sufficiency," like everyone else, through a job. They needed to get their act together, learn how to wind an alarm clock, get out there and get to work. But now that government has largely withdrawn its "handouts," now that the overwhelming majority of the poor are out there toiling in Wal-Mart or Wendy's—well, what are we to think of them? Disapproval and condescension no longer apply, so what outlook makes sense?

Guilt, you may be thinking warily. Isn't that what we're supposed to feel? But guilt doesn't go anywhere near far enough; the appropriate emotion is shame—shame at our *own* dependency, in this case, on the underpaid labor of others. When someone works for less pay than she can live on—when, for example, she goes hungry so that you can eat more cheaply and conveniently— then she has made a great sacrifice for you, she has made you a gift of some part of her abilities, her health, and her life. The "working poor," as they are approvingly termed, are in fact the major philanthropists of our society. They neglect their own children so that the children of others will be cared for; they live in substandard housing so that other homes will be shiny and perfect;

they endure privation so that inflation will be low and stock prices high. To be a member of the working poor is to be an anonymous donor, a nameless benefactor, to everyone else. As Gail, one of my restaurant coworkers put it, "you give and you give."

Someday, of course—and I will make no predictions as to exactly when— they are bound to tire of getting so little in return and to demand to be paid what they're worth. There'll be a lot of anger when that day comes, and strikes and disruption. But the sky will not fall, and we will all be better off for it in the end.

STRANGE FRUIT

Against
Lynching

From Southern Horrors

1892

Mobs lynched 4,743 people between 1882 and 1968, 70 percent of them black. Three men killed in March 1892 were friends of the African American journalist and writer Ida B. Wells (1862–1931), and this proximity to violence changed her perspective: previously she had accepted that anger about rape led to lynchings, but the death of her friends opened her eyes "to what lynching really was." She began to investigate the 728 lynchings that had taken place between 1882 and 1892 and wrote an editorial for the Memphis newspaper *Free Speech,* advising blacks to go west. Some two thousand blacks left Memphis.

Her editorial challenged the "old threadbare lie that Negro men assault white women." Wells was the first anti-lynching activist to discuss interracial sex, and outraged Memphis whites attacked the *Free Speech* office. Wells was in New York and responded by writing the pamphlet *Southern Horrors,* using the pen name "Exiled." The pamphlet is a combination of journalism, sociology, sarcastic sermonizing, and call to arms. It appeals to the press and pulpit, connects lynching to slavery, and advocates interracial marriage. Wells writes like a prosecutor, including times, places, and names for individual lynchings. She believed, as she said later, that figures could "speak for themselves." Unembellished fact countered the lies of the white press, and she summed up this approach in 1895: "Out of their own mouths shall the murderers be condemned." This approach also allows her to challenge stereotypes about emotive female writers. "The hour had come, where was the man?" asked one commentator in 1893, adding: "Unfortunately, the man was not forthcoming—but Miss Wells was!" Another assumed Wells *was* a man, and advised whites to "tie the wretch who utters these calumnies to a stake . . . and perform upon him a surgical operation with a pair of tailor's shears." Wells accompanies her hard facts with strategies to change the situation: boycotts of white businesses, exodus, self-protection, and investigation by black-owned newspapers. In another anti-lynching pamphlet she offered a five-point plan of action and asked readers to support the Blair Bill, a resolution coming before the House of Representatives in August 1894.

She continued her political lobbying, writing to President McKinley to ask him to take action against lynching. Wells was the first anti-lynching campaigner and the only black leader to focus on lynching for an extended period, and in 1895 she pointed to progress: "Governors of states, newspapers, senators and representatives and bishops of churches have all been compelled to take cognizance of the prevalence of this crime." She believed there was "an awakened conscience," and that lynching couldn't "flourish in the future."

Further reading: Edward Ayers, *Vengeance and Justice* (1984); Alfreda Duster, *Crusade for Justice* (1970).

Preface

This statement is not a shield for the despoiler of virtue, nor altogether a defense for the poor blind Afro-American Sampsons who suffer themselves to be betrayed by white Delilahs. It is a contribution to truth, an array of facts, the perusal of which it is hoped will stimulate this great American Republic to demand that justice be done though the heavens fall.

It is with no pleasure I have dipped my hands in the corruption here exposed. Somebody must show that the Afro-American race is more sinned against than sinning, and it seems to have fallen upon me to do so. The awful death-roll that Judge Lynch is calling every week is appalling, not only because of the lives it takes, the rank cruelty and outrage to the victims, but because of the prejudice it fosters and the stain it places against the good name of a weak race.

The Afro-American is not a bestial race. If this work can contribute in any way toward proving this, and at the same time arouse the conscience of the American people to a demand for justice to every citizen, and punishment by law for the lawless, I shall feel I have done my race a service. Other considerations are of minor importance.

Chapter III. The New Cry

The South resented giving the Afro-American his freedom, the ballot box and the Civil Rights Law. The raids of the Ku-Klux and White Liners to subvert reconstruction government, the Hamburg and Ellerton, S.C., the Copiah County, Miss., and the Layfayette Parish, La., massacres were excused as the natural resentment of intelligence against government by ignorance.

Honest white men practically conceded the necessity of intelligence murdering ignorance to correct the mistake of the general government, and the race was left to the tender mercies of the solid South. Thoughtful Afro-Americans with the strong arm of the government withdrawn and with the hope to stop such wholesale massacres urged the race to sacrifice its political rights for sake of peace. They honestly believed the race should fit itself for government, and when that should be done, the objection to race participation in politics would be removed.

But the sacrifice did not remove the trouble, nor move the South to justice.

One by one the Southern States have legally(?) disfranchised the Afro-American, and since the repeal of the Civil Rights Bill nearly every Southern State has passed separate car laws with a penalty against their infringement. The race regardless of advancement is penned into filthy, stifling partitions cut off from smoking cars. All this while, although the political cause has been removed, the butcheries of black men at Barnwell, S.C., Carrolton, Miss., Waycross, Ga., and Memphis, Tenn., have gone on; also the flaying alive of a man in Kentucky, the burning of one in Arkansas, the hanging of a fifteen-year-old girl in Louisiana, a woman in Jackson, Tenn., and one in Hollendale, Miss., until the dark and bloody record of the South shows 728 Afro-Americans lynched during the past eight years. Not fifty of these were for political causes; the rest were for all manner of accusations from that of rape of white women, to the case of the boy Will Lewis who was hanged at Tullahoma, Tenn., last year for being drunk and "sassy" to white folks.

These statistics compiled by the *Chicago Tribune* were given the first of this year (1892). Since then, not less than one hundred and fifty have been known to have met violent death at the hands of cruel bloodthirsty mobs during the past nine months.

To palliate this record (which grows worse as the Afro-American becomes intelligent) and excuse some of the most heinous crimes that ever stained the history of a country, the South is shielding itself behind the plausible screen of defending the honor of its women. This, too, in the face of the fact that only *one-third* of the 728 victims to mobs have been *charged* with rape, to say nothing of those of that one-third who were innocent of the charge. A white correspondent of the *Baltimore Sun* declares that the Afro-American who was lynched in Chestertown, Md., in May for assault on a white girl was innocent; that the deed was done by a white man who had since disappeared. The girl herself maintained that her assailant was a white man. When that poor Afro-American was murdered, the whites excused their refusal of a trial on the ground that they wished to spare the white girl the mortification of having to testify in court.

This cry has had its effect. It has closed the heart, stifled the conscience, warped the judgment and hushed the voice of press and pulpit on the subject of lynch law throughout this "land of liberty." Men who stand high in the esteem of the public for Christian character, for moral and physical courage, for devotion to the principles of equal and exact justice to all, and for great sagacity, stand as cowards who fear to open their mouths before this great outrage. They do not see that by their tacit encouragement, their silent acquiescence, the black shadow of lawlessness in the form of lynch law is spreading its wings over the whole country.

Men who, like Governor Tillman, start the ball of lynch law rolling for a certain crime, are powerless to stop it when drunken or criminal white toughs feel like hanging an Afro-American on any pretext.

Even to the better class of Afro-Americans the crime of rape is so revolting they have too often taken the white man's word and given lynch law neither the investigation nor condemnation it deserved.

They forget that a concession of the right to lynch a man for a certain crime, not only concedes the right to lynch any person for any crime, but (so frequently is the cry of rape now raised) it is in a fair way to stamp us a race of rapists and desperadoes. They have gone on hoping and believing that general education and financial strength would solve the difficulty, and are devoting their energies to the accumulation of both.

The mob spirit has grown with the increasing intelligence of the Afro-American. It has left the out-of-the-way places where ignorance prevails, has thrown off the mask and with this new cry stalks in broad daylight in large cities, the centers of civilization, and is encouraged by the "leading citizens" and the press.

Chapter V. The South's Position

Henry W. Grady in his well-remembered speeches in New England and New York pictured the Afro-American as incapable of self-government. Through him and other leading men the cry of the South to the country has been "Hands off! Leave us to solve our problem." To the Afro-American the South says, "the white man must and will rule." There is little difference between the Antebellum South and the New South.

Her white citizens are wedded to any method however revolting, any measure however extreme, for the subjugation of the young manhood of the race. They have cheated him out of his ballot, deprived him of civil rights or redress therefore in the civil courts, robbed him of the fruits of his labor, and are still murdering, burning and lynching him.

The result is a growing disregard of human life. Lynch law has spread its insidious influence till men in New York State, Pennsylvania and on the free Western plains feel they can take the law in their own hands with impunity, especially where an Afro-American is concerned. The South is brutalized to a degree not realized by its own inhabitants, and the very foundation of government, law and order, are imperiled.

Public sentiment has had a slight "reaction" though not sufficient to stop the crusade of lawlessness and lynching. The spirit of Christianity of the great M.E. Church was aroused to the frequent and revolting crimes against a weak people, enough to pass strong condemnatory resolutions at its General Conference in Omaha last May. The spirit of justice of the grand old party asserted itself sufficiently to secure a denunciation of the wrongs, and a feeble declaration of the belief in human rights in the Republican platform at Minneapolis, June 7. Some of the great dailies and weeklies have swung into line declaring that lynch law must go. The President of the United States issued a proclamation that it be not tolerated in the territories over which he has jurisdiction. Governor Northern and Chief Justice Bleckley of Georgia have proclaimed against it. The citizens of Chattanooga, Tenn., have set a worthy example in that they not only condemn lynch law, but her public men demanded a trial for Weems, the accused rapist, and guarded him while the trial was in progress. The trial only lasted ten minutes, and Weems chose to plead guilty and accept twenty-one years sentence, than invite the certain death which awaited him outside that cordon of police if he had told the truth and shown the letters he had from the white woman in the case.

Col. A. S. Colyar, of Nashville, Tenn., is so overcome with the horrible state of affairs that he addressed the following earnest letter to the *Nashville American.*

Nothing since I have been a reading man has so impressed me with the decay of manhood among the people of Tennessee as the dastardly submission to the mob reign. We have reached the unprecedented low level; the awful criminal depravity of substituting the mob for the court and jury, of giving up the jail keys to the mob whenever they are demanded. We do it in the largest cities and in the country towns; we do it in midday; we do it after full, not to say formal, notice, and so thoroughly and generally is it acquiesced in that the murderers have discarded the formula of masks. They go into the town where everybody knows them, sometimes under the gaze of the governor, in the presence of the courts, in the presence of the sheriff and his deputies, in the presence of the entire police force, take out the prisoner, take his life, often with fiendish glee, and often with acts of cruelty and barbarism which impress the reader with a degeneracy rapidly approaching savage life. That the State is disgraced but faintly expresses the humiliation which has settled upon the once proud people of Tennessee. The State, in its majesty, through its organized life, for which the people pay liberally, makes but one record, but one note, and that a criminal falsehood, "was hung by persons to the jury unknown." The murder at Shelbyville is only a verification of what every intelligent man knew would come, because with a mob a rumor is as good as a proof.

These efforts brought forth apologies and a short halt, but the lynching mania was raged again through the past three months with unabated fury.

The strong arm of the law must be brought to bear upon lynchers in severe punishment, but this cannot and will not be done unless a healthy public sentiment demands and sustains such action.

The men and women in the South who disapprove of lynching and remain silent on the perpetration of such outrages, are particeps criminis, accomplices, accessories before and after the fact, equally guilty with the actual lawbreakers who would not persist if they did not know that neither the law nor militia would be employed against them.

Chapter VI: Self-Help

In the creation of this healthier public sentiment, the Afro-American can do for himself what no one else can do for him. The world looks on with wonder that we have conceded so much and remain law-abiding under such great outrage and provocation.

To Northern capital and Afro-American labor the South owes its rehabilitation. If labor is withdrawn capital will not remain. The Afro-American is thus the backbone of the South. A thorough knowledge and judicious exercise of this power in lynching localities could many times effect a bloodless revolution. The white man's dollar is his god, and to stop this will be to stop outrages in many localities.

The Afro-Americans of Memphis denounced the lynching of three of their best citizens, and urged and waited for the authorities to act in the matter and bring the lynchers to justice. No attempt was made to do so, and the black men left the city by thousands, bringing about great stagnation in every branch of business. Those who remained so injured the business of the street car company by staying off the cars, that the superintendent, manager and treasurer called personally on the editor of the *Free Speech*, asked them to urge our people to give them their patronage again. Other business men became alarmed over the situation and the *Free Speech* was run away that the colored people might be more easily controlled. A meeting of white citizens in June, three months after the lynching, passed resolutions for the first time, condemning it. *But they did not punish the lynchers*. Every one of them was known by name, because they had been selected to do the dirty work, by some of the very citizens who passed these resolutions. Memphis is fast losing her black population, who proclaim as they go that there is no protection for the life and property of any Afro-American citizen in Memphis who is not a slave.

The Afro-American citizens of Kentucky, whose intellectual and financial improvement has been phenomenal, have never had a separate car law until now. Delegations and petitions poured into the Legislature against it, yet the bill passed and the Jim Crow Car of Kentucky is a legalized institution. Will the great mass of Negroes continue to patronize the railroad? A special from Covington, Ky., says:

Covington, June 13.—The railroads of the State are beginning to feel very markedly, the effects of the separate coach bill recently passed by the Legislature. No class of people in the State have so many and so largely attended ex-cursions as the blacks. All these have been abandoned, and regular travel is re-duced to a minimum. A competent authority says the loss to the various roads will reach $1,000,000 this year.

A call to a State Conference in Lexington, Ky., last June had delegates from every county in the State. Those delegates, the ministers, teachers, heads of se-cret and other orders, and the head of every family should pass the word around for every member of the race in Kentucky to stay off railroads unless obliged to ride. If they did so, and their advice was followed persistently the convention would not need to petition the Legislature to repeal the law or raise money to file a suit. The railroad corporations would be so effected they would in self-defense lobby to have the separate car law repealed. On the other hand, as long as the railroads can get Afro-American excursions they will al-ways have plenty of money to fight all the suits brought against them. They will be aided in so doing by the same partisan public sentiment which passed the law. White men passed the law, and white judges and juries would pass upon the suits against the law, and render judgment in line with their preju-dices and in deference to the greater financial power.

The appeal to the white man's pocket has ever been more effectual than all the appeals ever made to his conscience. Nothing, absolutely nothing, is to be gained by a further sacrifice of manhood and self-respect. By the right exercise of his power as the industrial factor of the South, the Afro-American can de-mand and secure his rights, the punishment of lynchers, and a fair trial for ac-cused rapists.

Of the many inhuman outrages of this present year, the only case where the proposed lynching did *not* occur, was where the men armed themselves in Jacksonville, Fla., and Paducah, Ky., and prevented it. The only times an Afro-American who was assaulted got away has been when he had a gun and used it in self-defense.

The lesson this teaches and which every Afro-American should ponder well, is that a Winchester rifle should have a place of honor in every black home, and it should be used for that protection which the law refuses to give. When the white man who is always the aggressor knows he runs as great risk of biting the dust every time his Afro-American victim does, he will have greater respect for Afro-American life. The more the Afro-American yields and cringes and begs, the more he has to do so, the more he is insulted, outraged and lynched.

The assertion has been substantiated throughout these pages that the press contains unreliable and doctored reports of lynchings, and one of the most necessary things for the race to do is to get these facts before the public. The people must know before they can act, and there is no educator to compare with the press.

The Afro-American papers are the only ones which will print the truth, and they lack means to employ agents and detectives to get at the facts. The race must rally a mighty host to the support of their journals, and thus enable them to do much in the way of investigation.

A lynching occurred at Port Jarvis, N.Y., the first week in June. A white and colored man were implicated in the assault upon a white girl. It was charged that the white man paid the colored boy to make the assault, which he did on the public highway in broad day time, and was lynched. This, too was done by "parties unknown." The white man in the case still lives. He was imprisoned and promises to fight the case on trial. At the preliminary examination, it developed that he had been a suitor of the girl's. She had repulsed and refused him, yet had given him money, and he had sent threatening letters demanding more.

The day before this examination she was so wrought up, she left home and wandered miles away. When found she said she did so because she was afraid of the man's testimony. Why should she be afraid of the prisoner! Why should she yield to his demands for money if not to prevent him exposing something he knew! It seems explainable only on the hypothesis that a *liaison* existed between the colored boy and the girl, and the white man knew of it. The press is singularly silent. Has it a motive? We owe it to ourselves to find out.

The story comes from Larned, Kansas, Oct. 1, that a young white lady held at bay until daylight, without alarming any one in the house, "a burly Negro" who entered her room and bed. The "burly Negro" was promptly lynched without investigation or examination of inconsistant stories.

A house was found burned down near Montgomery, Ala., in Monroe County, Oct. 13, a few weeks ago; also the burned bodies of the owners and melted piles of gold and silver.

These discoveries led to the conclusion that the awful crime was not prompted by motives of robbery. The suggestion of the whites was that "brutal lust was the incentive, and as there are nearly 200 Negroes living within a radius of five miles of the place the conclusion was inevitable that some of them were the perpetrators."

Upon this "suggestion" probably made by the real criminal, the mob acted upon the "conclusion" and arrested ten Afro-Americans, four of whom, they tell the world, confessed to the deed of murdering Richard L. Johnson and outraging his daughter, Jeanette. These four men, Berrell Jones, Moses Johnson, Jim and John Packer, none of them twenty-five years of age, upon this conclusion, were taken from jail, hanged, shot, and burned while yet alive the night of Oct. 12. The same report says Mr. Johnson was on the best of terms with his Negro tenants.

The race thus outraged must find out the facts of this awful hurling of men into eternity on supposition, and give them to the indifferent and apathetic country. We feel this to be a garbled report, but how can we prove it?

Near Vicksburg, Miss., a murder was committed by a gang of burglars. Of course it must have been done by Negroes, and Negroes were arrested for it. It is believed that two men, Smith Tooley and John Adams belonged to a gang controlled by white men and, fearing exposure, on the night of July 4, they were hanged in the Court House yard by those interested in silencing them. Robberies since committed in the same vicinity have been known to be by white men who had their faces blackened. We strongly believe in the innocence of these murdered men, but we have no proof. No other news goes out to the world save that which stamps us as a race of cutthroats, robbers and lustful wild beasts. So great is Southern hate and prejudice, they legally (?) hung poor little thirteen-year-old Mildrey Brown at Columbia, S.C., Oct. 7, on the circumstantial evidence that she poisoned a white infant. If her guilt had been proven unmistakably, had she been white, Mildrey Brown would never have been hung.

The country would have been aroused and South Carolina disgraced forever for such a crime. The Afro-American himself did not know as he should have known as his journals should be in a position to have him know and act.

Nothing is more definitely settled than he must act for himself. I have shown how he may employ the boycott, emigration and the press, and I feel that by a combination of all these agencies can be effectually stamped out lynch law, that last relic of barbarism and slavery. "The gods help those who help themselves."

Jesus Christ in Texas

<u>1920</u>

In 1899, the sociologist W. E. B. Du Bois (1868–1963) received word that the knuckles of a black sharecropper were on display in an Atlanta grocery, a few blocks from where he was walking. The shock pulled him off his feet. The sharecropper, Sam Hose, had allegedly killed his white employer during an argument over wages. Newspapers had promoted a lynching and Hose had been tortured to death before a mob of two thousand people. Men, women, and children had fought for souvenir pieces of his charred flesh, and were seen carrying bones through the Atlanta streets. Someone had presented the Georgia governor with a slice of Hose's heart.

Du Bois was working as a professor of economics and history at Atlanta University, believing the cure for the "Negro Problem" was "knowledge based on scientific investigation." But the Hose lynching shook his faith in dispassionate research: he felt "one could not be a calm, cool, and detached scientist while Negroes were lynched, murdered and starved." He wrote *The Souls of Black Folk* (1903), which at one point mentions a part of Atlanta "not far from where Sam Hose was crucified." In 1920 he wrote *Darkwater,* which includes a poem called "The Prayers of God." Here a white man takes part in a lynching, then fearfully asks God: "That black and riven thing—was it Thee?" The book also contained "Jesus Christ in Texas," again written from a white perspective. The black Christ figure in the story is Du Bois's challenge to the ideas of racial redemption that often infused white justifications of violence. Lynchings were performed as sacred rituals, sometimes led by white clergymen, and victims were often hung above water and or from trees. Like Countee Cullen's "Christ Recrucified" (1922), Walter White's *The Fire in the Flint* (1924), and Langston Hughes's "Christ in Alabama" (1931), all of which made the lynched victim into a black Christ, Du Bois's story stole the imagery of baptism and crucifixion from lynch mobs, and rewrote America's passion play for the Jim Crow South.

Further reading: David Levering Lewis, *W. E. B. Du Bois* (2000); Robert Zangrando, *The NAACP Crusade* (1980).

It was in Waco, Texas.

The convict guard laughed. "I don't know," he said, "I hadn't thought of that." He hesitated and looked at the stranger curiously. In the solemn twilight he got an impression of unusual height and soft, dark eyes. "Curious sort of acquaintance for the colonel," he thought; then he continued aloud: "But that nigger there is bad, a born thief, and ought to be sent up for life; got ten years last time—"

Here the voice of the promoter, talking within, broke in; he was bending over his figures, sitting by the colonel. He was slight, with a sharp nose.

"The convicts," he said, "would cost us $96 a year and board. Well, we can squeeze this so that it won't be over $125 apiece. Now if these fellows are driven, they can build this line within twelve months. It will be running by next April. Freights will fall fifty per cent. Why, man, you'll be a millionaire in less than ten years."

The colonel started. He was a thick, short man, with a clean-shaven face and a certain air of breeding about the lines of his countenance; the word millionaire sounded well to his ears. He thought—he thought a great deal; he almost heard the puff of the fearfully costly automobile that was coming up the road, and he said:

"I suppose we might as well hire them."

"Of course," answered the promoter.

The voice of the tall stranger in the corner broke in here:

"It will be a good thing for them?" he said, half in question.

The colonel moved. "The guard makes strange friends," he thought to himself. "What's this man doing here, anyway?" He looked at him, or rather looked at his eyes, and then somehow he felt a warming toward him. He said:

"Well, at least, it can't harm them; they're beyond that."

"It will do them good, then," said the stranger again.

The promoter shrugged his shoulders. "It will do us good," he said.

But the colonel shook his head impatiently. He felt a desire to justify himself before those eyes, and he answered: "Yes, it will do them good; or at any rate it won't make them any worse than they are." Then he started to say something else, but here sure enough the sound of the automobile breathing at the gate stopped him and they all arose.

"It is settled, then," said the promoter.

"Yes," said the colonel, turning toward the stranger again. "Are you going into town?" he asked with the Southern courtesy of white men to white men in a country town. The stranger said he was. "Then come along in my machine. I want to talk with you about this."

They went out to the car. The stranger as he went turned again to look back at the convict. He was a tall, powerfully built black fellow. His face was sullen, with a low forehead, thick, hanging lips, and bitter eyes. There was revolt written about his mouth despite the hang-dog expression. He stood bending over his pile of stones, pounding listlessly. Beside him stood a boy of twelve,—yellow, with a hunted, crafty look. The convict raised his eyes and they met the eyes of the stranger. The hammer fell from his hands.

The stranger turned slowly toward the automobile and the colonel introduced him. He had not exactly caught his name, but he mumbled something as he presented him to his wife and little girl, who were waiting.

As they whirled away the colonel started to talk, but the stranger had taken the little girl into his lap and together they conversed in low tones all the way home.

In some way, they did not exactly know how, they got the impression that the man was a teacher and, of course, he must be a foreigner. The long, cloak-like coat told this. They rode in the twilight through the lighted town and at last drew up before the colonel's mansion, with its ghost-like pillars.

The lady in the back seat was thinking of the guests she had invited to dinner and was wondering if she ought not to ask this man to stay. He seemed cultured and she supposed he was some acquaintance of the colonel's. It would be rather interesting to have him there, with the judge's wife and daughter and the rector. She spoke almost before she thought:

"You will enter and rest awhile?"

The colonel and the little girl insisted. For a moment the stranger seemed about to refuse. He said he had some business for his father, about town. Then for the child's sake he consented.

Up the steps they went and into the dark parlor where they sat and talked a long time. It was a curious conversation. Afterwards they did not remember exactly what was said and yet they all remembered a certain strange satisfaction in that long, low talk.

Finally the nurse came for the reluctant child and the hostess bethought herself:

"We will have a cup of tea; you will be dry and tired."

She rang and switched on a blaze of light. With one accord they all looked at the stranger, for they had hardly seen him well in the glooming twilight. The woman started in amazement and the colonel half rose in anger. Why, the man was a mulatto, surely; even if he did not own the Negro blood, their practised eyes knew it. He was tall and straight and the coat looked like a Jewish gabardine. His hair hung in close curls far down the sides of his face and his face was olive, even yellow.

A peremptory order rose to the colonel's lips and froze there as he caught the stranger's eyes. Those eyes,—where had he seen those eyes before? He remembered them long years ago. The soft, tear-filled eyes of a brown girl. He remembered many things, and his face grew drawn and white. Those eyes kept burning into him, even when they were turned half away toward the staircase, where the white figure of the child hovered with her nurse and waved goodnight. The lady sank into her chair and thought: "What will the judge's wife say? How did the colonel come to invite this man here? How shall we be rid of him?" She looked at the colonel in reproachful consternation.

Just then the door opened and the old butler came in. He was an ancient black man, with tufted white hair, and he held before him a large, silver tray filled with a china tea service. The stranger rose slowly and stretched forth his hands as if to bless the viands. The old man paused in bewilderment, tottered, and then with sudden gladness in his eyes dropped to his knees, and the tray crashed to the floor.

"My Lord and my God!" he whispered; but the woman screamed: "Mother's china!"

The doorbell rang.

"Heavens! here is the dinner party!" exclaimed the lady. She turned toward the door, but there in the hall, clad in her night clothes, was the little girl. She had stolen down the stairs to see the stranger again, and the nurse above was calling in vain. The woman felt hysterical and scolded at the nurse, but the stranger had stretched out his arms and with a glad cry the child nestled in them. They caught some words about the "Kingdom of Heaven" as he slowly mounted the stairs with his little, white burden.

The mother was glad of anything to get rid of the interloper, even for a moment. The bell rang again and she hastened toward the door, which the loitering black maid was just opening. She did not notice the shadow of the stranger as he came slowly down the stairs and paused by the newel post, dark and silent.

The judge's wife came in. She was an old woman, frilled and powdered into a semblance of youth, and gorgeously gowned. She came forward, smiling with extended hands, but when she was opposite the stranger, somewhere a chill seemed to strike her and she shuddered and cried:

"What a draft!" as she drew a silken shawl about her and shook hands cordially; she forgot to ask who the stranger was. The judge strode in unseeing, thinking of a puzzling case of theft.

"Eh? What? Oh—er—yes,—good evening," he said, "good evening." Behind them came a young woman in the glory of youth, and daintily silked, beautiful in face and form, with diamonds around her fair neck. She came in lightly, but stopped with a little gasp; then she laughed gaily and said:

"Why, I beg your pardon. Was it not curious? I thought I saw there behind your man"—she hesitated, but he must be a servant, she argued—"the shadow of great, white wings. It was but the light on the drapery. What a turn it gave me." And she smiled again. With her came a tall, handsome, young naval officer. Hearing his lady refer to the servant, he hardly looked at him, but held his gilded cap carelessly toward him, and the stranger placed it carefully on the rack.

Last came the rector, a man of forty, and well-clothed. He started to pass the stranger, stopped, and looked at him inquiringly.

"I beg your pardon," he said. "I beg your pardon,—I think I have met you?"

The stranger made no answer, and the hostess nervously hurried the guests on. But the rector lingered and looked perplexed.

"Surely, I know you. I have met you somewhere," he said, putting his hand vaguely to his head. "You—you remember me, do you not?"

The stranger quietly swept his cloak aside, and to the hostess' unspeakable relief passed out of the door.

"I never knew you," he said in low tones as he went.

The lady murmured some vain excuse about intruders, but the rector stood with annoyance written on his face.

"I beg a thousand pardons," he said to the hostess absently. "It is a great pleasure to be here,—somehow I thought I knew that man. I am sure I knew him once."

The stranger had passed down the steps, and as he passed, the nurse, lingering at the top of the staircase, flew down after him, caught his cloak, trembled, hesitated, and then kneeled in the dust.

He touched her lightly with his hand and said: "Go, and sin no more!"

With a glad cry the maid left the house, with its open door, and turned north, running. The stranger turned eastward into the night. As they parted a long, low howl rose tremulously and reverberated through the night. The colonel's wife within shuddered.

"The bloodhounds!" she said.

The rector answered carelessly:

"Another one of those convicts escaped, I suppose. Really, they need severer measures." Then he stopped. He was trying to remember that stranger's name.

The judge's wife looked about for the draft and arranged her shawl. The girl glanced at the white drapery in the hall, but the young officer was bending over her and the fires of life burned in her veins.

Howl after howl rose in the night, swelled, and died away. The stranger strode rapidly along the highway and out into the deep forest. There he paused and stood waiting, tall and still.

A mile up the road behind a man was running, tall and powerful and black, with crime-stained face and convicts' stripes upon him, and shackles on his legs. He ran and jumped, in little, short steps, and his chains rang. He fell and rose again, while the howl of the hounds rang louder behind him.

Into the forest he leapt and crept and jumped and ran, streaming with sweat; seeing the tall form rise before him, he stopped suddenly, dropped his hands in sullen impotence, and sank panting to the earth. A greyhound shot out of the woods behind him, howled, whined, and fawned before the stranger's feet. Hound after hound bayed, leapt, and lay there; then silently, one by one, and with bowed heads, they crept backward toward the town.

The stranger made a cup of his hands and gave the man water to drink, bathed his hot head, and gently took the chains and irons from his feet. By and by the convict stood up. Day was dawning above the treetops. He looked into the stranger's face, and for a moment a gladness swept over the stains of his face.

"Why, you are a nigger, too," he said.

Then the convict seemed anxious to justify himself.

"I never had no chance," he said furtively.

"Thou shalt not steal," said the stranger.

The man bridled.

"But how about them? Can they steal? Didn't they steal a whole year's work, and then when I stole to keep from starving—" He glanced at the stranger.

"No, I didn't steal just to keep from starving. I stole to be stealing. I can't seem to keep from stealing. Seems like when I see things, I just must—but, yes, I'll try!"

The convict looked down at his striped clothes, but the stranger had taken off his long coat; he had put it around him and the stripes disappeared.

In the opening morning the black man started toward the low, log farm-house in the distance, while the stranger stood watching him. There was a new glory in the day. The black man's face cleared up, and the farmer was glad to get him. All day the black man worked as he had never worked before. The farmer gave him some cold food.

"You can sleep in the barn," he said, and turned away.

"How much do I git a day?" asked the black man.

The farmer scowled.

"Now see here," said he. "If you'll sign a contract for the season, I'll give you ten dollars a month."

"I won't sign no contract," said the black man doggedly.

"Yes, you will," said the farmer, threateningly, "or I'll call the convict guard." And he grinned.

The convict shrank and slouched to the barn. As night fell he looked out and saw the farmer leave the place. Slowly he crept out and sneaked toward the house. He looked through the kitchen door. No one was there, but the supper was spread as if the mistress had laid it and gone out. He ate ravenously. Then he looked into the front room and listened. He could hear low voices on the porch. On the table lay a gold watch. He gazed at it, and in a moment he was beside it,—his hands were on it! Quickly he slipped out of the house and slouched toward the field. He saw his employer coming along the highway. He fled back in terror and around to the front of the house, when suddenly he stopped. He felt the great, dark eyes of the stranger and saw the same dark, cloak-like coat where the stranger sat on the doorstep talking with the mistress of the house. Slowly, guiltily, he turned back, entered the kitchen, and laid the watch stealthily where he had found it; then he rushed wildly back toward the stranger, with arms outstretched.

The woman had laid supper for her husband, and going down from the house had walked out toward a neighbor's. She was gone but a little while, and when she came back she started to see a dark figure on the doorsteps under the tall, red oak. She thought it was the new Negro until he said in a soft voice:

"Will you give me bread?"

Reassured at the voice of a white man, she answered quickly in her soft, Southern tones:

"Why, certainly."

She was a little woman, and once had been pretty; but now her face was drawn with work and care. She was nervous and always thinking, wishing, wanting for something. She went in and got him some cornbread and a glass of cool, rich buttermilk; then she came out and sat down beside him. She began, quite unconsciously, to tell him about herself,—the things she had done and had not done and the things she had wished for. She told him of her husband and this new farm they were trying to buy. She said it was hard to get niggers to work. She said they ought all to be in the chain-gang and made to work. Even then some ran away. Only yesterday one had escaped, and another the day before.

At last she gossiped of her neighbors, how good they were and how bad.

"And do you like them all?" asked the stranger.

She hesitated.

"Most of them," she said; and then, looking up into his face and putting her hand into his, as though he were her father, she said:

"There are none I hate; no, none at all."

He looked away, holding her hand in his, and said dreamily:

"You love your neighbor as yourself?"

She hesitated.

"I try—" she began, and then looked the way he was looking; down under the hill where lay a little, half-ruined cabin.

"They are niggers," she said briefly.

He looked at her. Suddenly a confusion came over her and she insisted, she knew not why.

"But they are niggers!"

With a sudden impulse she arose and hurriedly lighted the lamp that stood just within the door, and held it above her head. She saw his dark face and curly hair. She shrieked in angry terror and rushed down the path, and just as she rushed down, the black convict came running up with hands outstretched. They met in mid-path, and before he could stop he had run against her and she fell heavily to earth and lay white and still. Her husband came rushing around the house with a cry and an oath.

"I knew it," he said. "It's that runaway nigger." He held the black man struggling to the earth and raised his voice to a yell. Down the highway came the convict guard, with hound and mob and gun. They paused across the fields. The farmer motioned to them.

"He—attacked—my wife," he gasped.

The mob snarled and worked silently. Right to the limb of the red oak they hoisted the struggling, writhing black man, while others lifted the dazed woman. Right and left, as she tottered to the house, she searched for the stranger with a yearning, but the stranger was gone. And she told none of her guests.

"No—no, I want nothing," she insisted, until they left her, as they thought, asleep. For a time she lay still, listening to the departure of the mob. Then she rose. She shuddered as she heard the creaking of the limb where the body hung. But resolutely she crawled to the window and peered out into the moonlight; she saw the dead man writhe. He stretched his arms out like a cross, looking upward. She gasped and clung to the window sill. Behind the swaying body, and down where the little, half-ruined cabin lay, a single flame flashed up amid the far-off shout and cry of the mob. A fierce joy sobbed up through the terror in her soul and then sank abashed as she watched the flame rise. Suddenly whirling into one great crimson column it shot to the top of the sky and threw great arms athwart the gloom until above the world and behind the roped and swaying form below hung quivering and burning a great crimson cross.

She hid her dizzy, aching head in an agony of tears, and dared not look, for she knew.

Her dry lips moved:

"Despised and rejected of men."

She knew, and the very horror of it lifted her dull and shrinking eyelids. There, heaven-tall, earth-wide, hung the stranger on the crimson cross, riven and blood-stained, with thorn-crowned head and pierced hands. She stretched her arms and shrieked.

He did not hear. He did not see. His calm dark eyes, all sorrowful, were fastened on the writhing, twisting body of the thief, and a voice came out of the winds of the night, saying:

"This day thou shalt be with me in Paradise!"

The Lynching

1920

The Harlem Renaissance poet Claude McKay (1889–1948) dismantled the master's house with the master's tools: his variation on the Italian sonnet in this poem reminds readers that lynchings were carefully planned recreation and stylized rituals, and meets the perpetrators of tightly scripted lynchings on their own ground. Lynching had its own script: the corpse was displayed alongside written signs, or else participants took performance souvenirs. Ralph Ellison later explained that the goal of lynchers was to achieve "ritual purification," that lynching was a "ritual drama . . . led by a masked celebrant dressed in a garish costume who manipulated the numinous objects . . . associated with the rite." McKay wrote in the aftermath of the "Red Summer" of 1919, when 83 lynchings took place across America, many when race riots shook Chicago, Texas, D.C., and Arkansas, but also as the KKK reappeared in force, with its particularly stylized rituals.

McKay's poem is significant in the history of anti-lynching protest writing for three further reasons. First, like many protest writers, he makes the lynching victim into a Christ figure. Second, he challenges the myth of gentle Southern womanhood: white women watch the lynching with "eyes of steely blue." Soon after McKay published his poem, an increasing number of Southern white women joined the anti-lynching movement, angry at the Southern defense of lynching as the "protection" of white womanhood. Third, again like numerous anti-lynching protestors, he connects lynching to slavery: the "bright and solitary star" is the North star "that ever guided" slaves. Violence was no anomaly in American history, said Mary Church Terrell in 1904: "Lynching is the aftermath of slavery." The children in McKay's poem, "lynchers that were to be," are slavery's offspring.

McKay's legacy in the anti-lynching protest movement extended all the way to 2002, when *Without Sanctuary,* an exhibition of lynching photographs, opened in Atlanta. Alongside the images, and the lyrics to Billie Holiday's song "Strange Fruit" (1939), was one of McKay's sonnets. Displayed in the foyer, it was the first thing visitors to the exhibition saw.

Further reading: Phillip Dray, *At the Hands of Persons Unknown* (2002); Trudier Harris, *Exorcising Blackness* (1984).

His spirit is smoke ascended to high heaven.
His father, by the cruelest way of pain,
Had bidden him to his bosom once again;

The awful sin remained still unforgiven.
All night a bright and solitary star
(Perchance the one that ever guided him,
Yet gave him up at last to Fate's wild whim)
Hung pitifully o'er the swinging char.
Day dawned, and soon the mixed crowds came to view
The ghastly body swaying in the sun:
The women thronged to look, but never a one
Showed sorrow in her eyes of steely blue.

And little lads, lynchers that were to be,
Danced round the dreadful thing in fiendish glee.

From Big Boy Leaves Home

1936

Richard Wright (1908–1960) wrote his character Big Boy as a child of the Depression: there were 28 lynchings in 1933 alone, and in 1937 the author Erskine Caldwell wondered if the "defeated" white farmer of the rural south "released his pent-up emotions by lynching the black man." Big Boy is also a child of slavery; Wright's lynching story adapts the slave narrative theme of escaping on a train North. Wright, the grandson of slaves, was trying to break the link to the slave past, exclaiming in the epigraph to *Uncle Tom's Children* (where the story appeared), "Uncle Tom is dead!" But slavery casts a long shadow throughout the story. The lynch mob adapts a verse from the Civil War song "John Brown's Body," and the boys are trapped by a kind of determinism: the story sets up a series of mini-prophecies and, in fulfilling them, confirms that the boys remain "Uncle Tom's children."

Wright later explained that the South's environment was "too small to nourish human beings," and that life under Jim Crow was like "a thousand lynchings." In the story, this tight space is evoked by the hole where Big Boy hides from the lynchers. The snake in the hole recalls Frederick Douglass's warning in his 1852 speech, "The Meaning of July Fourth for the Negro": "Be warned! a horrible reptile is coiled up in your nation's bosom." The hiding place also symbolizes the ongoing absence of blacks from national culture and history, what Ralph Ellison once called the "whole unrecorded history" of blacks. But in that space Big Boy imagines a different history, complete with newspaper headlines, and in 1945, Ellison insisted that Wright had converted the black impulse toward "going-under-ground"—entering the hole—into "a will to confront the world."

Further reading: Sandra Gunnin, *Race, Rape and Lynching* (1996); Herbert Shapiro, *White Violence* (1988).

He made for the railroad, running straight toward the sunset. He held his left hand tightly over his heart, holding the hot pone of corn bread there. At times he stumbled over the ties, for his shoes were tight and hurt his feet. His throat burned from thirst; he had had no water since noon.

He veered off the track and trotted over the crest of a hill, following Bullard's Road. His feet slipped and slid in the dust. He kept his eyes straight ahead, fearing every clump of shrubbery, every tree. He wished it were night. If he could only get to the kilns without meeting anyone. Suddenly a thought came to him like a blow. He recalled hearing the old folks tell tales of blood-hounds, and fear made him run slower. None of them had thought of that. Spose blood-hounds wuz put on his trail? Lawd! Spose a whole pack of em, foamin n howlin, tore im t pieces? He went limp and his feet dragged. Yeah, thas whut they wuz gonna send after im, blood-hounds! N then thered be no way fer im t dodge! Why hadnt Pa let im take the shotgun? He stopped. He oughta go back n git the shotgun. And then when the mob came he would take some with him.

In the distance he heard the approach of a train. It jarred him back to a sharp sense of danger. He ran again, his big shoes sopping up and down in the dust. He was tired and his lungs were bursting from running. He wet his lips, wanting water. As he turned from the road across a plowed field he heard the train roaring at his heels. He ran faster, gripped in terror.

He was nearly there now. He could see the black clay on the sloping hillside. Once inside a kiln he would be safe. For a little while, at least. He thought of the shotgun again. If he only had something! Someone to talk to... Thas right! Bobo! Bobod be wid im. Hed almost fergot Bobo. Bobod bringa gun; he knowed he would. N tergether they could kill the whole mob. Then in the mawning theyd git inter Will's truck n go far erway, t Chicawgo . . .

He slowed to a walk, looking back and ahead. A light wind skipped over the grass. A beetle lit on his cheek and he brushed it off. Behind the dark pines hung a red sun. Two bats flapped against that sun. He shivered, for he was growing cold; the sweat on his body was drying.

He stopped at the foot of the hill, trying to choose between two patches of black kilns high above him. He went to the left, for there lay the ones he, Bobo, Lester, and Buck had dug only last week. He looked around again; the landscape was bare. He climbed the embankment and stood before a row of black pits sinking four and five feet deep into the earth. He went to the largest and peered in. He stiffened when his ears caught the sound of a whir. He ran back a few steps and poised on his toes. Six foot of snake slid out of the pit and went into coil. Big Boy looked around wildly for a stick. He ran down the slope, peering into the grass. He stumbled over a tree limb. He picked it up and tested it by striking it against the ground.

Warily, he crept back up the slope, his stick poised. When about seven feet from the snake he stopped and waved the stick. The coil grew tighter, the whir sounded louder, and a flat head reared to strike. He went to the right, and the flat head followed him, the blue-black tongue darting forth; he went to the left, and the flat head followed him there too.

He stopped, teeth clenched. He had to kill this snake. Jus had t kill im! This wuz the safest pit on the hillside. He waved the stick again, looking at the snake before, thinking of a mob behind. The flat head reared higher. With stick over shoulder, he jumped in, swinging. The stick sang through the air, catching the snake on the side of the head, sweeping him out of coil. There was a brown writhing mass. Then Big Boy was upon him, pounding blows home, one on top of the other. He fought viciously, his eyes red, his teeth bared in a snarl. He beat till the snake lay still; then he stomped it with his heel, grinding its head into the dirt.

He stopped, limp, wet. The corners of his lips were white with spittle. He spat and shuddered.

Cautiously, he went to the hole and peered. He longed for a match. He imagined whole nests of them in there waiting. He put the stick into the hole and waved it around. Stooping, he peered again. It mus be awright. He looked over the hillside, his eyes coming back to the dead snake. Then he got to his knees and backed slowly into the hole . . .

The view from his hole was fringed by the long tufts of grass. He could see all the way to Bullard's Road, and even beyond. The wind was blowing, and in the east the first touch of dusk was rising. Every now and then a bird floated past, a spot of wheeling black printed against the sky. Big Boy sighed, shifted his weight, and chewed at a blade of grass. A wasp droned. He heard number nine, far away and mournful.

The train made him remember how they had dug these kilns on long hot summer days, how they had made boilers out of big tin cans, filled them with water, fixed stoppers for steam, cemented them in holes with wet clay, and built fires under them. He recalled how they had danced and yelled when a stopper blew out of a boiler, letting out a big spout of steam and a shrill whistle. There were times when they had the whole hillside blazing and smoking. Yeah, yuh see, Big Boy wuz Casey Jones n wuz speedin it down the gleamin rails of the Southern Pacific. Bobo had number two on the Santa Fe. Buck wuz on the Illinoy Central. Lester the Nickel Plate. Lawd, how they sheveled the wood in! The boiling water would almost jar the cans loose from the clay. More and more pine-knots and dry leaves would be piled under the cans. Flames would grow so tall they would have to shield their eyes. Sweat would pour off their faces. Then, suddenly, a peg would shoot high into the air, and

Pssseeeezzzzzzzzzzzzzzzz . . .

Big Boy sighed and stretched out his arm, quenching the flames and scattering the smoke. Why didnt Bobo c mon? He looked over the fields; there was nothing but dying sunlight. His mind drifted back to the kilns. He remembered the day when Buck, jealous of his winning, had tried to smash his kiln. Yeah, that ol sonofabitch! Naw, Lawd! He didnt go t say the! Whut wuz he thinkin erbout? Cussin the dead! Yeah, po ol Buck wuz dead now. N Lester too. Yeah, it wuz awright fer Buck t smash his kiln. Sho. N he wished he hadnt socked ol Buck so hard the day. He wuz sorry fer Buck now. N he sho wished he hadnt cussed po ol Bucks ma, neither. Tha wuz sinful! Mabbe Gawd would git im fer that? But he didnt go t do it! Po Buck! Po Lester! Hed never treat anybody like the ergin, never . . .

Dusk was slowly deepening. Somewhere, he could not tell exactly where, a cricket took up a fitful song. The air was growing soft and heavy. He looked over the fields, longing for Bobo . . .

He shifted his body to ease the cold damp of the ground, and thought back over the day. Yeah, hed been dam right erbout not wantin t go swimmin. N ef hed followed his right min hed neverve gone n got inter all this trouble. At first hed said new. But shucks, somehow hed just went on wid the res. Yeah he shoulda went on t school the mawnin, like Ma told im t do. But, hell, who wouldnt git tireda awways drivin a guy t school! Tha wuz the big trouble awways drivin a guy t school! He wouldnt be in all this trouble now if it wuznt fer that Gawddam school! Impatiently, he took the grass out of his mouth and threw it away, demolishing the little red school house . . .

Yeah, if they had all kept still n quiet when the ol white woman showed-up, mabbe shedve went on off. But yuh never kin tell erbout these white folks. Mabbe she wouldntve went. Mabbe the white man woulda killed all of em! All fo of em! Yeah, yuh never kin tell erbout white folks. Then, ergin, mabbe the white woman woulda went on off n laffed. Yeah, mabbe the white man woulda said: *Yuh nigger bastards git t hell outta here! Yuh know Gawdam well yuh don berlong here!* N then they woulda grabbed their cloes n run like all hell . . . He blinked the white man away. Where wuz Bobo? Why didnt he hurry up n c mon?

He jerked another blade and chewed. Yeah, ef Pa had only let im have the shotgun! He could stan off a whole mob wid a shotgun. He looked at the ground as he turned a shotgun over in his hands. Then he leveled it at an advancing white man. Boooom! The man curled up. Another came. He reloaded quickly, and let him have what the other had got. He too curled up. Then another came. He got the same medicine. Then the whole mob swirled around him, and he blazed away, getting as many as he could. They closed in; but, by Gawd, he had done his part, hadnt he? N the newspapersd say: NIGGER KILLS DOZEN OF MOB BEFO LYNCHED! Er mabbe theyd say: TRAPPED NIGGER SLAYS TWENTY BEFO KILLED! He smiled a little. Tha wouldnt be so bad, would it? Blinking the newspaper away, he looked over the fields. Where wuz Bobo? Why didnt he hurry up n c mon?

He heard footsteps. Then voices came . . .

"We o'ughta kill ever black bastard in this country!"

"Waal, Jim got two of em, anyhow."

"But Bertha said there wuz *fo!*"

"Where in hell they hidin?"

"She said one of em wuz named Big Boy, or somethin like tha."

"We went t his shack lookin fer im."

"Yeah?"

"But we didnt fin im."

"These niggers stick tergether; they don never tell on each other."

"We looked all thu the shack n couldnt fin hide ner hair of im. Then we drove the ol woman n man out n set the shack on fire . . ."

"Jeesus! Ah wished Ah coulda been there!"

"Shoulda heard the ol nigger woman howl . . ."

"Hoalo!"

"C mon over!"

. . . Big Boy had no feelings now. He was waiting. He did not wonder if they were coming after him. He just waited. He did not wonder about Bobo. He rested his cheek against the cold clay, waiting.

A dog barked. He stiffened. It barked again. He balled himself into a knot at the bottom of the hole, waiting. Then he heard the patter of dog feet.

"Look!"

"Whuts he got?"

"Its a snake!"

"Yeah, the dogs foun a snake!"

"Gee, its a big one!"

"Shucks, Ah wish he could fin one of them sonofabitchin niggers!"

The voices sank to low murmurs. Then he heard number twelve, its bell tolling and whistle crying as it slid along the rails. He flattened himself against the clay. Someone was singing:

"We'll hang ever nigger t a sour apple tree . . ."

When the song ended there was hard laughter. From the other side of the hill he heard the dog barking furiously. He listened. There was more than one dog now. There were many and they were barking their throats out.

"Hush. Ah hear them dogs!"

"When theys barkin like the theys foun somethin!"

"Here they come over the hill!"

"WE GOT IM! WE GOT IM!"

There came a roar. Tha must be Bobo, tha mus be Bobo . . . In spite of his fear, Big Boy looked. The road, and half of the hillside across the road, were covered with men. A few were at the top of the hill, stenciled against the sky. He could see dark forms moving up the slopes. They were yelling.

"By Gawd, we got im!"

"C mon!"

"Where is he?"

"Theyre bringin im over the hill!"

"Ah got a rope fer im!"

"Say, somebody go n git the others!"

"Where is he? Cant we see im, Mister?"

"They say Berthas comin, too."

"Jack! Jack! Don leave me! Ah wanna see im!"

"Theyre bringin im over the hill, sweetheart!"

"AH WANNA BE THE FIRS T PUT A ROPE ON THA BLACK BASTARDS NECK!"

"Les start the fire!"

"Heat the tar!"

"Ah got some chains t chain im."

"Bring im over this way!"

"Chris, Ah wished Ah hada drink . . ."

Big Boy saw men moving over the hill. Among them was a long dark spot. Tha mus be Bobo; the mus be Bobo theys carryin . . . Theyll git im here. He oughta git up n run. He clamped his teeth and ran his hand across his forehead, bringing it away wet. He tried to swallow, but could not; his throat was dry.

They had started the song again:

"We'll hang ever nigger t a sour apple tree . . ."

There were women singing now. Their voices made the song round and full. Song waves rolled over the top of pine trees. The sky sagged low, heavy with clouds. Wind was rising. Sometimes cricket cries cut surprisingly across the mob song. A dog had gone to the utmost top of the hill. At each lull of the song his howl floated full into the night.

Big Boy shrank when he saw the first flame light the hillside. Would they see im here? Then he remembered you could not see into the dark if you were standing in the light. As flames leaped higher he saw two men rolling a barrel up the slope.

"Say, gimme a han here, will yuh?"

"Awright, heave!"

"C mon! Straight up! Git t the other end!"

"Ah got the feathers here in this pillar!"

"BRING SOME MO WOOD!"

Big Boy could see the barrel surrounded by flames. The mob fell back, forming a dark circle. Theyd fin im here! He had a wild impulse to climb out and fly across the hills. But his legs would not move. He stared hard, trying to find Bobo. His eyes played over a long, dark spot near the fire. Fanned by wind, flames leaped higher. He jumped. That dark spot had moved. Lawd, thas Bobo; thas Bobo . . .

He smelt the scent of tar, faint at first, then stronger. The wind brought it full into his face, then blew it away. His eyes burned and he rubbed them with his knuckles. He sneezed.

"LES GIT SOURVINEERS!"

He saw the mob close in around the fire. Their faces were hard and sharp in the light of the flames. More men and women were coming over the hill. The long, dark spot was smudged out.

"Everybody git back!"

"Look! Hes gotta finger!"

"C MON! GIT THE GALS BACK FROM THE FIRE!"

"He's got one of his ears, see?"

"Whuts the matter!"

"A woman fell out! Fainted, Ah reckon . . ."

The stench of tar permeated the hillside. The sky was black and the wind was blowing hard.

"HURRY UP N BURN THE NIGGER FO IT RAINS!"

Big Boy saw the mob fall back, leaving a small knot of men about the fire. Then, for the first time, he had a full glimpse of Bobo. A black body flashed in the light. Bobo was struggling, twisting; they were binding his arms and legs.

When he saw them tilt the barrel he stiffened. A scream quivered. He knew the tar was on Bobo. The mob fell back. He saw a tar-drenched body glistening and turning.

"THE BASTARDS GOT IT!"

There was a sudden quiet. Then he shrank violently as the wind carried, like a flurry of snow, a widening spiral of white feathers into the night. The flames leaped tall as the trees. The scream came again. Big Boy trembled and looked. The mob was running down the slopes, leaving the fire clear. Then he saw a writhing white mass cradled in yellow flame, and heard screams, one on top of the other, each shriller and shorter than the last. The mob was quiet now, standing still, looking up the slopes at the writhing white mass gradually growing black, growing black in a cradle of yellow flame.

"PO ON MO GAS!"

"Gimme a lif, will yuh!"

Two men were struggling, carrying between them a heavy can. They set it down, tilted it, leaving it so that the gas would trickle down to the hollowed earth around the fire.

Big Boy slid back into the hole, his face buried in clay. He had no feelings now, no fears. He was numb, empty, as though all blood had been drawn from him. Then his muscles flexed taut when he heard a faint patter. A tiny stream of cold water seeped to his knees, making him push back to a drier spot. He looked up; rain was beating in the grass.

"It's rainin!"

"C mon, les git t town!"

". . . don worry, when the fire git thu wid im hell be gone . . ."

"Wait, Charles! Don leave me; its slippery here . . ."

"Ahll take some of yuh ladies back in mah car . . ."

Big Boy heard the dogs barking again, this time closer. Running feet pounded past. Cold water chilled his ankles. He could hear raindrops steadily hissing.

Now a dog was barking at the mouth of the hole, barking furiously, sensing a presence there. He balled himself into a knot and clung to the bottom, his knees and shins buried in water. The bark came louder. He heard paws scraping and felt the hot scent of dog breath on his face. Green eyes glowed and drew nearer as the barking, muffled by the closeness of the hole, beat upon his eardrums. Backing till his shoulders pressed against the clay, he held his breath. He pushed out his hands, his fingers stiff. The dog yawped louder, advancing, his bark rising sharp and thin. Big Boy rose to his knees, his hands before him. Then he flattened out still more against the bottom, breathing lungsful of hot dog scent, breathing it slowly, hard, but evenly. The dog came closer, bringing hotter dog scent. Big Boy could go back no more. His knees were slipping and slopping in the water. He braced himself, ready. Then, he never exactly knew how—he never knew whether he had lunged or the dog had lunged—they were together, rolling in the water. The green eyes were beneath him, between his legs. Dognails bit into his arms. His knees slipped backward and he landed full on the dog; the dog's breath left in a heavy gasp. Instinctively, he fumbled for the throat as he felt the dog twisting between his knees. The dog snarled, long and low, as though gathering strength. Big Boy's hands traveled swiftly over the dog's back, groping for the throat. He felt dognails again and saw green eyes, but his fingers had found the throat. He choked, feeling his fingers sink; he choked, throwing back his head and stiffening his arms. He felt the dog's body heave, felt dognails digging into his loins. With strength flowing from fear, he closed his fingers, pushing his full weight on the dog's throat. The dog heaved again, and lay still . . . Big Boy heard the sound of his own breathing filling the hole, and heard shouts and footsteps above him going past.

For a long time he held the dog, held it long after the last footstep had died out, long after the rain had stopped.

Strange Fruit

1937, 1939

In 1935 the Jewish schoolteacher, union activist, and communist Abel Meeropol (1903–1986) saw a photograph of the 1930 lynching of Thomas Shipp and Abram Smith. The image haunted him for days and in response he wrote a poem, "Bitter Fruit," and set it to music. It was published in 1937 and regularly performed at leftist gatherings.

In January 1939 he played his song to the up-and-coming jazz singer Billie Holiday (1915–1959), at Café Society, an integrated nightclub in Greenwich Village. He remembered that Holiday only asked one question—what did "pastoral" mean? After years of performing her own version of the song around the country, encountering such violent audience responses that she was sometimes forced to leave town, Holiday had her own answer to this question. In 1958, when a young boy asked her, "What's a pastoral scene?" she apparently replied, "It means when they take a little nigger like you and snatch off his nuts and shove them down his goddamn throat . . . That's a goddamn pastoral scene."

It is rare that a protest movement does not have a protest song at its heart, and "Strange Fruit" was the anti-lynching movement's anthem. First performed by Holiday in late January 1939, at Café Society, it was a call to arms in a year of three lynchings, reports that 60 percent of Southerners believed lynching was justifiable, and the release of *Gone with the Wind:* the film that was later criticized for its "moonlight and magnolias" approach to the history of the South was sweeping the nation, but in "Strange Fruit" the smell of burning flesh accompanies the "scent of magnolias." It was the first time anyone had sung so explicitly about lynching, and people were gripped. "This is about a phonograph record which has obsessed me for two days," wrote a journalist in October 1939. "Even now, as I think of it, the short hair on the back of my neck tightens and I want to hit somebody." The record producer Ahmet Ertegun called the song "a declaration of war . . . the beginning of the civil rights movement," and the South African government banned it during apartheid. So troubling was Holiday's rendition that, in the 1980s, United Airlines removed the track from an in-flight entertainment album, and a North Carolina radio station still had it marked "Do not play." Other people embraced its power: in 2003, *Q Magazine* ranked it sixth in a list of one hundred songs that changed the world, and in 2002 an exhibition of lynching photographs, *Without Sanctuary,* featured the photograph that had haunted Meeropol, Meeropol's poem, and a recording of "Strange Fruit."

Further reading: Angela Davis, *Blues Legacies* (1998); David Margolick, *Strange Fruit* (2000).

Southern trees bear strange fruit,
Blood on the leaves and blood at the root,
Black bodies swinging in the southern breeze,
Strange fruit hanging from the poplar trees.

Pastoral scene of the gallant south,
The bulging eyes and the twisted mouth,
Scent of magnolias, sweet and fresh,
Then the sudden smell of burning flesh.

Here is fruit for the crows to pluck,
For the rain to gather, for the wind to suck,
For the sun to rot, for the trees to drop,
Here is a strange and bitter crop.

Bill for Negro Rights
and the Suppression of Lynching

<u>1934</u>

Nearly two hundred anti-lynching bills died in Congress between 1890 and 1960. One, the Costigan-Wagner Bill of 1935, proposed fines (not exceeding $5,000) and imprisonment (not exceeding five years) for any governmental body that failed to protect an individual against a mob—the same penalties imposed in kidnapping cases. Hoping to garner support for the bill, the National Association for the Advancement of Colored People (NAACP) organized the exhibition "An Art Commentary on Lynching." It ran in New York for two weeks through March 2, 1935, and on March 3 a second exhibition opened, "The Struggle for Negro Rights." This was organized by a coalition of left-wing organizations, including the League of Struggle for Negro Rights (LSNR), and offered its own legislation—a "Bill for Negro Rights." The proposed bill indicted lynchers for murder, punishable by death. It had little chance of passage, but the exhibition organizers wanted to make the point that the Costigan-Wagner bill did not go far enough. Both exhibitions asked visitors to support the associated bills.

The LSNR, author of the "Bill for Negro Rights," was the main African American branch of the Communist Party and a successor to the American Negro Labor Congress. Established in 1930, it campaigned for a separate black nation in the South, against police brutality, and against the Italian occupation of Ethiopia. It published the bill in a pamphlet that also included its "Program" and "Constitution." The program called for the death penalty for lynchers, the outlawing of the KKK, and the formation of self-defense organizations. It asked white workers to join in solidarity with black workers and to "cast to the winds the least stench of the slave market and the lynching post." Further connecting slavery and lynching, the program explained that the "same blow which struck off the shackles of chattel slavery . . . hammered on the chains of a new slavery." African Americans now faced "further enslavement" amid a "stifling lynch atmosphere."

The writer Langston Hughes, who composed anti-lynching poems like "Christ in Alabama" (1931) and "Lynching Song" (1936), became President of the League's National Council in 1934. The LSNR reached an official membership of 10,000 but disappeared after 1935 when the Communist Party joined with non-communist organizations to form the National Negro Congress.

To Abolish the Practice of Lynching of Negroes, and to Secure Full Equality and Civil Rights, throughout the United States of America

SECTION 1:—BE IT ENACTED BY THE SENATE AND HOUSE OF REPRESEN-TATIVES OF THE UNITED STATES OF AMERICA IN CONGRESS ASSEMBLED, that because the rights of the Negro people, although guaranteed by the Constitution of the United States of America, 13th, 14th and 15th Amendments, have been and are being systematically violated, as shown by: the denial of the rights of citizenship, the denial in many sections of the country of their right to vote, to serve on juries and to enjoy equal rights in courts of law, the system of peonage and slavery and chain gang widely practiced in the South, the wholesale frame-ups against innocent Negroes and other such oppressive practices, the fact that during the past fifty years more than 5,000 lynchings have taken place in the United States and with very little effort on the part of the Police or Judicial Authorities to apprehend or to punish the guilty parties; therefore it becomes necessary to adopt special measures to suppress the practice of lynching and to secure to the Negro people the full and free exercise of complete equal rights with every other section of the population.

SECTION 2:—Every person participating in a lynching is declared to be guilty of murder in the first degree, and upon conviction shall be punished by death. Lynching is defined as a violent assault, resulting in death or aggravated injury, directed against the victim because of supposed inferiority of the Negroes, and/or, because he or she is accused of a crime associated with such supposed inferiority, and/or, when such violent attacks are wholly or partly directed towards intimidating the Negro population to prevent them from claiming their rights, and/or, when such violence is directed towards preventing the free association of whites and Negroes and their joint activity in all phases of life. Such violent attack shall be considered a lynching whenever motivated by any or all of the above, whether the attacker or attackers are private individuals or officers of the law, or both, and whether or not such attack was directed against any particular individual. Participation in any attempted lynching shall be a felony, punishable by imprisonment for not less than one year.

SECTION 3:—Any official or official body of any subdivision of the United States government of any state, county, or municipality, who shall adopt or enforce any measure aimed at or resulting in, the denial of full equality of Negroes, is guilty of a malfeasance in office, and is subject to immediate removal and is guilty of a felony. In such category of prohibited measures are all so-called Jim-Crow laws and regulations which provide for segregation of, or discrimination against Negroes, which deprive them of the right to vote through the enacting of special qualifications which in practice result in depriving the

Negro of the franchise, which exclude them from jury lists or panels, and in practice result in the dismissal of persons from juries on account of being Negroes, which exclude Negroes from any employment or office, or which in any way directly or indirectly deprive the Negroes of their full and complete rights or participation in any phase of public life.

SECTION 4:—Any person who shall in his private capacity discriminate against Negroes, in employment or in the renting or other occupancy of any dwellings or business quarters, or who shall charge higher prices or rents to Negroes than to the general public, or who shall refuse to render to Negroes professional services which he or she normally offers to the public, shall be declared guilty of a misdemeanor, punishable by not less than six months in prison, and, upon a third repetition of the offense if guilty of a felony, punishable by not less than two years in prison, in both cases in addition to punitive damages payable to the person discriminated against.

Federal Law Is Imperative

1947

In 1946 Helen Gahagan Douglas (1900–1980), an ex-Broadway star and Democratic Congresswoman, read her "Democratic Credo" into the Congressional Record: "We, the members of this House, do not believe that Capitol Hill is a hill on which to kindle a fiery cross," said Douglas, "but rather one on which to display the shining Cross . . . the symbol of the Brotherhood of Man." The following year she took up this problem of the "fiery cross" and sponsored an anti-lynching bill. Just as the bill reached Congress, a lynch mob seized a young man from a North Carolina jail. The reporter Jack Bell asked Douglas about another lynching, in South Carolina, in the radio interview reprinted here.

Douglas's bill was one of three particularly high-profile attempts at anti-lynching legislation: the Dyer Bill came in 1918, and in 1935 campaigners tried to push through the Costigan-Wagner Bill. By the mid-1940s anti-lynching campaigners were seeking a new impetus in the international arena. Douglas had been a delegate to the United Nations and referred to the UN charter in the radio interview. Her focus on race relations also encompassed a fight for anti-discrimination employment laws and the introduction of a bill to add a condition to the Daughters of the American Revolution tax exemption so that the group couldn't deny commercial use of Constitution Hall for reasons of race. In 1946 she received the Scroll of Honor from the National Council of Negro Women.

Southern legislators blocked Douglas's bill, as they did in 1949 when she reintroduced it. In 1950 Douglas gave up her House seat to run for the Senate. Her opponent was Richard Nixon, who had come to prominence for his role on the House Un-American Activities Committee. He called Douglas a communist, won the election, and was elected U.S. vice president two years later. Lynching continued through the 1950s and beyond. But, ever hopeful, Douglas ended her 1982 autobiography: "There is still time for sane people to set things right. But time is running out." Here she echoes Charles Chesnutt's novel about racial violence, *The Marrow of Tradition* (1901), which ends with hope "nearly gone" and a warning to the future: "There's time enough, but none to spare."

Jack Bell: Mrs. Douglas, I notice you have introduced a second anti-lynching bill recently. What was the additional purpose?

Helen Gahagan Douglas: First let us re-read the Fourteenth Amendment of the Constitution: "nor shall any state deprive any person of life, liberty or property without the due process of law, nor deny to any person within its jurisdiction the equal protection of the laws." Last year's bill sought only to penalise state law enforcement officers, derelict in their duty. My bill Hr3618 this year, reflects our new obligations, born of the great role we played in the writing of the United Nations charter, which seeks to promote universal respect for, and observance of, human rights and fundamental freedoms for all without distinction as to race, language or religion. The bill provides that the federal government shall prosecute and punish persons who commit, or attempt to commit, violence against any person because of race, creed or colour.

Jack Bell: How would your bill apply to the recent Greenville, South Carolina case?

Helen Gahagan Douglas: Federal law is imperative, Mr. Bell, if we're going to stop lynching. The criminal prosecutions under my bill will be conducted in a federal district court. The significance of federal trial is manifold. I have deep sympathy with the local court officials who are victims of local prejudices and pressures on themselves as well as on their families. Often, they do the very best that they can, but that is no guarantee of justice under the present practices of local administrators. Under my bill, a federal judge and a federal prosecutor would have dealt in the Greenville case. Secondly, you would have been able to draw on half the state of South Carolina for a jury, instead of just the community of Greenville, which was immediately involved, and in which case you would have had a jury which wouldn't have reflected the immediate pressures of the community.

Jack Bell: Under your bill, Mrs. Douglas, the community where the abduction takes place and the community where the violence is actually committed would be subject to civil suit?

Helen Gahagan Douglas: Yes, Mr. Bell.

Jack Bell: What chances do you see for action on your bill in the House at the session?

Helen Gahagan Douglas: Before answering that question, I want to say that I just learned a few hours ago that Senator Wagner and Senator Morse had introduced a similar bill in the Senate this afternoon. In the house, I shall certainly urge the House judiciary committee, to which this bill has been referred, hold full and speedy hearings on this whole question of lynching. I also hope that they will report the bill out so that the members of the House have a chance to vote on this vital issue before congress recesses for the summer.

Jack Bell: Thank you, Representative Helen Gahagan Douglas.

Take a Stand against the Klan

1980

Ten days after John Brown's execution, the abolitionist George William Curtis insisted that Brown was "not buried but planted" and would spring up "a hundred-fold." By the 1970s, Brown had perhaps done just that. The radical left organization the Weather Underground named its journal *Osawatomie,* echoing Brown's nickname "Osawatomie Brown," printed Brown's picture in each issue, and published letters from the John Brown Book Club. One article claimed Brown as "a heroic American revolutionary . . . and guerrilla fighter." And in 1978, a white anti-racist group with connections to the Weather Underground began a national campaign against white supremacists and racist violence. Members named the group the John Brown Anti-Klan Committee (JBAKC). Lisa Roth, who cofounded the JBAKC, explained in a recent interview: "For most white anti-racists making the leap from ideas to action is a bit of a challenge. Brown was someone who really understood white privilege. He understood that this is nothing to feel guilty about, nobody chooses how they're born. But the way you relinquish your privilege is by fighting for those who have no privilege. Ultimately, Brown made the sacrifice of privilege."

In the late 1970s, Roth and others were working to support incarcerated Black Panthers and heard rumors that the KKK was organizing in New York State prisons. They drove to Albany, examined the New York State Klan incorporation papers, and discovered that the man who had incorporated the state chapter was the head of the guard unit at Napanoch prison. All those listed in the incorporation were guards there. In protest the JBAKC was born, soon developing into a national organization with local chapters mandated to educate and organize against the Klan. They set themselves in a tradition of anti-lynching protest, quoting the activist Ida B. Wells's description of white America's "reign of terror" in their pamphlets. Like Wells, one of the group's strategies was to list details of racist attacks, and they described twenty-four incidents of murders, rapes, beatings, arson attacks, and cross-burnings between June 1978 and May 1980. These were Klan attacks that paralleled and surpassed those of the Klan in Reconstruction, one JBAKC pamphlet asserted.

They used the term "Nazified Klan" to describe the ideological and organizational merger of the KKK and neo-Nazis, contributing theory as well as practice to the anti-racist movement. In California they clashed with Nazi skinheads, who called them the "James Brown Anti-Klan Committee"—"we always thought it amusing that they considered that a big insult," Roth remembers. The group produced a newspaper called *NO KKK, NO FASCIST USA!,* with a national circulation of 10,000, that covered racist tracking in schools, homophobia and AIDS, the dumping of nuclear waste on Native reservations, whites-only country clubs, political prisoners, and the "slave sport" of using inmates to train tracking dogs in Texas and Florida prisons. "We had a holistic world view," says Roth. "We took a lot of crap for not being a 'single issue' organization. But racism and white supremacy have a broad reach and a really meaningful analysis has to try to address the many aspects." Identifying themselves as anti-imperialists, the JBAKC viewed African Americans, Native Americans, Puerto Ricans, and Mexicans as oppressed colonies within the United States, and rejected calls for integration.

In 1988, the JBAKC member Terry Bisson retraced Brown's path through Lawrence, Osawatomie, and Harpers Ferry, Virginia, and wrote the novel *Fire on the Mountain*. One character in the novel says that if Harriet Tubman is "the Mother of Our Country and Frederick Douglass the Father," then Brown "is some kind of Godfather. Blood may be thicker than water, but politics is thicker than either." Bisson's preface notes that the novel is a counterfactual history: "a story of what might have happened if John Brown's raid had succeeded." In a sense, however, the JBAKC replaced counterfactuals with a new attempt to succeed.

"We need allies who are going to help us achieve a victory, not allies who are going to tell us to be non-violent. If a white man wants to be an ally, ask him what does he think of John Brown. You know what John Brown did? He went to war."—Malcolm X

To this day, John Brown remains a leading example of a white American willing to take up arms under the leadership of the Black liberation struggle in the fight against white supremacy. Because we believe his uncompromising opposition to the white supremacy and total commitment to Black liberation represent the only strategy to defeat the Ku Klux Klan and all forms of organized white supremacy, we take the name of the John Brown Anti-Klan Committee.

Principles of Unity—John Brown Anti-Klan Committee

I. Fight White Supremacy in All Its Forms! Death to the Klan! Support the Struggle of the Black Nation for Self-Determination! Support the Struggle to Free the Land! White supremacy has been a part of every counter-insurgency terror plan that the U.S. has developed. The struggle to free the land of the Black nation has been a fierce, life-and-death struggle of Black people for 400 years. The Black nation will win its freedom. The freeing of the land will shake the very foundations of U.S. society; the freeing of the land will defeat white supremacy. **II. Follow Black and Other Third World Leadership!** The struggle against the Klan is a life-and-death struggle, based on the antagonistic relationship between oppressed nations and U.S. imperialism. Our tasks as white people are defined by and grow out of the strategy and tasks set by the oppressed nations... The dominant history and practice of white people in this country has been to reject this leadership. John Brown was a white man who responded to the leadership of the Black Liberation Struggle and actively fought white supremacy. This is why we take the name John Brown Anti-Klan Committee, for it is only under Black and other Third World leadership that we can do our work correctly. **III. Support the Struggle of Third World People for Human Rights! Oppose White Supremacist Attacks!** We are committed to fighting attacks on Black and other Third World communities and to supporting the struggle to free prisoners-of-war, captured freedom fighters, and leaders of the oppressed nations. We are committed to fighting not only the Klan but also police terror, white vigilante attacks by the Jewish Defense League and other Zionist forces, white gangs, and all forms of organized white supremacy.

The Rise of the Ku Klux Klan

Nightriders terrorizing Black communities . . . Cross burnings and fire-bombings at the homes of Black families . . . Public rallies proclaiming the 'superiority' and 'rights' of white people . . . The South in the 1870s? No. The United States—North, South, East, and West—right now in 1980. Today, the U.S. is divided by a struggle which is so basic, so fundamental and so critical that its resolution will profoundly change forever the very nature of this country. The struggle of Black people against slavery, against genocide, and for the liberation of their people has shaped this country for more than 400 years. And for more than 400 years the U.S. government, its military and police forces, as well as organized white supremacist forces and large segments of the white population, have conspired to maintain the oppression and subjection of Black people. This conflict is as old as the history of the U.S., and has gone through such significant epochs as slavery, the Civil War and Reconstruction, the massive popular movements in the 1920's and again in the 1960's. The current period, however, is more critical than any earlier point in history—both because of the grave danger facing Black people as they fight against genocide and because the reconsolidation and growth of the Black liberation struggle is bringing the victory of the struggle for national liberation closer than ever . . . The rise of white supremacy in this period is in direct relationship to the decline of imperialism. Imperialism, a system that is based on the oppression and exploitation of entire nations, clearly has always relied upon white supremacy—the economic, political, and social enforcement of the "superiority" of white people. It was the basis of African slavery, which built this country; of the "Manifest Destiny" which meant the genocide of Native American people and the annexation of Mexican land as the U.S. expanded to the Pacific; of the "white man's burden" which justified the conquest of Puerto Rico, Hawaii, and the Philippines and continues to justify U.S. military intervention in every

part of the Third World. Inside the borders of this country, the rule of white supremacy has meant the rule of the lynch mob and killer cops; the super-exploi-
tation of Black labor on the land in the South and in industry North and
South; and the institutionalization of genocidal conditions of life for the entire
Black population. There has never been a time in the history of the U.S. when
white supremacy has not been dominant. But with the very real threat to the
continued existence of U.S. imperialism, white supremacy is more important
than ever—to maintain, protect and defend the white oppressor nation in
the face of the rise of national liberation struggles. The rise of the Ku Klux Klan
today is part of imperialism's answer to the contradiction it finds itself in. That
is, the contradiction between the continued oppression of Third World peoples and the threat that national liberation represents to the very existence of
imperialism. Serving the interests of U.S. imperialism, the Klan plays many
roles. In part it is a secret, armed organization which is part of the military response to the Black liberation struggle; it conducts terror campaigns against
the black community which "official" government forces cannot at this time
do. As such, the Klan plays an important role in counter-insurgency against,
the Black movement. There are growing numbers of Klan-cops, Klan-prison
guards, and Klansmen in the military.

The Strategy to Defeat the Klan

The Klan is more dangerous than ever. There should be no mistake about it—
the Klan has not 'reformed,' adopted a 'new image' or changed its program.
It is definitely operating more openly—holding public rallies, running for president etc.—but this is part of a self-conscious strategy to become the leadership of mass white-supremacist movements and the legitimate voice of white
Amerika. The Klan is actively organizing in high schools, in factories and communities all over the U.S. Klan leaders appear regularly on network television
and Klan propaganda has a wide distribution. The different Klan organizations
are clearly well-financed and are protected by the federal government and
courts. The Klan's right to speak and organize, when it is officially challenged
at all, is defended by the ACLU. Churches, civic and community organizations and 'liberals' in general are reluctant to speak out against the Klan. The
women's movement gave the Klan a platform at the International Women's
Year conference in Houston and has done nothing to oppose it since. Yet the
basic reality of the Klan has not changed. In the most recent period the Klan
has been responsible for the murders of Black people in Alabama; the murders of five members of the Communist Workers' Party in Greensboro, North
Carolina; the murders of at least two prisoners in New York state and attacks
on hundreds of prisoners throughout the country; the firebombings of dozens

of homes of Black families who "dare" to move into white communities and has held hundreds of rallies and cross burnings. On the border between the U.S. and Mexico—from Texas to California—the Klan assists the INS (Immigration and Naturalization Service) in the brutal repression of undocumented workers, patrolling the borders in gangs of armed white nightriders, terrorizing and murdering Chicanos and Mexicanos. The KKK today, as it has always been, is about one thing—white supremacy and genocide. Today, however, there is a strategy to defeat the Klan, a strategy that is led by the Black liberation struggle and a strategy in which all progressive white people must play a part . . . Taking a stand against the Klan is not a question of morality (although one could question the morality of refusing to do so). Rather, it is a question of urgent necessity, a question which will go a long way towards determining the role that white people can play in the future of this country. The Klan represents everything which is repressive, undemocratic, violent, and brutal about this society—it is the embodiment of white Amerika. The decline of U.S. imperialism affects every one of us. The material basis of white supremacy is threatened as the U.S. empire shrinks and crumbles. For Black and other Third World people this means heightened genocide. But it has a direct impact on the conditions and quality of life for white people in the U.S. as well. Economically, politically, and socially, conditions are deteriorating—schools, communities, cities are all in crisis. More and more, white working class people are finding it difficult to maintain or even approximate a standing of living which U.S. imperialism has always held out as its end of the bargain. And the threat of imperialist world war constantly hangs over us all. The Klan and other fascist movements can never solve the crisis in the U.S. in a way that benefits most Americans. But make not mistake about it—neither U.S. imperialism nor the system of white supremacy will crumble by their own weight. In fact, the more it is threatened, the more violent and repressive the system becomes. The Black liberation struggle along with other national liberation struggles inside the U.S. and as part of the worldwide anti-imperialist movement, represents the best hope for all of us to resolve the centuries-old contradictions and current crises in a direction which will mean a better society for all people. A self-conscious stand against the Klan and a serious commitment to fight white supremacy and support Black liberation is the way that we can participate in this process.

DEATH TO THE KLAN!
SUPPORT THE BLACK LIBERATION STRUGGLE!
DEFEAT U.S. IMPERIALISM AND WORLDWIDE WHITE SUPREMACY!

From AmeriKKKa 1998:
The Lynching of James Byrd

1998

It must have seemed like a time warp: thousands gathered at the funeral of a black man brutally lynched by several whites, just as thousands had gathered for the same reason forty-three years earlier. The earlier funeral was for Emmett Till, murdered in Mississippi in 1955, reportedly for whistling at a white woman. The second was for James Byrd, Jr., murdered in Texas in 1998 by three white men with ties to the Aryan Nation. Ranking behind only Mississippi and Georgia in the number of lynchings between 1882 and 1968, with 493 incidents, Texas is a big feature on the landscape of the "Amerikkka" described by Michael Slate (b. 1950) in the article reprinted here. Anti-racist activists characterized Byrd's murder as the worst racist hate crime since Till's, and Slate, a writer for *Revolution* (the magazine of the Revolutionary Communist Party), refers to antebellum America in order to show how little progress has been made. In response to the murder, Dread Scott, a revolutionary Maoist and a founding member of the Artists Network of Refuse & Resist!, produced a protest-art installation, *Historic Corrections,* that connected lynching to police brutality and the death penalty. In 2001 Scott mounted another protest installation, this time explicitly about the Byrd murder. Called *Jasper the Ghost,* it traced a historical line from slavery to lynching.

In May 2001, Texas signed into law the James Byrd Jr. Hate Crimes Act. This amended the previous hate crimes law to include targeting race, color, disability, religion, national origin or ancestry, age, and gender or sexual orientation. The last element was important because, four months after Byrd's death, Matthew Shepard, a gay student in Wyoming (a state without a hate crime law), was lynched and left for dead. The passerby who discovered him the next morning—unconscious, mutilated, burned, hypothermic, and tied to a fencepost—at first thought he was a scarecrow. Journalists pointed to the symbolism of the fencepost, calling Shepard's death a crucifixion. Shepard died a few days later, just as Terrence McNally's play *Corpus Christi* opened on Broadway. This featured a gay Christ-like Texan, an uncanny blend of Byrd and Shepard. The following year, McNally's preface to the published play observed: "Jesus Christ died again when Matthew Shepard did." But outside the theater during the play's first performance, religious activists protested the depiction of Jesus as a gay man. They didn't see the irony: a gay man had apparently just become Jesus.

I wanted to stand on a corner, in the middle of skyscrapers, open my mouth and let loose a roar from hell. I wanted to spit flames and burn Babylon to the ground. A horrible image was seared onto the lens of my eyes. A blacktop road in the rural Texas town of Jasper stretched out to the horizon. Little white chalk circles gave the road a weird polka dot pattern. A newscaster calmly explained that the circles marked the spots where pieces of James Byrd Jr., a 49-year-old Black man, were found . . .

On Saturday, June 6, James Byrd went to, and sang at, a couple of family get-togethers. At the end of the night he was walking home from his niece's bridal shower. Born and raised in Jasper, it seemed like everyone knew him. Although he was now divorced and lived alone, he was the father of three children. He had six sisters, and in his family he was known as "Toe" because he had lost one of his toes in a childhood injury. He was formerly a vacuum cleaner salesman who now depended on disability because of a crippling job-related injury to his left arm. And, like many Black people in Texas, or for that matter in the U.S. as a whole, James had done some prison time for minor crimes. His daughter described him as a "people person," "an entertainer always trying to tell jokes." Byrd's sister said he was one of those people who was always outgoing and friendly, somebody that everyone in town seemed to like. He often walked where he was going because he suffered from a medical disorder that brought on seizures and that prevented him from driving. So it helped that he was so well known and liked because people would often help him out by offering him a ride.

But there were some people among the 8,000 residents of Jasper who didn't like James Byrd, not because of anything he did or said but because of the color of his skin. On June 6 three of these beasts—supporters of the Ku Klux Klan complete with KKK tattoos and racist posters in their houses—offered him a ride. Who knows why James Byrd took that ride. Maybe it was because he recognized one of the men as somebody who had the same parole officer. Maybe he just never thought that there was any danger facing him in a town he thought he knew so well. But before the night was over, these modern-day slave catchers beat James Byrd senseless. They wrapped him in a chain and attached it to the back of their pick-up truck. Then they dragged James Byrd for three miles on this lonely blacktop country road. Byrd's body broke into 75 pieces. His torso was found in a ditch on the side of the road, at the end of a long trail of blood and near empty beer cans and a cigarette lighter that belonged to one of the killers—the lighter had the word "possum" inscribed on it along with a triangular symbol, which is a KKK symbol. James' head, neck and right arm were found more than a mile from his torso. Pieces of James Byrd, including his dentures, were scattered over more than 10,000 feet of roadway. Pieces of his body were lodged up in the underbody of the truck. His body was so grotesquely mauled that he could only be identified by his fingerprints . . .

The murder of James Byrd, Jr. didn't happen just because three white men got into a drunken rage. This was a crime birthed and nurtured in the cradle of AmeriKKKa. Lawrence Brewer, Sr., the father of one of the men who killed James Byrd, spoke to this as he repeatedly stressed his sympathy for the victim in this case, "If the color of your skin is gonna cause you to be killed, there is something wrong with society."

In the hours after hearing about the murder of James Byrd, Jr., I spoke to many friends about it. A lot of white friends expressed their horror and disgust at the murder. What they were saying reminded me of the Refuse & Resist! slogan: "I used to be a white American but I gave it up in the interests of humanity." A few Black friends... wanted to know if, in the face of all this—all the insane cruelty and hatred crammed into the murder of James Byrd Jr.—I still believed that things can and will change.

As I thought about my answer to this challenge, I was reminded of a statement Frederick Douglass made back in 1852 about the meaning of July 4th to the slave and how, in many ways, very little has changed over the last 150 years. At the end of this statement Douglass declared, "Go where you may, search where you will, roam through all the monarchies and despotisms of the old world, travel through South America, search out every abuse, and when you have found the last, lay your facts by the side of the every-day practices of this nation, and you will say with me, that, for revolting barbarity and shameless hypocrisy, America reigns without a rival."

AmeriKKKa may have no rivals, but its horrific oppression has produced hundreds of millions of enemies inside its borders and around the world. Can we really change things? Yes, a million times over, yes! More than that, we, the enemies of AmeriKKKa, have to do this. But it can only be done through our struggle, our all-out revolutionary struggle to completely overthrow this society, finally opening up the possibility of digging out all the sick and twisted diseases it gives rise to. And on that day, the story of James Byrd, Jr.—along with all the slave stories—will be told to the children to teach them why we must never again allow a society as sick as this one to torture humanity.

The Lynching of Thomas Shipp
and Abram Smith, 1930

<u>2000</u>

"The photographic art played as significant a role in the [lynching] ritual as torture or souvenir grabbing," explained the collector and curator James Allen (b. 1954) in 2000. Some lynchings were delayed until a photographer arrived, and participants in lynchings regularly posed with corpses and sent images to friends and family members as postcards, often with their own faces circled. Images were also sent to anti-lynching activists. John H. Holmes, a Unitarian minister in New York who had publicly condemned lynching, received one with the inscription: "This is the way we do them down here. The last lynching has not been put on card yet. Will put you on our regular mailing list. Expect one a month on average." But Allen's lynching photography exhibition, *Without Sanctuary,* with images taken between 1878 and 1960, provided a new context for the images by appropriating material never intended as protest.

   The exhibition's title refers to lynching victims and to the exhibit's own visitors: a violent history had invaded the sanctuary of galleries and museums. Previous exhibitions of

lynching photographs had included anti-lynching art, but all of the images in *Without Sanctuary* were taken as celebratory evidence and many include white faces staring out; the photographs seem like mirror images of the exhibition's white visitors. Some visitors felt forced to identify with the lynch mobs, others treated the experience as a mourning ritual, and still others felt it forced, necessarily, the history of lynching into public memory. One African American visitor observed: "We have always known about this. We are glad to see a museum can finally acknowledge the truth." Over 50,000 visitors viewed the exhibition in its first four months at the New-York Historical Society. Congressman John Lewis called lynching "an American holocaust" and said the exhibition was a call to "prevent anything like this from ever happening again."

In February 2005, Senators Mary Landrieu and George Allen put forward a resolution on lynching. A total of 4,742 victims were named and some two hundred descendants of victims were invited to witness the vote. Also present at the vote was the only known lynching survivor in the U.S., 91-year old James Cameron. He had narrowly missed being part of the photograph printed here—an image that inspired Abel Meeropol's anti-lynching song, "Strange Fruit" (1939) and was featured in *Without Sanctuary.* In August 1930, Cameron was arrested in Marion, Ind., and taken to the local jail with two other black men, Thomas Shipp and Abram Smith. All three were seized by a lynch mob, and Shipp and Smith were hanged in a public square before two thousand people. A photographer captured the moment, and later thousands of copies of the image were sold. When a rope was thrown over Cameron's head, someone called out that he was innocent. He was cut down, returned to jail, and eventually pardoned in 1993. Now the government asked *his* pardon. The resolution summed up the history of lynching and of anti-lynching protest, and added: "Whereas the recent publication of *Without Sanctuary* . . . helped bring greater awareness and proper recognition of the victims of lynching . . . the Senate [apologizes] for the failure . . . to enact anti-lynching legislation . . . and remembers the history of lynching, to ensure that these tragedies will be neither forgotten nor repeated." Ninety senators signed an oversized copy of the resolution and presented it to the curators of *Without Sanctuary.*

DUST TRACKS ON THE ROAD

The
Great
Depression

Migrant Mother

1936

In March 1936, the documentary photographer Dorothea Lange (1895–1965) was driving through California in the rain. She was heading home with boxes of exposed film ready to send to the Farm Security Administration (FSA). One of the most famous New Deal programs, the FSA provided loans and relocation assistance to farmers. It needed support to receive funding, and so the FSA's Historical Section documented the migrants' living conditions and federal programs' beneficial impact. Established in 1935 as the Resettlement Administration, renamed the Farm Security Administration in 1937, and active until 1943, among the photographers who contributed their images were Walker Evans, Gordon Parks, Marion Post Wolcott, Ben Shahn, and Lange. These photographers worked in the context of a documentary explosion that included the Federal Theatre's documentary plays and the Works Progress Administration's *American Guide* series, and against the backdrop of a massive movement for the rights of working people and anti-fascist agitation.

Lange had a capacity for empathy beyond most of her FSA colleagues and tried to give subjects her full attention. But on this rainy day she was ready to tune out. She passed a camp for seasonal agricultural workers and didn't stop. For the next 20 miles she argued with herself, then turned back, saying later, "I was following instinct." She'd spend only ten minutes at the camp but would emerge with the most famous of the FSA's 250,000 images.

Feeling drawn to a woman in a lean-to tent, Lange approached. The woman was 32 years old and a mother of seven. They had all had been living on birds and frozen vegetables for days. The pea crop was frozen and there was no work. Lange felt that the women "seemed to know that my pictures might help her, and so she helped me. There was a sort of equality about it." Her first shots included too much landscape or captured unsatisfactory facial expressions. So she asked two girls to lean on their mother's shoulder, their faces turned away, and told the mother to bring a hand to her face. Suddenly they were symbols of dependence and the photograph a classic Madonna-and-child image. Lange didn't try to photograph other migrants in the camp, believing she "had recorded the essence of my assignment." A few days later, she showed her photographs to the editor of the *San Francisco News*. He contacted government officials, who rushed 20,000 pounds of food to the camp, and the paper published Lange's images.

John Steinbeck was influenced by Lange's photographs: the FSA Historical Section chief Roy Stryker remembered him looking through the FSA files for days, inspired by the "tragic, beautiful faces," and some of Lange's photographs appeared in Steinbeck's essays. In 1941 the documentary filmmaker Pare Lorentz pointed to Lange and Steinbeck as the dominant forces in Depression-era protest: "If there are transient camps, and better working conditions, and a permanent agency seeking to help migratory workers," then "Lange, with her still pictures . . . and Steinbeck, with two novels, a play, and a motion picture, have done more for these tragic nomads than all the politicians of the country."

Further reading: Pete Daniel, *Official Images* (1987); Maren Stange, *Symbols of Ideal Life* (1989).

Farmer and Sons

1936

In 1936 the Farm Security Administration (FSA) photographer Arthur Rothstein (1915–1985) went to document the Dust Bowl. "It was a very difficult thing to show in pictures," he recalled. The worse drought in the climatological history of the country had hit the country in 1930. By 1934 it had turned the Great Plains into a desert. Vast dust storms swept a region extending from the Mississippi River Valley to the Rockies, North Dakota to Texas. In 1935, the government developed conservation programs, but the Dust Bowl would last ten years. Rothstein wanted to show that the drought affected people as well

as crops. In April 1936 he came across an Oklahoma farm and captured an image of a family fleeing a dust storm, the father struggling against the wind, the younger child abandoned, and the family divided. But there was no storm to flee. Rothstein worked with the family to achieve the effect, later insisting that the photographer was not only cameraman but "scenarist, dramatist, and director as well," that "deliberate distortion may actually add to [a photograph's] reality," and that the particular image encouraged legislation for soil conservation.

Rothstein wasn't the only artist who found the Depression hard to represent, as an article for *Life* magazine explained in 1938: "Depressions are hard to see because they consist of things not happening, of business not being done." Photographers had to picture *nothing*. "This was a very difficult thing to show in pictures," said Rothstein. His solution was to create *something*: the over-directed image spoke—ironically—to a national sense of indirection. The bent father and the son's shielded face give visual expression to a farmer's remark in Dorothea Lange and Paul Taylor's photography book *An American Exodus* (1939): "My boys have no more future than I have, so far as I can see ahead."

A month after taking his photograph, Rothstein found a bleached steer skull in South Dakota. He moved it onto cracked earth, created a shadow, and took five different photographs. One of these images quickly came to symbolize the drought, just as his Oklahoma image became a symbol of the dust storms. But this time a front-page editorial in a conservative newspaper claimed his image was government propaganda. Reporters dug through the FSA files and found Rothstein's negatives. Cartoonists drew him carrying the skull around the country and the FSA was challenged as fake. "If you have that goddamn skull," warned his supervisor, "hide it, for Christ's sake." So notorious was the image that in 1951 copies circulated on the Senate floor as politicians debated a composite photograph of a senator and the head of the U.S. Communist Party.

Further reading: Cara Finnegan, *Picturing Poverty* (2003); Michael Shapiro, *The Politics of Representation* (1988).

From The Grapes of Wrath

1939

"I have read a book recently," announced President Roosevelt in 1940, of *The Grapes of Wrath.* There were 500,000 Americans living between its covers, Roosevelt said: "I would like to see the California Columbia Basin devoted to [their] care." John Steinbeck (1902–1968) had produced a publishing sensation. By 1941 it had sold over 543,000 copies. *The New Republic* magazine placed it "very high in the category of the great angry books like *Uncle Tom's Cabin* that have roused a people to fight against intolerable wrongs." But some were roused to fight the book instead. It was ritually burned and publicly banned. As with *Uncle Tom's Cabin* (1852) and *Looking Backward* (1888), spinoffs were published, countered the protest. It went on to become an index of dissent in America, selling fewer copies in the 1980s, and more after the 2003 invasion of Iraq.

The novel draws on the language of scripture. Jim Casy (JC) is a Christ figure, with twelve disciples and a Judas in Connie. Casy dies with the words: "You don know what you're a doin'" (echoing Jesus on the cross). The ironically named Noah doesn't witness the flood and abandons the Joads' ark, and Rose of Sharon's baby is sent downriver as a dead Moses in a basket. These mythic resonances elevated the novel above the now-for-gotten proletarian novels of the period. Steinbeck's migrants are also strange descendants of America's frontiersmen, moving west to find no promised land. The westward movement of the novel draws on narrative conventions of inevitability: the characters are "caught in something larger than themselves," disaster is unstoppable, revolution is inevitable, and everything is ruled by the "the great fact" of history. Even Steinbeck's writing process reflected this teleology. He worked toward a definite end, noting in his journal that he was "fixed on the last scene . . . toward which the whole story moves." The novel's structure of alternating narrative chapters and inter-chapters adds to this in-evitability: events in inter-chapters precede the same events in narrative chapters. This structure implies that change will come with or without individual action, and raises the problem of agency within the protest tradition.

But Steinbeck believed an alternation between general and particular was a good pro-test strategy. He noted that the novel was designed to "hit the reader below the belt" by offering "the rhythms and symbols of poetry" which would "open him up" in order to fa-cilitate the introduction of "things on an intellectual level." In addition, the structure makes readers experience inevitability along with the migrants. Steinbeck told his editor he had done his "damndest . . . to make the reader participate in the actuality," because the reader's empathy matters: one change that Steinbeck did believe possible was in the human heart. He was calling for a spiritualized, private transformation. Like Harriet Beecher Stowe's readers, his must "see to it that *they feel right,*" as Stowe puts it in *Uncle Tom's Cabin* (1852). He filled the novel with different voices—dialect, communal stories, folk music, newsreels, ad copy, and the Old Testament—then trusted his readers to listen. Like the character Casy, they might "hear em an . . . feel em." Like the migrants in the novel who hear stories around a campfire, they might "became great through them."

Further reading: Richard Pells, *Radical Visions* (1973); Susan Suleiman, *Authoritarian Fictions* (1983).

Chapter 14

The western land, nervous under the beginning change. THE WESTERN STATES, nervous as horses before a thunder storm. The great owners, nervous, sensing a change, knowing nothing of the nature of the change. The great owners, striking at the immediate thing, the widening government, the growing labor unity; striking at new taxes, at plans; not knowing these things are results, not causes. Results, not causes; results, not causes. The causes lie deep and simply—the causes are a hunger in a stomach, multiplied a million times; a hunger in a single soul, hunger for joy and some security, multiplied a million times; muscles and mind aching to grow, to work, to create, multiplied a million times. The last clear definite function of man—muscles aching to work, minds aching to create beyond the single need—this is man. To build a wall, to build a house, a dam, and in the wall and house and dam to put something of Manself, and to Manself take back something of the wall, the house, the dam; to take hard muscles from the lifting, to take the clear lines and form from conceiving. For man, unlike any other thing organic or inorganic in the universe, grows beyond his work, walks up the stairs of his concepts, emerges ahead of his accomplishments. This you may say of man—when theories change and crash, when schools, philosophies, when narrow dark alleys of thought, national, religious, economic, grow and disintegrate, man reaches, stumbles forward, painfully, mistakenly sometimes. Having stepped forward, he may slip back, but only half a step, never the full step back. This you may say and know it and know it. This you may know when the bombs plummet out of the black planes on the market place, when prisoners are stuck like pigs, when the crushed bodies drain filthily in the dust. You may know it in this way. If the step were not being taken, if the stumbling-forward ache were not alive, the bombs would not fall, the throats would not be cut. Fear the time when the bombs stop falling while the bombers live—for every bomb is proof that the spirit has not died. And fear the time when the strikes stop while the great owners live—for every little beaten strike is proof that the step is being taken. And this you can know—fear the time when Manself will not suffer and die for a concept, for this one quality is the foundation of Manself, and this one quality is man, distinctive in the universe.

*   *   *

The Western States nervous under the beginning change. Texas and Oklahoma, Kansas and Arkansas, New Mexico, Arizona, California. A single family moved from the land. Pa borrowed money from the bank, and now the bank wants the land. The land company—that's the bank when it has land—wants tractors, not families on the land. Is a tractor bad? Is the power that turns the long furrows wrong? If this tractor were ours it would be good—not mine, but ours. If our tractor turned the long furrows of our land, it would be good. Not my land, but ours. We could love that tractor then as we have loved this land when it was ours. But this tractor does two things—it turns the land and turns us off the land. There is little difference between this tractor and a tank. The people are driven, intimidated, hurt by both. We must think about this.

One man, one family driven from the land; this rusty car creaking along the highway to the west. I lost my land, a single tractor took my land. I am alone and I am bewildered. And in the night one family camps in a ditch and another family pulls in and the tents come out. The two men squat on their hams and the women and children listen. Here is the node, you who hate change and fear revolution. Keep these two squatting men apart; make them hate, fear, suspect each other. Here is the anlage of the thing you fear. This is the zygote. For here "I lost my land" is changed; a cell is split and from its splitting grows the thing you hate—"We lost *our* land." The danger is here, for two men are not as lonely and perplexed as one. And from this first "we" there grows a still more dangerous thing: "I have a little food" plus "I have none." If from this problem the sum is "We have a little food," the thing is on its way, the movement has direction. Only a little multiplication now, and this land, this tractor are ours. The two men squatting in a ditch, the little fire, the side-meat stewing in a single pot, the silent, stone-eyed women; behind, the children listening with their souls to words their minds do not understand. The night draws down. The baby has a cold. Here, take this blanket. It's wool. It was my mother's blanket—take it for the baby. This is the thing to bomb. This is the beginning—from "I" to "we."

If you who own the things people must have could understand this, you might preserve yourself. If you could separate causes from results, if you could know that Paine, Marx, Jefferson, Lenin, were results, not causes, you might survive. But that you cannot know. For the quality of owning freezes you forever into "I," and cuts you off forever from the "we."

The Western States are nervous under the beginning change. Need is the stimulus to concept, concept to action. A half-million people moving over the country; a million more restive, ready to move; ten million more feeling the first nervousness.

And tractors turning the multiple furrows in the vacant land.

Chapter 28

They sat silent in the coal-black cave of vines. Ma said, "How'm I gonna know 'bout you? They might kill ya an' I wouldn' know. They might hurt ya. How'm I gonna know?"

Tom laughed uneasily, "Well, maybe like Casy says, a fella ain't got a soul of his own, but on'y a piece of a big one—an' then—"

"Then what, Tom?"

"Then it don' matter. Then I'll be all aroun' in the dark. I'll be ever'where—wherever you look. Wherever they's a fight so hungry people can eat, I'll be there. Wherever they's a cop beatin' up a guy, I'll be there. If Casy knowed, why, I'll be in the way guys yell when they're mad an'—I'll be in the way kids laugh when they're hungry an' they know supper's ready. An' when our folks eat the stuff they raise an' live in the houses they build—why, I'll be there. See? God, I'm talkin' like Casy. Comes of thinkin' about him so much. Seems like I can see him sometimes."

"I don' un'erstan'," Ma said. "I don' really know."

"Me neither," said Tom. "It's jus' stuff I been thinkin' about. Get thinkin' a lot when you ain't movin' aroun'. You got to get back, Ma."

"You take the money then."

He was silent for a moment. "Awright," he said.

"An', Tom, later—when it's blowed over, you'll come back. You'll find us?"

"Sure," he said. "Now you better go. Here, gimme your han'." He guided her toward the entrance. Her fingers clutched his wrist. He swept the vines aside and followed her out. "Go up to the field till you come to a sycamore on the edge, an' then cut acrost the stream. Good-by."

"Good-by," she said, and she walked quickly away. Her eyes were wet and burning, but she did not cry. Her footsteps were loud and careless on the leaves as she went through the brush. And as she went, out of the dim sky the rain began to fall, big drops and few, splashing on the dry leaves heavily . . .

Chapter 30

They came panting up to the rain-soaked barn and staggered into the open end. There was no door in this end. A few rusty farm tools lay about, a disk plow and a broken cultivator, an iron wheel. The rain hammered on the roof and curtained the entrance. Pa gently set Rose of Sharon down on an oily box. "God Awmighty!" he said.

Ma said, "Maybe they's hay inside. Look, there's a door." She swung the door on its rusty hinges. "They is hay," she cried. "Come on in, you."

It was dark inside. A little light came in through the cracks between the boards.

"Lay down, Rosasharn," Ma said. "Lay down an' res'. I'll try to figger some way to dry you off."

Winfield said, "Ma!" and the rain roaring on the roof drowned his voice. "*Ma!*"

"What is it? What you want?"

"Look! In the corner."

Ma looked. There were two figures in the gloom; a man who lay on his back, and a boy sitting beside him, his eyes wide, staring at the newcomers. As he looked, the boy got slowly up to his feet and came toward her. His voice croaked. "You own this here?"

"No," Ma said. "Jus' come in outa the wet. We got a sick girl. You got a dry blanket we could use an' get her wet clothes off?"

The boy went back to the corner and brought a dirty comfort and held it out to Ma.

"Thank ya," she said. "What's the matter'th that fella?"

The boy spoke in a croaking monotone. "Fust he was sick—but now he's starvin'."

"What?"

"Starvin'. Got sick in the cotton. He ain't et for six days."

Ma walked to the corner and looked down at the man. He was about fifty, his whiskery face gaunt, and his open eyes were vague and staring. The boy stood beside her. "Your pa?" Ma asked.

"Yeah! Says he wasn' hungry, or he jus' et. Give me the food. Now he's too weak. Can't hardly move."

The pounding of the rain decreased to a soothing swish on the roof. The gaunt man moved his lips. Ma knelt beside him and put her ear close. His lips moved again.

"Sure," Ma said. "You jus' be easy. He'll be awright. You jus' wait'll I get them wet clo'es off'n my girl."

Ma went back to the girl. "Now slip 'em off," she said. She held the comfort up to screen her from view. And when she was naked, Ma folded the comfort about her.

The boy was at her side again explaining, "I didn' know. He said he et, or he wasn' hungry. Las' night I went an' bust a winda an' stoled some bread. Made 'im chew 'er down. But he puked it all up, an' then he was weaker. Got to have soup or milk. You folks got money to git milk?"

Ma said, "Hush. Don' worry. We'll figger somepin out."

Suddenly the boy cried, "He's dyin', I tell you! He's starvin' to death, I tell you."

"Hush," said Ma. She looked at Pa and Uncle John standing helplessly gazing at the sick man. She looked at Rose of Sharon huddled in the comfort. Ma's eyes passed Rose of Sharon's eyes, and then came back to them. And the two women looked deep into each other. The girl's breath came short and gasping.

She said "Yes."

Ma smiled. "I knowed you would. I knowed!" She looked down at her hands, tight-locked in her lap.

Rose of Sharon whispered, "Will—will you all—go out?" The rain whisked lightly on the roof.

Ma leaned forward and with her palm she brushed the tousled hair back from her daughter's forehead, and she kissed her on the forehead. Ma got up quickly. "Come on, you fellas," she called. "You come out in the tool shed."

Ruthie opened her mouth to speak. "Hush," Ma said. "Hush and git." She herded them through the door, drew the boy with her; and she closed the squeaking door.

For a minute Rose of Sharon sat still in the whispering barn. Then she hoisted her tired body up and drew the comfort about her. She moved slowly to the corner and stood looking down at the wasted face, into the wide, frightened eyes. Then slowly she lay down beside him. He shook his head slowly from side to side. Rose of Sharon loosened one side of the blanket and bared her breast. "You got to," she said. She squirmed closer and pulled his head close. "There!" she said. "There." Her hand moved behind his head and supported it. Her fingers moved gently in his hair. She looked up and across the barn, and her lips came together and smiled mysteriously.

Hale County, Alabama

1936

In 1931, F. Scott Fitzgerald said the Jazz Age had ended two years earlier, adding: "It was borrowed time anyhow." The 1929 crash ended the biggest speculative binge in the nation's history. By 1932, the stock market had dropped 80 percent and unemployment was at 30 percent. The documentary photographer Walker Evans (1903–1975) confronted this sudden vacuum where the American dream used to be. His image of the young William Fields, reproduced here, evokes this anti-fairytale: the sheets form wings, making the child a fairy behind bars. The photograph, taken on assignment for *Fortune* magazine in Alabama in 1936 after the writer James Agee requested Evans as his collaborator on an article about tenant farmers in the South, was printed in Evans's image-text collaboration with Agee, *Let Us Now Praise Famous Men* (1941). It echoes Agee's descriptions in the book of an "angel nailed to the ground by its wings" and the "angelic possibility . . . savagely danced on." Acknowledging the national drama, Agee and Evans depicted its discarded stage props.

Evans had a literary sensibility, and believed photography could use diction, puns, and oxymora. He was also interested in the narrative continuity of film, and arranged his photographs for *Famous Men* as a collection of small series. Double-page spreads and image sequences move from fullness to emptiness, giving visual expression to the migrant exodus. Evans saw a vanishing America and wanted to "suggest people sometimes by their absence . . . I like to make you feel that an interior is *almost* inhabited by somebody." The image of the Fields family paired with an image of their empty kitchen is one example. The bowl on the wall in the second image echoes Mrs. Fields's head in the first; the chair leg echoes her bent leg and the bed leg; the V-shape and the wall's dark area echo the daughter's dirty dress; the stove echoes Mr. Fields's square posture; the pot's white interior echoes the son's open mouth; the plate on the shelf echoes the grandmother's head.

The collaboration protested conventional documentary texts that filled in all the gaps. *Famous Men* leaves work to be done by the reader: the echoes Evans created across photographs are an appeal to active memory, beyond passive spectatorship. We are challenged to engage—like a woman who arrived at the Farm Security Administration office and asked for an Evans image to give to her brother, a steel executive, intending to write across it: "*your* streets, *your* buildings . . . But *our* souls. God damn you."

Further reading: Robert Coles, *Doing Documentary Work* (1997); Clive Scott, *The Spoken Image* (1999).

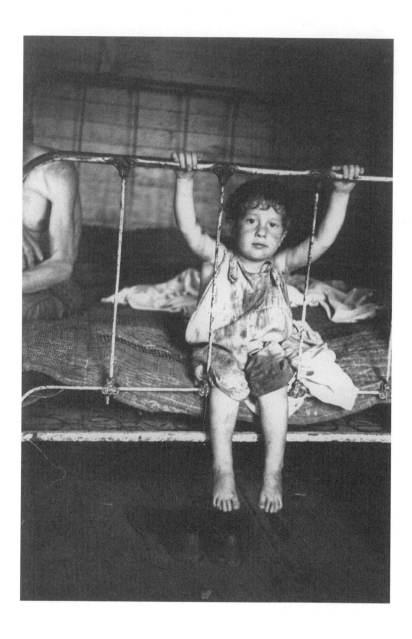

From Let Us Now Praise Famous Men

1941

The novelist and journalist James Agee (1905–1955) approached his 1936 trip to Alabama with characteristic gusto, a convincing Southern accent, and what Walker Evans, his collaborator on the trip, remembered as possession: he "worked in what looked like a rush and a rage" and talked until six in the morning. Agee was irresistible: "He won almost everybody in those families . . . even though some of the individuals were hardbitten," Evans recalled. Out of this experience came the image-text *Let Us Now Praise Famous Men,* an impassioned protest against impersonal documentary that tried to shake readers into a new awareness by violating all expectations of the form. Agee's decision not to write a more straightforward narrative also evolved out of guilt about the potential voyeurism of his project. In an unpublished passage reprinted following excerpts from the published text, he explains his circular, repetitive prose style as a response to this guilt and as an attempt to close the gap between readers and farmers—so that "a little might be set upon you of the unspeakable weight, and monotonies and cumulations, of the work itself."

Originally commissioned as an article for *Fortune* magazine about sharecroppers in the Deep South, the manuscript was ten times longer than any his editors had ever seen. They rejected it, and by the time Agee found a book publisher in 1941, the country was more interested in war than rural poverty. Early reviewers complained about Agee's "bad manners, exhibitionism, and verbosity." *Famous Men* sold 1000 copies and went out of print in 1948, only reissued in the 1960s, when the literature of the 1930s seemed to offer a radical heritage. To a new generation the book contained advice on how to overcome barriers between rich and poor, black and white. White activists helping with voter registration brought the book along to Mississippi, and Evans described the renewed appeal of Agee's "rebellion": it was "unquenchable, self-damaging, deeply principled, infinitely costly, and ultimately priceless."

Further reading: Carol Shloss, *In Visible Light* (1987); Alan Spiegel, *James Agee* (1998).

'It seems to me curious, not to say obscene and thoroughly terrifying, that it could occur to an association of human beings drawn together through need and chance and for profit into a company, an organ of journalism, to pry intimately into the lives of an undefended and appallingly damaged group of human beings, an ignorant and helpless rural family, for the purpose of parading the nakedness, disadvantage and humiliation of these lives before another group of human beings, in the name of science, of "honest journalism" (whatever that paradox may mean), of humanity, of social fearlessness, for money, and for a reputation for crusading and for unbias which, when skillfully enough qualified, is exchangeable at any bank for money (and in politics, for votes, job patronage, abelincolnism, etc.*; and that these people could be capable of meditating this prospect without the slightest doubt of their qualification to do an "honest" piece of work, and with a conscience better than clear, and in the virtual certitude of almost unanimous public approval. It seems curious, further, that the assignment of this work should have fallen to persons having so extremely different a form of respect for the subject, and responsibility toward it, that from the first and inevitably they counted their employers, and that Government likewise to which one of them was bonded, among their most dangerous enemies, acted as spies, guardians, and cheats,† and trusted no judgment, however authoritative it claimed to be, save their own: which in many aspects of the task before them was untrained and uninformed. It seems further curious that realizing the extreme corruptness and difficulty of the circumstances, and the unlikelihood of achieving in any untainted form what they wished to achieve, they accepted the work in the first place. And it seems curious still further that, with all their suspicion of and contempt for every person and thing to do with the situation, save only for the tenants and for themselves, and their own intentions, and with all their realization of the seriousness and mystery of the subject, and of the human responsibility they undertook, they so little questioned or doubted their own qualifications for this work.

All of this, I repeat, seems to me curious, obscene, terrifying, and unfathomably mysterious.

So does the whole course, in all its detail, of the effort of these persons to find, and to defend, what they sought: and the nature of their relationship with those with whom during the searching stages they came into contact; and the subtlety, importance, and almost intangibility of the insights or revelations or oblique suggestions which under different circumstances could never have materialized; so does the method of research which was partly evolved by them, partly forced upon them; so does the strange quality of their relationship with those whose lives they so tenderly and sternly respected, and so rashly undertook to investigate and to record.

So does the whole subsequent course and fate of the work: the causes for its non-publication, the details of its later acceptance elsewhere, and of its design;

---

* Money

† Une chose permise ne peut pas être pure. / L'illégal me va.—*Essai de Critique Indirecte*

the problems which confronted the maker of the photographs; and those which confront me as I try to write of it: the question, Who are you who will read these words and study these photographs, and through what cause, by what chance, and for what purpose, and by what right do you qualify to, and what will you do about it; and the question, Why we make this book, and set it at large, and by what right, and for what purpose, and to what good end, or none: the whole memory of the South in its six-thousand-mile parade and flowering outlay of the façades of cities, and of the eyes in the streets of towns, and of hotels, and of the trembling heat, and of the wide wild opening of the tragic land, wearing the trapped frail flowers of its garden of faces; the fleet flush and flower and fainting of the human crop it raises; the virulent, insolent, deceitful, pitying, infinitesimal and frenzied running and searching, on this colossal peasant map, of two angry, futile and bottomless, botched and overcomplicated youthful intelligences in the service of an anger and of a love and of an undiscernible truth, and in the frightening vanity of their would-be purity; the sustaining, even now, and forward moving, lifted on the lifting of this day as ships on a wave, above whom, in a few hours, night once more will stand up in his stars, and they decline through lamplight and be dreaming statues, of those, each, whose lives we knew and whom we love and intend well toward, and of whose living we know little in some while now, save that quite steadily, in not much possible change for better or much worse, mute, innocent, helpless and incorporate among that small-moted and inestimable swarm and pollen stream and fleet of single, irreparable, unrepeatable existences, they are led, gently, quite steadily, quite without mercy, each a little farther toward the washing and the wailing, the sunday suit and the prettiest dress, the pine box, and the closed clay room whose frailly decorated roof, until rain has taken it flat into oblivion, wears the shape of a ritual scar and of an inverted boat: curious, obscene, terrifying, beyond all search of dream unanswerable, those problems which stand thickly forth like light from all matter, triviality, chance, intention, and record in the body, of being, of truth, of conscience, of hope, of hatred, of beauty, of indignation, of guilt, of betrayal, of innocence, of forgiveness, of vengeance, of guardianship, of an indenominable fate, predicament, destination, and God . . .

"The communication is not by any means so simple. It seems to me now that to contrive techniques appropriate to it in the first place, and capable of planting it cleanly in others, in the second, would be a matter of years, and I shall probably try none of it or little, and that very tortured and diluted, at present. I realize that, with even so much involvement in explanations as this, I am liable seriously, and perhaps irretrievably, to obscure what would at best be hard enough to give its appropriate clarity and intensity; and what seems to me most important of all: namely, that these I will write of are human beings, living in this world, innocent of such twistings as these which are taking place over their heads; and that they were dwelt among, investigated, spied on, revered, and loved, by other quite monstrously alien human beings, in the employment of still others still more alien; and that they are now being looked into by still others, who have picked up their living as casually as if it were a book, and who were actuated toward this reading by various possible reflexes of sympathy, curiosity, idleness, et cetera, and almost certainly in a lack of consciousness, and conscience, remotely appropriate to the enormity of what they are doing.

If I could do it, I'd do no writing at all here. It would be photographs; the rest would be fragments of cloth, bits of cotton, lumps of earth, records of speech, pieces of wood and iron, phials of odors, plates of food and of excrement. Booksellers would consider it quite a novelty; critics would murmur, yes, but is it art; and I could trust a majority of you to use it as you would a parlor game.

A piece of the body torn out by the roots might be more to the point.

As it is, though, I'll do what little I can in writing. Only it will be very little. I'm not capable of it; and if I were, you would not go near it at all. For if you did, you would hardly bear to live.

As a matter of fact, nothing I might write could make any difference whatever. It would only be a "book" at the best. If it were a safely dangerous one it would be a "scientific" or "political" or "revolutionary." If it were really dangerous it would be "literature" or "religion" or "mysticism" or "art," and under one such name or another might in time achieve the emasculation of acceptance. If it were dangerous enough to be of any remote use to the human race it would be merely "frivolous" or "pathological," and that would be the end of that. Wiser and more capable men than I shall ever be have put their findings before you, findings so rich and so full of anger, serenity, murder, healing, truth, and love that it seems incredible the world were not destroyed and fulfilled in the instant, but you are too much for them: the weak in courage are strong in cunning; and one by one, you have absorbed and have captured and dishonored, and have distilled of your deliverers the most ruinous of all your poisons; people hear Beethoven in concert halls, or over a bridge game, or to relax; Cézannes are hung on walls, reproduced, in natural wood frames; van Gogh is the man who cut off his ear and whose yellows became recently popular in window decoration; Swift loved individuals but hated the human race; Kafka is a fad; Blake is in the Modern Library; Freud is a Modern Library Giant; Dovschenko's *Frontier* is disliked by those who demand that it fit the Eisenstein esthetic; *nobody* reads Joyce any more; Céline is a madman who has incurred the hearty dislike of Alfred Kazin, reviewer for the *New York Herald Tribune* book section, and is, moreover, a fascist; I hope I need not mention Jesus Christ, of whom you have managed to make a dirty gentile.

However that may be, this is a book about "sharecroppers," and is written for all those who have a soft place in their hearts for the laughter and tears inherent in poverty viewed at a distance, and especially for those who can afford the retail price; in the hope that the reader will be edified, and may feel kindly disposed toward any well-thought-out liberal efforts to rectify the unpleasant situation down South, and will somewhat better and more guiltily appreciate the next good meal he eats; and in the hope, too, that he will recommend this little book to really sympathetic friends, in order that our publishers may at least cover their investment and that just the merest perhaps) some kindly thought may be turned our way, and a little of your money fall to poor little us.'

'Above all else: in God's name don't think of it as Art.

Every fury on earth has been absorbed in time, as art, or as religion, or as authority in one form or another. The deadliest blow the enemy of the human soul can strike is to do fury honor. Swift, Blake, Beethoven, Christ, Joyce, Kafka, name me a one who has not been thus castrated. Official acceptance is the one unmistakable symptom that salvation is beaten again, and is the one surest sign of fatal misunderstanding, and is the kiss of Judas.

Really it should be possible to hope that this be recognized as so, and as a mortal and inevitably recurrent danger. It is scientific fact. It is disease. It is avoidable. Let a start be made. And then exercise your perception of it on work that has more to tell you than mine has. See how respectable Beethoven is; and by what right any wall in museum, gallery or home presumes to wear a Cézanne; and by what idiocy Blake or work even of such intention as mine is ever published and sold. I will tell you a test. It is unfair. It is untrue. It stacks all the cards. It is out of line with what the composer intended. All so much the better.

Get a radio or a phonograph capable of the most extreme loudness possible, and sit down to listen to a performance of Beethoven's Seventh Symphony or of Schubert's C-Major Symphony. But I don't mean just sit down and listen. I mean this: Turn it on as loud as you can get it. Then get down on the floor and jam your ear as close into the loudspeaker as you can get it and stay there, breathing as lightly as possible, and not moving, and neither eating nor smoking nor drinking. Concentrate everything you can into your hearing and into your body. You won't hear it nicely. If it hurts you, be glad of it. As near as you will ever get, you are inside the music; not only inside it, you are it; your body is no longer your shape and substance, it is the shape and substance of the music.

Is what you hear pretty? or beautiful? or legal? or acceptable in polite or any other society? It is beyond any calculation savage and dangerous and murderous to all equilibrium in human life as human life is; and nothing can equal the rape it does on all that death; nothing except anything, anything in existence or dream, perceived anywhere remotely toward its true dimension.'

Just a half-inch beyond the surface of this wall I face is another surface, one of the four walls which square and collaborate against the air another room, and there lie sleeping, on two iron beds and on pallets on the floor, a man and his wife and her sister, and four children, a girl, and three harmed boys. Their lamp is out, their light is done this long while, and not in a long while has any one of them made a sound. Not even straining, can I hear their breathing: rather, I have a not quite sensuous knowledge of a sort of suspiration, less breathing than that indiscernible drawing-in of heaven by which plants live, and thus I know they rest and the profundity of their tiredness, as if I were in each one of these seven bodies whose sleeping I can almost touch through this wall, and which in the darkness I so clearly see, with the whole touch and weight of my body: George's red body, already a little squat with the burden of thirty years, knotted like oakwood, in its clean white cotton summer union suit that it sleeps in; and his wife's beside him, Annie Mae's, slender, and sharpened through with bone, that ten years past must have had such beauty, and now is veined at the breast, and the skin of the breast translucent, delicately shriveled, and blue, and she and her sister Emma are in plain cotton shifts; and the body of Emma, her sister, strong, thick and wide, tall, the breasts set wide and high, shallow and round, not yet those of a full woman, the legs long thick and strong; and Louise's green lovely body, the dim breasts faintly blown between wide shoulders, the thighs long, clean and light in their line from hip to knee, the head back steep and silent to the floor, the chin highest, and the white shift up to her divided thighs; and the tough little body of Junior, hardskinned and gritty, the feet crusted with sores; and the milky and strengthless littler body of Burt whose veins are so bright in his temples; and the shriveled and hopeless, most pitiful body of Squinchy, which will not grow:

But it is not only their bodies but their postures that I know, and their weight on the bed or on the floor, so that I lie down inside each one as if exhausted in a bed, and I become not my own shape and weight and self, but that of each of them, the whole of it, sunken in sleep like stones; so that I know almost the dreams they will not remember, and the soul and body of each of these seven, and of all of them together in this room in sleep, as if they were music I were hearing, each voice in relation to all the others, and all audible, singly, and as one organism, and a music that cannot be communicated: and thus they lie in this silence, and rest . . .

Here at a center is a creature: it would be our business to show how through every instant of every day of every year of his existence alive he is from all sides streamed inward upon, bombarded, pierced, destroyed by that enormous sleeting of all objects forms and ghosts how great how small no matter, which surround and whom his senses take: in as great and perfect and exact particularity as we can name them:

This would be our business, to show them each thus transfixed as between the stars' trillions of javelins and of each the transfixions: but it is beyond my human power to do. The most I can do—the most I can hope to do—is to make a number of physical entities as plain and vivid as possible, and to make a few guesses, a few conjectures; and to leave to you much of the burden of realizing in each of them what I have wanted to make clear of them as a whole: how each is itself; and how each is a shapener.

We undertake not much yet some, to say: to say, what is his house: for whom does he work: under what arrangements and in what results: what is this work: who is he and where from, that he is now here; what is it his life has been and has done to him: what of his wife and of their children, each, for of all these each is a life, a full universe: what are their clothes: what food is theirs to eat: what is it which is in their senses and their minds: what is the living and manner of their day, of a season, of a year: what, inward and outward, is their manner of living; of their spending and usage of these few years' openness out of the black vast and senseless death; what is their manner of life:

All this, all such, you can see, it so intensely surrounds and takes meaning from a certain center which we shall be unable to keep steadily before your eyes, that should be written, should be listed, calculated, analyzed, conjectured upon, as if all in one sentence and spread suspension and flight or fugue of music: and that I shall not be able so to sustain it, so to sustain its intensity toward this center human life, so to yield it out that it all strikes inward upon this center at once and in all its intersections and in the meanings of its interrelations and interenhancements: it is this which so paralyzes me: yet one can write only one word at a time, and if these seem lists and inventories merely, things dead unto themselves, devoid of mutual magnetisms, and if they sink, lose impetus, meter, intension, then bear in mind at least my wish, and perceive in them and restore them what strength you can of yourself: for I must say to you, this is not a work of art or of entertainment, nor will I assume the obligations of the artist or entertainer, but is a human effort which must require human co-operation . . .

Work: 1 (from unpublished "Works" chapter)

If I had been born a tenant farmer's son, there would have been no question about it: no question of 'education', none of learning a skilled trade, none of

knowing except as the cloudiest kind of a dream the existence of a world different from that I was foundered in: even in my own world, all except those of
my own class would be strangers to me; they would move and appear in the
strangeness of people on a stage, or seen through a thick sheet of glass: there
would be no question about it, what dialect I was to use, what clothes I was to
wear, what was to go on in my mind, what I was going to eat all my life, what
sort of house I was to live in, what people I was to be at ease with, what sort of
girl I was to marry, what sort of life we were to have together, what sort of work
I was going to do; what sort of work she was going to do: above all else no question, no question at all, but what I *would* work, hard, with my hands, with my
body, with all my strength, learning my trade in my childhood and youth, and
working hard in my childhood and in my adolescence, and from the day of my
marriage on, working with all I had, that we might stay alive, and scarcely
better than staying alive, for that work, and helpless in my leisure.

That I was not born a tenant farmer's son is no doing of mine: nor is it any
doing of mine that I was born as I happened to be, among relative advantages.
But every human advantage is a theft: and the worst of it is, that by this theft
by which one gains, another is deprived; and that the one who is deprived is
the one who has earned what he is deprived of by hard and hopeless work, or
his children who must suffer for him. I feel intense guilt towards every such
man and woman and child alive; and I suggest that you need to feel it too; and
that that sense of guilt cannot possibly be intense enough, nor the wish to ex-
piate sufficient.

It is in the terms of this intensely felt guilt that I wish I could write of a tenant's work: in such a way as to break your back with it and your heart if I could:
this implies consciousness greater than they have. That consciousness has
been described near here as more limited than this, but still more: in such a
way that "innocent" of them though you are, you might go insane with shame
and with guilt that you are who you are, and that you are not what some one
of these persons is, who is living, while you are living. Good God, if I could
only make even this *guilt* what it is: not just some piece of pathology or of
metaphysics, but the literal thing it is, the literal thing. The literal fact that you
and they are living in the same earth. That because you are as you are, they are
as they are: living persons, each with as sacred a claim upon all existence as
your own: and that of this existence, they get what they get of it, and are made
what they are made, and you get and are made what you are . . .

Words can do anything: perhaps: hurried and green, however, I see no way
of making in words what human work is: each of whose thousands of gestures
should be transliterated into the bones of any one who reads, yet not even
only that: for besides, each such gesture, must be set in the whole meaning,
rhythm, tension and texture, of each individual life: so that I might write al-

most illimitably long, listing merely, not embodying, all those things which we who do not know this work, who are merely examining, must ask ourselves simultaneously to imagine, and to know the pressures of: and to know these pressures intimately in the exhaustions of individual lives; or to know, only for instance, to imagine, to try to compute, not lightly nor merely mentally but in our exact bodies, the sum and whole series, each by each and day upon day and year upon long solemnly draughted year, of each of these gestures and extensions of effort between pressures of need and deprivation in no hope and friendlessness, which just one such creature, Mrs. Gudger, has made, in the course of only twenty-seven years, that she now stands made as she is in the photograph in this book, the beautiful, and dreadful, and piteous, and irretrievable creation of what she has had to do: or merely, but again literally, to know the sum of these efforts as they are extended and reflexed upon the lives which comprise the living of one family, from the birth of each of two parents until they shall have sunk in death, leaving their children standing, saplings sprung fresh between thin roots, what energy, what incalculable expence and persistence of the hear[t]s has wrought up and spread and held and seeded this simple family flower: what energy, what straining and draining dry of all strength and love and hope, has composed even this one living generation of even this one shallow city of such flowers who in their grand and sterile field on this southern country are dedicated, making their landlords neither the happier nor the better nor more than a little the more rich, into the raising of the cotton plant, that they may by incidental hold the frayed string of existence together within each of them: and these unfolded backward upon all past generations into the sources, and spread in horizontals such that the planet and its cities are one glittering membrane of these unpaid agonies; and postulated upon the future into what hope of change: and driven against all minds that have ever searched or meditated and against all braveries which have acted the question which of its self is accusation, what is it you have done for this: and [done] into our hearts and brains who read or make record of this: by what ways and means and by what rights are you advantaged of this to differ from it in the least . . .

I have been aware that like one in a snowstorm I have been going in circles; and that has pleased rather than dismayed me, for each of the circles, such as it is, has been turned in obedience of an intense need and wish to make clear, however blind, and if as each has rounded past remembered landmarks any sense of dead and heavy weight and of oppressiveness has added itself upon you, then I am grateful, for it was in that hope that I kept on with the circlings: in the hope that by the slowly wound inane and earnest brutality and boredom of their reincidence a little might be set upon you of the unspeakable weight, and monotonies and cumulations, of the work itself: and in the hope that no task or process named or described could seem as merely one but as one of thousands in each person and of billions in the millions of them: but now I have come to where I must go into these singled particulars, and I myself am so dizzied, and so disturbed over my lack of proper space, that I do not know quite where or how to anchor: or whether I had better not discard all I have written on this subject, and try to make some more clean and succinct start.

Tom Joad

1940

Woody Guthrie (1912–1967), a folksinger and America's most famous Okie migrant, believed his songs could restore "the right amount of people to the right amount of land." When dust storms hit the Great Plains in 1935, he headed West with other refugees and began to write what he called "migratious songs." He sang them on picket lines and in union halls. "I've never once seen them fail," he said. "Our songs are singing history." In 1941 he wrote twenty-six songs protesting the Grand Coulee Dam in Oregon and played them on loudspeakers until, as he recalled, the authorities "shelled out the money and bought the bonds and brought the electricity over the hill to . . . run the factories. That's how things get done." His friend and fellow folksinger Pete Seeger noted: "I always believed that the right song at the right moment could change history."

On March 3, 1940, Guthrie played in a "Grapes of Wrath Evening" to benefit the John Steinbeck Committee for Agricultural Workers, and a few days later wrote his song "Tom Joad," after watching the movie of *The Grapes of Wrath* (1940). He noted: "the people back in Oklahoma haven't got two bucks to buy the book, or even thirty-five cents to see the movie, but the song will get to them and tell them what Preacher Casy said." Addressing *Daily Worker* readers, he wrote of the movie in his newspaper column: "It says you got to get together and have some meetins, and stick together, and raise old billy hell till you get your job, and get your farm back . . . Go to see *Grapes of Wrath,* pardner . . . You was the star in that picture."

Guthrie spoke warmly about John Steinbeck, believing the novelist "felt in his heart and knew in his head that us Okies was a lookin' for 'A Living WITH Labor.'" In return, Steinbeck observed: "The songs of the working people have always been their sharpest statement, and the one statement that cannot be destroyed," elsewhere claiming Guthrie as the voice of the people—"just a voice and a guitar. He sings the songs of a people and I suspect that he is, in a way, that people."

Guthrie's music and the folk revival formed a bridge between the literature of the early 20th-century labor movement and the literature of the civil rights movement, and also influenced the 1960s and 1970s peace movements: Bob Dylan wrote "Song to Woody" (1962) and "Last Thoughts on Woody Guthrie" (1973), and in a recent interview, the Vietnam war protest singer Country Joe McDonald echoed Steinbeck's assessment of Guthrie's authenticity: "Woody could write about Okies because he was one. It is the idea of a man of the people. Playing music of the people in his own way. Music that the people can relate to, that says what they can't say but what they feel. Woody did this and it enabled others to do it. That he was a genius at doing this is almost less important than him doing it."

Tom Joad got out of the old McAlester Pen;
There he got his parole.
After four long years on a man killing charge,
Tom Joad come a-walking down the road, poor boy,
Tom Joad come a-walking down the road.
Tom Joad, he met a truck driving man;
There he caught him a ride.
He said, "I just got loose from McAlester Pen
On a charge called homicide,
A charge called homicide."
That truck rolled away in a cloud of dust,
Tommy turned his face toward home.
He met Preacher Casey and they had a little drink,
But they found that his family they was gone,
He found that his family they was gone.
He found his mother's old-fashioned shoe,
Found his daddy's hat.
And he found little Muley and Muley said,
"They've been tractored out by the cats,
They've been tractored out by the cats."
Tom Joad walked down to the neighbor's farm,
Found his family.
They took Preacher Casey and loaded in a car,
And his mother said, "We've got to get away."
His mother said, "We've got to get away."
Now the twelve of the Joads made a mighty heavy load,
But Grandpa Joad did cry.
He picked up a handful of land in his hand,
Said: "I'm stayin' with the farm till I die.
Yes, I'm stayin' with the farm till I die."
They fed him short ribs and coffee and soothing syrup;
And Grandpa Joad did die.
They buried Grandpa Joad by the side of the road,
Grandma on the California side,
They buried Grandma on the California side.
They stood on a mountain and they looked to the west,

And it looked like the promised land.
That bright green valley with a river running through,
There was work for every single hand, they thought,
There was work for every single hand.
The Joads road away to the jungle camp,
There they cooked a stew.
And the hungry little kids of the jungle camp
Said: "We'd like to have some, too."
Said: "We'd like to have some, too."
Now a deputy sheriff fired loose at a man,
Shot a woman in the back.
Before he could take his aim again
Preacher Casey dropped him in his tracks.
Preacher Casey dropped him in his tracks.
They handcuffed Casey and they took him in jail,
And then he got away.
And he met Tom Joad on the old river bridge,
And these few words he did say, poor boy,
These few words he did say:
"I preached for the Lord a mighty long time,
Preached about the rich and the poor.
Us workin' folks is all get together,
'Cause we ain't got a chance anymore.
We ain't got a chance anymore."
Now the deputies come and Tom and Casey run
To the bridge where the water run down.
But the vigilante thugs hit Casey with a club,
They laid Preacher Casey on the ground, poor Casey,
They laid Preacher Casey on the ground.
Tom Joad he grabbed that deputy's club,
Hit him over the head.
Tom Joad took flight in the dark rainy night,
And a deputy and a preacher lying dead, two men,
A deputy and a preacher lying dead.
Tom run back where his mother was asleep;
He woke her up out of bed.
Then he kissed goodbye to the mother that he loved,
Said what Preacher Casey said, Tom Joad,
He said what Preacher Casey said.
"Ever'body might be just one big soul,
Well it looks that a-way to me.

Everywhere that you look, in the day or night,
That's where I'm a-gonna be, Ma,
That's where I'm a-gonna be.
Wherever little children are hungry and cry,
Wherever people ain't free.
Wherever men are fightin' for their rights,
That's where I'm gonna be, Ma.
That's where I'm gonna be."

From 12 Million Black Voices

1941

In 1940 the editor and photographer Edwin Rosskam (1919–1985) spent three weeks collaborating with the author Richard Wright, for whom the Federal Writers' Project was a training ground. Their collaboration became an illustrated folk history and a sociological study of black migration. "Wright really knew that stuff cold," said Rosskam. "I don't know if many white men had the opportunity to see it the way we saw it." Wright contributed text and Rosskam selected images for the book, mostly from the Farm Security Administration (FSA) archives.

But this project was different from earlier Depression-era image-texts. The FSA Historical Section chief Roy Stryker had tried to "show the city people what it's like to live on the farm," believing the FSA "introduced Americans to America." Wright wanted to remind Americans of their invisible population—the twelve million black voices—and show the city, as well as the "farm." He and Rosskam portray black struggles against what they call "the Bosses of the Buildings," as well as "the Lords of the Land," and explore where the migrants went when they left the land.

Wright had observed Depression-era artists struggling to depict the chaos of the 1930s. Now he explains the abrupt transitions of black history as the situation of Depression America writ large. *12 Million Black Voices* reveals the wider American culture: "We are you, looking back at you from the dark mirror of our lives," he writes. Protest literature functioned best, Wright thought, as the story of Everyman and all men. The book prompted investigation of Wright as a communist, but Rosskam observed: "I don't think anyone can describe where information starts and education stops, and propaganda begins . . . they overlap."

For his part, Rosskam uses image-pairings to construct his protest message. He had explained in 1939 that "the new unit is the double-page spread," and in the double-page spread printed here, a child in white in the first image is echoed by a white cross in the second, his posture forming the cross of door-frame and arm. The black strip on the cross echoes the child's black forearm. The Jesus in a loincloth behind the cross has his legs in the same pose as the child, right over left. Poised on the doorstep, the child is the man "struggling to be born," about to feel the "heavy toll [of] death," from Wright's preceding text. On the brink of birth he is sacrificed to the white world—doomed like Christ. Rosskam builds an echo-chamber space beyond the "kitchenette" prisons and invites readers to enter, and to make protest connections.

We are the children of the black sharecroppers, the first-born of the city tenements.

We have tramped down a road three hundred years long. We have been shunted to and fro by cataclysmic social changes.

We are a folk born of cultural devastation, slavery, physical suffering, unrequited longing, abrupt emancipation, migration, disillusionment, bewilderment, joblessness, and insecurity—all enacted within a *short* space of historical time!

There are millions of us and we are moving in all directions. All our lives we have been catapulted into arenas where, had we thought consciously of invading them, we would have hung back. A sense of constant change has stolen silently into our lives and has become operative in our personalities as a law of living.

There are some of us who feel our hurts so deeply that we find it impossible to work with whites; we feel that it is futile to hope or dream in terms of American life. Our distrust is so great that we form intensely racial and nationalistic organizations and advocate the establishment of a separate state, a forty-ninth state, in which we black folk would live.

There are even today among us groups that forlornly plan a return to Africa.

There are others of us who feel the need of the protection of a strong nation so keenly that we admire the harsh and imperialistic policies of Japan and ardently hope that the Japanese will assume the leadership of the "darker races."

As our consciousness changes, as we come of age, as we shed our folk swaddling-clothes, so run our lives in a hundred directions.

Today, all of us black folk are not poor. A few of us have money. We make it as the white folk make theirs, but our money-making is restricted to our own people. Many of us black folk have managed to send our children to school, and a few of our children are now professional and business men whose standards of living approximate those of middle-class whites. Some of us own small businesses; others devote their lives to law and medicine.

But the majority of us still toil on the plantations, work in heavy industry, and labor in the kitchens of the Lords of the Land and the Bosses of the Buildings.

The general dislocation of life during the depression caused many white workers to learn through chronic privation that they could not protect their standards of living so long as we blacks were excluded from their unions. Many hundreds of thousands of them found that they could not fight successfully for increased wages and union recognition unless we stood shoulder to shoulder with them. As a consequence, many of us have recently become members of steel, auto, packing, and tobacco unions.

In 1929, when millions of us black folk were jobless, many unemployed white workers joined with us on a national scale to urge relief measures and adequate housing. The influence of this united effort spread even into the South where black and white sharecroppers were caught in the throes of futile conflict.

The fears of black and white lessened in the face of the slowly widening acceptance of an identity of interests. When the depression was at its severest, the courts of many cities, at the instigation of the Bosses of the Buildings, sent armed marshals to evict our jobless black families for their inability to pay rent for the rotting kitchenettes. Organized into groups, we black folk smashed the marshals' locks, picked up the paltry sticks of furniture, and replaced the evicted families. Having hurdled fear's first barrier, we found that many white workers were eager to have us in their organizations, and we were proud to feel that at last our strength was sufficient to awaken in others a desire to work with us. These men differed from those whom we had known on the plantations; they were not "po' white trash." We invited them into our homes and broke our scanty bread with them, and this was our supreme gesture of trust. In this way we encountered for the first time in our lives the full effect of those forces that tended to reshape our folk consciousness, and a few of us stepped forth and accepted within the confines of our personalities the death of our

old folk lives, an acceptance of a death that enabled us to cross class and racial lines, a death that made us free.

Not all black folk, however, reacted to the depression in this manner. There were hundreds of thousands of us who saw that we bought our groceries from white clerks, that we paid our insurance to white agents, that we paid our rent to white realtors, that our children were taught in school by white teachers, that we were served in hospitals by white doctors, that we asked jobs of white bosses, that we paid our fares on busses and street cars to white conductors; in short, that we had no word to say about anything that happened in our lives. In 1935, inarticulate black men and women, filled with a naive, peasant anger, rioted in Harlem's business district and wrought a property damage of more than $2,000,000!

But our most qualitatively significant progress was organized and conducted through peaceful channels. In many large cities there were sturdy minorities of us, both black and white, who banded together in disciplined, class-conscious groups and created new organs of action and expression. We were able to seize nine black boys in a jail in Scottsboro, Alabama, lift them so high in our collective hands, focus such a battery of comment and interpretation upon them, that they became symbols to all the world of the plight of black folk in America.

If we had been allowed to participate in the vital processes of America's national growth, what would have been the texture of our lives, the pattern of our traditions, the routine of our customs, the state of our arts, the code of our laws, the function of our government! Whatever others may say, we black folk say that America would have been stronger and greater!

Standing now at the apex of the twentieth century, we look back over the road we have traveled and compare it with the road over which the white folk have traveled, and we see that three hundred years in the history of our lives are equivalent to two thousand years in the history of the lives of whites! The many historical phases which whites have traversed voluntarily and gradually during the course of Western civilization we black folk have traversed through swift compulsion. During the three hundred years we have been in the New World, we have experienced all the various types of family life, all the many adjustments to rural and urban life, and today, weary but still eager, we stand ready to accept more change.

Imagine European history from the days of Christ to the present telescoped into three hundred years and you can comprehend the drama which our consciousness has experienced! Brutal, bloody, crowded with suffering and abrupt transitions, the lives of us black folk represent the most magical and meaningful picture of human experience in the Western world. Hurled from our native African homes into the very center of the most complex and highly industrialized civilization the world has ever known, we stand today with a consciousness and memory such as few people possess.

We black folk, our history and our present being, are a mirror of all the manifold experiences of America. What we want, what we represent, what we endure is what America *is*. If we black folk perish, America will perish. If America has forgotten her past, then let her look into the mirror of our consciousness and she will see the *living* past living in the present, for our memories go back, through our black folk of today, through the recollections of our black parents, and through the tales of slavery told by our black grandparents, to the time when none of us, black or white, lived in this fertile land.

The differences between black folk and white folk are not blood or color, and the ties that bind us are deeper than those that separate us. The common road of hope which we all have traveled has brought us into a stronger kinship than any words, laws, or legal claims.

Look at us and know us and you will know yourselves, for *we* are *you,* looking back at you from the dark mirror of our lives!

What do we black folk want?

We want what others have, the right to share in the upward march of American life, the only life we remember or have ever known.

The Lords of the Land say: "We will not grant this!"

We answer: "We ask you to grant us nothing. We are winning our heritage, though our toll in suffering is great!"

The Bosses of the Buildings say: "Your problem is beyond solution!"

We answer: "Our problem is being solved. We are crossing the line you dared us to cross, though we pay in the coin of death!"

The seasons of the plantation no longer dictate the lives of many of us; hundreds of thousands of us are moving into the sphere of conscious history.

We are with the new tide. We stand at the crossroads. We watch each new procession. The hot wires carry urgent appeals. Print compels us. Voices are speaking. Men are moving! And we shall be with them.

From The Sweet Flypaper of Life

1955

Like much great protest literature, the photo-text collaboration of the photographer Roy DeCarava (b. 1919) and the writer Langston Hughes (1902–1967) confronts the question of erasure or exclusion. The fictional autobiography opens with a telegram from God calling the narrator, Mary Bradley, to heaven. Like the people around her in Harlem, she is "passing," echoing numerous 1930s photo-texts about exodus and vanishing. Bradley doesn't even appear in a photograph until the last page of the book, when she finally declares: "Here I am." This assertion of presence comes just as the book ends and she slips into silence: Hughes was developing the idea of a deferred and vanished presence, as established in his poem "Harlem: A Dream Deferred" (1951). *The Sweet Flypaper of Life* also continues the 1930s theme of the "dream" turned nightmare, or the anti-fairytale. One of DeCarava's images shows a black girl in a white dress, with an advertisement for a product called "Prince Albert" on the wall behind her. The poster is torn, so that it reads "Princ." The fairy-tale is incomplete, the prince as absent as the final "e." An empty cart in the shadows and an advertisement for the "All-Star" car suggest a missing carriage.

But in response to death Bradley has revealed her life, and the book's present-tense narration establishes a living presence that counters the erasure. DeCarava's captioned headshots echo the technique of 1930s photo-texts focused on people's faces, and echo the Depression-era archival impulse. Just as Native American writers fought the idea of the vanishing Indian, slave narratives established black humanity, Ralph Ellison confronted black invisibility in his novel *Invisible Man* (1952), and gay liberationists chanted, "We're Here, We're Queer," so *The Sweet Flypaper of Life* asserts: "I am here."

This world is like a crossword puzzle in the *Daily News*—some folks make the puzzles, others try to solve them . . . Every so often, ever so once in a while, somedays a woman gets a chance to set in her window for a minute and look out. New York is not like back down South with not much happening outside. In Harlem something is happening all the time, people are going every which-a-way. No matter which way you look, up or down, somebody is always headed somewhere, something is happening . . . Some have been where they are going. And some can't make up their minds which way to go: And some ain't going no place at all. But it's nice to see young folks all dressed up going somewhere—maybe to a party.

But it's sad if you ain't invited: It's too bad they're no front porches in Harlem: Almost nothing except stoops to set on . . . Yet there is so much to see in Harlem! . . . Somebody almost passing . . . Yes, you can set in your window anywhere in Harlem and see plenty . . . But back windows ain't much good for looking out. I never did like looking backwards nohow. I always did believe in looking out front—looking ahead—which is why I's worried about Rodney: What do you reckon's out there in them streets for that boy? He's my grandchild, but he seems more like my son . . . I would not choose not girl for Rodney, as I would not want no one to choose a man for me. But our janitor: his wife is dead. Do you reckon I'm too old to get married again? When I were sick he came upstairs to see me, and he said, "Miss Mary, I hear tell you's down—but with no intentions of going out," I said, "You're right! I done got my feet caught in the sweet flypaper of life—and I'll be dogged if I want to get loose" . . . well, if I do say so, I'm as a good as new—back on my feet again and still kicking—with no intentions of signing any messages from St. Peter writing me to "come home." When I get through with my pots and pans . . . ever once in a while, I put on my best clothes. Here I am.

From The Other America

1962

Tom Hayden, the leader of Students for a Democratic Society (SDS), claimed that the socialist and writer Michael Harrington (1928–1989) was almost the only person over 30 trusted by his generation. Like SDS members and other 1960s New Leftists, Harrington challenged the rhetoric of New Deal liberals. In 1958 John Kenneth Galbraith's *The Affluent Society* had expressed the tenets of this liberalist prosperity. Responding to Galbraith, the economist Leon Keyserling noted that a quarter of American families had annual incomes of less than $4,000. The *Commentary* editor Anatole Shub asked Harrington to write on poverty, and Harrington developed his articles into *The Other America.*

Confronting America's blind faith in its continued economic growth, the book examines the failure of New Deal legislation and compares poverty in the 1960s and the 1930s. It describes "the strangest poor in the history of mankind"—25 percent of America's population. This statistic, Harrington says, should prompt outrage. Although the poverty gap was widening, he insists that the dream of abolishing poverty is within reach. He defines poverty absolutely, in terms of what America *could* be, noting that his standard of comparison is "not how much worse things used to be," but "how much better they could be if only we were stirred."

The book was read by millions. President Kennedy's economic adviser gave him a copy and in November 1963 Kennedy launched his "war on poverty." Announcing the Economic Opportunity Act of 1964, President Johnson echoed Harrington's belief: "for the first time in our history, it is possible to conquer poverty." Harrington was appointed to work with the Office of Economic Opportunity. But increased government spending barely covered the Vietnam war. The "war on poverty" was funded at less than one percent of the federal budget. Harrington went on to found the Democratic Socialist Organizing Committee, serving as chair from 1973 until he died in 1989. At one point he shared the post with the social critic Barbara Ehrenreich, who lived in the "other America" while researching her book *Nickel and Dimed* (2001). Harrington was an influence on Ehrenreich, but she insisted in a recent interview: "I wanted to do something very different, something that didn't include the notion of 'the other.' I was never comfortable with Harrington's idea that the poor are 'different.'"

This book is a description of the world in which these people live; it is about the other America. Here are the unskilled workers, the migrant farm workers, the aged, the minorities, and all the others who live in the economic underworld of American life. In all this, there will be statistics, and that offers the opportunity for disagreement among honest and sincere men. I would ask the reader to respond critically to every assertion, but not to allow statistical quibbling to obscure the huge, enormous, and intolerable fact of poverty in America. For, when all is said and done, that fact is unmistakable, whatever its exact dimensions, and the truly human reaction can only be outrage. As W. H. Auden wrote:

> Hunger allows no choice
> To the citizen or the police;
> We must love one another or die.

The millions who are poor in the United States tend to become increasingly invisible. Here is a great mass of people, yet it takes an effort of the intellect and will even to see them . . .

That the poor are invisible is one of the most important things about them. They are not simply neglected and forgotten as in the old rhetoric of reform; what is much worse, they are not seen.

One might take a remark from George Eliot's *Felix Holt* as a basic statement of what this book is about:

> there is no private life which has not been determined by a wider public life, from the time when the primeval milkmaid had to wander with the wanderings of her clan, because the cow she milked was one of a herd which had made the pasture bare. Even in the conservatory existence where the fair Camellia is sighed for by the noble young Pineapple, neither of them needing to care about the frost or rain outside, there is a nether apparatus of hot-water pipes liable to cool down on a strike of the gardeners or a scarcity of coal.
>
> And the lives we are about to look back upon do not belong to those conservatory species; they are rooted in the common earth, having to endure all the ordinary chances of past and present weather.

Forty to 50,000,000 people are becoming increasingly invisible. That is a shocking fact. But there is a second basic irony of poverty that is equally important: if one is to make the mistake of being born poor, he should choose a time when the majority of the people are miserable too.

J. K. Galbraith develops this idea in *The Affluent Society*, and in doing so defines the "newness" of the kind of poverty in contemporary America. The old poverty, Galbraith notes, was general. It was the condition of life of an entire society, or at least of that huge majority who were without special skills or the luck of birth. When the entire economy advanced, a good many of these people gained higher standards of living. Unlike the poor today, the majority poor of a generation ago were an immediate (if cynical) concern of political leaders.

The old slums of the immigrants had the votes; they provided the basis for labor organizations; their very numbers could be a powerful force in political conflict. At the same time the new technology required higher skills, more education, and stimulated an upward movement for millions.

Perhaps the most dramatic case of the power of the majority poor took place in the 1930's. The Congress of Industrial Organizations literally organized millions in a matter of years. A labor movement that had been declining and confined to a thin stratum of the highly skilled suddenly embraced masses of men and women in basic industry. At the same time this acted as a pressure upon the Government, and the New Deal codified some of the social gains in laws like the Wagner Act. The result was not a basic transformation of the American system, but it did transform the lives of an entire section of the population.

In the thirties one of the reasons for these advances was that misery was general. There was no need then to write books about unemployment and poverty. That was the decisive social experience of the entire society, and the apple sellers even invaded Wall Street. There was political sympathy from middle-class reformers; there were an élan and spirit that grew out of a deep crisis.

Some of those who advanced in the thirties did so because they had unique and individual personal talents. But for the great mass, it was a question of being at the right point in the economy at the right time in history, and utilizing that position for common struggle. Some of those who failed did so because they did not have the will to take advantage of new opportunities. But for the most part the poor who were left behind had been at the wrong place in the economy at the wrong moment in history.

These were the people in the unorganizable jobs, in the South, in the minority groups, in the fly-by-night factories that were low on capital and high on labor. When some of them did break into the economic mainstream—when, for instance, the CIO opened up the way for some Negroes to find good industrial jobs—they proved to be as resourceful as anyone else. As a group, the other Americans who stayed behind were not originally composed primarily of individual failures. Rather, they were victims of an impersonal process that selected some for progress and discriminated against others.

Out of the thirties came the welfare state. Its creation had been stimulated by mass impoverishment and misery, yet it helped the poor least of all. Laws like unemployment compensation, the Wagner Act, the various farm programs, all these were designed for the middle third in the cities, for the organized workers, and for the upper third in the country, for the big market farmers. If a man works in an extremely low-paying job, he may not even be covered by social security or other welfare programs. If he receives unemployment compensation, the payment is scaled down according to his low earnings.

One of the major laws that was designed to cover everyone, rich and poor, was social security. But even here the other Americans suffered discrimination. Over the years social security payments have not even provided a subsistence level of life. The middle third have been able to supplement the Federal pension through private plans negotiated by unions, through joining medical insurance schemes like Blue Cross, and so on. The poor have not been able to do so. They lead a bitter life, and then have to pay for that fact in old age.

Indeed, the paradox that the welfare state benefits those least who need help most is but a single instance of a persistent irony in the other America. Even when the money finally trickles down, even when a school is built in a poor neighborhood, for instance, the poor are still deprived. Their entire environment, their life, their values, do not prepare them to take advantage of the new opportunity. The parents are anxious for the children to go to work; the pupils are pent up, waiting for the moment when their education has complied with the law.

Today's poor, in short, missed the political and social gains of the thirties. They are, as Galbraith rightly points out, the first minority poor in history, the first poor not to be seen, the first poor whom the politicians could leave alone . . .

Even more explosive is the possibility that people who participated in the gains of the thirties and the forties will be pulled back down into poverty. Today the mass-production industries where unionization made such a difference are contracting. Jobs are being destroyed. In the process, workers who had achieved a certain level of wages, who had won working conditions in the shop, are suddenly confronted with impoverishment. This is particularly true for anyone over forty years of age and for members of minority groups. Once their job is abolished, their chances of ever getting similar work are very slim.

It is too early to say whether or not this phenomenon is temporary, or whether it represents a massive retrogression that will swell the numbers of the poor. To a large extent, the answer to this question will be determined by the political response of the United States in the sixties. If serious and massive action is not undertaken, it may be necessary for statisticians to add some old-fashioned, pre-welfare-state poverty to the misery of the other America.

Poverty in the 1960's is invisible and it is new, and both these factors make it more tenacious. It is more isolated and politically powerless than ever before. It is laced with ironies, not the least of which is that many of the poor view progress upside-down, as a menace and a threat to their lives. And if the nation does not measure up to the challenge of automation, poverty in the 1960's might be on the increase.

Poverty Is a Crime

1972

"You can see anything you want in her," said the Farm Security Administration Historical Section chief Roy Stryker of Dorothea Lange's subject in "Migrant Mother" (1936). "She is immortal." Lange's subject certainly achieved immortality in the protest tradition: in 1939 the artist Diana Thorne made a lithograph called "The Spanish Mother, Terror of 1938," based on Lange's image; in 1964 a Latin American magazine adapted Lange's photograph for its cover; in 1972, the Black Panther Party (BPP) made the family black. In 1966 the art critic George Elliott explained that Lange's photograph was "a work of art with its own message rather than its maker's . . . a great, perfect, anonymous image [that] is a trick of grace."

The BPP often explored the rhetorical power of mother-and-child images. In 1968 Ruth-Marion Baruch made a photograph called "Black Panther Mother and Baby Jesus X," and in 1969 the *Black Panther* newspaper praised "the art coming out of the struggle in Vietnam," especially "a picture of a mother holding her baby" which expressed "the victorious spirit" that would "fight from one generation to the next." Captioned "poverty is a crime and our people are victims," the BPP's adaptation of Lange's "Migrant Mother" image, itself a symbol of intergenerational connection, was another connection "from one generation to the next"—from protest in the Depression era to protest in the 1960s.

The need to revisit the Depression continued. Late 20th-century photographers re-photographed Walker Evans's Alabama sharecroppers and Arthur Rothstein's figures in "Farmer and Sons." And in 1983, historians sought the real identity of Lange's iconic figure. She was one quite human Florence Thompson, and she had become gravely ill. The *New York Times* reprinted Lange's famous photograph and announced: "Decades after her careworn, resolute face became a symbol of the grinding poverty of the Depression, Florence Thompson's children are asking for help to save their mother's ebbing life." A month later the appeal had raised $15,000.

THE DUNGEON
SHOOK

Civil Rights
and
Black Liberation

Montgomery:
Reflections of a Loving Alien

1956

At the funeral of Rosa Parks (1913–2005) in November 2005, Bill Clinton said that when he first met Parks he thought of Abraham Lincoln's purported comment to Harriet Beecher Stowe: "So this is the little lady who started the great war." The civil-rights war is often considered to have begun on December 1, 1955, when Parks was arrested for violating Montgomery's bus segregation laws. She was sitting in the first seat of the "colored section" of a bus, and the white section was full. The white driver asked her to give up her seat and she refused. Parks, a 42-year-old seamstress, "was tired of being pushed around," as she recalled; "I was not tired physically . . . the only tired I was, was tired of giving in." Martin Luther King, Jr., called her "a victim of . . . the forces of destiny," though Parks *had* resisted segregation before and was the National Association for the Advancement of Colored People (NAACP) secretary in Montgomer he sntp e;

Another important character in the Montgomery story was Edgar D. Nixon, a former NAACP state president. On the night of December 1, after Parks's arrest, he thought, "Why not ask the Negroes in Montgomery to stand up and be counted?" He had long believed that "one person could kindle a spark that might cause others to see light and work." The following day he helped form the Montgomery Improvement Association, which elected King as president, adopted the official slogan "Justice without Violence," and distributed a leaflet asking African Americans to stay off the buses. King was initially reluctant to join Nixon but decided God was using Montgomery as a proving ground. Over the next 381 days, 75 percent of the bus company's business, some 50,000 black riders, boycotted its buses. In April 1956 King proclaimed: "In Montgomery we walk in a new way . . . The Southern Negro has come of age, politically and morally," and on December 20, 1956, the Supreme Court declared Montgomery's bus segregation illegal. The poet Gwendolyn Brooks paid tribute to Nixon: "He induced, it seems, Reverend King to take his place as chider, cherisher, champion."

Throughout the bus boycott, supporters referred to the Declaration of Independence, the "unfinished business" of the Civil War, and the civil disobediences of the Industrial Workers of the World. They compared Montgomery to Lexington and Concord. Some suggested that America's fight against communism abroad was hampered by racial oppression at home. In the magazine piece reprinted here, Robert Granat, a subsistence farmer, sees an integrated society on the horizon. "Why would we criticize if we had no hope, if we did not love?" he asks, echoing James Baldwin's famous statement of 1955: "I love America more than any other country in this world, and, exactly for this reason, I insist on the right to criticize her perpetually."

Further reading: Rosa Parks, *My Story* (1992); Jo Ann Robinson, *The Montgomery Bus Boycott* (1987).

I am a native American, brought up in America, living in America. I am not a member of the Communist Party or of any subversive group, nor have I been since 1925. (Prior to this I was not born). Although I don't have to register with the government, or carry identification papers (yet), I am an alien nonetheless, as much as if I had been born on Lenin's desk. But I am a reluctant alien. Despite a real desire for integration and citizenship, I become more and more alienated every day.

Maybe you know the story about the little boy whose mother took him to see Santa Claus in Macy's.

"And what would you like me to bring you for Christmas, sonny?" old Santa Claus said, chucking the child under the chin.

"An electric train," the boy said.

Next they went to Gimbel's and visited the Santa Claus there.

"And what would you like me to bring you for Christmas, sonny?" old Santa Claus said, chucking the child under the chin.

"You bastard," the boy said, "I *knew* you'd forget."

What does one do when one has seen through Santa Claus? It would take more than the ordinary psychiatrist to re-erect a crumpled myth. (Though for a fee he would certainly try).

What does one do when one has seen through *Life* and *Time?* Nothing! You can't make what has become transparent opaque again. Alienation is setting in. If you are lucky you'll hold out and there's hope for you. If you're unlucky your personality will begin to split, you'll become an alcholic, a criminal, a suicide, a madman, a fanatic. Isolation is not the pleasantest sensation in the world.

To be alienated from the culture you would like to love is like losing your beloved to a fat rich old man—the same kind of pain.

How to Praise?

One longs ardently to identify himself with his surroundings. He would like, if he is a poet, to sing paeans, like Whitman. There is no joy like loving, like praising. But what is one going to write his love poems to? A fast buck? The eight millionth Mercury? A thirty-six inch bust? A hero who rose to preside over fifteen corporations at the age of twenty-two? Carbonated shaving soap? A woman who knows all the brand names?

Only God and nature, in abstract, or in manifest forms, are worth a poem. But this is a physiological civilization. The doctors are our high priests, the ad-men our philosophers, the men of quantity our heroes.

So what is there left to do? We who desire to love are obliged to excoriate. Be-cause we must at least be honest or else we are really lost. Yet from our isola-tion, rejecting and rejected, we look on and continue to love and to hope. Why would we criticize, if we had no hope, if we did not love?

The alien for whom there *is* hope believes that behind him he has a tradition of alienation. And beyond him he has Truth, God if you like. And, he can con-ceive of God in any way that is natural to him. This alien, this loving alien—he can love because he is not consumed by self-pity—knows that all this rampag-ing materialism, all this perverse pragmatism, this enthronement of expedi-ency, demonstrates to the people, who have forgotten, that no good can come of it, that it is a shameful and lying way for men to live and can lead only to de-struction. The loving alien knows that this isn't the first time that men and women with a weakness for integrity have been alienated. He accepts his posi-tion and makes the best of it. He knows that he can best serve the people by guarding his integrity and by constantly training himself to be worthy of his insight.

Self-interest, ignorance, depravity are all pretty much the same everywhere everytime. Darkness is darkness, the bottom is the bottom. But to measure the height of a structure one looks at the top, not the bottom. Humanity is as tall as its tallest men. Christianity is as great as Christ. America is as great as Jeffer-son and Lincoln and Thoreau. The twentieth century is as great as Gandhi and Schweitzer.

Revolution with a Future

The world, Gide said, will be saved by the few. Don't wait for the revolution, Frost said, the only revolution that's coming is the one-man revolution.

That's it, the one-man revolution. One by one by one. Until maybe on some morning inconceivably far away the whole world will have saved itself from its ignorance. One by one by one. This is the only revolution that has a future.

So there's hope, there's meaning in alienation. The alien is the yeast in the social dough . . . the alien, that is, the reluctant alien, who would rather not be one, who would rather identify himself completely with the environment in which his life must be lived.

My generation, the one born in the twenties, produced more aliens than the one before it. We were alienated singly, one at a time and place, unknown even to each other. We could see that capitalism is wrong. It shifts the emphasis to external circumstances and to hell with the inner effects; it shifts the values from effort to reward, from quality to quantity. The generation before mine, in the 1930's especially, may have been hoodwinked by the idea of Communism. But my generation scarcely got a chance to get disillusioned. We saw that Communism was just capitalism with different pants on. We rejected both of these colossi.

Blackboard Jungle

The alienation of the generation after mine is more pointed. They seem to become aware at ten years of age of things we discovered at twenty. Whereas we were characterized by apathy, half-heartedness, nihilism and confusion, they are more violent in their rejection. We felt a little guilty, they do not. They smoke reefers, they rob, they are at home in violence.

These children of our future: what's going to help them and us? An alien can see this more clearly than the school principals and the probation officers. Not more playgrounds, not more amusements. In a society too busy grubbing for funds to pay for its luxuries; in a society seduced by the ad-man's glittering set of values; they get in society's way. There is no time. What do the ad-men say to do for the kids? Buy them off, get them stuff, give them fun. This, of course, is a lie. What they need is to be loved—recognized would be a better word—to have a useful function in society. The kids know what's up, and the aliens are on the increase. We may be producing a whole generation of aliens, though not necessarily loving ones. How to spread love and respect and a sense of value is our problem.

Even Henry Luce has admitted at times that the popular respect for enterprise and work, which gave this country its vitality, is now changing into a respect for consumption and rewards. It's still o.k. to get something by working for it. But if you can get it without working, by cheating in an accepted way, better yet. This is the order of the day. The students terrorizing their teachers have got this straight.

The Emperor is obviously naked. The social fathers never say a mumbling word, either because they fear, or are truly ignorant, or else for craftier reasons. But the little boys in the juvenile courts shout right out. Something stinks!

The Way Back

For myself, I must confess that I believe in God. I am aware of God in two of his aspects. First, in the orderliness and beauty of the universe, the infinite array of marvels, from the mathematics of galaxies to the workings of my central nervous system, from the beauty of grasshoppers to the beauty of the mother and offspring. Secondly, since to be aware only of his forms would not be enough, I am also aware of him internally. I feel him as a need to act with love; to act without selfishness, as a yearning for a pure joy that the senses and the mind don't have the power to give me. I feel him as an inner knowledge of perfection and a hunger after it.

I don't think things are rotten beyond saving. I think it is possible that without the slaughter of most of us we can learn to reject the scientist as holy-man, the ad-man as philosopher, the super seller and the super-buyer as folk heroes. There is more hope in the genes of this country than in any other in history, except possibly India. The spirit of freedom is still there. We've got it and many others less radical have got it. But we drowse and make payments on our new refrigerators, while the bully-boys of active ignorance are out scrimmaging.

Keep alive, you loving aliens, keep hard and keep pushing at the truth. Don't let hate take you over and petrify your souls. Act with love and guard your integrity. We are coming into a season that breeds prophets. For inevitably, whenever the people get lost, men are born to point the way back. And out of the aliens, the prophets will come. Not the prophets of doom and destruction, but prophets of the way of love and peace, pointing to a positive integrated society where only fear, exploitation and hate will be alien.

My Dungeon Shook

1962

In 1963, the writer James Baldwin (1924–1987) was heralded as a 20th-century Frederick Douglass and the voice of African Americans. His book *The Fire Next Time* hit the bestseller lists and he began to advise President Kennedy, as Douglass had President Lincoln. But, while Baldwin called the writer a "disturber of the peace" and was active in the civil rights movement, he rejected the term "spokesman," explaining that to be the "representative of some thirteen million people," like fellow protest artist Richard Wright, was a "false responsibility . . . and impossible."

Instead Baldwin believed that he had to "excavate and recreate history," and that this meant recreating his own experience. There had been no language for the "horrors of the American Negro's life," he said—the "privacy of his experience" had been denied—and so Baldwin wrote confessional autobiography. *The Fire Next Time* is a highly personal call to intimacy and love. He asks blacks and whites to create America's consciousness "like lovers" in order to "end the racial nightmare." The love he proposes is mystical, and he writes as prophet throughout, in the tradition of David Walker, Harriet Beecher Stowe, Eugene Debs and Martin Luther King, Jr. He offers a narrative of conversion, like Upton Sinclair in *The Jungle* (1906) and John Steinbeck at the end of *The Grapes of Wrath* (1939)—though while Steinbeck secularizes religious experience, Baldwin sanctifies society. Art is spiritual expression, divinity is more important than doctrine, and self-will and God's will are intertwined.

As the nation's conscience Baldwin holds up what he calls "the rainbow sign," his vision of a harmoniously blended society. This vision of interdependence means, as he put it in 1961, that "one cannot deny the humanity of another without diminishing one's own: in the face of one's victim, one sees oneself." In the book's first part, "My Dungeon Shook," Baldwin uses the letter form to bridge the distance between self and other. It suggests a continuing involvement from a place of racial exile in America, and asks each individual reader to become the letter's addressee. The letter also connects Baldwin's past and present selves. It is addressed to his nephew and namesake, who was the same age as Baldwin's autobiographical self in the opening of the book's second part; but it is also a letter to his younger self—from James to Jimmy.

Further reading: David Leeming, *James Baldwin* (1994); Horace Porter, *Stealing the Fire* (1989).

Dear James:

I have begun this letter five times and torn it up five times. I keep seeing your face, which is also the face of your father and my brother. Like him, you are tough, dark, vulnerable, moody—with a very definite tendency to sound truculent because you want no one to think you are soft. You may be like your grandfather in this, I don't know, but certainly both you and your father resemble him very much physically. Well, he is dead, he never saw you, and he had a terrible life; he was defeated long before he died because, at the bottom of his heart, he really believed what white people said about him. This is one of the reasons that he became so holy. I am sure that your father has told you something about all that. Neither you nor your father exhibit any tendency towards holiness: you really *are* of another era, part of what happened when the late E. Franklin Frazier called "the cities of destruction." You can only be destroyed by believing that you really are what the white world calls a *nigger.* I tell you this because I love you, and please don't forget it.

I have known both of you all your lives, have carried your Daddy in my arms and on my shoulders, kissed and spanked him and watched him learn to walk. I don't know if you've known anybody from that far back; if you've loved anybody that long, first as an infant, then as a child, then as a man, you gain a strange perspective on time and human pain and effort. Other people cannot see what I see whenever I look into your father's face, for behind your father's face as it is today are all those other faces which were his. Let him laugh and I see a cellar your father does not remember and a house he does not remember and I hear in his present laughter his laughter as a child. Let him curse and I remember him falling down the cellar steps, and howling, and I remember, with pain, his tears, which my hand or your grandmother's so easily wiped away. But no one's hand can wipe away those tears he sheds invisibly today, which one hears in his laughter and in his speech and in his songs. I know what the world has done to my brother and how narrowly he has survived it. And I know, which is much worse, and this is the crime of which I accuse my country and my countrymen, and for which neither I nor time nor history will ever forgive them, that they have destroyed and are destroying hundreds of thousands of lives and do not know it and do not want to know it. One can be, indeed one must strive to become, tough and philosophical concerning destruction and death, for this is what most of mankind has been best at since we have heard of man. (But remember: *most* of mankind is not *all* of mankind.) But it is not permissible that the authors of devastation should also be innocent. It is the innocence which constitutes the crime.

Now, my dear namesake, these innocent and well-meaning people, your countrymen, have caused you to be born under conditions not very far removed from those described for us by Charles Dickens in the London of more than a hundred years ago. (I hear the chorus of the innocents screaming, "No! This is not true! How *bitter* you are!"—but I am writing this letter to *you*, to try to tell you something about how to handle *them*, for most of them do not yet really know that you exist. I *know* the conditions, under which you were born, for I was there. Your countrymen were *not* there, and haven't made it yet. Your grandmother was also there, and no one has ever accused her of being bitter. I suggest that the innocents check with her. She isn't hard to find. Your country-men don't know that *she* exists, either, though she has been working for them all their lives.)

Well, you were born, here you came, something like fourteen years ago: and though your father and mother and grandmother, looking about the streets through which they were carrying you, staring at the walls into which they brought you, had every reason to be heavyhearted, yet they were not. For here you were, Big James, named for me—you were a big baby, I was not—here you were: to be loved. To be loved, baby, hard, at once, and forever, to strengthen you against the loveless world. Remember that: I know how black it looks to-day, for you. It looked bad that day, too, yes, we were trembling. We have not stopped trembling yet, but if we had not loved each other none of us would have survived. And now you must survive because we love you, and for the sake of your children and your children's children.

This innocent country set you down in a ghetto in which, in fact, it in-tended that you should perish. Let me spell out precisely what I mean by that, for the heart of the matter is here, and the root of my dispute with my country. You were born where you were born, and faced the future that you faced be-cause you were black and *for no other reason*. The limits of your ambition were, thus, expected to be set forever. You were born into a society which spelled out with brutal clarity, and in as many ways as possible, that you were a worthless human being. You were not expected to aspire to excellence: you were ex-pected to make peace with mediocrity. Wherever you have turned, James, in your short time on this earth, you have been told where you could go and what you could do (and *how* you could do it) and where you could do it and whom you could marry. I know that your countrymen do not agree with me about this, and I hear them saying, "You exaggerate." They do not know Har-lem, and I do. So do you. Take no one's word for anything, including mine—but trust your experience. Know whence you came. If you know whence you came, there is really no limit to where you can go. The details and symbols of your life have been deliberately constructed to make you believe what white people say about you. Please try to remember that what they believe, as well as what they do and cause you to endure, does not testify to your inferiority but to their inhumanity and fear. Please try to be clear, dear James, though the storm which rages about your youthful head today, about the reality which lies behind the words *acceptance* and *integration*. There is no reason for you to try to become like white people and there is no basis whatever for their impertinent assumption that *they* must accept *you*. The really terrible thing, old buddy, is that *you* must accept *them*. And I mean that very seriously. You must accept them and accept them with love. For these innocent people have no other hope. They are, in effect, still trapped in a history which they do not understand; and until they understand it, they cannot be released from it. They have had to believe for so many years, and for innumerable reasons, that black men are inferior to white men. Many of them, indeed, know better, but, as you will discover, people find it very difficult to act on what they know. To act is to be committed, and to be committed is to be in danger. In this case, the danger, in the minds of most white Americans, is the loss of identity. Try to imagine how you would feel if you woke up one morning to find the sun shining and all the stars aflame. You would be frightened because it is out of the order of nature. Any upheaval in the universe is terrifying because it so profoundly attacks one's sense of one's own reality. Well, the black man has functioned in the white man's world as a fixed star, as an immovable pillar: and as he moves out of his place, heaven and earth are shaken to their foundations. You, don't be afraid. I said that it was intended that you should perish in the ghetto, perish by never being allowed to go behind the white man's definitions, by never being allowed to spell your proper name. You have, and many of us have, defeated this intention; and, by a terrible law, a terrible paradox, those innocents who believed that your imprisonment made them safe are losing their grasp of reality. But these men are your brothers—your lost, younger brothers. And if the word *integration* means anything, this is what it means: that we, with love, shall force our brothers to see themselves as they are, to cease fleeing from reality and begin to change it. For this is your home, my friend, do not be driven from it; great men have done great things here, and will again, and we can make America what America must become. It will be hard, James, but you come from sturdy, peasant stock, men who picked cotton and dammed rivers and built railroads, and in the teeth of the most terrifying odds, achieved an unassailable and monumental dignity. You come from a long line of poets, some of the greatest poets since Homer. One of them said, *The very time I thought I was lost, My dungeon shook and my chains fell off.*

You know, and I know, that the country is celebrating one hundred years of freedom one hundred years too soon. We cannot be free until they are free. God bless you, James, and Godspeed.

Your uncle, James

From Letter from Birmingham Jail

1963

On Good Friday, 1963, the Baptist minister Martin Luther King, Jr. (1929–1968) led fifty-three African Americans on a protest march through Birmingham, Alabama. After all the protesters were arrested, eight white clergymen published a letter calling such demonstrations unwise, untimely, and extreme. King responded from jail with the letter excerpted here. Based in part on his sermon of 1956, "Paul's Letter to the American Christians," it justifies the need for nonviolent civil disobedience against unjust laws.

His letter follows the pattern of *exordium* (introduction), *exposito* (exposition), *confirmatio* (argument), *confutatio* (rebuttal) and *peroratio* (conclusion), though woven together around the clergymen's points. He establishes goodwill, mentions his reputation and common-knowledge facts, relentlessly defines and redefines the clergymen's terms, and works out cause and effect. Only after laying a groundwork of logic and philosophy, does he shift to pathos and personal appeal.

King always used the Bible as an instrument of liberty and infused his speeches with the language of the black church and slave spirituals. His letter appeals to moral authorities in the Jewish and Christian traditions (one of the eight people he was addressing was a rabbi). He calls on the theologians Reinhold Niebuhr, Augustine, Aquinas, Martin Buber, and Paul Tillich, and quotes or refers to Daniel 3, Matthew 5:44, and Galatians 6:17. He explains he was "compelled" to act, like the apostle Paul, and sets the demonstration in an American but also a Christian tradition of civil disobedience. He adds new characters to the American pantheon of heroes—like James Meredith, who in 1962 had become the first black student to attend the University of Mississippi. Then he ends with a call to action.

Two months later, President Kennedy introduced a civil rights bill—in response, he said, to "cries for equality" from the streets of Birmingham. King's letter had explained that "the creation of tension" was "part of the work of the nonviolent-resister." Now Kennedy echoed him: "Redress is sought in the streets, in . . . protests which create tensions." King continued to write and speak on civil rights and was awarded the Nobel Peace Prize in 1964. In April 1968 he went to Memphis, Tennessee, to support a strike by the city's sanitation workers. On April 3, he gave his "I've Been to the Mountaintop" speech: "Like anybody, I would like to live a long life," he said. "But I'm not concerned about that now . . . I have seen the promised land . . . I may not get there with you." The following day, exactly a year after he'd spoken out against the Vietnam war in "A Time to Break Silence," he was killed by a sniper's bullet as he stepped onto his motel balcony. Another 46 people died in riots that erupted across 125 cities.

Further reading: Taylor Branch, *Parting the Waters* (1988); Clayborne Carson, *The Auto-biography of Martin Luther King, Jr.* (1998).

April 16, 1963

My Dear Fellow Clergymen:

While confined here in the Birmingham city jail, I came across your recent statement calling my present activities "unwise and untimely" . . . I am in Birmingham because injustice is here. Just as the prophets of the eighth century B.C. left their villages and carried their "thus saith the Lord" far beyond the boundaries of their home towns, and just as the Apostle Paul left his village of Tarsus and carried the gospel of Jesus Christ to the far corners of the Greco-Roman world, so am I compelled to carry the gospel of freedom beyond my own home town. Like Paul, I must constantly respond to the Macedonian call for aid.

Moreover, I am cognizant of the interrelatedness of all communities and states. I cannot sit idly by in Atlanta and not be concerned about what happens in Birmingham. Injustice anywhere is a threat to justice everywhere. We are caught in an inescapable network of mutuality, tied in a single garment of destiny. Whatever affects one directly, affects all indirectly. Never again can we afford to live with the narrow, provincial "outside agitator" idea. Anyone who lives inside the United States can never be considered an outsider anywhere within its bounds . . . You may well ask: "Why direct action? Why sit-ins, marches and so forth? Isn't negotiation a better path?" You are quite right in calling, for negotiation. Indeed, this is the very purpose of direct action. Nonviolent direct action seeks to create such a crisis and foster such a tension that a community which has constantly refused to negotiate is forced to confront the issue. It seeks so to dramatize the issue that it can no longer be ignored. My citing the creation of tension as part of the work of the nonviolent-resister may sound rather shocking. But I must confess that I am not afraid of the word "tension." I have earnestly opposed violent tension, but there is a type of constructive, nonviolent tension which is necessary for growth. Just as Socrates felt that it was necessary to create a tension in the mind so that individuals could rise from the bondage of myths and half-truths to the unfettered realm of creative analysis and objective appraisal, so must we see the need for nonviolent gadflies to create the kind of tension in society that will help men rise from the dark depths of prejudice and racism to the majestic heights of understanding and brotherhood.

The purpose of our direct-action program is to create a situation so crisis-packed that it will inevitably open the door to negotiation. I therefore concur with you in your call for negotiation. Too long has our beloved Southland been bogged down in a tragic effort to live in monologue rather than dialogue . . . We know through painful experience that freedom is never voluntarily given by the oppressor; it must be demanded by the oppressed. Frankly, I have yet to engage in a direct-action campaign that was "well timed" in the view of those who have not suffered unduly from the disease of segregation. For years now I have heard the word "Wait!" It rings in the ear of every Negro with piercing familiarity. This "Wait" has almost always meant "Never." We must come to see, with one of our distinguished jurists, that "justice too long delayed is justice denied."

We have waited for more than 340 years for our constitutional and God-given rights. The nations of Asia and Africa are moving with jet-like speed toward gaining political independence, but we stiff creep at horse-and-buggy pace toward gaining a cup of coffee at a lunch counter. Perhaps it is easy for those who have never felt the stinging dark of segregation to say, "Wait." But when you have seen vicious mobs lynch your mothers and fathers at will and drown your sisters and brothers at whim; when you have seen hate-filled policemen curse, kick and even kill your black brothers and sisters; when you see the vast majority of your twenty million Negro brothers smothering in an airtight cage of poverty in the midst of an affluent society; when you suddenly find your tongue twisted and your speech stammering as you seek to explain to your six-year-old daughter why she can't go to the public amusement park that has just been advertised on television, and see tears welling up in her eyes when she is told that Funtown is closed to colored children, and see ominous clouds of inferiority beginning to form in her little mental sky, and see her beginning to distort her personality by developing an unconscious bitterness toward white people; when you have to concoct an answer for a five-year-old son who is asking: "Daddy, why do white people treat colored people so mean?"; when you take a cross-country drive and find it necessary to sleep night after night in the uncomfortable corners of your automobile because no motel will accept you; when you are humiliated day in and day out by nagging signs reading "white" and "colored"; when your first name becomes "nigger," your middle name becomes "boy" (however old you are) and your last name becomes "John," and your wife and mother are never given the respected title "Mrs."; when you are harried by day and haunted by night by the fact that you are a Negro, living constantly at tiptoe stance, never quite knowing what to expect next, and are plagued with inner fears and outer resentments; when you are forever fighting a degenerating sense of "nobodiness"—then you will understand why we find it difficult to wait. There comes a time when the cup of endurance runs over, and men are no longer willing to be plunged into the abyss of despair. I hope, sirs, you can understand our legitimate and unavoidable impatience.

You express a great deal of anxiety over our willingness to break laws. This is certainly a legitimate concern. Since we so diligently urge people to obey the Supreme Court's decision of 1954 outlawing segregation in the public schools, at first glance it may seem rather paradoxical for us consciously to break laws. One may well ask: "How can you advocate breaking some laws and obeying others?" The answer lies in the fact that there are two types of laws: just and unjust. I would be the first to advocate obeying just laws. One has not only a legal but a moral responsibility to obey just laws. Conversely, one has a moral responsibility to disobey unjust laws. I would agree with St. Augustine that "an unjust law is no law at all."

Now, what is the difference between the two? How does one determine whether a law is just or unjust? A just law is a man-made code that squares with the moral law or the law of God. An unjust law is a code that is out of harmony with the moral law. To put it in the terms of St. Thomas Aquinas: An unjust law is a human law that is not rooted in eternal law and natural law. Any law that uplifts human personality is just. Any law that degrades human personality is unjust. All segregation statutes are unjust because segregation distort the soul and damages the personality. It gives the segregator a false sense of superiority and the segregated a false sense of inferiority. Segregation, to use the terminology of the Jewish philosopher Martin Buber, substitutes an "I-it" relationship for an "I-thou" relationship and ends up relegating persons to the status of things. Hence segregation is not only politically, economically and sociologically unsound, it is morally wrong and awful. Paul Tillich said that sin is separation. Is not segregation an existential expression of man's tragic separation, his awful estrangement, his terrible sinfulness? Thus it is that I can urge men to obey the 1954 decision of the Supreme Court, for it is morally right; and I can urge them to disobey segregation ordinances, for they are morally wrong . . .

Of course, there is nothing new about this kind of civil disobedience. It was evidenced sublimely in the refusal of Shadrach, Meshach and Abednego to obey the laws of Nebuchadnezzar, on the ground that a higher moral law was at stake. It was practiced superbly by the early Christians, who were willing to face hungry lions and the excruciating pain of chopping blocks rather than submit to certain unjust laws of the Roman Empire. To a degree, academic freedom is a reality today because Socrates practiced civil disobedience. In our own nation, the Boston Tea Party represented a massive act of civil disobedience.

We should never forget that everything Adolf Hitler did in Germany was "legal" and everything the Hungarian freedom fighters did in Hungary was "illegal." It was "illegal" to aid and comfort a Jew in Hitler's Germany. Even so, I am sure that, had I lived in Germany at the time, I would have aided and comforted my Jewish brothers. If today I lived in a Communist country where certain principles dear to the Christian faith are suppressed, I would openly advocate disobeying that country's antireligious laws . . .

In your statement you assert that our actions, even though peaceful, must be condemned because they precipitate violence. But is this a logical assertion? Isn't this like condemning a robbed man because his possession of money precipitated the evil act of robbery? Isn't this like condemning Socrates because his unswerving commitment to truth and his philosophical inquiries precipitated the act by the misguided populace in which they made him drink hemlock? Isn't this like condemning Jesus because his unique God-consciousness and never-ceasing devotion to God's will precipitated the evil act of crucifixion? We must come to see that, as the federal courts have consistently affirmed, it is wrong to urge an individual to cease his efforts to gain his basic constitutional rights because the quest may precipitate violence. Society must protect the robbed and punish the robber . . . You speak of our activity in Birmingham as extreme. At first I was rather disappointed that fellow clergymen would see my nonviolent efforts as those of an extremist. I began thinking about the fact that I stand in the middle of two opposing forces in the Negro community. One is a force of complacency, made up in part of Negroes who, as a result of long years of oppression, are so drained of self-respect and a sense of "somebodiness" that they have adjusted to segregation; and in part of a few middle class Negroes who, because of a degree of academic and economic security and because in some ways they profit by segregation, have become insensitive to the problems of the masses. The other force is one of bitterness and hatred, and it comes perilously close to advocating violence. It is expressed in the various black nationalist groups that are springing up across the nation, the largest and best-known being Elijah Muhammad's Muslim movement. Nourished by the Negro's frustration over the continued existence of racial discrimination, this movement is made up of people who have lost faith in America, who have absolutely repudiated Christianity, and who have concluded that the white man is an incorrigible "devil."

I have tried to stand between these two forces, saying that we need emulate neither the "do-nothingism" of the complacent nor the hatred and despair of the black nationalist. For there is the more excellent way of love and nonviolent protest. I am grateful to God that, through the influence of the Negro church, the way of nonviolence became an integral part of our struggle.

If this philosophy had not emerged, by now many streets of the South would, I am convinced, be flowing with blood. And I am further convinced that if our white brothers dismiss as "rabble-rousers" and "outside agitators" those of us who employ nonviolent direct action, and if they refuse to support our nonviolent efforts, millions of Negroes will, out of frustration and despair, seek solace and security in black-nationalist ideologies a development that would inevitably lead to a frightening racial nightmare.

Oppressed people cannot remain oppressed forever. The yearning for freedom eventually manifests itself, and that is what has happened to the American Negro. Something within has reminded him of his birthright of freedom, and something without has reminded him that it can be gained. Consciously or unconsciously, he has been caught up by the *Zeitgeist,* and with his black brothers of Africa and his brown and yellow brothers of Asia, South America and the Caribbean, the United States Negro is moving with a sense of great urgency toward the promised land of racial justice. If one recognizes this vital urge that has engulfed the Negro community, one should readily understand why public demonstrations are taking place. The Negro has many pent-up resentments and latent frustrations, and he must release them. So let him march; let him make prayer pilgrimages to the city hall; let him go on freedom rides and try to understand why he must do so. If his repressed emotions are not released in nonviolent ways, they will seek expression through violence; this is not a threat but a fact of history. So I have not said to my people: "Get rid of your discontent." Rather, I have tried to say that this normal and healthy discontent can be channeled into the creative outlet of nonviolent direct action. And now this approach is being termed extremist.

But though I was initially disappointed at being categorized as an extremist, as I continued to think about the matter I gradually gained a measure of satisfaction from the label. Was not Jesus an extremist for love: "Love your enemies, bless them that curse you, do good to them that hate you, and pray for them which despitefully use you, and persecute you." Was not Amos an extremist for justice: "Let justice roll down like waters and righteousness like an ever-flowing stream." Was not Paul an extremist for the Christian gospel: "I bear in my body the marks of the Lord Jesus." Was not Martin Luther an extremist: "Here I stand; I cannot do otherwise, so help me God." And John Bunyan: "I will stay in jail to the end of my days before I make a butchery of my conscience." And Abraham Lincoln: "This nation cannot survive half slave and half free." And Thomas Jefferson: "We hold these truths to be self-evident, that all men are created equal . . ." So the question is not whether we will be extremists, but what kind of extremists we will be. Will we be extremists for hate or for love? Will we be extremists for the preservation of injustice or for the extension of justice? In that dramatic scene on Calvary's hill three men were crucified. We must never forget that all three were crucified for the same crime—the crime of extremism. Two were extremists for immorality, and thus fell below their environment. The other, Jesus Christ, was an extremist for love, truth and goodness, and thereby rose above his environment. Perhaps the South, the nation and the world are in dire need of creative extremists . . .

We will reach the goal of freedom in Birmingham, and all over the nation, because the goal of America is freedom. Abused and scorned though we may be, our destiny is tied up with America's destiny. Before the pilgrims landed at

Plymouth, we were here. Before the pen of Jefferson etched the majestic words of the Declaration of Independence across the pages of history, we were here. For more than two centuries our forebears labored in this country without wages; they made cotton king; they built the homes of their masters while suffering gross injustice and shameful humiliation—and yet out of a bottomless vitality they continued to thrive and develop. If the inexpressible cruelties of slavery could not stop us, the opposition we now face will surely fail. We will win our freedom because the sacred heritage of our nation and the eternal will of God are embodied in our echoing demands.

Before closing I feel impelled to mention one other point in your statement that has troubled me profoundly. You warmly commended the Birmingham police force for keeping "order" and "preventing violence." I doubt that you would have so warmly commended the police force if you had seen its dogs sinking their teeth into unarmed, nonviolent Negroes. I doubt that you would so quickly commend the policemen if you were to observe their ugly and inhumane treatment of Negroes here in the city jail; if you were to watch them push and curse old Negro women and young Negro girls; if you were to see them slap and kick old Negro men and young boys; if you were to observe them, as they did on two occasions, refuse to give us food because we wanted to sing our grace together. I cannot join you in your praise of the Birmingham police department.

It is true that the police have exercised a degree of discipline in handing the demonstrators. In this sense they have conducted themselves rather "nonviolently" in public. But for what purpose? To preserve the evil system of segregation. Over the past few years I have consistently preached that nonviolence demands that the means we use must be as pure as the ends we seek. I have tried to make clear that it is wrong to use immoral means to attain moral ends. But now I must affirm that it is just as wrong, or perhaps even more so, to use moral means to preserve immoral ends. Perhaps Mr. Connor and his policemen have been rather nonviolent in public, as was Chief Pritchett in Albany, Georgia but they have used the moral means of nonviolence to maintain the immoral end of racial injustice. As T. S. Eliot has said: "The last temptation is the greatest treason: To do the right deed for the wrong reason."

I wish you had commended the Negro sit-inners and demonstrators of Birmingham for their sublime courage, their willingness to suffer and their amazing discipline in the midst of great provocation. One day the South will recognize its real heroes. They will be the James Merediths, with the noble sense of purpose that enables them to face jeering, and hostile mobs, and with the agonizing loneliness that characterizes the life of the pioneer. They will be old, oppressed, battered Negro women, symbolized in a seventy-two-year-old woman in Montgomery, Alabama, who rose up with a sense of dignity and with her people decided not to ride segregated buses, and who responded with ungrammatical profundity to one who inquired about her weariness: "My feets is tired, but my soul is at rest." They will be the young high school and college students, the young ministers of the gospel and a host of their elders, courageously and nonviolently sitting in at lunch counters and willingly going to jail for conscience' sake. One day the South will know that when these disinherited children of God sat down at lunch counters, they were in reality standing up for what is best in the American dream and for the most sacred values in our Judaeo-Christian heritage, thereby bringing our nation back to those great wells of democracy which were dug deep by the founding fathers in their formulation of the Constitution and the Declaration of Independence . . . Let us all hope that the dark clouds of racial prejudice will soon pass away and the deep fog of misunderstanding will be lifted from our fear-drenched communities, and in some not too distant tomorrow the radiant stars of love and brotherhood will shine over our great nation with all their scintillating beauty.

Yours for the cause of Peace and Brotherhood,
Martin Luther King, Jr.

Civil Rights March on Washington, D.C.

1963

During the civil rights movement, the rhetoric and reality of constrained space loomed large. From the Montgomery bus boycott and Freedom Rides, to attempts at integrating public schools and lunch counter sit-ins, activists did battle for physical and civic space. Martin Luther King, Jr., protested the "airtight cage of poverty" and the experience of being "locked within the narrow walls of opportunity," and photographers depicted spatial limitations as well—as in the image reproduced here of demonstrators crowded behind a storm fence. The image's power and poignancy also come from the presence of the abandoned shoe, and the word "right" on a sign torn in half on the ground.

The camera was an important tool of the movement. Some leaders took photographs themselves, like Wyatt Walker and Andrew Young of the Southern Christian Leadership Conference (SCLC) or James Forman and Robert Zellner of the Student Nonviolent Coordinating Committee (SNCC). The SCLC supported photographers of the Movement, and the SNCC enlisted and trained a dozen. Photographs appeared as posters and were printed in pamphlets and displayed in freedom houses. Charles Moore, Gordon Parks, and Frank Dandridge photographed the movement for *Life* magazine, and Moneta Sleet, Jr., worked for *Ebony.*

Marion Trikosko, a staff photographer for *U.S. News and World Report,* took this photograph at the March on Washington for Jobs and Freedom on August 28, 1963. On June 19, President Kennedy had sent Congress a civil rights bill, and the Washington demonstration, organized principally by A. Philip Randolph, Bayard Rustin, and King (who delivered his famous "I Have a Dream" speech during the rally), was partly intended to pressure through this bill. It was the largest political demonstration in the United States to date, with estimates of the crowd size ranging from 200,000 to 500,000. Press coverage was more extensive than for any previous political demonstration; another photographer is even visible within Trikosko's image. The following year, King explained the importance of the camera to the movement: "The brutality with which officials would have quelled the black individual became impotent when it could not . . . remain unobserved," he explained. "It was caught—as a fugitive from a penitentiary . . . in gigantic circling spotlights. It was imprisoned in a luminous glare revealing the naked truth to the whole world." Imprisoning whites within a "penitentiary," photographers helped invert American society's negative space.

Further reading: Steven Kasher, *Appeal to This Age* (1995); Ernest C. Withers, *Pictures Tell the Story* (2000).

From The Ballot or the Bullet

1964

To white Americans, Martin Luther King, Jr., seemed the civil rights movement's undis-
puted leader. But Malcolm X (1925–1965), a Muslim minister and a national spokesman
for the Nation of Islam, was another contender. Born Malcolm Little, he converted to the
Black Muslim religion while in prison for armed robbery. Upon release he became a
spokesman for Elijah Muhammad, the leader of the Nation of Islam, and a minister of the
faith. They fell out, and when Malcolm remarked that John F. Kennedy's assassination was
"chickens coming home to roost," Muhammad banned him from speaking in public. In
1964 Malcolm declared independence from the Nation of Islam and formed Muslim
Mosque, Inc. Decrying King's rhetorical use of the word "we" to include whites, he suggested that King was the faithful "house negro" to his rebellious "field negro," and developed what he called the "gospel" of black nationalism. Eldridge Cleaver, Huey Newton,
and Stokely Carmichael then translated this into the ideology of Black Power.

Malcolm's speech "The Ballot or the Bullet" is a full explication of black nationalism as
the route to racial equality. Its original audience was young urban blacks, frustrated
by what they saw as King's futile gradualism. Malcolm frequently criticized King's philosophy of nonviolence, instead advocating "whatever means necessary" to achieve equality. These means included violence (though generally only in response to violence): "If
you're going to get yourself a .45 and start singing 'We Shall Overcome,' I'm with you,"
Malcolm once said. This prompted comparisons between Malcolm and the 19th-century
slave rebel Nat Turner, and in 1965 the social activist Ossie Davis added that Malcolm
stood in relation to the "'responsible' civil rights leaders, just about where John Brown
stood in relation to the 'responsible' abolitionist in the fight against slavery."

Malcolm was in the tradition of the urban street speaker. He would use phrases like
"what's good for the goose is good for the gander," while King described "radiant stars
of love and brotherhood . . . with all their scintillating beauty." But writers in the Black
Arts Movement, the artistic branch of the Black Power movement, heard a saxophone
solo in Malcolm's voice: "What I liked most about Malcolm was his sense of poetry," said
Larry Neal in 1970. "Because I was not reared in the Black church . . . I did not have ready
access to the rhetorical strategies of Martin Luther King . . . [But Malcolm] reminded
many of us of the music of Charlie Parker and John Coltrane—a music that was a central
force in the emerging ethos of the Black artistic consciousness." Malcolm was killed while
speaking in Harlem, on February 21, 1965. The Black Arts poet Amiri Baraka wrote "A
Poem for Black Hearts" (1965): "For Malcolm's / pleas for your dignity, black men, for
your life."

Further reading: Michael Dyson, *Making Malcolm* (1996); Alex Haley, *The Autobiography of Malcolm X* (1965).

1964 threatens to be the most explosive year America has ever witnessed. The most explosive year. Why? It's also a political year. It's the year when all of the white politicians will be back in the so-called Negro community jiving you and me for some votes. The year when all of the white political crooks will be right back in your and my community with their false promises, building up our hopes for a letdown, with their trickery and their treachery, with their false promises which they don't intend to keep. As they nourish these dissatisfactions, it can only lead to one thing, an explosion; and now we have the type of black man on the scene in America today—I'm sorry, Brother Lomax—who just doesn't intend to turn the other cheek any longer.

Don't let anybody tell you anything about the odds are against you. If they draft you, they send you to Korea and make you face 800 million Chinese. If you can be brave over there, you can be brave right here. These odds aren't as great as those odds. And if you fight here, you will at least know what you're fighting for.

I'm not a politician, not even a student of politics; in fact, I'm not a student of much of anything. I'm not a Democrat. I'm not a Republican, and I don't even consider myself an American. If you and I were Americans, there'd be no problem. Those Honkies that just got off the boat, they're already Americans; Polacks are already Americans; the Italian refugees are already Americans. Everything that came out of Europe, every blue-eyed thing, is already an American. And as long as you and I have been over here, we aren't Americans yet.

Well, I am one who doesn't believe in deluding myself. I'm not going to sit at your table and watch you eat, with nothing on my plate, and call myself a diner. Sitting at the table doesn't make you a diner, unless you eat some of what's on that plate. Being here in America doesn't make you an American. Being born here in America doesn't make you an American. Why, if birth made you American, you wouldn't need any legislation; you wouldn't need any amendments to the Constitution; you wouldn't be faced with civil-rights filibustering in Washington, D.C., right now. They don't have to pass civil-rights legislation to make a Polack an American

No, I'm not an American. I'm one of the 22 million black people who are the victims of Americanism. One of the 22 million black people who are the victims of democracy, nothing but disguised hypocrisy. So, I'm not standing here speaking to you as an American, or a patriot, or a flag-saluter, or a flag-waver—no, not I. I'm speaking as a victim of this American system. And I see America through the eyes of the victim. I don't see any American dream; I see an American nightmare . . . So it's time in 1964 to wake up. And when you see them coming up with that kind of conspiracy, let them know your eyes are open. And let them know you—something else that's wide open too. It's got to be the ballot or the bullet. The ballot or the bullet. If you're afraid to use an expression like that, you should get on out of the country; you should get back in the cotton patch; you should get back in the alley. They get all the Negro vote, and after they get it, the Negro gets nothing in return. All they did when they got to Washington was give a few big Negroes big jobs. Those big Negroes didn't need big jobs, they already had jobs. That's camouflage, that's trickery, that's treachery, window-dressing. I'm not trying to knock out the Democrats for the Republicans. We'll get to them in a minute. But it is true; you put the Democrats first and the Democrats put you last . . . You and I in America are faced not with a segregationist conspiracy, we're faced with a government conspiracy. Everyone who's filibustering is a senator—that's the government. Everyone who's finagling in Washington, D.C., is a congressman—that's the government. You don't have anybody putting blocks in your path but people who are a part of the government. The same government that you go abroad to fight for and die for is the government that is in a conspiracy to deprive you of your voting rights, deprive you of your economic opportunities, deprive you of decent housing, deprive you of decent education. You don't need to go to the employer alone, it is the government itself, the government of America, that is responsible for the oppression and exploitation and degradation of black people in this country. And you should drop it in their lap. This government has failed the Negro. This so-called democracy has failed the Negro. And all these white liberals have definitely failed the Negro.

So, where do we go from here? First, we need some friends. We need some new allies. The entire civil-rights struggle needs a new interpretation, a broader interpretation. We need to look at this civil-rights thing from another angle— from the inside as well as from the outside. To those of us whose philosophy is black nationalism, the only way you can get involved in the civil-rights struggle is give it a new interpretation. That old interpretation excluded us. It kept us out. So, we're giving a new interpretation to the civil-rights struggle, an interpretation that will enable us to come into it, take part in it. And these handkerchief-heads who have been dillydallying and pussy footing and compromising—we don't intend to let them pussyfoot and dillydally and compromise any longer.

How can you thank a man for giving you what's already yours? How then can you thank him for giving you only part of what's already yours? You haven't even made progress, if what's being given to you, you should have had already. That's not progress. And I love my Brother Lomax, the way he pointed out we're right back where we were in 1954. We're not even as far up as we were in 1954. We're behind where we were in 1954. There's more segregation now than there was in 1954. There's more racial animosity, more racial hatred, more racial violence today in 1964, than there was in 1954. Where is the progress?

And now you're facing a situation where the young Negro's coming up. They don't want to hear that "turn-the-other-cheek" stuff, no. In Jacksonville, those were teenagers, they were throwing Molotov cocktails. Negroes have never done that before. But it shows you there's a new deal coming in. There's new thinking coming in. There's new strategy coming in. It'll be Molotov cocktails this month, hand grenades next month, and something else next month. It'll be ballots, or it'll be bullets. It'll be liberty, or it will be death. The only difference about this kind of death—it'll be reciprocal. You know what is meant by "reciprocal"? That's one of Brother Lomax's words. I stole it from him. I don't usually deal with those big words because I don't usually deal with big people. I deal with small people. I find you can get a whole lot of small people and whip hell out of a whole lot of big people. They haven't got anything to lose, and they've got every thing to gain. And they'll let you know in a minute: "It takes two to tango; when I go, you go."

The black nationalists, those whose philosophy is black nationalism, in bringing about this new interpretation of the entire meaning of civil rights, look upon it as meaning, as Brother Lomax has pointed out, equality of opportunity. Well, we're justified in seeking civil rights, if it means equality of opportunity, because all we're doing there is trying to collect for our investment. Our mothers and fathers invested sweat and blood. Three hundred and ten years we worked in this country without a dime in return—I mean without a dime in return. You let the white man walk around here talking about how rich this country is, but you never stop to think how it got rich so quick. It got rich because you made it rich.

You take the people who are in this audience right now. They're poor. We're all poor as individuals. Our weekly salary individually amounts to hardly anything. But if you take the salary of everyone in here collectively, it'll fill up a whole lot of baskets. It's a lot of wealth. If you can collect the wages of just these people right here for a year, you'll be rich—richer than rich. When you look at it like that, think how rich Uncle Sam had to become, not with this handful, but millions of black people. Your and my mother and father, who didn't work an eight-hour shift, but worked from "can't see" in the morning until "can't see" at night, and worked for nothing, making the white man rich, making Uncle Sam rich. This is our investment. This is our contribution, our blood.

Not only did we give of our free labor, we gave of our blood. Every time he had a call to arms, we were the first ones in uniform. We died on every bat-tlefield the white man had. We have made a greater sacrifice than anybody who's standing up in America today. We have made a greater contribution and have collected less. Civil rights, for those of us whose philosophy is black na-tionalism, means: "Give it to us now. Don't wait for next year. Give it to us yes-terday, and that's not fast enough." . . . Whenever you demonstrate against segregation, whether it is segregated education, segregated housing, or any-thing else, the law is on your side, and anyone who stands in the way is not the law any longer. They are breaking the law; they are not representatives of the law. Any time you demonstrate against segregation and a man has the audacity to put a police dog on you, kill that dog, kill him, I'm telling you, kill that dog. I say it, if they put me in jail tomorrow, kill that dog. Then you'll put a stop to it. Now, if these white people in here don't want to see that kind of action, get down and tell the mayor to tell the police department to pull the dogs in. That's all you have to do. If you don't do it, someone else will.

If you don't take this kind of stand, your little children will grow up and look at you and think "shame." If you don't take an uncompromising stand, I don't mean go out and get violent; but at the same time you should never be nonvi-olent unless you run into some nonviolence. I'm nonviolent with those who are nonviolent with me. But when you drop that violence on me, then you've made me go insane, and I'm not responsible for what I do. And that's the way every Negro should get. Any time you know you're within the law, within your legal rights, within your moral rights, in accord with justice, then die for what you believe in. But don't die alone. Let your dying be reciprocal. This is what is meant by equality. What's good for the goose is good for the gander.

When we begin to get in this area, we need new friends, we need new allies. We need to expand the civil-rights struggle to a higher level—to the level of human rights. Whenever you are in a civil-rights struggle, whether you know it or not, you are confining yourself to the jurisdiction of Uncle Sam. No one from the outside world can speak out in your behalf as long as your struggle is a civil-rights struggle. Civil rights comes within the domestic affairs of this country. All of our African brothers and our Asian brothers and our Latin-American brothers cannot open their mouths and interfere in the domestic af-fairs of the United States. And as long as it's civil rights, this comes under the jurisdiction of Uncle Sam . . . Uncle Sam's hands are dripping with blood, drip-ping with the blood of the black man in this country. He's the earth's number-one hypocrite. He has the audacity—yes, he has—imagine him posing as the leader of the free world. The free world! And you over here singing "We Shall Overcome." Expand the civil-rights struggle to the level of human rights. Take it into the United Nations, where our African brothers can throw their weight on our side, where our Asian brothers can throw their weight on our side, where our Latin-American brothers can throw their weight on our side, and where 800 million Chinamen are sitting there waiting to throw their weight on our side.

Let the world know how bloody his hands are. Let the world know the hypocrisy that's practiced over here. Let it be the ballot or the bullet. Let him know that it must be the ballot or the bullet.

When you take your case to Washington, D.C., you're taking it to the criminal who's responsible; it's like running from the wolf to the fox. They're all in cahoots together. They all work political chicanery and make you look like a chump before the eyes of the world. Here you are walking around in America, getting ready to be drafted and sent abroad, like a tin soldier, and when you get over there, people ask you what are you fighting for, and you have to stick your tongue in your cheek. No, take Uncle Sam to court, take him before the world . . .

Right now, in this country, if you and I, 22 million African-Americans— that's what we are—Africans who are in America. You're nothing but Africans. Nothing but Africans. In fact, you'd get farther calling yourself African instead of Negro. Africans don't catch hell. You're the only one catching hell. They don't have to pass civil-rights bills for Africans. An African can go anywhere he wants right now. All you've got to do is tie your head up. That's right, go anywhere you want. Just stop being a Negro. Change your name to Hoogagagooba. That'll show you how silly the white man is. You're dealing with a silly man. A friend of mine who's very dark put a turban on his head and went into a restaurant in Atlanta before they called themselves desegregated. He went into a white restaurant, he sat down, they served him, and he said, "What would happen if a Negro came in here? And there he's sitting, black as night, but because he had his head wrapped up the waitress looked back at him and says, "Why, there wouldn't no nigger dare come in here."

So, you're dealing with a man whose bias and prejudice are making him lose his mind, his intelligence, every day. He's frightened. He looks around and sees what's taking place on this earth, and he sees that the pendulum of time is swinging in your direction. The dark people are waking up. They're losing their fear of the white man. No place where he's fighting right now is he winning. Everywhere he's fighting, he's fighting someone your and my complexion. And they're beating him. He can't win any more. He's won his last battle. He failed to win the Korean War. He couldn't win it. He had to sign a truce. That's a loss . . . You've got to have heart to be a guerrilla warrior, and he hasn't got any heart . . . The political philosophy of black nationalism is being taught in the Christian church. It's being taught in the NAACP. It's being taught in CORE meetings. It's being taught in SNCC Student Nonviolent Coordinating Committee meetings. It's being taught in Muslim meetings. It's being taught where nothing but atheists and agnostics come together. It's being taught everywhere. Black people are fed up with the dillydallying, pussyfooting, compromising approach that we've been using toward getting our freedom. We want freedom now, but we're not going to get it saying "We Shall Overcome." We've got to fight until we overcome . . . The social philosophy of black nationalism only means that we have to get together and remove the evils, the vices, alcoholism, drug addiction, and other evils that are destroying the moral fiber of our community. We our selves have to lift the level of our community, the standard of our community to a higher level, make our own society beautiful so that we will be satisfied in our own social circles and won't be running around here trying to knock our way into a social circle where we're not wanted. So I say, in spreading a gospel such as black nationalism, it is not designed to make the black man re-evaluate the white man—you know him already—but to make the black man re-evaluate himself. Don't change the white man's mind—you can't change his mind, and that whole thing about appealing to the moral conscience of America—America's conscience is bankrupt. She lost all conscience a long time ago. Uncle Sam has no conscience.

They don't know what morals are. They don't try and eliminate an evil because it's evil, or because it's illegal, or because it's immoral; they eliminate it only when it threatens their existence. So you're wasting your time appealing to the moral conscience of a bankrupt man like Uncle Sam. If he had a conscience, he'd straighten this thing out with no more pressure being put upon him. So it is not necessary to change the white man's mind. We have to change our own mind. You can't change his mind about us. We've got to change our own minds about each other. We have to see each other with new eyes. We have to see each other as brothers and sisters. We have to come together with warmth so we can develop unity and harmony that's necessary to get this problem solved ourselves . . . It's time for you and me to stop sitting in this country, letting some cracker senators, Northern crackers and Southern crackers, sit there in Washington, D.C., and come to a conclusion in their mind that you and I are supposed to have civil rights. There's no white man going to tell me anything about my rights. Brothers and sisters, always remember, if it doesn't take senators and congressmen and presidential proclamations to give freedom to the white man, it is not necessary for legislation or proclamation or Supreme Court decisions to give freedom to the black man. You let that white man know, if this is a country of freedom, let it be a country of freedom; and if it's not a country of freedom, change it . . . No, if you never see me another time in your life, if I die in the morning, I'll die saying one thing: the ballot or the bullet, the ballot or the bullet . . . The black nationalists aren't going to wait. Lyndon B. Johnson is the head of the Democratic Party. If he's for civil rights, let him go into the Senate next week and declare himself. Let him go in there right now and declare himself. Let him go in there and denounce the Southern branch of his party. Let him go in there right now and take a moral stand—right now, not later. Tell him, don't wait until election time. If he waits too long, brothers and sisters, he will be responsible for letting a condition develop in this country which will create a climate that will bring seeds up out of the ground with vegetation on the end of them looking like something these people never dreamed of. In 1964, it's the ballot or the bullet.

On Civil Rights

1963

Senator Edward Kennedy calls this speech by John F. Kennedy (1917–1963), and President Kennedy's speech to Congress eight days later proposing legislation that became the 1964 Civil Rights Act, "landmarks of the civil rights movement." The legislation was one of his brother's "greatest legacies," Senator Kennedy says, and he believes their brother Robert Kennedy would feel the same way.

In 1960 the Civil Rights Commission found that 57 percent of African American housing was judged unacceptable, that African Americans found it nearly impossible to get mortgages, and that African American life expectancy was seven years lower than whites' while African American infant mortality was twice that of whites. The Senator recalls that his two older brothers were hands-on civil rights activists as early as October 1960: "Jack and Bobby responded swiftly when Dr. Martin Luther King was arrested with other demonstrators for taking seats at a segregated restaurant in Atlanta . . . Jack called Coretta Scott King to offer his moral support and promised to work for Dr. King's release. Bobby called the judge, and was able to obtain Dr. King's release the next day." He adds: "In those early days of the civil rights movement, just a week before the Presidential election, Nixon opted to remain silent on the issue."

Kennedy's address makes it clear that the legislation was proposed in response to civil rights protest, and the Senator remembers that his brother felt "strongly compelled to take action": the laws "were inspired by the civil rights movement," by the "sacrifices [of] dedicated leaders at every level of American society who marched, protested, and organized." The speech came a month after the Southern Christian Leadership Conference's "Children's Campaign" in Birmingham, and two months after King's "Letter from Birmingham Jail." The Senator notes that when King was in jail in Birmingham, President Kennedy and his cabinet members "privately called corporate leaders with subsidiaries in Birmingham, urging them to negotiate with Dr. King to try to settle the civil rights issues he'd raised in the city."

In this speech, Kennedy puts the act in its Cold War context. The Senator explains that, while the issue of civil rights was important to his brother on its own terms, it obviously had a global context: "As the American people became more focused on promoting basic human rights for our citizens, it was inevitable that these goals would shape our view of oppression and the denial of human rights in other nations." President Kennedy also refers to Lincoln's Emancipation Proclamation. This was a way to insist, the Senator says, that "too many years had passed without a genuine national commitment to eliminate the stain of slavery."

Congress was still debating the Civil Rights bill when Kennedy was assassinated in Dallas on November 22, 1963. Lyndon Johnson used the shock of Kennedy's death to push forward the legislation and by January 1964, 68 percent of the population supported its passage. In July 1964 Johnson signed the bill. The Senator believes that the act brought not just "a change in the law, but a change in attitudes," that it "helped change America not just legally, but in terms of our ideal of equality, of opportunity for all," and that it "defined a new and lasting national commitment to get serious about ending the injustice of segregation and racial oppression." But he acknowledges that "civil rights is still the great unfinished business of America." Citing the lyrics of the 1968 song about Lincoln, King, and Kennedy, "Abraham, Martin, and John," the Senator concludes: "we'll be free . . . it's gonna be *one day.*"

This afternoon, following a series of threats and defiant statements, the presence of Alabama National Guardsmen was required on the University of Alabama to carry out the final and unequivocal order of the United States District Court of the Northern District of Alabama. That order called for the admission of two clearly qualified young Alabama residents who happened to have been born Negro. That they were admitted peacefully on the campus is due in good measure to the conduct of the students of the University of Alabama, who met their responsibilities in a constructive way.

I hope that every American, regardless of where he lives, will stop and examine his conscience about this and other related incidents. This Nation was founded by men of many nations and backgrounds. It was founded on the principle that all men are created equal, and that the rights of every man are diminished when the rights of one man are threatened.

Today we are committed to a worldwide struggle to promote and protect the rights of all who wish to be free. And when Americans are sent to Viet-Nam or West Berlin, we do not ask for whites only. It ought to be possible, therefore, for American students of any color to attend any public institution they select without having to be backed up by troops. It ought to be possible for American consumers of any color to receive equal service in places of public accommodation, such as hotels and restaurants and theaters and retail stores, without being forced to resort to demonstrations in the street, and it ought to be possible for American citizens of any color to register to vote in a free election without interference or fear of reprisal. It ought to be possible, in short, for every American to enjoy the privileges of being American without regard to his race or his color. In short, every American ought to have the right to be treated as he would wish to be treated, as one would wish his children to be treated. But this is not the case.

The Negro baby born in America today, regardless of the section of the Nation in which he is born, has about one-half as much chance of completing a high school as a white baby born in the same place on the same day, one-third as much chance of completing college, one-third as much chance of becoming a professional man, twice as much chance of becoming unemployed, about one-seventh as much chance of earning $10,000 a year, a life expectancy which is seven years shorter, and the prospects of earning only half as much.

This is not a sectional issue. Difficulties over segregation and discrimination exist in every city, in every State of the Union, producing in many cities a rising tide of discontent that threatens the public safety. Nor is this a partisan issue. In a time of domestic crisis men of good will and generosity should be able to unite regardless of party or politics. This is not even a legal or legislative issue alone. It is better to settle these matters in the courts than on the streets, and new laws are needed at every level, but law alone cannot make men see right.

We are confronted primarily with a moral issue. It is as old as the scriptures and is as clear as the American Constitution. The heart of the question is whether all Americans are to be afforded equal rights and equal opportunities, whether we are going to treat our fellow Americans as we want to be treated. If an American, because his skin is dark, cannot eat lunch in a restaurant open to the public, if he cannot send his children to the best public school available, if he cannot vote for the public officials who will represent him, if, in short, he cannot enjoy the full and free life which all of us want, then who among us would be content to have the color of his skin changed and stand in his place? Who among us would then be content with the counsels of patience and delay? One hundred years of delay have passed since President Lincoln freed the slaves, yet their heirs, their grandsons, are not fully free. They are not yet freed from the bonds of injustice. They are not yet freed from social and economic oppression. And this Nation, for all its hopes and all its boasts, will not be fully free until all its citizens are free.

We preach freedom around the world, and we mean it, and we cherish our freedom here at home, but are we to say to the world, and much more importantly, to each other that this is the land of the free except for the Negroes; that we have no second-class citizens except Negroes; that we have no class or caste system, no ghettoes, no master race except with respect to Negroes?

Now the time has come for this Nation to fulfill its promise. The events in Birmingham and elsewhere have so increased the cries for equality that no city or State or legislative body can prudently choose to ignore them. The fires of frustration and discord are burning in every city, North and South, where legal remedies are not at hand. Redress is sought in the streets, in demonstrations, parades, and protests which create tensions and threaten violence and threaten lives.

We face, therefore, a moral crisis as a country and as a people. It cannot be met by repressive police action. It cannot be left to increased demonstrations in the streets. It cannot be quieted by token moves or talk. It is time to act in the Congress, in your State and local legislative body and, above all, in all of our daily lives. It is not enough to pin the blame of others, to say this a problem of one section of the country or another, or deplore the fact that we face. A great change is at hand, and our task, our obligation, is to make that revolution, that change, peaceful and constructive for all. Those who do nothing are inviting shame as well as violence. Those who act boldly are recognizing right as well as reality.

Next week I shall ask the Congress of the United States to act, to make a commitment it has not fully made in this century to the proposition that race has no place in American life or law. The Federal judiciary has upheld that proposition in the conduct of its affairs, including the employment of Federal personnel, the use of Federal facilities, and the sale of federally financed housing. But there are other necessary measures which only the Congress can provide, and they must be provided at this session. The old code of equity law under which we live commands for every wrong a remedy, but in too many communities, in too many parts of the country, wrongs are inflicted on Negro citizens and there are no remedies at law. Unless the Congress acts, their only remedy is in the street. I am, therefore, asking the Congress to enact legislation giving all Americans the right to be served in facilities which are open to the public—hotels, restaurants, theaters, retail stores, and similar establishments. This seems to me to be an elementary right. Its denial is an arbitrary indignity that no American in 1963 should have to endure, but many do.

I have recently met with scores of business leaders urging them to take voluntary action to end this discrimination and I have been encouraged by their response, and in the last two weeks over 75 cities have seen progress made in desegregating these kinds of facilities. But many are unwilling to act alone, and for this reason, nationwide legislation is needed if we are to move this problem from the streets to the courts.

I am also asking the Congress to authorize the Federal Government to participate more fully in lawsuits designed to end segregation in public education. We have succeeded in persuading many districts to desegregate voluntarily. Dozens have admitted Negroes without violence. Today a Negro is attending a State-supported institution in every one of our 50 States, but the pace is very slow. Too many Negro children entering segregated grade schools at the time of the Supreme Court's decision nine years ago will enter segregated high schools this fall, having suffered a loss which can never be restored. The lack of an adequate education denies the Negro a chance to get a decent job.

The orderly implementation of the Supreme Court decision, therefore, cannot be left solely to those who may not have the economic resources to carry the legal action or who may be subject to harassment. Other features will also be requested, including greater protection for the right to vote. But legislation,

I repeat, cannot solve this problem alone. It must be solved in the homes of every American in every community across our country. In this respect I want to pay tribute to those citizens North and South who have been working in their communities to make life better for all. They are acting not out of a sense of legal duty but out of a sense of human decency. Like our soldiers and sailors in all parts of the world they are meeting freedom's challenge on the firing line, and I salute them for their honor and their courage.

My fellow Americans, this is a problem which faces us all—in every city of the North as well as the South. Today there are Negroes unemployed, two or three times as many compared to whites, inadequate in education, moving into the large cities, unable to find work, young people particularly out of work without hope, denied equal rights, denied the opportunity to eat at a restaurant or lunch counter or go to a movie theater, denied the right to a decent education, denied almost today the right to attend a State university even though qualified. It seems to me that these are matters which concern us all, not merely Presidents or Congressmen or Governors, but every citizen of the United States. This is one country. It has become one country because all of us and all the people who came here had an equal chance to develop their talents.

We cannot say to ten per cent of the population that you can't have that right; that your children cannot have the chance to develop whatever talents they have; that the only way that they are going to get their rights is to go into the streets and demonstrate. I think we owe them and we owe ourselves a better country than that. Therefore, I am asking for your help in making it easier for us to move ahead and to provide the kind of equality of treatment which we would want ourselves; to give a chance for every child to be educated to the limit of his talents. As I have said before, not every child has an equal talent or an equal ability or an equal motivation, but they should have an equal right to develop their talent and their ability and their motivation, to make something of themselves.

We have a right to expect that the Negro community will be responsible, will uphold the law, but they have a right to expect that the law will be fair, that the Constitution will be color blind, as Justice Harlan said at the turn of the century. This is what we are talking about and this is a matter which concerns this country and what it stands for, and in meeting it I ask the support of all our citizens.

From The American Promise

1965

This speech to Congress by President Johnson (1908–1973) points to the unkept promises of the Declaration of Independence and the Emancipation Proclamation. Existing federal anti-discrimination laws had never overcome state officials' resistance to the Fifteenth Amendment. In the 1890s, some states enacted disenfranchising laws: poll taxes, literacy tests, and disqualification of voters for "crimes of moral turpitude." White supremacist groups practiced violent intimidation, and election districts were gerrymandered. By 1910 nearly all black citizens in the former Confederate states were disenfranchised. In 1965, only a third of eligible African Americans, as opposed to two-thirds of eligible whites, were registered in these states.

Martin Luther King, Jr., desperately wanted the voting rights legislation to be enacted and planned a march in its support from Selma to Montgomery on March 7, 1965. But Johnson, who had advised King against the demonstration, called him to Washington, D.C., for a meeting. Six hundred marchers crossed the bridge over the Alabama River and were attacked on the other side by two hundred troopers and deputized "possemen" with clubs and tear gas. Seventeen marchers were hospitalized and a Boston minister died. Americans watched the televised violence and thousands headed to Selma to help the voter registration drive. Johnson gave his speech on March 15, and on March 21 the demonstration began again, with federal protection. On August 5, Congress passed the bill, parts of which follow the language of the Fifteenth Amendment. It provided for unprecedented federal intervention and ended the use of literacy requirements for voting in six states. Most southern states opened voter registration lists to blacks and control passed to the Justice Department in sixty-two counties that remained resistant. In Mississippi, black voting enrollment went from 6 percent in 1965 to 44 percent by 1968.

Johnson's speech acknowledges civil rights protest as the driving force behind the legislation, and he paid further tribute to protestors in an address of June 4, 1965. But the civil rights movement had been a training ground for several prominent antiwar protesters, and as Johnson escalated the Vietnam war effort between 1964 and 1968—sometimes using the language of his voting rights speech to explain America's presence in Vietnam ("We are there because we have a promise to keep . . . And I intend to keep that promise")—protesters turned against him. In 1966 the Student Nonviolent Coordinating Committee noted: "16% of the draftees from this country are Negroes called on to stifle the liberation of Vietnam, to preserve a 'democracy' which does not exist for them at home." King noted in 1967 that the Vietnam war had destroyed his Poverty Program, much as it came to hinder Johnson's Great Society program. In the wake of the My Lai massacre, Johnson's description in his voting rights speech of the "scars on the hopeful face of a young child" seemed painfully ironic.

At times history and fate meet at a single time in a single place to shape a turning point in man's unending search for freedom. So it was at Lexington and Concord. So it was a century ago at Appomattox. So it was last week in Selma, Alabama. There, long-suffering men and women peacefully protested the denial of their rights as Americans. Many were brutally assaulted. One good man, a man of God, was killed. There is no cause for pride in what has happened in Selma. There is no cause for self-satisfaction in the long denial of equal rights of millions of Americans. But there is cause for hope and for faith in our democracy in what is happening here tonight. For the cries of pain and the hymns and protests of oppressed people have summoned into convocation all the majesty of this great Government—the Government of the greatest Nation on earth. Our mission is at once the oldest and the most basic of this country: to right wrong, to do justice, to serve man.

In our time we have come to live with moments of great crisis. Our lives have been marked with debate about great issues; issues of war and peace, issues of prosperity and depression. But rarely in any time does an issue lay bare the secret heart of America itself. Rarely are we met with a challenge, not to our growth or abundance, our welfare or our security, but rather to the values and the purposes and the meaning of our beloved Nation. The issue of equal rights for American Negroes is such an issue. And should we defeat every enemy, should we double our wealth and conquer the stars, and still be unequal to this issue, then we will have failed as a people and as a nation. For with a country as with a person, "What is a man profited, if he shall gain the whole world, and lose his own soul?" There is no Negro problem. There is no Southern problem. There is no Northern problem. There is only an American problem. And we are met here tonight as Americans—not as Democrats or Republicans—we are met here as Americans to solve that problem.

This was the first nation in the history of the world to be founded with a purpose. The great phrases of that purpose still sound in every American heart, North and South: "All men are created equal"—"government by consent of the governed"—"give me liberty or give me death." Well, those are not just clever words, or those are not just empty theories. In their name Americans have fought and died for two centuries, and tonight around the world they stand there as guardians of our liberty, risking their lives. Those words are a promise to every citizen that he shall share in the dignity of man. This dignity cannot be found in a man's possessions; it cannot be found in his power, or in his position. It really rests on his right to be treated as a man equal in opportunity to all others. It says that he shall share in freedom, he shall choose his leaders, educate his children, and provide for his family according to his ability and his merits as a human being.

To apply any other test—to deny a man his hopes because of his color or race, his religion or the place of his birth—is not only to do injustice, it is to deny America and to dishonor the dead who gave their lives for American freedom. Our fathers believed that if this noble view of the rights of man was to flourish, it must be rooted in democracy. The most basic right of all was the right to choose your own leaders. The history of this country, in large measure, is the history of the expansion of that right to all of our people.

Many of the issues of civil rights are very complex and most difficult. But about this there can and should be no argument. Every American citizen must have an equal right to vote. There is no reason which can excuse the denial of that right. There is no duty which weighs more heavily on us than the duty we have to ensure that right. Yet the harsh fact is that in many places in this country men and women are kept from voting simply because they are Negroes. Every device of which human ingenuity is capable has been used to deny this right. The Negro citizen may go to register only to be told that the day is wrong, or the hour is late, or the official in charge is absent. And if he persists, and if he manages to present himself to the registrar, he may be disqualified because he did not spell out his middle name or because he abbreviated a word on the application. And if he manages to fill out an application he is given a test. The registrar is the sole judge of whether he passes this test. He may be asked to recite the entire Constitution, or explain the most complex provisions of State law. And even a college degree cannot be used to prove that he can read and write. For the fact is that the only way to pass these barriers is to show a white skin.

Experience has clearly shown that the existing process of law cannot overcome systematic and ingenious discrimination. No law that we now have on the books—and I have helped to put three of them there—can ensure the right to vote when local officials are determined to deny it. In such a case our duty must be clear to all of us. The Constitution says that no person shall be kept from voting because of his race or his color. We have all sworn an oath before God to support and to defend that Constitution. We must now act in obedience to that oath. On Wednesday I will send to Congress a law designed to eliminate illegal barriers to the right to vote . . . This bill will strike down restrictions to voting in all elections—Federal, State, and local—which have been used to deny Negroes the right to vote. This bill will establish a simple, uniform standard which cannot be used, however ingenious the effort, to flout our Constitution. It will provide for citizens to be registered by officials of the United States Government if the State officials refuse to register them. It will eliminate tedious, unnecessary lawsuits which delay the right to vote. Finally, this legislation will ensure that properly registered individuals are not prohibited from voting . . . To those who seek to avoid action by their National Government in their own communities; who want to and who seek to maintain purely local control over elections, the answer is simple: Open your polling places to all your people. Allow men and women to register and vote whatever the color of their skin. Extend the rights of citizenship to every citizen of this land. There is no constitutional issue here. The command of the Constitution is plain. There is no moral issue. It is wrong—deadly wrong—to deny any of your fellow Americans the right to vote in this country. There is no issue of States rights or national rights. There is only the struggle for human rights. I have not the slightest doubt what will be your answer.

The last time a President sent a civil rights bill to the Congress it contained a provision to protect voting rights in Federal elections. That civil rights bill was passed after eight long months of debate. And when that bill came to my desk from the Congress for my signature, the heart of the voting provision had been eliminated. This time, on this issue, there must be no delay, no hesitation and no compromise with our purpose. We cannot, we must not, refuse to protect the right of every American to vote in every election that he may desire to participate in. And we ought not and we cannot and we must not wait another eight months before we get a bill. We have already waited a hundred years and more, and the time for waiting is gone. So I ask you to join me in working long hours—nights and weekends, if necessary—to pass this bill. And I don't make that request lightly. For from the window where I sit with the problems of our country I recognize that outside this chamber is the outraged conscience of a nation, the grave concern of many nations, and the harsh judgment of history on our acts. But even if we pass this bill, the battle will not be over. What happened in Selma is part of a far larger movement which reaches into every section and State of America. It is the effort of American Negroes to secure for themselves the full blessings of American life. Their cause must be our cause too. Because it is not just Negroes, but really it is all of us, who must overcome the crippling legacy of bigotry and injustice. And we shall overcome.

As a man whose roots go deeply into Southern soil I know how agonizing racial feelings are. I know how difficult it is to reshape the attitudes and the structure of our society. But a century has passed, more than a hundred years, since the Negro was freed. And he is not fully free tonight. It was more than a hundred years ago that Abraham Lincoln, a great President of another party, signed the Emancipation Proclamation, but emancipation is a proclamation and not a fact. A century has passed, more than a hundred years, since equality was promised. And yet the Negro is not equal. A century has passed since the day of promise. And the promise is unkept. The time of justice has now come. I tell you that I believe sincerely that no force can hold it back. It is right in the eyes of man and God that it should come. And when it does, I think that day will brighten the lives of every American. For Negroes are not the only victims. How many white children have gone uneducated, how many white families have lived in stark poverty, how many white lives have been scarred by fear, because we have wasted our energy and our substance to maintain the barriers of hatred and terror? So I say to all of you here, and to all in the Nation to-night, that those who appeal to you to hold on to the past do so at the cost of denying you your future. This great, rich, restless country can offer opportunity and education and hope to all: black and white, North and South, share-cropper and city dweller. These are the enemies: poverty, ignorance, disease. They are the enemies and not our fellow man, not our neighbor. And these enemies too, poverty, disease and ignorance, we shall overcome . . .

As we meet here in this peaceful, historic chamber tonight, men from the South, some of whom were at Iwo Jima, men from the North who have carried Old Glory to far corners of the world and brought it back without a stain on it, men from the East and from the West, are all fighting together without regard to religion, or color, or region, in Viet-Nam. Men from every region fought for us across the world 20 years ago. And in these common dangers and these common sacrifices the South made its contribution of honor and gallantry no less than any other region of the great Republic—and in some instances, a great many of them, more. And I have not the slightest doubt that good men from everywhere in this country, from the Great Lakes to the Gulf of Mexico, from the Golden Gate to the harbors along the Atlantic, will rally together now in this cause to vindicate the freedom of all Americans. For all of us owe this duty; and I believe that all of us will respond to it. Your President makes that request of every American.

The real hero of this struggle is the American Negro. His actions and protests, his courage to risk safety and even to risk his life, have awakened the conscience of this Nation. His demonstrations have been designed to call attention to injustice, designed to provoke change, designed to stir reform. He has called upon us to make good the promise of America. And who among us can say that we would have made the same progress were it not for his persistent bravery, and his faith in American democracy. For at the real heart of battle for equality is a deep-seated belief in the democratic process. Equality depends not on the force of arms or tear gas but upon the force of moral right; not on recourse to violence but on respect for law and order . . .

My first job after college was as a teacher in Cotulla, Texas, in a small Mexican-American school. Few of them could speak English, and I couldn't speak much Spanish. My students were poor and they often came to class without breakfast, hungry. They knew even in their youth the pain of prejudice. They never seemed to know why people disliked them. But they knew it was so, because I saw it in their eyes. I often walked home late in the afternoon, after the classes were finished, wishing there was more that I could do. But all I knew was to teach them the little that I knew, hoping that it might help them against the hardships that lay ahead. Somehow you never forget what poverty and hatred can do when you see its scars on the hopeful face of a young child. I never thought then, in 1928, that I would be standing here in 1965. It never even occurred to me in my fondest dreams that I might have the chance to help the sons and daughters of those students and to help people like them all over this country. But now I do have that chance—and I'll let you in on a secret—I mean to use it. And I hope that you will use it with me.

This is the richest and most powerful country which ever occupied the globe. The might of past empires is little compared to ours. But I do not want to be the President who built empires, or sought grandeur, or extended dominion. I want to be the President who educated young children to the wonders of their world. I want to be the President who helped to feed the hungry and to prepare them to be taxpayers instead of taxeaters. I want to be the President who helped the poor to find their own way and who protected the right of every citizen to vote in every election. I want to be the President who helped to end hatred among his fellow men and who promoted love among the people of all races and all regions and all parties. I want to be the President who helped to end war among the brothers of this earth . . .

Beyond this great chamber, out yonder in 50 States, are the people that we serve. Who can tell what deep and unspoken hopes are in their hearts tonight as they sit there and listen. We all can guess, from our own lives, how difficult they often find their own pursuit of happiness, how many problems each little family has. They look most of all to themselves for their futures. But I think that they also look to each of us.

Above the pyramid on the great seal of the United States it says—in Latin— "God has favored our undertaking." God will not favor everything that we do. It is rather our duty to divine His will. But I cannot help believing that He truly understands and that He really favors the undertaking that we begin here tonight.

Black Art

1966

Often accused of using shock value and expressing anti-Semitism, the Marxist anti-imperialist poet Amiri Baraka (b. 1934) claims that these criticisms come from his saying "what is not being said, what is taboo, or opposed to the status quo." After the assassination of Malcolm X in 1965, Baraka changed his name from LeRoi Jones, moved from Greenwich Village to Harlem, opened the Black Arts Repertory Theatre/School, focused on community art, and transformed himself from a Beat poet into a black nationalist. "Black Art" is partially directed at the Beat poet Allen Ginsberg, Baraka's old friend, who replied in 1968: "Leroi I been done you wrong, I'm just an old Uncle Tom in disguise all along."

Malcolm's assassination also sparked into existence the Black Arts Movement (BAM), led by Baraka, Larry Neal, and others. BAM poets believed that political action would come through artistic expression, and Neal noted that the movement, which stressed cultural heritage, the beauty of blackness, and a "Black Aesthetic," was "the aesthetic and spiritual sister of the Black Power concept." BAM poets believed that social and political action would come through artistic expression: BAM was "an attempt to capture the minds of the people, to . . . direct them," said Baraka in a recent interview. He also puts the movement on a continuum with the Harlem Renaissance and calls it "a version of Mao's Cultural Revolution, a form of the Indigisme of Haiti, the Negrismo of Latin America, literally a sorting out and repositioning of cultural meanings." His own experimental poetry subverts these cultural meanings: if "white" and "black" are conventional signifiers for "good" and bad," then Baraka uses the terms differently, celebrating what he calls "black magic."

The activist poet can "tell what side you're on . . . by your art," Baraka says. "Art sez Mao is the ideological reflection of the world." Baraka also points to Bertolt Brecht's Theater of Instruction, noting that "ethics and aesthetics are one." The greatest evil is "to see us stupid in the world or stupid to the world. If poetry is not to tell us something . . . then it serves what purpose?" He adds, "All art is political. It takes a stand, wants to convince you one way or another. Those who claim art should not be political are making a political statement." No literature exists in a vacuum and any suggestion to the contrary means "only to have us look away from the real world so that 'the pleasure of the text' is a titillation of empty sensuality. All's well in the big house while the great majority . . . suffer out of sight."

Poems are bullshit unless they are
teeth or trees or lemons piled
on a step. Or black ladies dying
of men leaving nickel hearts
beating them down. Fuck poems
and they are useful, wd they shoot
come at you, love what you are,
breathe like wrestlers, or shudder
strangely after pissing. We want live
words of the hip world live flesh &
coursing blood. Hearts Brains
Souls splintering fire. We want poems
like fists beating niggers out of Jocks
or dagger poems in the slimy bellies
of the owner-jews. Black poems to
smear on girdlemamma mulatto bitches
whose brains are red jelly stuck
between 'lizabeth taylor's toes. Stinking
Whores! We want "poems that kill."
Assassin poems, Poems that shoot
guns. Poems that wrestle cops into alleys
and take their weapons leaving them dead
with tongues pulled out and sent to Ireland. Knockoff
poems for dope selling wops or slick halfwhite
politicians Airplane poems, rrrrrrrrrrrrrrrr
rrrrrrrrrrrrrrr . . . tuhtuhtuhtuhtuhtuhtuhtuh
. . . rrrrrrrrrrrrrrr . . . Setting fire and death to
whities ass. Look at the Liberal
Spokesman for the jews clutch his throat
& puke himself into eternity . . . rrrrrrrr
There's a negroleader pinned to
a bar stool in Sardi's eyeballs melting
in hot flame Another negroleader
on the steps of the white house one
kneeling between the sheriff's thighs
negotiating coolly for his people.
Agggh . . . stumbles across the room . . .
Put it on him, poem. Strip him naked
to the world! Another bad poem cracking
steel knuckles in a jewlady's mouth
Poem scream poison gas on beasts in green berets

Clean out the world for virtue and love,
Let there be no love poems written
until love can exist freely and
cleanly. Let Black People understand
that they are the lovers and the sons
of lovers and warriors and sons
of warriors Are poems & poets &
all the loveliness here in the world
We want a black poem. And a
Black World.
Let the world be a Black Poem
And Let All Black People Speak This Poem
Silently
or LOUD

Panther Power

1989

"It's time to fight back that's what Huey said," rapped Tupac Shakur (1971–1996) in his posthumously released song "Changes" (1998). Referring to the Black Panther Huey Newton, the song expresses a post–civil rights philosophy: "The old way wasn't working so it's on us to do what we gotta do." As Newton and the Black Panthers had pointed out, the black agenda after 1965 needed to move beyond civil rights reform. Tupac, the son of two Black Panthers, who sometimes said he could easily have been a preacher, picked up where the Black Panther Party had left off.

His songs question Abraham Lincoln's motives for signing the Emancipation Proclamation and lay out the legacy of slavery and racism: poverty, wage-slavery, mass incarceration, privatized prison labor, death row, and police violence. Other hip-hop artists compared police officers to slave overseers. KRS-One's "Sound of Da Police" (1993) observes: "They both ride horses, after 400 years I've got no choices." The history of black oppression is unbroken in Onyx's "Getto Mentalitee" (1995) as well: "They traded in the white sheets, for badges and blue suits." White supremacy has just changed its costume.

James Baldwin once wrote, "It is only in his music . . . that the Negro in America has been able to tell his story." Spirituals and blues had long been a form of black protest, and hip-hop emerged as the late 20th century's protest music in the wake of "Black Power" anthems like James Brown's "Say It Loud—I'm Black and I'm Proud" (1968). It began as rap music in the 1970s, when deejays at parties would speak words over the beats of rock, disco, and soul tracks, and was born at a particular moment: during Reaganism, amid shrinking job and housing markets, and as racial profiling, police brutality, and mandatory minimum sentencing made African Americans "prisoners of war," as some activists put it. Revolutionary and reactionary, serious and playful, hip-hop responded to a whole culture of oppression and became a culture itself, extending beyond rap to incorporate break dancing, deejaying, graffiti, and fashion, and ultimately becoming a tool deployed in the name of marketing and conspicuous consumption. Noting this shift, the rap artist Chopmaster J released Tupac's *Lost Tapes* in 2000, which included "Panther Power." Tupac, a hyper-representation of urban outlaw manhood, had been killed in a drive-by shooting in September 1996, amid a highly publicized East Coast–West Coast hip-hop rivalry. Now the liner notes to *Lost Tapes* read: "I thought that Tupac's fans would like to hear what his first recordings sounded like back when . . . socially conscious themes ruled Hip-Hop."

As real as it seems the American Dream
Ain't nothing but another calculated scheme
To get us locked up, shot up, back in chains
To deny us of the future, rob our names
Kept our history a mystery but now I see
The American Dream wasn't meant for me
Cause lady liberty's a hypocrite, she lied to me
Promised freedom, education, and equality
Never gave me nothing but slavery
And now look at how dangerous you made me
Calling me a mad man cause I'm strong and bold
With this gumbo of knowledge of the lies you told
Promise me emancipation and a free nation
All you gave my people was starvation
The fathers of this country never cared for me
They kept our ancestors shackled up in slavery
Uncle Sam never did a damn thing for me
Except lie about the facts in my history
Now I'm sitting here mad cause I'm unemployed
But the government's glad cause they enjoy
When my people are down so they can screw us around
Time to change the government now, panther power
[chorus]
Panther power
Panther power
Panther power
Coming straight from the place that resides within
Go toe to toe with a panther and you just can't win
Self proclaimed best suppressed the rich
The rich get richer and the poor take less
The American Dream was an American nightmare
You kept my people down and refused to fight fair
The Ku Klux Klan tried to keep us out
With signs that state "No Blacks Allowed"
With intimidation and segregation
Once would wait for our freedom
But now we're impatient
Blacks, the others, they yell sell out,
Freedom, equality, then I'll yell out
"Don't you ever be ashamed of what you are
It's ya panther power that makes you a star"

Panther power [chorus]
My Mother never let me forget my history
Hoping I was set free, chains never put on me
Wanted to be more than just free
Had to know the true facts about my history
I couldn't settle for being a statistic
Couldn't survive in this capitalistic government
Cause it was meant to hold us back with ignorance,
Drugs, sneak attacks in my community
They killed our unity
But when I charged them, tried to claim immunity
I strike America like a case of heart disease
Panther power is running through my arteries
Try to stop me homeboy you'll get clawed to death
Cause I'll be fighting for my freedom till my dying breath
Do you remember that's what I'm asking you?
You think you're living free, don't make me laugh at you
Open your eyes realize you've been locked in chains
Said you wasn't civilized and stole your name
Cause some time has passed we seem to all forget
There's no liberty for me and you we ain't free yet
Panther power [chorus]

Ten Point Program

2001

By the late 1970s, the Black Panther Party (BPP) had fallen apart. Founded in 1966, the party had articulated new goals for the civil rights movement after the passage of the Civil Rights and Voting Rights Acts of 1964 and 1965. It called for "Black Power" and an end to police brutality, ran breakfast programs, offered free health clinics, conducted sickle-cell anemia testing, pushed for better housing, and developed free legal aids and transportation of visiting family members to prisons. It had five thousand members at its peak. But the party's energy and support were diminished by internal disputes, infiltration by covert government operations, and the deaths of twenty-eight party members in clashes with police.

In the early 1990s, a new generation of activists announced the return of the BPP. The New African American Vanguard Movement, founded in 1994, revised the BPP's original Ten Point Program of 1966 to include new demands for religious tolerance and an end to military aggression. The Black Panther Collective (BPC), also founded in 1994, kept the BPP's Ten Point Program intact. BPC members refer to Tupac Shakur and point to the protest writers Elizabeth Cady Stanton, Eugene V. Debs, and Ida B. Wells as evidence of an effective radical tradition in America. They locate the BPP and the BPC in that tradition.

But the most high-profile of these new Panther groups is the New Black Panther Party (NBPP), registered in 1991. The party, which follows a radical black nationalist philosophy, rewrote the original BPP platform in 2001: "black community" is now "Black nation," "racist" is "wicked racist," "decadent" is "devilish and decadent," and the Constitution is a "white law." While the BPP had quoted the Declaration of Independence, the NBPP ends its platform: "History has proven that the white man is absolutely disagreeable to get along with in peace." Acknowledging the feminist movement that gained ground between 1966 and 2001, the new document uses "herstory" and "person" throughout. The platform marks further shifts in the protest agenda, addressing issues of black-on-black violence, military jails, and political prisoners. The NBPP calls for independent African-centered schools, more trade with Africa, and its own provisional government. It asks black police officers to be black first and officers second.

The NBPP is strongly anti-Zionist, and is often accused of anti-Semitism. It voiced support for the black nationalist poet Amiri Baraka during the controversy over his poem "Somebody Blew Up America" (2001), which asked: "Who told 4000 Israeli workers at the Twin Towers to stay home . . .?" Original BPP members have condemned the NBPP and filed a lawsuit to stop them from using the Panther name, with one former

Panther, David Hilliard, noting that the original party had operated with love for blacks, not hatred of whites.

What the New Black Panthers Want
What the New Black Panthers Believe

1. We want freedom. We want the power to practice self-determination, and to determine the destiny of our community and THE BLACK NATION. We believe in the spiritual high moral code of our Ancestors. We believe in the truths of the Bible, Quran, and other sacred texts and writings. We believe in MAAT and the principles of NGUZO SABA. We believe that Black People will not be free until we are able to determine our Divine Destiny.

2. We want full employment for our people and we demand the dignity to do for ourselves what we have begged the white man to do for us. We believe that since the white man has kept us deaf, dumb and blind, and used every "dirty trick" in the book to stand in the way of our freedom and independence, that we should be gainfully employed until such time we can employ and provide for ourselves. We believe further in: POWER IN THE HANDS OF THE PEOPLE! WEALTH IN THE HANDS OF THE PEOPLE! ARMS IN THE HANDS OF THE PEOPLE!

3. We want tax exemption and an end to robbery of THE BLACK NATION by the CAPITALIST. We want an end to the capitalistic domination of Africa in all of its forms: imperialism, criminal settler colonialism, neo-colonialism, racism, sexism, zionism, Apartheid and artificial borders. We believe that this wicked racist government has robbed us, and now we are demanding the overdue debt of reparations. A form of reparations was promised 100 years ago (forty acres and a mule) as restitution for the continued genocide of our people and to in meaningful measure and repair the damage for the AFRICAN HOLOCAUST (Maangamizo/ Maafa). We believe our people should be exempt from ALL TAXATION as long as we are deprived of equal justice under the laws of the land and the overdue reparations debt remains unpaid. We will accept payment in fertile and minerally rich land, precious metals, industry, commerce and currency. As genocide crimes continue, people's tribunals must be set up to prosecute and to execute. The "Jews" were given reparations. The Japanese were given reparations. The Black, the Red and the Brown Nations must be given reparations. The American white man owes us reparations. England owes us reparations. France owes us reparations, Spain and all of Europe. Africa owes us reparations and repatriation. The Arabs owe us reparations. The "Jews" owe us reparations. All have taken part in the AFRICAN HOLOCAUST and the slaughter of 600 million of our people over the past 6,000 years in general and 400 years in particular. We know that this is a reasonable and just demand that we make at this time in history.

4. We want decent housing, fit for shelter of human beings, free health-care (preventive and maintenance). We want an end to the trafficking of drugs and to the biological and chemical warfare targeted at our people. We believe since the white landlords will not give decent housing and quality health care to our Black Community, the housing, the land, the social, political and economic institutions should be made into independent UUAMAA "New African Communal/Cooperatives" so that our community, with government reparations and aid (until we can do for ourselves) can build and make drug free, decent housing with health facilities for our people.

5. We want education for our people that exposes the true nature of this devilish and decadent American society. We want education that teaches us our true history/herstory and our role in the present day society. We believe in an educational system that will give our people "a knowledge of self." If we do not have knowledge of self and of our position in society and the world, then we have little chance to properly relate to anything else.

6. We want all Black Men and Black Women to be exempt from military service. We believe that Black People should not be forced to fight in the military service to defend a racist government that holds us captive and does not protect us. We will not fight and kill other people of color in the world who, like Black People, are being victimized by the white racist government of America. We will protect ourselves from the force and violence of the racist police and the racist military, "by any means necessary."

7. We want an immediate end to POLICE HARASSMENT, BRUTALITY and MURDER of Black People. We want an end to Black-on-Black violence, "snitching," cooperation and collaboration with the oppressor. We believe we can end police brutality in our community by organizing Black self-defense groups (Black People's Militias/Black Liberation Armies) that are dedicated to defending our Black Community from racist, fascist, police/military oppression and brutality. The Second Amendment of white America's Constitution gives a right to bear arms. We therefore believe that all Black People should unite and form an "African United Front" and arm ourselves for self-defense.

8. We want freedom for all Black Men and Black Women held in international, military, federal, state, county, city jails and prisons. We believe that all Black People and people of color should be released from the many jails and prisons because they have not received a fair and impartial trial. 'Released' means 'released' to the lawful authorities of the Black Nation.

9. We want all Black People when brought to trial to be tried in a court by a jury of their peer group or people from their Black Communities, as defined by white law of the Constitution of the United States. We believe that the courts should follow their own law, if their nature will allow (as stated in their Constitution of the United States) so that Black People will receive fair trials. The 6th Amendment of the United States Constitution gives a man/woman a right to an impartial trial, which has been interpreted to be a "fair" trial by one's "peer" group. A "peer" is a person from a similar economic, social, religious, geographical, environmental, historical and racial background. To do this, the court will be forced to select a jury from the Black Community from which the Black defendant came. We have been and are being tried by all white juries that have no understanding of the "average reasoning person" of the Black Community.

10. WE DEMAND AN END TO THE RACIST DEATH PENALTY AS IT IS APPLIED TO BLACK AND OPPRESSED PEOPLE IN AMERICA. WE DEMAND FREEDOM FOR ALL POLITICAL PRISONERS OF THE BLACK RED AND BROWN NATION! We want land, bread, housing, education, clothing, justice and peace. And, as our political objective, we want **NATIONAL LIBERATION** in a separate state or territory of our own, here or elsewhere, "a liberated zone" ("New Africa" or Africa), and a plebiscite to be held throughout the BLACK NATION in which only we will be allowed to participate for the purposes of determining our will and DIVINE destiny as a people. **FREE THE LAND! "UP YOU MIGHTY NATION! YOU CAN ACCOMPLISH WHAT YOU WILL!" BLACK POWER!** History has proven that the white man is absolutely disagreeable to get along with in peace. No one has been able to get along with the white man. All the people of color have been subjected to the white man's wrath. We believe that his very nature will not allow for true sharing, fairness, equity and justice. Therefore, to the Red Man and Woman, to the Yellow and to the Brown, we say to you **"THE SAME RABID DOG THAT BIT YOU, BIT US TOO!" ALL POWER TO THE PEOPLE!**

9

A PROBLEM THAT
HAD
NO NAME

Second-Wave
Feminism

TILLIE OLSEN

I Stand Here Ironing

<u>1956</u>

Tillie Olsen (b. 1913) tries to save women's history from oblivion. In the early 1970s she published historical lists of women writers, and in 1972 she persuaded the Feminist Press to republish Rebecca Harding Davis's novella *Life in the Iron Mills* (1861), which was long out of print. "Literary history and the present are dark with silences," she wrote in *Silences* (1978), and her particular focus was "the mute inglorious Miltons . . . those whose waking hours are all struggle for existence; the barely educated; the illiterate; women." The narrator's sense that she will "never total it all," in "I Stand Here Ironing," points to hidden, missing stories of lives forgotten or never known.

Olsen writes about silence from personal experience. "I have had special need to learn all I could of this over the years, myself so nearly remaining mute," she noted, describing the deafening silence of a potential interrupted by motherhood. Olsen raised children and worked for money while her writing gasped for air: "It is no accident that the first work I considered publishable began: 'I stand here ironing.'" But Emily, in the early second-wave feminist story reprinted here, is part of a new generation of women, one who might believe that she is "more than this dress on the ironing board."

Second-wave feminism is associated with the New Left, but Olsen is Old Left. She belongs to a socialist-feminist literary tradition, like Charlotte Perkins Gilman and Crystal Eastman. In the 1930s she worked on women's rights, health, and education within the Communist Party, and debated the role of women in society. As a Jewish socialist feminist she tries to bridge the category divides of race, class, and sex, and to "recognize what is common between us," but she believes that the oppression of women is the worst oppression of all: "an oppression entangled through with human love, human need."

Olsen is sometimes accused of pessimism. But she insists that she writes with hope. History is full of resistance, she says: "Why is it that the resistance movements . . . get obliterated from consciousness? . . . The fact that human beings do not put up forever with misery . . . but act is a fact which every human being should know about." Elsewhere she adds, "It's not unremittingly grim to know that we haven't changed enough things yet . . . I have a lot of belief in us."

Further reading: Constance Coiner, *Better Red* (1995); Mara Faulker, *Protest and Possibility* (1993).

I stand here ironing, and what you asked me moves tormented back and forth with the iron.

"I wish you would manage the time to come in and talk with me about your daughter. I'm sure you can help me understand her. She's a youngster who needs help and whom I'm deeply interested in helping."

"Who needs help?" Even if I came what good would it do? You think because I am her mother I have a key, or that in some way you could use me as a key? She has lived for nineteen years. There is all that life that has happened outside of me, beyond me.

And when is there time to remember, to sift, to weigh, to estimate, to total? I will start and there will be an interruption and I will have to gather it all together again. Or I will become engulfed with all I did or did not do, with what should have been and what cannot be helped.

She was a beautiful baby. The first and only one, of our five that was beautiful at birth. You do not guess how new and uneasy her tenancy in her now-loveliness. You did not know her all those years she was thought homely, or see her poring over her baby pictures, making me tell her over and over how beautiful she had been—and would be, I would tell her—and was now, to the seeing eye. But the seeing eyes were few or nonexistent. Including mine.

I nursed her. They feel that's important nowadays. I nursed all the children, but with her, with all the fierce rigidity of first motherhood, I did like the books said. Though her cries battered me to trembling and my breasts ached with swollenness, I waited till the clock decreed.

Why do I put that first? I do not even know if it matters, or if it explains anything.

She was a beautiful baby. She blew shining bubbles of sound. She loved motion, loved light, loved color and music and textures. She would lie on the floor in her blue overalls patting the surface so hard in ecstasy her hands and feet would blur. She was a miracle to me, but when she was eight months old I had to leave her daytimes with the woman downstairs to whom she was no miracle at all, for I worked or looked for work and for Emily's father, who "could no longer endure" (he wrote in his good-by note) "sharing want with us."

I was nineteen. It was the pre-relief, pre-WPA world of the depression, I would start running as soon as I got off the streetcar, running up the stairs, the place smelling sour, and awake or asleep to startle awake, when she saw me she would break into a clogged weeping that could not be comforted, a weeping I can yet hear.

After a while I found a job hashing at night so I could be with her days, and it was better. But it came to where I had to bring her to his family and leave her.

It took a long time to raise the money for her fare back. Then she got chicken pox and I had to wait longer. When she finally came, I hardly knew her, walking quick and nervous like her father, looking like her father, thin, and dressed in a shoddy red that yellowed her skin and glared at the pock marks. All the baby loveliness gone.

She was two. Old enough for nursery school they said, and I did not know then what I know now—the fatigue of the long day, and the lacerations of group life in the nurseries that are only parking places for children.

Except that it would have made no difference if I had known. It was the only place there was. It was the only way we could be together, the only way I could hold a job.

And even without knowing, I knew. I knew the teacher that was evil because all these years it has curdled into my memory, the little boy hunched in the corner, her rasp, "why aren't you outside, because Alvin hits you? That's no reason, go out coward." I knew Emily hated it even if she did not clutch and implore "don't go Mommy" like the other children, mornings.

She always had a reason why we should stay home. Momma, you look sick, Momma. I feel sick Momma, the teachers aren't there today, they're sick. Momma there was a fire there last night. Momma it's a holiday today, no school, they told me.

But never a direct protest, never rebellion. I think of our others in their three-, four-year-oldness—the explosions, the tempers, the denunciations, the demands—and I feel suddenly ill. I stop the ironing. What in me demanded that goodness in her? And what was the cost, the cost to her of such goodness?

The old man living in the back once said in his gentle way: "You should smile at Emily more when you look at her." What *was* in my face when I looked at her? I loved her. There were all the acts of love.

It was only with the others I remembered what he said, so that it was the face of joy, and not of care or tightness or worry I turned to them—but never to Emily. She does not smile easily, let alone almost always as her brothers and sisters do. Her face is closed and somber, but when she wants, how fluid. You must have seen it in her pantomimes, you spoke of her rare gift for comedy on the stage that rouses a laughter out of the audience so dear they applaud and applaud and do not want to let her go.

Where does it come from, that comedy? There was none of it in her when she came back to me that second time, after I had had to send her away again. She had a new daddy now to learn to love, and I think perhaps it was a better time. Except when we left her alone nights, telling ourselves she was old enough.

"Can't you go some other time Mommy, like tomorrow?" she would ask. "Will it be just a little while you'll be gone?"

The time we came back, the front door open, the clock on the floor in the hall. She rigid awake. "It wasn't just a little while. I didn't cry. I called you a little, just three times, and then I went downstairs to open the door so you could come faster. The clock talked loud, I threw it away, it scared me what it talked."

She said the clock talked loud that night I went to the hospital to have Susan. She was delirious with the fever that comes before red measles, but she was fully conscious all the week I was gone and the week after we were home when she could not come near the baby or me.

She did not get well. She stayed skeleton thin, not wanting to eat, and night after night she had nightmares. She would call for me, and I would sleepily call back, "you're all right, darling, go to sleep, it's just a dream," and if she still called, in a sterner voice, "now go to sleep Emily, there's nothing to hurt you." Twice, only twice, when I had to get up for Susan anyhow, I went in to sit with her.

Now when it is too late (as if she would let me hold and comfort her like I do the others) I get up and go to her at her moan or restless stirring. "Are you awake? Can I get you something?" And the answer is always the same: "No, I'm all right, go back to sleep Mother."

They persuaded me at the clinic to send her away to a convalescent home in the country where "she can have the kind of food and care you can't manage for her, and you'll be free to concentrate on the new baby." They still send children to that place. I see pictures on the society page of sleek young women planning affairs to raise money for it, or dancing at the affairs, or decorating Easter eggs or filling Christmas stockings for the children.

They never have a picture of the children so I do not know if they still wear those gigantic red bows and the ravaged looks on the every other Sunday when parents can come to visit "unless otherwise notified"—as we were notified the first six weeks.

Oh it is a handsome place, green lawns and tall trees and fluted flower beds. High up on the balconies of each cottage the children stand, the girls in their red bows and white dresses, the boys in white suits and giant red ties. The parents stand below shrieking up to be heard and the children shriek down to be heard, and between them the invisible wall "Not To Be Contaminated by Parental Germs or Physical Affection."

There was a tiny girl who always stood hand in hand with Emily. Her parents never came. One visit she was gone. "They moved her to Rose Cottage," Emily shouted in explanation. "They don't like you to love anybody here."

She wrote once a week, the labored writing of a seven-year-old. "I am fine. How is the baby. If I write my leter nicly I will have a star. Love." There never was a star. We wrote every other day, letters she could never hold or keep but only hear read—once. "We simply do not have room for children to keep any personal possessions," they patiently explained when we pieced one Sunday's shrieking together to plead how much it would mean to Emily to keep her letters and cards.

Each visit she looked frailer. "She isn't eating," they told us. (They had runny eggs for breakfast or mush with lumps, Emily said later, I'd hold it in my mouth and not swallow. Nothing ever tasted good, just when they had chicken.)

It took us eight months to get her released home, and only the fact that she gained back so little of her seven lost pounds convinced the social worker.

I used to try to hold and love her after she came back, but her body would stay stiff, and after a while she'd push away. She ate little. Food sickened her, and I think much of life too. Oh she had physical lightness and brightness, twinkling by on skates, bouncing like a ball up and down up and down over the jump rope, skimming over the hill; but these were momentary.

She fretted about her appearance, thin and dark and foreign-looking at a time when every little girl was supposed to look or thought she should look a chubby blond replica of Shirley Temple. The doorbell sometimes rang for her, but no one seemed to come and play in the house or be a best friend. Maybe because we moved so much.

There was a boy she loved painfully through two school semesters. Months later she told me how she had taken pennies from my purse to buy him candy. "Licorice was his favorite and I brought him some every day, but he still liked Jennifer better'n me. Why Mommy why?" A question I could never answer.

School was a worry to her. She was not glib or quick in a world where glibness and quickness were easily confused with ability to learn. To her overworked and exasperated teachers she was an over-conscientious "slow learner" who kept trying to catch up and was absent entirely too often.

I let her be absent, though sometimes the illness was imaginary. How different from my now-strictness about attendance with the others. I wasn't working. We had a new baby, I was home anyhow. Sometimes, after Susan grew old enough, I would keep her home from school, too, to have them all together.

Mostly Emily had asthma, and her breathing, harsh and labored, would fill the house with a curiously tranquil sound. I would bring the two old dresser mirrors and her boxes of collections to her bed. She would select beads and single earrings, bottle tops and shells, dried flowers and pebbles, old postcards and scraps, all sorts of oddments; then she and Susan would play Kingdom, setting up landscapes and furniture, peopling them with action.

Those were the only times of peaceful companionship between her and Susan. I have edged away from it, that poisonous feeling between them, that terrible balancing of hurts and needs I had to do between the two, and did so badly, those earlier years.

Oh there are conflicts between the others too, each one human, needling, demanding, hurting, taking—but only between Emily and Susan, no, Emily toward Susan that corroding resentment. It seems so obvious on the surface, yet it is not obvious. Susan, the second child, Susan, golden and curly haired and chubby, quick and articulate and assured, everything in appearance and manner Emily was not; Susan, not able to resist Emily's precious things, losing or sometimes clumsily breaking them; Susan telling jokes and riddles to company for applause while Emily sat silent (to say to me later: that was *my* riddle,

Mother, I told it to Susan); Susan, who for all the five years' difference in age was just a year behind Emily in developing physically.

I am glad for that slow physical development that widened the difference between her and her contemporaries, though she suffered over it. She was too vulnerable for that terrible world of youthful competition, of preening and parading, of constant measuring of yourself against every other, of envy, "If I had that copper hair," or "If I had that skin . . ." She tormented herself enough about not looking like the others, there was enough of the unsureness, the having to be conscious of words before you speak, the constant caring—what are they thinking of me? what kind of an impression am I making—there was enough without having it all magnified unendurably by the merciless physical drives.

Ronnie is calling. He is wet and I change him. It is rare there is such a cry now. That time of motherhood is almost behind me when the ear is not one's own but must always be racked and listening for the child cry, the child call. We sit for a while and I hold him, looking out over the city spread in charcoal with its soft aisles of light. "Shuggily" he breathes. A funny word, a family word, inherited from Emily, invented by her to say comfort.

In this and other ways she leaves her seal, I say aloud. And startle at my saying it. What do I mean? What did I start to gather together, to try and make coherent? I was at the terrible, growing years. War years. I do not remember them well. I was working, there were four smaller ones now, there was not time for her. She had to help be a mother, and housekeeper, and shopper. She had to set her seal. Mornings of crisis and near hysteria trying to get lunches packed, hair combed, coats and shoes found, everyone to school or Child Care on time, the baby ready for transportation. And always the paper scribbled on by a smaller one, the book looked at by Susan then mislaid, the homework not done. Running out to that huge school where she was one, she was lost, she was a drop; suffering over the unpreparedness, stammering and unsure in her classes.

There was so little time left at night after the kids were bedded down. She would struggle over books, always eating (it was in those years she developed her enormous appetite that is legendary in our family) and I would be ironing, or preparing food for the next day, or writing V-mail to Bill, or tending the baby. Sometimes, to make me laugh, or out of her despair, she would imitate happenings or types at school.

I think I said once: "Why don't you do something like this in the school amateur show?" One morning she phoned me at work, hardly understandable through the weeping: "Mother, I did it. I won, I won; they gave me first prize; they clapped and clapped and wouldn't let me go."

Now suddenly she was Somebody, and as imprisoned in her difference as in anonymity.

She began to be asked to perform at other high schools, even in colleges, then at city and state-wide affairs. The first one we went to, I only recognized her that first moment when thin, shy, she almost drowned herself into the curtains. Then: Was this Emily? the control, the command, the convulsing and deadly clowning, the spell, then the roaring, stamping audience, unwilling to let this rare and precious laughter out of their lives.

Afterwards: You ought to do something about her with a gift like that—but without money or knowing how, what does one do? We have left it all to her, and the gift has as often eddied inside, clogged and clotted, as been used and growing.

She is coming. She runs up the stairs two at a time with her light graceful step, and I know she is happy tonight. Whatever it was that occasioned your call did not happen today.

"Aren't you ever going to finish the ironing, Mother? Whistler painted his mother in a rocker. I'd have to paint mine standing over an ironing board." This is one of her communicative nights and she tells me everything and nothing as she fixes herself a plate of food out of the icebox.

She is so lovely. Why did you want me to come in at all? Why were you concerned? She will find her way.

She starts up the stairs to bed. "Don't get me up with the rest in the morning." "But I thought you were having midterms." "Oh, those," she comes back in and says quite lightly, "in a couple of years when we'll all be atom-dead they won't matter a bit."

She has said it before. She believes it. But because I have been dredging the past, and all that compounds a human being is so heavy and meaningful in me, I cannot endure it tonight.

I will never total it all now. I will never come in to say: She was a child seldom smiled at. Her father left me before she was a year old. I worked her first six years when there was work, or I sent her home and to his relatives. There were years she had care she hated. She was dark and thin and foreign-looking in a world where the prestige went to blondness and curly hair and dimples, slow where glibness was prized. She was a child of anxious, not proud, love. We were poor and could not afford for her the soil of easy growth. I was a young mother, I was a distracted mother. There were the other children pushing up, demanding. Her younger sister was all that she was not. She did not like me to touch her. She kept too much in herself, her life was such she had to keep too much in herself. My wisdom came too late. She has much in her and probably nothing will come of it. She is a child of her age, of depression, of war, of fear.

Let her be. So all that is in her will not bloom—but in how many does it? There is still enough left to live by. Only help her to believe—help make it so there is cause for her to believe that she is more than this dress on the ironing board, helpless before the iron.

From The Feminine Mystique

1963

In 1997 the feminist poet Adrienne Rich offered a manifesto for protest literature: "I believe in art's social presence—as breaker of official silences." Betty Friedan (1921–2006) broke one of these silences, debunked a mystery, and named "the problem that has no name," as she puts it in *The Feminine Mystique.* The "feminine mystique" is an erasure of women's identity, a pedestal keeping women down, and the myth that female fulfilment comes from domestic responsibilities. The mystique was part of the social fabric, like the yellow wallpaper of Charlotte Perkins Gilman's famous 1892 story. Friedan's book points to the lost ideals of women's rights, vanquished since Gilman and feminism's first wave, becoming the founding document of *second*-wave feminism. Published after President Kennedy established the Commission on the Status of Women in December 1961, and in the same year that the Commission issued a report that revealed widespread discrimination against women in the workplace, *The Feminine Mystique* sold millions. Excerpts appeared in *Good Housekeeping* and *Ladies Home Journal,* two of the magazines that apparently perpetuated the "feminine mystique." Women said it changed their lives, and described their conversion experiences as the "click" of sudden recognition.

Though framed as social research, *The Feminine Mystique* relies heavily on Friedan's personal stories and is part conversion narrative. Friedan presents herself as a victim of the mystique: "It has to change your whole life: it certainly changed mine," she said elsewhere. Her frustrated suburban housewife persona is only partly based in fact—Friedan had a career as a labor journalist—but she recognized the power of speaking from the inside. She focuses on middle-class women and life in the suburbs, as well as unhealthy forms of masculinity, and the social and psychological roots of women's oppression. Then, after naming a problem, Friedan pondered its solution. She felt women needed something new to affirm before rejecting the old. Looking at the civil rights movement, she wondered if women might build their own political movement. In June 1966, she met with female delegates attending a conference of the Commission on the Status of Women. The delegates were frustrated by the government's failure to act on the Commission's findings. Friedan scribbled NOW on a napkin—spelling out a solution—and drafted the first sentence of the statement of purpose for the National Organization for Women (NOW).

Further reading: Susan Hartmann, *From Margin to Mainstream* (1989); Daniel Horowitz, *Betty Friedan* (1998).

The problem lay buried, unspoken, for many years in the minds of American women. It was a strange stirring, a sense of dissatisfaction, a yearning that women suffered in the middle of the twentieth century in the United States. Each suburban wife struggled with it alone. As she made the beds, shopped for groceries, matched slipcover material, ate peanut butter sandwiches with her children, chauffeured Cub Scouts and Brownies, lay beside her husband at night—she was afraid to ask even of herself the silent question—"Is this all?"

For over fifteen years there was no word of this yearning in the millions of words written about women, for women, in all the columns, books and articles by experts telling women their role was to seek fulfillment as wives and mothers. Over and over women heard in voices of tradition and of Freudian sophistication that they could desire no greater destiny than to glory in their own femininity. Experts told them how to catch a man and keep him, how to breastfeed children and handle their toilet training, how to cope with sibling rivalry and adolescent rebellion; how to buy a dishwasher, bake bread, cook gourmet snails, and build a swimming pool with their own hands; how to dress, look, and act more feminine and make marriage more exciting; how to keep their husbands from dying young and their sons from growing into delinquents. They were taught to pity the neurotic, unfeminine, unhappy women who wanted to be poets or physicists or presidents. They learned that truly feminine women do not want careers, higher education, political rights—the independence and the opportunities that the old-fashioned feminists fought for. Some women, in their forties and fifties, still remembered painfully giving up those dreams, but most of the younger women no longer even thought about them. A thousand expert voices applauded their femininity, their adjustment, their new maturity. All they had to do was devote their lives from earliest girlhood to finding a husband and bearing children.

By the end of the nineteen-fifties, the average marriage age of women in America dropped to 20, and was still dropping, into the teens. Fourteen million girls were engaged by 17. The proportion of women attending college in comparison with men dropped from 47 per cent in 1920 to 35 percent in 1958. A century earlier, women had fought for higher education; now girls went to college to get a husband. By the mid-fifties, 60 per cent dropped out of college to marry, or because they were afraid too much education would be a marriage bar. Colleges built dormitories for "married students," but the students were almost always the husbands. A new degree was instituted for the wives—"Ph.T." (Putting Husband Through) . . .

Gradually I came to realize that the problem that has no name was shared by countless women in America. As a magazine writer I often interviewed women about problems with their children, or their marriages, or their houses, or their communities. But after a while I began to recognize the telltale signs of this other problem. I saw the same signs in suburban ranch houses and split-levels on Long Island and in New Jersey and Westchester County; in colonial houses in a small Massachusetts town; on patios in Memphis; in suburban and city apartments; in living rooms in the Midwest. Sometimes I sensed the problem, not as a reporter, but as a suburban housewife, for during this time I was also bringing up my own three children in Rockland County, New York. I heard echoes of the problem in college dormitories and semi-private maternity wards, at PTA meetings and luncheons of the League of Women Voters, at suburban cocktail parties, in station wagons waiting for trains, and in snatches of conversation overheard at Schrafft's. The groping words I heard from other women, on quiet afternoons when children were at school or on quiet evenings when husbands worked late, I think I understood first as a woman long before I understood their larger social and psychological implications.

Just what was this problem that has no name? What were the words women used when they tried to express it? Sometimes a woman would say "I feel empty somehow . . . incomplete." Or she would say, "I feel as if I don't exist." Sometimes she blotted out the feeling with a tranquilizer. Sometimes she thought the problem was with her husband, or her children, or that what she really needed was to redecorate her house, or move to a better neighborhood, or have an affair, or another baby. Sometimes, she went to a doctor with symptoms she could hardly describe: "A tired feeling . . . I get so angry with the children it scares me . . . I feel like crying without any reason." (A Cleveland doctor called it "the housewife's syndrome.") A number of women told me about great bleeding blisters that break out on their hands and arms. "I call it the housewife's blight," said a family doctor in Pennsylvania. "I see it so often lately in these young women with four, five and six children who bury themselves in their dishpans. But it isn't caused by detergent and it isn't cured by cortisone." . . .

Can the problem that has no name be somehow related to the domestic routine of the housewife? When a woman tries to put the problem into words, she often merely describes the daily life she leads. What is there in this recital of comfortable domestic detail that could possibly cause such a feeling of desperation? Is she trapped simply by the enormous demands of her role as modern housewife: wife, mistress, mother, nurse, consumer, cook, chauffeur; expert on interior decoration, child care, appliance repair, furniture refinishing, nutrition, and education? Her day is fragmented as she rushes from dishwasher to washing machine to telephone to dryer to station wagon to supermarket, and delivers Johnny to the Little League field, takes Janey to dancing class, gets the lawnmower fixed and meets the 6:45. She can never spend more than 15 minutes on any one thing; she has no time to read books, only magazines; even if she had time, she has lost the power to concentrate. At the end of the day, she is so terribly tired that sometimes her husband has to take over and put the children to bed.

This terrible tiredness took so many women to doctors in the 1950's that one decided to investigate it. He found, surprisingly, that his patients suffering from "housewife's fatigue" slept more than an adult needed to sleep—as much as ten hours a day—and that the actual energy they expended on housework did not tax their capacity. The real problem must be something else, he decided—perhaps boredom. Some doctors told their women patients they must get out of the house for a day, treat themselves to a movie in town. Others prescribed tranquilizers. Many suburban housewives were taking tranquilizers like cough drops. "You wake up in the morning, and you feel as if there's no point in going on another day like this. So you take a tranquilizer because it makes you not care so much that it's pointless."

It is easy to see the concrete details that trap the suburban housewife, the continual demands on her time. But the chains that bind her in her trap are chains in her own mind and spirit. They are chains made up of mistaken ideas and misinterpreted facts, of incomplete truths and unreal choices. They are not easily seen and not easily shaken off.

How can any woman see the whole truth within the bounds of her own life? How can she believe that voice inside herself, when it denies the conventional, accepted truths by which she has been living? And yet the women I have talked to, who are finally listening to that inner voice, seem in some incredible way to be groping through to a truth that has defied the experts.

I think the experts in a great many fields have been holding pieces of that truth under their microscopes for a long time without realizing it. I found pieces of it in certain new research and theoretical developments in psychological, social and biological science whose implications for women seem never to have been examined. I found many clues by talking to suburban doctors, gynecologists, obstetricians, child-guidance clinicians, pediatricians, high-school guidance counselors, college professors, marriage counselors, psychiatrists and ministers—questioning them not on their theories, but on their actual experience in treating American women, I became aware of a growing body of evidence, much of which has not been reported publicly because it does not fit current modes of thought about women—evidence which throws into question the standards of feminine normality, feminine adjustment, feminine fulfillment, and feminine maturity by which most women are still trying to live.

I began to see in a strange new light the American return to early marriage and the large families that are causing the population explosion; the recent movement to natural childbirth and breastfeeding; suburban conformity, and the new neuroses, character pathologies and sexual problems being reported by the doctors. I began to see new dimensions to old problems that have long been taken for granted among women: menstrual difficulties, sexual frigidity, promiscuity, pregnancy fears, childbirth depression, the high incidence of emotional breakdown and suicide among women in their twenties and thirties, the menopause crises, the so-called passivity and immaturity of American men, the discrepancy between women's tested intellectual abilities in childhood and their adult achievement, the changing incidence of adult sexual orgasm in American women, and persistent problems in psychotherapy and in women's education.

If I am right, the problem that has no name stirring in the minds of so many American women today is not a matter of loss of femininity or too much education, or the demands of domesticity. It is far more important than anyone recognizes. It is the key to these other new and old problems which have been torturing women and their husbands and children, and puzzling their doctors and educators for years. It may well be the key to our future as a nation and a culture. We can no longer ignore that voice within women that says: "I want something more than my husband and my children and my home." . . .

The search for identity is not new, however, in American thought—though in every generation, each man who writes about it discovers it anew. In America, from the beginning, it has somehow been understood that men must thrust into the future; the pace has always been too rapid for man's identity to stand still. In every generation, many men have suffered misery, unhappiness, and uncertainty because they could not take the image of the man they wanted to be from their fathers. The search for identity of the young man who can't go home again has always been a major theme of American writers. And it has always been considered right in America, good, for men to suffer these agonies of growth, to search for and find their own identities. The farm boy went to the city, the garment-maker's son became a doctor, Abraham Lincoln taught himself to read—these were more than rags-to-riches stories. They were an integral part of the American dream. The problem for many was money, race, color, class, which barred them from choice—not what they would be if they were free to choose.

Even today a young man learns soon enough that he must decide who he wants to be. If he does not decide in junior high, in high school, in college, he must somehow come to terms with it by twenty-five or thirty, or he is lost. But this search for identity is seen as a greater problem now because more and more boys cannot find images in our culture—from their fathers or other men—to help them in their search. The old frontiers have been conquered, and the boundaries of the new are not so clearly marked. More and more young men in America today suffer an identity crisis for want of any image of man worth pursuing, for want of a purpose that truly realizes their human abilities.

But why have theorists not recognized this same identity crisis in women? In terms of the old conventions and the new feminine mystique women are not expected to grow up to find out who they are, to choose their human identity. Anatomy is woman's destiny, say the theorists of femininity; the identity of woman is determined by her biology.

But is it? More and more women are asking themselves this question. As if they were waking from a coma, they ask, "Where am I . . . what am I doing here?" For the first time in their history, women are becoming aware of an identity crisis in their own lives, a crisis which began many generations ago, has grown worse with each succeeding generation, and will not end until they, or their daughters, turn an unknown corner and make of themselves and their lives the new image that so many women now so desperately need.

In a sense that goes beyond any one woman's life, I think this is the crisis of women growing up—a turning point from an immaturity that has been called femininity to full human identity. I think women had to suffer this crisis of identity, which began a hundred years ago, and have to suffer it still today, simply to become fully human . . .

Who knows what women can be when they are finally free to become themselves? Who knows what women's intelligence will contribute when it can be nourished without denying love? Who knows of the possibilities of love when men and women share not only children, home, and garden, not only the fulfillment of their biological roles, but the responsibilities and passions of the work that creates the human future and the full human knowledge of who they are? It has barely begun, the search of women for themselves. But the time is at hand when the voices of the feminine mystique can no longer drown out the inner voice that is driving women on to become complete.

Statement of Purpose

1966

The Civil Rights Act of 1964 banned sex and race discrimination in employment, but the feminist writer Betty Friedan believed sex discrimination was not being taken seriously by the Equal Opportunity Commission. In 1966, along with twenty-six women and one man, she established the National Organization for Women (NOW). They invited more men to join; Friedan criticized feminists who made "a false analogy with obsolete or irrelevant ideologies of . . . race separatism." Unlike American Indian Movement activists and gay liberationists, Friedan's interest in civil rights protest as a parallel movement to her own did not extend to the separatist philosophy of black nationalists. Ti-Grace Atkinson protested this approach, called for separatism, and left NOW to form The Feminists.

NOW's Statement of Purpose calls for equality, respect, and the chance to fulfill human potential. It attacks educators and the mass media, as Friedan had in *The Feminine Mystique* (1963). NOW led the Women's Strike for Equality in August 1970, and afterward 80 percent of American adults reported an awareness of the women's movement. It publicized issues in the media and lobbied legislatures on job discrimination, maternity leave, tax deductions for child care expenses, day care, job training, and violence against women. Friedan stepped down as president in 1970, "to come to new terms with the political as well as the personal, in my own life." But she retained a high profile within the feminist movement, and in 1973 she controversially attacked those in NOW who were "pushing lesbianism."

The other primary author of NOW's Statement of Purpose, Pauli Murray, took issue with a different strategy: NOW's support for the Equal Rights Amendment (ERA). Murray had worked with Martin Luther King, Jr., in the early 1960s, and while Friedan took positive inspiration from the civil rights movement, Murray found it a negative spur. Black women were crucial at a grass-roots level but overlooked for leadership positions; Murray used the phrase "Jane Crow" to name a "conjunction" of two oppressions, gender and race. This conjunction meant she couldn't support NOW's push for the ERA: "I cannot allow myself to be fragmented into Negro at one time, woman at another," she explained in 1967; "I must find a unifying principle in all of these movements."

Further reading: Maryann Barakso, *Governing NOW* (2004); Sara Evans, *Personal Politics* (1979).

We, men and women who hereby constitute ourselves as the National Organization for Women, believe that the time has come for a new movement toward true equality for all women in America, and toward a fully equal partnership of the sexes, as part of the world-wide revolution of human rights now taking place within and beyond our national borders.

The purpose of NOW is to take action to bring women into full participation in the mainstream of American society now, exercising all the privileges and responsibilities thereof in truly equal partnership with men.

We believe the time has come to move beyond the abstract argument, discussion and symposia over the status and special nature of women which has raged in America in recent years; the time has come to confront, with concrete action, the conditions that now prevent women from enjoying the equality of opportunity and freedom of choice which is their right, as individual Americans, and as human beings.

NOW is dedicated to the proposition that women, first and foremost, are human beings, who, like all other people in our society, must have the chance to develop their fullest human potential. We believe that women can achieve such equality only by accepting to the full the challenges and responsibilities they share with all other people in our society, as part of the decision-making mainstream of American political, economic and social life.

We organize to initiate or support action, nationally, or in any part of this nation, by individuals or organizations, to break through the silken curtain of prejudice and discrimination against women in government, industry, the professions, the churches, the political parties, the judiciary, the labor unions, in education, science, medicine, law, religion and every other field of importance in American society.

Enormous changes taking place in our society make it both possible and urgently necessary to advance the unfinished revolution of women toward true equality, now. With a life span lengthened to nearly 75 years it is no longer either necessary or possible for women to devote the greater part of their lives to child-rearing; yet childbearing and rearing which continues to be a most important part of most women's lives—still is used to justify barring women from equal professional and economic participation and advance.

Today's technology has reduced most of the productive chores which women once performed in the home and in mass-production industries based upon routine unskilled labor. This same technology has virtually eliminated the quality of muscular strength as a criterion for filling most jobs, while intensifying American industry's need for creative intelligence. In view of this new industrial revolution created by automation in the mid-twentieth century, women can and must participate in old and new fields of society in full equality—or become permanent outsiders.

Despite all the talk about the status of American women in recent years, the actual position of women in the United States has declined, and is declining, to an alarming degree throughout the 1950's and 60's. Although 46.4% of all American women between the ages of 18 and 65 now work outside the home, the overwhelming majority—75%—are in routine clerical, sales, or factory jobs, or they are household workers, cleaning women, hospital attendants. About two-thirds of Negro women workers are in the lowest paid service occupations. Working women are becoming increasingly—not less—concentrated on the bottom of the job ladder. As a consequence full-time women workers today earn on the average only 60% of what men earn, and that wage gap has been increasing over the past twenty-five years in every major industry group. In 1964, of all women with a yearly income, 89% earned under $5,000 a year; half of all full-time year round women workers earned less than $3,690; only 1.4% of full-time year round women workers had an annual income of $10,000 or more.

Further, with higher education increasingly essential in today's society, too few women are entering and finishing college or going on to graduate or professional school. Today, women earn only one in three of the B.A.'s and M.A.'s granted, and one in ten of the Ph.D.'s.

In all the professions considered of importance to society, and in the executive ranks of industry and government, women are losing ground. Where they are present it is only a token handful. Women comprise less than 1% of federal judges; less than 4% of all lawyers; 7% of doctors. Yet women represent 51% of the U.S. population. And, increasingly, men are replacing women in the top positions in secondary and elementary schools, in social work, and in libraries—once thought to be women's fields.

Official pronouncements of the advance in the status of women hide not only the reality of this dangerous decline, but the fact that nothing is being done to stop it. The excellent reports of the President's Commission on the Status of Women and of the State Commissions have not been fully implemented. Such Commissions have power only to advise. They have no power to enforce their recommendation; nor have they the freedom to organize American women and men to press for action on them. The reports of these commissions have, however, created a basis upon which it is now possible to build. Discrimination in employment on the basis of sex is now prohibited by federal law, in Title VII of the Civil Rights Act of 1964. But although nearly one-third of the cases brought before the Equal Employment Opportunity Commission during the first year dealt with sex discrimination and the proportion is increasing dramatically, the Commission has not made clear its intention to enforce the law with the same seriousness on behalf of women as of other victims of discrimination. Many of these cases were Negro women, who are the victims of double discrimination of race and sex. Until now, too few women's organizations and official spokesmen have been willing to speak out against these dangers facing women. Too many women have been restrained by the fear of being called "feminist." There is no civil rights movement to speak for women, as there has been for Negroes and other victims of discrimination. The National Organization for Women must therefore begin to speak.

WE BELIEVE that the power of American law, and the protection guaranteed by the U.S. Constitution to the civil rights of all individuals, must be effectively applied and enforced to isolate and remove patterns of sex discrimination, to ensure equality of opportunity in employment and education, and equality of civil and political rights and responsibilities on behalf of women, as well as for Negroes and other deprived groups.

We realize that women's problems are linked to many broader questions of social justice; their solution will require concerted action by many groups. Therefore, convinced that human rights for all are indivisible, we expect to give active support to the common cause of equal rights for all those who suffer discrimination and deprivation, and we call upon other organizations committed to such goals to support our efforts toward equality for women.

WE DO NOT ACCEPT the token appointment of a few women to high-level positions in government and industry as a substitute for serious continuing effort to recruit and advance women according to their individual abilities. To this end, we urge American government and industry to mobilize the same resources of ingenuity and command with which they have solved problems of far greater difficulty than those now impeding the progress of women.

WE BELIEVE that this nation has a capacity at least as great as other nations, to innovate new social institutions which will enable women to enjoy the true equality of opportunity and responsibility in society, without conflict with their responsibilities as mothers and homemakers. In such innovations, America does not lead the Western world, but lags by decades behind many European countries. We do not accept the traditional assumption that a woman has to choose between marriage and motherhood, on the one hand, and serious participation in industry or the professions on the other. We question the present expectation that all normal women will retire from job or profession for 10 or 15 years, to devote their full time to raising children, only to reenter the job market at a relatively minor level. This, in itself, is a deterrent to the aspirations of women, to their acceptance into management or professional training courses, and to the very possibility of equality of opportunity or real choice, for all but a few women. Above all, we reject the assumption that these problems are the unique responsibility of each individual woman, rather than a basic social dilemma which society must solve. True equality of opportunity and freedom of choice for women requires such practical, and possible innovations as a nationwide network of child-care centers, which will make it unnecessary for women to retire completely from society until their children are grown, and national programs to provide retraining for women who have chosen to care for their children full-time.

WE BELIEVE that it is as essential for every girl to be educated to her full potential of human ability as it is for every boy—with the knowledge that such education is the key to effective participation in today's economy and that, for a girl as for a boy, education can only be serious where there is expectation that it will be used in society. We believe that American educators are capable of devising means of imparting such expectations to girl students. Moreover, we consider the decline in the proportion of women receiving higher and professional education to be evidence of discrimination. This discrimination may take the form of quotas against the admission of women to colleges, and professional schools; lack of encouragement by parents, counselors and educators; denial of loans or fellowships; or the traditional or arbitrary procedures in graduate and professional training geared in terms of men, which inadvertently discriminate against women. We believe that the same serious attention must be given to high school dropouts who are girls as to boys.

WE REJECT the current assumptions that a man must carry the sole burden of supporting himself, his wife, and family, and that a woman is automatically entitled to lifelong support by a man upon her marriage, or that marriage, home and family are primarily woman's world and responsibility—hers, to dominate—his to support. We believe that a true partnership between the sexes demands a different concept of marriage, an equitable sharing of the responsibilities of home and children and of the economic burdens of their support. We believe that proper recognition should be given to the economic and social value of homemaking and child-care. To these ends, we will seek to open a reexamination of laws and mores governing marriage and divorce, for we believe that the current state of "half-equity" between the sexes discriminates against both men and women, and is the cause of much unnecessary hostility between the sexes.

WE BELIEVE that women must now exercise their political rights and responsibilities as American citizens. They must refuse to be segregated on the basis of sex into separate-and-not-equal ladies' auxiliaries in the political parties, and they must demand representation according to their numbers in the regularly constituted party committees—at local, state, and national levels—and in the informal power structure, participating fully in the selection of candidates and political decision-making, and running for office themselves.

IN THE INTERESTS OF THE HUMAN DIGNITY OF WOMEN, we will protest, and endeavor to change, the false image of women now prevalent in the mass media, and in the texts, ceremonies, laws, and practices of our major social institutions. Such images perpetuate contempt for women by society and by women for themselves. We are similarly opposed to all policies and practices—in church, state, college, factory, or office—which, in the guise of protectiveness, not only deny opportunities but also foster in women self-denigration, dependence, and evasion of responsibility, undermine their confidence in their own abilities and foster contempt for women.

NOW WILL HOLD ITSELF INDEPENDENT OF ANY POLITICAL PARTY in order to mobilize the political power of all women and men intent on our goals. We will strive to ensure that no party, candidate, president, senator, governor, congressman, or any public official who betrays or ignores the principle of full equality between the sexes is elected or appointed to office. If it is necessary to mobilize the votes of men and women who believe in our cause, in order to win for women the final right to be fully free and equal human beings, we so commit ourselves.

WE BELIEVE THAT women will do most to create a new image of women by acting now, and by speaking out in behalf of their own equality, freedom, and human dignity—not in pleas for special privilege, nor in enmity toward men, who are also victims of the current, half-equality between the sexes—but in an active, self-respecting partnership with men. By so doing, women will develop confidence in their own ability to determine actively, in partnership with men, the conditions of their life, their choices, their future and their society.

Women's Liberation Has a Different
Meaning for Blacks

1970

"Womanist is to feminist as purple is to lavender," wrote the feminist author Alice Walker, explaining that "womanist" referred to a feminist of color who fought for all oppressed men and women. Professional, liberal white women championed one kind of feminism in the 1960s, but a more diverse group of women, many of whom had encountered varying degrees of sexism from black nationalists and civil rights activists, led another part of the movement. Black feminists stressed the interconnection of race, gender, and class, and challenged the assumption that black women needed white feminists to explain sexist oppression for them. Many objected that white, middle-class women presented their experiences as universal. "The oppression of women knows no ethnic or racial boundaries, true, but that does not mean it is identical within those boundaries," wrote the poet and essayist Audre Lorde in 1979. Along with the literature of Lorde and Walker, Toni Cade's *The Black Woman* (1970) and Toni Morrison's *The Bluest Eye* (1970) were important texts of black feminism.

Black feminist groups formed in parallel with the National Conference of Puerto Rican Women (founded 1972), the Mexican American Woman's Association (also formed in 1972), and Women of All Red Nations, founded in 1974 by women's rights activists in the American Indian Movement. In 1968 Francis Beal and other members of the Student Nonviolent Coordinating Committee's Women's Caucus formed the Third World Women's Alliance, the first black feminist group of second-wave feminism. In 1973, Black Women Organized for Action was founded in San Francisco, and the National Black Feminist Organization was founded in New York. The Combahee River Collective, a black lesbian feminist group, was founded in 1974.

Renee Ferguson (b. 1949), now an NBC reporter, was a *Washington Post* intern when she wrote this article in 1970 discussing the "priorities of black women versus the priorities of white women." These different priorities were evident in groups' agendas. Like the National Organization for Women (NOW), black feminist organizations worked on reproductive rights, abortion access, child care, and welfare rights. But their priorities also included protesting forced sterilization, rape, police brutality, union busting, and imperialism. Lorde explained that "for nonwhite women in this country, there [are] . . . three times the number of unnecessary eventrations, hysterectomies and sterilizations as for white women; three times as many chances of being raped, murdered, or assaulted."

White feminist groups did eventually address the diversity of women's oppression. But tensions arose when NOW's white leaders declined to support Shirley Chisholm's candidacy for the presidential nomination in 1972. Chisholm, the first African American woman elected to Congress, told NOW and others: "If you can't support me, get out of my way."

Further reading: Cynthia Burack, *Healing Identities* (2004); Elizabeth Spelman, *Inessential Woman* (1988).

The women's liberation movement touches some sensitive nerves among black women—but they are not always the nerves the movement seems to touch among so many whites.

At a time when some radical white feminists are striving for a different family structure, many black women are trying to stabilize their families. They are making a special effort, in a great number of cases, to assume the wife and mother role more effectively. Whether a black woman feels that she can relate to the women's liberation movement and the extent to which she is or is not involved in it may well depend on her age and her experiences.

Dr. Anna Hedgeman, for instance, who takes pride in the fact that she lived in Harlem for most of the 30 years she has lived in New York, is a strong advocate of the women's liberation movement. She believes that there is no way in which black women in America are uninvolved in the movement. "We as Afro-American women have to face the problems of total discrimination in our society," Dr. Hedgeman says. "We have the extra burden of being women. But if you just review the problems that women face you need only substitute the word Afro-American people for the word women and you have the same problems—job discrimination, want ads that discriminate and false stereotypes."

On the other hand, Howard University senior and Student Association Secretary Pamely Preston doesn't think that the women's liberation movement has any meaning for black women. "As far as I'm concerned the women's liberation movement is trite, trivial and simple. It's just another white political fad," Miss Preston says. "Black people have some of the same problems that they had when they were first brought to this country. That's what we've got to deal with." If the relatively modest turnout of black women for the recent Woman's Liberation Day demonstrations is any indication of the black women's interest in the movement, then perhaps Miss Preston's attitude is indicative of the way most black women feel.

These vastly differing attitudes raise a real question about the extent to which the women's liberation movement means very much to black women. Do black women and white women have the same social, economic and political priorities and problems and how do they affect the status of the women's liberation movement in the minds of black women?

In a 1963 article which appeared in the *Washington Post*, the president of the National Council of Negro Women, Dorothy Height, said, "A Negro woman has the same kind of problems as other women, but she can't take the same things for granted. For instance, she has to raise children who seldom have the same sense of security that white children have when they see their father accepted as a successful member of the community. A Negro child's father is ignored as though he doesn't exist."

The instability of the black inner-city family has been the subject of concern and study by sociologists for years . . . Local singer Marjorie Barnes in citing the problems of the instability of black families as one of her main reasons for non-involvement in the women's liberation movement, says, "I don't think that black women can afford to be competitive with their men—especially now. Competing with them for jobs would just add to the problem that already exists. Black women have been able to find work when their husbands couldn't and have often been the head of the family not because they wanted to be but out of economic necessity. Some of those women's lib girls are asking for jobs that black men haven't been able to get." Miss Barnes adds, "Black women have the additional problem of raising their children in crime ridden neighbourhoods and they've got to see to it that their children receive a decent basic education. Most black women don't have time to take up white middle class cause women's lib unless they're trying to hide from the realities of the struggle for black liberation."

During a recent interview Miss Height, who served as a member of President Kennedy's commission on the status of women and who has been working actively for women's liberation for many years, explained the lack of black involvement in the movement this way: "A few days ago we observed the fiftieth anniversary of women's suffrage, but in 1965 black women had to work for the passage of a voting rights act in order to make it possible for millions of black people to have their right to vote protected. I think that it is not that black women are not interested in the liberation of women, but many people have not recognized that everyone has to work for the liberation of black people—men and women."

Even those black women who vehemently oppose the women's liberation movement agree that some of the political and social reforms for which the movement is working and have helped achieve will help black women. They agree that abortion reform and free child care centers would be of considerable value to black women. And they acknowledge the fact that a strong woman's lobby helped pass the New York State abortion reform law, which will have a positive effect on halting the heretofore growing rate of New York hospital emergency cases of black and other minority-group women who attempt to perform self-induced abortions. They were also unable to deny the fact that black women are the victims of stereotypes but possibly more hurtful.

When asked to describe the black stereotypical woman Miss Preston replies, "Black women are pictured by some segments of white society and even by some black men as loud, obstinate, domineering, emasculating and generally immoral—that old Sapphire image. In contrast white women are stereotyped as blue-eyed, virtuous, to-be-put-on-a-pedestal types. But I don't think it's going to take any women's liberation movement to remove those stereotypes.

Miss Height believes that the main black stereotype of black women pictures them as the domineering matriarch. "There is a complete denial by this society of the fact that since the slave ships brought the black woman to this country she has had to hold the family together," Miss Height says. "She has been forced into a position of responsibility. These stereotypes have even caused the black male to think that he is dominated. The whole culture downgrades women. White women aren't treated as real human beings. They must be subservient to the male and are at his mercy for being called either beautiful and dumb or smart and aggressive. The black woman has had to struggle against being a person of great strength. She has had to demonstrate the skill to cope with that has happened to the whole black family. Black women have had to make for themselves services that white women have been able to take for granted. We had to take care of our own teen-age mothers when white women had Florence Crittendon homes over the years. Our children had to carry the door key around their necks because there were no day care centers for black working mothers."

Another important issue of the women's liberation movement has been sexual exploitation. White women are rebelling against advertising that insults women and magazines that depict women as nonthinking, bosomy bundles of sexiness placed on earth for the benefit of the *Playboy Magazine* centerfold and the prurient interests of men. To black women, the term sexual exploitation has a completely different meaning. Dr. Hedgeman describes the sexual exploitation of black women through the mass media. "We just weren't even there. We've had the greater sexual exploitation because we were ignored. We've not been seen. It's only been in the past couple of years that even the ads recognized the fact that we use toothpaste. And since then we've been used in the same stupid ways as women have always been used. In addition to that, Afro-American women have been sexually abused. During slavery we were chattel, breeders and often times at the mercy of slave owners. That was a form of sexual exploitation that affects us even today."

Perhaps the lack of involvement of black women in the women's liberation movement can best be explained in terms of priorities. The priorities of black women versus the priorities of white women.

Obviously the first priority of virtually all black people is the elimination of racial prejudice in America—in effect the liberation of black people. Second in importance is the black family problem of establishing a decent way of life in America as it exists today. When racism in America is eliminated, then perhaps the black family's stability problem will disappear and more black women will be able to give first priority to the elimination of oppression because of sex.

For the Equal Rights Amendment

1970

In this speech, Shirley Chisholm (1924–2005) tells Congress that it is not too late to complete the Founding Fathers' unfinished work. An amendment outlawing sex discrimination was also the unfinished work of one of feminism's founding mothers: Alice Paul had first proposed the Equal Rights Amendment (ERA) in 1923. Introducing it on the 75th anniversary of the 1848 Seneca Falls "Declaration of Sentiments," Paul had warned: "If we keep on this way they will be celebrating the 150th anniversary of the 1848 Convention without being much further advanced in equal rights than we are." Like advocates for the Civil Rights Act in the early 1960s, Chisholm believed equality before the law would begin a process of attitude change. Women would no longer feel inferior, and men would find it harder to perpetuate myths of male superiority. The House and Senate passed the ERA in October 1971 and March 1972, but it needed ratification by 38 states. Indiana was the 35th and last state to ratify, in 1977, the year that Paul died. The deadline for ratification passed in 1979.

Chisholm had become the first black woman in Congress in 1968. She got there, she said, in spite of two "handicaps," but called sex a worse handicap than race. She often compared feminism to the civil rights movement, noting that shame of race had become pride, and so should shame of sex. In 1972 she entered the Democratic presidential primaries, later explaining: "The next time a woman runs . . . she will be taken seriously . . . I ran because somebody had to do it first." She caused further controversy when she visited rival candidate George Wallace, a segregationist Alabama governor, in the hospital during the campaign after he was left paralyzed by an assassination attempt. When Chisholm arrived at the hospital, Wallace asked her, "What are your people going to say?" She replied, "I know what they're going to say. But I wouldn't want what happened to you to happen to anyone." Wallace cried.

Further reading: Kenneth Karst, *Belonging to America* (1989); Jane Mansbridge, *Why We Lost the ERA* (1986).

Mr. Speaker, House Joint Resolution 264, before us today, which provides for equality under the law for both men and women, represents one of the most clear-cut opportunities we are likely to have to declare our faith in the principles that shaped our Constitution. It provides a legal basis for attack on the most subtle, most pervasive, and most institutionalized form of prejudice that exists. Discrimination against women, solely on the basis of their sex, is so widespread that is seems to many persons normal, natural and right.

Legal expression of prejudice on the grounds of religious or political belief has become a minor problem in our society. Prejudice on the basis of race is, at least, under systematic attack. There is reason for optimism that it will start to die with the present, older generation. It is time we act to assure full equality of opportunity to those citizens who, although in a majority, suffer the restrictions that are commonly imposed on minorities, to women.

The argument that this amendment will not solve the problem of sex discrimination is not relevant. If the argument were used against a civil rights bill, as it has been used in the past, the prejudice that lies behind it would be embarrassing. Of course laws will not eliminate prejudice from the hearts of human beings. But that is no reason to allow prejudice to continue to be enshrined in our laws—to perpetuate injustice through inaction.

The amendment is necessary to clarify countless ambiguities and inconsistencies in our legal system. For instance, the Constitution guarantees due process of law, in the 5th and 14th amendments. But the applicability of due process of sex distinctions is not clear. Women are excluded from some State colleges and universities. In some States, restrictions are placed on a married woman who engages in an independent business. Women may not be chosen for some juries. Women even receive heavier criminal penalties than men who commit the same crime. What would the legal effects of the equal rights amendment really be? The equal rights amendment would govern only the relationship between the State and its citizens—not relationships between private citizens. The amendment would be largely self-executing, that is, and Federal or State laws in conflict would be ineffective one year after date of ratification without further action by the Congress or State legislatures.

Opponents of the amendment claim its ratification would throw the law into a state of confusion and would result in much litigation to establish its meaning. This objection overlooks the influence of legislative history in determining intent and the recent activities of many groups preparing for legislative changes in this direction.

State labor laws applying only to women, such as those limiting hours of work and weights to be lifted would become inoperative unless the legislature amended them to apply to men. As of early 1970 most States would have some laws that would be affected. However, changes are being made so rapidly as a result of Title VII of the Civil Rights Act of 1964, it is likely that by the time the equal rights amendment would become effective; no conflict in State laws would remain.

In any event, there has for years been great controversy as to the usefulness to women of these State labor laws. There has never been any doubt that they worked a hardship on women who need or want to work overtime and on women who need or want better paying jobs, and there has been no persuasive evidence as to how many women benefit from the archaic policy of the laws. After the Delaware hours law was repealed in 1966, there were no complaints from women to any of the State agencies that might have been approached.

Jury service laws not making women equally liable for jury service would have been revised. The selective service law would have to include women, but women would not be required to serve in the Armed Forces where they are not fitted any more than men are required to serve. Military service, while a great responsibility, is not without benefits, particularly for young men with limited education or training.

Since October 1966, 246,000 young men who did not meet the normal mental or physical requirements have been given opportunities for training and correcting physical problems. This opportunity is not open to their sisters. Only girls who have completed high school and meet high standards on the educational test can volunteer. Ratification of the amendment would not permit application of higher standards to women.

Survivorship benefits would be available to husbands of female workers on the same basis as to wives of male workers. The Social Security Act and the civil service and military service retirement acts are in conflict. Public schools and universities could not be limited to one sex and could not apply different admission standards to men and women. Laws requiring longer prison sentences for women than men would be invalid, and equal opportunities for rehabilitation and vocational training would have to be provided in public correctional institutions. Different ages of majority based on sex would have to be harmonized. Federal, State, and other governmental bodies would be obligated to follow nondiscriminatory practices in all aspects of employment, including public school teachers and State university and college faculties.

What would be the economic effects of the equal rights amendment? Direct economic effects would be minor. If any labor laws applying only to women still remained, their amendment or repeal would provide opportunity for women in better-paying jobs in manufacturing. More opportunities in public vocational and graduate schools for women would also tend to open up opportunities in better jobs for women.

Indirect effects could be much greater. The focusing of public attention on the gross legal, economic, and social discrimination against women by hearings and debates in the Federal and State legislatures would result in changes in attitude of parents, educators, and employers that would bring about substantial economic changes in the long run.

Sex prejudice cuts both ways. Men are oppressed by the requirements of the Selective Service Act, by enforced legal guardianship of minors, and by alimony laws. Each sex, I believe, should be liable when necessary to serve and defend this country. Each has a responsibility for the support of children.

There are objections raised to wiping out laws protecting women workers. No one would condone exploitation. But what does sex have to do with it? Working conditions and hours that are harmful to women are harmful to men; wages that are unfair for women are unfair for men. Laws setting employment limitations on the basis of sex are irrational, and the proof of this is their inconsistency from State to State. The physical characteristics of men and women are not fixed, but cover two wide spans that have a great deal of overlap. It is obvious, I think, that a robust woman could be more fit for physical labor than a weak man. The choice of occupation would be determined by individual capabilities, and the rewards for equal work should be equal.

This is what it comes down to: artificial distinctions between persons must be wiped out of the law. Legal discrimination between the sexes is, in almost every instance, founded on outmoded views of society and the pre-scientific beliefs about psychology and physiology. It is time to sweep away these relics of the past and set further generations free of them.

Federal agencies and institutions responsible for the enforcement of equal opportunity laws need the authority of a Constitutional amendment. The 1964 Civil Rights Act and the 1963 Equal Pay Act are not enough; they are limited in their coverage—for instance, one excludes teachers, and the other leaves out administrative and professional women. The Equal Employment Opportunity Commission has not proven to be an adequate device, with its power limited to investigation, conciliation, and recommendation to the Justice Department. In its cases involving sexual discrimination, it has failed in more than one-half. The Justice Department has been even less effective. It has intervened in only one case involving discrimination on the basis of sex, and this was on a procedural point. In a second case, in which both sexual and racial discrimination were alleged, the racial bias charge was given far greater weight.

Evidence of discrimination on the basis of sex should hardly have to be cited here. It is in the Labor Department's employment and salary figures for anyone who is still in doubt. Its elimination will involve so many changes in our State and Federal laws that, without the authority and impetus of this proposed amendment, it will perhaps take another 194 years. We cannot be party to continuing a delay. The time is clearly now to put this House on record for the fullest expression of that equality of opportunity which our founding fathers professed. They professed it, but they did not assure it to their daughters, as they tried to do for their sons.

The Constitution they wrote was designed to protect the rights of white, male citizens. As there were no black Founding Fathers, there were no founding mothers—a great pity, on both counts. It is not too late to complete the work they left undone. Today, here, we should start to do so.

In closing I would like to make one point. Social and psychological effects will be initially more important than legal or economic results. As Leo Kanowitz has pointed out:

Rules of law that treat of the sexes per see inevitably produce far-reaching effect upon social psychological and economic aspects of male-female relations beyond the limited confines of legislative chambers and courtrooms. As long as organized legal systems, at once the most respected and most feared of social institutions, continue to differentiate sharply, in treatment or in words, between men and women on the basis of irrelevant and artificially created distinctions, the likelihood of men and women coming to regard one another primarily as fellow human beings and only secondarily as representatives of another sex will continue to be remote. When men and women are prevented from recognizing one another's essential humanity by sexual prejudices, nourished by legal as well as social institutions, society as a whole remains less than it could otherwise become.

Letter to Betty Friedan

1963

Second-wave feminists said the personal was political. But the feminist historian Gerda Lerner (b. 1920) made the personal historical. Focused on the intersections of race, class, and sex discrimination, she has spent decades writing history that might authorize and emancipate women, asserting in 1994 that women were "deprived of their own history, and that held them back."

Lerner was an early voice of third-wave feminism. In a private letter to Betty Friedan, printed here, she points out that Friedan's bestselling book, *The Feminine Mystique* (1963), doesn't address the problems of working-class women. Friedan wrote about white suburban women and didn't acknowledge that sexism changes in combination with racism or poverty. Her book lists statistics that hide poor whites, blacks, and lesbians (60 percent of women drop out of college to marry, three in ten women dye their hair blond, fourteen million women are engaged by age seventeen). Lerner anticipates the public criticisms of later feminists, who would note that domestic drudgery continues even when middle-class women enter the workplace and hire domestic help: a female household worker was more likely to be black than white. Other feminists added that Friedan had glamorized work; many women worked out of necessity, regarding full-time homemaking as an unaffordable ideal. "She did not tell readers whether it was more fulfilling to be a maid, a babysitter, a factory worker, a clerk, or a prostitute, than to be a leisure class housewife," said bell hooks in 1984.

The Feminine Mystique claims that myths of female identity are the barrier to gender equality, and tries to restore what Friedan calls "the firm core of self or 'I.'" In her letter, Lerner explains that this idea ignores the source of working women's problems and their institutional solutions. Working-class women had taken a different path to feminism and developed a politics of community. Unionized women were vocal in the 1930s and postwar decades, demanding child care, equal pay, and an end to sexual harassment. Women in the labor movement opened doors to traditionally male trades. Lerner's work, both before and after she wrote this letter, shows how the practical became ideological, the personal became collective, and the collective changed women's history. In 2003 she helped found Historians against the War, this time making the historical political.

I have just finished reading your splendid book and want to tell you how excited and delighted I am with it. You have done a most important job which desperately needed doing, I am sure it will unsettle a great many smug certainties, cause a lot of healthy doubts, and, I hope, will stir up controversy. The "experts" of the feminine mystique have had it their way for far too long . . . The more controversy the better, for the sooner people will begin to think of new solutions. You have done for women what Rachel Carson did for birds and trees . . . I have one reservation about your treatment of your subject: you address yourself solely to the problems of middle class, college-educated women. This approach was one of the shortcomings of the suffrage movement for many years and has, I believe, retarded the general advance of women. Working women, especially Negro women, labor not only under the disadvantages imposed by the feminine mystique, but under the more pressing disadvantages of economic discrimination. To leave them out of consideration of the problem or to ignore the contributions they can make toward its solution, is something we simply cannot afford to do. By their desperate need, by their numbers, by their organizational experience (if trade union members), working women are most important in reaching *institutional* solutions to the problems of women. It is my belief, that one of the most insidious results of the feminine mystique is that it led women to believe that their problems could be solved on the basis of the individual family. This is, in fact, a serious retrogression, for American women learned before the turn of the century that community solutions to their problems were more important and far-reaching than the best individual solutions. I have in mind, for a future program, not only the fine educational scheme you suggested, but a system of social reforms (daycare centers, maternity benefits, communized household services), which would bring our social services up to a standard already taken for granted in many European and Scandinavian countries.

AUDRE LORDE

Poetry Is Not a Luxury

<u>1977</u>

Audre Lorde (1934–1992) once asserted that literature's beauty had to serve the purpose of change, that "the question of social protest and art is inseparable." Her work involved "the transformation of silence into language and action," because the poet realized, "If I cannot air this pain and alter it, I will surely die of it." Poetry was not a luxury.

Lorde wanted people to *feel,* to realize that some parts of their lives didn't allow for love and joy, and then ask why this was so. This last question would lead to change. Her focus on feeling prompted the criticism that she confirmed the stereotype of emotional black women, at a time when black nationalists like Amiri Baraka were calling for gender separation. "We could never be equals," insisted Baraka in 1970; "Nature has not provided thus." Lorde countered these criticisms by insisting that rationality just moved people from place to place but that "if you don't honor those places, then the road is meaningless."

She wanted to be voice for the voiceless and "give name to the nameless," as she puts it in the essay reprinted here. "What I am writing is . . . about the lives of many voiceless people," she added later. She sought a feminist utopia in herself, where a plurality of identities (black, female, mother, lesbian) might coexist. Connecting the pieces of her self, she imagined a community. But while the black poet June Jordan and others sought community through an equation of gender with race, explaining that differences had the same meaning, Lorde acknowledged each difference as unique. Community didn't mean "a shedding of our differences," she emphasized. Instead she asked everyone to define themselves—or else they would be defined by others. In speaking for the voiceless, she tried to empower them to speak, and to replace division with self-definition.

The quality of light by which we scrutinize our lives has direct bearing upon the product which we live, and upon the changes which we hope to bring about through those lives. It is within this light that we form those ideas by which we pursue our magic and make it realized. This is poetry as illumination, for it is through poetry that we give name to those ideas which are—until the poem—nameless and formless, about to be birthed, but already felt. That distillation of experience from which true poetry springs births thought as dream births concept, as feeling births idea, as knowledge births (precedes) understanding.

As we learn to bear the intimacy of scrutiny and to flourish within it, as we learn to use the products of that scrutiny for power within our living, those fears which rule our lives and form our silences begin to lose their control over us.

For each of us as women, there is a dark place within, where hidden and growing our true spirit rises, "beautiful/and tough as chestnut/stanchions against (y)our nightmare of weakness/" and of impotence.

These places of possibility within ourselves are dark because they are ancient and hidden; they have survived and grown strong through that darkness. Within these deep places, each one of us holds an incredible reserve of creativity and power, of unexamined and unrecorded emotion and feeling. The woman's place of power within each of us is neither white nor surface; it is dark, it is ancient, and it is deep.

When we view living in the european mode only as a problem to be solved, we rely solely upon our ideas to make us free, for these were what the white fathers told us were precious.

But as we come more into touch with our own ancient, non-european consciousness of living as a situation to be experienced and interacted with, we learn more and more to cherish our feelings, and to respect those hidden sources of our power from where true knowledge and, therefore, lasting action comes.

At this point in time, I believe that women carry within ourselves the possibility for fusion of these two approaches so necessary for survival, and we come closest to this combination in our poetry. I speak here of poetry as a revelatory distillation of experience, not the sterile word play that, too often, the white fathers distorted the word *poetry* to mean—in order to cover a desperate wish for imagination without insight.

For women, then, poetry is not a luxury. It is a vital necessity of our existence. It forms the quality of the light within which we predicate our hopes and dreams toward survival and change, first made into language, then into idea, then into more tangible action. Poetry is the way we help give name to the nameless so it can be thought. The farthest horizons of our hopes and fears are cobbled by our poems, carved from the rock experiences of our daily lives.

As they become known to and accepted by us, our feelings and the honest exploration of them become sanctuaries and spawning grounds for the most radical and daring of ideas. They become a safe-house for that difference so necessary to change and the conceptualization of any meaningful action. Right now, I could name at least ten ideas I would have found intolerable or incomprehensible and frightening, except as they came after dreams and poems. This is not idle fantasy, but a disciplined attention to the true meaning of "it feels right to me." We can train ourselves to respect our feelings and to transpose them into a language so they can be shared. And where that language does not yet exist, it is our poetry which helps to fashion it. Poetry is not only dream and vision; it is the skeleton architecture of our lives. It lays the foundations for a future of change, a bridge across our fears of what has never been before.

Possibility is neither forever nor instant. It is not easy to sustain belief in its efficacy. We can sometimes work long and hard to establish one beachhead of real resistance to the deaths we are expected to live, only to have that beachhead assaulted or threatened by those canards we have been socialized to fear, or by the withdrawal of those approvals that we have been warned to seek for safety. Women see ourselves diminished or softened by the falsely benign accusations of childishness, of nonuniversality, of changeability, of sensuality. And who asks the question: Am I altering your aura, your ideas, your dreams, or am I merely moving you to temporary and reactive action? And even though the latter is no mean task, it is one that must be seen within the context of a need for true alteration of the very foundations of our lives.

The white fathers told us: I think, therefore I am. The Black mother within each of us—the poet—whispers in our dreams: I feel, therefore I can be free. Poetry coins the language to express and charter this revolutionary demand, the implementation of that freedom.

However, experience has taught us that action in the now is also necessary, always. Our children cannot dream unless they live, they cannot live unless they are nourished, and who else will feed them the real food without which their dreams will be no different from ours? "If you want us to change the world someday, we at least have to live long enough to grow up!" shouts the child.

Sometimes we drug ourselves with dreams of new ideas. The head will save us. The brain alone will set us free. But there are no new ideas still waiting in the wings to save us as women, as human. There are only old and forgotten ones, new combinations, extrapolations and recognitions from within ourselves—along with the renewed courage to try them out. And we must constantly encourage ourselves and each other to attempt the heretical actions that our dreams imply, and so many of our old ideas disparage. In the forefront of our move toward change, there is only poetry to hint at possibility made real. Our poems formulate the implications of ourselves, what we feel within and dare make real (or bring action into accordance with), our fears, our hopes, our most cherished terrors.

For within living structures defined by profit, by linear power, by institutional dehumanization, our feelings were not meant to survive. Kept around as unavoidable adjuncts or pleasant pastimes, feelings were expected to kneel to thought as women were expected to kneel to men. But women have survived. As poets. And there are no new pains. We have felt them all already. We have hidden that fact in the same place where we have hidden our power. They surface in our dreams, and it is our dreams that point the way to freedom. Those dreams are made realizable through our poems that give us the strength and courage to see, to feel, to speak, and to dare.

If what we need to dream, to move our spirits most deeply and directly toward and through promise, is discounted as a luxury, then we give up the core—the fountain—of our power, our womanness; we give up the future of our worlds.

For there are no new ideas. There are only new ways of making them felt—of examining what those ideas feel like being lived on Sunday morning at 7 A.M., after brunch, during wild love, making war, giving birth, mourning our dead—while we suffer the old longings, battle the old warnings and fears of being silent and impotent and alone, while we taste new possibilities and strengths.

The Female and the Silence of a Man

1989

June Jordan (1936–2002) believed that poetry was political action. "Poetry means taking control of the language of your life," she wrote in 1995. "Good poems can . . . build a revolution in which speaking and listening to somebody becomes the first and last purpose to every social encounter." Poetry was power, she added, but also trust. It required a trustworthy use of language, and could be the basis for a "democratic state in which the people can trust the names they have invented for themselves and for each other." Her sonnet printed here renamed the experience of W. B. Yeats's Leda, and directly addressed the question of trust.

Jordan, an African American bisexual activist, revises Yeats's 1924 sonnet "Leda and the Swan," turning his description of "loosening thighs," with its suggestion of consensual sex, into the unambiguously violent: "He tears the slender legs apart." Yeats's swan had held Leda "upon his breast," and Jordan's rapist now "lacerates her breasts." She replaces the swan's "white rush" with "the soft last bastion of her trust." This revisionist mythmaking offers alternative models of female identity. In other poems, Jordan entered into a dialogue with American history as well, writing on Phillis Wheatley, Sojourner Truth, and Fannie Lou Hamer.

Feminists have long seen Yeats's poem as a rape fantasy. They've noted that Leda is degraded, reduced to body parts, and subjected to a poetics of hate. But according to Yeats, his poem was inspired by the relationship between colonial Britain and violated Ireland. A peace activist since the Vietnam War, Jordan also wrote about imperialist violence and expanded on Yeats's metaphor of nation-rape in her "Poem about My Rights" (1980): "South Africa penetrating into Namibia . . . whether it's about the sanctity of my vagina or the sanctity of my national boundaries . . . I have been raped."

[cf. W. B. Yeats' "Leda and the Swan"]

And now she knows: The big fist shattering her face.
Above, the sky conceals the sadness of the moon.
And windows light, doors close, against all trace
of her: She falls into the violence of a woman's ruin.

How should she rise against the plunging of his lust?
She vomits out her teeth. He tears the slender legs apart.

The hairy torso of his rage destroys the soft last bastion
　　of her trust.
He lacerates her breasts. He claws and squeezes out her
　Heart.

She sinks into a meadow pond of lilies and a swan.
She floats above an afternoon of music from the trees.
She vanishes like blood that people walk upon.
She reappears: A mad *bitch* dog that reason cannot seize;
A fever withering the river and the crops:
A lovely girl protected by her cruel / incandescent energies.

From The Morning After

1993

Katie Roiphe (b. 1969) writes on the morning after feminism. In part, her book's title refers to her own postfeminism. Fashioning herself as an Alice at a mad women's-studies tea party, Roiphe claims that feminists have blown date rape out of proportion and created a "nonexistent" epidemic with false statistics. She observes that date rape is often just "bad sex" for which women refuse to take responsibility, and insists that focusing on "victimhood" makes women passive. The book, which was met with both outrage and celebration from reviewers, disparages protectionism and the ideology of Take Back the Night demonstrations and warns of a backlash: "Feminists . . . will conjure up the sexist beast if they push far enough."

Roiphe's feminism is one of several third-wave feminisms. In 1990, taking a different approach, Judith Butler called the moment "postfeminist" but embraced this as a chance to end the "binarism of sex." Feminists had constructed woman as a coherent subject, thereby reifying gender dynamics. Calling for a "variable construction of identity," Butler anticipated Leslie Feinberg's novel of transgender identity, *Stone Butch Blues* (1993). Another feminism has come from the grassroots. The Women's Health Action Mobilization was founded in 1989, inspired by the street protests of ACT UP, and the Third Wave Foundation was founded in 1993, combining local protests with political advocacy. Some grassroots organizations bridged the generation gap: the 1990s riot grrls groups used the techniques of 1970s consciousness-raising, and the third-wave publication *Feminista!* continued second-wave feminists' work against pornography.

Roiphe's book notwithstanding, marital rape became a crime in all states in 1993. In 1994, the Violence against Women Act included funding for services for victims of rape and violence. And in 1998, *The Vagina Monologues* put the topic of violence against women back in the spotlight. Second-waver Gloria Steinem described a journey of "truth telling" that women had been on for thirty years, whose destination was Eve Ensler's play. The monologues repeat the word "vagina" 128 times: "What a long and blessed way from a hushed 'down there,'" Steinem noted. But pro-sex feminists claimed Ensler's "sex-fearing feminism" set the movement back. Roiphe had protested rape-crisis feminism because it portrayed women as victims, and Ensler perhaps further essentialized female identity: the monologues call vaginas "our center . . . our motor," seemingly a throwback to the "down there" generation.

In an essay entitled "Nonviolent Sexual Coercion," psychologists Charlene Muelenhard and Jennifer Schrag include the remarks "He said he'd break up with me if I didn't," "He said I was frigid," and "He said everyone's doing it" in the category of verbal coercion. They go on to explain that "a woman with low self-esteem might feel that if she refuses her partner's sexual advances she will lose him, and her value will be lessened because she is no longer associated with him."[1] This is a portrait of the cowering woman, knocked on her back by the barest feather of peer pressure. Solidifying this image of women into policy implies an acceptance of the passive role. By protecting women against verbal coercion, these feminists are promoting the view of women as weak-willed, alabaster bodies, whose virtue must be protected from the cunning encroachments of the outside world. The idea that women can't withstand verbal or emotional pressure infantilizes them. The suggestion lurking beneath this definition of rape is that men are not just physically but intellectually and emotionally more powerful than women. Printing pamphlets about verbal coercion institutionalizes an unacceptable female position.

We should not nurture this woman on her back, her will so mutable, so easily shaped; we should not support her in her passivity. We are not this woman on her back. We do not have the mind of an eleven-year-old in the body of a twenty-year-old. All competent female college students are compromised by the association of gullibility, low self-esteem, and the inability to assert ourselves with our position in relation to men. We should not be pressured and intimidated by words like "I'll break up with you if you don't"—and anyone who is intimidated should be recognized as the exception, not the rule. Allowing verbal coercion to constitute rape is a sign of tolerance toward the ultra-feminine stance of passivity. The brand of "low self-esteem" these psychologists describe should not be tolerated, it should be changed. Whether or not we feel pressured, regardless of our level of self-esteem, the responsibility for our actions is still our own.

Imagine men sitting around in a circle talking about how she called him impotent and how she manipulated him into sex, how violated and dirty he felt afterward, how coercive she was, how she got him drunk first, how he hated his body and couldn't eat for three weeks afterward. Imagine him calling this rape. Everyone feels the weight of emotional pressure at one time or another. The question is not whether people pressure each other, but how that pressure is transformed in our mind and culture into full-blown assault. There would never be a rule or a law, or even a pamphlet or peer-counseling group, for men who claimed to have been emotionally raped or verbally pressured into sex. And for the same reasons—assumptions of basic competence, free will, and strength of character—there should be no such rules or groups or pamphlets for women.

A manners guide from 1848 warns young women about the perils of verbally coercive men:

> The more attractive his exterior, the more dangerous he is as a companion for a young and inexperienced girl, and the more likely to dazzle and bewilder her mind. . . . He can with a subtlety almost beyond the power of her detection, change her ordinary views of things, confuse her judgements, and destroy her rational confidence in discriminating the powers of her own mind.[2]

The fear of verbal coercion, then, does not have its origins in modern feminism. The idea that young girls will be swayed, their judgment overturned, their mind dazzled and bewildered, by the sheer force of masculine logic has been included in date-rape pamphlets for more than a century.

Any value there may be in promoting this idea about female passivity and gullibility is eclipsed by its negative effects. Feminist educators should keep track of the images they project: women can't take care of themselves, they can't make their own decisions with a clear head.

In discussing rape, campus feminists often slip into an outdated, sexist vocabulary. "Rape" is a dangerous word. As Susan Sontag has warned us about illness, we have to be careful of rape as metaphor. The sheer physical fact of rape has always been loaded with cultural meaning. Throughout history, women's bodies have been seen as property, as chaste objects, as virtuous vessels to be "dishonored," "ruined," "defiled." Their purity or lack of purity has been a measure of value for the men to whom they belonged.

Shakespeare's Lucrece is "spotted, spoiled, corrupted" after her rape.[3] The tragic dimensions of Lucrece's personal trauma have more to do with conceptions of honor, virtue, and chastity than her own visceral experience. Lucrece worries about the shadow the rape will cast on her husband's reputation. Shakespeare's Titus Andronicus kills his daughter after she has been raped. Her virtue was so important, so vital, that once she was ravished, her life was worth nothing. Rape-crisis feminists reproduce the idea that there is something vulnerable to be taken or lost, that there is something pure to be violated.

"Politically, I call it rape whenever a woman has sex and feels violated," writes Catharine MacKinnon.[4] The language of virtue and violation reinforces stereotypes. It backs women into old corners. Younger feminists share MacKinnon's vocabulary and the accompanying assumptions about women's bodies. In one student's account of date rape in the *Rag*, she talks about the anguish of being "defiled."[5] Another student writes of her feelings after being raped, "I long to be innocent again." With such anachronistic constructions of the female body, with all their assumptions about female purity, these young women frame their experience of rape in archaic, sexist terms.

Combating myths about rape is one of the central missions of the leaders of the rape-crisis movement. They spend money and energy trying to break down myths like "She asked for it." But with all their noise about rape myths, rape-crisis feminists are generating their own. If you look at the scenes described in the plays, the poems, the pamphlets, the Take Back the Night speak-outs, the stories told are loss-of-innocence stories. We all know this plot: I trusted him—I thought people were good—then I realized—afterward I knew. The rape, or sexual assault, is the moment of the fall. It is the isolated instant when, in one victim's words, they "learn to hate."

Take Back the Night marches are propelled by this myth of innocence lost. All the talk about empowering the voiceless dissolves into the image of the naive girl child who trusts the rakish man. This is a plot that reaches back centuries. It is the plot that propels Samuel Richardson's eighteenth-century epistolary novel *Clarissa*. After hundreds of pages chronicling the minute details of her plight, her seduction and resistance, her break from her family, Clarissa is raped by the duplicitous Robert Lovelace. Afterward she refuses to eat and fades toward a very virtuous, very religious death. Her coffin is finally returned to her father's house. More than a thousand pages are devoted to the story of her fall from innocence, a weighty event by eighteenth-century standards. But did these twentieth-century girls, raised on Madonna videos and the six o'clock news, really trust that people were good until they themselves were raped? Maybe. Were these girls, raised on horror movies and glossy Hollywood sex scenes, really as innocent as all that? Maybe. But maybe the myth of lost innocence is a trope—convenient, appealing, politically effective.

As long as we're taking back the night, we might as well take back our own purity. Sure, we were all kind of innocent, playing in the sandbox with bright red shovels, boys too. We can all look back through the tumultuous tunnel of adolescence on a honey-glazed childhood, with simple rules and early bed-times. (We don't have to look at parents fighting, at sibling struggles, at casting out one best friend for another in the Darwinian playground—this is not the innocence lost, this is the innocence we never had.)

The idea of a fall from childhood grace, pinned on one particular moment—a moment over which we had no control, much lamented—gives our lives a compelling narrative structure. It's easy to see why the seventeen-year-old likes it. It's easy to see why the rape-crisis feminists like it. It's a natural human impulse put to political purpose. But in generating and perpetuating these kinds of myths we should keep in mind that myths surrounding female innocence have been used to keep women inside and behind veils. They have been used to keep them out of work and in labor . . .

One day I was looking through my mother's bookshelves, and I found her old, battered copy of Germaine Greer's feminist classic, *The Female Eunuch*. The pages were dog-eared, and whole passages were marked with penciled notes. It was 1971 when Germaine Greer fanned the fires with *The Female Eunuch,* and it was 1971 when my mother read it, brand-new, explosive, a tough and sexy terrorism for the early stirrings of the feminist movement.

Today's rape-crisis feminists threaten to create their own version of the desexualized woman Greer complained of twenty years ago . . .

From Catharine MacKinnon to the protestors against the *Sports Illustrated* swimsuit issue to more mainstream theorists of sexual harassment, feminists are on the front lines of sexual regulation. Much of today's feminism in its most popular forms provides yet another source of repression, in the Freudian sense; feminism increasingly sides with "civilization," not its wild, edgy "discontents." Which is to say that feminism has come more and more to represent sexual thoughts and images censored, behavior checked, fantasies regulated. In my late-adolescent idiom, feminism was not about rebellion, but rules; it was not about setting loose, as it once was, it was about reining in.

As I looked out my window, at people in robes darting through the streets, grandmothers carrying flowers, I tried to picture the summer ahead. The plot came to me, strangely enough, in the voice of Susan Minot, Tama Janowitz, Jay McInerney, and others of their ilk: I move to a small walk-up in the East Village, with a bathtub in the kitchen. I get a job as a receptionist in a doctor's office and get picked up at a bar by a rich, older man who owns an art gallery and takes me to glamorous parties. He treats me like dirt. I stay with him, I don't know why. I curl up in bed at the end of the day. He calls, I go out with him again—what else is there to do?

The sound of the cars below broke my train of thought. I had caught myself in the middle of an unappealing fantasy of passivity: being carried along by fate, listening to the tarot cards, floating numb. What was I thinking? At the most uncharted moments in our lives we reach instinctively for the stock plots available to our generation, as trashy and clichéd as they may be. In the fifties it was love and marriage, or existentialism and Beat poetry in smoky bars. Now, if you're a woman, there's another role readily available: that of the sensitive female, pinched, leered at, assaulted daily by sexual advances, encroached upon, kept down, bruised by harsh reality. Among other things, feminism has given us this. A new stock plot, a new identity spinning not around love, not marriage, not communes, not materialism this time, but passivity and victimhood. This is not what I want, not even as a fantasy.

Notes

1. Charlene L. Muelenhard and Jennifer L. Schrag, "Nonviolent Sexual Coercion," in Andrea Parrot and Laurie Bechhofer, eds., *Acquaintance Rape: The Hidden Crime* (New York: John Wiley, 1991), 123.

2. T. S. Arthur, *Advice to Young Ladies* (Boston: Phillips and Sampson, 1848), 151.
3. William Shakespeare (ed. Maurice Evans), *The Narrative Poems* (London: Penguin, 1989), 142.
4. Catharine MacKinnon, *Feminism Unmodified* (Cambridge: Harvard University Press, 1987), 82.
5. *Rag,* May 1991.

Women Don't Riot

1998

"We really do have a lot more to concentrate on beside the pathology of white wimmin," insisted doris davenport in 1980. From the 1960s onwards, women of color protested the racist, ethnocentric, and classist assumptions of mainstream feminists. "Assimilation within a solely western-european herstory is not acceptable," warned Audre Lorde in 1979, and in 1981 Cherríe Moraga claimed that the "commitment to women in the feminist movement" had grown to be "exclusive and reactionary." Instead, Moraga and Gloria Anzaldúa formulated "Third World feminism." In 1979 they announced a women's retreat: "We want to express to all women . . . the experiences which divide us as feminists," they wrote; "we want to examine incidents of intolerance, prejudice, and denial of differences within the feminist movement." And in 1981 they called for a "broad-based U.S. women of color movement capable of spanning borders of nation and ethnicity."

Part of this movement, Ana Castillo (b. 1954) began to write protest literature in the late 1970s, calling herself a "Chicana protest poet." Chicana feminism emerged during the Chicano Movement of 1965–1975, when Mexican American activists sought to define their cultural and political identity. Disenfranchised within a movement that neglected gender, and ignored by white feminists, Chicanas protested their double oppression—Castillo observed that she was "demeaned, misunderstood, objectified, and excluded by the politics of those men with whom I had aligned myself on the basis of our mutual subjugation as Latinos in the United States."

Castillo focuses on the interconnected inequalities of race, class, gender, and sexuality as they affect women of Mexican descent in the United States, and in 1994 coined the term "Xicanisma," meaning a Chicana feminism that demonstrated an "ever present consciousness of our interdependence specifically rooted in our culture and history." It was a feminism "based on wholeness not dualisms," she said. "Men are not . . . our 'other.'" Castillo's poetry challenges the binaries of black-white, masculine-feminine, straight-gay, issuing what she calls in the poem reprinted here a "third-millennium call." Like many of her poems, it engages what Moraga calls "the real work of women of color feminism." This work, Moraga said in 2002, is to "become warriors of conscience and action who resist . . . poverty, cultural assimilation, child abuse, motherless mothering, gentrification, mental illness, welfare cuts, the prison system, racial profiling, immigrant and queer bashing, invasion and imperialism at home and at war." After the protest movements of civil rights, feminism, gay liberation, and Native American rights, Castillo continues to foreground the racism, sexism, and homophobia in American society, and to take back a denied history.

(For N.B.S.)

Women don't riot,
not in maquilas in Malaysia, Mexico, or Korea,
not in sweatshops in New York or El Paso.
They don't revolt
in kitchens, laundries, or nurseries.
Not by the hundreds or thousands, changing
sheets in hotels or in laundries
when scalded by hot water,
not in restaurants where they clean and clean
and clean their hands raw.

Women don't riot, not sober and earnest,
or high and strung out, not of any color,
any race, not the rich, poor,
or those in between. And mothers of all kinds
especially don't run rampant through the streets.

In college those who've thought it out
join hands in crucial times, carry signs,
are dragged away in protest.
We pass out petitions, organize a civilized vigil,
return to work the next day.

We women are sterilized, have more children
than they can feed,
don't speak the official language,
want things they see on TV,
would like to own a TV—
women who were molested as children
raped,
beaten,
harassed, which means
every last one sooner or later;
women who've defended themselves
and women who can't or don't know how
we don't—won't ever rise up in arms.

We don't storm through cities,
take over the press, make a unified statement,
once and for all: A third-millennium call—
from this day on no more, not me, not my daughter,
not her daughter either.

Women don't form a battalion, march arm in arm
across continents bound
by the same tongue, same food or lack thereof,
same God, same abandonment,
same broken heart,
raising children on our own, have
so much endless misery in common
that must stop
not for one woman or every woman,
but for the sake of us all.

Quietly, instead, one and each takes the offense,
rejection, bureaucratic dismissal, disease
that should not have been, insult,
shove, blow to the head,
a knife at her throat.
She won't fight, she won't even scream—
taught as she's been
to be brought down as if by surprise.
She'll die like an ant beneath a passing heel.
Today it was her. Next time who.

THE WORD
IS OUT

Gay
Liberation

From Howl

1956

"Stonewall didn't just happen," declared the Homosexuals Intransigent! president Craig Schoonmaker in 1979. "Gay Liberation rose at Stonewall from a launch pad created 20 years earlier by men of inspiring courage who dared, in the Fifties, to speak the unspeakable." Allen Ginsberg (1926–1997) was one of those men; his long poem "Howl," which rejects rigid form and restrictive content, shattered the stifling silence of the 1950s. He first unleashed "Howl" at a gathering in San Francisco, in October 1955. When Lawrence Ferlinghetti's press, City Lights, published the poem in 1956, Ferlinghetti was brought to trial on charges of obscenity. But after a widely publicized case, the judge ruled that "Howl" was not obscene, and the way was opened for more literature of homosexual love and sex.

Halfway through Ginsberg's first reading of "Howl" in 1955, his friend and fellow Beat writer Jack Kerouac began chanting "Go! Go!"—the poem was a communal, oral event, breaking down the dichotomies of oral/written and individual/community. "Howl," like Ginsberg's own fluid sexuality and persona, also broke down dichotomies of male/female, sacred/profane, madness/sanity, mystical/everyday. Ginsberg then bridged another divide, between the 1940s–1950s Beats and the 1960s radicals: he marched for civil rights, against the Vietnam war, and with the Black Panthers.

"Howl," with its long catalogues, revises Walt Whitman's euphoric lists in *Leaves of Grass* (1855), and one passage directly echoes it. Whitman had written, "I make holy whatever I touch or am touched from," and Ginsberg writes, "The tongue and cock and hand and asshole holy!" Whitman was more than a footnote in gay history, though summoned here in Ginsberg's "Footnote" to "Howl." Ginsberg later made the same observation of Whitman that activists made of Ginsberg: "Whitman opened up a lot of political space, simply by changing poetry from a very fixed and classical form, to an open form that anybody could participate in." He even claimed Whitman as a lover four times removed.

Other gay liberationists looked back to Whitman, claiming him as a prophet of gay rights, and his poems were read aloud at Gay Liberation Front meetings in the early 1970s. Whitman's promise, "I shall . . . filter and fibre your blood," was then resonant for AIDS protest writers: in Tony Kushner's play *Perestroika* (1991), the Angel echoes Whitman ("I stop down the road, waiting for you"), and in 1997 the activist Jack Nichols, who edited *GAY*, America's first gay weekly newspaper, from 1969 to 1973, observed, "I can hear him now, speaking in the midst of the AIDS crisis, he who once traversed bloody battlefields as a male nurse."

Further reading: Nicholas Edsall, *Toward Stonewall* (2003); Michael Schumacher, *Dharma Lion* (1994).

I saw the best minds of my generation destroyed by madness, starving hysterical naked,

dragging themselves through the negro streets at dawn looking for an angry fix,

angelheaded hipsters burning for the ancient heavenly connection to the starry dynamo in the machinery of night,

who poverty and tatters and hollow-eyed and high sat up smoking in the supernatural darkness of cold-water flats floating across the tops of cities contemplating jazz,

who bared their brains to Heaven under the El and saw Mohammedan angels staggering on tenement roofs illuminated,

who passed through universities with radiant cool eyes hallucinating Arkansas and Blake-light tragedy among the scholars of war,

who were expelled from the academies for crazy & publishing obscene odes on the windows of the skull,

who cowered in unshaven rooms in underwear, burning their money in wastebaskets and listening to the Terror through the wall,

who got busted in their pubic beards returning through Laredo with a belt of marijuana for New York,

who ate fire in paint hotels or drank turpentine in Paradise Alley, death, or purgatoried their torsos night after night

with dreams, with drugs, with waking nightmares, alcohol and cock and endless balls,

incomparable blind streets of shuddering cloud and lightning in the mind leaping toward poles of Canada & Paterson, illuminating all the motionless world of Time between . . .

. . . . .

who broke down crying in white gymnasiums naked and trembling before the machinery of other skeletons,

who bit detectives in the neck and shrieked with delight in policecars for committing no crime but their own wild cooking pederasty and intoxication,

who howled on their knees in the subway and were dragged off the roof waving genitals and manuscripts,

who let themselves be fucked in the ass by saintly motorcyclists, and screamed with joy,

who blew and were blown by those human seraphim, the sailors, ca-
resses of Atlantic and Caribbean love,
who balled in the morning in the evenings in rosegardens and the
grass of public parks and cemeteries scattering their semen freely to
whomever come who may . . .

Stonewall Documents

1969–1970

Allen Ginsberg stopped by Christopher Street two nights after the Stonewall riots and spoke to the activists there. "Gay power! Isn't that great!" he remarked. "It's about time we did something to assert ourselves." He told a journalist afterward, "the guys there were so beautiful—they've lost that wounded look that fags all had 10 years ago."

Stonewall was a spontaneous rebellion, not organized by any group in particular. On June 27, 1969, at around midnight, eight New York City police officers raided the Stonewall Inn, a gay bar on Christopher Street in Greenwich Village. They served a warrant for selling liquor without a license, and ordered patrons to leave. Black, white, and Latino drag queens threw bricks and bottles, and the Tactical Patrol Force arrived to help the police officers. A crowd outside swelled to more than 500. Over the next few days hundreds of gays and lesbians arrived in Sheridan Square. Several factors had come together: antiwar protestors and feminists were making themselves heard; the hippie movement advocated sexual liberation; and the civil rights movement provided a model of oppressed minorities fighting back. In 1970 the activist Leo Skir observed, "This time *our* time had come." It was, he said, "like the black woman who wouldn't give up her bus seat . . . we're not going back to the Closet, the back-of-the-bus." And, echoing Martin Luther King, Jr.'s "I Have a Dream" speech, Don Jackson announced in 1969: "I have a recurring daydream. I imagine a place where gay people can be free . . . freedom at last."

Homophile organizations had existed before Stonewall. But the Gay Liberation Front (GLF), which formed in the wake of the riots, was the most ambitious and radical gay rights group to date. Its members considered themselves to be to gay liberation what the Black Panthers were to black liberation, and also took inspiration from antiwar protestors. On Christmas Eve 1969, members of the New York GLF handed out a flyer in Sheridan Square: "Homosexual men and women have served willingly in every one of America's wars . . . we fought and bled and we died beside our straight brothers and sisters. [Yet we] are denied our birthright and are branded criminals for claiming the right to the self-determination of our own bodies." But the GLF meetings often featured heated arguments over the group's responsibility to other protest movements, and certain members' support of the antiwar effort and the Panthers forced a split. In December 1969, twelve New York members formed the Gay Activist Alliance, which was exclusively focused on gay liberation.

Further reading: Martin Duberman, *Stonewall* (1993); Jim Kepner, *Rough News* (1998).

Homophile Youth Movement Flier

GET THE MAFIA AND THE COPS OUT OF GAY BARS. The nights of Friday, June 27, 1969 and Saturday, June 28, 1969 will go down in history as the first time that thousands of Homosexual men and women went out into the streets to protest the intolerable situation which has existed in New York City for many years—namely, the Mafia (or syndicate) control of this city's Gay bars in collusion with certain elements in the Police Dept. of the City of New York. The demonstrations were triggered by a Police raid on the Stonewall Inn late Friday night, June 27th. The purported reason for the raid was the Stonewall's lack of a liquor license. Who's kidding whom here? Can anybody really believe that an operation as big as the Stonewall could continue for almost three years just a few blocks from the 6th Precinct house without having a liquor license? No! The Police have known about the Stonewall operation all along. What's happened is the presence of new "brass" in 6th Precinct which has vowed to "drive the fags out of the Village."

Many of you have noticed one of the signs which the "management" of the Stonewall has placed outside stating "Legalize Gay bars and lick the problem. Judge Kenneth Keating (a former US Senator) ruled in January, 1968 that even close dancing between Homosexuals is legal. Since that date there has been nothing legal, per se, about a Gay bar. What is illegal about New York City's Gay bars today is the Mafia (or syndicate) stranglehold on them. Legitimate Gay businessmen are afraid to open decent Gay bars with a healthy social atmosphere (as opposed to the hell-hole atmosphere of places typified by the Stonewall) because of fear of pressure from the unholy alliance of the Mafia and elements in the Police Dept. who accept payoffs and protect the Mafia monopoly.

We at the Homophile Youth Movement (HYMN) believe that the only way this monopoly can be broken is through the action of Homosexual men and women themselves. We obviously cannot rely on the various agencies of government who for years have known about this situation but who have refused to do anything about it.

Therefore we urge the following: 1) That Gay businessmen step forward and open Gay bars that will be run legally with competitive pricing and a healthy social atmosphere. 2) That Homosexual men and women boycott places like the Stonewall. The only way, it seems, that we can get the criminal elements out of gay bars is simply to make it unprofitable for them. 3) That the Homosexual citizens of New York City, and concerned Heterosexuals, write to Mayor Lindsay demanding a thorough investigation and effective action to correct this intolerable situation.

Gay Liberation Front Flier

DO YOU THINK HOMOSEXUALS ARE REVOLTING? YOU BET YOUR SWEET ASS WE ARE. We're going to make a place for ourselves in the revolutionary movement. We challenge the myths that are screwing up this society. MEETING: Thursday, July 24th, 6:30 PM at Alternate U, 69 West 14th Street at Sixth Avenue.

Mattachine Society Leaflet

HOMOSEXUALS ARE COMING TOGETHER AT LAST. To examine how we are oppressed and how we oppress ourselves. To fight for gay control of gay businesses. To publish our own newspaper. To these and other radical ends.

Student Homophile League Manifesto

A RADICAL MANIFESTO: THE HOMOPHILE MOVEMENT MUST BE RADICAL-IZED!

1) We see the persecution of homosexuality as part of a general attempt to oppress all minorities and keep them powerless. Our fate is linked with these minorities; if the detention camps are filled tomorrow with blacks, hippies and other radicals, we will not escape that fate, all our attempts to dissociate ourselves from them notwithstanding. A common struggle, however, will bring common triumph.

2) Therefore we declare our support as homosexuals or bisexuals for the struggles of the black, the feminist, the Spanish-American, the Indian, the Hippie, the Young, the Student, and other victims of oppression and prejudice.

3) We call upon these groups to lend us their support and encourage their presence with NACHO and the homophile movement at large.

4) Our enemies, an implacable, repressive governmental system; much of organized religion, business and medicine, will not be moved by appeasement or appeals to reason and justice, but only by power and force.

5) We regard established heterosexual standards of morality as immoral and refuse to condone them by demanding an equality which is merely the common yoke of sexual repression.

6) We declare that homosexuals, as individuals and members of the greater community, must develop homosexual ethics and esthetics independent of, and without reference to, the mores imposed upon heterosexuality.

7) We demand the removal of all restriction on sex between consenting persons of any sex, of any orientation, of any age, anywhere, whether for money or not, and for the removal of all censorship.

8) We call upon the churches to sanction homosexual liaisons when called upon to do so by the parties concerned.

9) We call upon the homophile movement to be more honestly concerned with youth rather than trying to promote a mythical, non-existent "good public image."

10) The homophile movement must totally reject the insane war in Viet Nam and refuse to encourage complicity in the war and support of the war machine, which may well be turned against us. We oppose any attempts by the movement to obtain security clearances for homosexuals, since these contribute to the war machine.

11) The homophile movement must engage in continuous political struggle on all fronts.

12) We must open the eyes of homosexuals on this continent to the increasingly repressive nature of our society and to the realizations that Chicago may await us tomorrow.

Statement and Editorial from *Come out!*

Gay Liberation Front is a revolutionary group of homosexual women and men formed with the realization that complete sexual liberation for all people cannot come about unless existing social institutions are abolished. We reject society's attempt to impose sexual roles and definitions of our nature. We are stepping outside these roles and simplistic myths. We are going to be who we are. At the same time, we are creating new social forms and relations, that is, relations based upon sisterhood, cooperation, human love and uninhibited sexuality. Babylon has forced us to commit ourselves to one thing . . . revolution.

Come out for freedom! Come out now! Power to the people! Gay power to the gay people! Come out of the closet before the door is nailed shut! COME OUT, a newspaper for the homosexual community, dedicates itself to the joy, the humor, and the dignity of the homosexual female and male. Come-out has COME OUT to fight for the freedom of the homosexual; to give voice to the rapidly growing militancy within our community; to provide a public forum for the discussion and clarification of methods and actions necessary to end our oppression. COME-OUT has COME OUT indeed for "life, liberty and the pursuit of happiness."

Make no mistake about our oppression: it is real, it is visible, it is demonstrable. In New York a homosexual is legitimate as an individual but illegitimate as a participant in a homosexual act. Hell, every homosexual and lesbian in this country survives solely by sufferance, not by law or even that cold state of grace known as tolerance. Our humanity is questioned, our choice of housing is circumscribed, our employment is tenuous, our friendly neighborhood tavern is a Mafioso-on-the-job training school for dum-dum hoods. It is just such grievances as these which have sparked the revolutionary movements of history.

Through mutual respect, action, and education COME OUT hopes to unify both the homosexual community and other oppressed groups into a cohesive body of people who do not find the enemy in each other.

We will not be gay bourgeoisie, searching for the sterile "American Dream" of the ivy-covered cottage and the good corporation job, but neither will we tolerate the exclusion of homosexuals from any area of American life.

Because our oppression is based on sex and the sex roles which oppress us from infancy, we must explore these roles and their meanings. We must recognize and make others recognize that being homosexual says only one thing: emotionally you prefer your own sex. It says nothing about your worth, your value as a human being. Does society make a place for us . . . as a man? A woman? A homosexual or lesbian? How does the family structure effect us? What is sex? What does it mean? What is love? As homosexuals, we are in a unique position to examine these questions from a fresh point of view. You'd better believe we are going to do so—that we are going to transform the society at large through the open realization of our own consciousness.

Item in *San Francisco Free Press*

IN THE STREETS FOR THE REVOLUTION. Nothing is more pathetic as a Black who denies his culture and tries to pass for white . . . unless it's one of our Gay brothers who denies his Gayness to get along in the straight plastic culture. Both have become less than men and sunk to the level of imitations. Luckily for the souls of Black folk they have awakened to their beauty and cultural integrity in time. Luckily, also, for the Blacks, racial differences make passing difficult. Unluckily for us passing is the easiest thing in the world. . . . We have had confrontations with all kinds of Auntie Toms who are comfortable living half lives as imitation men and sucking up to the Almighty Dollar to make up for the parts of their lives that are missing. We have seen the effect of years of oppression—poor, tired, sickly imitation men and women who would continue their own oppression and the oppression of their brothers and sisters. We've seen the society in which we live . . . We will build the new society in the streets, not by giving up on our brothers and sisters who have accepted their oppression, but by continuing to hammer at the chains that bind all of us. The new world will be built by new people who are in the open, free of chains; by proud men and women of all colors . . . by men and women who know love and live it. And it begins in the streets.

Editorial in *Homosexual Renaissance*

Homosexuals can effectively demand respect from others only if we first respect ourselves—*as* homosexuals. That requires that we admit to ourselves that we are homosexual . . . Say it! aloud: "I am homosexual." Shout it, whisper it. Laugh it, cry it. State it, proclaim it, confess it in sobs, but *say* it: "I am homosexual." Say it today, say it tomorrow, say it the day after that. Say it when you wake up, when you go to bed, when you find yourself thinking of someone of your own sex. Say it as often as you need to until you realize that it is true and that the fact that it is true forces you to adjust your attitudes and actions to make the very best of your life as a homosexual. "I am homosexual." Not "Leonardo da Vinci was homosexual," but "*I* am homosexual." Not "Gore Vidal is homosexual," but "*I* am homosexual." Not "one man of every six, one woman of every eight is homosexual," but "*I* am homosexual." Not even "some of the finest, most beautiful, and most talented people in the world are homosexual," but "*I* am homosexual."

Steve Kuromiya in *Philadelphia Free Press*

We came battle-scarred and angry to topple your sexist, racist, hateful society. We came to challenge the incredible hypocrisy of your serial monogamy, your oppressive sexual role-playing, your nuclear family, your Protestant ethic, apple pie and Mother. We came to New York holding hands and kissing, openly and proudly, waving 15-foot banners and chanting 'HO-HO-HOMOSEXUAL!' In one fell swoop, we came to destroy by our mere presence your labels and stereotypes with which you've oppressed us for centuries. And we came with love and open hearts to challenge your hate and secrecy.

From Refugees from Amerika:
A Gay Manifesto

<u>1969</u>

If the gay liberation movement began on the East Coast with the Stonewall riots, it began on the West Coast with the publication of "Refugees from Amerika." Carl Wittman (1943–1986) was an antiwar and civil rights activist, previously the national secretary of Students for a Democratic Society. His influential manifesto links the gay rights struggle to other protest movements and acknowledges the inspiration of civil rights activism. He examines the daily realities of gay childhood and adulthood and instructs gay people to end self-oppression and begin self-determination.

Written before Stonewall, though not published until later, "Refugees from Amerika" grew out of numerous discussions and meetings on gay rights. Wittman wrote it for gay people, to continue discussion, also hoping that straight people might read it and understand. He notes that San Francisco was a refugee camp, a self-protective ghetto that bred self-hatred and exploitation, and offers a vision of a free, self-governed territory. The idea of a free territory was as popular within the gay liberation movement as it was among black radicals: L. Craig Schoonmaker, the leader of Homosexuals Intransigent!, suggested migration to certain city neighborhoods and the takeover of election districts to create gay majorities; and the activist Don Jackson wanted to take over Alpine County, in California, and turn it into a "Stonewall Nation."

"Refugees from Amerika" quickly became a blueprint for gay activism, if not for a gay colony. It was taken up by the Gay Liberation Front, and one Marxist group, The Red Butterfly, responded to Wittman's manifesto by quoting Herbert Marcuse's *Eros and Civilization:* "Today the fight for Eros, the fight for life, is the political fight." The personal was now political. Wittman had painted the art of the possible. A line from Gwendolyn Brooks's poem "In Montgomery" (1971) aptly describes his manifesto's power: "To make a might of a movement you need a Resolution."

Further reading: John D'Emilio, *Sexual Politics* (1983); Jeffrey Escoffier, *American Homo* (1998).

San Francisco is a refugee camp for homosexuals. We have fled here from every part of the nation, and like refugees elsewhere, we came not because it is so great here, but because it was so bad there. By the tens of thousands, we fled small towns where to be ourselves would endanger our jobs and any hope of a decent life; we have fled from blackmailing cops, from families who disowned or 'tolerated' us; we have been drummed out of the armed services, thrown out of schools, fired from jobs, beaten by punks and policemen.

And we have formed a ghetto, out of self-protection. It is a ghetto rather than a free territory because it is still theirs. Straight cops patrol us, straight legislators govern us, straight employers keep us in line, straight money exploits us. We have pretended everything is OK, because we haven't been able to see how to change it—we've been afraid.

In the past year there has been an awakening of gay liberation ideas and energy. How it began we don't know; maybe we were inspired by black people and their freedom movement; we learned how to stop pretending from the hip revolution. Amerika in all its ugliness has surfaced with the war and our national leaders. And we are revulsed by the quality of our ghetto life.

Where once there was frustration, alienation, and cynicism, there are new characteristics among us. We are full of love for each other and are showing it; we are full of anger at what has been done to us. And as we recall all the self-censorship and repression for so many years, a reservoir of tears pours out of our eyes. And we are euphoric, high, with the initial flourish of a movement . . . Our group consciousness will evolve as we get ourselves together—we are only at the beginning.

I. On Orientation

1. WHAT HOMOSEXUALITY IS: Nature leaves undefined the object of sexual desire. The gender of that object is imposed socially. Humans originally made homosexuality taboo because they needed every bit of energy to produce and raise children: survival of species was a priority. With overpopulation and technological change, that taboo continued only to exploit us and enslave us.

As kids we refused to capitulate to demands that we ignore our feelings toward each other. Somewhere we found the strength to resist being indoctrinated, and we should count that among our assets. We have to realize that our loving each other is a good thing, not an unfortunate thing, and that we have a lot to teach straights about sex, love, strength, and resistance.

Homosexuality is *not* a lot of things. It is not a makeshift in the absence of the opposite sex; it is not a hatred or rejection of the opposite sex; it is not genetic; it is not the result of broken homes except inasmuch as we could see the sham of American marriage. *Homosexuality is the capacity to love someone of the same sex.*

2. BISEXUALITY: Bisexuality is good; it is the capacity to love people of either sex. The reason so few of us are bisexual is because society made such a big stink about homosexuality that we got forced into seeing ourselves as either

straight or non-straight. Also, many gays got turned off to the ways men are supposed to act with women and vice-versa, which is pretty fucked-up. Gays will begin to turn on to women when 1) it's something that we do because we want to, and not because we should, and 2) when women's liberation changes the nature of heterosexual relationships . . .

3. HETEROSEXUALITY: Exclusive heterosexuality is fucked up. It reflects a fear of people of the same sex, it's anti-homosexual, and it is fraught with frustration. Heterosexual sex is fucked up too; ask women's liberation about what straight guys are like in bed. Sex is aggression for the male chauvinist; sex is obligation for the traditional woman . . .

II. On Women

1. LESBIANISM: It's been a male-dominated society for too long, and that has warped both men and women. So gay women are going to see things differently from gay men; they are going to feel put down as women, too. Their liberation is tied up with both gay liberation and women's liberation . . .

2. MALE CHAUVINISM: All men are infected with male chauvinism—we were brought up that way. It means we assume that women play subordinate roles and are less human than ourselves. (At an early gay liberation meeting one guy said, "Why don't we invite women's liberation—they can bring sandwiches and coffee.") It is no wonder that so few gay women have become active in our groups.

Male chauvinism, however, is not central to us. We can junk it much more easily than straight men can. For we understand oppression. We have largely opted out of a system which oppresses women daily—our egos are not built on putting women down and having them build us up. Also, living in a mostly male world we have become used to playing different roles, doing our own shit-work. And finally, we have a common enemy: the big male chauvinists are also the big anti-gays.

But we need to purge male chauvinism, both in behavior and in thought among us. Chick equals nigger equals queer. Think it over.

3. WOMEN'S LIBERATION: They are assuming their equality and dignity and in doing so are challenging the same things we are: the roles, the exploitation of minorities by capitalism, the arrogant smugness of straight white male middle-class Amerika. They are our sisters in struggle . . . We must come to know and understand each other's style, jargon and humor.

III. On Roles

1. MIMICRY OF STRAIGHT SOCIETY: We are children of straight society. We still think straight: that is part of our oppression. One of the worst of straight

concepts is inequality. Straight (also white, English, male, capitalist) thinking views things in terms of order and comparison. A is before B, B is after A; one is below two is below three; there is no room for equality. This idea gets extended to male/female, on top/on bottom, spouse/not spouse, heterosexual/homo-sexual, boss/worker, white/black and rich/poor. Our social institutions cause and reflect this verbal hierarchy. This is Amerika.

We've lived in these institutions all our lives. Naturally we mimic the roles. For too long we mimicked these roles to protect ourselves—a survival mecha-nism. Now we are becoming free enough to shed the roles which we've picked up from the institutions which have imprisoned us. *"Stop mimicking straights, stop censoring ourselves."*

2. MARRIAGE: Marriage is a prime example of a straight institution fraught with role playing. Traditional marriage is a rotten, oppressive institu-tion . . . Gay people must stop gauging their self-respect by how well they mimic straight marriages . . . To accept that happiness comes through find-ing a groovy spouse and settling down, showing the world that "we're just the same as you" is avoiding the real issues, and is an expression of self-hatred.

3. ALTERNATIVES TO MARRIAGE: People want to get married for lots of good reasons, although marriage won't often meet those needs or desires. We're all looking for security, a flow of love, and a feeling of belonging and be-ing needed.

These needs can be met through a number of social relationships and living situations. Things we want to get away from are: 1. exclusiveness, propertied attitudes toward each other, a mutual pact against the rest of the world; 2. promises about the future, which we have no right to make and which prevent us from, or make us feel guilty about, growing; 3. inflexible roles, roles which do not reflect us at the moment but are inherited through mimicry and inabil-ity to define equalitarian relationships.

We have to define for ourselves a new pluralistic, role-free social structure for ourselves . . .

4. GAY 'STEREOTYPES': The straight's image of the gay world is defined largely by those of us who have violated straight roles. There is a tendency among 'homophile' groups to deplore gays who play visible roles—the queens and the nellies. As liberated gays, we must take a clear stand. 1) Gays who stand out have become our first martyrs. They came out and withstood disap-proval before the rest of us did. 2) If they have suffered from being open, it is straight society whom we must indict, not the queen.

5. CLOSET QUEENS: This phrase is becoming analogous to 'Uncle Tom.' To pretend to be straight sexually, or to pretend to be straight socially, is probably the most harmful pattern of behavior in the ghetto . . . If we are liberated we are open with our sexuality. Closet queenery must end. *Come out* . . .

IV. On Oppression

. . . A lot of 'movement' types come on with a line of shit about homosexuals not being oppressed as much as blacks or Vietnamese or workers or women. We don't happen to fit into their ideas of class or caste. Bull! When people feel oppressed, they act on that feeling. We feel oppressed. Talk about the priority of black liberation or ending imperialism over and above gay liberation is just anti-gay propaganda.

1. PHYSICAL ATTACKS: We are attacked, beaten, castrated and left dead time and time again. There are half a dozen known unsolved slayings in San Francisco parks in the last few years. "Punks," often of minority groups who look around for someone under them socially, feel encouraged to beat up on "queens" and cops look the other way. That used to be called lynching . . .

2. PSYCHOLOGICAL WARFARE: Right from the beginning we have been subjected to a barrage of straight propaganda. Since our parents don't know any homosexuals, we grow up thinking that we are alone and different and perverted. Our school friends identify 'queer' with any non-conformist or bad behavior. Our elementary school teachers tell us not to talk to strangers or accept rides. Television, billboards and magazines put forth a false idealization of male/female relationships, and make us wish we were different, wish we were 'in.' In family living class we're taught how we're supposed to turn out. And all along, the best we hear if anything about homosexuality is that it's an unfortunate problem.

3. SELF-OPPRESSION: As gay liberation grows, we will find our uptight brothers and sisters, particularly those who are making a buck off our ghetto, coming on strong to defend the status quo. This is self oppression: 'don't rock the boat'; 'things in SF are OK'; 'gay people just aren't together'; 'I'm not oppressed.' These lines are right out of the mouths of the straight establishment. A large part of our oppression would end if we would stop putting ourselves and our pride down.

4. INSTITUTIONAL: Discrimination against gays is blatant, if we open our eyes. Homosexual relationships are illegal, and even if these laws are not regularly enforced, they encourage and enforce closet queenery. The bulk of the social work psychiatric field looks upon homosexuality as a problem, and treats us as sick. Employers let it be known that our skills are acceptable as long as our sexuality is hidden. Big business and government are particularly notorious offenders.

The discrimination in the draft and armed services is a pillar of the general attitude towards gays . . . Hell, no, we won't go, of course not, but we can't let the army fuck us over this way, either.

V. On Sex

. . . I like to think of good sex in terms of playing the violin: with both people on one level seeing the other body as an object capable of creating beauty when they play it well; and on a second level the players communicating through their mutual production and appreciation of beauty. As in good music, you get totally into it—and coming back out of that state of consciousness is like finishing a work of art or coming back from an episode of an acid or mescaline trip. And to press the analogy further: the variety of music is infinite and varied, depending on the capabilities of the players, both as subjects and as objects. Solos, duets, quartets (symphonies, even, if you happen to dig Romantic music!) are possible. The variations in gender, response, and bodies are like different instruments. And perhaps what we have called sexual 'orientation' probably just means that we have not yet learned to turn on to the total range of musical expression . . .

VI. On Our Ghetto

We are refugees from Amerika. So we came to the ghetto—and as other ghettos, it has its negative and positive aspects. Refugee camps are better than what preceded them, or people never would have come. But they are still enslaving, if only that we are limited to being ourselves there and only there.

Ghettos breed self-hatred. We stagnate here, accepting the status quo. The status quo is rotten. We are all warped by our oppression, and in the isolation of the ghetto we blame ourselves rather than our oppressors . . . Our ghetto certainly is more beautiful and larger and more diverse than most ghettos, and is certainly freer than the rest of Amerika. That's why we're here. But it isn't ours. Capitalists make money off of us, cops patrol us, government tolerates us as long as we shut up, and daily we work for and pay taxes to those who oppress us.

To be a free territory, we must govern ourselves, set up our own institutions, defend ourselves, and use our own energies to improve our lives. The emergence of gay liberation communes, and our own paper is a good start. The talk about gay liberation coffee shop/dance hall should be acted upon. Rural retreats, political action offices, food cooperatives, a free school, unalienating bars and after hours places—they must be developed if we are to have even the shadow of a free territory.

VII. On Coalition

. . . face it: we can't change Amerika alone: Who do we look to for collaboration?

1. WOMEN'S LIBERATION: summarizing earlier statements, 1) they are our closest ally; we must try hard to get together with them. 2) a lesbian caucus is probably the best way to attack gay guys' male chauvinism, and challenge the straightness of women's liberation; 3) as males we must be sensitive to their developing identities as women, and respect that; if we know what *our* freedom is about, *they* certainly know what's best for *them.*

2. BLACK LIBERATION: This is tenuous right now because of the uptightness and supermasculinity of many black men (which is understandable). Despite that, we must support their movement, particularly when they are under attack from the establishment; we must show them that we mean business; and we must figure out which our common enemies are: police, city hall, capitalism.

3. CHICANOS: Basically the same problem as with blacks: trying to overcome mutual animosity and fear, and finding ways to support them. The extra problem of super up-tightness and machismo among Latin cultures, and the traditional pattern of Mexicans beating up "queers" can be overcome: we're both oppressed, and by the same people at the top.

4. WHITE RADICALS AND IDEOLOGUES: We can look forward to coalition and mutual support with radical groups if they are able to transcend their anti-gay and male chauvinist patterns. We support radical and militant demands when they arise, e.g. Moratorium, People's Park; but only as a group; we can't compromise or soft-peddle our gay identity . . .

5. HIP AND STREET-PEOPLE: A major dynamic of rising gay lib sentiment is the hip revolution within the gay community. Emphasis on love, dropping out, being honest, expressing yourself through hair and clothes, and smoking dope are all attributes of this. The gays who are the least vulnerable to attack by the establishment have been the freest to express themselves on gay liberation . . .

6. HOMOPHILE GROUPS: 1) reformist or pokey as they sometimes are, they are our brothers. They'll grow as we have grown and grow. Do not attack them in straight or mixed company. 2) ignore their attack on us. 3) cooperate where cooperation is possible without essential compromise of our identity.

Conclusion: An Outline of Imperatives for Gay Liberation

1. Free ourselves: come out everywhere; initiate self defense and political activity; initiate counter community institutions.

2. Turn other gay people on: talk all the time; understand, forgive, accept.

3. Free the homosexual in everyone: we'll be getting a good bit of shit from threatened latents: be gentle, and keep talking & acting free.

4. We've been playing an act for a long time, so we're consummate actors. Now we can begin *to be,* and it'll be a good show!

The Women's Liberation
and Gay Liberation Movements

1970

"We saw the maleness . . . pushing us to walls" writes the African American poet Gwendolyn Brooks in "Malcolm X" (1968). Brooks's description of uber-masculinity typified representations of both Malcolm and the Black Panther Party (BPP)—termed supermasculine by Carl Wittman in his manifesto "Refugees from Amerika" (1970). Some called the BPP a cult of black masculinity and black power an assertion of patriarchy. The lesbian poet Audre Lorde later observed: "The existence of Black lesbian and gay people was not even allowed to cross the public consciousness of Black America."

In the early 1970s, the Gay Liberation Front (GLF) was keen to align itself with revolutionary movements. It confronted in some black liberationists a racial machismo that had mutated into a homophobic hostility to coalition. Journalists for GAY, America's first gay weekly newspaper, protested H. Rap Brown's use of the word "faggot" and Eldridge Cleaver's statement that "Homosexuality is a sickness." But GLF members persisted with coalition building. Some spoke in support of the Panther 21 in May 1970, Jim Fouratt telling the crowd, "We call upon every radical here today to Off the word faggot . . . there will only be a revolution when all oppressed people work together." In August 1970, the BPP leader Huey Newton (1942–1989) announced in the letter reprinted here that he was willing to work with the gay liberation and women's movements toward common revolutionary goals. He invited GLF members to attend the BPP's Revolutionary People's Constitutional Convention of September 1970.

The GLF and the Gay Activist Alliance went on to form affiliated groups for African Americans. Lesbians were prominent in the black feminist group Combahee River Collective, which described in 1977 the "interlocking" system of "racial, sexual, heterosexual, and class oppression." The National Coalition of Black Gays was founded in 1978, and the first Black Lesbian and Gay Pride March took place in 1991. Black gay activists still take inspiration from Newton's letter as well as from James Baldwin's 1985 statement: "We are all androgynous . . . each of us, helplessly and forever, contains the other—male in female, female in male, white in black and black in white. We are a part of each other."

Further reading: Keith Boykin, *One More River* (1996); bell hooks, *We real cool* (2004).

During the past few years strong movements have developed among women and among homosexuals seeking their liberation. There has been some uncertainty about how to relate to these movements.

Whatever your personal opinions and your insecurities about homosexuality and the various liberation movements among homosexuals and women (and I speak of the homosexuals and women as oppressed groups), we should try to unite with them in a revolutionary fashion. I say "whatever your insecurities are" because as we very well know, sometimes our first instinct is to want to hit a homosexual in the mouth, and want a woman to be quiet. We want to hit a homosexual in the mouth because we are afraid that we might be homosexual; and we want to hit the women or shut her up because we are afraid that she might castrate us, or take the nuts that we might not have to start with.

We must gain security in ourselves and therefore have respect and feelings for all oppressed people. We must not use the racist attitude that the White racists use against our people because they are Black and poor. Many times the poorest White person is the most racist because he is afraid that he might lose something, or discover something that he does not have. So you're some kind of a threat to him. This kind of psychology is in operation when we view oppressed people and we are angry with them because of their particular kind of behavior, or their particular kind of deviation from the established norm.

Remember, we have not established a revolutionary value system; we are only in the process of establishing it. I do not remember our ever constituting any value that said that a revolutionary must say offensive things towards homosexuals, or that a revolutionary should make sure that women do not speak out about their own particular kind of oppression. As a matter of fact, it is just the opposite: we say that we recognize the women's right to be free. We have not said much about the homosexual at all, but we must relate to the homosexual movement because it is a real thing. And I know through reading, and through my life experience and observations that homosexuals are not given freedom and liberty by anyone in the society. They might be the most oppressed people in the society. And what made them homosexual? Perhaps it's a phenomenon that I don't understand entirely. Some people say that it is the decadence of capitalism. I don't know if that is the case; I rather doubt it. But whatever the case is, we know that homosexuality is a fact that exists, and we must understand it in its purest form: that is, a person should have the freedom to use his body in whatever way he wants.

That is not endorsing things in homosexuality that we wouldn't view as revolutionary. But there is nothing to say that a homosexual cannot also be a revolutionary. And maybe I'm now injecting some of my prejudice by saying that "even a homosexual can be a revolutionary." Quite the contrary, maybe a homosexual could be the most revolutionary. When we have revolutionary conferences, rallies, and demonstrations, there should be full participation of the gay liberation movement and the women's liberation movement. Some groups might be more revolutionary than others. We should not use the actions of a few to say that they are all reactionary or counterrevolutionary, because they are not. We should deal with the factions just as we deal with any other group or party that claims to be revolutionary. We should try to judge, somehow, whether they are operating in a sincere revolutionary fashion and from a really oppressed situation. (And we will grant that if they are women they are probably oppressed.) If they do things that are unrevolutionary or counterrevolutionary, then criticize that action. If we feel that the group in spirit means to be revolutionary in practice, but they make mistakes in interpretation of the revolutionary philosophy, or they do not understand the dialectics of the social forces in operation, we should criticize that and not criticize them because they are women trying to be free. And the same is true for homosexuals. We should never say a whole movement is dishonest when in fact they are trying to be honest. They are just making honest mistakes. Friends are allowed to make mistakes. The enemy is not allowed to make mistakes because his whole existence is a mistake, and we suffer from it. But the women's liberation front and gay liberation front are our friends, they are our potential allies, and we need as many allies as possible.

We should be willing to discuss the insecurities that many people have about homosexuality. When I say "insecurities," I mean the fear that they are some kind of threat to our manhood. I can understand this fear. Because of the long conditioning process which builds insecurity in the American male, homosexuality might produce certain hang-ups in us. I have hang-ups myself about male homosexuality. But on the other hand, I have no hang-up about female homosexuality. And that is a phenomenon in itself. I think it is probably because male homosexuality is a threat to me and female homosexuality is not. We should be careful about using those terms that might turn our friends off. The terms "faggot" and "punk" should be deleted from our vocabulary, and especially we should not attach names normally designed for homosexuals to men who are enemies of the people, such as Nixon or Mitchell. Homosexuals are not enemies of the people.

We should try to form a working coalition with the gay liberation and women's liberation groups. We must always handle social forces in the most appropriate manner. And this is really a significant part of the population, both women, and the growing number of homosexuals, that we have to deal with.

ALL POWER TO THE PEOPLE!

From Street Theater

1982

"I cover my political points ironically," said Doric Wilson (b. 1939) in a recent interview; "I bury them in sugar or wickedness." The end result is an audience "laughing and being indoctrinated without knowing it, laughing and agreeing." Wilson's satirical approach means he has avoided writing about AIDS, even when AIDS plays became a main sub-genre of gay theater in the 1980s; empathy and shock value were better approaches than humor to the topic of AIDS, he thought.

Wilson, who in 1974 cofounded "The Other Side of Silence," the first professional the-ater company in New York City to deal openly with the gay experience, is cautious about the very term "gay theater." Though he is put in that tradition, he insists that it's a "political-technical term." The fact that a play has a gay character doesn't make it gay theater, he says—rather, gay theater specifically "calls attention to the fact that this is the-ater ignored in the mainstream."

Street Theater explores pre-Stonewall drag culture and gay street life. The layered iden-tities of its characters critique the reduction of gay identity to a set of stereotypes: Sey-mour is an actor playing a gay man playing a straight police officer playing a hippy, and Wilson describes the play's "panorama of drags, dykes, leathermen, flower children, vice cops and cruisers" as a Whitmanesque "army of lovers." It's a vision of unity across differ-ence; collapsing the barrier between cast and audience, characters address the audience members directly. Wilson observes, "At the end of *Street Theater,* the audience wants to get up and riot . . . get up and join the people on stage." In some performances, audi-ence members have joined the cast on stage for the play's last scene, which is reprinted here. Wilson's solution to the problem of homophobia is united resistance.

Wilson sorts protest literature into three camps. One kind fails, like Euripides's *Trojan Women* (415 BC): "It's probably one of the greatest statements about war ever written. The Athenians were terribly moved by it," he says. "Nevertheless, they went off to war and lost." There's another kind that succeeds—Wilson cites Harriet Beecher Stowe's *Uncle Tom's Cabin* (1852): "It helped activate the abolitionist movement. The fact that melodra-mas were made of it is proof of its success." The third kind fails *and* succeeds; here Wilson points to Tony Kushner's *Angels in America* (1990, 1991). As for his own protest literature, Wilson doesn't think it has ever prompted rebellion, but rather has reenforced existing re-bellion. He writes because he can't "accept the status quo," though never as a political mouthpiece: "my muse would sit in a corner and continue to sleep until the last spring she had." A participant in the Stonewall riots, he also writes to insist upon historical re-sponsibility: even his characters "only find resolution when they begin to understand that." Believing that America has no interest in the past and sensing history slipping by, Wilson wrote *Street Theater* as a record of Stonewall—what he calls "a D-day in gay history."

Further reading: Stephen Bottoms, *Playing Underground* (2004); John Clum, *Acting Gay* (1992).

Stonewall 1969. In two acts.

Characters: Murfino, a thug. Jack, heavy leather, keys left, C.B., a politically incorrect lesbian, Heather, a flower child, Seymour, a vice cop, Ceil, a street queen, Donovan, apparently a pedestrian, Sidney, in the closet, Boom Boom, a street queen, Timothy, new in town, Michael, in analysis, Donald, noncommittal, Jordan, a student radical, Gordon, a new-left liberal
Time: the present (and then late evening, the 27th of June, 1969)
Scene: a performance space (and then Christopher Street)

from Act One

C.B.: We all know who's behind the raids.
Boom Boom: Fanny Spellman?
Jack: She's too busy waging her war in Vietnam—
Ceil: —to worry her beads over us.
Boom Boom: It's the real estate interests.
C.B.: They want to clear us queers out of the Village—
Jack: —to make way for the hetero high-rises.
Ceil: Whoever's behind it—
Boom Boom: —they can't keep shoving it to us.
Jack: Who's gonna stop them?
C.B.: We could.
Ceil: "We" who?
Boom Boom: Us.
C.B.: There's enough of us.
Boom Boom: If we all band together—
Ceil: Together?
Jack: You can't find two faggots who agree on the recipe for cheese fondue.
Boom Boom: Wouldn't it be beautiful?
C.B.: An army of lovers.
Ceil: I can already hear the bitching.

from Act Two

C.B.: (Standing firm.) This street belongs to us.
   (The chant stops.)
Donovan: (Nightstick at ready.) Yeah?
Ceil: (Joining C.B.) Us and our friends.
Seymour: (Nightstick at ready.) Says who?
Boom Boom: (Joining C.B. & Ceil.) Says me.
Jack: (Joining C.B., Ceil & Boom Boom.) And me.
Timothy: (Joining C.B., Ceil, Boom Boom & Jack.) Me, too.
Jordan: (Joining C.B., Ceil, Boom Boom, Jack & Timothy.) That includes—
Gordon: (Joining C.B., Ceil, Boom Boom, Jack & Timothy.)—us.
Heather: (Joining the gathering crowd.) Look who's united!
Murfino: (Taking refuge behind the cops, clutching the Stonewall sign like a
   security blanket.) We don't want no trouble on this street.
Ceil: (To Donald, beginning a new chant, the tone of which is welcoming and
   slightly giddy with new found potency.) Join us.
Donald: (Taking refuge behind the cops.) You're only making it harder on the
   rest of us!
Boom Boom: (To Michael, taking up the chant.) Join us.
Michael: (Taking refuge behind the cops.) You're an impediment to my rapid
   recovery.
Jack: (To Donald, taking up the chant.) Join us.
Donald: Sick . . . and sad . . . and . . . and . . .
Jack: Pathetic?
C.B.: (To Sidney, taking up the chant.) Join us.
Sidney: (Struggling his way through the crowd.) You don't understand—
Timothy & Heather: (To Sidney, taking up the chant.) Join us.
Seymour: (To Sidney.) Don't listen to them.
Jordan & Gordon: (To Sidney, taking up the chant.) Join us.
Sidney: —I'd be risking everything.
Jack: (To Sidney, taking up the chant.) Join us.
Sidney: (Caught in the middle between the cops and the crowd.) I have a pro-
   fessional career—
Boom Boom: (To Sidney, taking up the chant.) Join us.
Sidney: (To Timothy, trying to justify.)—elderly parents.
Ceil: Believe me, Miss Thing, you ain't got nothing left to lose.
Jack leading the others: (To Seymour.) Out of the closets—
Seymour: (To Jack.) You aren't proving anything.
Jack leading the others: (To Seymour.)—into the streets.
Seymour: No!

Jack leading the others: (To Seymour.) Out of the closets—

Seymour: Never!!

Jack leading the others: (To Seymour.)—into the streets.

Seymour: No way!!!

Jack leading the others: (To Seymour.) Out of the closets—

Seymour: (Swinging his nightstick at Jack with the full fury of self-hate.) You faggots are revolting!!!!*

   (Reacting without thinking, Sidney grabs the nightstick from Seymour. With horror he realizes what he has done and almost immediately his fear transforms to exhilaration.)

Sidney: (Brandishing the nightstick at Seymour with joy and pride.) You bet your sweet ass we are!*

   (Flashing red lights illuminate a grouping worthy of a statue in Sheridan Square. Blackout.)

---

* Graffiti from the front of the Stonewall Inn, the morning of June 28th, 1969.

Read My Lips

Still/Here

1988, 1994

President Reagan didn't speak publicly about the AIDS crisis until October 1987. By this point, 59,572 AIDS cases had been reported. In response to this silence, a group of gay men in New York began the SILENCE = DEATH Project in 1985. Their posters instructed: "Turn anger, fear, grief into action." In 1987 some 300 people—including members of the SILENCE = DEATH Project, the Lavender Hill Mob, and the Lesbian and Gay Antidefamation League—founded the New York chapter of the AIDS Coalition to Unleash Power, or ACT UP. By 1990, ACT UP had more than 100 chapters worldwide.

Many ACT UP members had a background in theater, and the group's demonstrations were often a form of street theater. In June 1987 they sponsored a concentration camp float in the Gay Pride March in Washington, consisting of protestors in a wire cage accompanied by more protestors in military costume. Explaining that theatrical protest was a form of civil disobedience, ACT UP produced a "Civil Disobedience Manual" in 1988 that referred to a long tradition of civil disobedience—Henry David Thoreau, suffragist protest, the Montgomery bus boycott, and Vietnam draft resistance. It quoted Frederick

Douglass: "Power concedes nothing without a demand." Many members came from the art world too, and used art to confront demoralizing media images of people with AIDS, often borrowing from advertising techniques. One of ACT UP's most famous icons was the pink triangle assigned to gay men by the Nazis, but now turned upside down. ACT UP also returned to the 1940s for the "Read My Lips" poster, held by a protester in the postcard image reproduced here. It borrows from George Bush's promise made during the Republican primaries, "Read my lips: no new taxes." Like the inverted triangle, it is a form of appropriation art.

ACT UP distributed medical information about new drugs and worked with the Food and Drug Administration (FDA) to create a fast track for HIV drugs. The activist Larry Kramer warned: "If we do not get these drugs, you will see an uprising the likes of which you have never seen since the Vietnam War." In April 1992, the FDA proposed an accelerated approval program, and in 1997 Congress codified it. But drugs remained expensive, and as ACT UP's activism slowed down, the group was accused of not fighting for working-class AIDS victims.

ACT UP's images are part of an AIDS protest movement that also encompasses visual art and performance, like the 1994 dance piece "Still/Here." In the wake of his partner's death from AIDS in 1988, the African American dancer and choreographer Bill T. Jones (b. 1952) traveled the country for two years, conducting "Survival Workshops" with terminally ill people. He asked participants to express themselves in one gesture. In the final piece, dancers recite these participants' names and the explanations they had given for their movements, and then perform their gestures. "Still/Here" made the untouchable body erotic, and offered protest voices when silence equaled death.

From Angels in America

1990, 1991

Tony Kushner (b. 1956) claims an aversion to artists who confuse their work with activism. He explained in a recent interview that he can't write with the intention of preaching, or with an idea that his art is protest. Instead he leaves this to others—"to use my plays as they will." But he does believe that audiences have a hunger for political discussion, and wants his plays to be "of use to progressive people." The playwright is a political provocateur and should believe that art can start revolutions because all theater is political, says Kushner, whose play *Angels in America* challenges the public discourse that aimed a rhetoric of blame at gay men during the early days of the AIDS crisis. The play also confronts Reaganomics, global warming, the end of idealism, and the death of God.

Kushner believes that playwriting is impossible without hope, but insists that his work is not a fortune cookie. He embraces the inherent uncertainties of theater and tries to insert doubt, mediating between order and chaos, risk and responsibility. He protests moral oppositions and tries to make his audiences feel vulnerable, to acknowledge suffering, and to see the world differently. Combining formal realism and fantasy, his plays challenge what he calls the "illusion-reality paradigm." Capitalist politics tries to hide the wires, "the human labor that produced the effect," but "what's great about theatre is that it never can do that successfully . . . [You're] saying, 'It's an angel! I'm seeing an angel!' Then you're saying, 'It's a woman in a silly wig and fly wires,' and that doubleness is the kind of consciousness that citizens of capitalism need to survive, and are constantly being winnowed away from." He also uses humor to unsettle audience expectation: in his plays, terror and comedy, the tragic and the ludicrous, are never far apart.

Kushner sees theater as ritual and discipline, like religion, noting that "certain forms of ritual practice can transform one's consciousness through gesture and through design and through ritual." But after transformation must come action. In spite of the angels in his play, Kushner believes that we must solve the problems on earth ourselves—perhaps even force a rapture: "How else should an angel land on earth but with the utmost difficulty?" he wrote in 1992. "If we are to be visited by angels we will have to call them down with sweat and strain."

Millennium Approaches, Act III, Scene 2

The next day. Split scene: Louis and Belize in a coffee shop. Prior is at the outpatient clinic at the hospital with Emily, the nurse; she has him on a pentamidine IV drip.

Louis: Why has democracy succeeded in America? Of course by succeeded I
mean comparatively, not literally, not in the present, but what makes for
the prospect of some sort of radical democracy spreading outward and
growing up? Why does the power that was once so carefully preserved at
the top of the pyramid by the original framers of the Constitution seem
drawn inexorably downward and outward in spite of the best effort of the
Right to stop this? I mean it's the really hard thing about being Left in this
country, the American Left can't help but trip over all these petrified little
fetishes: freedom, that's the worst; you know, *Jeane Kirkpatrick* for God's
sake will go on and on about freedom and so what does that mean, the
word freedom, when she talks about it, or human rights; you have Bush
talking about human rights, and so what are these people talking about,
they might as well be talking about the mating habits of Venusians, these
people don't begin to know what, ontologically, freedom is or human
rights, like they see these bourgeois property-based Rights-of-Man-type
rights but that's not enfranchisement, not democracy, not what's implicit,
what's potential within the idea, not the idea with blood in it. That's just
liberalism, the worst kind of liberalism, really, bourgeois tolerance, and
what I think is that what AIDS shows us is the limits of tolerance, that it's
not enough to be tolerated, because when the shit hits the fan you find out
how much tolerance is worth. Nothing. And underneath all the tolerance is
intense, passionate hatred.

Belize: Uh huh.

Louis: Well don't you think that's true?

Belize: Uh huh. It is.

Louis: Power is the object, not being tolerated. Fuck assimilation. But I mean
in spite of all this the thing about America, I think, is that ultimately we're
different from every other nation on earth, in that, with people here of every race, we can't. . . . Ultimately what defines us isn't race, but politics. Not
like any European country where there's an insurmountable fact of a kind
of racial, or ethnic, monopoly, or monolith, like all Dutchmen, I mean
Dutch people, are well, Dutch, and the Jews of Europe were never Europe-
ans, just a small problem. Facing the monolith. But here there are so many
small problems, it's really just a collection of small problems, the monolith
is missing. Oh, I mean, of course I suppose there's the monolith of White
America. White Straight Male America.

Belize: Which is not unimpressive, even among monoliths.

Louis: Well, no, but when the race thing gets taken care of, and I don't mean
to minimalize how major it is, I mean I know it is, this is a really, really incredibly racist country but it's like, well, the British. I mean, all these blue-
eyed pink people. And it's just weird, you know, I mean I'm not all that Jew-

ish-looking, or . . . well, maybe I am but, you know, in New York, everyone is . . . well, not everyone, but so many are but so but in England, in London I walk into bars and I feel like Sid the Yid, you know I mean like Woody Allen in *Annie Hall,* with the payess and the gabardine coat, like never, never anywhere so much—I mean, not actively despised, not like they're Germans, who I think are still terribly anti-Semitic, and racist too, I mean black-racist, they pretend otherwise but, anyway, in London, there's just . . . and at one point I met this black gay guy from Jamaica who talked with a lilt but he said his family'd been living in London since before the Civil War—the American one—and how the English never let him forget for a minute that he wasn't blue-eyed and pink and I said yeah, me too, these people are anti-Semites and he said yeah but the British Jews have the clothing business all sewed up and blacks there can't get a foothold. And it was an incredibly awkward moment of just. . . . I mean here we were, in this bar that was gay but it was a *pub,* you know, the beams and the plaster and those horrible little, like, two-day-old fish and egg sandwiches—and just so British, so *old,* and I felt, well, there's no way out of this because both of us are, right now, too much immersed in this history, hope is dissolved in the sheer age of this place, where race is what counts and there's no real hope of change—it's the racial destiny of the Brits that matters to them, not their political destiny, whereas in America . . .

Belize: Here in America race doesn't count.

Louis: No, no, that's not. . . . I mean you *can't* be hearing that . . .

Belize: I . . .

Louis: It's—look, race, yes, but ultimately race here is a political question, right? Racists just try to use race here as a tool in a political struggle. It's not really about race. Like the spiritualists try to use that stuff, are you enlight- ened, are you centered, channeled, whatever, this reaching out for a spiri- tual past in a country where no indigenous spirits exist—only the Indians, I mean Native American spirits and we killed them off so now, there are no gods here, no ghosts and spirits in America, there are no angels in America, no spiritual past, no racial past, there's only the political, and the decoys and the ploys to maneuver around the inescapable battle of politics, the shifting downwards and outwards of political power to the people . . .

Belize: POWER to the People! AMEN! *(Looking at his watch) OH MY GOOD- NESS!* Will you look at the time, I gotta . . .

Perestroika, Act II, Scene 2

Belize: You have been spending too much time alone.

Prior: Not by choice. None of this by choice.

Belize: This is . . . worse than nuts, it's . . . well, don't migrate, don't mingle,

that's . . . malevolent, some of us didn't exactly *choose* to migrate, know
what I'm saying . . .

Prior (Overlapping): I hardly think it's appropriate for you to get *offended*, I
didn't invent this shit it was *visited* on me . . .

Belize (Overlapping on "offended"): But it *is* offensive or at least monumentally
confused and it's not . . . *visited*, Prior. By who? It *is* from you, what else is
it?

Prior: Something else.

Belize: That's crazy.

Prior: Then I'm crazy.

Belize: No, you're . . .

Prior: Then it was an angel.

Belize: It was *not* an . . .

Prior: Then I'm crazy. The whole world is, why not me?

It's 1986 and there's a *plague*, half my friends are dead and I'm only
thirty-one, and every goddamn morning I wake up and I think Louis is next
to me in the bed and it takes me long minutes to remember . . . that this is
real, it isn't just an impossible, terrible dream, so maybe yes I'm flipping out.

Belize (Angry): You better not. You better fucking not flip out.

This is not dementia. And this is not real. This is just you, Prior, afraid of
what's coming, afraid of time. But see that's just not how it goes, the world
doesn't spin backwards. Listen to the world, to how fast it goes.

*(They stand silently, listening, and the sounds of the city grow louder and louder,
filling the stage—sounds of traffic, whistles, alarms, people, all very fast and very
complex and very determinedly moving ahead.)*

Belize: That's New York traffic, baby, the sound of energy, the sound of time.
Even if you're hurting, it can't go back.

There's no angel. You hear me? For me? I can handle anything but not
this happening to you.

Angel's voice:

Whisper into the ear of the World, Prophet,

Wash up red in the tide of its dreams,

And billow bloody words into the sky of sleep.

Prior: Maybe I am a prophet. Not just me, all of us who are dying now. Maybe
we've caught the virus of prophecy. Be still. Toil no more. Maybe the world
has driven God from Heaven, incurred the angels' wrath.

I believe I've seen the end of things. And having seen, I'm going blind, as
prophets do. It makes a certain sense to me.

Angel's voice:

FOR THIS AGE OF ANOMIE: A NEW LAW! Delivered this night, this silent
night, from Heaven, Oh Prophet, to You.

Prior: I hate heaven. I've got no resistance left. Except to run.

Perestroika, Epilogue: Bethesda (February 1990)

Prior, Louis, Belize and Hannah sitting on the rim of the Bethesda Fountain in Central Park. It's a bright day, but cold.
   Prior is heavily bundled, and he has thick glasses on, and he supports himself with a cane. Hannah is noticeably different—she looks like a New Yorker, and she is reading the New York Times. *Louis and Belize are arguing. The Bethesda Angel is above them all.*

Louis: The Berlin Wall has fallen. The Ceauçescus are out. He's building democratic socialism. The New Internationalism. Gorbachev is the greatest political thinker since Lenin.
Belize: I don't think we know enough yet to start canonizing him. The Russians hate his guts.
Louis: Yeah but. Remember back four years ago? The whole time we were feeling everything everywhere was stuck, while in Russia! Look! Perestroika! The Thaw! It's the end of the Cold War! The whole world is changing! Overnight!
Hannah: I wonder what'll happen now in places like Yugoslavia.
Prior (To audience): Let's just turn the volume down on this, OK?
   They'll be at it for hours. It's not that what they're saying isn't important, it's just . . .
   This is my favorite place in New York City. No, in the whole universe. The parts of it I have seen.
   On a day like today. A sunny winter's day, warm and cold at once. The sky's a little hazy, so the sunlight has a physical presence, a character. In autumn, those trees across the lake are yellow, and the sun strikes those most brilliantly. Against the blue of the sky, that sad fall blue, those trees are more light than vegetation. They are Yankee trees, New England transplants. They're barren now. It's January 1990. I've been living with AIDS for five years. That's six whole months longer than I lived with Louis.
Louis: Whatever comes, what you have to admire in Gorbachev, in the Russians is that they're making a leap into the unknown. You can't wait around for a theory. The sprawl of life, the weird . . .
Hannah: Interconnectedness . . .
Louis: Yes.
Belize: Maybe the sheer size of the terrain.
Louis: It's all too much to be encompassed by a single theory now.
Belize: The world is faster than the mind.
Louis: That's what politics is. The world moving ahead. And only in politics does the miraculous occur.

Belize: But that's a theory.

Hannah: You can't live in the world without an idea of the world, but it's living that makes the ideas. You can't wait for a theory, but you have to have a theory.

Louis: Go know. As my grandma would say.

Prior (Turning the sound off again): This angel. She's my favorite angel.

I like them best when they're statuary. They commemorate death but they suggest a world without dying. They are made of the heaviest things on earth, stone and iron, they weigh tons but they're winged, they are engines and instruments of flight.

This is the angel Bethesda. Louis will tell you her story.

Louis: Oh. Um, well, she was this angel, she landed in the Temple square in Jerusalem, in the days of the Second Temple, right in the middle of a working day she descended and just her foot touched earth. And where it did, a fountain shot up from the ground.

When the Romans destroyed the Temple, the fountain of Bethesda ran dry.

Prior: And Belize will tell you about the nature of the fountain, before its flowing stopped.

Belize: If anyone who was suffering, in the body or the spirit, walked through the waters of the fountain of Bethesda, they would be healed, washed clean of pain.

Prior: They know this because I've told them, many times. Hannah here told it to me. She also told me this:

Hannah: When the Millennium comes . . .

Prior: Not the year two thousand, but the Capital M Millennium . . .

Hannah: Right. The fountain of Bethesda will flow again. And I told him I would personally take him there to bathe. We will all bathe ourselves clean.

Louis: Not literally in Jerusalem, I mean we don't want this to have sort of Zionist implications, we . . .

Belize: Right on.

Louis: But on the other hand we *do* recognize the right of the state of Israel to exist.

Belize: But the West Bank should be a homeland for the Palestinians, and the Golan Heights should . . .

Louis: Well not *both* the West Bank and the Golan Heights, I mean no one supports Palestinian rights more than I do but

Belize (Overlapping): Oh yeah right, Louis, like not even the Palestinians are more devoted than . . .

Prior: I'm almost done.

The fountain's not flowing now, they turn it off in the winter, ice in the pipes. But in the summer it's a sight to see. I want to be around to see it. I plan to be. I hope to be.

This disease will be the end of many of us, but not nearly all, and the dead will be commemorated and will struggle on with the living, and we are not going away. We won't die secret deaths anymore. The world only spins forward. We will be citizens. The time has come.

Bye now.

You are fabulous creatures, each and every one.

And I bless you: *More Life*.

The Great Work Begins.

Dyke Manifesto

1993

In 1992, six women in New York decided that protest groups like ACT UP were overlooking lesbians. Gay liberation and feminist groups had long been criticized for ignoring and stereotyping lesbians, prompting the formation of lesbian feminist organizations like Radicalesbians and The Furies during the early 1970s. Now deciding to form a new group, the six women named it the Lesbian Avengers. On June 26, they handed out eight thousand fliers announcing a meeting, and on July 7, fifty women met at New York's Lesbian and Gay Community Services Center to officially launch the group, described as "a post-ACT UP lesbian movement."

The Avengers also believed that existing gay liberation and AIDS awareness groups were too focused on political ideals: they wanted to develop grassroots lesbian activism and use "direct action" to raise lesbian visibility. They advised against stale strategies like chanting or picketing, and noted that listening to speakers was disempowering. Instead they performed street theater, threw papier-mâché bombs, ate fire, and wore superhero capes. In June 1993 they organized a "Dyke March" and rolled a huge bed filled with lesbians down Fifth Avenue. But they also stressed the mundane realities of activist organizing—fundraising, photocopying, and constructing phone trees. Beyond the fun of protest, the Avengers wanted to teach lesbians how to become effective organizers.

The Avengers helped defeat Proposition One, an anti-gay initiative on Idaho's November 1994 ballot. They marched against the death penalty, protested domestic violence, and held "eat-outs" to protest fat phobia. But by 1995, they were drowned out by the mainstream's focus on same-sex marriage and gays in the military. One of their last high-profile protests came in February 1995, when five members climbed onto the reception desk of Exodus International, a Christian organization devoted to "curing" homosexuality. After they released one thousand crickets, an Exodus International administrator called the police to report "There are lesbians here with bugs." One Avenger told the press: "If anyone deserves a plague of Biblical proportions right now, it's the Radical Right." This language echoed the Avengers' claim in their "Dyke Manifesto" ("We are the apocalypse"): a mini-apocalypse, complete with locusts, had descended on Exodus International just as the Avengers themselves began to implode.

lesbian avengers **DYKE MANIFESTO** lesbian avengers
CALLING ALL LESBIANS

WAKE UP! WAKE UP! WAKE UP!

IT'S TIME TO GET OUT OF THE BEDS, OUT OF THE BARS AND INTO
THE STREETS.
IT'S TIME TO SEIZE THE POWER OF *DYKE* LOVE, *DYKE* VISION,
DYKE ANGER
DYKE INTELLIGENCE, *DYKE* STRATEGY.
TIME TO ORGANIZE AND IGNITE. TIME TO GET TOGETHER AND FIGHT
WE'RE INVISIBLE, SISTERS, AND IT'S NOT SAFE—NOT IN OUR HOMES,
NOT IN THE STREETS, NOT ON THE JOB, NOT IN THE COURTS
WHERE ARE THE *OUT* LESBIAN LEADERS?
IT'S TIME FOR A FIERCE LESBIAN MOVEMENT
AND THAT'S *YOU:* THE ROLE MODEL, THE VISION, THE DESIRE.

WE NEED YOU

BECAUSE WE'RE NOT WAITING FOR THE RAPTURE.
WE ARE THE APOCALYPSE
We'll be your dream and their nightmare.

LESBIAN POWER

LESBIAN AVENGERS BELIEVE IN CREATIVE ACTIVISM: LOUD, BOLD,
SEXY, SILLY, FIERCE, TASTY AND DRAMATIC. ARREST OPTIONAL.
THINK DEMONSTRATIONS ARE A GREAT TIME AND GREAT PLACE TO
CRUISE WOMEN.
LESBIAN AVENGERS DON'T HAVE PATIENCE FOR POLITE POLITICS.
ARE BORED WITH THE BOYS. THINK OF STINK BOMBS AS ALL-SEASON
ACCESSORIES. *Don't have a position on fur.*
LESBIAN AVENGERS THINK CONFRONTATION FOSTERS GROWTH AND
STRONG BONES. BELIEVE IN RECRUITMENT. NOT BY THE ARMY; NOT
OF STRAIGHT WOMEN. DON'T MIND HANDCUFFS AT ALL.
LESBIAN AVENGERS DO BELIEVE HOMOPHOBIA IS A FORM
OF MISOGYNY.
LESBIAN AVENGERS ARE NOT CONTENT WITH GHETTOS: WE WANT
YOUR HOUSE, YOUR JOB. YOUR FREQUENT FLYER MILES. WE'LL SELL
YOUR JEWELRY TO SUBSIDIZE OUR MOVEMENT.

LESBIAN AVENGERS DON'T BELIEVE IN THE FEMINIZATION OF POVERTY. WE DEMAND UNIVERSAL HEALTH INSURANCE AND HOUSING. WE DEMAND FOOD AND SHELTER FOR ALL HOMELESS LESBIANS.
LESBIAN AVENGERS ARE THE 13TH STEP.
LESBIAN AVENGERS THINK *girl gangs are the wave of the future.*

LESBIAN SEX

LESBIAN AVENGERS BELIEVE IN TRANSCENDENCE IN ALL STATES, INCLUDING COLORADO AND OREGON. THINK SEX IS A DAILY LIBERATION. GOOD ENERGY FOR ACTIONS,
LESBIAN AVENGERS CRAVE, ENJOY, EXPLORE, SUFFER FROM NEW IDEAS ABOUT RELATIONSHIPS: SLUMBER PARTIES, POLYGAMY (WHY GET MARRIED ONLY ONCE?). PERSONAL ADS, AFFINITY GROUPS.
LESBIAN AVENGERS ARE OLD-FASHIONED, PINE, LONG, WHINE, STAY IN BAD RELATIONSHIPS. GET MARRIED BUT DON'T WANT TO DOMESTICATE OUR PARTNERS.
LESBIAN AVENGERS USE LIVE ACTION WORDS: *lick, waltz, eat, fuck, kiss, bite, give it up, hit the dirt.*
LESBIAN AVENGERS LIKE JINGLES. SUBVERSION IS OUR PERVERSION.

LESBIAN ACTIVISM

LESBIAN AVENGERS *scheme and scream,* THINK ACTIONS MUST BE LOCAL, REGIONAL, NATIONAL, GLOBAL, COSMIC.
LESBIAN AVENGERS THINK CLOSETED LESBIANS, QUEER BOYS AND SYMPATHETIC STRAIGHTS SHOULD SEND US MONEY. BELIEVE DIRECT ACTION IS A KICK IN THE FACE.
LESBIAN AVENGERS PLAN TO TARGET HOMOPHOBES OF EVERY STRIPE AND INFILTRATE THE CHRISTIAN RIGHT.

TOP 10 AVENGER QUALITIES
(IN DESCENDING ORDER)
10. COMPASSION
9. LEADERSHIP
8. NO BIG EGO
7. INFORMED
6. FEARLESSNESS

5. RIGHTEOUS ANGER

4. FIGHTING SPIRIT

3. PRO SEX

2. GOOD DANCER

1. ACCESS TO RESOURCES (XEROX MACHINES)

THE LESBIAN AVENGERS

WE RECRUIT

From Stone Butch Blues

1993

In 1992, the activist Anne Waldman called for "an androgynous poetics . . . a poetics of transformation beyond gender." The following year, Leslie Feinberg (b. 1949) offered just that. The novel *Stone Butch Blues* protests the idea of biology as destiny, tracing the journey of Jess Goldberg, a transgendered "butch," toward what Waldman had imagined as the place where "we are not defined by our sexual positions as men or women in bed or on the page."

Feinberg, a transgender activist and writer, explores W. E. B. Du Bois's concept of double consciousness. In the novel, Jess reads a passage from *The Souls of Black Folk* (1903): "this sense of always looking at one's self through the eyes of others." Gay liberationists had long proposed that staying in the closet was akin to racial passing, sometimes alluding to Du Bois, and after taking male hormones, Jess notes: "I could see my *passing* self, but even I could no longer see the more complicated me beneath the surface." Jess looks in the mirror and can't recognize the image: "I didn't get to explore being a he-she . . . I simply became a he—a man without a past."

Feinberg restores this past through the historical protest tradition. Jess encounters "an old slave dance," James Baldwin's essays, and Malcolm X's speeches, realizing "There's lots of us who are on the outside and we don't want to be." Then, coming across a book called *Gay American History,* Jess confesses, "I want to know about history. I have all this new information about people like me down the ages, but I don't know anything about the ages." Beginning to live on the inside of the gay liberation movement, Jess enters through its history.

The police van was backed right up to the door of the club. The cops roughed us up as they shoved us in. Some of the drag queens bantered nervously on the way to the precinct, making jokes to relieve the tension. I rode in silence.

We were all put together in one huge holding cell. My cuffed hands felt swollen and cold from lack of circulation. I waited in the cell. Two cops opened the door. They were laughing and talking to themselves. I wasn't listening. "What do you want, a fucking invitation? Now!" one of them commanded.

"C'mon, Jesse," a cop taunted me, "let's have a pretty smile for the camera. You're such a pretty girl. Isn't she pretty, guys?" They snapped my mug shot. One of the cops loosened my tie. As he ripped open my new dress shirt, the sky blue buttons bounced and rolled across the floor. He pulled up my T-shirt, exposing my breasts. My hands were cuffed behind my back. I was flat up against a wall.

"I don't think she likes you, Gary," another cop said. "Maybe she'd like me better." He crossed the room. My knees were wobbling. *Lt. Mulroney,* that's what his badge read. He saw me looking at it and slapped me hard across the face. His hand clamped on my face like a vise. "Suck my cock," he said quietly.

There wasn't a sound in the room. I didn't move. No one said anything. I almost got the feeling it could stay that way, all action frozen, but it didn't. Mulroney was fingering his crotch. "Suck my cock, bulldagger." Someone hit the side of my knee with a nightstick. My knees buckled more from fear than pain. Mulroney grabbed me by the collar and dragged me several feet away to a steel toilet. There was a piece of unflushed shit floating in the water. "Either eat me or eat my shit, bulldagger. It's up to you." I was too frightened to think or move.

I held my breath the first time he shoved my head in the toilet. The second time he held me under so long I sucked in water and felt the hard shape of the shit against my tongue. When Mulroney pulled my head back out of the toilet I spewed vomit all over him. I gagged and retched over and over again.

"Aw shit, fuck, get her out of here," the cops yelled to each other as I lay heaving.

"No," Mulroney said, "handcuff her over there, on top of the desk."

They lifted me and threw me on my back across the desk and handcuffed my hands over my head. As one cop pulled off my trousers I tried to calm the spasms in my stomach so I wouldn't choke to death on my own vomit.

"Aw, ain't that cute, BVD's," one cop called out to another. "Fuckin' pervert."

I looked at the light on the ceiling, a large yellow bulb burning behind a metal mesh. The light reminded me of the endless stream of television westerns I saw after we moved up north. Whenever anyone was lost in the desert the only image shown was a glaring sun—all the beauty of the desert reduced to that one impression. Staring at that jail light bulb rescued me from watching my own degradation: I just went away.

I found myself standing in the desert. The sky was streaked with color. Every shift of light cast a different hue across the wilderness: salmon, rose, lavender. The scent of sage was overpowering. Even before I saw the golden eagle gliding in the updraft above me, I heard it scream, as clearly as if it had come from my own throat. I longed to soar in flight with the eagle, but I felt rooted to the earth. The mountains rose to meet me. I walked toward them, seeking sanctuary, but something held me back.

"Fuck it," Mulroney spat. "Turn her over, her cunt's too fuckin' loose."

"Jeez Lieutenant, how come these fuckin' bulldaggers don't fuck men and they got such big cunts?"

"Ask your wife," Mulroney said. The other cops laughed.

I panicked. I tried to return to the desert but I couldn't find that floating opening between the dimensions I'd passed through before. An explosion of pain in my body catapulted me back.

I was standing on the desert floor again, but this time the sands had cooled. The sky was overcast, threatening to storm. The air pressure was unbearable. It was hard to breathe. From a distance I heard the eagle scream again. The sky was growing as dark as the mountains. Wind blew through my hair.

I closed my eyes and turned my face up to the desert sky. And then, finally, it released—the welcome relief of warm rain down my cheeks.

Ruth offered me a cookie she'd just decorated. "It's still warm so it's soft. It's gingerbread. Try it. Just a bite." I rediscovered taste. "We're making cookies to take to friends who are stuck in the hospital with AIDS."

Up until that moment I had felt as though the epidemic was taking place a million miles away from me. "Can I go with?" I asked.

Ruth sighed heavily. "Yes, if you want to."

Tanya offered me a mug. "This is Tanya's killer eggnog. If this don't give you the holiday spirit nothing will."

Ruth wiped her hands on her apron. "Take it easy with that stuff."

Tanya made a face at her. "Don't listen to her. Just cause she's a friend of Bill W's doesn't mean we all have to hang out with him."

"We're going out to a drag club later tonight. You want to come?" Esperanza asked. I looked at Ruth. She smiled and shrugged.

"I'll teach you to bump and grind on the dance floor, honey," Tanya said.

I laughed. "I'll show you a thing or two on the dance floor."

"Lord have mercy," Tanya fanned herself with her large hand. "Kill me now."

Esperanza smiled. "I'll teach you an old slave dance, the merengue."

I remembered Ruth's present. "I'll be right back," I said. When I lugged the heavy rectangular present into her living room Ruth sat down heavily on the couch as though she'd been hit with bad news. "It's for you," I smiled.

"Open it, girl," Tanya urged.

Ruth chewed her lip. "You shouldn't have."

All my love was in my smile. "Oh, hush."

She sighed, opened the paper carefully, folded it, and put it aside. When Ruth took the cover off the sewing machine she gasped. I could tell by the way her fingers trailed across the machine how happy it made her. "I'll make you a suit," she whispered.

I beamed. "Really?" Ruth nodded and bit her knuckles. She stood up and walked over to the half-decorated evergreen. "These are for you," she handed me two flat packages.

The first was a book called *Gay American History*. My hands trembled as I leafed through the pages.

"Look," Ruth took the book from my hands and turned to the index. "Remember I told you about what I read in a drag magazine about how people like us used to be honored? Look at this whole section about Native societies. But, wait, look at this." She flipped the pages. "This whole part is about women like you who lived as men." Tears clouded my vision.

Esperanza looked at the title and shook her head. "I wish we weren't always lumped into gay."

"Hush," Ruth shook her head. She handed me a package wrapped in red tissue paper. "Open this." Inside was a watercolor of a face filled with emotion, looking up at a host of stars. It was a beautiful face, a face I'd never seen before. It was my face.

"Let me see that, honey," Tanya reached for it. "Ooh, Rum. That's nice. That looks just like him."

"Ruth," I chewed my lip. "Do I really look like this?"

She nodded and smiled through her tears. "When I thought you might die, I started to sketch your face. I wanted something more than my memories of you to remain. Your eyes were closed, but I could shut my own and remember the way the color of your eyes changes in the light."

Ruth sat down next to me on the couch. We put our arms around each other and rocked. Esperanza and Tanya sat on the floor near us.

My chin ached and trembled. "You know," I told them, "I've been searching for you all for such a long time. I can't believe I've finally found you." I squeezed Ruth tightly in my arms as we both cried.

Esperanza rested her hand on my thigh. "Do you know what my name means?"

I shook my head. "No, but it sure is pretty."

She smiled and looked me at me with a sure, unwavering expression. "Esperanza," she explained—"it means hope."

It was hot that night, almost too unbearable to sleep. The air pressure and humidity made it difficult to breath. Thunder rumbled in the distance. I thought about how my life was changing, in little ways and big ways.

And I thought about Theresa. I'd never written that letter she'd asked me for. Could I write it someday soon? What would I say? Where could I send it?

The rain pelted my windows. As I fell asleep thinking about the letter, lightning bolts streaked the sky. During the night I had this dream:

I walked across a vast field. Women and men and children stood on the edges of the field looking at me, smiling and nodding. I headed toward a small round hut near the edge of the woods. I had a feeling I had been in this place before.

There were people who were different like me inside. We could all see our reflections in the faces of those who sat in this circle. I looked around. It was hard to say who was a woman, who was a man. Their faces radiated a different kind of beauty than I'd grown up seeing celebrated on television or in magazines. It's a beauty one isn't born with, but must fight to construct at great sacrifice.

I felt proud to sit among them. I was proud to be one of them.

A fire burned in the center of our gathering. One of the oldest in the circle caught my eyes. I didn't know if she was a man or a woman at birth. She held up an object. I understood I was supposed to accept the realness of this object. I looked more closely. It was the ring that the Dineh women gifted me with as an infant.

I felt an urge to leap to my feet, to plead for the ring to be returned to me. I restrained the impulse.

She pointed to the circle the ring cast on the ground. I nodded, acknowledging that the shadow was as real as the ring. She smiled and waved her hand in the space between the ring and its shadow. Isn't this distance also real? She indicated our circle. I looked at the faces around me. I followed the shadow of her hand against the wall of the hut, seeing for the first time the shadows surrounding us.

She called me to the present. My mind slipped back to the past, forward to the future. Aren't these connected, she asked wordlessly?

I felt my whole life coming full circle. Growing up so different, coming out as a butch, passing as a man, and then back to the same question that had shaped my life: woman or man?

The sound of a street argument, born of frustration, woke me from sleep. I didn't want to come back to this world. I struggled to return to the dream, but I was wide awake. It was near dawn. I unlocked the bedroom window and crawled out on the fire escape. The cool air felt good. I closed my eyes.

I recalled the night Theresa and I broke up, how I stared into the night sky, straining for a glimpse of my own future. If I could send a message back in time to that young butch sitting on a milk crate, it would be this: My neighbor, Ruth, asked me recently if I had my life to live all over again would I make the same decisions? "Yes," I answered! unequivocally, "yes."

I'm so sorry it's had to be this hard. But if I hadn't walked this path, who would I be? At the moment I felt at the center of my own life, the dream still braided like sweet-grass in my memory.

I remembered Duffy's challenge. *Imagine a world worth living in, a world worth fighting for.* I closed my eyes and allowed my hopes to soar.

I heard the beating of wings nearby. I opened my eyes. A young man on a nearby rooftop released his pigeons, like dreams, into the dawn.

Goodridge v. Department of Public Health

2003

In 1989 Thomas Stoddard predicted that gay people would "earn the right" to marry "sooner than most of us imagine." He cited the economic and practical advantages of legal marriage, and explained that the issue was not the desirability of marriage, but rather the *right* to marry. The same year Paula Ettelbrick protested the idea of "emphasizing our sameness to married heterosexuals in order to obtain this 'right.'" It meant "mimicking all that is bad about the institution of marriage in our effort to appear to be the same," and would outlaw gay and lesbian sex outside of marriage. There would still be a "two-tier system of the 'haves' and the 'have nots.'" In 1999 Michael Warner called the desire for legal same-sex marriage a "false consciousness," the same force in history that meant "young men have marched gaily off to be slaughtered on behalf of deities and nations."

This debate came to a head in November 2003, when the Massachusetts Supreme Judicial Court rejected the Commonwealth's claim that the primary purpose of marriage was procreation and held that a ban on same-sex marriage violated the Massachusetts Constitution, which forbids the creation of second-class citizens. The court order went into effect in May 2004. Hundreds of couples were legally married in Massachusetts, and the ruling set off legal battles across the country. But some activists have been surprised by the focus on same-sex marriage, calling it a far less urgent issue than AIDS or homophobic violence. Less divisive within the activist community was another high-profile case of 2003 *(Lawrence v. Texas),* this time addressing the issue of sodomy. In 1998 two men were charged with violating Texas's anti-sodomy statute, and in 2002 they filed a petition with the Supreme Court. The statute was struck down, and the decision invalidated similar sodomy laws across the United States.

MARSHALL, C. J. Marriage is a vital social institution. The exclusive commitment of two individuals to each other nurtures love and mutual support; it brings stability to our society. For those who choose to marry, and for their children, marriage provides an abundance of legal, financial, and social benefits. In return it imposes weighty legal, financial, and social obligations. The question before us is whether, consistent with the Massachusetts Constitution, the Commonwealth may deny the protections, benefits, and obligations conferred by civil marriage to two individuals of the same sex who wish to marry. We conclude that it may not. The Massachusetts Constitution affirms the dignity and equality of all individuals. It forbids the creation of second-class citizens. In reaching our conclusion we have given full deference to the arguments made by the Commonwealth. But it has failed to identify any constitutionally adequate reason for denying civil marriage to same-sex couples . . . Barred access to the protections, benefits, and obligations of civil marriage, a person who enters into an intimate, exclusive union with another of the same sex is arbitrarily deprived of membership in one of our community's most rewarding and cherished institutions. That exclusion is incompatible with the constitutional principles of respect for individual autonomy and equality under law . . . For decades, indeed centuries, in much of this country (including Massachusetts) no lawful marriage was possible between white and black Americans. That long history availed not when the Supreme Court of California held in 1948 that a legislative prohibition against interracial marriage violated the due process and equality guarantees of the Fourteenth Amendment, Perez v. Sharp, 32 Cal. 2d 711, 728 (1948), or when, nineteen years later, the United States Supreme Court also held that a statutory bar to interracial marriage violated the Fourteenth Amendment, Loving v. Virginia, 388 U.S. 1 (1967).[16] As both Perez and Loving make clear, the right to marry means little if it does not include the right to marry the person of one's choice, subject to appropriate government restrictions in the interests of public health, safety, and welfare. See Perez v. Sharp, supra at 717 ("the essence of the right to marry is freedom to join in marriage with the person of one's choice"). See also Loving v. Virginia, supra at 12. In this case, as in Perez and Loving, a statute deprives individuals of access to an institution of fundamental legal, personal, and social significance—the institution of marriage—because of a single trait: skin color in Perez and Loving, sexual orientation here. As it did in Perez and Loving, history must yield to a more fully developed understanding of the invidious quality of the discrimination . . . In their complaint the plaintiffs request only a declaration that their exclusion and the exclusion of other qualified same-sex couples from access to civil marriage violates Massachusetts law. We declare that barring an individual from the protections, benefits, and obligations of civil marriage solely because that person would marry a person of the same sex violates the Massachusetts Constitution.

GREANEY, J. (concurring). I agree with the result reached by the court, the remedy ordered, and much of the reasoning in the court's opinion. In my view, however, the case is more directly resolved using traditional equal protection analysis. (a) Article 1 of the Declaration of Rights, as amended by art. 106 of the Amendments to the Massachusetts Constitution, provides: "All people are born free and equal and have certain natural, essential and unalienable rights; among which may be reckoned the right of enjoying and defending their lives and liberties; that of acquiring, possessing and protecting property; in fine, that of seeking and obtaining their safety and happiness. Equality under the law shall not be denied or abridged because of sex, race, color, creed or national origin" . . . I am hopeful that our decision will be accepted by those thoughtful citizens who believe that same-sex unions should not be approved by the State. I am not referring here to acceptance in the sense of grudging acknowledgment of the court's authority to adjudicate the matter. My hope is more liberating. The plaintiffs are members of our community, our neighbors, our coworkers, our friends. As pointed out by the court, their professions include investment advisor, computer engineer, teacher, therapist, and lawyer. The plaintiffs volunteer in our schools, worship beside us in our religious houses, and have children who play with our children, to mention just a few ordinary daily contacts. We share a common humanity and participate together in the social contract that is the foundation of our Commonwealth. Simple principles of decency dictate that we extend to the plaintiffs, and to their new status, full acceptance, tolerance, and respect. We should do so because it is the right thing to do. The union of two people contemplated by G.L.c. 207 "is a coming together for better or for worse, hopefully enduring, and intimate to the degree of being sacred. It is an association that promotes a way of life, not causes; a harmony in living, not political faiths; a bilateral loyalty, not commercial or social projects. Yet it is an association for as noble a purpose as any involved in our prior decisions." Griswold v. Connecticut, 381 U.S. 479, 486 (1965). Because of the terms of art. 1, the plaintiffs will no longer be excluded from that association.

FROM SAIGON TO BAGHDAD

The Vietnam War
and Beyond

I-Feel-Like-I'm-Fixin'-To-Die-Rag

<u>1965</u>

Country Joe McDonald (b. 1942), the lead singer of the band Country Joe and the Fish, sometimes claims that his music stopped the Vietnam war. The claim, like the band's music, is tongue-in-cheek. But the "Rag" *is* the definitive antiwar song of the Vietnam era; "the melody underneath all the protest," as Vietnam veteran and writer Tim O'Brien put it in a recent interview. "I tried to write music that was a sound track for my era," McDonald says. "My music was music to work by, be it soldiering or antiwar work." He claims that a soldier once died singing the line from the "Rag," "Whoopee! We're all going to die."

"Good protest music must be entertaining or else it is just propaganda," adds McDonald. His song is an unlikely marriage of biting lyrics and jaunty tune. Within the antiwar movement, the absurd was a weapon of protest against the war's twilight-zone logic: one line from the song ("you know that peace can only be won / When we've blown 'em all to kingdom come") echoes the expressed desire of General Curtis 'Bombs Away' LeMay to "bomb Vietnam back to the stone age." It also foreshadows an unattributed comment, likely made after the 1968 Tet offensive, that "we had to destroy the village in order to save it." Absurdist protest humor likewise infused the Yippies' attempt to levitate the Pentagon in 1967 and nominate a pig for President in 1968, and the carnival aspects of the 1969–1970 Chicago Conspiracy Trial, when a marshal had to hold McDonald's mouth shut to stop him from singing on the witness stand.

The "Rag" reached a wide audience in 1967 (on the album *I Feel Like I'm Fixin' To Die*) and a mass audience in 1970 (through the film and recordings of the Woodstock festival). The music of Country Joe and the Fish was a fulcrum between folk music and burgeoning psychedelic music: they imbued the new sound with folk's political sensibilities. Their credibility as key creators of this sound meant their political messages reached audiences with little time for folk, which seemed increasingly divorced from the new underground rock culture. McDonald also gained credibility because he couldn't be dismissed as a hippy peacenik. He had been in the military and maintained close links with Vietnam Veterans against the War, noting recently: "I felt a comradeship with the soldiers and tried to write from their point of view. I have never felt that I was apart from those I wrote about." He combined antiwar radicalism with respect for soldiers: "Now movements all say 'support the troops,' and this is largely due to myself and others driving home the message that soldiers are not responsible for war."

This stance echoed Woody Guthrie's fusion of populism, egalitarianism, and patriotism. But during the war it put McDonald out of step with some peace activists, who viewed his support for troops with suspicion. They didn't love him, he remembers, like they loved the folk singer Pete Seeger, whose music was "nice." Because of "my using the fuck word, my lack of blaming the soldiers, and playing rock and roll, I was not asked to do much by the peace movement." He was "no Bob Dylan": "Bob did not say 'kiss my ass' and 'fuck.' My legacy is gangster rap . . . Tupac's song 'Only God Can Judge Me,' is the greatest modern protest poetry I have ever heard." McDonald concludes that another "legacy of Vietnam protest is contemporary antiwar protest." Though the "war on terror" is a new challenge for those who write about war, it is just "another war like Vietnam."

Further reading: Lee Andresen, *Battle Notes* (2000); Jerome Rodnitzky, *Minstrels* (1976).

Well, come on all of you, big strong men,
Uncle Sam needs your help again.
He's got himself in a terrible jam
Way down yonder in Vietnam
So put down your books and pick up a gun,
We're gonna have a whole lotta fun.
[Chorus]
And it's one, two, three,
What are we fighting for?
Don't ask me, I don't give a damn,
Next stop is Vietnam;
And it's five, six, seven,
Open up the pearly gates,
Well there ain't no time to wonder why,
Whoopee! We're all gonna die.

Come on Wall Street, don't be slow,
Why man, this is war au-go-go
There's plenty good money to be made
By supplying the Army with the tools of its trade,
But just hope and pray that if they drop the bomb,
They drop it on the Viet Cong.
[Chorus]

Well, come on generals, let's move fast;
Your big chance has come at last.
Now you can go out and get those reds
'Cause the only good commie is the one that's dead
And you know that peace can only be won
When we've blown 'em all to kingdom come.
[Chorus]

Come on mothers throughout the land,
Pack your boys off to Vietnam.
Come on fathers, and don't hesitate
To send your sons off before it's too late.
And you can be the first ones in your block
To have your boy come home in a box.
[Chorus]

Advent 1966

1966

Denise Levertov (1923–1997) dwells on the wartime horror of multiplied, burning children. "Advent" anticipates Ron Haeberle's famous photograph of the My Lai massacre (1968), with its piles of children, rather than Nick Ut's image of an individualized child fleeing a napalm strike (1972). The children in Levertov's poem have lost all individuality. Their names are forgotten, their sexes unknown. Her "clear caressive sight" is blurred.

This is her *poetic* sight. To Levertov, war seemed an attack on order and so on poetry. She believed there could be no poetry without order in the world, and no order in the world without poetry. Her trademark mystic, prayer-like poetry sought harmony amid war's chaos, and she equated peacemaking with poem writing, but the broken lines in "Advent" acknowledge the pressure on her form. In part, Levertov emphasizes the war's impact on poetry because she hadn't seen war firsthand, and so wrote instead about the bleeding of words and the disordering of poetry—exploring the crisis of language, representation, and vision. This was a theme for other antiwar writers: in 1966 Allen Ginsberg professed to be "almost in tears to know how to speak the right language" when "almost all our language has been taxed by war."

Like many poets, Levertov combined this battle for meaning and language with an attempt to use language as a weapon against war. Protest poets held readings, contributed to anthologies like *A Poetry Reading against the Vietnam War* (1966), *Where Is Vietnam?* (1967), *Out of the Shadow of War* (1968), and *Poetry against the War* (1972), and took part in Angry Arts Week in February 1967. In 1974 the poet Kirby Congdon announced: "Good bye poets / who think art is separated from politics . . . who think poetry an escape . . . And Hello poets . . . who still call / over our own torments."

Further reading: Peter Middleton, *Revelation and Revolution* (1981); Audrey Rodgers, *Denise Levertov* (1993).

Because in Vietnam the vision of a Burning Babe
is multiplied, multiplied,
                    the flesh on fire
not Christ's, as Southwell saw it, prefiguring
the Passion upon the Eve of Christmas,

but wholly human and repeated, repeated,
infant after infant, their names forgotten,

Their sex unknown in the ashes,
set alight, flaming but not vanishing,
not vanishing, as his vision but lingering.

cinders upon the earth or living on
moaning and stinking in hospitals three abed;

because of this my strong sight,
my clear caressive sight, my poet's sight I was given
that it might stir me to song,
is blurred.
                      There is a cataract filming over
my inner eyes. Or else a monstrous insect
has entered my head, and looks out
from my sockets with multiple vision,

seeing not the unique Holy Infant
burning sublimely, an imagination of redemption,
furnace in which souls are wrought into new life,
but, as off a beltline, more, senseless figures aflame.

And this insect (who is not there—
it is my own eyes do my seeing, the insect
is not there, what I see is there)
will not permit me to look elsewhere,

or if I look, to see except dulled and unfocused
the delicate, firm whole flesh of the still unburned.

From Why Are We in Vietnam?

<u>1967</u>

As the gap widened between fantasy and reality in official reports of the Vietnam war, Norman Mailer (b. 1923) and others developed the genre of New Journalism, which focused on the untenable division between fact and fiction. Mailer used obscenity to expose further the limits of official language, observing of the response to *Why Are We In Vietnam?*: "the American corporation executive . . . was perfectly capable of burning unseen women and children in the Vietnamese jungles, yet felt a large displeasure . . . at the generous use of obscenity in literature . . . was America the first great power to be built on bullshit?" The book protests the language of warrior masculinity as well. As antiwar protestors noted of politicians and the press, alongside the official language of mechanical process ("taking out a target," "mopping up") was the language of hunting ("soldiers captured a prize," "squads found their quarry"). And so Mailer makes no mention of Vietnam until the end of the novel, the passage excerpted here. Instead the narrator, D.J., plays at hunting on the frontier of "America's last unspoiled wilderness" before leaving for Vietnam—the next frontier. In Alaska he commits animal "murder of the soldieriest sort." The novel ends with D.J. "off to see the wizard in Vietnam." The movie of *The Wizard of Oz* was released in 1939 as another war began, one in which Mailer had served (in the South Pacific and later with the occupation forces in Japan). Mailer suggests that, having seen America's true war lurking in the fibers of its culture, D.J. will find the wizard in Vietnam is just a little man behind a curtain.

Warrior masculinity drives the novel's characters throughout, and America's warrior mentality continued beyond the Vietnam war: civilians began to attend combat schools, and two million military rifles were sold between the war's end and 1989. Just as D.J. fought the war before he got there, so Americans have refought the war since they lost it. In 2003 Mailer observed the Iraq invasion and returned to the question he had originally asked in his novel's title, writing the book *Why Are We At War?* (2003). In *The Armies of the Night* (1968), his nonfiction novel about the 1967 protest march on the Pentagon, he had answered the question "Why are we in Vietnam?": "the expression of brutality offers a definite if temporary relief to the schizophrenic," and "the center of America might be insane." And in 2003, the answer was insanity again: "the idea that we . . . will dominate the obstacles," our "mad-eyed mystique."

Further reading: Loren Baritz, *Backfire* (1985); Milton Bates, *The Wars We Took to Vietnam* (1996).

Terminal Intro Beep and Out

A ring of vengeance like a pitch of the Saracen's sword on the quiver (what a movie was that, madame!) rings out of the air as if all the woe and shit and parsimony and genuine greed of all those fucking English, Irish, Scotch and European weeds, transplanted to North America, that sad deep sweet beauteous mystery land of purple forests, and pink rock, and blue water, Indian haunts from Maine to the shore of Californ, all gutted, shit on, used and blasted, man, cause a weed thrives on a cesspool, piss is its nectar, shit all ambrosia, and those messages at night—oh, God, let me hump the boss' daughter, let me make it, God, all going up through the M.E.F. cutting the night air, giving a singe to the dream field, all the United Greedies of America humping up that old rhythm, turning the dynamo around, generating, just cut through that magnetism and go, boy, and God got to give it to the Greedies, cause get a man greedy enough and he got the guts to go—go, go, Gutsy Hyde—so the Devil feeding them from one side and God having to juice man from the other, and whoa, whoa, but no, it will not slow, and these messages zoom across the lands, M.E.F. on call, at night—check on this, idiot expert technologue!—the ionization layer rises, the interference is less, the radio messages go further, zoom, zoom, zoom, like pneumatic tubes going back to the lap of Hiram Harden, President and Head of Head's Dept. Store right up there, Endicott Mountains, Brooks Range, and an hour before sunrise as all those North America shit heads stir in their sleep, digesting the messages they sent out and got back, beginning to smog the predawning air with their psychic glug, glut and exudations, not to mention all the funeral parlors cooling out in the premature morn from the M.E.F. all through the night screams and wails of corpses exhumed, excavated, flushed, sponged, spiced, finger-fucked, flayed, sewn, pushed, cut and shoved, not to mention sliced loose from their organs and petrified man in embalming juice—every undertaker worth his junked-out gunk has a secret formula—formaldehyde, do not relinquish your secret ceremonies, your treasure chests, your Paris gardens where the vestal virgins partouse in your juice, no, sir, never forget the living, the dead, and the just dead are fighting up all those square root of minus one bands in the M.E.F. mystery kc frequently kill your cycles, and as morning comes on, one hour before dawn, they are scheming in their sleep, getting practical, getting ready to get up, yawn, cough, fart, shoot a little piss, just generally fuck up that M.E.F. band, and so, friends, the ionization layer (first cousin to static in telepathic affairs) comes down again like a cloud, and intercranial communication is muffled, no mean matter, cause at Brooks Range, on the edge of the great snow-white parabolic reflector, sitting in the silent resonant electric hum of the still, there is a rub in the air like your hair on edge or coitus all interruptus with electric coils of gas in your bowel, pain in your balls, and hate in your ding, yes, discomfort as the ionization layer settles back and the hills is full of static charge. And when the shit was over in the Moe Henry and Obungekat Safari Group bunkhouse on Dolly Ding Bat Lake and the ice pinnacles of the Brooks Range was murmuring the word from ice shield to parabolic vale, "m.e.f., m.e.f., roger and out, it's morning, come in, m.e.f.," why, Rusty and Luke and the guides and boys and packers and medium assholes all got into the planes to go on back to Fairbanks and led the way into the new life smack right up here two years later in my consciousness, D.J. here at this grope dinner in the Dallas ass manse, given in my honor, D.J., I thank you, because tomorrow Tex and me, we're off to see the wizard in Vietnam. Unless, that is, I'm a black-ass cripple Spade and sending from Harlem. You never know. You never know what vision has been humping you through the night. So, ass-head America contemplate your butt. Which D.J. white or black could possibly be worse of a genius if Harlem or Dallas is guiding the other, and who knows which? This is D.J., Disc Jockey to America turning off. Vietnam, hot dam.

Saigon

Napalm

1968, 1972

On February 2, 1968, the *New York Times* printed a photograph on its front page show-ing a South Vietnamese general executing a Vietcong suspect in civilian clothes. The im-age, taken by Eddie Adams (1933–2004) for the Associated Press, is beautiful, with a soft-focus background, a flexed forearm, and devil-horn tufts of hair. And it is simple, just two men and an execution, no complex maneuvers or jargon. A speechwriter for President Johnson noted the power of this simplicity, which revealed "the unethical quality of a war in which a prisoner is shot at point-blank range," and so he "put aside the confidential ca-bles . . . fed up with the optimism that seemed to flow without stopping."

Adams's timing was perfect: he clicked his shutter just as General Loan pulled the trig-ger. His timing was perfect in another sense: the image came three days into the Tet Of-fensive, and after five years of antiwar agitation and organization. Protest dominated the

front pages, while the government tried to write off protestors as un-American cowards. After the image was reprinted across the world, Gallup opinion polls showed the greatest shift ever recorded: between February and March 1968, opposition to the war jumped from 25 to 40 percent, and support dwindled from 60 to 40 percent.

On June 9, 1972, an image of a child fleeing her village after an accidental napalm bombing appeared in every American newspaper. It too is beautiful, with full contrast and smoky backdrop, and an expression on a boy's face in the foreground like a Greek tragic mask. The image suggested Vietnam was a plundered, female country, and the idea of napalm eating away flesh echoed widespread fears that the war was eroding America's foundations. Like Adams, this photographer, Nick Ut (b. 1951), reaches for shock value: the central child, Kim Phuc, is stretched out as though crucified. He also calls for empathy: Phuc links the children (the boy on her right extends an arm to the left, and the boy on her left extends an arm to the right), forming an almost-complete chain of humanity and inviting the viewer to complete the connection.

Further reading: Jerry Lembcke, *The Spitting Image* (1998); Elaine Scarry, *The Body in Pain* (1985).

From Dispatches

1967–1969, 1977

Michael Herr (b. 1940) believed Vietnam was *"the* story," and wasn't "being told in any true way." In 1967, at the age of 27, he went to cover the war for *Esquire* magazine, later expanding his articles into the book *Dispatches.* His belief that the true story of the war was untold echoed a growing public unease with official representations of the war's progress. Public relations campaigns offered exaggerated statistics, and jargon drained language of meaning: *Dispatches* recounts that heavy casualties were described as light, ambushes as tactical ploys. Disregarding place names and maps, Herr seeks instead the "secret history . . . under the fact-figure crossfire."

Protesting official representations of the war, Herr chose New Journalism for his own representation. Defined by Tom Wolfe in 1967, New Journalism blurred the distinction between fact and fiction, subject and narrator. As history became fiction in Vietnam, so fiction became history, and Herr communicates this hall-of-mirrors process. Conventional journalism couldn't evoke the ambience of Vietnam, the surreal descent into insanity and the dope and dementia giddiness.

Herr uses a filmic style to express the idea that Vietnam had become a movie, approached by politicians like a Western, and fought by cowboy Generals. One marine in *Dispatches* hates the movie he's in, and Herr compares life to film a dozen times. Treating war as a movie, Herr addresses the problem of voyeurism head-on, but the New Journalistic focus on his own subjectivity allows him to become a participant rather than a mere observer. Invited to be more than voyeurs ourselves, we might breathe the exhausted mantra of Herr's last lines: "Vietnam, Vietnam, Vietnam. We've all been there."

Further reading: William Hammond, *Reporting Vietnam* (1998); Donald Ringnalda, *Fighting and Writing* (1994).

There wasn't a day when someone didn't ask me what I was doing there. Sometimes an especially smart grunt or another correspondent would even ask me what I was *really* doing there, as though I could say anything honest about it except "Blah blah blah cover the war" or "Blah blah blah write a book." Maybe we accepted each other's stories about why we were there at face value: the grunts who "had" to be there, the spooks and civilians whose corporate faith had led them there, the correspondents whose curiosity or ambition drew them over. But somewhere all the mythic tracks intersected, from the lowest

John Wayne wetdream to the most aggravated soldier-poet fantasy, and where they did I believe that everyone knew everything about everyone else, every one of us there a true volunteer. Not that you didn't hear some overripe bull-shit about it: Hearts and Minds, Peoples of the Republic, tumbling dominoes, maintaining the equilibrium of the Dingdong by containing the ever en-croaching Doodah; you could also hear the other, some young soldier speak-ing in all bloody innocence, saying, "All that's just a *load*, man. We're here to kill gooks. Period." Which wasn't at all true of me. I was there to watch.

Talk about impersonating an identity, about locking into a role, about irony: I went to cover the war and the war covered me; an old story, unless of course you've never heard it. I went there behind the crude but serious belief that you had to be able to look at anything, serious because I acted on it and went, crude because I didn't know, it took the war to teach it, that you were as re-sponsible for everything you saw as you were for everything you did. The prob-lem was that you didn't always know what you were seeing until later, maybe years later, that a lot of it never made it in at all, it just stayed stored there in your eyes. Time and information, rock and roll, life itself, the information isn't frozen, you are.

Sometimes I didn't know if an action took a second or an hour or if I dreamed it or what. In war more than in other life you don't really know what you're doing most of the time, you're just behaving, and afterward you can make up any kind of bullshit you want to about it, say you felt good or bad, loved it or hated it, did this or that, the right thing or the wrong thing; still, what happened happened.

Coming back, telling stories, I'd say, "Oh man I was scared," and, "Oh God I thought it was all over," a long time before I knew how scared I was really sup-posed to be, or how clear and closed and beyond my control "all over" could become. I wasn't dumb but I sure was raw, certain connections are hard to make when you come from a place where they go around with war in their heads all the time . . .

Prayers in the Delta, prayers in the Highlands, prayers in the Marine bunkers of the "frontier" facing the DMZ, and for every prayer there was a counter-prayer—it was hard to see who had the edge. In Dalat the emperor's mother sprinkled rice in her hair so the birds could fly around her and feed while she said her morning prayers. In wood-paneled, air-conditioned chapels in Sai-gon, MACV padres would fire one up to sweet muscular Jesus, blessing ammo dumps and 105's and officers' clubs. The best-armed patrols in history went out after services to feed smoke to people whose priests could let themselves burn down to consecrated ash on street corners. Deep in the alleys you could hear small Buddhist chimes ringing for peace, *hoa bien;* smell incense in the middle of the thickest Asian street funk; see groups of ARVN with their families waiting for transport huddled around a burning prayer strip. Sermonettes came over Armed Forces radio every couple of hours, once I heard a chaplain from the 9th Division starting up, "Oh Gawd, help us learn to live with Thee in a more dynamic way in these perilous times, that we may better serve Thee in the struggle against Thine enemies. . . ." Holy war, long-nose jihad like a face-off between one god who would hold the coonskin to the wall while we nailed it up, and another whose detachment would see the blood run out of ten generations, if that was how long it took for the wheel to go around.

And around. While the last falling-off contacts were still going on and the last casualties being dusted off, Command added Dak To to our victory list, a reflexive move supported by the Saigon press corps but never once or for a minute by reporters who'd seen it going on from meters or even inches away, and this latest media defection added more bitterness to an already rotten mix, leaving the commanding general of the 4th to wonder out loud and in my hearing whether we were or weren't all Americans in this thing together. I said I thought we were. For sure we were.

"*. . . Wow I love it in the movies when they say like, 'Okay Jim, where do you want it?'*"

"*Right! Right! Yeah, beautiful, I don't want it at all! Haw, shit . . . where do you fucking want it?*"

Mythopathic moment; *Fort Apache,* where Henry Fonda as the new colonel says to John Wayne, the old hand, "We saw some Apache as we neared the Fort," and John Wayne says, "If you saw them, sir, they weren't Apache." But this colonel is obsessed, brave like a maniac, not very bright, a West Point aristo wounded in his career and his pride, posted out to some Arizona shithole with only marginal consolation: he's a professional and this is a war, the only war we've got. So he gives the John Wayne information a pass and he and half his command get wiped out. More a war movie than a Western, Nam paradigm, Vietnam, not a movie, no jive cartoon either where the characters get smacked around and electrocuted and dropped from heights, flattened out and frizzed black and broken like a dish, then up again and whole and back in the game, "Nobody dies," as someone said in another war movie . . .

One night I woke up and heard the sounds of a firefight going on kilometers away, a "skirmish" outside our perimeter, muffled by distance to sound like the noises we made playing guns as children, KSSSHH KSSSHH; we knew it was more authentic than BANG BANG, it enriched the game and this game was the same, only way out of hand at last, too rich for all but a few serious players. The rules now were tight and absolute, no arguing over who missed who and who was really dead; *No fair* was no good, *Why me?* the saddest question in the world.

Well, good luck, the Vietnam verbal tic, even Ocean Eyes, the third-tour Lurp, had remembered to at least say it to me that night before he went on the job. It came out dry and distant, I knew he didn't care one way or the other, maybe I admired his detachment. It was as though people couldn't stop themselves from saying it, even when they actually meant to express the opposite wish, like, "Die, motherfucker." Usually it was only an uninhabited passage of dead language, sometimes it came out five times in a sentence, like punctuation, often it was spoken flat side up to telegraph the belief that there wasn't any way out; tough shit, *sin loi,* smack it, good luck. Sometimes, though, it was said with such feeling and tenderness that it could crack your mask, that much love where there was so much war. Me too, every day, compulsively, good luck: to friends in the press corps going out on operations, to grunts I'd meet at firebases and airstrips, to the wounded, the dead and all the Vietnamese I ever saw getting fucked over by us and each other, less often but most passionately to myself, and though I meant it every time I said it, it was meaningless. It was like telling someone going out in a storm not to get any on him, it was the same as saying, "Gee, I hope you don't get killed or wounded or see anything that drives you insane." You could make all the ritual moves, carry your lucky piece, wear your magic jungle hat, kiss your thumb knuckle smooth as stones under running water, the Inscrutable Immutable was still out there, and you kept on or not at its pitiless discretion. All you could say that wasn't fundamentally lame was something like, "He who bites it this day is safe from the next," and that was exactly what nobody wanted to hear.

After enough time passed and memory receded and settled, the name itself became a prayer, coded like all prayer to go past the extremes of petition and gratitude: Vietnam Vietnam Vietnam, say again, until the word lost all its old loads of pain, pleasure, horror, guilt, nostalgia. Then and there, everyone was just trying to get through it, existential crunch, no atheists in foxholes like you wouldn't believe. Even bitter refracted faith was better than none at all, like the black Marine I'd heard about during heavy shelling at Con Thien who said, "Don't worry, baby, God'll think of something." . . .

I keep thinking about all the kids who got wiped out by seventeen years of war movies before coming to Vietnam to get wiped out for good. You don't know what a media freak is until you've seen the way a few of those grunts would run around during a fight when they knew that there was a television crew nearby; they were actually making war movies in their heads, doing little guts-and-glory Leatherneck tap dances under fire, getting their pimples shot off for the networks. They were insane, but the war hadn't done that to them. Most combat troops stopped thinking of the war as an adventure after their first few firefights, but there were always the ones who couldn't let that go, these few who were up there doing numbers for the cameras. A lot of correspondents weren't much better. We'd all seen too many movies, stayed too long in Television City, years of media glut had made certain connections difficult. The first few times that I got fired at or saw combat deaths, nothing really happened, all the responses got locked in my head. It was the same familiar violence, only moved over to another medium; some kind of jungle play with giant helicopters and fantastic special effects, actors lying out there in canvas body bags waiting for the scene to end so they could get up again and walk it off. But that was some scene (you found out), there was no cutting it.

A lot of things had to be unlearned before you could learn anything at all, and even after you knew better you couldn't avoid the ways in which things got mixed, the war itself with those parts of the war that were just like the movies, just like *The Quiet American* or *Catch-22* (a Nam standard because it said that in a war everybody thinks that everybody else is crazy), just like all that combat footage from television ("We're taking fire from the treeline!" "Where?" "There!" *"Where?"* "Over *there!"* "Over WHERE?" "Over THERE!!" Flynn heard that go on for fifteen minutes once; we made it an epiphany), your vision blurring, images jumping and falling as though they were being received by a dropped camera, hearing a hundred horrible sounds at once—screams, sobs, hysterical shouting, a throbbing inside your head that threatened to take over, quavering voices trying to get the orders out, the dulls and sharps of weapons going off (Lore: When they're near they whistle, when they're really near they crack), the thud of helicopter rotors, the tinny, clouded voice coming over the radio, "Uh, that's a Rog, we mark your position, over." And out. Far out.

April 30, 1975

1975

"Auden said that 'poetry makes nothing happen,'" remarked the poet John Balaban (b. 1943) in a recent interview; "but sometimes it can." During the Vietnam war, Balaban set out into the Vietnamese countryside to tape oral poetry, intending to translate "all its humane beauty" and make something happen: he thought the translations might affect how people saw the Vietnamese, and so change Americans' attitudes toward the war. He believes that to know another culture is to know our own, and that to know our own is to not repeat the errors that drove the country uncomprehendingly to war. Through learning about Vietnam's literature he glimpsed another possible society, and began to write "out of a sense of injustice, a sense of things gone disastrously wrong and the possibility of one's own implication in that injustice." He believes that writing well is a moral gesture, that knowledge results in action: "the clearest statement of the problem is the solution to the problem."

Balaban was a registered conscientious objector. Between 1967 and 1969 he lived in a South Vietnamese community and taught linguistics at a university. He noticed that the Vietnamese used poetry in their daily speech, and would ask farmers to sing their favorite poems for him to record. Many of his recordings have firefights in the background. After his university was bombed during the 1968 Tet offensive, he began work as a field representative for the Committee of Responsibility, which brought war-wounded children to the United States for treatment. The Vietnamese child Bui Ngoc Huong, to whom "April 30, 1975" is dedicated, had his lower face blown away by a landmine. It took five years of surgery in Philadelphia to construct a workable mouth for him, and he lived with Balaban during his convalescence before returning to his village.

Nixon declared a ceasefire on January 15, 1973, and by the end of March most American troops had left Vietnam. North and South Vietnamese fought until 1975, and Saigon fell in late April 1975. Balaban heard that Bui Ngoc Huong had been killed at a roadblock, just as he was beginning work on "April 30, 1975," his poem about the war's last day. Huong tried to flee, but was shot: "he had gotten very tall as a teenager on American food," Balaban explains, "so they took him for a fleeing American soldier." This background to the poem resonates with Balaban's whole approach to protest literature: just as he helped rebuild Huong's mouth, so he has tried to restore Vietnamese voices.

Like much protest literature about the Vietnam war, Balaban's poem emphasizes the violence of American culture and the likelihood of more warfare. But reading 21st-century antiwar poetry has confirmed for Balaban that the poetry of the Vietnam war has an aesthetic legacy. "Once, walking with David Ignatow and Robert Bly . . . I voiced skepticism about the enduring value of the protest poetry of the war. Bly berated me saying that I didn't understand that a 'whole new genre was being written.' Now I think he was right." At first he didn't think the analogies drawn between the two wars were accurate, but changed his mind: "Just as we were ignorant of the abiding aspirations of the Vietnamese, we failed to have a clue about what the Iraqis might want." America has entered another "period of conscience and responsibility," Balaban says. As in Vietnam, "we are made a story and a byword through the world," and "testimony is required of each of us."

In 2003 Balaban published his poem "Collateral Damage" on the Poets against the War website in protest against the War in Iraq.

(for Bui Ngoc Huong)

The evening Nixon called his last troops off
the church bells tolled across our states.
We leaned on farmhouse porch pilings, our eyes
wandering the lightning bug meadow thick with mist,
and counted tinny peals clanking out
through oaks around the church belltower.
You asked, "Is it peace, or only a bell ringing?"

This night the war has finally ended.
My wife and I sit on a littered park bench
sorting out our shared and separate lives
in the dark, in silence, before a quiet pond
where ducks tug slimy papers and bits of soggy bread.
City lights have reddened the bellies of fumed clouds
Like trip flares scorching skies over a city at war.

In whooshing traffic at the park's lit edge,
red brake lights streak to sudden halts:
a ski-masked man staggers through lanes,
maced by a girl he tried to mug.
As he crashes to curb under mercury lamps,
a man snakes towards him, wetting lips,
twirling the root of his tongue like a dial.

Some kids have burnt a bum on Brooklyn Bridge.
Screaming out of sleep: he flares the causeway.
And the war returns like figures in a dream.
In Vietnam, pagodas chime their bells.
"A Clear Mind spreads like the wind.
By the Lo waterfalls, free and high,
you wash away the dust of life."

From How to Tell a True War Story

1987

"Everything I've ever written is protest literature," said Tim O'Brien (b. 1946) in a recent interview. "Like I write in *If I Die n a Combat Zone*—'someday I plan to strike back.' My protest writing comes out of a sense of personal outrage, feeling helpless yet determined to strike back." In 1969 O'Brien went to Vietnam as an infantryman. He notes that his military service was a bad thing he did for love: he knew the war was a mistake but, when his draft notice arrived, he couldn't bear the rejection of friends, family, and country. His need for love conquered conscience, he says. Now, though, his writing is a call to conscience: "I could write analytic essays, but fiction is qualitatively different. "It puts the reader *into* the story, collapses the distance that you still feel even with a movie—the story up there on a screen. In a story you build your own pictures of people, and then you realize that the book has become part of you." His work humanizes friends and enemies alike and he describes this "empathy" as "the solution to the problem my work confronts."

O'Brien notes that he tells lies to get at the truth, that "story truths" reveal "happening truths." Even during the war these different truths interacted: "Those of us fighting took stories out there of gallantry and heroism, and America always being right; a cartoon, comic-book version of American history. We hauled a storybook psyche to Vietnam. And the stories didn't apply." O'Brien has spent thirty-five years protesting this comic-book version of history, seeking an explanation for how he ended up in Vietnam. He dwells in the time of returning, carrying the war as a burden and putting memory at the heart of his work: "My writing protests national and cultural erasure, the attempt to simply put the past behind us and 'heal.'" The public continues to forget: "When the Abu Ghraib images quickly faded from the national scene, I was reminded of how quickly the images of the My Lai massacre were forgotten, how we were told that it was the system was to blame. 'That's war for you,' they said—'That's *crime* for you,' I wanted to say. It was written off as an aberration, like Abu Ghraib." Americans are endlessly asked to forget, but "sometimes picking at a scab is helpful. The role of the artist is to uphold a sense of personal and national honesty, and keep a culture remembering." Stories can save us, he concludes, pointing to the last story in *The Things They Carried* (1990), his collection that includes the story excerpted here, which ends: "I'm skimming across the surface of my own history . . . and when I take a high leap into the dark and come down thirty years later, I realize it is as Tim trying to save Timmy's life with a story."

A true war story is never moral. It does not instruct, nor encourage virtue, nor suggest models of proper human behavior, nor restrain men from doing the things they have always done. If a story seems moral, do not believe it. If at the end of a war story you feel uplifted, or if you feel that some small bit of rectitude has been salvaged from the larger waste, then you have been made the victim of a very old and terrible lie. There is no rectitude whatsoever. There is no virtue. As a first rule of thumb, therefore, you can tell a true war story by its absolute and uncompromising allegiance to obscenity and evil . . . You can tell a true war story if it embarrasses you. If you don't care for obscenity, you don't care for the truth; if you don't care for the truth, watch how you vote. Send guys to war, they come home talking dirty . . . In any war story, but especially a true one, it's difficult to separate what happened from what seemed to happen. What seems to happen becomes its own happening and has to be told that way. The angles of vision are skewed. When a booby trap explodes, you close your eyes and duck and float outside yourself. When a guy dies, like Curt Lemon, you look away and then look back for a moment and then look away again. The pictures get jumbled; you tend to miss a lot. And then afterward, when you go to tell about it, there is always that surreal seemingness, which makes the story seem untrue, but which in fact represents the hard and exact truth as it *seemed.*

In many cases a true war story cannot be believed. If you believe it, be skeptical. It's a question of credibility. Often the crazy stuff is true and the normal stuff isn't, because the normal stuff is necessary to make you believe the truly incredible craziness.

In other cases you can't even tell a true war story. Sometimes it's just beyond the telling . . . You can tell a true war story by the way it never seems to end. Not then, not ever . . . In a true war story, if there's a moral at all, it's like the thread that makes the cloth. You can't tease it out. You can't extract the meaning without unraveling the deeper meaning. And in the end, really, there's nothing much to say about a true war story, except maybe "Oh."

True war stories do not generalize. They do not indulge in abstraction or analysis.

For example: War is hell. As a moral declaration the old truism seems perfectly true, and yet because it abstracts, because it generalizes, I can't believe it with my stomach. Nothing turns inside.

It comes down to gut instinct. A true war story, if truly told, makes the stomach believe.

How do you generalize?

War is hell, but that's not the half of it, because war is mystery and terror and adventure and courage and discovery and holiness and pity and despair and longing and love. War is nasty; war is fun. War is thrilling; war is drudgery. War makes you a man; makes you dead.

The truths are contradictory. It can be argued, for instance, that war is grotesque. But in truth war is also beauty. For all its horror, you can't help but gape at the awful majesty of combat. You stare out at tracer rounds unwinding through the dark like brilliant red ribbons. You crouch in ambush as a cool, impassive moon rises over the nighttime paddies. You admire the fluid symmetries of troops on the move, the great sheets of metal-fire streaming down from a gunship, the illumination rounds, the white phosphorus, the purply orange glow of napalm, the rocket's red glare. It's not pretty, exactly. It's astonishing. It fills the eye. It commands you. You hate it, yes, but your eyes do not. Like a killer forest fire, like cancer under a microscope, any battle or bombing raid or artillery barrage has the aesthetic purity of absolute moral indifference—a powerful, implacable beauty—and a true war story will tell the truth about this, though the truth is ugly.

To generalize about war is like generalizing about peace. Almost everything is true. Almost nothing is true. At its core, perhaps, war is just another name for death, and yet any soldier will tell you, if he tells the truth, that proximity to death brings with it a corresponding proximity to life. After a firefight, there is always the immense pleasure of aliveness. The trees are alive. The grass, the soil—everything. All around you things are purely living, and you among them, and the aliveness makes you tremble. You feel an intense, out-of-the skin awareness of your living self—your truest self, the human being you want to be and then become by the force of wanting it. In the midst of evil you want to be a good man. You want decency. You want justice and courtesy and human concord, things you never knew you wanted. There is a kind of largeness to it, a kind of godliness. Though it's odd, you're never more alive than when you're almost dead. You recognize what's valuable. Freshly, as if for the first time, you love what's best in yourself and in the world, all that might be lost. At the hour of dusk you sit at your foxhole and look out on a wide river turning pinkish red, and at the mountains beyond, and although in the morning you must cross the river and go into the mountains and do terrible things and maybe die, even so, you find yourself studying the fine colors on the river, you feel wonder and awe at the setting of the sun, and you are filled with a hard, aching love for how the world could be and always should be, but now is not.

Mitchell Sanders was right. For the common soldier, at least, war has the feel—the spiritual texture—of a great ghostly fog, thick and permanent. There is no clarity. Everything swirls. The old rules are no longer binding, the old truths no longer true. Right spills over into wrong. Order blends into chaos, hate into love, ugliness into beauty, law into anarchy, civility into savagery.

The vapors suck you in. You can't tell where you are, or why you're there, and the only certainty is absolute ambiguity.

In war you lose your sense of the definite, hence your sense of truth itself, and therefore it's safe to say that in a true war story nothing is absolutely true.

Often in a true war story there is not even a point, or else the point doesn't hit you until, say, twenty years later, in your sleep, and you wake up and shake your wife and start telling the story to her, except when you get to the end you've forgotten the point again. And then for a long time you lie there watching the story happen in your head. You listen to your wife's breathing. The war's over. You close your eyes. You smile and think, Christ, what's the *point?* . . . You can tell a true war story by the questions you ask. Somebody tells a story, let's say, and afterward you ask, "Is it true?" and if the answer matters, you've got your answer.

For example, we've all heard this one. Four guys go down a trail. A grenade sails out. One guy jumps on it and takes the blast and saves his three buddies.

Is it true?

The answer matters.

You'd feel cheated if it never happened. Without the grounding reality, it's just a trite bit of puffery, pure Hollywood, untrue in the way all such stories are untrue. Yet even if it did happen—and maybe it did, anything's possible even then you know it can't be true, because a true war story does not depend upon that kind of truth. Absolute occurrence is irrelevant. A thing may happen and be a total lie; another thing may not happen and be truer than the truth. For example: Four guys go down a trail. A grenade sails out. One guy jumps on it and takes the blast, but it's a killer grenade and everybody dies anyway. Before they die, though, one of the dead guys says, "The fuck you do *that* for?" and the jumper says, "Story of my life, man," and the other guy starts to smile but he's dead.

That's a true story that never happened . . .

You can tell a true war story if you just keep on telling it.

And in the end, of course, a true war story is never about war. It's about sunlight. It's about the special way that dawn spreads out on a river when you know you must cross that river and march into the mountains and do things you are afraid to do. It's about love and memory. It's about sorrow. It's about sisters who never write back and people who never listen.

Speak Out
LAWRENCE FERLINGHETTI

Poem of War
JIM HARRISON

Poem of Disconnected Parts
ROBERT PINSKY

2003, 2003, 2005

In January 2003, Laura Bush invited poets to take tea in the White House Rose Garden to discuss Emily Dickinson, Langston Hughes, and Walt Whitman. The poet Sam Hamill received an invitation. In response, he e-mailed fifty other poets, explaining that he'd received the invitation just as he'd heard about President Bush's proposed "Shock and Awe" attack on Iraq, and that he wanted to "reconstitute a Poets against the War movement like the one organized to speak out against the war in Vietnam." He asked poets to forward his e-mail and help compile a protest anthology to present to Laura Bush. He received fifteen hundred responses within three days. Laura Bush shut down the symposium, and Poets against the War helped organize hundreds of poetry readings instead. The activist Anne Waldman launched the "Poetry Is News Coalition" and held a "Counter-Intelligence Symposium," saying, "I am reminded these days of the American/Vietnam wars . . . This is a *war for the imagination.*" Some 66,000 people signed a "Not in Our Name Statement of Conscience," which asserted, "We . . . draw on the many examples of resistance and conscience from the past of the United States: from those who fought slavery . . . to those who defied the Vietnam war."

Hamill created a website for the poems, and by March 1, 2003, more than 13,000 poems were posted. He delivered them to Congress and many entered the Congressional Record. Lawrence Ferlinghetti (b. 1919), who wrote antiwar poems in the 1960s, contributed the first poem printed here. In 2004 Robert Bly, who had written protest poems against the Vietnam war, put together a collection entitled *The Insanity of Empire: A Book of Poems against the Iraq War,* and in 2005, some 15,000 people signed the "New Not in Our Name Statement of Conscience," which declared: "The movement against the war in Vietnam never won a presidential election. But it blocked troop trains, closed induction centers, marched, spoke to people door to door—and it helped to stop a war." Antiwar protest art also included Michael Moore's *Fahrenheit 9/11* (2004), the highest grossing documentary film to date, and Green Day's hit album *American Idiot* (2004).

Another poet invited to the White House event was the former Poet Laureate Robert

Pinsky (b. 1940). He replied to the invitation: "In our current political situation I am unwilling to participate in a Washington event that invokes an 'American voice' in the singular . . . in the house of authority I mistrust, on the verge of a questionable war . . . the more so when I remember the candid, rebellious, individualistic voices of Dickinson, Whitman, Langston Hughes." In July 2005, the *Washington Post* invited Pinsky to help compose a "new Pledge of Allegiance" for their features page. He declined, replying: "I don't believe that I got much from chanting sentences of allegiance . . . My classmates and I would have been better off . . . if the teacher had read a different passage from *Leaves of Grass* each morning." That same month Pinsky wrote "Poem of Disconnected Parts," published here for the first time. In an interview he explained: "In this time of immense American power, military and economic, in the wake of an American invasion of Iraq . . . do I not have particular, urgent responsibilities?" He is angry at the government much of the time and when he thinks about how that anger relates to poetry, he imagines his task as "reopening and questioning metaphors." He's trying to be an expert not in foreign policy, but rather in "the contradictions and reversals of language": "Great rhetoric may talk as though there is only politics. Great erotic passion may talk as though there is only eros. Poetry, in contrast with these, somehow acknowledges or implies the All . . . It excludes nothing. Irritably, it looks beyond everything." Poetry doesn't describe the world as it is, but tries to "bring about by words the world as it potentially, maybe essentially, can be."

Laura Bush's symposium was reminiscent of President Johnson's "White House Festival of the Arts," scheduled for June 1965. Then as now, poets declined the invitation. The Poetry against the War readings were also reminiscent of New York's "Angry Arts Week" of 1967. And, like Hamill's original e-mail, Waldman's remark, and the "Not in Our Name" statements, dozens of poems submitted to Poets against the War explicitly link Iraq and Vietnam. Like the protest literature of the Vietnam war, some allude to movie Westerns: in the poem by Jim Harrison (b. 1937) printed here, Clint Eastwood whispers, "George, they were only movies."

Speak Out

LAWRENCE FERLINGHETTI/2003

And a vast paranoia sweeps across the land
And America turns the attack on its Twin Towers
Into the beginning of the Third World War
The war with the Third World

And the terrorists in Washington
Are shipping out the young men
To the killing fields again

And no one speaks

And they are rousting out

All the ones with turbans
And they are flushing out
All the strange immigrants

And they are shipping all the young men
To the killing fields again

And no one speaks

And when they come to round up
All the great writers and poets and painters
The National Endowment of the Arts of Complacency
Will not speak

While all the young men
Will be killing all the young men
In the killing fields again

So now is the time for you to speak
All you lovers of liberty
All you lovers of the pursuit of happiness
All you lovers and sleepers
Deep in your private dream
Now is the time for *you* to speak
O silent majority!

Poem of War

JIM HARRISON/2003

The old rancher of seventy-nine years
said while branding and nutting young bulls
with the rank odor of burned hairs and flesh
in the air, the oil slippery red nuts
plopping into a galvanized bucket,
"this smells just like Guadalcanal."

The theocratic cowboy forgetting Viet Nam rides
into town on a red horse. He's praying to himself
not God, though the two are confused
in the heat of vengeance. The music
is the thump of derricks, the computerized
lynch mob geek dissonance. Clint Eastwood
whispers from an alley, "George, they

were only movies." Shock and Awe.
God is only on God's side. War prayers
swim in their tanks of pus like poisoned
frogs in algae laden ponds. The red horse
he rides is the horse of blasphemy. Jesus
leads a flower laden donkey across the Red Sea
in the other directions, his nose full of the stink
of corpses. Buddha and Mohammed offer
cool water from a palm's shade while young
men die in the rocket's red glare
and in the old men's hard puckered dreams
René Char asked, "Who stands on the gangplank
directing operations, the captain or the rats?"
Whitman said, "so many young throats
choked on their own blood." God says nothing.

Poem of Disconnected Parts
ROBERT PINSKY/2005

At Robben Island the political prisoners studied.
They coined the motto *Each one Teach one.*

In Argentina the torturers demanded the prisoners
Address them always as *"Profesor."*

Many of my friends are moved by guilt, but I
Am a creature of shame, I am ashamed to say.

Culture the lock, culture the key. Imagination
That calls boiled sheep heads "Smileys."

The first year at Guantánamo, Abdul Rahim Dost
Incised his Pashto poems into styrofoam cups.

"The Sangomo says in our Zulu culture we do not
Worship our ancestors: we consult them."

Becky is abandoned in 1902 and Rose dies giving
Birth in 1924 and Sylvia falls in 1951.

Still falling still dying still abandoned in 2005
Still nothing finished among the descendants.

I support the War says the comic it's just the Troops
I'm against: can't stand those Young People.

Proud of the fallen, proud of her son the bomber.
Ashamed of the government. Skeptical.

After the Klansman was found Not Guilty one juror
Said she just couldn't vote to convict a pastor.

So who do you write for? I write for dead people:
For Emily Dickinson, for my grandfather.

"The Ancestors say the problem with your Knees
Began in your Feet. It could move up your Back."

But later the Americans gave Dost not only paper
And pen but books. Hemingway, Dickens.

Old Aegyptius said Whoever has called this Assembly,
For whatever reason—it is a good in itself.

O avid shades who regard my offering, O stained earth.
There are many fake Sangomos. This one is real.

Coloured prisoners got different meals and could wear
Long pants and underwear, Blacks got only shorts.

No he says he cannot regret the three years in prison:
Otherwise he would not have written those poems.

I have a small-town mind. Like the Greeks and Trojans.
Shame. Pride. Importance of looking bad or good.

Did he see anything like the prisoner on a leash? Yes,
In Afghanistan. In Guantánamo he was isolated.

Our enemies "disassemble" says the President.
Not that anyone at all couldn't mis-speak.

The *profesores* created nicknames for torture devices:
The Airplane. The Frog. Burping the Baby.

Not that those who behead the helpless in the name
Of God or tradition don't also write poetry.

Guilts, metaphors, traditions. Hunger strikes.
Culture the penalty. Culture the escape.

What could your children boast about you? What
Will your father say, down among the shades?

The Sangomo told Marvin, "You are crushed by some
Weight. Only your own Ancestors can help you."

Who Would Jesus Torture?

2004

"What I am doing is the essence of what it means to be American," explained the activist and artist Clinton Fein (b. 1964), in a recent interview; "America's history is rich with people who went against the grain . . . dissent is the most powerful tool America has, and ensuring its protection is the most patriotic thing an American can do." He's part of a satiric protest tradition that extends from Philip Freneau to Doric Wilson. His photomontages are also part of a graphic-design protest tradition that includes ACT UP's posters (cited by Fein as "unbelievably successful, smart, nimble, and creative").

Fein, who was raised in South Africa under apartheid and came to America in 1986, battles for First Amendment rights. On January 30, 1997, he filed a lawsuit against Attorney General Janet Reno, challenging the constitutionality of the Communications Decency Act. Signed into law by Clinton in February 1996, this act made it a felony to communicate anything "indecent with the intent to annoy." At the same time Fein launched his infamous website, Annoy.com. The case reached the Supreme Court, which decided that communications, even if intended to "annoy," were protected by the Constitution. It was a landmark victory for First Amendment rights. But after 9/11, Fein felt alone in using those rights. "I was astounded at how few artists there were who were doing or saying anything even remotely political," he said; "too many artists were deafeningly silent during a time when it would have been helpful for them to speak out."

Fein resists the idea that "art and literature exist in a vacuum, and particularly that text is obligated to evoke pleasure." Critiquing a culture of fear and the Bush administration's "Shock and Awe" military policy, his art is calculated to shock. Technology is his weapon: he digitally alters images and subversively collages fragments, so that Condoleezza Rice becomes Marie Antoinette, Bin Laden the Statue of Liberty. The performance art of his continually published images parallel and challenge an amnesiac 24-hour news cycle, and he notes that the Internet best accommodates contemporary protest: although antiwar protestors didn't manage to stop the Iraq war, the Internet allowed them to mobilize huge demonstrations.

He believes that if the mainstream media were allowed to show what was really going on in Iraq, "America would be pulling out of there within a month, and Bush would be facing impeachment." He watches the media deal with the legacy of the Vietnam war: the resistance to the word "quagmire"; the Pentagon's refusal to allow images of returning coffins; the decision to "embed" journalists in Iraq, which Fein calls "the single most brilliant censorship strategy I have ever seen." In 2004 Fein himself faced censorship when a printing company destroyed two of his images days before an exhibition opening. One, reproduced here, was "Who Would Jesus Torture?," which the company felt would offend Christians.

It pictures President Bush with a missile as his phallus, recalling Maj. T. J. "King" Kong straddling a missile at the end of the movie *Dr. Strangelove* (1964). In the background is an Abu Ghraib image of a prisoner receiving a simulated blowjob: Fein used this "to add the sexual dimension that seemed to be glaringly obvious in the Abu Ghraib imagery— the elephant in the room." The elephants in the image represent three notions: a refusal to state the obvious; Republicans; and a circus elephant who killed her trainer in 1916. Attempts to electrocute or shoot her failed, and she was hung. Fein's image comments further on the death penalty: Lynndie England, the soldier punished for her role in the incident, sits on an electric chair, and Donald Rumsfeld and John Ashcroft strap Saddam Hussein into another. This asks "how exactly America thinks it retains the moral highroad to even condemn the torture being perpetrated in its name, when it still executes people." The outstretched arm of an Iraqi, from another Abu Ghraib image, provides the question Bush is trying to balance, which Fein formulates as: "Would killing Lynndie England and Saddam Hussein equal the damage wrought by the torturing of the Iraqis by both Saddam Hussein and the Americans?"

The crucifixion imagery echoes Nick Ut's famous photograph "Napalm" (1972). Fein echoed that photograph to debunk the idea that one kind of violence is worse than another: "Whether you're running naked screaming with napalm covering your body, or being forced to climb onto a human pyramid of naked prisoners, all represent violence. There's no screaming of 'baby killers' at active duty service members, yet babies have hardly been spared the horror of tons of depleted uranium dumped on them." Struck by the lack of outraged public response to the Abu Ghraib images, he concluded that a "combination of communications allowing instant gratification, collective attention deficit disorder, information glut, and an unwillingness to confront who we are in those grainy photos, all combined to defuse their impact." So he tried to make the images into something that might rival the protest art of the Vietnam war.

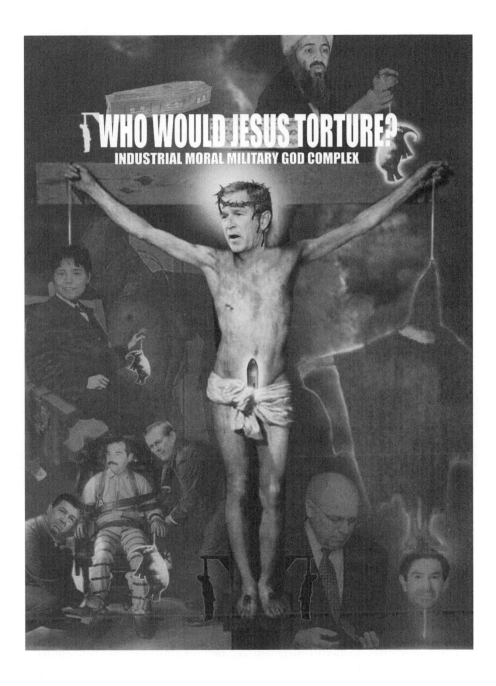

From Born on the Fourth of July

1976, 2005

Ron Kovic (b. 1946) remembers that *Born on the Fourth of July* (1976) came like an explosion. He worked until his fingers hurt and finished most of the book in two months, in 1974, exactly a decade after he'd first left for Vietnam. Kovic, who was left paralyzed after a war injury, wanted to explain why he had eventually opposed the war—an opposition that landed him in jail twelve times and earned him the label "Communist traitor"—and marched with Vietnam Veterans Against the War (VVAW). The book was made into an Academy Award–winning film directed by Oliver Stone in 1989. It was the second film in Stone's Vietnam trilogy, which includes *Platoon* (1986) and *Heaven and Earth* (1993).

VVAW now tries to teach the lessons of Vietnam and stop further wars. It opposes the Iraq war, noting that the Bush administration's justifications are as misguided as those used to send its members to Southeast Asia. VVAW recently inspired the formation of a group called Iraq Veterans Against the War, who were visible at the 2004 Democratic Convention, just as Kovic had made a controversial appearance at the 1976 convention. And Kovic is back protesting a new war. He had come back from Vietnam and pieced together a book from the wreckage—a salvaging process, like numerous protest writers who have stitched their literature from the material of earlier protest movements. His memoir had focused on the legacy of the Vietnam war, the veteran experience, and the changing relationship between protestors and government. Now, in a new introduction to the book, excerpted here, he identifies a new legacy of the Vietnam war: "the mirror image of another Vietnam unfolding." The ghosts of Vietnam rise up from the sands of Iraq. Yet again, he has the mission of "shouting from the highest rooftops, warning the American people . . . pleading for an alternative": it's a mantra and a manifesto for American protest literature.

For the past two years we have been involved in a tragic and senseless war in Iraq. As of this writing, over 1,500 Americans have died and more than 11,000 have been wounded, while tens of thousands of innocent Iraqi civilians, many of them women and children, have been killed.

I have watched in horror the mirror image of another Vietnam unfolding. So many similarities, so many things said that remind me of that war thirty years ago which left me paralyzed for the rest of my life. Refusing to learn from our experiences in Vietnam, our government continues to pursue a policy of deception, distortion, manipulation, and denial, doing everything it can to hide from the American people their true intentions and agenda in Iraq. The flag-draped caskets of our dead begin their long and sorrowful journeys home hidden from public view, while the Iraqi casualties are not even considered worth counting—some estimate as many as 100,000 have been killed so far.

The paraplegics, amputees, burn victims, the blinded and maimed, shocked and stunned, brain damaged and psychologically stressed, now fill our veterans hospitals. Most of them were not even born when I came home wounded to the Bronx V.A. in 1968. The same lifesaving medical-evacuation procedures that kept me alive in Vietnam are bringing home a whole new generation of severely maimed from Iraq.

Post-traumatic stress disorder (PTSD), which afflicted so many of us after Vietnam, is just now beginning to appear among soldiers recently returned from the current war. For some, the agony and suffering, the sleepless nights, anxiety attacks, and awful bouts of insomnia, loneliness, alienation, anger, and rage, will last for decades, if not their whole lives. They will be trapped in a permanent nightmare of that war, of killing another man, a child, watching a friend die . . . fighting against an enemy that can never be seen, while at any moment someone—a child, a woman, an old man, anyone—might kill you. These traumas return home with us and we carry them, sometimes hidden, for agonizing decades. They deeply impact our daily lives, and the lives of those closest to us.

To kill another human being, to take another life out of this world with one pull of a trigger, is something that never leaves you. It is as if a part of you dies with them. If you choose to keep on living, there may be a healing, and even hope and happiness again—but that scar and memory and sorrow will be with you forever.

Some of these veterans are showing up at homeless shelters around our country, while others have begun to courageously speak out against the senselessness and insanity of this war and the leaders who sent them there. During the 2004 Democratic Convention, returning soldiers formed a group called Iraq Veterans Against the War, just as we marched in Miami in August of 1972 as Vietnam Veterans Against the War. Still others have refused deployment to Iraq, gone to Canada, and begun resisting this immoral and illegal war.

For months leading up to the invasion of Iraq, citizens here in the United States and around the world marched and demonstrated in growing opposition to our government's reckless plan to launch an attack. I proudly participated in protests in Los Angeles, San Francisco, and Washington, D.C., doing countless interviews and speaking out wherever people would listen to me. Many prominent world leaders, including Nelson Mandela and Pope John Paul II, began to raise their voices against the terrible and ill-fated foreign policy. This extraordinary opposition culminated on February 15, 2003, when more than 30 million citizens in over 100 nations participated in the most massive demonstration on behalf of peace in the history of the world. Never before had so many human beings come together before a war had even begun to say no to the insanity and madness.

Many of us promised ourselves long ago that we would never allow what happened to us in Vietnam to happen again. We had an obligation, a responsibility as citizens, as Americans, as human beings, to raise our voices in protest. We could never forget the hospitals, the intensive care wards, the wounded all around us fighting for their lives, those long and painful years after we came home, those lonely nights. There were lives to save on both sides, young men and women who would be disfigured and maimed, mothers and fathers who would lose their sons and daughters, wives and loved ones who would suffer for decades to come if we did not do everything we could to stop the forward momentum of this madness. We sensed it very early and very quickly. We saw the same destructive patterns reasserting themselves all over again as our leaders spoke of "bad guys" and "evil-doers," "imminent threats" and "mushroom clouds," attempting to frighten and intimidate the American people into supporting their agenda.

The Bush administration seems to have learned some very different lessons than we did from Vietnam. Where we learned of the deep immorality and obscenity of that war, they learned to be even more brutal, more violent and ruthless, i.e., "shock and awe." Sadly, the war on terror has become a war of terror. Where we learned to be more open and honest, to be more truthful, to expose, to express, to shatter the myths of the past, they seem to have learned the exact opposite—to hide, to censor, to fabricate, to mislead and deceive—to perpetuate those myths.

Instead of being intimidated or frightened, many of us became more outraged and more determined than ever to stop these ignorant, arrogant men and women who never saw the things we saw, never had to grieve over the loss of their bodies or the bodies of their sons and daughters, never had to watch as so many friends and fellow veterans were destroyed by alcoholism and drugs, homelessness, imprisonment, neglect and rejection, torture, abandonment and betrayal, in the painful aftermath of the war. These leaders have never experienced the tears, the dread and rage, the feeling that there is no God, no country, nothing but the wound, the horrifying memories, the shock, the guilt, the shame, the terrible injustice that took the lives of more than 58,000 Americans and over two million Vietnamese.

We had to act. We had to speak.

I am no longer the 28-year-old man, six years returned from the war in Vietnam, who sat behind that typewriter in Santa Monica in the fall of 1974. I am nearly 60 now. My hair and beard are almost completely white. The nightmares and anxiety attacks have all but disappeared, but I still do not sleep well at night. I toss and turn in increasing physical pain. But I remain very positive and optimistic. I am still determined to rise above all of this. I know my pain and the horrors of my past will always be with me, but perhaps not with the same force and fury of those early years after the war.

I have learned to forgive my enemies and forgive myself. It has been very difficult to heal from the war while living in America, and I have often dreamed of moving to neutral ground, another country. Yet I have somehow made a certain peace, even in a nation that so often still seems to believe in war and the use of violence as a solution to its problems. There has been a reckoning, a renewal. The scar will always be there, a living reminder of that war, but it has also become something beautiful now, something of faith and hope and love.

I have been given an opportunity to move through that dark night of the soul to a new shore, to gain an understanding, a knowledge, an entirely different vision. I now believe I have suffered for a reason, and in many ways I have found that reason in my commitment to peace and nonviolence. My life has been a blessing in disguise, even with the pain and great difficulty that my physical disability continues to bring. It is a blessing to be able to speak on behalf of peace, to be able to reach such a great number of people.

I saw firsthand what our government's terrible policy had wrought. I endured; I survived and understood. The one gift I was given in that war was an awakening. I became a messenger, a living symbol, an example, a man who learned that love and forgiveness are more powerful than hatred, who has learned to embrace all men and women as my brothers and sisters. No one will ever again be my enemy, no matter how hard they try to frighten and intimidate me. No government will ever teach me to hate another human being. I have been given the task of lighting a lantern, ringing a bell, shouting from the highest rooftops, warning the American people and citizens everywhere of the deep immorality and utter wrongness of this approach to solving our problems, pleading for an alternative to this chaos and madness, this insanity and brutality. We must change course.

I truly feel that this beautiful world has given me back so much more than it has taken from me. So many others that I knew are gone, and gone way too young. I am grateful to be alive after all these years and all that I've been through. I am thankful for every day. Life is so precious.

Afterword

I read "protest literature" as a teenager—John Steinbeck's *The Grapes of Wrath* (1939), Upton Sinclair's *Boston* (1928)—without distinguishing it from any other kind of literature. But there was clearly something about this kind of writing that held a special attraction for me. Only later did I realize that even the aesthetic element (which some people think is all one should care about) was enhanced for me by the fact that it was a *political* act thrust into the social struggles of our time.

Now, reading Zoe Trodd's provocative examination of this genre, I am forced to examine the question: how exactly (or even roughly) does protest literature do what I assume it is meant to do? How does it change the world? Or, more modestly, how does it enhance the social consciousness of a reader, moving him or her to think about injustice and even to act against it?

I can think of several ways in which such writing has these effects that I am talking about. And I must add that I am not distinguishing between fiction and nonfiction, not just because protest literature exists in both forms, but also because the line between the two is not clear: fiction may give you vital fact, and nonfiction is in its own way an imaginative reconstruction of reality.

The most obvious—and therefore often overlooked—contribution to social change that literature can make is simply to inform people of something they know nothing about, to startle them with new information into reaching for something that was previously beyond their vision. When Upton Sinclair wrote *The Jungle* (1906), what he told about the meat packing industry—both the conditions of the people who worked there, and the quality of meat that made its way into American kitchens—provoked such concern as to cause Congress to pass the Meat Inspection Act of 1906. Rachel Carson's *The Sea Around Us* (1951) and *The Silent Spring* (1962) led millions of people to think, for the first time, about their natural environment and sparked not only national legislation, but the beginnings of a social movement.

But there are other situations where we *believe* we know something, but don't *really* know it in a visceral way; we don't know it emotionally to the point where it moves us to action. White people in the United States always 'knew' that black people were discriminated against. Certainly that was true of the white students in my classes at Boston University. Only when these students read Malcolm X's *Autobiography* (1965), or Richard Wright's *Black Boy*

(1945), or the poems of Countee Cullen and Langston Hughes, were they confronted with the reality of black life. They had no idea why black people might be so angry, and were not only confused but made fearful by that anger. The prose of Malcolm X, or of James Baldwin, made them, for the first time, *understand*.

As a young man, I knew (or thought I knew), that black people were treated as inferiors, discriminated against in a hundred different ways. One day I picked up a book of poems by Countee Cullen, poet of the Harlem Renaissance, and read a poem called "Incident" (1925). He recalls a trip to Baltimore. He was eight years old, sitting on a bus, when a white boy, about his own age, stuck out his tongue and called him "nigger." The poem's last lines are: "I traveled all through Baltimore, from May until December, but of all the things that happened there, that's all that I remember." Those lines reached deep inside me. For the first time I understood what it must be like to be humiliated because of your color. And after all, humiliation is a universal experience—beyond color.

Or, here's another example of what I mean by *really* knowing something: everyone knows war is hell, but unless you have been inside a war, it remains an abstraction, the numbers of the dead just numbers, the crosses in the cemetery just crosses. But there is a literature of war which brings you up short, makes you think for the first time about what it's truly, truly like—in such a way as to revolt, nauseate, and turn you against war no matter what lofty justifications come from the mouths of authority.

That was the effect on me as a young man, reading Dalton Trumbo's novel *Johnny Got His Gun* (1939). Here was war, brought home to me in a way I had never experienced. The stump of a young American is found in the no-man's-land of World War I. It is a torso without arms or legs, unable to see or hear, but the heart is still beating and the brain is still working. It is brought onto a hospital bed, and the novel then consists of the thoughts going on within that brain, and the finally successful struggle to communicate with the outside world.

Then generals arrive to pin a medal on his chest. They ask him: "What do you want?" The response: "Take me into the schoolhouses all the schoolhouses in the world . . . Take me wherever there are parliaments and diets and congresses and chambers of statesmen. I want to be there when they talk about honor and justice and making the world safe for democracy and fourteen points and the self determination of peoples . . . But before they . . . give the order for all the little guys to start killing each other let the main guy rap his gavel on my case and point down at me and say here gentlemen is the only issue before this house and that is are you for this thing or are you against it."

I was in a war, bombing cities in Europe during World War II. And yet, I didn't really understand what I was doing, and what was happening to the human beings below. Flying six miles above the ground, releasing my bombs, I could hear no screams, see no blood and no mangled corpses of children. Modern warfare can remove even combatants from the human effects of their actions. I reacted to the bombing of Hiroshima as I had reacted to my own bombing missions—with a coldness of which I am still ashamed.

And then I read John Hersey's *Hiroshima* (1946). He talked to the survivors of the atomic bomb—people with limbs missing, sockets for eyes, their skin horrible to look at. For the first time I understood bombing, and from that time on I have never accepted the glib apologies for "accidents," the talk about "collateral damage," the references to "smart" bombs, the explanations of why it was necessary to "shock and awe" the entire population of a city in order to rid it of its tyrant.

There is still another way in which literature can affect our social consciousness. The literature of the absurd creates bizarre and unreal situations which upset our ways of thinking about the world. Novels like Mark Twain's *A Connecticut Yankee in King Arthur's Court* (1889) move outside the boundaries of 'rational' thought, and compel us to make a radical break from the orthodoxies that have confined us. We doubt our assumptions.

I think of Voltaire's *Candide* (1759). How many thousands of sermons are preached every Sunday where, in the midst of a world in pain, we are assured by the Pangloss in the pulpit that it is God's will? Or I think of Joseph Heller's equally absurdist *Catch-22* (1961), in particular the scene in the Italian brothel where the old man tells Yossarian that the Italians will win, because they are so "weak," while the Americans will lose because they are so "strong." An absurd statement; but if you don't immediately dismiss it, these words may haunt you, and make you think like you haven't thought before, as the *Tao Te Ching* does in its own way.

Ultimately, protest literature should move people to think more broadly, feel more deeply, and begin to act; perhaps alone at first, but then with others. It works on the supposition that social change comes through the combined and cumulative actions of many people, even if they do not know one another or are not aware of one another's existence. If this is so, then Kurt Vonnegut's comment, in *Timequake* (1997), is appropriate. He has been asked many times, he says, why he bothers writing. He responds that he writes to tell the reader: "I care about the same things you care about. You are not alone."

Protest literature says to the reader, have hope—you are not alone. And if it does nothing but that, it has done something profoundly important.

Sources

Philip Freneau, "A Political Litany": First published in the American press in 1775; rept. in Fred Lewis Pattee, ed., *The Poems of Philip Freneau, Poet of the American Revolution* (Princeton: The University Library, 1902–1907), III: 141.

Thomas Paine, *Common Sense: Addressed to the Inhabitants of America on the Following Interesting Subjects, Written by an Englishman* (Philadelphia: R. Bell, 1776).

John Witherspoon, "The Dominion of Providence over the Passions of Men: A Sermon Preached at Princeton, on the 17th of May, 1776" (Philadelphia: R. Aitken, 1776).

Declaration of Independence: "The Unanimous Declaration of the Thirteen United States of America, July 4, 1776," National Archives.

J. Hector St. John de Crèvecoeur, *Letters from an American Farmer* (London: T. Davies, 1782), Letter IX.

George Evans, "The Working Men's Party Declaration of Independence," *Working Men's Advocate* (New York), 1829; rept. in *Mechanic's Free Press* (Philadelphia), December 26, 1829.

Seneca Falls Declaration of Sentiments: Written July 16, 1848, and presented at the Seneca Falls convention on woman's rights, July 19, 1848. Printed in national newspapers, July 1848, and in Elizabeth Cady Stanton, *A History of Woman Suffrage* (Rochester: Fowler and Wells, 1889), I:70–71.

Henry David Thoreau, "Resistance to Civil Government": Originally a lecture delivered January 26, 1848. First published in Elizabeth Peabody, ed., *Aesthetic Papers* (New York: Putnam, 1849). Published as "On the Duty of Civil Disobedience" in *A Yankee in Canada with Anti-Slavery and Reform Papers* (Boston: Ticknor and Fields, 1866).

John Brown, "Provisional Constitution and Ordinances for the People of the United States, May 8, 1858" (Hamilton, Canada, 1858), reprinted in full in Zoe Trodd and John Stauffer, eds., *Meteor of War: The John Brown Story* (2004), 109–120.

Daniel De Leon, "Declaration of Interdependence," in *The People* (New York), June 30, 1895. See *slp.org/pdf/mbrmtrls/slp_const.pdf* for the Constitution of the Socialist Labor Party, adopted at the National Convention in New York, July 1904 (accessed 08/05/05).

Tecumseh, speech to Governor William Harrison, delivered August 11, 1810. Different versions of this translated speech exist: see also Edward Eggleston, *Techumseh and the Shawnee Prophet* (1878), 182–186, and *Governors Messages and Letters*, vol. 1 (Indiana Historical Commission, 1922), 463–467.

William Apess, "An Indian's Looking-Glass for the White Man," in *The Experiences of Five Christian Indians of the Pequot Tribe* (Boston: James B. Dow, 1833)

Lydia Sigourney, "Indian Names," in *Select Poems by Mrs. L. H. Sigourney* (Philadelphia: Parry and McMillan, 1856), 258–260.

Charles Eastman, *From the Deep Woods to Civilization: Chapters in the Autobiography of an Indian* (Boston: Little, Brown, 1916).

Black Elk and John G. Neihardt, *Black Elk Speaks: Being the Life Story of a Holy Man of the Oglala Sioux* (University of Nebraska Press, 1932). Copyright © 1932, 1959, 1972 by

John G. Neihardt. © 1961 by the John G. Neihardt Trust. © 2000 by the University of
Nebraska Press. Reprinted by permission of the University of Nebraska Press.

Dee Brown, *Bury My Heart at Wounded Knee: An Indian History of the American West* (New
York: Holt, Rinehart & Winston, 1970). Copyright by The Dee Brown LLC. Reprinted
by permission of Sterling Lord Literistic, Inc.

Birgil Kills Straight and Richard LaCourse, "What Is the American Indian Movement?"
American Indian Press Association, issued in 1973. See *aimovement.org* for the American
Indian Movement, and *usinfo.state.gov/usa/infousa/society/landmark/indian.pdf* for the
1968 Indian Civil Rights Act (both accessed 09/01/05). Reprinted by permission of the
American Indian Movement Grand Governing Council.

Roland Winkler, "American Indians and Vietnamese" poster. Library of Congress Prints and
Photographs Division.

Mary Crow Dog with Richard Erdoes, *Lakota Woman* (New York: Grove Weidenfeld, 1990).
Copyright © 1990 by Mary Crow Dog and Richard Erdoes. Used by permission of
Grove/Atlantic, Inc.

Sherman Alexie, "The Exaggeration of Despair," in *The Summer of Black Widows* (Brooklyn,
N.Y.: Hanging Loose Press, 1996). © 1996 by Sherman Alexie. Reprinted by permission
of Hanging Loose Press.

David Walker, *Appeal, in four articles; together with a preamble, to the coloured citizens of the
world, but in particular, and very expressly, to those of the United States of America, written in
Boston, state of Massachusetts, September 28, 1829,* 3d and last ed. (Boston: D. Walker,
1830).

Harriet Beecher Stowe, *Uncle Tom's Cabin, or, Life among the Lowly* (Boston: J. P. Jewett,
1852).

Frederick Douglass, "The Meaning of July Fourth for the Negro": Excerpt from a speech
published as *Oration, Delivered in Corinthian Hall, Rochester, July 5, 1852.* Rept. in *The
Frederick Douglass Papers, Series One* (New Haven: Yale University Press, 1979–1992),
2:359–388.

John Brown, prison letters, October 21–December 2, 1859: Published in the national press;
rept. in Zoe Trodd and John Stauffer, eds., *Meteor of War: The John Brown Story* (New
York: Brandywine, 2004), 134–159.

Harriet Jacobs, *Incidents in the Life of a Slave Girl, Written By Herself,* edited by Lydia Maria
Child (Boston: Published for the Author, 1861).

Emancipation Proclamation and Constitutional Amendments: National Archives. Lincoln
read the first draft of the Proclamation to Cabinet members on July 22, 1862, and issued the preliminary version on September 22, which specified that the final document would take effect January 1, 1863. Thirteenth Amendment passed by Congress
January 31, 1865, ratified December 6, 1865; Fourteenth Amendment passed by Congress June 13, 1866, ratified July 9, 1868; Fifteenth Amendment passed by Congress
February 26, 1869, ratified February 3, 1870.

Ralph Chaplin, "Solidarity Forever," in *I.W.W. Songs: To Fan the Flames of Discontent* (Chicago: I.W.W. Publishing Bureau, 1917), 26.

James Baldwin, "Everybody's Protest Novel," in *Notes of a Native Son* (Boston: Beacon Press,
1955).

Still from *The Defiant Ones,* directed by Stanley Kramer. Lomitas Productions, Inc., and AC
Curtleigh Productions, Inc. Reprinted by permission of Metro Goldwyn Mayer.

Kevin Bales, *Disposable People: New Slavery in the Global Economy* (Berkeley: University of
California Press, 1999). Reprinted by permission of the University of California Press.
Bales's comments in the headnote are from an interview with Zoe Trodd (05/04/05).

Wendell Phillips, "Shall Women Have the Right to Vote?": Speech at Woman's Rights Convention, Worcester, Mass., October 15, 1851. Published as a pamphlet, *Freedom for Women: Speech of Wendell Phillips, Esq. at the Convention Held at Worcester, October 15 and 16, 1851* (Syracuse: Woman's Rights Tracts, 1852). This version from the pamphlet *Shall Women Have the Right to Vote?* (Philadelphia: Equal Franchise Society of Pennsylvania, 1910).

Lydia Maria Child, "Women and Suffrage," published in *The Independent,* January 17, 1867.

National Woman Suffrage Association, *Declaration and Protest of the Women of the United States, July 4th, 1876* (Philadelphia: NWSA, 1876), 1–4. Also printed in Elizabeth Cady Stanton et al., eds., *History of Woman Suffrage* (New York: NAWSA, 1881–1922), III: 31–34.

Elizabeth Cady Stanton, "Solitude of Self": Excerpts from address delivered before the United States Congressional Committee on the Judiciary, January 18, 1892. Published in *Woman's Journal,* January 23, 1892, and in Elizabeth Cady Stanton et al., eds., *History of Woman Suffrage* (New York: Fowler & Wells, 1881–1922), IV: 189–195.

Charlotte Perkins Gilman, "The Yellow Wallpaper," first published in *New England Magazine* 5 (January 1892): 647–656.

Mary Church Terrell, "Frederick Douglass": Excerpts from a speech at the 60th anniversary celebration of the Seneca Falls Convention, 1908, in *Centennial Anniversary of Seneca County and Auxiliary Paper* (Seneca Falls: Seneca Falls Historical Society, 1908), 54–58.

Jane Addams, "Why Women Should Vote," *Ladies' Home Journal* 27 (January 1910), 21–22.

Charlotte Perkins Gilman, *Herland,* first serialized in *The Forerunner* 6 (1915), a journal edited by Gilman.

Nineteenth Amendment and Equal Rights Amendments: Nineteenth Amendment passed by Congress June 4, 1919, ratified August 18, 1920, in the Center for Legislative Archives, Washington D.C. Equal Rights Amendment: Senate Joint Resolution No. 21 of December 10, 1923, House Joint Resolution No. 75 of December 13, 1923. Reworded Equal Rights Amendment proposed in Congress, 1943, in the *National Woman's Party Papers, 1913–1974* (Glenn Rock: Microfilming Corporation of America, 1977–1978).

Crystal Eastman, "Now We Can Begin": Speech delivered in New York, September 1920, published in *The Liberator,* December 1920.

Rebecca Harding Davis, *Life in the Iron Mills:* first edition published in *The Atlantic Monthly,* April 1861.

Edward Bellamy, *Looking Backward 2000–1887* (Boston: Houghton Mifflin, 1888).

Jacob Riis, *How the Other Half Lives* (New York: Charles Scribner, 1890), chapters 4, 11, and 25. Image from chapter 6 showing unauthorized immigration lodgings in a Bayard Street tenement in New York City from the Library of Congress, Prints and Photographs Division.

Upton Sinclair, *The Jungle* (New York: Doubleday, Page and Company, 1906).

Lewis Hine, "Sadie Pfeifer, 48 inches high, has worked half a year. One of the many small children at work in Lancaster Cotton Mills. Nov. 30, 1908. Location: Lancaster, South Carolina," Library of Congress, Prints and Photographs Division. "Making Human Junk," montage poster published in *Child Labor Bulletin* 3 (1914–1915) and in Hine's pamphlet "The High Cost of Child Labor" (1915). Library of Congress Prints and Photographs Division, National Child Labor Committee Collection.

Ignatius Donnelly, "The People's Party Platform": Presented at the People's Party's first national convention in Omaha on July 4, 1892, and published in the *Omaha Morning World-Herald,* July 5, 1892. Also known as the "Populist Party Platform" and the "Omaha Platform."

Food and Drugs Act and Meat Inspection Act, both effective June 30, 1906. From the U.S. Food and Drug Administration Archives.

Eugene V. Debs, statement to the court, September 18, 1918, published as *Debs' Address to the Jury, and Statement to the Court* (Chicago: National Office, Socialist Party, 1918).

William (Big Bill) Haywood, "Farewell, Capitalist America!" in *Bill Haywood's Book: The Autobiography of William D. Haywood* (New York: International Publishers, 1929).

Barbara Ehrenreich, *Nickel and Dimed: On (Not) Getting By in America* (New York: Metropolitan Books, 2001). © 2001 by Barbara Ehrenreich. Reprinted by permission of Henry Holt and Company, LLC, and International Creative Management, Inc. Comments by Ehrenreich in the headnote are from an interview with Zoe Trodd (07/28/05).

Ida B. Wells, *Southern Horrors: Lynch Law in All Its Phases,* parts published in the *New York Age,* June 1892, and expanded version by The New York Age Print, October 1892.

W. E. B. Du Bois, "Jesus Christ in Texas," in *Darkwater: Voices from within the Veil* (New York: Harcourt, Brace and Howe, 1920).

Claude McKay, "The Lynching," first published in Odgen Nash, ed., *Cambridge Magazine* (Summer 1920), and then in Claude McKay, *Harlem Shadows* (New York: Harcourt, Brace and Company, 1922).

Richard Wright, "Big Boy Leaves Home," in *The New Caravan* (1936). Rept. in Richard Wright, *Uncle Tom's Children.* Copyright 1936 by Richard Wright. Copyright 1964 by Ellen Wright. Reprinted by permission of HarperCollins Publishers.

Abel Meeropol and Billie Holiday, "Strange Fruit": Written by Abel Meeropol as a poem, "Bitter Fruit," published in the *New York Teacher,* January 1937, under the pseudonym Lewis Allan. First performed as "Strange Fruit" by Billie Holiday at the Café Society, Greenwich Village, January 1939, and first recorded by Billie Holiday & Her Orchestra in New York, April 20, 1939 for Commodore Records, reaching no. 16 on the charts in July 1939. Words and music by Lewis Allan. Copyright © 1939 (renewed) by Music Sales Corporation (ASCAP). International copyright secured. All rights outside the United States controlled by Edward B. Marks Music Company. All rights reserved. Reprinted by permission.

Helen Gahagan Douglas, "Federal Law Is Imperative": Transcript of radio interview by reporter Jack Bell, Washington, D.C., 1947. Audio recording in National Archives and Records Administration.

League of Struggle for Negro Rights, "Bill for Negro Rights and the Suppression of Lynching." Published in the pamphlet *Equality, Land and Freedom: A Program for Negro Liberation* (New York: League of Struggle for Negro Rights, 1934), 27–30. Redrafted and revised on the basis of a document carried to Washington, D.C., by the "Free the Scottsboro Boys" marchers on May 8, 1933, and presented to Congress.

The John Brown Anti-Klan Committee, "Take a Stand against the Klan," from *The Dividing Line of the 80s: Take a Stand Against the Klan—A Pamphlet on the Fight against White Supremacy* (New York: John Brown Anti-Klan Committee, 1980). Comments by Lisa Roth in the headnote are from an interview with Zoe Trodd and Jeff Rakover (08/20/05).

Michael Slate, "AmeriKKKa 1998: The Lynching of James Byrd," *Revolutionary Worker* [later *Revolution*] 962 (June 21, 1998).

"The Lynching of Thomas Shipp and Abram Smith, 1930": Photograph taken on August 7, 1930, in Marion, Indiana, by an unknown photographer. Library of Congress, Prints and Photographs Division. Published in James Allen et al., eds., *Without Sanctuary: Lynching Photography in America* (Santa Fe: Twin Palms, 2000), plate 31.

Dorothea Lange, "Migrant Mother," March 1936, published in *Survey Graphic,* September

1936. FSA caption: "Destitute pea pickers in California. Mother of seven children. Age thirty-two. Nipomo, California." FSA-OWI, Library of Congress.

Arthur Rothstein, "Farmer and sons walking in the face of a dust storm. Cimarron County, Oklahoma, April 1936." FSA-OWI, Library of Congress.

John Steinbeck, *The Grapes of Wrath* (New York: The Viking Press, 1939). Copyright 1939, renewed © 1967 by John Steinbeck. Used by permission of Viking Penguin, a division of Penguin Group (USA) Inc. and Penguin Books Ltd.

Walker Evans, "Sharecropper Bud Fields and his family at home, Hale County, Alabama, 1936"; "Corner of kitchen in Bud Fields' home, Hale County, Alabama, 1936"; "William Fields, Hale County, Alabama, 1936." FSA-OWI, Library of Congress.

James Agee and Walker Evans, *Let Us Now Praise Famous Men* (Boston: Houghton Mifflin, 1941). Copyright 1941 by James Agee and Walker Evans. Copyright © renewed 1969 by Mia Fritsh Agee and Walker Evans. Reprinted by permission of Houghton Mifflin Company. All rights reserved. Unpublished "Works" chapter, James Agee Collection, Harry Ransom Humanities Research Center, University of Texas at Austin: 6: 12–15, typescript and carbon copy typescript with corrections, n.d. © 1972 The James Agee Trust, reprinted with the permission of the Wylie Agency Inc.

Woody Guthrie, "Tom Joad": Lyrics as recorded by Woody Guthrie, RCA Studios, Camden, N.J., April 26, 1940; released on Woody Guthrie, *Dust Bowl Ballads*, RCA Studios, July 1940. To the tune of "John Hardy," a traditional English outlaw ballad. Words and music by Woody Guthrie. © Copyright 1960 (renewed) 1963 (renewed) Ludlow Music, Inc., New York, N.Y. Used by permission. Comments by Joe McDonald in the headnote are from an interview with Zoe Trodd and Geoff Trodd (08/21/05).

Richard Wright and Edwin Rosskam, *12 Million Black Voices* (New York: Viking, 1941). Edwin Rosskam, "Negro family and their home in one of the alley dwelling sections, Washington, D.C." (1941), and Russell Lee, "During the services at storefront Baptist church on Easter Sunday, Chicago, Illinois" (1941). FSA-OWI, Library of Congress.

Roy DeCarava and Langston Hughes, *The Sweet Flypaper of Life* (New York: Simon and Schuster, 1955). Reprinted by permission of Harold Ober Associates Incorporated.

Michael Harrington, *The Other America: Poverty in the United States* (New York: Macmillan, 1962). Copyright © 1962, 1969, 1981 by Michael Harrington; copyright renewed © 1990 by Stephanie Harrington. Reprinted with the permission of Scribner, an imprint of Simon & Schuster Adult Publishing Group. Comments by Barbara Ehrenreich in the headnote are from an interview with Zoe Trodd (07/28/05).

Malik, image captioned "Poverty is a crime, and our people are the victims," *The Black Panther Party Newsletter* 9:8 (1972). Reprinted by permission of the Dr. Huey P. Newton Foundation.

Robert Granat, "Montgomery: Reflections of a Loving Alien," *Liberation* (April 1956), 1:2, special issue titled "Montgomery, Alabama, 'Our Struggle.'" Contributor's note read: "Robert Granat does subsistence-farming in New Mexico, where he raises chilli."

James Baldwin, "My Dungeon Shook": Originally published in *The Progressive* as "A Letter to My Nephew" © 1962 by James Baldwin. Copyright renewed. Collected in *The Fire Next Time* (New York: The Dial Press, 1963), published by Vintage Books. Reprinted by arrangement with the James Baldwin Estate.

Martin Luther King, Jr., "Letter from Birmingham Jail,": First published in *The Christian Century*, June 12, 1963, and as a pamphlet by the American Friends Committee. This excerpt is from King's revised version, in *Why We Can't Wait* (New York: Harper & Row, 1964). Reprinted by arrangement with the Estate of Martin Luther King Jr., c/o Writers House as agent for the proprietor, New York, N.Y. Copyright 1963 Martin Luther King Jr., copyright renewed 1991 Coretta Scott King.

Marion S. Trikosko, "Civil Rights March on Washington, D.C." Library of Congress Prints and Photographs Division.

Malcolm X, "The Ballot or the Bullet": Speech delivered April 3, 1964, at Cory Methodist Church, Cleveland, Ohio. Published in *Malcolm X Speaks* (New York: Pathfinder Press, 1989). For audio see americanrhetoric.com/speeches/malcolmxballot.htm (accessed 07/02/05). Copyright © 1965, 1989 by Betty Shabazz and the Pathfinder Press. Reprinted by permission.

John F. Kennedy, "On Civil Rights": "Radio and Television Report to the American People on Civil Rights," June 11, 1963. National Archives, Presidential Papers. For audio see jfklibrary.org/j061163.htm, and for Civil Rights Act see usinfo.state.gov/usa/infousa/laws/majorlaw/civilr19.htm (both accessed 06/04/05). Comments by Senator Ted Kennedy in the headnote are from an interview with Zoe Trodd (11/01/05).

Lyndon B. Johnson, "The American Promise": Excerpts from an address to a Joint Session of Congress, March 15, 1965, which was broadcast nationally. National Archives, Presidential Papers. For audio see hpol.org/lbj/voting and for Voting Rights Act see ourdocuments.gov (both accessed 06/04/05).

Amiri Baraka, "Black Art," *Liberator* (1966); rept. in Amiri Baraka (LeRoi Jones), *Black Magic: Collected Poetry 1961–1967* (Indianapolis: Bobbs-Merrill, 1969). Copyright LeRoi Jones 1969. Reprinted by permission of the author. Comments by Baraka in the headnote are from an interview with Zoe Trodd (08/20/05).

Tupac Shakur, "Panther Power": Written and recorded in 1989, and first released on *The Lost Tapes* (2000), then *Resurrection* (2003). For audio clips, see 2paclegacy.com (accessed 09/01/05). Reprinted by permission of Notting Dale Songs Inc. (ASCAP). Copyright © 1997 by Universal Music Corporation (ASCAP). Used by permission. All rights reserved. Written by Ray Tyson, published by Trapped Music. Used by permission.

The New Black Panther Party, "Ten Point Program": Issued by Malik Zulu Shabazz, Chairman of the New Black Panther Party, adapted by the NBPP from Huey Newton's "The Black Panther Party: Platform and Program" (October 1966). For original BPP platform see blackpanther.org/TenPoint.htm (accessed 06/04/05).

Tillie Olsen, "I Stand Here Ironing," in *Tell Me a Riddle* (Philadelphia: J. B. Lippincott, 1961). Copyright 1956, 1957, 1960, 1961 by Tillie Olsen. Reprinted by permission of the Elaine Markson Literary Agency.

Betty Friedan, *The Feminine Mystique* (New York: W. W. Norton, 1963). Copyright © 1983, 1974, 1973, 1963 by Betty Friedan. Used by permission of W. W. Norton & Company, Inc.

National Organization for Women, "Statement of Purpose": Drafted June 1966, by Betty Friedan and Pauli Murray. Reprinted by permission of the National Organization for Women. Notice: this is a historic document, which was adopted at NOW's first National Conference in Washington, D.C., on October 29, 1966. The words are those of the 1960s, and do not reflect current language or NOW's current priorities.

Renee Ferguson, "Women's Liberation Has a Different Meaning for Blacks": Published as "Just another white political fad—women's liberation has a different meaning for blacks," in *The Washington Post,* October 3, 1970, A18. Reprinted by permission of the author.

Shirley Chisholm, "For the Equal Rights Amendment": Address to Congress, August 10, 1970. 91st Congress, 2nd session, Congressional Record, National Archives.

Gerda Lerner, excerpts from letter to Betty Friedan, February 6, 1963, in the Friedan Collection, Schlesinger Library, Radcliffe Institute, Cambridge, Mass., box 20a, folder 715, BF-SLRC. Reprinted by permission of the author.

Audre Lorde, "Poetry Is Not a Luxury": First published in *Chrysalis* 3 (1977); rept. in Audre Lorde, *Sister Outsider: Essays and Speeches* (Trumansburg, N.Y.: The Crossing Press, 1984). Copyright © 1977 by the estate of Audre Lorde, published by permission of the Charlotte Sheedy Literary Agency, Inc.

June Jordan, "The Female and the Silence of a Man": First published in *Naming our Destiny: New and Selected Poems* (New York: Thunder's Mouth Press, 1989). Copyright June Jordan. Reprinted by permission of the June M. Jordan Literary Estate Trust, www.junejordan.com. For Yeats's 1924 poem see yeatsvision.com/History.html (accessed 09/09/05).

Katie Roiphe, *The Morning After: Sex, Fear, and Feminism on Campus* (Boston: Little, Brown, 1993). Copyright © 1993 by Katie Roiphe. Reprinted by permission of International Creative Management, Inc.

Ana Castillo, "Women Don't Riot," from *I Ask the Impossible: Poems* (New York: Anchor Books, 2001). Copyright © 2001 by Ana Castillo. Published by Anchor Books, a division of Random House, Inc. Reprinted by permission of Susan Bergholz Literary Services, New York. All rights reserved.

Allen Ginsberg, "Howl": first read publicly by Ginsberg on October 7, 1955, at the Six Gallery in San Francisco. Published in *Howl and Other Poems* (San Francisco: City Light Books, 1956); rept. in *Collected Poems 1947–1980* (New York: Harper & Row, 1984). For audio of Ginsberg reading "Howl" see archive.org (accessed 09/05/05). Copyright © 1955 by Allen Ginsberg. Reprinted by permission of HarperCollins Publishers. Copyright © Allen Ginsberg, 1987. Reproduced by permission of Penguin Books Ltd.

Stonewall Documents: Homophile Youth Movement, "GET THE MAFIA AND THE COPS OUT OF GAY BARS," undated New York flier (early July 1969). Graffiti on the Stonewall Inn, June 28, 1969, and Gay Liberation Front, "DO YOU THINK HOMOSEXUALS ARE REVOLTING?", New York flier, July 17, 1969. Mattachine Society, "HOMOSEXUALS ARE COMING," New York leaflet, July 27, 1969. Student Homophile League, "A RADICAL MANIFESTO," in *Gay Power* 2, August 28, 1969. "First GLF Statement" and "Editorial I" in *Come out!: New York Gay Liberation Front Newspaper,* September 1969. "IN THE STREETS FOR THE REVOLUTION," *San Francisco Free Press,* November 1–14. L. Craig Schoonmaker and Homosexuals Intransigent!, editorial in *Homosexual Renaissance* 1, November 12, 1969. Steve Kuromiya, *Philadelphia Free Press,* July 27, 1970. For visual icons of the Gay Liberation Movement, see myweb.lsbu.ac.uk/~stafflag/icons.html (accessed 09/01/05).

Carl Wittman, "Refugees from Amerika: A Gay Manifesto": Drafted and circulated amongst friends in 1968, finished May 1969, and first published in the *San Francisco Free Press,* December 22, 1970.

Huey P. Newton, "A Letter from Huey to the Revolutionary Brothers and Sisters About the Women's Liberation and Gay Liberation Movements," first printed in the *Black Panther,* August 21, 1970, and the *Berkeley Tribe,* September 5–12, 1970. Reprinted by permission of the Dr. Huey P. Newton Foundation.

Doric Wilson, *Street Theater: The Twenty-Seventh of June, 1969 in Two Acts,* premiered February 18, 1982, at Theatre Rhinoceros, San Francisco; published in 1983 (New York: TNT

Classics). Reprinted by permission of the author. Comments by Wilson in the headnote are from an interview with Jeff Rakover and Zoe Trodd (07/08/05).

ACT UP, "Read My Lips": Postcard of ACT UP activists at the Democratic National Convention in Atlanta, Georgia, in 1988, holding Gran Fury's poster, "Read My Lips" (National Library of Medicine). Photograph from "Still," the first act of "Still/Here," a two-act, evening-length performance by the Bill T. Jones/Arnie Zane Dance Company, which debuted on November 30, 1994, at the Brooklyn Academy of Opera House (image by Beatriz Schiller).

Tony Kushner, *Angels in America, Part One: Millennium Approaches* copyright © 1992, 1993 by Tony Kushner. *Part Two: Perestroika* copyright © 1992, 1994, 1995 by Tony Kushner. *Angels in America, A Gay Fantasia on National Themes* is published and used by permission of Theatre Communications Group. Comments by Kushner in the headnote are from an interview with Zoe Trodd (03/31/05).

Lesbian Avengers, "Dyke Manifesto," by Anne-Christine D'Adesky, Kathy Danger, Brenda Miller, Carrie Moyer, and Ana Simo, in *Lesbian Avenger Handbook* (1993). Expanded version of a broadsheet written by Ana Simo, Kat Campbell, and Lisa Springer, distributed at the Dyke March to the White House, on April 24, 1993, before the Third Lesbian and Gay March on April 25.

Leslie Feinberg, *Stone Butch Blues* (Ithaca: Firebrand Books, 1993). Copyright by Leslie Feinberg. Reprinted by permission of Sterling Lord Literistic, Inc.

Goodridge v. Department of Public Health: Excerpts from Massachusetts Supreme Judicial Court, slip opinions and orders: Hillary Goodridge & others [FN1] v. Department of Public Health & another. [FN2] SJC-08860, November 18, 2003. Administrative Office of the Trial Court.

Country Joe and the Fish, "I-Feel-Like-I'm-Fixin'-To-Die-Rag": written and recorded in 1965; first released in October 1965, on the EP "Talking Issue *Rag Baby*." For audio see countryjoe.com/rag.htm (accessed 09/01/05). © 1965 Alkatraz Corner Music Co. BMI. Words and Music by Joe McDonald. Used by permission. Comments by McDonald in the headnote are from an interview with Zoe Trodd and Geoff Trodd (08/21/05).

Denise Levertov, "Advent 1966," first published in *The Nation* (1966), rept. in *Poems, 1968–1972* (New York: New Directions, 1972). Copyright © 1965, 1966, 1967, 1968, 1969, 1970, 1971 by Denise Levertov Goodman. Copyright © 1970, 1971, 1972, 1987 by Denise Levertov. Reprinted by permission of New Directions Publishing Corp.

Norman Mailer, *Why Are We in Vietnam?* (New York: Putnam, 1967). © 1967 by Norman Mailer. Reprinted by permission of Henry Holt and Company, LLC, and the Wylie Agency.

Eddie Adams, "Saigon: Execution of a Suspected Viet Cong Terrorist," taken February 1, 1968, published in the *New York Times* on February 2, four columns wide on the front page, with the headline: "Street Clashes Go On in Vietnam, Foe Still Holds Parts of Cities; Johnson Pledges Never to Yield," and reprinted worldwide. Nick Ut, "Villagers Fleeing a Napalm Strike, Village of Trang Bang," taken June 8, 1972, published in newspapers across America on June 9, and on the cover of *Time* in late June. AP/Wide World Photos.

Michael Herr, *Dispatches* (New York: Knopf, 1977). First published in part as a series of articles for *Esquire* (1967–1969). Copyright 1977 Michael Herr. Reprinted by permission of Donadio & Olson, Inc.

John Balaban, "April 30, 1975": Published in *The Nation*, October 25, 1975, 29; rept. in *Blue Mountain* (Unicorn Press, 1982). Reprinted by permission of the author. Comments by Balaban in the headnote are from an interview with Zoe Trodd (07/13/05).

Tim O'Brien, "How to Tell a True War Story": Published in *Esquire,* October 1987, 208–212; rept. in *The Things They Carried* (Boston: Houghton Mifflin, 1990). Copyright © 1990 by Tim O'Brien. Reprinted by permission of Houghton Mifflin Company and HarperCollins Publishers Ltd. All rights reserved. Comments in the headnotes by Tim O'Brien are from an interview with Zoe Trodd (07/12/05); by Country Joe, from an interview with Zoe Trodd and Geoff Trodd (08/20/05).

Lawrence Ferlinghetti, "Speak Out": First published in the *San Francisco Chronicle,* February 14, 2003. Reprinted by permission of City Lights Booksellers & Publishers.

Jim Harrison, "Poem of War," dated February 13, 2003. Reprinted by permission of the author.

Robert Pinsky, "Poem of Disconnected Parts": Written in July 2005, published here for the first time. Reprinted by permission of the author. Comments by Pinsky in the headnote are from an interview with Zoe Trodd (08/03/05). Letters to Laura Bush and the *Washington Post* provided by the author (07/05/05).

Clinton Fein, "Who Would Jesus Torture?" Created in 2004, intended for a Clinton Fein exhibition entitled "Numb and Number," opened October 7, 2004, at the Toomey Tourell Gallery in San Francisco; destroyed by Zazzle, a Palo Alto–based printing company, before the opening. Courtesy of Toomey Tourell Gallery. Reprinted by permission of Clinton Fein. All quoted comments by Fein are from an interview with Zoe Trodd (09/20/05). For Clinton Fein art and editorials see *clintonfein.com;* for Fein's online forum and commentary website see *annoy.com;* for Abu Ghraib images see *cbc.ca/news/photogalleries/iraqprisonabuse* (all accessed 09/01/05).

Ron Kovic, *Born on the Fourth of July* (New York: McGraw-Hill, 1976). New introduction from 2005 edition (New York: Akashic Books, 2005). Reprinted by permission of Akashic Books.

Acknowledgements

This book would not have been possible without the skill, wisdom, and imagination of Jennifer Snodgrass—I couldn't have asked for a better editor.

I'd like to acknowledge the invaluable feedback of Michael Kazin, Paul Lauter, and Howard Zinn. For their assistance, I'm grateful to Robert Dana, John A. Collins in Harvard's Government Documents Collection, Paul Sprecher at the James Agee Trust, Katie Friis at the Bill T. Jones/Arnie Zane Dance Company, Lisa Roth of the John Brown Anti-Klan Committee, and Beth Haugland and Tony Marks in the U.S. Senate.

John Balaban, Kevin Bales, Amiri Baraka, "Country" Joe McDonald, Barbara Ehrenreich, Clinton Fein, Senator Edward Kennedy, Tony Kushner, Tim O'Brien, Robert Pinsky, Lisa Roth, and Doric Wilson were generous and patient with interviews.

Thanks are due to my research assistant Jeff Rakover (who did superb work on ACT UP and Doric Wilson in particular), and my students Adam Clark Estes, Sabrina Forte, Kyle Cooper Frisina, Michael Grynbaum, Kendall Kulper, Chase Mahoney, Nathaniel Naddaff-Hafrey, Stephen Narain, and Ann Mary Olson. I also want to thank Steve Biel, Marcia Dambry, Miguel de Baca, Danielle de Feo, Peter Ellison, Karen Flood, Henry Louis Gates, Jr., Margot Gill, Jean Gooder, Robin Kelsey, James Kloppenberg, Christine McFadden, Josie McQuail and the North East MLA, Luke Menand, Onora O'Neill, Adoyo Owuor and the Zamani Foundation, Dale Riley, Jennifer Roberts, Erin Royston, Yael Schacher, Tom Rob Smith, and Werner Sollors. Further warm thanks to Robert Pinsky for being a dark angel on my shoulder, Teddy Kennedy for a scholarship and his continued encouragement, Christopher Le Coney (the real thing), Alex Williamson for technicolor inspiration, and Kevin Bales for being a co-conspirator and fellow traveler.

I want to thank three friends and colleagues in particular. All three were part of this book from start to finish. Timothy Patrick McCarthy, a 21st-century James Baldwin. I met Tim, the dungeon shook, and my chains fell off. John McMillian, far from a nattering nabob of negativity, who burns like a fabulous yellow roman candle (the best kind of person, Kerouac said). Tim and John's brilliant anthology, *The Radical Reader* (2003), is a vital counterpart to *American Protest Literature*. And John Stauffer, Camerado. This book seeks the protest-self he describes in *Listening to Cement* (2000) as one of "sincerity and wonder, subtlety and nuance," that "refuses to lie still [and] is polymorphous . . . an aesthetic self that is large and contains multitudes."

Finally, thanks to my sister, the incomparably special Bee, my genius brother, Gabe, who did great research for this book, and my mother, Lyn Jenkinson-Trodd, pilgrim soul. But most of all, thanks to my father, Geoff Trodd, who wrote about Country Joe with me and critiqued the book manuscript. Throughout my whole life he has called (with apologies to Whitman): "Allons, the road is before us! It is safe—I have *trodd* it— my own feet have *trodd* it well—be not detain'd!" Hope this book is a step along the way, Dad.

Index

RACHEL WHITEREAD EMBANKMENT

SETTING OUT PAPER BOX

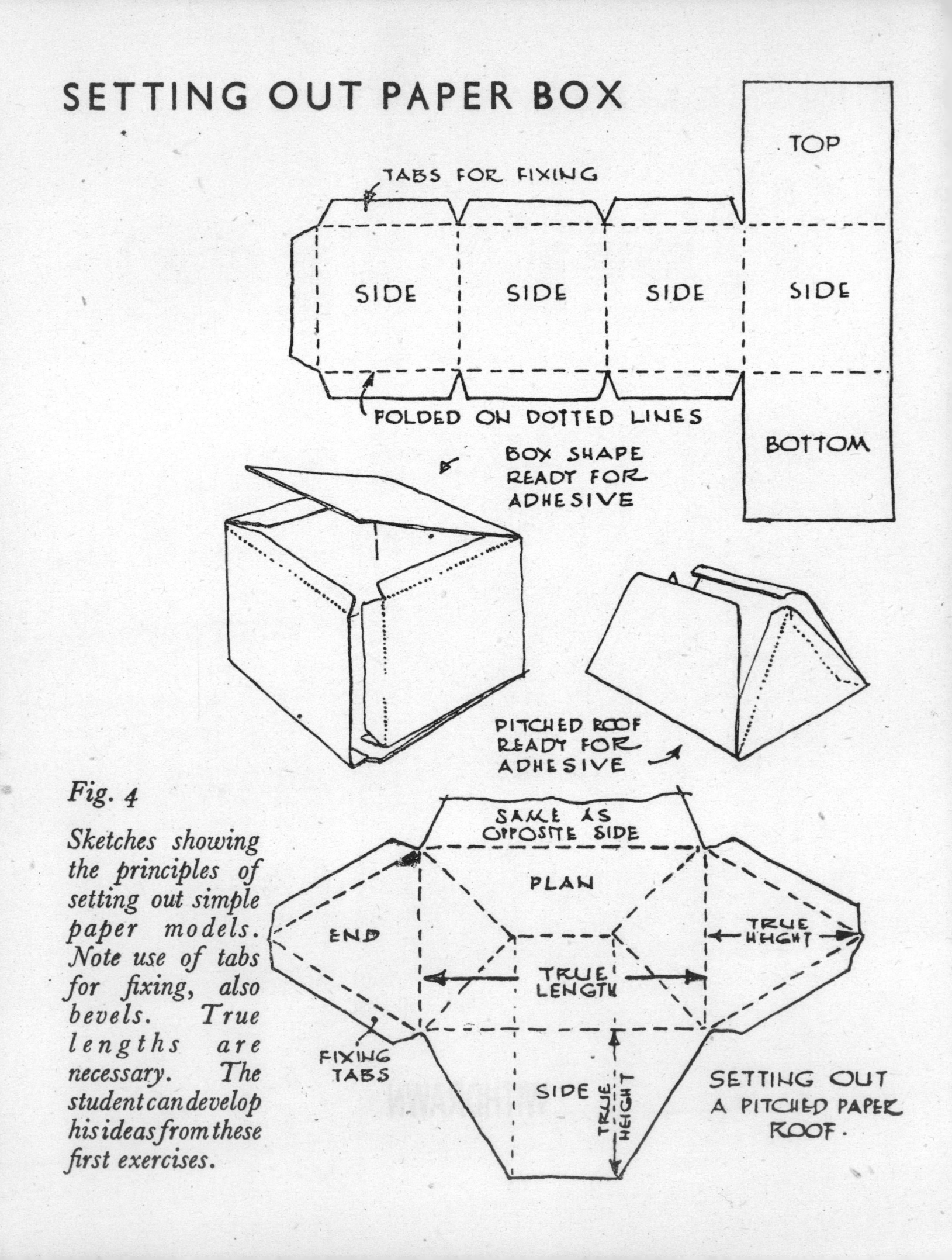

TABS FOR FIXING

SIDE SIDE SIDE SIDE

FOLDED ON DOTTED LINES

TOP

BOTTOM

BOX SHAPE
READY FOR
ADHESIVE

PITCHED ROOF
READY FOR
ADHESIVE

Fig. 4

Sketches showing the principles of setting out simple paper models. Note use of tabs for fixing, also bevels. True lengths are necessary. The student can develop his ideas from these first exercises.

SAME AS OPPOSITE SIDE

PLAN

END

TRUE HEIGHT

TRUE LENGTH

FIXING TABS

SIDE

TRUE HEIGHT

TRUE HEIGHT

SETTING OUT A PITCHED PAPER ROOF.